The Russian Empire and the World, 1700–1917

The Russian Empire and the World, 1700–1917

The Geopolitics of Expansion and Containment

John P. LeDonne

1,20,368,367

New York   Oxford

OXFORD UNIVERSITY PRESS

1997

Oxford University Press

Oxford   New York
Athens   Auckland   Bangkok   Bogota
Bombay   Buenos Aires   Calcutta   Cape Town
Dar es Salaam   Delhi   Florence   Hong Kong   Istanbul
Karachi   Kuala Lumpur   Madras   Madrid   Melbourne
Mexico City   Nairobi   Paris   Singapore
Taipei   Tokyo   Toronto

and associated companies in
Berlin   Ibadan

Copyright © 1997 by Oxford University Press, Inc.

Published by Oxford University Press, Inc.
198 Madison Avenue, New York, New York 10016

Library of Congress Cataloging-in-Publication Data

LeDonne, John P., 1935–
The Russian empire and the world, 1700–1917 : the geopolitics of
expansion and containment / John LeDonne.
p. cm.   Includes bibliographical references and index.
ISBN 0-19-510926-0   ISBN 0-19-510927-9 (pbk.)
1. Russia—Foreign relations—1689–1801.   2. Russia—Foreign relations—1801–1917.
3. Geopolitics—Russia. I. Title.
DK145.L43   1996
325'.32'094709033—dc20   96-4235

1 3 5 7 9 8 6 4 2

Printed in the United States of America
on acid-free paper

For Jean-Michel,
    who showed the way

Contents

Maps

Preface

This book has a dual purpose. It is intended to be, first of all, a comprehensive survey of the major events in the history of tsarist Russian foreign relations between 1700, when the Northern War with Sweden began, and 1917, when the Romanov dynasty collapsed. The history of Russian diplomacy has been neglected for a number of reasons: the year 1917 remained for many years the great divide in Russian history, since it was assumed that Soviet foreign policy was guided by the tenets of Marxism-Leninism and showed little or no continuity with its predecessor, and the emphasis on social history consigned foreign policy to a scholarly limbo, especially after the 1960s.

More than thirty years ago, Ivo Lederer edited a collection of essays on Russian foreign policy; Taras Hunczak followed suit with another collection twelve years later. Barbara Jelavich published in 1964 the first short survey of Russia's foreign relations from 1814 to 1914, expanded later to include the Soviet period. These three basic books have been out of print for many years. We now have another short general survey by David MacKenzie, Dietrich Geyer's study for the period from 1860 to 1914, and William Fuller's analysis of Russian strategy from the seventeenth century to 1914. This book begins in 1700, a more appropriate date than 1801 or 1814, when the goals and methods of Russian foreign policy had become well established. It might be argued that the eighteenth century was a century of empire-building, and that it was not until 1815 that the Russian Empire, completed but for the annexation of Central Asia and the Amur valley, took its place alongside the other great powers of Europe as a major player in international relations. But such neglect of the eighteenth century ignores the valuable lessons we may learn from Russia's intensive relations with Sweden, Poland, and Turkey.

This book is also an interpretation of Russian foreign policy. Any interpretation makes use of concepts developed in other disciplines, and I acknowledge the influence of four great scholars. One was Sir Halford Mackinder, who read before the Royal Geographical Society in January 1904—only two years after the Anglo-Japanese alliance completed the encirclement of the Russian Empire and three years before the historic Anglo-Russian agreement on their respective spheres of influence—a paper entitled "The Geographical Pivot of History." In that paper, Mackinder established the importance of a "pivot area," consisting of areas of continental and Arctic drainage including the basin of the Volga and the Siberian rivers, and identified it as the heart of a powerful Eurasian empire of the future. The pivot area later became the "Heartland," when Mackinder expanded his original concept in 1919 to include an immense area from the Elbe River to beyond Lake Baikal. The Heartland was flanked by a European and a Monsoon Coastland, separated by a land bridge called "Arabia." The concept has been much criticized for a variety of reasons, but its resilience remains the best proof of its value.[1] It has been of basic importance in helping me place the history of Russian foreign policy in a geopolitical context.

The second influence was that of Admiral Alfred Mahan, whose books became classics and offered a general theory of sea power that has not lost its importance three generations later. Mackinder and Mahan were contemporaries, and their views were complementary, and not incompatible, as is sometimes believed. The "evangelist of sea power,"[2] with the history and achievements of the British Empire as a model, was convinced the future belonged to the maritime powers, of which he had reason to believe the United States would soon become the leader. Sea powers moved freely across the oceans. In peacetime they sought control of the river mouths because these were extensions of the sea into the hinterland of the coastal cities. They sought free trade and followed an "open door" policy of commercial access, as they built up a global economy for the greater good of all. In wartime their navies took the offensive and bottled up the warships and merchantmen of their enemy in its home ports in order to seize overseas markets without opposition. They denied the enemy the use of the sea and destroyed its revenue from colonial trade. While Mackinder visualized Russian expansion toward the perimeter of the Heartland, Mahan believed implicitly that Russia should be contained within the Heartland. Mackinder discovered the geopolitical context of Russian expansion; Mahan conceptualized Britain's policy of containing it.

Mackinder did not write a history of Russian expansion, he only established the physical framework within which it took place. To understand the dynamism of international relations within the Heartland, I borrowed from Geoffrey Parker the concept of "core area." Parker believes there were core areas in the Ile de France, Castile, Brandenburg, Austria, Muscovy, and the Turkish Straits, around which powerful dynasties built nation states and empires. While I retained Parker's criteria to define core areas, I expanded their number to include Sweden, Poland, and Persia within the Heartland; Britain, China, and Japan in the Coastlands. In such a perspective, an expanding Russian core area faced in 1700 four core areas—Sweden, Poland, Turkey, and Persia—that had passed their prime and were entering a period of decline, during which they found themselves unable to resist in the long run the expansion of Russia's dynamic power. In the east, China was an expanding power from the 1650s to the 1800s but then slowly declined in the course of the nineteenth century; it became the sick man of Asia to the same extent that Turkey had already become the sick man of Europe. On the other land, the rise of Russia coincided with the emergence of Austria and Prussia, whose own dynamism worked to contain Russia's expansion and block access to the Heartland's periphery; of France, which sought to create a community of interests against both Russia and Austria; of Britain, which replaced France after 1815 and became the only global power capable of containing Russian expansion; and of Japan, with a mission to block Russia's access to the Pacific. The interaction between Russia and these eight powers set the pulse of international relations within the Heartland and between the Heartland and the Coastlands.

Finally, I have been much influenced by Owen Lattimore's studies of the frontier. Lattimore's interest was China and its relations with the nomads of Inner Asia's borderlands—Manchuria, Mongolia, Sinkiang, and Tibet. The great value of these studies lies in Lattimore's ability to go beyond a descriptive narrative to work out a theory of the frontier as a succession of zones beginning along China's periphery and extending to the outer limits of the nomadic world. Lattimore saw territorial expansion as the product of an accumulation of energy seeking release after the completion of a preliminary stage of "state" building. Such expenditure of energy raised the question of "a line of an optimum of conquest" beyond which further expansion became counterproductive. It was not hard to see that Parker's and Lattimore's concepts were complementary: "core areas" are not contiguous but are separated by territories that can easily be described as "frontiers."

I have borrowed freely from these four authors and have used and modified their concepts to work out a geopolitical model that describes and explains the methods and goals of Russian foreign policy between 1700 and 1917. The story of Russian expansion takes place against the background of a slow but inexorable change in the balance of power within the Heartland. It is the story of a struggle between a rising Russia and declining core areas for the control of frontiers separating them; of a persistent attempt to destabilize, partition, and even annex those declining core areas in order eventually to occupy the entire Heartland. And it is the story of the determination of the Germanic and maritime powers to prevent that expansion from reaching the Heartland's periphery.

I anticipate objections. I greatly emphasize the importance of geographic factors in the shaping and evolution of Russian foreign policy, and expose myself to the accusation of geographic determinism. The Russians knew their geography; so did the Prussians, the Austrians, the French, and the British. They also knew that geography conditioned their national existence, their past, and their future. Geography did not determine foreign policy in the sense of being the only factor taken into consideration in its shaping, but it conditioned the formulation of such a policy by narrowing the range of options. Geography certainly determined England's existence as a sea power and conditioned its policymakers to develop policies based on that fundamental fact. Geography certainly created the French (and Chinese) strategic dilemma—was France primarily a sea or a land power? And it imposed on the Germans the often agonizing question whether Germany belonged to the east or to the west; or, in the terminology used here, whether Germany was primarily a Coastland or a Heartland power.

Geography determined the paths of Russian expansion. Rivers created corridors of expansion that channeled Russia's advance along clear paths and determined its political, strategic, and commercial objectives; before the construction of railroads there was hardly any substitute for a riverbank for soldiers or merchants. It is this belief in the primacy of geography that convinced me that a chronological discussion of Russia's foreign policy was not the best way to emphasize the remarkable consistency of its goals and methods. A chronological presentation was bound to give excessive importance—some of the works just cited show this only too well—to Russia's relations with Europe and to a lesser extent with the Ottoman Empire, and to neglect Russia's relations with Persia and China and the world of the steppe, at least until some major events such as the conquest of Central Asia and the advance into Manchuria seemed to "redress the balance." The result was always to create a false sense of priorities and to render fashionable the concept of a pendulum movement in Russia's policy, in fact, a cliché born of an optical illusion. That is why I chose to study the Russian advance in chronological order but in three separate theaters ("frontiers") in order to show the internal dynamism of each theater, independently of events taking place in others at the same time. The example cited most often to illustrate the pendulum movement is the presumed shift in Russian policy from the Balkans to the Far East after the Bulgarian fiasco in the 1880s. But the Russians had been pursuing a forward policy in the Far East since the arrival of Muravev in Irkutsk in 1847. Incidentally, it was he and not Witte who laid the foundations of a Russian empire in the region. The advance into the valley of the Amur, the founding of Vladivostok, the emergence of Japan, the Kuril agreement of 1875, and the increasing competition in Korea had kept the Russians very active, in fact just as active as in Central Asia and the Balkans. There was no shift of the pendulum in the 1890s, only the continuation of a forward policy that was already nearly fifty years old but was reaching the stage when major decisions needed to be taken.

It will be objected that personalities are given little prominence in the story presented here. Personalities are important when we examine short-term developments such as diplomatic crises and military campaigns. Conflicting views expose the strengths and weaknesses of the participants, their vested interests, their rivalries. But when the crises are over and the dust settles again, it generally appears that what has actually been done takes its place in a long-range process marked by consistency of methods and purpose. Such a long-range process has little to do with personalities. One can argue that Catherine's foreign policy, despite its exceptional achievements, showed no originality. It achieved what Anna Ivanovna's foreign policy attempted but could not achieve, because a complex of cir-cumstances—diplomatic, military, and economic—had made the realiza-tion of those goals premature. If Rumiantsev had commanded the Russian army in 1738, he might have been no more successful than Münnich or Lacy. One can glorify Witte as the architect of Russian expansion in the Far East, but that expansion was made possible by the increasing inability of the Manchu dynasty to keep its hold on the frontier zones and by the scramble for concessions that followed the Opium War. Both developments had little to do with personalities. If Witte and Sir Henry Parkes had never lived, Russian and British policy would most likely have been the same in the long run. If Izvolsky rather than Sazonov had been foreign minister in 1915, would the Russian stand on the Straits have been any different?

To question, if not to deny, the critical importance of personalities would seem to imply the existence of some sinister master plan of Russian expansion, worked out at some indefinite date in the past and carried out in masterly fashion, stage after stage by individuals who were the prison-ers of their geographic environment. I would never claim that such a mas-ter plan—some "Testament of Peter I"[3]—ever existed, but I do claim that geography so restricted the range of options that there were few alternatives most of the time, and none very often. For example, once it was established that Russia must tap, for fiscal reasons, the resources of the Central Asian trade with India, geography determined that the Hindu Kush must be reached from the Ural River via the Aral Sea, then via the Amu Darya to Khiva and Bukhara. It followed that a military, administra-tive, and commercial headquarters had to be established on the edge of the frontier, and Orenburg was founded (in different places before the final choice was made). Then it became imperative to protect the security of the caravans, and that could be done only by implanting a Russian presence in the Kazakh steppe. And the determination to reach "India" also enhanced the importance of Persia, located between Astrakhan and the Hindu Kush, and required the creation of a military, naval, and com-mercial infrastructure on the eastern shore of the Caspian. Once geogra-phy had determined "how to get there," a nexus of interests and external circumstances would determine the opportunity of each stage of the advance toward that goal. Russian expansion was not the result of a

master plan, but the timely decision of each move on a predetermined
geographic path, made by leading individuals on the spot who knew what
their predecessors had intended and what was expected of them.

But what of the ultimate goal of Russian expansion? Catherine II is
reported to have told her secretary Gavril Derzhavin (not for publication): "If I could live 200 years, the whole of Europe would be brought
under Russian rule," and "I shall not die before I have ejected the Turks
from Europe, broken the insolence of China, and established trade relations with India."[4] If "the whole of Europe" is modified to mean "the
whole of Germanic Europe"—which may have been Catherine's real
intention—then the empress (and the Russian political establishment)
had a clear geopolitical vision of Russia's objective, a vision determined by
geography. The objective was no less than the unification of the Heartland under Russian rule from the Elbe to Manchuria. In that vision, river
basins formed large hinterlands of river mouths, and hinterlands combined to form the basin of the sea into which those rivers drained. The
Dvina, the Niemen, the Vistula, and the Oder had vast hinterlands oriented
toward the Baltic Sea; the valleys of the Danube, the Dniestr, the Bug,
the Dniepr, the Don, and the Kuban shaped the hinterland of the Black
Sea. And the Amu and Syr Darya converging toward the Aral Sea also
belonged, like the Volga and the Ural, to the basin of the Caspian. The
basins of those three seas abutted the Heartland's periphery. Either from
the headwaters or from the mouths, depending on the case, Russian
expansion was carried in the direction of that periphery, which the Russians, in their wildest dreams, considered the ideal outer limit of a world
administered or controlled from Petersburg. Catherine was speaking the
language not only of politics but also of geography.

And in fact, most of her geopolitical program was realized in various
stages before 1917. Russia did establish its hegemony in the Baltic basin in
the eighteenth century, and over the Germanic powers during the first half
of the nineteenth, before the rise of German power forced it to withdraw.
Russia failed to reach the periphery of the Balkans, but nearly unified the
basin of the Black Sea when it reached the Straits and the Anatolian coast
(on paper) in 1915-1916; it had reached the approaches to the Zagros
Mountains and the Hindu Kush and was penetrating the Gobi Desert. In
East Asia alone had it crossed the Heartland's periphery, and then only to
fail to develop its possessions on the Sea of Okhotsk and the Sea of Japan.
One can therefore claim that the geopolitical horizon of Russian statesmen was the Heartland's periphery, and that on the eve of the Revolution
much of Catherine's geopolitical vision was becoming reality.

The history of Russia's foreign relations has often been presented in a
one-dimensional format, the Russians expanding and encountering here
and there the resistance of various powers. Since this book is not so much
a history as an analysis of Russia's policies, the containment of Russian
expansion needed to be treated separately. The last two parts discuss
containment as pursued by the Germanic powers within the Heartland

and by the Coastland powers along the Heartland's periphery. Russian expansion is thus placed in a global, or nearly global, context that brings out the dynamism of international relations both within the Heartland and between Heartland and Coastland. It is hardly necessary to add that the history of Imperial Russia's foreign policy repeated itself during the Soviet period, the United States assuming after 1945 the mission and the burden of the Germanic and Coastland powers to block Soviet expansion across the Heartland's periphery. And it may well be asked whether today's Russia, reduced to its 1650 borders in much of the three frontiers, will not seek once again to restore in the Heartland a hegemony to which it had become accustomed in the heyday of Imperial and Soviet Russia.

The spelling of geographical names follows the *Times Atlas of the World* (8th comprehensive edition, 1990), with few exceptions. Dates conform to the Gregorian calendar, which was eleven days ahead of the Julian, or old-style, calendar in the eighteenth century; twelve days in the nineteenth; and thirteen days in the twentieth. Thus, the Empress Elizabeth, who died on December 24, 1761, is said to have died in January 1762.

Cambridge, Massachusetts   J. P. L.
June 1996

Acknowledgments

It is a pleasant duty to express, once again, my gratitude to Marc Raeff for his continuous intellectual support and his readiness to discuss the several complex issues I have raised in my work (even though he does not fully agree with some of them) with an interest and impartiality of which only a rich and generous mind is capable. In preparing this manuscript for publication I have benefited greatly from those who read it, in its entirety or only parts of it, and helped me correct errors of fact and interpretation: Toshiyuki Akizuki, James Flynn, John Gagliardo, Beatrice Manz, Kimitaka Matsuzato, Firouzeh Mostashari, Mark O'Connor, and Sally Paine. I owe a special debt to James Cracraft and thank Richard Wortman for organizing a workshop at the Harriman Institute, Columbia University, in the fall of 1993 to discuss the concepts developed in this book. Whatever errors remain are my own.

It is another pleasant duty to acknowledge the financial support of the National Endowment for the Humanities; the Kennan Institute, Wilson Center, and its director, Blair Ruble; the Slavic Research Center of Hokkaido University and its then director, Shugo Minagawa; the Ecole des Hautes Etudes in Paris and Wladmir Berelowitch; and of course the Russian Research (now Davis) Center, Harvard University, and its director, Timothy Colton. My work there was always greatly facilitated by the encouragement, direct and indirect, of Edward Keenan, both teacher and friend. And I do not forget Adam Ulam, the former director of the Russian Center, and Priscilla McMillan, a wise and trusted friend.

A final word of thanks to Ruth Mathewson for her matchless editing talents, to Jeff Pike for his skillful rendition of the maps, and to Nancy Lane and Thomas LeBien of Oxford University Press, who welcomed the manuscript and piloted it through the mysterious process that turns a manuscript into a book.

Geopolitics as a policy science has the merit of requiring analysts and commentators to stand back from the detail of contemporary debate and ask "What does it mean?"

C. Gray, *The Geopolitics of the Nuclear Era*, ix

The Russian Empire
and the World,
1700–1917

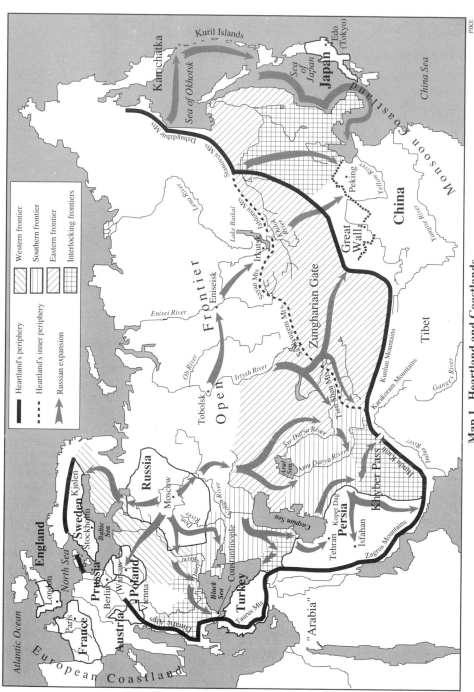

Map 1. Heartland and Coastlands

Introduction

Heartland, Core Areas, Frontiers

The Russian Empire, even at the time of its greatest territorial extent, was never conterminous with the Heartland. To reach its periphery was the ultimate goal of Russian foreign policy, the inability to do so a constant source of frustration. The Heartland was fated to remain the mirror image of Russia's unfulfilled ambitions.

It consisted of four maritime basins. One was the immense area of Arctic drainage watered by the Ob, the Enisei, the Lena, and their tributaries. Much of it consisted of what Mackinder called the Great Lowland between the Ob and the Enisei.[1] The second was the area of continental drainage consisting of the basin of the Caspian and Aral seas, both large inland seas, fed by the Volga, the Ural, the Syr, and Amu Daryas. The basin of the Black Sea was the third; it drained the Don, the Dniepr, and the Danube, and the excess of its sweet water fed the Mediterranean through the Turkish Straits. Finally, the Baltic drained the Oder (Odra), the Vistula (Wisła), and the Neva, and the countless streams of Sweden and Finland.

The Heartland was a continuous plain from west to east, barely interrupted by the Ural Mountains, from the Baltic to the Enisei, beyond which the Central Siberian Plateau announced the great chains separating Siberia from the Pacific. It was likewise a continuous plain from the Barents Sea to the Plateau of Persia (Iran) and the mountains of the Caucasus. One of its major characteristics was its continental climate, with hot summers and a snow cover during most of the winter. The Baltic Sea, its largely sweet waters icebound for various lengths of time from the Gulf of Finland to the Sound, was not the usual warming agent, and remained far

1

removed from the moderating influence of the Gulf Stream. Even the Black Sea, whose coastal waters freeze almost everywhere, belonged to the zone of continental climate, and the traveler who crossed the Turkish Straits from the warm waters of the Aegean entered a new world that to the ancient Greeks appeared inhospitable and ominous.

The great forests of northern Russia and Siberia and the deserts of Inner Asia also enclosed the steppe or grazing lands that began on the Dniestr and formed a broad zone stretching past Kiev, Tobolsk, and Tomsk to the foothills of the Altai Mountains, only to reappear beyond Lake Baikal in the Mongolian upland all the way to the Great Khingan of Manchuria. That zone was for centuries the world of the nomad, an equal threat to the Russian lands, the more settled world of Anatolia and Persia, the oasis societies of Inner Asia, and the walled cities of China, but also an opportunity, a conduit for trade, and a source of leaders and soldiers. The creation of the Russian Empire marked the victory of the forest settler over the nomad, a victory sealed in the tacit Russo-Chinese alliance that destroyed the last steppe empire in 1757.

One cannot describe the Heartland without seeking to determine its boundary, a task before which the historian and the geographer rebel—a simple dividing line can only run roughshod across a physical and human landscape of diversity and contrast—but it must be done for the sake of clarity, if Russian foreign policy is to be placed in an intelligible context.

The Heartland's western boundary followed the crest line of the Kjølen that separates Sweden from Norway and gave Sweden a Baltic, Norway an Atlantic, destiny. The Varangians from Sweden went east to seek the overland route to Constantinople; the Vikings from Norway went west to England and Normandy and later on to the Mediterranean. The Kjølen always constituted a barrier to movement; Swedes and Norwegians never had much affinity for each other, as the union of 1815–1905 was to show. The boundary then ran through Denmark facing both the Baltic and the Atlantic, a place of transit, and therefore of trade. It reached Hamburg and followed the valley of the Elbe, the great historical divide since Roman days. The western Slavs had once stopped on the Saale, one of the Elbe's left-bank tributaries, and the Germanic expansion into Slavic lands—the famous *Drang nach Osten*—had begun on the Elbe. Beyond the river there stretched a different landscape and different patterns of rural and urban settlement. The Elbe flowed into the North Sea; all the rivers west of it belonged to the European Coastland; all its eastern cousins flowed into the Baltic. South of Dresden, the boundary followed the corridor between the Erzgebirge and the Sudeten Mountains, skirted the Czech-Moravian upland, and followed the Moravian corridor to the Danube west of Vienna. The Austrian capital faced both east and west, but the Bohemian lands faced west, drained as they were by the Elbe (Labe) and its tributaries, the Moldau (Vltava) and Berounka. South of Vienna, the boundary curled around the foothills of the eastern Alps to reach the Adriatic Sea at Trieste and Fiume (Rijeka), gateways of Austria and the Hungarian plain.

The southern boundary of the Heartland followed the Dinaric Alps, massive folds of bare limestone, then turned sharply north and east past the Pindus Mountains to follow the southern skirt of the Rhodope chain, merging with the climatic boundary between continental and Mediterranean climate. The narrow coastland, except the swampy lowland of Albania, had no hinterland. Spalato (Split) and Ragusa (Dubrovnik) looked to Italy, and once belonged to the dominion of Venice. Greece faced southward, but the valley of the Danube faced east, toward the Black Sea. The boundary then crossed the Sea of Marmara into Anatolia past the coastal plain of the Aegean and followed the southern fold of the Taurus (Toros) Mountains of Turkey and the Zagros Mountains past the great desert of central Persia and the Makran to merge imperceptibly with the Hindu Kush to the Pamirs, the "roof of the world." This immense arc of mountains from the Dinaric Alps to the Pamirs had one characteristic feature that truly made it the physical boundary of the Heartland: the mountains run in folds parallel to the coast, making passage extremely difficult, and drop to the coastline, creating a barren environment inimical to human settlement. Only the Hindu Kush formed a porous barrier, its passes linking the interior with northern India on the margin of the Monsoon Coastland.

The eastern boundary presented an even more formidable barrier. It was also more complex. From the Pamirs, an inner boundary ran along the Tien Shan Mountains and across the corridor separating them from the Mongolian Altai, where countless hordes of nomads had begun their journey toward the Black Sea. It then followed the Saylyugem and Sayan ranges past Lake Baikal, then the Iablonoi, Stanovoi, and Dzhugdzhur ranges, the latter a nearly impassable watershed between the valley of the Lena and the Sea of Okhotsk. An outer boundary followed the southern edge of the Taklimakan and Gobi deserts and linked up with the Iablonoi range along the watershed separating the basin of Lake Baikal from that of the Amur, including into the Heartland the Turkic peoples of modern Sinkiang and the Western Mongols of Outer Mongolia.

Such was the Heartland within which Russia proceeded to build an empire, a framework that determined the directions of Russian expansion, imposed limitations beyond which Russia could seldom go, and even compelled it to withdraw when it managed to break through.

Core areas are defined by their location, their social and political organization, and their drive for hegemony. A core area emerges as a marginal development at the junction between the territory of two parent cultures. It emerges when an acceleration of centrifugal forces seeks to strike out an independent course in a location well suited to the exercise of power. Such a location is likely to be a center of hydrographic convergence or divergence. Power and authority can radiate from it along river networks or sea lanes, and it draws traders, churchmen, and soldiers in search of fame, wealth, and power. A combination of factors—an ambitious ruling group, political opportunities, economic incentives, population pressures, clashing cultural and religious claims—creates enough internal energy to support the formation of a distinct political system and give it an aggressive ideology.

Such a system may be a centralized and militarized one in land-based core areas, or a decentralized and mercantile one in island core areas. In either case, the emerging core area possesses an ideology embodying "simplistic and fundamentalist attitudes"[2] shaping the world view of an intolerant political elite, such as we find, for example, in early Christianity, in Islam, in Protestantism and Catholicism, and in the secular assumptions of the Enlightenment and Social Darwinism. This elite seeks to achieve political unity, linguistic and cultural homogeneity to justify its rule and make it legitimate. More often than not, the process of internal unification includes a violent phase, even a civil war, in which the energy devoted to core area formation is not spent but renews itself and then focuses on expansion into the territory of first one parent culture and then the other, in an attempt to capture their political, economic, and cultural centers. The expansionist drive creates its own "logic of unity,"[3] a forward movement toward "natural" boundaries, a term without an easy definition but one representing a complex of obstacles establishing "an optimum of conquest."[4] The core area remains an organism in search of an elusive equilibrium with other core areas.

The Russian core area developed on the peripheries of Orthodox and Latin Christendom, of the Golden Horde and Byzantium. The Volga-Oka mesopotamia was its center of hydrographic divergence toward the basin of continental drainage, and the proximity of the sources of the Northern and Western Dvinas, the Dniepr, and the Don placed it at the edge of the basins of the Arctic Ocean, the Baltic Sea, and the Black Sea. The core area was born in the taiga zone of deciduous trees and slowly expanded toward the skirt of the Central Upland. It "ended" where the world of the nomad "began," in the boundless steppe. Its princely house, a vassal of the Mongol khan who resided near Astrakhan, remained for more than three centuries at the mercy of nomadic raids from the steppe. It developed a siege mentality and fundamentalist attitudes, immensely reinforced by the close association between the Church and the ruling house, and inherited universalist claims from the Byzantine and Mongol empires. By 1600, the Russian core area had a social system increasingly dominated by the enserfment of the population to a ruling class of nobles who formed the backbone of the Russian army and the main support of a highly centralized autocratic government. The civil war known as the Time of Troubles consecrated the victory of that system and released new energies for empire-building. The annexation of Novgorod had already given it a northern boundary running along the edge of the east Baltic plain; that of Kazan and Astrakhan a southern one between the wooded steppe and the treeless steppe stretching to the Black Sea and the Caucasus.

Along the inner periphery of the Heartland, as if guarding its approaches from both Russia and the Coastland powers, were four core areas. The Swedish core area developed as the northernmost margin of the Scandinavian world dominated by Denmark. In medieval times and until 1660, Denmark controlled both shores of the Sound and the southern tip of the Scandinavian peninsula, its richest part. Sweden stood at the junction of the Germanic and Finnish worlds, of Germanic and Slavic civilizations, of Latin and Orthodox Christendom. It always faced east, and Finland was its first colony. The Baltic Sea was its zone of hydrographic convergence, the drainage basin of the Oder, the Vistula, the Western Dvina, and the Neva. The revolution of 1523 against Denmark and the election of Gustav Vasa as Sweden's first king took place soon after Luther's act of defiance against Catholic Rome. Lutheranism became the fighting faith of the new dynasty, strengthening everywhere the power of the king by preaching the virtues of unconditional obedience. An army of free but disciplined peasants supplied by the best iron industry in Europe became the king's instrument to complete the unification of the Swedish core area.

The original Polish lands, watered by the Oder and the Vistula, had once been the westernmost margin of the Slavic advance, at the junction with the Germanic lands. To thwart the threat of the Germans' eastward drive, the Poles adopted Latin Christianity and became its easternmost fringe facing the Orthodox lands. Religious antagonism gave Polish Catholicism an exceptional militancy and helped the Poles develop a national consciousness strong enough to overcome certain structural weaknesses. Poland never had a true hydrographic center. Its unity was hampered by the tension between the north-south axis of its river network and the east-west corridors formed by its latitudinal geological and ecological zones. Poland remained a country kept together by its crusading spirit. By the mid-sixteenth century, a brilliant Jagiellon dynasty (1378–1572) had forged against the Germans, the Ottoman Turks, and the Russians a Polish core area in the east European plain between the Oder, the Niemen, and the Dniestr.

The Anatolian upland and the Taurus Mountains stood at the junction of the Turkish and Byzantine worlds, of Islam and Orthodox Christendom, of nomadic and sedentary civilizations. The Bosphorus and the Dardanelles—the intersection of trade routes between the Crimea and the Mediterranean, between the East, the Balkans, and Europe—was its natural hydrographic center. The Turks, of nomadic origin, who had gradually become sedentary during their westward advance from Central Asia, gained control of the Straits after the conquest of Constantinople (Istanbul) in 1453. Their Ottoman dynasty completed the unification of Anatolia in the 1520s and took Baghdad, the capital of Islam's Caliphate, in 1534. Their religious ideology was Sunni Orthodoxy, their political system an autocracy supported by a slave army of converted Christians from the Balkans and Georgia and a crusading clergy.

The Persian core area, like the Polish, possessed no hydrographic center: much of Persia is a desert. Its capital changed many times, until the choice fell on Isfahan (Esfahan) in the sixteenth century. It owed its identity as a core area to the distinctive ethnic self-consciousness of its people hemmed in between the Arab and the Turkic world, ensconced in the coastal plain between the Caspian Sea and the Elburz Mountains, scattered in the valleys of the Zagros Mountains and the upland of Khorasan. This self-consciousness was reinforced by the adoption of Shi'ism, a minority confession of Islam with which Sunni Orthodoxy remained almost permanently at war. Its own structural weaknesses explain the constant factional strife and tribal separatism. Nevertheless, the Safavid dynasty, founded in 1502, was an autocracy supported by a tribal nobility, an intolerant clergy, and an army of converted slaves.

Core areas with their relatively well-defined territorial base, characteristic political and social systems, and military ideology are separated by frontiers. A boundary refers to a line, but a frontier is a succession of zones, a "historical structure of zones which varies from time to time."[5] Zones are of various kinds. Some are physical and ecological, others economic and cultural. They support human communities with different patterns of settlement, different ethnic structures and social organizations, different religious beliefs. Zones, like core areas, do not have clear boundaries, have no "edge, but shade off into a margin of uncertainty."[6] Mountains, rivers, mixed soils, and vegetation act like filters that separate but also foster penetration and exchange. Marginal zones may in rare cases become core areas, but their essential characteristic is that they do not possess the necessary combination of hydrographic network, sturdy political organization, social discipline, ideological conformity and fiscal resources to become core areas. Therefore, they are destined to remain the playground for the ambitions of rival core areas propelled by their inner dynamism to incorporate them into the core area's empire.

The frontier being a succession of zones at various distances from two core areas, each core area borders on a proximate zone, followed by intermediate zones, and its ultimate zone is also the opposite core area's proximate zone. Proximate zones determine the vital interests of a core area, and intermediate zones help maintain a balance between conflicting ambitions, until a core area's advance into the frontier leaves a single zone, the last defense of the rival core area's territorial integrity. The advance creates two frontiers: the zones incorporated into the core area's empire constitute an inner frontier, the others become an outer frontier. It also raises the question of a limit of "an optimum of conquest" beyond which empire-building becomes counterproductive, when the inner frontier becomes a factor of dissension instead of consolidation.

A core area in the process of empire-building needs to define its policy toward the frontier zones. Its policy toward the inner frontier is an internal matter—whether to assimilate or to institute various degrees of autonomy. Toward the outer frontier zones it has a choice between a close-border policy and a forward policy.

The term *close-border policy* was coined by the British on their Northwest Frontier separating Afghanistan from present-day Pakistan.[7] The term is not quite appropriate, because a border, or a boundary, can never close hermetically. A close-border policy drew a "red line" on the map across passes and hills, beyond which military parties were forbidden to go even in hot pursuit. On the other hand, the line did not keep the hill men from crossing into British-held territory to plunder and kill. It established only an artificial boundary separating related human communities. The policy was one of exclusion, separating an indigenous society from the intrusive society of the white man; it assumed the recognition of a line of an optimum of conquest, a perimeter beyond which expansion was neither feasible nor profitable, and reflected a willingness to stop the expenditure of energy that had made possible the creation of the core area and its transformation into an emerging empire. Two historical examples come to mind—the Roman Empire and its *limes* along the Rhine and the Danube from the North Sea to the Black Sea; and Tokugawa Japan and its policy of exclusion for 250 years. But a close-border policy was ill adapted to the needs of an expanding core area because "the limits of an empire created by the ruthless assertion of an active principle could not be safely defined by resting passively on the line of a negative, defensive, containing Frontier."[8] The Roman Empire that built the *limes* had reached its largest territorial extent. Japan was an island, and its policy of exclusion was a recognition of internal weakness.

A fortress-fleet strategy[9] at sea is the equivalent of a close-border policy on land. It assumes that the purpose of a fleet, with its supply depots and berthing installations, is not to project power beyond the proximate zone of the empire but to guard an invisible "red line" against intrusions by foreign ships. It seeks not so much to gain possession of straits to the wide oceans as to prevent entry by foreign ships in order eventually to transform the proximate maritime zone into an inner frontier zone of the empire.

By contrast, a forward policy denies the existence of a linear boundary except for purely administrative purposes, and actively intervenes in the frontier zones. The purpose of the intervention is to give the core area's dynamism an expanding field of action as well as to neutralize any actual or potential threat from communities with different ways of life and uncertain allegiance, often manipulated by the no less dynamic ambitions of the opposite core area.

This policy takes various forms. It establishes friendly relations with the "men of power"[10] in the proximate and even intermediate zones, instead of ignoring them and as a result remaining in the dark about their intentions and capabilities. It seeks to gain the right to mediate their disputes, thereby establishing influence in their tribal councils; to turn the tribal leaders outward; to redirect their energies away from raids into the core area; to give them a stake in transforming the zone they occupy into an outer defensive zone of the core area. And, in the last resort, it sends punitive expeditions to impress tribal leaders with the might of the core area government.

A forward policy is most effective when a core area is expanding, because the frontier, by its very nature a battleground between core areas, retains unity in all its diversity. Such a policy makes use of that diversity and interdependence to destabilize the entire frontier and pave the way for the incorporation of one frontier zone after another into the expanding empire. It is thus a policy of inclusion: fostering social interaction and the integration of local elites into the ruling elite of the core area; subverting the independence of the frontier zones in the name of political conservatism. The process of annexation is gradual. A frontier zone becomes a sphere of influence, shading into a protectorate when the ruling elite loses the ability to control its destiny and then becomes a satellite or a colony. The zone is then ready for incorporation into the inner frontier of the empire. The process is repeated in the next zone, each intermediate zone of the outer frontier becoming in turn a proximate zone before passing into the inner frontier.

A forward policy has a counterpart in the fleet-in-being strategy. Such a strategy concentrates naval forces in a maritime proximate zone in order to seize the straits—the "passes" in the landman's language—leading to the high seas. The straits are channels through which the core area projects power across great distances, protects its merchant marine, and in the event of war, sinks enemy warships on the high seas. It is an offensive strategy in which the sea is a dynamic and boundless frontier. However, as in all human affairs, these two policies are not mutually exclusive. They merely provide broad alternatives to guide policymakers as they direct their core area's advance into the frontier.

Russia and Its Three Frontiers

This brief outline shows that a frontier separated Russia from each of the four core areas. These four frontiers can conveniently be reduced to two—a Western and a Southern Frontier. A third, or Eastern, Frontier separated Russia from the Chinese core area. China belonged not to the Heartland but to the Monsoon Coastland, and must be considered among the containing powers, but its long continental boundary with the nomadic world, symbolized by the Great Wall, made it Russia's natural rival for the control of an immense frontier stretching from the Kazakh steppe to Manchuria.

By 1600, Poland was at the height of its power and Sweden was about to reach it. The catalyst of Polish and Swedish expansion in the eastern Baltic had been the weakening of the Teutonic Order, whose jurisdiction had once stretched from Brandenburg to the Gulf of Finland. Poland crushed the Order in 1410 and again in 1466, when it received easternmost Pomerania (Pomerelia), west of the Vistula, and the territory of Kulm (Chełmo), east of it. The grand master of the Order became the vassal of the Polish king. Estland passed under Swedish overlordship in 1546, and in 1561 a master of the Order in Mitava (Jelgava) broke away to become a vassal of Poland and received his domain, Kurland, back as a fief from the king. That same year, the remainder of Livonia—Livland—was incorporated into the Polish Empire[11] as another fief of the Polish crown. Eight years later, in 1569, Poland annexed three more zones,

Volhynia, Podolia, and the left bank of the Dniepr, into the Polish kingdom (*Korona*), and the Grand Duchy of Lithuania was associated with
the kingdom in a single and indivisible empire. Sweden was likewise
expanding eastward. Finland, including Karelia, was proclaimed a grand
duchy of the emerging Swedish Empire in 1581, thereby transforming
the Gulf of Bothnia and the Gulf of Finland into a Swedish waterway.
Only a part of Ingria remained under Moscow's jurisdiction.

Such was the situation in 1600. The Russian civil war that followed the
death of Boris Godunov in 1605 precipitated a Swedish and Polish intervention. The Swedes occupied Ingria and took Novgorod, but abandoned the city when they made peace with Russia at Stolbovo in 1617. At
that time, the Swedish high command drew a line of an optimum of conquest running from Gdov on Lake Peipus (Chud) to Lake Ladoga, bringing the entire Neva into the Swedish domain and cutting off Russia from
the Gulf of Finland. As a result, the entire Russo-Swedish frontier was
incorporated into the Swedish Empire. Sweden reached the height of its
power during the reign of Gustav Adolf (1611–1632). The Protestant
king made war on the Catholic king of Poland to settle once and for all
the latter's claim to the Swedish crown (the two crowns had been united
between 1587 and 1599) and annexed Livonia with Riga in 1621.

Meanwhile, the Poles had invaded the Russian core area itself and
occupied Moscow in 1610. The son of the Polish king was elected tsar,
raising the possibility of a future union of the two crowns. But a
national movement forced the Poles to withdraw and elected Mikhail
Romanov, the first tsar of a new dynasty, in 1613. Peace was made in
1618, the Poles retaining Smolensk. From then on, however, the
energy accumulated during the formation of the core area and further
stimulated by the national revival would generate an expansionist
impulse directed for the most part against the Polish Empire. The Russians would fight the Poles zone by zone in their common frontier
until the final destruction of the Polish Empire in 1795.

The Russian advance into the frontier began with the Cossack revolt on
the left bank of the Dniepr. The zone was one of transition between the
more settled population of the right bank, the Zaporozhian Cossacks, and
the nomadic Tatars of the Crimea. Religious and social enmity kept Poles
and Cossacks apart, and the Orthodox Cossacks were not above forming
ephemeral alliances with the infidel Tatars against their Catholic overlords.
The revolt broke out in 1648 and was not crushed until 1651. Its leadership
then turned to Moscow. Moscow imposed a protectorate on the left bank
and forced the Poles to withdraw behind the Dniepr in 1654.

Moscow built on its first victory by challenging Poland in Bielorussia.
The Thirteen Years War (1654–1667) was joined by the Swedes, who
penetrated deep into Poland but were forced to negotiate by the success of
their other enemies, including Russia, and the death of their king, whose
heir was a boy of 4. The peace of Oliva (Oliwa) near Danzig (Gdansk)
partitioned Livonia, the Poles obtaining so-called Polish Livonia, the

southeastern corner of Livonia with Dünaburg (Dvinsk-Daugavpils) and Drissa on the Dvina. The Swedes made peace with Russia at Kardis (between Reval and Derpt-Tartu) in 1661, confirming the settlement of Stolbovo. The Poles, however, remained at war with Russia until 1667, when the "truce" of Andrusovo near Smolensk showed Poland's inability to resist the Russian advance. Moscow was forced to relinquish Vitebsk and Polotsk—the chief cities of Bielorussia on the Dvina—and Polish Livonia, but gained Smolensk and a broad swath of land from the source of the Dvina to the Desna. Poland had to recognize the loss of the Left Bank. Kiev and its triangular lowland on the right bank formed by the Dniepr, the Teterev, and the Ros was ceded to Russia for two years, but was never returned. The Thirteen Years War had brought about the first partition of the Polish Empire.

The Southern Frontier combined two frontiers, the Russo-Turkish and the Russo-Persian. The formation of the Turkish core area reached completion in the 1360s, when the corps of janissaries was created, and Sultan Murad IV made Adrianople his capital. The Ottomans captured Sofia in 1382 and imposed their will on the entire Balkan peninsula after the great battle of Kosovo in 1389. Bulgaria was divided into *sanjaks* (provinces) under a governor general in Sofia. Wallachia became a tributary of the Porte in 1391. The capital was moved from Tirgoviste to Bucharest in 1698. Moldavia, centered in Jassy (Iasi), fought over by the Ottomans and the Poles, began to pay tribute in 1513. Both principalities retained their institutions, headed by a *hospodar* (governor) elected by a council of *boyars* (landowners) and confirmed by the Ottoman government. The Crimean khanate had recognized Turkish suzerainty in 1478, and its khan became the instrument of a forward policy designed to destabilize the Russian core area and keep the entire frontier between the Central Upland and the Black Sea in permanent turmoil. East of the Black Sea, most of Armenia and western Georgia fell under Ottoman control—but also retained their native institutions—during the first half of the sixteenth century. By 1600, the Ottomans dominated the entire Russo-Turkish frontier.

The same expenditure of energy that propelled the Russian advance into the Western Frontier was directed against the Ottomans in the seventeenth century, but the Ottoman Empire was still much stronger than the Polish, and distances and the climate maintained insuperable logistical obstacles. Moscow tightened its control of the Cossack zone between the Dniepr and the Volga. The Don Cossacks were placed under the jurisdiction of the *prikaz* of Foreign Affairs in 1623, and the ancestors of the Slobodskie Cossacks under the *voevoda* (governors) of Chuguev in the 1630s. These cossacks became Moscow's first line of defense against the Crimean Tatars, and the establishment of a protectorate over the hetmanate on the left bank in the 1650s completed the incorporation of the Cossack zone into Russia's defensive and offensive perimeter. Joined by their cousins from the lower Dniepr (Zaporozhians), these "frontier men"—similar to the *Grenzleute* of the Austrian Military Frontier in Croatia-Slavonia—

were turned outward to carry Moscow's fight into the intermediate frontier zones. The Ottomans retaliated by tightening their control of the Crimean khan. The khanate, protected by the waterless and treeless steppe, remained inaccessible to Russian power, and the two expeditions of 1687 and 1689 ended in failure.

Georgia and Armenia formed a zone where the Russo-Turkish, Russo-Persian, and Turco-Persian frontiers overlapped. Eastern Georgia—Kartlia and Kakhetia with Tiflis (Tbilisi) as its capital—the Armenian upland punctured by Lake Sevan, and the Mugan depression, watered by the Kura and the Araks, all belonged to the valley of the Caspian. The Caspian was a Persian sea until the development of Astrakhan as a Russian naval base in the eighteenth century. It was also Persia's proximate zone. East of the Caspian, the Turkmen tribal lands, in and around the Karakum Desert between the Ustyurt upland, the Kopet Dag, the Amu Darya, and the foothills of the Hindu Kush, formed an additional zone. A third was the territory between the Amu and Syr Daryas with the Kyzylkum Desert, the home of the Khiva, Bukhara, and Kokand khanates, facing the Tien Shan Mountains. At its eastern end, the Russo-Persian frontier interlocked with the Indo-Persian and the Indo-Russian frontier, making Afghanistan, like Georgia and Armenia, one of the most strategically sensitive areas on the periphery of the Heartland. Such areas are sometimes called by geopolitical writers "forward points of growth" (*Wachstumspitzen*) or "proruptions,"[12] because they enable the power that controls them to expand into two or more contiguous frontiers, thereby maximizing its strategic possibilities. In the Southern Frontier, they offered Russia an opportunity to break through the Heartland's boundary into the Coastland areas.

While the Ottomans were building an empire around the Black Sea, Persia fell under the rule of Timur (Tamerlane), who had established his power base in Samarkand, in the third frontier zone. His death in 1405 was followed by nearly a century of internecine wars during which three power centers developed in Persia—Tabriz, Fars, and Herat. Nonetheless, the devastation paved the way for a revival focused on Ardabil, a center of Shi'ism, east of Tabriz, where the Safavid dynasty was born in 1502, when Ismail I took the title of shah. Persia and the Turkmen zone were soon united under his rule, but the khanates between the Amu and Syr Darya that had long been under Persia's cultural influence remained under their Uzbek rulers of Turco-Mongol stock and Sunni faith. The Ottomans saw a threat to their hegemony in the rise of a Shi'ite dynasty, conquered Azerbaijan, and annexed Eastern Georgia. Their empire reached its apogee under Suleiman the Magnificent, the son-in-law of a Russian priest, and the peace of 1555 confirmed the annexation of Georgia, Azerbaijan, and Armenia, including Erzerum, a strategic point on the caravan route from Trebizond (Trabzon) to Tabriz.

Persian fortunes revived under Shah Abbas (1587–1629). With an army manned, like the Ottoman janissaries, with enslaved Christians from Georgia and Armenia, he defeated the Ottomans near Lake Urmia (Orumiyeh), west of Tabriz, in 1606, and rolled them back beyond Erivan and Kars. The peace of 1639 restored Eastern Georgia, most of Armenia, and Azerbaijan to the Persian Empire. The remainder of the seventeenth century was taken up with the struggle over Kandahar, south of the Hindu Kush. Northern India was then under the rule of the Mughal dynasty, whose greatest emperor, Akbar (1556–1605), was a contemporary of Shah Abbas. Both the Safavid and the Mughal rulers sought the allegiance of the Afghan tribes and were rivals for the control of the passes into northern India. Persia was finally able to reach a modus vivendi with a Ghilzai chief, Mir Vais, who remained virtually independent until his death in 1715.

Russia's relations with Persia remained distant until the eighteenth century. The English had once sought a passage to India across Muscovy and Persia but the hazards were too great. It was rumored that when the shah learned that the Russian treasury was empty in 1613, he had loaned 7000 rubles to Tsar Mikhail. By 1670, there was a colony of Persian merchants in Moscow, and Astrakhan had long been the entrepôt of Persian trade. Russian traders had their own warehouses in Shemakha. Russo-Persian relations were not yet dominated by strategic considerations; they remained commercial and peaceful.

The Eastern, or Russo-Chinese, Frontier consisted of three segments. The Turkestan segment began along the Ural River, rose gently toward the Kazakh upland, rested along the Mongolian Altai, and curled around the Taklimakan Desert to the Pamirs, on the Heartland's periphery. Its southern boundary was the Ustyurt upland and the Syr Darya; in the north it went as far as the Tobol and Irtysh rivers, in the Great Lowland of Siberia. The Mongolian segment stretched from Zungharia to the Great Khingan, divided by the Gobi Desert that prolongs the Mongolian Altai between a northern upland well watered by the Selenga and its tributaries and a southern dry steppe. The Pacific segment included the valleys of the Amur and the Liao. Each segment contained a highway into China: along the Silk Road via Bukhara, Samarkand, Kokand, Osh, Kashgar (Kashi), and Lanchow (Landzhou); the valley of the Selenga and the caravan route via Urga (Ulan Bator) to Peking, crossing the Great Wall at Kalgan (Zhangjiaokou); along the Ingoda and the Shilka and the upper Amur, from which a first portage took the travelers to the Nonni (Nen) and the Sungari and a second to the Liao and on to Shankaikuan (Shanhaiguan), the eastern end of the Great Wall.

The sixteenth century witnessed the rise of the Swedish, Polish, Ottoman, and Persian empires; it was a century of decline for the Ming dynasty (1368–1644). The dynasty had been unable to conquer the Manchus, the Mongols, and the Uighurs, but they all recognized Chinese overlordship. Envoys from frontier tribes brought tribute to Peking and kowtowed before the emperor to express their group allegiance to a dynasty that believed it ruled not only China but the entire known world. Nevertheless, the frontier remained a permanent source of insecurity, and the periodic weakening of the Chinese core area emboldened tribal warriors to form hostile confederations among themselves and even to strike at China itself. The Western Mongols were the most restless, but, as the hold of the Ming on their frontier weakened in the second half of the sixteenth century, a dangerous enemy arose in Manchuria, where an ambitious ruler proclaimed a new dynasty in 1616.

That same year, the Russians, who had overthrown the rule of various Mongol khans since the "conquest" of Siberia by Ermak in 1581, sent their first embassy to the leader (Altyn Khan) of the Western Mongols, whose capital was at the time near the upper reaches of the Enisei, on the periphery of the Heartland. Tomsk, well within it on a tributary of the Ob, became the center of the Russo-Mongol-Chinese trade. Twenty years later, in 1636, the opening in Mukden (Shenyang), the Manchu headquarters, of formal relations with the Eastern Mongols went a long way to transform the ethnic zones of the frontier into a succession of political territories over which the Manchus, who took Peking and proclaimed their dynasty (1644–1911) the successor of the Ming, would have to fight the Russians from the Irtysh to the Pacific.

The Manchus faced two dangers in their steppe frontier—the rise of the Zunghars and the expansion of the Russians. The Zunghars were seeking in the seventeenth century to transform a loose confederation of Western Mongol tribes, among which they were the most powerful, into a steppe empire between the Sayan Mountains and Lake Koko Nor (Qinghai Hu). They found a dynamic and capable leader in Galdan (r. 1671–1697), who established himself in Kashgaria in the 1670s where he could collect substantial revenue from the overland trade on the Silk Road. He then moved against the Eastern Mongols in 1688, at the very time a Russian embassy was about to begin negotiations with the Manchus.

Meanwhile, the Russians had been expanding toward the Pacific. They founded Irkutsk on Lake Baikal and Albazin on the Amur in 1651. Five years later, they established a base at Nerchinsk, near the confluence of the Nercha with the Ingoda, where the lead and silver mines had already attracted the Manchus. The appointment of a *voevoda* was an event of capital importance, because Nerchinsk soon became the headquarters of the Russian presence east of Lake Baikal, beyond the Heartland, in the basin of the Pacific. The Russians were beginning to lay claim to the first zone of the Manchurian frontier. The prize was the Amur River. The Manchus, who had achieved a temporary victory over Galdan in 1681, returned in force and seized Albazin in 1685. Their determination had already induced the Russians to seek a settlement. That same year, Moscow appointed Fedor Golovin minister plenipotentiary to meet the Manchus in Selenginsk. He arrived there in October 1687. It was symbolic that the town stood on the very periphery of the Heartland.

Containment

Russian expansion naturally provoked resistance. The exercise of power over any length of time is certain to bring about the emergence of a countervailing power in an endless contest of wills that is the essence of life itself. Containment takes various forms. It may be imposed by an insuperable physical obstacle. The Kunlun Mountains, the desolate highlands of Tibet, and the Himalayas beyond them would have blocked Russian expansion toward Lhasa and India even if the Russians had succeeded in establishing themselves in Kashgaria. Containment is also the expression of a certain balance of forces at any given time, as long as opposite core areas are capable of defending their position in their respective frontiers. If Russian foreign policy during the Imperial period is understood as the steady and consistent application of power to dislodge the Swedes, the Poles, the Turks, the Persians, and the Chinese from the frontier zones, the story of containment is the story of the efforts by these five core areas to slow down Russia's attempts to profit from the shift of a certain balance of power in the Heartland that was nevertheless inexorably turning against them. By their very presence and the existence of extensive commitments in the frontier zones, they kept checking the Russian advance. They attempted domestic reforms to modernize their society and institutions, but their inadequate resources and conservative reluctance to face the consequences of modernization—because reforms threatened to destroy the political order in which they had a vital interest—placed them at an increasingly dangerous disadvantage vis-à-vis their giant rival.

Containment need not be only a policy of resisting the advance of a dynamic power; Russia encountered much more than the resistance of declining powers. Containment is also a dynamic policy to commit superior resources to redress a shifting balance within the frontier zones and secure a new equilibrium within the Heartland as a whole. One detects a certain resemblance between this type of containment and both a close-border and a forward policy. Containment drew a "red line" along the Heartland's periphery and by the application of naval power backed by superior resources blocked the exits through the straits and access to the global economy of the maritime powers. It also intervened within the Heartland to strengthen the resources of the declining core areas and even claimed that their integrity had become a vital interest.

Six core areas were able in the eighteenth and nineteenth centuries to pursue such a dynamic policy. Two, Prussia-Germany and Austria, were continental powers within the Heartland, guarding its approaches from the east. Prussia began as the northern margin ("march") of the Holy Roman Empire, on the left bank of the Elbe, facing the eastern Slavs across the Heartland's boundary. Its early mission was to settle the lands beyond the Elbe and christianize their inhabitants. Expansion to the Oder created a "middle march," and beyond, a "new march." The three marches were later joined to form the margraviate of Brandenburg. Eastward expansion gave Brandenburg a strategic position straddling the Elbe and the Oder, a center of hydrographic divergence toward the Baltic and landward toward Bohemia and Moravia. Nevertheless, Brandenburg remained a bleak marchland of sandy soils and pine forests without natural borders in the east and inevitably drawn eastward by the logic of its initial expansion. It developed an extensive agriculture manned by cheap labor under the tight supervision of an entrepreneurial nobility of Junkers, the social backbone of the country.

The disintegration of the Teutonic Order after 1561 made the duchy of East Prussia (its capital was Königsberg) a prime attraction for Brandenburg. The marriage of the Elector with the daughter of the last duke in 1594 brought with it the annexation of the country following the duke's death in 1618. The Thirty Years War (1618–1646) left the new country at the mercy of Sweden. The Elector's Protestantism served him well, however, and placed him on the winning side. The Treaty of Westphalia (1648) gave him eastern Pomerania (*Hinterpommern*), but western Pomerania (*Vorpommern*), west of the Oder with the strategic fortress of Stettin (Szczecin), went to Sweden. The eastern end of Pomerania (Pomerelia) to the Vistula remained in Poland. By annexing East Prussia and gaining access to the sea, Brandenburg-Prussia became the enemy of Poland and Sweden, but a potential ally and enemy of Russia. In return for military support against France in the War of the Spanish Succession (1701–1714), the Holy Roman Emperor allowed the Elector to be crowned king in January 1701.

The historic core of Austria—the "eastern march"—was the valley of the Danube between the Enns and the Morava, abutting from the east the Heartland's boundary. Its mission was to convert the southern Slavs to Latin Christianity, to contain the Magyars within the plain of Hungary, and eventually to become the shield of Christendom against Ottoman expansion. Its Habsburg dynasty combined until 1806 the crown of the Holy Roman Empire with that of Austria proper. The dual title created often incompatible responsibilities, a strategic dilemma. The structural alignment of the Danube valley is from west to east, and the location of the Austrian lands within the Heartland gave Austria an eastern destiny. But the emperor was also king of the Germans with responsibilities stretching from Pomerania to the Netherlands, from the Baltic to the Alps. These responsibilities became the source of a bitter conflict with the Hohenzollern kings of Brandenburg-Prussia.

Momentous events drew Austria eastward during the sixteenth and seventeenth centuries. The Ottomans defeated the Hungarians at the battle of Mohacs on the Danube in 1526, and appeared before Vienna in 1529. Forced to lift the siege, they retreated, leaving behind a truncated kingdom of Hungary bordering on Turkish Hungary and the Ottoman possessions in the Balkans. Their retreat set the Austrian agenda in the east—rolling back the Turkish menace to southern Germany. But the champion of Islam proved to be a stubborn enemy, and it was not until the Ottoman defeat before Vienna in 1683 that Austria gained the upper hand. Leopold I (1658–1705) created a Danubian monarchy by conquering the Hungarian plain and imposing the Habsburgs as kings of Hungary. At the Peace of Karlowitz (Sremski Karlovci) of 1699, the Porte accepted the loss of Turkish Hungary—with the exception of the *banat* (border province) of Temesvàr (Timişoara)—of Transylvania to the arc of the Carpathian Mountains, of Slavonia and Croatia to the Adriatic. The gains transformed Austria into a potential ally and enemy of Russia—ally against the Ottomans in a great continental Christian crusade to expel them from Europe; enemy in the lower Danube beyond the Carpathians, where the ultimate zones of the Russo-Turkish, Austro-Turkish, and Austro-Russian frontier interlocked.

In Mackinder's geopolitical vision, the Heartland was flanked by the European Coastland in the west and the Monsoon Coastland in the east, separated by "Arabia"[13]—Egypt, the Arabian Peninsula, and Mesopotamia. The two coastlands had much in common. Their climates ranged from temperate to warm and humid; their rich soils supported much higher population densities than anywhere in the Heartland. They were regions of intensive agriculture and profitable trade on the edge of vast oceanic basins. All the major rivers of the European Coastland except the Rhone flowed north and west toward the Atlantic; the Indus and the Ganges drew the whole of northern India toward the Indian Ocean; the Yangtse and the Yellow River linked the foothills of the Himalayas with the Pacific. They were all navigable, often on the greater part of their course, and drew the highlands everywhere outward toward the sea.

Rivers and seas generated faster, more reliable, and more profitable exchanges, and the two coastlands discovered at the dawn of the modern age that their products were complementary—spices and "colonial" goods were exchanged for textiles and other manufactures. "Arabia" was the land bridge between them, an easy portage between the Mediterranean and the Indian Ocean. The Red Sea began a step away from the Mediterranean; the Persian Gulf extended the Indian Ocean deep inland, and its channel merged with the valley of the Euphrates from which goods were transshipped to the Mediterranean coast. The Arabs, with their base in "Arabia," went west and east, and Islam linked Gibraltar with the mouth of the Indus. In 1690, Britain laid the foundations of Calcutta in the estuary of the Ganges. From there, it went on to impose its dominion over its predecessors, Portugal and Holland. The powers of the European Coastland had been forging a permanent chain of maritime links with the Monsoon Coastland while the Russians were crossing the Heartland in the direction of the Pacific. All the elements of the future rivalry between Heartland and Coastland were in place by 1700.

France and England were the two powers of the European Coastland capable of containing Russian expansion. France arose on the margin of the Roman and Germanic world, between the Rhine and the Atlantic. Its core area developed around the Ile de France in the valley of the Seine and within easy reach of the Loire and Rhone valleys. Its monarchy was formed in the crucible of the Hundred Years War (1337–1453), fought with England for the control of the mouths of the Seine, Loire, and Garonne and for their hinterlands. The long and victorious war with England and the wars of religion 100 years later (1562–1598) released an immense amount of energy that went into the consolidation of the monarchy and expansion toward "natural boundaries"—the Pyrennes, the Rhine, and the Alps—and intervention elsewhere in the Coastland. France reached the apogee of its power during the reign of Louis XIV (1643–1715).

The logic of its initial expansion after 1453 eventually gave priority to expansion toward the periphery of the Heartland. Its goal was to break the power of the Habsburgs of Spain and Austria. The settlement of 1556 terminated the compact uniting the two branches and made Spain, and later, after 1659, Austria, the chief enemy of France. Their enmity would determine the course of continental politics for a century. The Peace of Westphalia forged a natural alliance between France, Sweden, and Prussia against Austria. It also completed the French network of alliances that began with the Franco-Polish alliance of 1524 and the Franco-Ottoman alliance of 1535, six years after the first appearance of the Turks before Vienna. However, the policy of encircling—containing—Austria had the effect of making France Russia's natural enemy, since France's friends were Russia's enemies. On the other hand, in the event of a radical shift in the balance of power in the Germanic world, the very fact that Russia and France were "flanking powers"[14] also made them natural allies.

Conquered by Rome to eliminate the risk that a sea power might rise off the Gallic coast, England was a plain, bounded in the north and west by mountainous terrain separating it from Wales and Scotland. Its center of hydrographic divergence was the Thames River, facing the continent. The withdrawal of Roman power was followed by waves of invasion, until William the Conqueror, a vassal of the French king in Normandy, established a powerful monarchy. His successors of the House of Plantagenet turned back into the France of their origin by uniting under their leadership the lower basins of the Seine, Loire, and Garonne, setting off an inevitable conflict with the Valois dynasty of France.

The expulsion of England from the continent in 1453 had two major consequences. It compelled England to focus on internal construction, constitutional and social. The Reformation created a militant Anglican Church and a no less militant Puritanism. England and Wales were united in 1536, and the accession of the Stuart House in 1603 united the crowns of England and Scotland. It was not until the Glorious Revolution of 1688 that major domestic issues received a satisfactory settlement; only then could the English core area turn to the task of empire-building, in a second and no less bitter conflict with France for hegemony in the European Coastland.

The creation of a core area in nearly complete isolation from international politics also compelled England to see itself as a sea power with strategic interests of a primarily commercial nature. The Hundred Years War had taught the decisive importance of holding straits and the mouths of rivers, and much later, in the nineteenth century, it would become an axiom of British policy that the Sound, the Strait of Gibraltar, and the Turkish Straits, together with Flanders and Denmark, either must be under British control or must remain in friendly hands. The lure of the eastern trade took British traders to Russia beginning in 1533, in a never very successful attempt to reach Persia, Central Asia, and China overland. The British, who looked to Russia as another colonial country, received exclusive privileges for their merchants, and sought to achieve a monopoly of the Russian trade with the European Coastland while refusing every Russian request for an alliance against the Swedes, the Poles, and the Turks. This refusal, together with the execution of Charles I, brought that trade to an end in 1649 for fifteen years. Meanwhile, the British mercantile establishment had been directing its energy and resources to the development of the Cape route to India. The East India Company was founded in 1600, and British traders won a favored position at the Mughal Court. By 1700, Anglo-Russian relations remained distant but Bombay and Calcutta were becoming flourishing commercial outposts, leading British power toward the Persian Gulf and the China Sea.

China was the dominant power in the Monsoon Coastland. It was the most permanent core area in the world, with the longest continuous history. Its hydrographic network of three main rivers flowing into the China Sea; its intensive agriculture of irrigated fields, setting it off sharply from the highlands and deserts surrounding it in the west; its distinctive society of walled cities, sedentary farmers, and ruling class of landowners and officials; its distinctive civilization of rigid Confucian precepts mitigated by the gentler teachings of Buddhism and Taoism—all these factors combined to form a core area of exceptional strength.

But there is no great strength without great weaknesses. Despite its extensive coastline and geographic eastward orientation, China followed a maritime destiny only on a number of isolated occasions. The existence of powerful nomadic confederations along its western and northern borders forced China to look landward and fostered a defensive mentality; the Great Wall was the perfect embodiment of a close-border policy. An overwhelming political and social conservatism contained the seeds of its own destruction, and nomadic pressures accelerated a recurrent process of internal decay. Thus, Chinese history was characterized by imperial expansion—until a balance of power was reached with the "northern barbarians"—and by contraction under the combined effect of nomadic pressure and internal loss of energy—completed, on occasions, when the nomads conquered the core area itself. In the history of Russo-Chinese relations, a triumphant Manchu China played the role of containing power from the last quarter of the seventeenth century to the 1840s, when the arrival of the "western barbarians" from the European Coastland destabilized the core area and facilitated a Russian advance into the Chinese Empire.

Japan's case was truly unique. Like Britain at the other end of the Heartland, it was a maritime core area. It developed at the margin of the Chinese world from which it derived its Confucianism and Buddhism and even its written language. During the Ashikaga shogunate (1338–1573), based in Kyoto, it developed its own indigenous military culture, its own religious beliefs centered on Zen Buddhism and Shintoism, its own feudal landowning structure. It possessed its own center of hydrographic convergence—the Inland Sea and the Tsushima Strait linking it with Korea and the mainland. The emergence of the Tokugawas was a marginal development within a marginal development—the Kanto plain was a distant and swampy land in the late sixteenth century—but the foundations of modern Japan were laid there during the Tokugawa shogunate (1603–1867). Japan's experience was unique because it involved a suspension, one might even say a mutilation, of the expansionist impulse after 1636, when the shoguns closed Japanese ports and forbade contact with foreigners. Russia and Japan knew each other from a distance, but there could be no Russo-Japanese frontier until the Russians appeared in force on the shores of the Pacific.

The geopolitical context of Russian foreign policy during the two centuries under consideration (1700–1917) should now be clear. "The domain of geopolitics," it has been said, "is concerned with conflict and change, evolution and revolution, attack and defense, the dynamics of the territorial spaces and of the political forces struggling on them for survival."[15] Its goal is the establishment by a space-conscious ruling elite of political objectives within definite spatial configurations and the determination of ways by which to reach these objectives. Geography created a permanent framework that channeled Russian expansion into well-defined drainage basins—the Baltic, the Black Sea, the Caspian and Aral internal seas, and the Pacific. But geography also contained Russia behind an extensive physical barrier difficult to reach and well nigh impossible to cross effectively. Spatial configurations conditioned if not altogether determined the direction and nature of Russian expansion and exposed its limits, so that boundaries advanced and retreated within static regional frameworks, giving Russian foreign policy great continuity in goals and methods. They also imposed on the Russian leadership a belief in autarky as the goal of economic policy. Space consciousness fostered centrifugal tendencies, but the permanence of insuperable physical obstacles created a centripetal drag that partly neutralized those tendencies, giving Russian expansion a slow but steady momentum.

The boundary of the Heartland, flanked by the Coastlands in east and west, ran along the Kjølen; the Elbe valley; a continuous chain of mountain folds running parallel to the Adriatic, Mediterranean, and Persian Gulf; one great desert; and more mountains blocking access to a barren sea. Its power center was the Russian core area, where tsars and ruling elite built during the sixteenth century a fortress stretching from the Dniepr and Dvina to Lake Baikal in a continuous and well-irrigated lowland. As the Russian core area gathered strength and accumulated energy after the debilitating experience of the Time of Troubles, it encountered the countervailing power of five core areas arranged in a semicircle from the Baltic to the Pacific. They had passed their prime, however, and four of them—Sweden, Poland, Turkey, and Persia—were entering a period of slow inner disintegration. Their decline was brought about by their inability to modernize their social, economic, and political institutions and military organization without losing their independence, while a combination of size, economic resources, military power, and disciplined organization kept giving Russia a decisive advantage. The resulting change in the balance of power stimulated Russian expansion and induced a steady retrenchment of the rival core areas. The battles were fought over the frontier zone separating the Russian from those rival core areas. The methods were everywhere remarkably similar and consistent—the destabilization of the frontier by exploiting local opposition; the incorporation of the elites of the zones into an Imperial ruling elite; and the destabilization of the core area itself. The logic of Russian expansion pointed toward the annexation of the core areas until the empire would become conterminous with the Heartland.

Such expansion, led by the global ambitions of a multinational Imperial elite against the background of a steady deterioration, beginning in the eighteenth century, of the balance of power within the Heartland, was bound to create both resistance and a countermovement to contain that expansion. The collapse of Sweden and Poland paved the way for the emergence of the Germanic powers' role as guardians blocking access to the western boundary of the Heartland. The Russian advance into the frontier zones of the Ottoman Empire and Persia reached its decisive stage when Britain became ready to fight to block the exits from the Heartland in the Southern Frontier. And the collapse of China was more than compensated by the emergence of Japanese power to block Russian access to the East China Sea. The complicated process by which Imperial Russia expanded at the expense of some core areas and was contained by others after 1700 is the story of this book.

I

RUSSIA AND ITS WESTERN FRONTIER

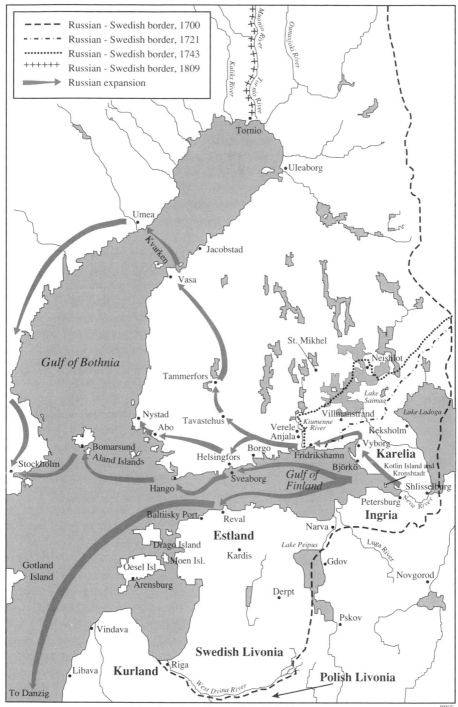

Legend:
- – – – Russian - Swedish border, 1700
- – · – · Russian - Swedish border, 1721
- ········ Russian - Swedish border, 1743
- ++++++ Russian - Swedish border, 1809
- ➤ Russian expansion

Muonio River
Ounasjoki River
Kaliks River
Tornio River

Tornio

Uleaborg

Umea

Kvarken

Jacobstad

Vasa

Gulf of Bothnia

St. Mikhel

Neishlot

Lake Saimaa

Lake Ladoga

Tammerfors

Villmanstrand

Nystad
Abo

Tavastehus

Verele
Anjala

Kiumenne River

Keksholm

Vyborg

Karelia

Bomarsund
Aland Islands

Borgo

Fridrikshamn

Björkö

Stockholm

Helsingfors

Sveaborg

Gulf of Finland

Kotlin Island and Kronshtadt

Hango

Shlisselburg

Petersburg

Neva River

Baltiisky Port

Reval

Narva

Ingria

Gotland Island

Drago Island
Moen Isl.

Kardis

Lake Peipus

Gdov

Luga River

Novgorod

Oesel Isl.

Estland

Arensburg

Derpt

Pskov

Vindava

Swedish Livonia

Libava

Riga

Kurland

West Dvina River

Polish Livonia

To Danzig

Map 2.   The Russo-Swedish Frontier

PIKE

22

1

The Destabilization of the Core Areas, 1700–1768

The First Round, 1700–1721

The major thrust of Russian foreign policy after the truce of Andrusovo (1667) was directed against the Southern Frontier, for the acquisition of Kiev strengthened a logic of expansion along the Dniepr in the direction of the Black Sea. The failure of the Turks before Vienna in 1683 seemed to show that the time had come to roll them back from their Balkan and Black Sea frontiers. The result was a "natural" Austro-Russian alliance in which Russia's goal would be the conquest of the Crimea and Azov, the Ottomans' strongest outposts in the Black and Azov seas. The Russians failed in the Crimea. They took Azov in July 1696, but Azov was worthless without Kerch that controlled the exit to the Black Sea. One of the purposes of Peter I's grand tour of Europe (March 1697–September 1698) was to gain the support of the Coastland powers against the Ottomans, a hopeless task since France was strong in the eastern Mediterranean and the Ottomans were its ally. In January 1699, Austria, having defeated the Ottomans without Russian help, made a separate peace at Karlowitz, leaving the Russians on their own to make peace as best they could.

The grand tour opened the eyes of the tsar and his entourage to the wealth of the Coastland, a wealth largely based on the colonial trade. It confirmed the wisdom of Peter's father, Alexei Mikhailovich, who had been willing to allow certain well-filtered Western influences into the Muscovite world and had invited Western mercenaries to create a more effective Russian army to fight both the Poles and the Turks. Peter's determination to open up Russia on a much wider scale, to redirect Russia's trade (carried largely in British and Dutch bottoms), and to tap its revenue to help finance the transformation of Russia into an imperial power exposed the inanity of a forward policy toward the Southern Frontier at the time and created instead a strategic interest in the Baltic, where Russia had followed a largely close-border policy since 1617. The time was ripe. Charles XI of Sweden died in April 1697, leaving a son of 15 years, the soon-to-be-famous Charles XII. Denmark and Poland formed an offensive alliance against Sweden in September 1699 to regain Skåne for Denmark and Livonia for Poland; Russia joined it in November. The broker was Johann Patkul, a nobleman from Livonia, where the Russo-Swedish, Russo-Polish, and Polono-Swedish frontiers interlocked, one of those "proruptions" from which Russia could hope to dominate one day both the Baltic and Poland, and even Prussia.

Denmark and Poland declared war on Sweden in March 1700, inaugurating the so-called Northern War that would last for twenty years. Denmark was quickly defeated, and Poland would have to lift the siege of Riga in August, at the very time Russia entered the war, after having received the news that peace had been concluded with the Ottomans. The first encounter took place before Narva, where Peter hoped to cut the first zone of the frontier in two, isolating the Swedes from Karelia. It was a Russian disaster. Charles XII had succeeded in defeating his three enemies one by one. But the great commander underestimated Russia's rising might and the determination of its tsar. This was a war for control of the Russo-Swedish frontier and not a rerun of his predecessors' wars against Denmark and Poland.

Instead of exploiting his victory and making the first zone an impassable barrier to the Gulf of Finland, Charles XII left only a reserve force in Livonia, Ingria, and Karelia. He hoped it would not only block access to the Gulf but also secure the Swedish position in Finland and keep Stockholm invincible. In addition, Livonia was Sweden's grain basket. The king directed all his energies against Augustus II of Poland in a last attempt to end in Sweden's favor the old rivalry of the two core areas for hegemony in the Baltic. In February 1704, he compelled the Polish Diet to depose Augustus and elect in his place Stanislas Leszczynski. His obsession with Poland allowed the Russians to take Noteburg, renamed Shlisselburg (Petrokrepost), where the Neva leaves Lake Ladoga, and Nineshants, where it enters the Gulf of Finland, in 1703; they took Narva and Derpt in Livonia in 1704. The founding of Petersburg in July 1703 was tantamount to a declaration that Russia had annexed the proximate zone of the frontier. Charles XII, while unbeaten on the battlefield, had lost the war.

From then on, Poland and the Russo-Polish frontier became the main theater of war between Russian and Swedish forces. The Russians were gradually forced to withdraw deeper into the frontier and the Swedes established a forward position at Grodno in Lithuania. The offensive began in June 1708. The Swedes crossed the Berezina on their way to Mogilev, vainly expecting to find reinforcements and supplies from Livonia, before launching an offensive against Moscow: the relief force had been defeated on the Lesna River near Brest-Litovsk in September. Charles XII was forced to change his plan and turn south into the Ukraine in search of supplies and reinforcements from the Cossacks of the Hetmanate. Instead, he found himself checkmated before Poltava, where he suffered a crushing defeat in July 1709. To escape capture, he had to flee to Bendery, in Ottoman-held territory.

The Russians went on the offensive, switching to a forward policy seeking not only to occupy the entire Western Frontier but also to destabilize the Swedish and Polish core areas. Riga fell in May 1710, Vyborg and Keksholm (Priozersk) in June. The entire proximate zone was now in Russian control. A land and sea invasion of Finland began in 1712, but it took two years to occupy the lake district; the Swedish fleet was annihilated at the battle of Hangö in July 1714. The Gulf of Bothnia was in Russian hands, together with the Åland Islands (Ahvenanmaa), within striking distance of Stockholm. Prussia entered the war and took Stralsund and Wismar, after gaining Stettin by negotiation the previous year. The Russians invaded Poland and crossed it on their way to Denmark, where a Russo-Danish force would prepare an invasion of Sweden across the Sound. The invasion never took place, because the Danes began to fear the emergence of Russian power in the Baltic. An invasion of the Swedish core area across the Sound and the Gulf of Bothnia was certain to result in the partition of Sweden, and the Danes suspected the Russians would take Stockholm and Karlskrona, Sweden's naval headquarters, and gain hegemony in the Baltic.

The tsar, dissatisfied with his allies, withdrew from northern Germany and began negotiations with Charles XII in May 1718. The king had returned in November 1714, in no mood to make peace. He kept forgetting Russia was his main enemy and struck at the Danes in Norway, then part of Denmark, where he was killed in December 1718. His younger sister and successor, Ulrica Leonora, understood that Sweden's greatest loss would be that of Livonia and the Gulf of Finland, and sought to continue the war, but the extraordinary energy unleashed by the war was transforming Russia into the Baltic's superpower. Its industries and shipyards were turning out guns and ships at a rate the French consul in Petersburg found overwhelming. There was no choice but to make peace. Negotiations began at Nystad (Uusikaupunki) in April 1721, and peace was signed in August.

Three issues dominated the Russo-Swedish agenda. The Treaty of Nystad recognized Russia's acquisition "by force of arms" of Swedish Livonia, Estonia, and Ingria, with all the islands from the Kurland border to Petersburg, including Oesel (Saarema), Drago (Hiiumaa), and Moen (Muhu) as well as Kotlin in the Gulf of Finland. A naval base (Kronshtadt) was already being built on Kotlin island—its purpose was to defend the new capital of the Russian empire against a naval attack. It also became the headquarters of one of the two squadrons of the new

Baltic fleet—the other was at Reval (Tallin). The prize city was Riga near the mouth of the Dvina; it gave Russia control of the east Baltic trade and of Riga's hinterland in the Russo-Polish frontier, all the way to the Pripyat marshes.

In these former Swedish provinces, except Ingria, Russia promised to maintain "the rights and privileges" of the Germanic nobility and townsmen and to recognize the Lutheran religion, provided the Germans accepted the free exercise of the Greek Orthodox faith. It also pledged to reverse the fiscally aggressive policy of Charles XI, known as the *Reduktion,* in which the Swedish treasury had sought to recover lands it claimed had been illegally acquired by the nobility. By deferring to the superior interest of the men of power, including their right to enserf the peasantry—a right not recognized in Sweden and Finland and one the Swedish monarchy had begun to challenge—the Russians gained the Germanic nobility's support and established durable foundations for Russian rule. They also acquired Karelia with Vyborg, the important fortress that had long been Sweden's forward position in the zone, but returned the lake district and the Åland Islands. From then on, Sweden's position in the Baltic became a hostage to Russia's goodwill—the coastal plain of southern Finland, the Åland Islands, and the Swedish coastline were at the mercy of a Russian attack.

Russia had won the war, and the momentum of the Russian advance could not simply stop at a linear boundary. The victory compelled Russia to seek to consolidate its newly won hegemony in the Baltic by destabilizing the Swedish core area for the purpose of transforming it into a Russian protectorate. Such a protectorate, together with a Russo-Danish alliance based on Denmark's traditional hatred of Sweden, would go a long way toward making the Baltic a closed sea, extending Russian influence to the boundary of the Heartland, and enabling Russia to develop a fortress-fleet strategy behind which it could safely destabilize Poland and keep Prussia in check.

The overweening ambition of Charles XII and the sacrifices it had imposed had exhausted Sweden, destroyed its empire, and discredited its absolute monarchy. A reaction had set in immediately after the king's death, and the Riksdag—the Swedish Parliament—had made it a point to elect Ulrica Leonora queen of Sweden in January 1719 and to insist on drawing up a constitution. It vested the executive power in a council that ruled with the monarch and, when the Riksdag was not in session, in a secret committee consisting of representatives from the clergy, the nobility, and the burghers; the peasant estate was consulted in matters of taxation. In a country where venality was widespread and the nobility as fractious as anywhere, the Constitution of 1720 was certain to create disorder and offer opportunities to paralyze the operations of the government. It was in that year that the Riksdag transferred the crown to the queen's consort, Frederick I (r. 1720–1751) of Hesse-Kassel, a foreigner less likely to appeal to Swedish national sentiment against the Riksdag's incompetence.

The Treaty of Nystad gave Russia the means to put considerable pressure on Sweden. Instead of cutting off the country from its grain basket in Livonia or permitting it to continue an unlimited and vital trade, it allowed Sweden to purchase every year 50,000 rubles worth of rye duty-free in Riga, Reval, and Arensburg (Kingissep) on Oesel Island on condition the skippers offered proof the grain was intended for consumption in Sweden. Such purchases would be discontinued, however, if "important reasons" induced the Russian government to impose a general prohibition on grain exports. The treaty also contained an ambiguous clause, pledging Russia not to interfere, or "assist anyone, in any manner, directly or indirectly," to interfere, in Sweden's domestic affairs. But it also required Russia "to prevent all that is contrary" to the settlement of 1720.[1] In other words, the treaty established Russia as the guarantor of Swedish liberties established by the Constitution of 1720 and gave it the right to intervene against any attempt to restore the absolute monarchy. Russia gained a license to keep Sweden in a state of permanent turmoil.

A territorial agreement in the Russo-Swedish frontier and an international settlement giving Russia much leverage on Sweden—these were the two major achievements of the Nystad negotiations. A third issue did not find its way into the treaty because it did not require an immediate solution and was kept by Russia as a sword of Damocles over the Swedish monarchy. It was the complicated and messy question of Schleswig-Holstein.

As Russia broke through the Western Frontier and claimed a role in the concert of European nations represented by the Germanic and Coastland powers, Peter sought to anchor the Romanov dynasty in the network of European dynasties. The states of the Holy Roman Empire offered excellent opportunities for dynastic marriages to exercise influence and apply power both within and beyond the Heartland. The first was that of his son Alexei with Charlotte of Brunswick-Wolfenbüttel, a principality west of the Elbe, in October 1711; the second that of his niece, Ekaterina Ivanovna, with the duke of Mecklenburg, east of it, in April 1716.

Schleswig and Holstein were two territories straddling the Eider River, bounded in the north by Denmark along the Kongeå River, in the south by a line running from Hamburg to Fehmarn island, just west of Mecklenburg. They were Scandinavia's land bridge to the continent. Their possession would give Denmark a role in the Holy Roman Empire, while at the same time giving Sweden an opportunity to encircle Denmark and improve its communications with its holdings on the Baltic coast of northern Germany. When the ducal line of Schleswig died out in 1459, the Danish king had gotten himself elected duke of Schleswig and count of Holstein by the combined nobility of both, on condition that the two territories would remain "forever undivided." However, after 1658 the Danish monarchy had to contend with the claims of the ducal house of Holstein-Gottorp. The family was based in Kiel in Holstein and Gottorp (Gottorf) in Schleswig and claimed to be the legitimate ruler of both lands, a medieval hodgepodge of properties held, some by the monarchy, others by the ducal house, yet others as common property by both houses. When Sweden and Denmark were at war, the dukes sided with the Swedes. When they made peace in 1720, Denmark acquired the ducal lands in Schleswig and incorporated them into the royal lands. The result was the dukes' undying hatred of Denmark.

Duke Frederick IV had married in 1698 Hedwig of Sweden, Charles XII's elder sister and heir to the Swedish throne should the king remain childless. The duke died in 1702. Denmark's decisive victory over Sweden at Tønning on the estuary of the Eider in 1713 left his son, Charles Frederick, at Denmark's mercy. The regent sought Russian support, offering to marry Charles Frederick to the tsar's daughter, Anna Petrovna—he was 14 and she was 6. The marriage did not take place until May 1725, but its possibility was used by Peter to threaten to impose a Russian candidate on the Swedish throne. The threat failed, and the Riksdag had already ignored Hedwig's higher claims in 1719 when it elected her younger sister Ulrica Leonora. But the "Schleswig-Holstein question" was only beginning.

Sweden was not the only loser of the Russo-Swedish war. The Polish Empire was an even greater victim. Much of the war had been fought on its territory, and Charles XII, as if animated by the same perversity that made him neglect the Baltic provinces, had seemed intent on doing the Russians' work in Poland. The country was devastated; its trade, credit, and towns in ruins; its Saxon dynasty discredited. By neglecting the fact that the war had been for Russia a war for the control of the Western Frontier, Charles XII had brought disaster to the two core areas, Sweden and Poland. Augustus II was not represented at Nystad; he had become irrelevant.

Three issues assumed fundamental importance in Russo-Polish relations during the first two decades of the eighteenth century: the selection of the king, the treatment of non-Catholics, and so-called "Polish liberties."

The Polish crown had been elective since the end of the Jagiellon dynasty in 1572, and Poles would choose their kings at times from outside Poland in a consistent attempt to keep the crown weak. Thus, Poland became the outstanding exception among the rising core areas of the continent, whose kings succeeded in concentrating in their hands the command of the army, the collection of revenue, and the legislative power. The Poles had chosen the elector of Saxony as king of Poland from among eighteen candidates in June 1697. He had assumed the dynastic name of Augustus II and would reign until 1733. His interests were divided between those of Saxony and those of Poland, and these did not always coincide. He was the tsar's ally during the war, in a vain attempt to recover Livonia. Charles XII had him deposed in February 1704, but in the summer of 1709, after Poltava, Charles's candidate, Stanislas Leszczynski, had to flee, and Augustus was reinstated with Russian support. It was Russia's first intervention in the selection of a king of Poland.

Augustus was soon faced with a revolt in his adopted country. The Polish magnates, a class of large and fiercely independent landowners who were the main beneficiaries of the crown's weakness, resented the predatory policies of their Saxon king and the depredations of his troops quartered on the country. In 1715, they formed a "confederation" with their brethren in Lithuania and rose up against the king. Confederations had a long and respectable history. They were temporary associations of nobles for the purpose of putting through a specific project, here to oppose the king's arbitrary power by force of arms. The confederates received none of the expected support from Sweden or Turkey and were forced by the Russian ambassador, Grigorii Dolgorukii, to make peace with Augustus. Saxon troops left the country, but were replaced by Russian troops awaiting developments in northern Germany. Russia insisted that Augustus not make the kingship hereditary in his house, for every election gave it a chance to apply pressure and win supporters. The settlement of January 1717 was ratified under duress by the Polish Diet; it guaranteed that the choice of Augustus' successor would require Russian approval. Poland was becoming a Russian protectorate.

Russia's influence was also growing in Kurland, its proximate zone in the Russo-Polish frontier. After the expulsion of the Swedes, the duke, Frederick William, was given a wife in October 1710—Anna Ivanovna, a niece of the tsar, and the sister of the future Ekaterina of Mecklenburg. The duke died on his way back from Petersburg in January 1711, and the ducal crown passed to his uncle Ferdinand, who chose to remain in Danzig at a relatively safe distance from Russian power. Anna remained in Mitava (Elblaga), Kurland's capital, until February 1730, when she was chosen empress of Russia, but effective power gradually passed into the hands of a Russian resident.

Elsewhere in the frontier, religious turbulence invited the Russian advance. The Counter-Reformation had stopped the progress of Protestantism in Poland but not eradicated it. There remained a large Protestant minority in the Polish core area and a large Orthodox minority—in some places even a majority—in the frontier zones. There, the religious struggle was complicated by the existence of the Uniate Church, created in the wake of the Union of Brest in 1596—it retained its Slavic liturgy but recognized the supremacy of Rome. The term *dissident* was originally given to the Protestant minority, but was later extended to include the Orthodox and the Uniates. The rise of religious intolerance in the seventeenth century, when Poland found itself on the defensive during the Thirteen Years War and the Cossack uprising, forced even the magnates who had embraced Protestantism as a form of protest against their Catholic kings to renounce it. Dissidents lost the right to have their clergy and were barred from occupying official positions.

The Northern War, social dislocation, and humiliation aggravated intolerance, and the Diet of 1717 passed legislation banning dissidents from its ranks, prohibiting the formation of confederations for the defense of religious rights, and placing mixed marriages under the provisions of canon law. Although the same legislation guaranteed the dissidents the inviolability of their property and equality with Catholics before the courts, in fact it declared open season against them, as mobs inflamed by greed and religious fanaticism turned to violence against the Orthodox, their churches, and their monasteries. The religious question in the frontier became inseparable from the larger question of the allegiance of the men of power in Bielorussia and Lithuania, who resisted the continued attempts of the Polish kings to create a hereditary monarchy. Such turbulence could not but disturb the Russians, who saw themselves as the champions of Orthodoxy against Latin Christendom and Islam, but they refrained from using their trump card against Poland—military intervention from Livonia and Smolensk and a boycott of Lithuanian exports through Riga. Winding down the Northern War and preparing for war with Persia absorbed all their attention. Nonetheless, the support given to the Orthodox bishop in Mogilev was tantamount to a promise of better things to come.

The third issue, around which Russia's policy would eventually crystallize, was that of "Polish liberties." The heart of these liberties was an intense distrust of the king's executive power and the so-called *liberum veto*. At his election, the new Polish king had to accept a *pactum conventum*, a kind of bilateral contract between him and "society," the nobility that made up the "Polish nation." It severely circumscribed his powers. The liberum veto, first invoked in 1652, was based on the assumption of the absolute equality of every Polish nobleman—a single negative vote vetoed the measure being debated by the Diet and dissolved the Diet as well. Such a suicidal method created chaos and invited foreign intervention. A "confederated" Diet that lifted the unanimity rule was the only way to prevent a total breakdown of governmental life.

The conservative defense of Polish liberties was ideally suited to favor a subversive policy to destabilize the Polish core area in Russia's favor. The settlement of 1717 reduced the Polish army to 24,000 men, while the Russians could easily concentrate twice that number on the border of the Polish Empire. A partition of Poland was suggested at least four times by the Prussian king during Peter's reign and, in 1721, by Augustus himself, ready to purchase the right to become hereditary king of Poland by giving away Lithuania and Bielorussia. Russia had a natural interest in opposing partition because a Russian protectorate over the entire Polish Empire would bring Russian power to the Oder. Russian prospects had never looked brighter in the Western Frontier.

The Second Round, 1721–1743

As often happens after a long war, the former enemies drew together, in a tacit understanding that the war had created a new and mutually acceptable balance between them, at least for a while. In February 1724, Russia and Sweden signed a defensive alliance to ward off for twelve years a hypothetical attack by a "Christian power" in Europe—it excluded an

Ottoman attack on Russia and was directed against Denmark and Prussia. It pledged Sweden to commit 10,000 troops and eight ships, Russia 16,000 troops and twelve ships, to the common defense. A secret article pledged the two parties to use their good offices in Copenhagen to help the Holstein-Gottorp house recover its lands in Schleswig, "that dangerous source of infinite troubles."[2] In December, the matrimonial contract between Duke Charles Frederick and Anna Petrovna spelled out Russian intentions toward the ducal house. The Russo-Swedish rapprochement had been facilitated by the Riksdag's decision in November 1723, when it became certain the king would have no children, to transfer the Swedish crown to the duke, Hedwig's son, at the king's death. In the contract, Anna renounced her rights to the Russian crown, but Tsar Peter reserved the right to select their son, if they should have one, to succeed to the Russian throne. A son was born in February 1728, named Charles Peter; he would later become Russian emperor as Peter III (1761–1762). The alliance and the contract raised the possibility of a union of the three crowns of Schleswig-Holstein, Sweden, and Russia that would consolidate Russia's hegemony in the Baltic, leave Denmark defenseless, and contain Prussia, whose policy of territorial aggrandizement was beginning to raise fears in Sweden and Poland.

These imperial ambitions were such a destabilizing factor in the entire basin of the Baltic—they would take Russian power to the boundary of the Heartland—that they brought about a reaction to counterbalance Russia's growing weight. Russia could use the old hatred between Danes and Swedes and side with one against the other, but its ambitions threatened to bring about a stiffening of resistance by both, in alliance with a containing power of the Coastland. Catherine I, Anna Petrovna's mother, who succeeded her husband Peter I in January 1725, did not conceal her hatred of Denmark, and insisted in February that it must return the ducal lands in Schleswig seized in 1720. The duke and Anna were married four months later. A Russian attack on Denmark was seriously contemplated in 1726, but a British squadron appeared before Reval in May as a warning that Britain would oppose a defeat of Denmark that would give Russia a preponderant influence in the Sound. The empress died in May 1727, two months after Sweden and Denmark joined Britain, France, and Prussia in the Union of Hanover directed against Russia. Russia had to abandon the duke's cause. The imbroglio had taught a significant lesson: any Russian attempt to subdue the Swedish core area and establish influence in Denmark would go beyond the limit of an optimum of conquest and trigger the containment policy of the Coastland powers.

Beginning in 1727, Russia began to face the growing opposition of those in Sweden who refused to accept the Nystad settlement and felt Sweden had a chance to regain the Baltic provinces, especially Karelia with Vyborg. They also wanted to cancel the agreement of November 1723 and promise the crown to a British prince. The leading figure in the Swedish government until the late 1730s was Count Arvid Horn, elected chairman of the Riksdag in September 1726. He led Sweden into the Union of Hanover and distrusted Russia, but felt prudence was the better part of wisdom. The major task of the Russian resident, Mikhail Bestuzhev-Riumin (who had been Anna Ivanovna's "guardian" in Mitava) was to distribute significant sums among the members of the Swedish political establishment to keep Horn on the path of moderation. Some discounted the alliance of 1724 and toyed with the idea of provoking Russia to make war, thereby bringing about an Anglo-French intervention on Sweden's side. The country's poverty and fiscal constraints were Bestuzhev's best allies.

Nevertheless, Sweden began to edge toward confrontation with Russia. The turning point was the Polish succession crisis of 1733 during which Russia imposed its candidate on the Polish throne with a demonstration of military power. The intervention caused fear in Stockholm that Russia might some day attempt a similar coup in Sweden. In October 1734, Sweden and Denmark buried their differences and formed a defensive alliance against Russia in accordance with Britain's desire to strengthen the defenses of the Heartland's boundary. Although the alliance of 1724 was renewed at Russia's request, the decision evoked some "important reflections,"[3] including the sneer that Russia must have valid reasons to seek Sweden's reassurance so soon after abandoning the Persian provinces it had cost so much effort to conquer. A dangerous shift was taking place in Swedish policy that would soon lead to a fatal underestimation of Russian power.

Bestuzhev openly interfered in Swedish politics; there was discrimination against Swedish subjects in Russia; and the export of Livonian grain was banned. France, true to its traditional alliance with Sweden, sent a new ambassador at the end of 1737 with an offer of subsidies, and the Riksdag began a long session to discuss them in May 1738. Horn was forced out of office in December, and Swedish politics became polarized between those who favored industrial development, a more aggressive commercial policy, and war with Russia to regain the Baltic provinces and those, chiefly the higher nobility and the coastal towns, that had everything to fear from a war with Russia. The partisans of war with Russia were called the Hats, and they would dominate Swedish politics until the 1760s. Their leader in 1739 was Count Karl Gyllenborg. Their opponents were called the Caps; Horn remained their leader. The Riksdag disbanded in May 1739, after putting the army and fleet on a war footing.

Russia was at war with Turkey at the time, and the Porte invited Sweden to join an offensive alliance against the common enemy. Negotiations were conducted in 1738, during which Sweden expressed readiness to ship 20,000 muskets to the Ottoman forces. One Swedish officer, a Major Malcom Sinclair (Sinkler), who sat on the secret committee between the sessions of the Riksdag, offered to travel to Constantinople and spy on Russian troop movements along the way. Bestuzhev found out and advised Petersburg to kidnap (*anlevirovat'*) him. On the way back, in June 1739, he was seized and murdered on orders of Marshal Münnich, the Russian commander in chief, and his dispatches were stolen. The murder caused outrage in Stockholm, where it was the common assumption that Bestuzhev had instigated it. The Turko-Swedish alliance was signed in December, but came too late—the Russians and the Ottomans had made peace in September. By then, the Russo-Swedish antagonism had reached a dangerous pitch, and the Swedes were ready for war at the first opportunity.

While the Hats were getting ready for a war to roll back Russian power in the Russo-Swedish frontier, the Polish monarchy had already withdrawn from its ultimate zone in the Russo-Polish frontier. The consequences of a marital alliance with the Romanov house were becoming obvious. A frontier creates centrifugal forces that draw a core area forward toward its rival as long as the superior side can compel, or take advantage of, a shift in the balance of power in the frontier. It can also create centripetal forces as the men of power in the proximate and intermediate zones begin to transfer their allegiance to the stronger core area. The phenomenon had already been noticeable during the Northern War, when the Germanic nobility, motivated by a social ideology inimical to the principles of the Swedish monarchy, switched their allegiance to Russia because the tsar pledged to maintain their rights and privileges, the foundation of their political, economic, and social power in Livonia. Those men of power in Lithuania who resented Poland's ascendancy could always count on the support of their distant cousins in the ruling elite of the Russian core area to support their yearnings for autonomy. Moreover, the great families of Volhynia and Podolia, the Potockis and Lubomirskis, among others, looked favorably to the growth of Russian influence in Poland to counter the ambitions of other powerful families like the Czartoryskis.

Russia's concern over the treatment of dissidents was relegated to the second plan at the end of 1725, as the succession question in Kurland approached a critical stage. Duke Ferdinand was childless, the last member of the Kettler house that had become a vassal of Poland in 1561. Poland was ready to claim Kurland as an intestate legacy and incorporate it into the Polish Empire, either as an intrinsic part of Poland, like Volhynia and Podolia, or as a separate appanage of the king. Berlin also had claims on the duchy, because it had once belonged to the Teutonic Order; Berlin could invoke the precedent of 1618, when Brandenburg had inherited Prussia. However, neither claim could compete with the fact that Anna Ivanovna and a Russian resident were still in Mitava.

If Anna was to marry again, the candidate would have to be acceptable to Russia. The most serious was Maurice of Saxony, a natural son of Augustus II, who had the advantage of being favored by Anna and the disadvantage of being unacceptable to Petersburg. Nevertheless, he was elected by the Kurland Diet as the presumptive heir of Ferdinand. Catherine I was not to be deterred, and threatened in June 1726 to send

20,000 troops into Kurland if the Diet refused to cancel the election and elect a more suitable candidate. None was to be found, even with Russia's promise to Berlin in December 1732 that it would support the candidacy of the Prussian king's second son following the death of Duke Ferdinand. But that was not to be. The Polish succession crisis broke out in 1733, and the new king of Poland, the oldest son of Augustus II, had to recognize, in return for Russia's support, the election of Anna's favorite, Ernst von Bühren (Biron), a Kurlander who had brightened her lonesome days in Mitava, as presumptive heir. Biron moved with Anna to Petersburg in 1730, and Ferdinand died in 1737. A Russian resident would remain in Mitava until 1795. Poland's ultimate zone in the Russo-Polish frontier had ceased to be a sphere of influence; it had become a full-fledged Russian protectorate.

The Kurland question was obviously part of the larger Polish question. Anticipating the death of Augustus II, Petersburg and Berlin had sought to reach a preliminary agreement on a candidate for the Polish throne acceptable to both. In August 1726 and again in September 1730, they had agreed that the Saxon dynasty had outlived its usefulness, because the restlessness of Augustus II and his persistent desire to establish a hereditary monarchy in Poland—it would strengthen the Polish core area—was a threat to his neighbors and a violation of Polish liberties. Therefore his successor should be a native Pole (Piast), because the interests of his house would no longer be intertwined with those of a foreign power. Moreover, the choice of a Pole was certain to aggravate the rivalries between the leading families, thereby benefiting Polish liberties, which flourished on domestic strife. Unfortunately, the only likely Polish candidate was expected to be the same Stanislas Leszczynski whom the Swedes had imposed in Warsaw in September 1704 and who had to flee in 1709. He had become a protégé of the French Court, and his daughter Maria, by an extraordinary stroke of good luck, had become queen of France in the spring of 1725. French support doomed his candidacy from the start in both Berlin and Petersburg. Both capitals had also agreed in September 1730 that the dissidents, Protestant and Orthodox, had to be protected by "the strongest proposals and remonstrances"[4] in Warsaw, a convenient pretext to intervene in the succession question at the propitious moment.

Augustus II died in February 1733 and Stanislas declared his candidacy. He was supported by Tadeusz Potocki, the primate of Poland, who exercised the king's power during an interregnum and was the leader of a powerful French faction. He also had the support of the Swedes and the Turks, France's traditional allies. General Peter Lacy (Lassi), the Russian governor of Livland in Riga, was instructed to warn the Poles that the election of Stanislas would be considered a casus belli. Prussia chose to remain neutral, and the Lithuanian magnates convinced Russia that the son of Augustus was the only alternative. Both Russia and France spent considerable sums to secure enough supporters for their respective candidates, and Lassi's troops even entered Poland at the beginning of August to explain Russia's intentions. Nevertheless, Stanislas was elected in September, and Russia immediately declared war. A week later, Russian troops had reached the suburbs of Warsaw, forcing Stanislas to flee, and demanded a new election. A "confederation" of obedient nobles elected Augustus III king of Poland. He would reign for thirty years.

Russia's intervention precipitated a polarization of Polish politics. Some powerful families, like the Potockis with their large properties in Volhynia and Podolia, remained the great defenders of Polish liberties—but Russia had become their guarantor. The Czartoryskis, now convinced that only internal reforms could strengthen Poland's hand, turned to Russia. Here was the germ of the tragic misunderstanding that would seal Poland's fate in the 1760s. The lesson of the succession crisis was that men of power on both sides had to turn to Russia in their pursuit of irreconcilable aims. After 1733, the Polish core area had been so destabilized that its real ruler was the Russian resident, a man from the frontier, Hermann von Keyserling, a nobleman from Livonia.

It was not until the summer of 1741 that the Hats in Sweden realized Russia was in the throes of a political crisis following the death of the Empress Anna in October 1740. The king declared war in July, referring to the ban on Livonian shipments of grain to Sweden, Bestuzhev's threats, and the assassination of Major Sinclair. Gyllenborg, the Hats' leader, welcomed the war that promised to restore to Sweden "its former power, glory, and credit." Petersburg expressed surprise that Sweden had declared war without first trying to settle Russo-Swedish differences, "an unheard-of thing in Christendom, even among the most savage nations."[5] The surprise was justified. A month later, in August, the small force of 3000 men the Swedes had been able to put in the field at the time was routed at Villmanstrand (Lappeenranta) on Lake Saimaa, on the Russian side of the lake district, by a Russian army three times that number commanded by the same Peter Lacy (now a field marshal) who had led Russian troops into Poland eight years earlier.

The Swedish objective was limited, however. There could be no question of defeating Russia on the battlefield. The Swedes were seeking to take advantage of the factional struggle in Russia to obtain the return of at least Karelia and Vyborg, overlooking the fact that even this objective was unrealistic because Karelia commanded the approaches to Petersburg. The establishment of the Imperial capital in what had been the proximate zone of the Russo-Swedish frontier was tantamount to including that zone into the core area itself, and the question of Karelia was no longer negotiable. Sweden's objective appeared quite clearly from the proclamation issued by the commander in chief in Finland. It declared that the Russo-Swedish enmity had been caused by the policy of the "foreign ministers who have dominated Russia for some years" and called on Russians to free themselves from their "cruel yoke."[6] With the support of the French ambassador in Petersburg, the Swedes were seeking to bring about the overthrow of Anna Leopoldovna's government and the dismissal of Andrei (Heinrich) Osterman, who had been the leading figure of the Russian government in the 1730s and consistently hostile to Sweden. Elizabeth, it was hoped, would welcome Swedish support in return for territorial concessions.

They miscalculated, however. Elizabeth, like the Romanovs in 1613, embodied a movement of national defiance, now directed against not only the "Germans" but the Swedes as well. She suspended hostilities, but negotiations foundered on Russia's refusal to give up Karelia. She then returned to war in March 1742 with an appeal to the Finns to secede from Sweden, so that Finland may become a "barrier" against Sweden's hostile intentions. If the Finns refused, Russia would destroy Finland "by fire and sword." They did refuse, but Finland was spared this ultimate calamity by the capitulation early in September of the Swedish army and fleet block-aded in Helsingfors (Helsinki). The Caps briefly returned to power, and peace was signed at Åbo (Turku), Finland's capital, in August 1743.

The Treaty of Åbo compelled Sweden to recognize, as it had at Nystad in 1721, the loss of its Baltic provinces from Livonia to Karelia. It retained the provision allowing Sweden to purchase 50,000 rubles worth of grain a year in Livonia. It also gave Russia a slice of the lake district including the province of Kiumenne (Kymijoki), so that the new bound-ary would run along the Kiumenne River, cut across Lake Saimaa, curl around Neishlot (Nyslott—Savonlinna), then run parallel to the old boundary to Arkhangelsk province. Russia promised to respect local "rights and privileges" and the Lutheran religion but insisted on equal rights for Greek Orthodoxy. The gains were substantial—Russia incorpo-rated the three fortresses of Fredrikshamn (Hamina), Villmanstrand, and Neishlot forming Sweden's last defense perimeter in Finland, but also its forward positions for an attack on Petersburg.

The Russians, however, gave up their right under Article 7 of the Treaty of Nystad to interfere in Swedish internal affairs in order "to pre-vent all that is contrary" to the settlement of 1720. The reason was the impending succession to the Swedish throne. Ulrica Leonora died in November 1741; her husband, King Frederick, was not expected to live long. According to the settlement of 1723, confirmed after Ulrica's death, the crown would pass to Charles Peter of Holstein-Gottorp, who was 13 years old in 1741. But in November 1742, the Empress Elizabeth, who was unmarried, invoked the matrimonial contract of December 1724 and chose him as her heir. The impossibility of joining the three crowns of Holstein, Sweden, and Russia without provoking a major war with Denmark and possibly the Coastland powers required a compromise. Charles Peter moved to Petersburg and was renamed Petr Federovich. He was also required to renounce his rights to the Swedish crown. Elizabeth then demanded, in return for this concession, for giving up Article 7, and for the retrocession of the greater part of Finland occupied by her troops, that her candidate be recognized by the Riksdag. He was Adolf Frederick, the first cousin of Charles Frederick, who had died in 1739, and the current duke of Holstein-Gottorp. The Danes threatened war, and the Baltic world was treated to the spectacle of Russian troops landing near Stockholm at the beginning of 1744 to protect the capital against a possible Danish attack. Adolf Frederick became king of Sweden in 1751.

The war had shown Sweden's inability to reverse the settlement of 1721. It demonstrated Russia's ability to project decisive power not only in the frontier but in the Swedish core area itself. It seemed that the Russo-Swedish enmity would now come to an end, but that could not be until the entire frontier had fallen under Russian control. Only then could Sweden abandon its Baltic ambitions and find comfort in the status of a neutral power between Russia and the Coastland powers determined to block Russia's access to the Heartland's boundary.

The Diplomatic Offensive, 1743–1768

Adolf Frederick married in 1744 the strong-willed sister of Frederick II of Prussia. The union was certain to raise Prussian influence in Stockholm and, since Prussia and France were allies, to bring Sweden into a power bloc hostile to Russia. It was likely to encourage the supporters of the monarchy in the army, the clergy, the peasantry, and the lower nobility—the coalition that had supported Gustav Adolf's brand of absolutism in the seventeenth century—in the belief a restoration was possible. Despite the renewal of the Russo-Swedish alliance in June 1745, the Hats continued to accept French subsidies and even concluded a defensive alliance with Prussia in May 1747. They also negotiated with the Ottomans. Petersburg was convinced they had learned nothing and that a grand coalition, led by the Prussian king who had just deprived Austria of Silesia, its richest province, was being formed to roll back Russian influence in the Baltic.

Only the resulting apprehension can explain the crisis of 1749. The preceding year, in April, a new Russian envoy had been appointed to Stockholm. He was Nikita Panin, "un esprit inquiet qui n'aimait pas la Suéde."[7] He saw his mission as designed to prevent the restoration of the absolute monarchy, to bring about the overthrow of the Hat ministry, and to surround the crown prince with "good patriots" who would tie his hands. King Frederick was ill and might die. In January 1749, Bestuzhev instructed Panin to give a first warning that Russia would not tolerate the restoration of absolutism. In May, Panin announced that, in accordance with Article 7 of the Treaty of Nystad, Russian troops were ready to cross into Finland to defend "Swedish liberties" (*shvedskaia vol'nost'*) and that Swedes who resisted would be treated as "traitors to their fatherland" and enemies of Russia. The Russian case had no legal justification—Article 7 was not repeated in the Treaty of Åbo—but that was irrelevant, because the crisis had been manufactured to frighten the Swedes. In October, Panin offered to negotiate an international convention that would guarantee the existing form of government. It would undercut the Hats' objection that Russia had no legal right to intervene in Swedish domestic affairs by turning the issue into a multinational one, justifying Russian intervention. The Swedes refused. In June 1750, the Russian government announced that there were already 27,000 Russian troops in Finland, that an additional 40,000 were about to be sent, and that 110 galleys were ready to leave Petersburg, Reval, and Fredrikshamn for an attack on Sweden. The threats were never carried out and the crisis petered out. The king died in March 1751, and the succession took place without incident. Russia had made its position clear.

Five years later, Poland became embroiled in the Russo-Prussian war (1756–1763). Those who argued in Poland before the war began that the country must stay out of a war that did not serve its interests forgot that Russo-Polish relations had become part of the broader question of Russia's relations with the Germanic powers. The aim of the war was to destroy Prussia, the Austrians engaging the Prussians in the valley of the Elbe, the Russians in the valley of the Oder. The leading men of power in Warsaw—the Czartoryskis, Poniatowskis, Branickis, Oginskis, Lubomirskis, and others—readily agreed in the fall of 1756, subject to ratification by the Diet, to the passage of Russian troops, hoping they would "protect" Poland. Their perception of the conflict was more realistic—they already realized Poland had moved into the Russian orbit. Mikhail Bestuzhev, on his way to France in the spring of 1757, tried to convince other magnates to enter the war on Russia's side; he appealed to their honor and their greed in the event of a Prussian defeat, to their fears in the event of a Prussian victory. They refused, arguing that Russia would not allow a Prussian revenge on Poland.

In the summer of 1757, Mikhail Volkonsky, the new envoy to Warsaw, announced Russia's intention to continue the policy of maintaining the status quo in Poland and keeping domestic strife under control. The weakening of the Saxon dynasty—Augustus III was old and despondent, having lost his possessions to Frederick II—was beginning to release dangerous centrifugal forces in the Polish political establishment. In an effort to contain those forces, Volkonsky tried to get the magnates to agree to maintain the Saxon dynasty on the Polish throne. He came, however, at the wrong time, and had to face a chorus of complaints against the behavior of Russian troops in Lithuania—buying all the grain for their stores and interfering with shipping on the Niemen—and rising tensions between Uniates and Orthodox. The situation worsened as Russian troops moved toward the Oder and retreated after each campaign behind the Vistula to take up their winter quarters. As they moved at will back and forth across Poland, they left garrisons at strategic points on or near the Vistula—Elbing (Elblag), Marienburg (Malbrok), Tczew, Grudziants, and Thorn (Torun)—and Poznan on the Warta. Poland became an occupied country and the Vistula the new forward perimeter of the Russian Empire. The war left a legacy in the Russian military high command: a conviction that the occupation of the Russo-Polish frontier alone could end the political, social, and religious turmoil so detrimental to the maintenance of a stable boundary for the Russian core area, and that the Vistula might, after all, become a line of an optimum of conquest.

Most wars bring about a territorial settlement of sorts, and Russia was likely to seek "compensations" in Poland for its war effort. It showed a renewed interest in Kurland. To prevent Augustus from making a separate peace with Prussia, it was agreed that his third son, Charles, would become duke of Kurland. Since "Kurlanders had grown used to regarding their dukes as governors appointed in Petersburg,"[8] the Kurland Diet made no objections, and Charles was invested by his father in December 1758. However, Elizabeth still refused to depose Biron and confirm Charles. Her hesitancy was part of a larger plan. Russia intended to separate Prussia from Brandenburg at the end of the war, then negotiate an agreement with Poland according to which Charles would receive Prussia as an appanage in exchange for Poland's accepting Russia's annexation of Kurland, as well as Volhynia and Podolia ("Polish Russia"). The plan showed an intention to complete the annexation of Livonia, begun in 1721. Another more ambitious plan sought to incorporate East Prussia into the Russian Empire and to occupy Danzig. Polish and Lithuanian trade depended on the Vistula and the Niemen—Danzig and Memel (Klaipeda) controlled the mouths of both rivers. The argument that Poland might not consent to being cut off from the Baltic was met with the retort that there was nothing it could do about it. The war with Prussia was bringing about a radical reassessment of Russian attitudes toward Poland. Partition was in the air.

The war exposed the decrepitude of Sweden. There was an irresolute king and a strong-willed but unpopular queen, sister of the hated king of Prussia; there were political parties and cliques for sale to France, Britain, and Russia; there was a court party, the butt of ridicule and contempt. Such was the Sweden which Russia, having done more than its share to destabilize, sought to draw into the war against Prussia with a gift of 10,000 *chetverti* (about 60,000 bushels) of grain as famine relief for an impoverished country. Sweden did enter the war in March 1757, but could not gather up the strength to attack the Prussians from its base in Swedish Pomerania. It remained a helpless spectator.

The war did not end as Elizabeth hoped it would. She died in December 1761, and Charles Peter succeeded her as Peter III. His admiration of the Prussian king led him to abandon all of Russia's gains. Nevertheless, the war confirmed the rising might of Russia, and his wife and successor, Catherine II (1762–1796), a German princess with close ties to the Holstein-Gottorp house, would put it to good use. The war also dealt a death blow to the status quo in Poland and Sweden.

Russia's new self-confidence, earned on the battlefield against a king considered the military genius of the age, soon found its expression in the so-called Northern Accord or Northern System. Its architect was Nikita

Panin, the former ambassador to Stockholm and now the major figure in shaping Russian foreign policy. The Northern Accord was not a policy of peace. It sought no less than to achieve, under the cover of an international agreement, the subjection of Sweden and Poland to Russia's dominion, thereby extending Russian influence to the boundary of the Heartland and incorporating the entire Western Frontier into the Russian Empire.

To achieve such an ambitious goal without resorting to war, Russia needed allies and found them in Prussia and Denmark. Although Prussia was saved from disaster at the last minute, the invasion of Brandenburg and Cossack depredations had taught the king a lesson that would continue to haunt him until his death in August 1786. He was anxious to secure an alliance that would not only allow him to spread his influence in the German states against Austria but also to become Russia's partner in the basin of the Baltic. The alliance was signed in April 1764.

Denmark's support required a settlement of the Schleswig-Holstein question. Let us recapitulate: Denmark had annexed the ducal lands in Schleswig in 1720, but the annexation was never recognized by the dukes. Denmark had been neutral during the war, but had stationed troops in Holstein as a preventive move against a possible attack by Frederick II on Hamburg and Lübeck. The Danish decision had angered Peter III who, as duke of Holstein-Gottorp, had reason to fear the Danes might annex the ducal properties in Holstein as well. He was determined to go to war against Denmark, but his assassination stopped the venture. The Danes, like the Prussians, had been frightened by Russia's willingness to use force, and now sought better ties. Catherine II accepted in March 1765 and again in April 1767 for herself and for her son, Paul (9 years of age in 1765), the annexation of 1720. She also renounced their right to the ducal possessions in Holstein in exchange for the two duchies of Oldenburg and Delmenhorst, just west of the Weser River, acquired by Denmark a century before. As a result, both Schleswig and Holstein found themselves once again united under the Danish king, whose sovereignty would no longer be challenged.

In the Northern Accord, Panin intended Denmark and Prussia to play the role of "active" powers in close alliance with Russia. The "passive" powers were Sweden, Poland, and Saxony. In dividing the members of the northern alliance into two camps, the Russians were pairing enemies from both groups—Denmark, Sweden's secular enemy; Poland, the object of Prussia's envy because its partition would link Brandenburg with Prussia; Saxony, that so temptingly filled the gap between Brandenburg and Bohemia where Frederick II had taken the war with Austria in 1756. Russia and Denmark would checkmate Sweden and make the Baltic into a closed sea; Russia and Prussia would place Poland in a deadly vise. There was something diabolical in Panin's plan, and that may be why Frederick, who liked to keep his options open but had little room to maneuver, pretended it was "too complicated"[9] for him. The Accord was never formalized in a quadruple agreement, because the interests of the passive powers were obviously incompatible with those of their intended masters. If it eventually failed, it was not for that reason, however, but because of the dramatic shift in the direction of Russian foreign policy after the first Turkish war of Catherine's reign (1768–1774). As an alliance of six powers (to which Panin intended to invite Britain, but it is not clear for what purpose) it was an unrealistic hope; as a device to ensure Russian domination of Sweden and Poland it was a forceful expression of Russian ambitions. Geopolitics teaches that space is a vision and a program. The basin of the Baltic was an ideal ground to test the means to transform a vision into political reality.

Russia's Polish policy acquired from the very beginning of Catherine's reign a forcefulness and sense of purpose unseen since the days of the Empress Anna. Catherine refused to let Charles of Saxony remain on Kurland's ducal throne, and in the summer of 1762 reinstated Biron, newly returned from Siberia. He arrived in Mitava in January 1763, and Charles fled ignominiously. His father, Augustus III, died in October, when the Russians had already decided, in agreement with Prussia, to do away with the Saxon house in Warsaw. They could not find a native candidate for the Polish throne in 1733. Now they found one in Stanislas Poniatowski, a nephew of the Czartoryski brothers, who had been Catherine's lover during his stay as Polish envoy to Petersburg between 1755 and 1758. A massive deployment of troops along the frontier in the fall of 1763 announced Russia's intention to support Stanislas to the full, and a confederation was formed in Lithuania to push the election in the Diet. He was elected in August 1764, the last king of Poland, with Russian troops in Warsaw to stave off any opposition.

The election ushered in the last stage in the disintegration of Poland. Bound to Catherine by his enormous debts and recent memories, the king had to promise to support her "just intentions." The issue of Polish liberties now came to a head. The Czartoryskis, in the hour of their long awaited success, were given to understand that their proposed reforms—abolition of the liberum veto and an increase in the size of the army—were unacceptable. The most violent source of discord between them and their Russian patrons remained the dissidents. It was brought to a head in July 1765 by the Orthodox bishop of Bielorussia, at the instigation of Catherine, who had summoned him to Moscow in the fall of 1762 to discuss the state of the Orthodox Church in Poland. The bishop submitted a list of grievances to the Polish king, who rejected them. The Czartoryskis were "very stubborn" in their refusal to annul the restrictions placed on the dissidents in 1717, but the days of Russian patience were over. Nikolai Repnin, Panin's nephew, who had arrived as Russian envoy in 1764 "with instructions which can only be described as a carefully drafted plan for destroying the republic," went on the offensive, and ordered in October the arrest of the opponents of a compromise, including a Catholic bishop. His stance forced the Poles to accept in February 1768 a treaty placing "Polish liberties" under Russian guarantee "for all time to come"[10] and conferring on the dissidents full civil and political rights.

Such a policy was bound to cause a backlash in a proud people. A confederation led by Jozef Pulaski was formed in the small Turco-Polish border town of Bar; it had once been called "the bastion of Podolia." Repnin ordered the crushing of the confederates. Despite orders to stay within fifteen miles of the border, some Russian troops pursued a group of confederates across border. The Ottomans, already impatient at the increasing deployment of Russian troops in Poland, declared war in October, and the Russians countered at the end of November.

A similar drama was unfolding in Sweden. The real meaning of the Northern Accord became evident when the three "active" powers—Russia, Prussia, and Denmark—pledged to support the oligarchic constitution of 1720. As in Poland, leading political families were for sale to foreign powers in a common orgy of national treason. Huge sums were spent during the Riksdag session of 1765–1766. The Caps returned to power, at the beck and call of the Russian ambassador, who became their treasurer and adviser. That Karlskrona, the naval headquarters, was their political base became a subject of great concern, and Gustav, the first crown prince to have been born in Sweden since Charles XII, warned that anarchy and corruption were leading Sweden down the Polish path. Russia, however, lacked the powerful levers at its disposal in Poland. It was impossible to move large numbers of troops to Sweden short of a general war. There were no dissidents. The monarchy, while weak, was hereditary, and an ambitious crown prince was waiting in the wings. Russia's policy of destabilizing Sweden had been a success, but it was about to suffer a decisive reversal.

2

The Showdown, 1769–1796

Russo-Polish Relations, 1769–1791

The Polish succession crisis of 1763–1764 made it possible to "settle" to Russia's satisfaction the old issues of "Polish liberties" and the rights of dissidents. The issue of Russian fugitives and deserters could not escape attention. The effect of tens of thousands of fugitives crossing into the valleys of the Dvina and the Dniepr was to advance the boundary of the Russian core area into the proximate zone of the Russo-Polish frontier, to create a "fringe of settlement"[1] preparing the way for its eventual transformation, not even into an inner frontier zone of the Russian Empire but into an extension of the core area itself. An awareness of these demographic changes, joined with military considerations that have always led the Russians to look for rivers as boundaries (they were the only physically distinctive feature in an otherwise uniform landscape) were behind the memorandum submitted by General Zakhar Chernyshev, Russia's "war minister," in October 1763. The general recommended taking advantage of the king's death by sending troops into eastern Bielorussia—the eastern fringe of the proximate zone—and then demanding from the new king and the magnates the cession of the fringe along the Dvina and the Drut´. He was certain such a correction of the old boundary would remove causes of enmity between the two countries. No decision was made at the time, but the annexation of the frontier's proximate zone was obviously being taken seriously at the highest levels of the Russian government.

Polish confederates also crossed into Hungary in search of refuge from pursuing Russian troops. To stem the flow and prevent incidents, and also to stop the progress of an epidemic of plague from the Balkans, Vienna

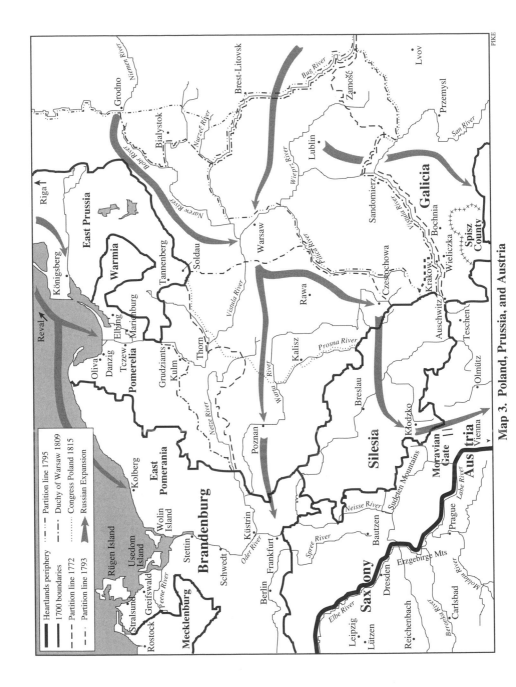

Map 3. Poland, Prussia, and Austria

44

imposed in February 1769 a military cordon around the Polish county of Spisz (Zips) in the foothills of the Tatra Mountains. To keep the confederates out of Prussian territory, Frederick II ordered troops along the Polish border with East Prussia, but took no further action. In May 1770, the Austrian envoy in Berlin reminded the Prussian king that the acquisition of Pomerelia ("Polish" or "West Prussia") separating Brandenburg from East Prussia would at long last unite the two major parts of his domain, a reminder that left the king "a little pensive."[2] In August, Austria extended the cordon into Galicia all the way to the Vistula, including Wieliczka and Bochnia—the richest salt mines in all Central Europe and a major source of revenue for the Polish crown. The move brought the Austrians opposite Kraków. The confederates, still at work, announced the deposition of King Stanislas in October. In retaliation, Prussian and Austrian troops entered Poland. In December, Vienna announced the re-incorporation of the county of Spisz into Hungary; it had been ceded to Poland in 1412.

These Austrian moves cannot be divorced from the rising concern in Vienna with the scope of Russian territorial ambitions in Moldavia and Wallachia, on the eastern fringe of Hungary. Russia was at war with the Ottomans and, as an ally of Prussia, was on unfriendly terms with Austria. The prospect of a Russian victory between the Dniestr and the Danube raised the question of "compensations" for the Germanic powers. Austria would seek compensation in Poland to balance Russian gains in the valley of the Danube. Russo-Polish relations, it bears repeating, had become part of the larger question of Russia's relations with the Germanic powers, whose mission remained the containment of Russian expansion.

The Austrian move activated Prussian policy. The king's brother, Prince Henry, who had been traveling in Sweden, arrived in Moscow in October. Somewhat to his surprise, he found in January 1771 that Catherine II was ready to discuss the possibility of partition. After his return to Berlin, he convinced the king, who gave his ambassador in Petersburg instructions to begin negotiations. The talks went smoothly, but the Russians rejected the Prussian claim to Danzig. The city controlled the entire Vistula trade, and its annexation would give Prussia, along with considerable customs revenues, a stranglehold on the Polish hinterland. Russia had insisted since the beginning of the eighteenth century that Danzig must remain a free city. Like the Austrians, the Prussians claimed compensations—the Russo-Prussian treaty of 1764 required them to subsidize the Russian war effort against the Turks. The Austrians found out about the secret negotiations in June. By then, the Russians had abandoned their claims in Moldavia and Wallachia; they now demanded compensations in Poland to match Austrian acquisitions. The Austrians had no choice but to agree to the principle of a tripartite partition in January 1772, two days after the completion of the separate Russo-Prussian negotiations in which Prussia gave up its claim to Danzig. They bargained hard, however, to obtain the largest share, despite Maria Theresa's qualms about partitioning a Christian country, and a final agreement was not reached until July. The tripartite convention was signed in Petersburg in August.

The partition gave Russia Polish Livonia and moved the boundary along the Dvina, the Ulla, the Drut´, and the Dniepr—Chernyshev's goal in 1763. It gave Russia the watershed between the Dvina and the Dniepr and the control of Bielorussian trade with the Baltic and the Black Sea, to which Russia was about to gain access when peace was made with the Ottomans. It created shorter interior lines from which to project power into Lithuania and Poland proper. Prussia gained Pomerelia and the Netze (Noteć) valley west of the Vistula. East of it, Prussia incorporated the palatinates of Marienburg and Kulm—but without Thorn—and the bishopric of Warmia, the deep enclave that had given East Prussia its particular configuration. Brandenburg and East Prussia were now linked to form a continuous Prussian state stretching from the Elbe to the Niemen. Austria annexed Galicia. The new boundary began at Auschwitz (Oświęcin), followed the Vistula past Sandomierz to the confluence of the San, then a straight line to Zamość, thence to the Western Bug separating Galicia from Volhynia and Podolia (the Right-Bank Ukraine). It continued past Zbarazh to and along the "Podgorze" (Zbruch), a tributary of the Dniestr. The size of the respective shares appears in Table 2.1.

In this first partition, Russia advanced into the frontier, the Germanic powers into the core area. The partition was not a success for Russian foreign policy; it must even be accounted a failure. It had been Russia's goal since Peter I to keep Poland weak, its institutions destabilized in the name of Polish liberties, while the Russian envoy in Warsaw, like the resident in Mitava, went about transforming both core area and frontier into a protectorate, the last stage before their incorporation into the Russian Empire. There had been a Saxon king in Warsaw; there was now a native Pole; there might be, at the proper time, a Russian tsar. However, geography, circumstances, and the containment policy of the Germanic powers were forcing Russia to abandon its long-range goal. It was Panin's view that "Poland must remain in perpetuity, even after partition, an intermediate power between the partitioning powers capable of preventing the collision of their

Table 2.1 The Partition of 1772

	Area[a]	Population[b]
Poland-Lithuania (1771)	**733.5**	**12.25**
Russian share	93.0	1.30
Prussian share	36.3	0.58
Austrian share	81.9	2.65
Remainder	**522.3**	**7.72**

[a]In thousands of square kilometers.
[b]In millions of inhabitants.

interests"; however, a momentum had been started that eventually gave Catherine II the entire frontier but deprived her of the prize.

If the Poles harbored illusions that Russia still regarded Poland as a partner in its foreign policy, rather than a playground for the settlement of its differences with Austria and Prussia, these were dissipated in 1787. Russia was then getting ready for another war with the Ottomans to dislodge them from the shores of the Black Sea west of the Dniepr. Catherine II undertook a long journey down the Dniepr to the Crimea and met King Stanislas at Kanev, south of Kiev, in May. The king offered to join the war at the head of a Polish army of 20,000 men in exchange for Russia's agreement to increase his royal prerogatives and the size of the Polish armed forces in peacetime. He also expected a large Russian subsidy. Seemingly unaware of Poland's weakness, he asked, in addition, for territorial compensations for the losses of 1772, including the annexation of Bessarabia and part of Moldavia, and a port on the Black Sea. With Danzig at the mercy of Prussian obstructionism, Bessarabia would be an outlet to the sea for products of southern Poland and Podolia. The fact that Bessarabia was also coveted by Russia and Austria made the king's offer totally unrealistic. The Russians were in no hurry to obtain the assistance of the Polish army, and their answer was not received in Warsaw until June 1788, when the war was already in progress. The offer of an "alliance" was accepted, but the Polish contingent was reduced to 12,000 men and would have to serve under Russian generals. Poland would receive no territorial compensations, and constitutional reform was unacceptable. Neither Prussia nor Austria would have accepted the alliance anyway—Austria, because it had been the driving force behind the first partition and wanted no rival in the Danube valley; Prussia, because it was then on unfriendly terms with Russia, and Russia could not afford an even more hostile Prussia in its rear in the midst of a war with the Ottomans.

In the meantime, Potemkin, who was also governor general of "New Russia" and the Crimea, had made "immense purchases" of land in the Right-Bank Ukraine, where his strongest supporters were the Potockis and Branickis, the great magnates of the region and the enemies of Stanislas and the "Family" (the name widely given to the Czartoryskis). Early in 1788, he sent to Petersburg a plan to raise a militia in Volhynia and Podolia for action against the Ottomans under his own command. It was suspected there was more than met the eye. After the war, Potemkin, a devout Orthodox, might turn against his Catholic supporters, rouse the Orthodox Ukrainian population, and make himself ruler of the Right Bank between the Pripyat marshes and the Dniestr—a repeat of Khmelnitsky's feat on the left bank in the 1640s. It would be another partition of Poland, in alliance with Prussia, to which Potemkin was willing to abandon Danzig. Austria, no doubt, would find additional compensations in Poland proper. Catherine II could not countenance such an ambitious project while Russia was at war not only with the Ottomans but the

Swedes as well. Austria's cooperation was necessary on the battlefield, but it led straight to the second partition four years later.

The shock administered in 1772 had convinced many Poles of the need to overcome the destructive strife among the magnates and their opposition to constitutional reform. A beginning was made in the right place—education. A central commission carried out fundamental reform in schools and in the two universities in Kraków and Vilno, secularizing and modernizing an educational system that had been the property of the Jesuit order, now abolished. The embodiment of the national revival was the Great Diet or Four-Year Diet that met in October 1788. By consent of all parties, it "confederated" in order to legislate effectively. A feeling of intense hatred against Russia moved the deputies to close the major institutions of government, the existence of which had been guaranteed by Russia to keep the Polish government in a state of permanent paralysis. The Diet went on to debate drastic reforms in all areas of political life. The news of the French Revolution electrified Poland in the fall of 1789. A new constitution was drafted in December but was not voted on by the Diet for more than a year—on May 3, 1791. Its major achievement was to abolish Polish liberties—the liberum veto and the elective monarchy.

The reform movement was a head-on challenge to Russia's position in Poland, but Russia had to tolerate it until the end of the war with the Ottomans in January 1792. Meanwhile, in their euphoria the Poles expected the Russians to accept the reforms as they had Swedish reforms in 1772, overlooking the crucial differences in the situation of the two countries. They added insult to injury by demanding the withdrawal of Russian troops from the frontier, including the Right Bank linking Kiev with the theater of war, and the Russians had to acquiesce in May 1789. The reform movement seemed especially dangerous to Russia because it received unexpected support from Prussia.

Russian foreign policy had been traditionally pro-Austrian because of a common interest in expelling the Ottomans from the southern Ukraine and the valley of the Danube. Catherine II's rapprochement with Prussia had been an interlude, and the Russo-Turkish war that ended in 1774 had brought about a renewal of friendly ties with Austria. In the climate of pathological hatred pervading Austro-Prussian relations, Russia's move caused rancor in Berlin. Frederick II had felt the power of Russian arms and learned he could not afford to provoke the Russians. His nephew and successor, Frederick William II, was less cautious, and chose to take advantage of Russia's military commitments against Sweden and Turkey to advance Prussian interests in Poland. If the Russians had ignored, or rejected, the possibility of strengthening the Polish core area against Prussia after 1772, the Prussians now decided to support the Polish reform movement in a frontal attack on Russia's position in Poland.

In December 1789, the Prussian king offered an alliance to Poland, knowing full well that Catherine had made it known many times that "she would pardon anything except [a Polish] alliance with Prussia."[3] He also offered to negotiate a commercial treaty that appealed to Polish interests, because the vast bulk of Polish foreign trade already had to pass through the territory annexed by Prussia in 1772. The alliance was signed in March 1790, pledging mutual assistance in case of attack. Its crucial provision was a promise of good offices and, if they failed, of assistance, to prevent interference by a third power in the affairs of Poland and Kurland. It had to be assumed that both Russia and Austria would insist on the maintenance of Polish liberties as soon as the Turkish war was over. The Prussian king's move was therefore no less than an ambitious new policy to guarantee Polish reforms, transform Poland into a Prussian protectorate, and turn it outward against Russia and Austria. He had already signed an alliance with the Ottomans in January requiring the Porte to negotiate at the peace conference with Russia and Austria the return to Poland of Austria's share in the partition. The alliance also pledged Prussia to come to the assistance of Turkey and Poland in case of an attack by Vienna or Petersburg. In August, the Diet agreed to begin negotiations in Constantinople for an alliance against Russia.

Much of the Prussian zeal had its origin in the expected support of Britain, which opposed Russia's gains on the Black Sea, and Britain went so far as to prepare for war with Russia in March 1791. However, Britain backed down at the last minute, leaving Prussia in the lurch at the very time the Poles were pushing the Constitution of May 3 through the Diet. Prussia then reversed course and abandoned the Polish cause in June. It would return to its traditional policy of supporting Polish liberties, now in alliance with a resentful Russia. The sorry episode confirmed the sad truth that relations with Poland remained part of the larger question of Russia's relations with the Germanic powers.

While Prussian diplomacy was moving toward war, Russia's policy was moving toward the acceptance of a second partition. Potemkin was then the commander in chief of the Russian army against the Ottomans, and kept his headquarters at Jassy in Moldavia, beyond the Dniestr. His fertile imagination had suggested the formation of an autonomous principality under his rule, combining Moldavia and Wallachia—provided the Russians could wrest them from the Ottomans. Galicia and Podolia were Moldavia's hinterland, and Potemkin's ambitions in Moldavia meshed very well with his ambitions in the Right-Bank Ukraine. In March 1790, he returned to his 1788 plan and recommended the outright annexation of the three palatinates of Kiev, Bratslav, and Podolia, the most fertile provinces of the Polish Empire, drawing a new boundary along a line from Khotin on the Dniestr to the confluence of the Drut´ with the Dniepr. Volhynia might also be added, bringing the entire frontier south of the Pripyat marshes into the Russian Empire. The plan was approved in April. The annexation would complement that of the Ochakov steppe, Russia's major demand from the Ottomans; open up a new corridor of expansion from the Dniepr in the direction of the Danube and the Carpathian Mountains; and break the land connection between Poland

and the Ottoman Empire that had given the Porte a justification for opposing the Russians in Poland.

The Constitution of May 3 polarized reformers and traditionalists. The Russians had always been consistent in their insistence on maintaining Polish liberties. Their determination was strengthened by the connection they saw between the Polish reform movement and the French Revolution. The constitution became a "Jacobin constitution," an imminent danger to the conservative order in Poland, Sweden, and the entire Western Frontier, and even, given enough time, Russia itself. That was intolerable. But the Revolution also offered a golden opportunity to deflect Prussian and Austrian ambitions westward and to place the Germanic powers at the forefront of the struggle against revolutionary France, while Russia gained a free hand in Poland. The Russians had only to find a party to do their work in Poland. Catherine II showed a keen understanding of frontier politics when she declared a party would always be found when needed. And indeed, the constitution had barely been proclaimed when Felix Potocki proposed to Potemkin a confederation of the Right-Bank palatinates to overthrow it. He was joined by Seweryn Rzewuski and Ksaveri Branicki. The three formed the so-called confederation of Targowica in Podolia. The empress approved it, but its implementation was delayed by Potemkin's death in October and the final negotiations with the Ottomans. Peace was made at Jassy in January 1792. The stage was now set for Russia's revenge.

Russo-Baltic Relations, 1769–1791

In the meantime, Russia had remained faithful to its no less consistent policy to destabilize the Swedish core area as well. The Russo-Prussian treaty of April 1764 had been the foundation of the Northern Accord; it had pledged both countries to defend the Constitution of 1720 against any "turbulent party" seeking to upset the peace of the north. When Russia went to war with the Ottomans, it had cause to fear the restoration of monarchical power and the return of an aggressive Swedish policy in alliance with France that had always supported the Ottomans. Prussia pledged in October 1769 that it would make a diversion in Swedish Pomerania in the event of a Swedish attack on Russia and an overthrow of the Swedish government. This Prussian commitment complemented the Russo-Danish alliance of March 1765, pledging Denmark to attack Sweden in Skåne.

Russia, Prussia, and Denmark—the "active powers" in the Northern Accord—had a common interest in supporting "Swedish liberties." Internal disintegration was certain to lead to an eventual partition of the Swedish Empire—the Danes regaining control of both shores of the Sound and Skåne, the Prussians expelling the Swedes from northern Germany, the Russians removing the threat to Petersburg from the large naval base the Swedes had been building at Sveaborg (Suomenlinna), off Helsingfors. A constellation of powers was emerging, similar to the

Russo-Austrian-Prussian ring surrounding Poland. A partition would incorporate Finland and the Gulf of Bothnia into the inner frontier of the empire, strengthen Russian hegemony in the Baltic, and place a Russian viceroy in Stockholm. But Russia's control of Swedish naval bases would also enable it to project naval power against Copenhagen, Stettin, and Königsberg (and Danzig) and effectively transform the Baltic into a closed sea. No wonder some realistic observers were surprised at the blindness of the Danes who, in their hatred of the Swedes—a hatred as intense as that between Prussia and Austria—were willing to ignore the consequences of a partition. Greed motivated the Danes and the Prussians to pursue their short-term interests. Realism should have taught them that only an alliance of the maritime powers—France, Britain, and Denmark—with Prussia could guarantee the "equilibrium of the North."

The corruption of Swedish political life had reached such an extent by the late 1760s that a showdown was becoming inevitable between those who felt Sweden had to save its honor and those who, like the Polish magnates, had no honor left to save and sold themselves to the French, the British, and the Russians. Some were even ready to invite the Russians into Sweden in the name of Swedish liberties. Russian policy toward both Sweden and Poland had rested on a paradox since the beginning of the century—the conservative defense of tradition served to justify a subversive policy of conquest. It was no less a paradox that those most devoted to the protection of civil liberties should have turned themselves into agents of a power so consistently dedicated to their eradication everywhere.

When the new French ambassador, the comte de Vergennes, arrived in Stockholm in 1771, he was shocked to see that the venality exceeded anything he had seen in Constantinople, his previous post. He wrote that the Swedish nation had only one goal—"to obtain the greatest advantage from its prostitution."[4] The Russian ambassador, Count Ivan Osterman (son of the famous Osterman of the 1730s), regularly asked for more than 200,000 rubles before the election of a new Riksdag to support "well intentioned" candidates in five provinces and 106 towns, not including Stockholm. The money was given mostly to the Caps to keep Sweden on a pro-Russian course, to neutralize the influence of rivals, and to secure the appointment of officers devoted to the maintenance of Swedish liberties. Vergennes' appointment alarmed Petersburg—he had been Russia's determined opponent in Constantinople and was destined to become one of the greatest foreign ministers of France. His arrival signaled a change of course in French foreign policy, from support of the Hats and Swedish liberties together with an aggressive stance toward Russia, to support for the restoration of a strong monarchy. France was now willing to outbid the Russian ambassador to reach that goal.

The crown prince had been active in the 1760s garnering supporters of a restoration and preparing public opinion. Rumors had been planted among the peasantry and townsmen that Russia, in alliance with Britain and Denmark, had bought half of the leadership with a view to transforming

Sweden into a Russian province. In January 1770, an agreement had been reached between the Court party and the Hats to revise the constitution, giving the king greater power in legislation and appointments, but it had been kept secret to avoid a political storm. In November, the crown prince had gone to France incognito to gain support for his cause. There the news reached him in February 1771 that King Adolf Frederick had died of a stroke. Sweden was a hereditary monarchy, and the succession could not afford Russia an opportunity to intervene. Nor was there any reason at first: the crown prince, now Gustav III, was still bound by the Constitution of 1720, and was determined to bide his time. The turning point was the partition of Poland, which became known in Stockholm in August 1772. Gustav, certain that Russia, now free in Poland and seeming about to conclude peace with the Ottomans, would turn its full force against Sweden and impose a partition, immediately rallied his supporters in the army, announced the abolition of the constitution, and proclaimed the "restoration" of the monarchy. There were no incidents, and the Stockholm populace acclaimed the change of government.

The attention shifted to Petersburg, because neither Denmark nor Prussia would move without Russia's leading the way. Catherine II was in a quandary. The coup challenged the fundamental assumptions of Russian policy in Sweden, and her credibility was at stake. She tried to stir up opposition in Stockholm and find a party of influential people, as she always did in Poland, but could not find any. The opposition had been silenced by the king's victory, which brought back memories of Sweden's past greatness. There was yet no secessionist movement in Finland, and confederations were unknown. During the winter of 1772–1773, Russia prepared for war and partition—Prussia to get Pomerania, Russia and Denmark to share Sweden between themselves.

But events in faraway Moldavia were forcing Catherine's hand. Russians and Turks had been meeting at Fokshany (Focşani) since July 1772 to end the war. News of the Polish partition stiffened Ottoman resistance to Russian demands—a partition of the Ottoman Empire was obviously one of Russia's objectives—and the similarity between the dissidents in Poland and the Christians in the Balkans was unmistakable. Negotiations broke down, resumed, and broke down again, and Catherine had to face the unpleasant fact that all available Russian forces would have to be concentrated against the Turks when war resumed in the spring of 1773. Russia could not afford a war on the Danube and in the Baltic at the same time, what with the Austro-Prussian antagonism always threatening to cause additional difficulties. Catherine decided to cut her losses and accepted the overthrow of Swedish liberties. In the Polish and Swedish empires, Russia had been forced to abandon its maximum program—a protectorate over both and their eventual annexation.

Nevertheless, the question needs to be asked whether the issue of Swedish liberties had not been a false issue all along. Charles XII had been an exceptional opponent, and it had taken twenty years to destroy the

Swedish hegemony in the Baltic. But memories die hard. Russia would not believe even two generations later that Sweden could no longer be a military rival; Sweden, that it had lost its chance forever. A dispassionate observer, the British envoy to Petersburg, had reported in March 1750 his conversation with Chancellor Bestuzhev-Riumin on the occasion of a similar crisis. He had told Bestuzhev he could not see what harm a change in the form of government could do to Russia; that without Charles XII's "wild expedition" the Russians would not be the masters of the "fine provinces" now in their possession; that there were "many Charles XII" in Sweden; and that if one should come back and make war, Russia would have a good chance to get the remainder of Finland. The chancellor had smiled and agreed it was true.[5]

The restoration revitalized Swedish foreign policy, and Gustav III set about reasserting Sweden's role in the Baltic. That could be done only by challenging Denmark or Russia, and perhaps even both. The Swedes knew that while their hold on Finland was weak, the Danes were vulnerable in Norway. The kings of Denmark had ruled Norway since 1442, but the two countries were separated by the Skagerrak Strait, and the Swedes could easily cut off communications between Copenhagen and Oslo from their base in Göthenburg (Göteborg). Charles XII had been killed in 1718 leading an expedition into Norway. During the eighteenth century, prosperity developed a national consciousness in Norway, where peasants were free, as in Sweden and Finland, while they were serfs in Denmark. As Swedish hopes to recover the Baltic provinces grew dimmer with the passage of time, the possibility to obtain "compensations" in Norway became more attractive, and influential voices began to be heard calling for a westward reorientation of Swedish foreign policy, across the Kjølen toward the Coastland and the Atlantic. In November 1779, for example, the Swedish ambassador to France and a noted literary figure, Gustav Creutz, called on his king to annex Norway.

Although it was in Russia's interest to turn Sweden outward, such a policy would be incompatible with the Russo-Danish rapprochement. Close relations became even more necessary after Gustav's coup, with all its unknown implications. Moreover, with the outbreak of the American Revolution in April 1775, Britain was taking an aggressive stand toward neutral shipping, and it was not the time to talk war in the Baltic when unity was essential. The Russo-Danish defensive alliance of August 1773 bound the two powers to assist each other in the event of a Swedish attack—Denmark with 12,000 troops and fifteen ships, Russia with 20,000 men and ten ships. It also confirmed the July agreement by which Grand Duke Paul, who had reached his majority in September, formally accepted the settlement of 1767. He ceded the two duchies of Oldenburg and Delmenhorst to Frederick August, the Protestant bishop of Lübeck and titular head of the cadet line of the Holstein-Gottorp house. From then on, the Russian emperor would remain supreme head (*verkhovnyi shef*) of the house, but the actual administration of its properties was transferred to the cadet line. The agreement finally brought an end to a complicated question that had poisoned Russo-Danish relations since the 1720s. Ten years later, at the end of the American revolutionary war in 1783, when the Swedes got ready for war—they planned to pin the Danes in Jutland while a Swedish army would cross into Norway—Catherine made it clear Russia would not stand for it. Her threat was persuasive because Sweden's rear was vulnerable in Finland.

Britain's interference with neutral shipping, based on the assumption that any goods destined for the enemy, even if carried in neutral ships, was liable to confiscation as contraband of war, caused a backlash among the Baltic powers. Twenty years earlier, in 1759, a Professor Martin Hupner of Copenhagen University had published a famous book claiming a neutral flag protected the goods against seizure and that a port could not be considered blockaded by a simple declaration of a belligerent power, thereby exposing any ship bound for it to seizure, but must be effectively closed to shipping by enemy warships. Britain rejected these contentions, but the Danish foreign minister, Andreas Bernstorf, convinced Catherine II to stand up for these principles. Such was the ideological origin of the Russian Declaration of Armed Neutrality of March 1780. The Swedes, too, had an interest in protecting their merchantmen. Gustav III's minister of commerce, Johan Liljencrants (Westerman), worked hard to develop a Swedish merchant marine in order to take advantage of the growing Baltic and North Sea trade, stimulated by war in America. Russia signed with Denmark in July and with Sweden in August two maritime conventions embodying Hupner's ideas. The three powers pledged to coordinate the naval protection of their ships and agreed that the Baltic was a closed sea to be kept out of international conflicts, not only during the present war but in the future as well. Russia was laying the foundation of a fortress-fleet strategy, seeking to close off the Baltic to British naval penetration. This ambition was bound to fail so long as both shores of the Sound remained controlled by two different powers whose mutual distrust and enmity could not be overcome whatever treaties and conventions might say.

And indeed, the American war was barely over when the restless Swedish king threatened to upset the "equilibrium of the North." His determination to modernize the Swedish government, to introduce fiscal reforms, to tame the nobility yearning for the golden age of Swedish liberties, and to control the civil service with his agents, generated much opposition in a country proud of its political pluralism. Foreign adventure is often a safety valve against domestic unrest. Russia's refusal to support Sweden against Denmark created resentment in Stockholm, and the ghost of Charles XII returned to exhort the Swedes who refused to accept Russia's hegemony in the Baltic. Soon after the coup, the king had decided to strengthen Sweden's offensive capacity in the Gulf of Finland, building up Sveaborg from which ships of the line would harass the Russian navy while a galley flotilla would land troops in Karelia and Estonia. New docks, the largest in the world, were built at Karlskrona.

The Russians were aware of Swedish intentions to force the issue in Finland, the intermediate zone of the Russo-Swedish frontier. In 1786, General Alexander Suvorov was sent to inspect the terrain. During the Riksdag session, the Russian envoy, Count Andrei Razumovsky, returned to tradition by openly siding with the opposition and inviting its members to meet at his house. More ominously, the Russians began to show interest in the nascent Finnish secessionist movement. The growth of Petersburg as the capital of a mighty empire was creating a gravitational pull on Finland. Large numbers of peasants, artisans, and domestics left for the Russian capital. Local men of power, resentful of the domination of Finland from Åbo, could not fail to be attracted by an empire where their cousins from the Germanic nobility of Livonia were making brilliant careers. Rumors were already circulating that a Colonel Jakob Sprengtporten had given the Russians the Swedish war plans. As in 1739 and 1772, Sweden needed to find Russia engaged in a war with the Ottomans, and one was about to begin, in August 1787. The Turco-Swedish alliance of 1739 was still on the books and had never been tested.

The third Russo-Swedish war of the century resulted, like the second (1741–1743), from a massive underestimation of Russian power. It was a gamble that the commitment of the Russian army to the Turkish front would leave Russia defenseless in Finland and Petersburg dangerously exposed to a Swedish surprise attack. It is possible, had their high command been less incompetent, that the Swedes might have invested Petersburg and forced the court to flee, but such a Pyrrhic victory would not have forced the enemy to make peace and would certainly have exposed the Swedes to the full fury of a Russian revenge at the end of the Turkish war. The Danes, despite their alliance with Russia, took little part in the war. They had always been torn between their short- and long-term interests. A partition of Sweden was always attractive, but the growth of Russian power was threatening. Preoccupation with land reform and the emancipation of the peasantry provided a good excuse for making only a token show of force. Even that—a small offensive from Norway against Göthenburg in September 1788—had to be stopped when Britain and Prussia, set to contain Russian expansion, threatened Denmark with a war on two fronts. Catherine's anger at Sweden's treacherous attack and Denmark's equivocation, together with Anglo-Prussian hostility, would go a long way to explain the harsh and uncompromising tone of Russian foreign policy from 1791 to 1796.

When the Swedish fleet left harbor in June 1788, the crews did not know they were going to war, and hostilities began with a ruse: a party of Swedish soldiers dressed in Russian uniforms attacked Swedish outposts from the Russian side in Karelia. Gustav III demanded the recall of Razumovsky, the return of the Baltic provinces, the acceptance of Swedish mediation in Russia's war with the Ottomans, and the disarmament of the warships the Russians were planning to send through the Sound to the Mediterranean to support their operations on land. Such war aims were unrealistic unless the Swedes could win a decisive victory. But they failed before Neishlot, even under the king's personal command, and retreated in August after a Swedish squadron was blockaded in Sveaborg, its communications with Karlskrona cut off by the Russians. A year later, in July 1789, another Swedish squadron sent out on a rescue mission was forced back to Karlskrona, and in August the Swedes were defeated at sea near Rochensalm, south of Fredrikshamn. Weather conditions restricted naval operations in the eastern Baltic to the summer months, and hostilities did not resume until May 1790, when the Swedes, commanded by the king's brother, Charles, duke of Södermanland, failed before Reval and Vyborg. The land war was not going better for the Swedes, who had to give up St. Mikhel (Mikkeli) in the lake district in July. Faced with the failure of his offensive war and unable to resist a Russian counteroffensive, the king sued for peace.

The war had not received unconditional support in Sweden, and the long tradition of staffing the officer corps with individuals who distrusted the monarchy had planted pockets of opposition to Gustav III in the Swedish army. Sweden's aggression and the devious ways by which it was launched had angered a number of officers, who formed a conspiracy known as the Anjala League (after a small Finnish town) in July 1788. Confederations had never been part of Swedish liberties, but the league resembled a Polish confederation in at least three ways: it sought to reduce the powers of the king to make war and peace; it was based in the frontier and called for Finnish autonomy within the Swedish Empire; it sought Russian support. But Catherine II was resolved not to play the Finnish card at this time, because the Turkish war and Anglo-Prussian hostility counseled prudence in the Baltic and the best form of prudence was to insist on maintaining the status quo ante bellum. On the other hand, the war placed the Finnish question on the agenda of Russia's Baltic policy—it exposed the potential vulnerability of Petersburg to a successful surprise attack, and that threat would dominate Russian thinking until the annexation of Finland in 1809.

Wars generally strengthen the executive power, and Gustav III felt strong enough during the Riksdag session of 1789 to push through the so-called Act of Union and Security. It abolished the council that had continued to rule with the king after 1772 and gave the king full powers over the appointment of officials and the exclusive right to propose legislation. Sweden became a dictatorship supported by Britain and Prussia. The king then turned against the seditious officers and sent members of the Anjala League to prison. But the restoration of the absolute monarchy did not bring victory in the field. On the contrary, it was followed by the peace of Verele (Werälä), near the Kiumenne River, in August 1790. The Russians tried to restore Article 7 of the Treaty of Nystad (it had given them an opportunity to interfere in Swedish affairs) on the grounds that every state must see to it that dangerous changes do not take place in the political constitutions of its neighbors. The claim was difficult to justify, because the coup of 1789 had abolished Swedish liberties and Sweden would have to accept Russia's right to overthrow its king from the Stockholm embassy. Britain made known its objections, and the Russians conceded the point.

The treaty was concluded "in a hurry" and probably remains one of the shortest on record. The Russians withdrew behind their prewar boundaries and the Swedes retained the right to purchase 50,000 rubles worth of grain duty-free in Russia's Baltic ports, provided the grain was destined for domestic consumption. Russia accepted implicitly the failure of its destabilization policy and the restoration of absolutism. When Peter von der Pahlen was sent to Stockholm on a special mission before the restoration of diplomatic relations, he was instructed "to use his eyes and ears but not to mix in anything."[6] That may have been the major achievement of the war, and it was a Swedish victory. Yet there was something ominous in the transfer of Otto von Stackelberg, Russia's "viceroy" in Warsaw, to Stockholm in 1791. Sweden was made to feel that Russia's concessions at Verele should not be misunderstood.

Gustav III had lost his war against Russia, and Sweden's position in Finland was weaker than ever. He could not hope to gain compensations in Norway without Russian support. He had lost the considerable subsidies France had been paying Sweden for a century, as the revolution channeled French energies into Germany and Italy. Only Russia could provide financial assistance to an exhausted Swedish treasury. And the king, paradoxically, found himself in need of Russian support for his own political survival when a financial crisis combined with popular anger at Sweden's performance during the war to create an explosive situation. On the other hand, Russia needed Sweden against the Anglo-Prussian combination. At the height of the crisis with Britain during the winter of 1790–1791, Russia demanded that Denmark close the Sound to British warships, but the Danes, on the periphery of the Heartland, were beginning to realize how vulnerable they were to British demands backed by an invincible fleet. Russia could not afford a hostile Sweden as the ground began to shake under the old network of alliances. A destabilization policy was becoming less realistic. A powerful Russia needed to be at peace with a weakened Sweden in order to maintain the new equilibrium of the North in Russia's favor. The Russo-Swedish defensive alliance of October 1791 was part of a broad offensive to create a "Triple Alliance of the North," the diplomatic complement of a fortress-fleet strategy. It also gave Russia a free hand in Poland.

Partitions and Humiliations, 1792–1796

The Turkish war was barely over in January 1792 when Catherine II ordered Nikolai Repnin—the same Repnin who had intervened so forcefully in Poland between 1764 and 1768 and had been one of the most assertive commanders in the war—to prepare for an invasion of Poland through the Right-Bank Ukraine. In Petersburg, the shaping of an uncompromising Polish policy passed into the hands of the new favorite, Platon Zubov. Prussia and Austria were informed of Russia's plans, but were encouraged to fight the French Revolution in the German lands west of the Elbe, leaving Russia free to concentrate its energy on extirpating

"Jacobinism" in Poland. Russian troops invaded Poland in May, and King Stanislas capitulated in July. The second partition was formalized in the Russo-Prussian convention of January 1793. It was justified by the "imminent and universal danger" created by the "spirit of insurrection and innovation" in Poland and by Russia's need to compensate for the large expenditures needed to keep its armed forces at their present "formidable level."[7] The new Russian boundary began at Druia on the Dvina near the Kurland border, followed the Naroch and Dubrova rivers, passed slightly to the west of Pinsk, and continued across the Pripyat marshes into the Right-Bank Ukraine in a straight line to the Zbruch, where it met the Austrian border of 1772. It then followed the Dniestr and the boundary of the Ottoman Empire to the Ochakov steppe annexed from the Turks in 1792. The Russian share included the whole of Bielorussia as well as most of Volhynia and Podolia, three of the six zones of the Russo-Polish frontier. The Left Bank had been annexed in 1667, Polish Livonia in 1772. There remained only Lithuania proper. On the other hand, Prussia's share included most of the original lands of the Polish core area—Great Poland and the duchy of Poznan—as well as Danzig. Its boundary followed a line running from Silesia past Czestochowa and Rawa to Soldau (Działdowo) on the East Prussian border. The actual annexation took place in April. The Russian share was by far the larger, but Prussia's was substantial (Table 2.2).

Since the intervention had taken place in the name of Polish liberties and the partition had been justified by the need to restore order and legality, the two powers insisted that the Diet must ratify the convention. Russia's representatives, General Otto von Igelström and Jakob von Sievers, both from Livonia of Swedish ancestry, and the Prussian envoy used every means at their disposal to coerce local assemblies to select deputies who would raise no questions. The new Diet met in Grodno, far from mutinous Warsaw, in June. The king was persuaded to go, but Catherine instructed Sievers to consider himself "the head of the country."[8] The Diet formally annulled the Constitution of May 3; reduced the Polish army to 18,000 men; restored the elective monarchy and the liberum veto; and ratified the partition with Russia in July, with Prussia in

Table 2.2   The Partition of 1793

	Area[a]	Population[b]
Poland-Lithuania (1792)	**522.3**	**7.72**
Russian share	250.2	3
Prussian share	57.1	1
Remainder	**215**	**3.72**

[a]In thousands of square kilometers.
[b]In millions of inhabitants.

September, at a so-called "dumb session"; the motion was declared carried when all the deputies remained silent.

Russia then imposed on the Diet an unequal treaty of alliance in October that removed whatever remained of Polish independence. In the event of Russia being at war with a European power, the Polish army would have to serve under a Russian commander in chief. Poland relinquished the capacity to form any "connection or transaction" with a foreign power except in concert with the Russian government. Last but not least, the Polish-Lithuanian nobility was given in Russia the same rights as the Russian nobility, and the Russian nobility in Poland-Lithuania the same rights as the local nobility. This clause was crucial, but by no means exceptional. It represented no less than an attempt to incorporate the men of power in both frontier and core area—what was left of it—into the Russian Imperial elite and to transform frontier and core area into an inner frontier of the Russian Empire. The destabilization policy had paid handsome dividends, and one can well understand why the Swedes had been so concerned.

The second partition did not end the Polish "spirit of insurrection." On the contrary. Nobles and burghers in the capital and larger towns launched a conspirational movement against the Russians. The uprising began in Ostrołenka and Kraków in March 1794. Warsaw rose in April; Igelström was taken by surprise, and half the Russian garrison was killed, wounded, or taken prisoner. The rest withdrew and Igelström was recalled in disgrace. The uprising spread to Lithuania and Volhynia, and found a leader in Tadeusz Kościuszko. The insurgents fought for the restoration of the Constitution of May 3 and even promised land and freedom to the peasantry. The Russians were slow to respond. Their forces had been withdrawn after the partition to Livonia and the Right Bank, and they counted on the Prussians to crush the rebellion in Warsaw. The Prussians failed, however, even with their king in command, and had to lift the siege of the capital in September. By then, the Russians were counterattacking. Repnin occupied Lithuania and was appointed governor general in Slonim in October; Suvorov was sent from the Right Bank with orders to take Warsaw. Kościuszko was defeated and taken prisoner in October; Warsaw surrendered in November. The uprising was over, and Russia had crushed it with minimal Prussian and Austrian help.

There could no longer be any question of retaining even the shadow of Polish "independence." The policy of destabilization had now outlived its usefulness, and its only alternative was a final partition. By May, even before the Russian counterattacks began, Alexander Bezborodko, Catherine's chief secretary and a man from the Left Bank, had marked out the respective shares of the three partitioning powers. The Austrians were more than a willing partner—they had been kept out of the second partition, and their appetite for compensations had grown accordingly. Petersburg was getting used to its new role not only of mediator between the Germanic powers but also of balancer between Berlin and Vienna. The need for Austrian support, as Catherine began to contemplate the possibility of another war with the Ottomans, drew Russia and Austria together. The empress, who had carried out the second partition in alliance with Prussia behind Austria's back, decided to carry out the third with Austria and to impose a joint settlement on Prussia.

The Russians and Austrians reached agreement in November 1794, paving the way for the convention of January 1795 to partition Poland. Austria recognized the partition of 1793 and abandoned its claims beyond the Bug, in the Russo-Polish frontier. It annexed all Polish lands between the Pilica, the Vistula, and the Bug and a line running from the upper Bug to the source of the Zbruch. It also recognized Russia's annexation of Lithuania along a line from Brest-Litovsk to Grodno and along the Niemen to the East Prussian border. The annexation of Lithuania (and of the district of Polangen) entailed the annexation of Kurland. Biron had died in 1769 and been succeeded by his son Peter, who was forced to abdicate in April. Petersburg appointed yet another Baltic German, Peter von der Pahlen (who had been sent to Stockholm in 1790), governor general in Mitava. The entire Russo-Polish frontier had been incorporated into the inner frontier of the Russian Empire.

Prussia had been kept in the dark, and decided to force the issue with Austria. It withdrew from the war with France in April and moved its forces into Poland and in Bohemia. In August, when war seemed inevitable, Vienna notified Berlin of the existence of the January agreement. Faced with the certainty of war with both Austria and Russia, Prussia acceded to the agreement in October. It also gained some concessions. It annexed Warsaw and Praga, the city's right-bank suburb, the salient between the Bug and the Vistula, and a wedge of land on the Silesian border. It had to accept the loss of Sandomierz and Kraków. The shares of the three powers appear in Table 2.3.

Poland and its empire had ceased to exist. King Stanislas abdicated in November 1796 and later went to live in Petersburg, where he died in 1798.

The year had begun as inauspiciously in Sweden as it had in Poland. One month before the proclamation of the confederation of Targowica,

Table 2.3 The Partition of 1795

	Area[a]	Population[b]
Poland-Lithuania (1794)	**215**	**3.72**
Russian share	120	1.20
Prussian share	48	1.02
Austrian share	47	1.50
Total	**215**	**3.72**

[a]In thousands of square kilometers.
[b]In millions of inhabitants.

in March, Gustav III had died of wounds suffered at the hand of an officer who had taken it upon himself to express the growing opposition to the king's dictatorial ways and to strike a blow for Swedish liberties. As Robert Bain wrote, "the political importance of Sweden died with him,"[9] and the country was about to enter the last stage of its imperial decline. His son Gustav was only 13, and the reins of government passed to his paternal uncle, Charles, duke of Södermanland, as regent. The duke had commanded the Swedish army during the war of 1788–1790, and was strongly anti-Russian. He regarded the agreement of October 1791 as "a dangerous pact of servitude,"[10] similar to those "defensive alliances" Russia had signed with Poland from time to time since the beginning of the eighteenth century. His policy was to return to the old alliance with France that had been for so long the bedrock of Swedish foreign policy. Unfortunately, the France of 1792 was revolutionary France, and the influence of the revolution in Warsaw had already become the main justification of Russia's massive intervention in Poland. From Petersburg, it seemed that when one head of the revolutionary hydra was about to be cut down in the Polish capital, another was sprouting in Stockholm.

The shift in Swedish policy was all the more threatening because the regent had brought back from exile Baron Gustav Reuterholm, who had belonged to the most extreme opposition to Gustav III and was known for his Jacobin sympathies. Reuterholm became the regent's chief adviser, and he believed Sweden still had a chance to recover Karelia. Russia saw the appointment as a challenge no less decisive than the Constitution of May 3. Stackelberg, the new Russian envoy, fresh from Warsaw, forgot he had crossed the Baltic and, perhaps confused by the fact that Russia had followed a destabilization policy in both Warsaw and Stockholm, exhibited the same overbearing behavior in the Swedish capital. He so offended the regent that Catherine had to recall him, and he left Sweden in May 1793 without even a farewell audience. Catherine retaliated by cutting off the subsidies promised in 1791, declaring they made no sense in the context of a growing Swedish rapprochement with France and Swedish intrigues against Russian interests in Warsaw and Constantinople. A new Russian envoy, no better choice, did not arrive until March 1794. Sergei Rumiantsev had been envoy to Berlin from 1786 to 1788, where his haughtiness and hostility to Prussia had also led to his recall. He could not expect to be successful in Stockholm. The regent, Reuterholm, and the Court made his life so unbearable that he had to leave five months later. Both Russia and Sweden were obviously fighting a war of nerves while Poland was being partitioned across the Baltic, but the war exposed the limitations of Russian policy. To be effective, a destabilization policy must be backed by credible military threats and must find a favorable environment. Russia's commitments in Poland and the Southern Frontier dictated caution in the Baltic, and so the absolute monarchy remained firmly established in Stockholm.

Relations were further embittered by the delicate negotiations over the prospective marriage of the king's heir, Gustav. If the regent and Reuterholm were anti-Russian, the regency was divided between partisans of the Russian alliance and those of the more traditional French alliance. Soon after Gustav III's death, an unofficial proposal was made to Petersburg to arrange for 1796, when Gustav would reach his majority, a marriage with Alexandra, the daughter of Grand Duke Paul and granddaughter of Catherine II. The envoy sent to Petersburg in October 1793 to congratulate the future Alexander I on his marriage with Elizabeth of Baden was empowered to begin formal negotiations for a marital contract. The announcement that Reuterholm would come to Petersburg to sign it made the Russians suspicious, but it was agreed that Gustav could not come to the Russian capital to meet his bride because Swedish law forbade a king to leave his country before his majority, and that Alexandra would be formally promised the exercise of her Orthodox religion in Lutheran Sweden. However, the regent, spurred by his anti-Russian advisers, announced publicly, and without even consulting Gustav, the engagement of the young heir to the princess of Mecklenburg. The engagement was celebrated in November 1795, and prayers were ordered in all churches for the health of the future queen.

Gustav, however, declared that he did not want that marriage, forcing the regent to promise Catherine in April 1796 that it would not take place. In August, in an attempt to mend relations, the regent and Gustav traveled to Petersburg incognito—a compromise with Swedish law. The king, only two months away from his majority, showed the rudeness and stubbornness that would make his reign a political disaster. When the contract was about to be signed, he refused to give the guarantee of Alexandra's religious freedom, and none of Catherine's dignified pleading would change his mind. Negotiations broke down, and the two Swedes returned to Stockholm in September. Gustav IV was inaugurated on November 1. It was widely believed at the time that his insulting behavior was the cause of the stroke that killed the empress two weeks later.

The contrast with Poland could not be greater. Not only had Russia's policy to destabilize Sweden failed ignominiously, but the empress had been humiliated in her own capital. However, the Russians still had a trump card—in Finland.

3

Denouement and Epilogue, 1796–1917

Russo-Baltic Relations, 1796–1815

Paul I, the new Russian emperor, had been tutored by Nikita Panin in the 1760s, and had a strong interest in reviving a Northern Accord. His dislike of the deceased Potemkin made him a natural opponent of a policy focused mainly on relations with the Ottoman Empire. Moreover, the continuously rising tide of the French Revolution and the emergence of Napoleon compelled Russia to take a more active part in the conservative struggle against international subversion instead of leaving that task to Prussia and Austria. This new focus on the Baltic sector and on the struggle with Napoleon during the reigns of Paul I (1796–1801) and Alexander I (1801–1825) was bound to have important consequences for Russo-Swedish and Russo-Polish relations.

Paul did not have his mother's patience, and the question of Alexandra's marriage was quickly settled. A last effort was made to obtain Gustav's religious guarantee, but he answered that he no longer wished to marry an Orthodox bride. Russia withdrew its envoy in March 1797, Sweden recalled its ambassador, and diplomatic relations were broken off. The two rulers having made their point, the time had come to face the future.

French expansionism created two theaters of international conflict, separate yet overlapping. One was the conflict between Britain and France for hegemony in the European Coastland; the other was a conflict between France and the Germanic powers and eventually Russia alone for hegemony within the Heartland between the Elbe, the Niemen, and the Bug. As a result, the four core areas—Prussia, Austria, Sweden, and Poland (partitioned between Prussia and Austria)—were transformed for the duration of the conflict into a succession of zones of an extended Franco-Russian frontier, and Russia's relations with them were submerged into the larger question of its relations with France and Britain.

The Anglo-French conflict at sea played havoc with neutral shipping, as it had in the past, during the Seven Years War and the war of American independence. As a result, Denmark and Sweden signed in March 1797 a treaty of armed neutrality, placing their warships under a single command to protect their merchantmen against British and French privateers. The move had little effect, and the continued denial of the rights of neutral shipping finally brought Russia into the fray. Russia entered the war with France in the fall of 1798. Gustav IV made his second visit to Petersburg and renewed in October 1799 the alliance of 1791, with the additional provision that 10,000 Swedish troops would join a Russian corps being shipped to Holland for action against the French. The alliance contained an implicit defense of armed neutrality, but it was not until December 1800 that Russia joined Denmark and Sweden (and Prussia) in a renewal of the Declaration of Armed Neutrality, first proclaimed in March 1780.

The immediate background of the Russian move was the tsar's abrupt reversal of course in the wake of Napoleon's victories and British intransigence over Malta. Russia found itself unofficially at war with Britain, and a declaration of armed neutrality was a hostile act on Russia's part, since the country was no longer neutral. Although the text of the convention of December 1800 made no reference to the Baltic's being a closed sea, that assertion had been very much part of the system of armed neutrality followed successfully during the American war. Britain could not help seeing another Russian attempt to project naval power in the Sound and even beyond, in the Coastland. It struck first, and a naval demonstration off Copenhagen at the end of March 1801 forced Denmark to leave the system of armed neutrality and recognize Britain's right to visit Danish ships on the high seas. The demonstration also served as a warning to Russia. In June, Alexander I abandoned the system, leaving Sweden in the lurch.

The next six years were dominated by the great conflict for hegemony in Central Europe, pitting Napoleon against the Prussians, the Austrians, and the Russians. Alliances shifted on the spur of the moment, and the suspicion of one another's motives became endemic, but the conservative coalition Catherine II had begun to forge in the Heartland continued to grow. During that time, Sweden's role was downgraded to that of a Russian satellite, drawn into the conflict against its own best interests. Gustav IV had been in touch with French emigrés who inspired in him a blind hatred of Napoleon. He joined the coalition against France in 1805, but its defeat two years later spelled the loss of Sweden's last possessions in Germany—Swedish Pomerania with Stralsund and Rügen Island. In fact, the Swedes had little room to maneuver. The enormous growth of Russian power in the Baltic after 1796 had made their hold on Finland a hostage to Russia's restraint. In 1803, a petty incident provoked by

Gustav IV on the Russo-Finnish border had brought about a forceful demonstration on land and at sea, and the king had been forced to yield.

The incident, however, revived Russian fears of a Swedish attack on Petersburg—fears never forgotten since the treacherous attack of 1788—at a time when Russian forces were engaged in Central Europe. The magnitude of the Napoleonic threat was forcing Russia to look on the security of its Finnish rear as an imperative necessity. During a discussion following the incident, Alexander I had asked the commanding general of the engineers, General Johann (Peter) van Suchtelen, to describe the optimum boundary between Russia and Sweden. The general had drawn a line across the length of the Gulf of Bothnia from Tornio to the Åland Islands, and insisted, much to the tsar's surprise at the size of the proposed annexation, that there was no other secure border. A consensus was emerging in the military establishment that the time had come to complete the incorporation of the entire Russo-Swedish frontier into the inner frontier of the Russian Empire.

The wars of 1805–1807 ended with a Russian defeat and the peace of Tilsit (Sovetsk) in July 1807. Russia had to recognize French supremacy in Europe and join the Continental System by which Napoleon hoped to close the entire Atlantic and Baltic coast to British trade. Its corollary was the closure of the Sound to British ships and the ships of other powers that refused to join the blockade. The Franco-Russian alliance forced Denmark and Sweden against the wall: it was agreed at Tilsit that if they did not close their ports by December 1, they would be treated as enemy powers by France and Russia.

The Danes had refused to join the coalition, hoping neutrality would save them from the British and the French. Tilsit made neutrality impossible, and it was known France intended to occupy Denmark and seize Elsinore (Helsingør), the customs house where the Danish king collected the Sound dues. Russia would attack Sweden across Finland. Again, Britain struck first, and a violent bombardment of Copenhagen in September forced the Danes to surrender their entire fleet. However, the British action threw the Danes into the French camp, where they would stay until 1814.

There remained Sweden. Gustav IV refused to join the Continental System, and 50,000 Russian troops were massed along the Finnish border at the end of the year. Napoleon gave Russia a free hand to conquer Finland in order to compel Swedish compliance, and even contemplated a joint Franco-Danish operation in Skåne. The fourth and last Russo-Swedish war was about to begin.

And yet, there was no eagerness in Russia to begin that war. One reason was Alexander's reluctance to fight his wife's brother-in-law. Gustav IV, after his unpleasant experience in Russia, had married in October 1797 Friederike of Baden, the sister of the tsar's wife. A second was Russian distrust of Napoleon's motives, notably in Poland, further stimulated by the unseemly haste with which the French ambassador kept urging the tsar to go to war. A third was the unpopularity of the Continental System in Russia. And finally, Russia had been at war with the Ottomans since the end of 1806, reviving the traditional apprehension about a war on two fronts separated by enormous distances.

Nevertheless, operations began in February 1808, when the Russians crossed into Finland without declaring war in a last attempt to convince Gustav IV of the error of his ways. The Swedes were unprepared, and the Russian advance met with little resistance. Tavastehus (Hämeenlinna), an important road junction on the western edge of the lake district, was taken a few weeks later. In March, the Russians landed on the Åland Islands and even Gotland. When Gustav still refused to join the Continental System, Russia declared war and announced the annexation of Finland. Sveaborg surrendered in April, and southern Finland was once again (as in 1714) in Russian hands. There remained northern Finland (Ostrobothnia), never yet conquered. The Swedes kept the Russians on the defensive in that desolate country through the summer, but withdrew with the onset of winter. Uleåborg (Oulu) capitulated in November, and the entire eastern coast of the Gulf of Bothnia passed under Russian occupation. The second stage of the war began—the invasion of Sweden itself.

The invasion was planned from three directions. A first force would take Tornio, seize Swedish stores of provisions, and advance in the coastal plain of Sweden in the direction of Umeå. A second would cross the Gulf of Bothnia on the ice, hopping from one island to the next in the Kvarken Strait facing Umeå and linking up with the first force. The third would cross from the Åland Islands, and the three forces would then converge on Stockholm. At no time since Peter I had such an ambitious land and sea operation been launched against Sweden, and in 1809 Russia's superiority was overwhelming. The first and second forces were on their way to success when dissatisfaction with Gustav IV's erratic behavior led a group of officers to depose him in March 1809. Alexander arrived in Åbo a few days after the coup and refused to accept an armistice. Unable to stop the Russian invasion, the Swedes capitulated and made peace at Fredrikshamn in September. Meanwhile, a new constitution had been promulgated in May that in some ways marked a return to that of 1720— it greatly reduced the king's power—and in June, the Riksdag, riding a wave of disgust with the king, chose his uncle, the former regent, to succeed him as Charles XIII (1809–1818).

The peace treaty compelled Sweden to join the Continental System and close its ports to British trade. It retained the old provision allowing Sweden to buy 50,000 rubles worth of grain duty-free for domestic consumption except when a poor harvest required the suspension of Russian grain exports. It confirmed the annexation of the Åland Islands and moved the boundary of the Russian Empire to the Tornio River and its tributary, the Muonio, both descended from the Kjølen. During the negotiations the Russians had insisted on drawing the boundary considerably farther west, along the Kalix River, but Alexander I agreed to withdraw along the Tornio River as a gesture of goodwill. Even with this considerable concession, Sweden lost 26 percent of its population and 40 percent of its territory. Suchtelen's project had been fully carried out. A Russian military presence on the Åland Islands, in Vasa (Vaasa), and in Tornio exposed the entire coastal plain of Sweden along the Gulf of Bothnia and Stockholm itself to a Russian attack. The Russo-Swedish frontier had been fully incorporated into the inner frontier of the Russian Empire, and any future Russo-Swedish war would have to be fought on Swedish soil. But there would be no other war. Russia recognized implicitly in 1809 that it had reached a line of an optimum of conquest, although it would later try, unsuccessfully, to get around the northern end of the Kjølen and reach the North Atlantic coast in Finnmark. Suchtelen was appointed ambassador to Stockholm with instructions not to take sides in Swedish internal affairs, because it was no longer in Russia's interest to further weaken its long-time opponent. Two centuries of Russo-Swedish antagonism were coming to an end.

Russia's desire to dampen rancor in Sweden after such a staggering defeat was motivated, not by disinterested generosity, but by the need to gain Swedish support in the struggle against Napoleon. Tilsit had created no real peace, and the Franco-Russian rivalry in Poland, Prussia, Austria, and the Southern Frontier already raised the specter of war. Russia needed allies to resist the French advance into the Heartland where its vital interests were most directly threatened, and the assistance of those powers to contain Napoleon within the Coastland.

The years 1810–1811 marked the transition to the new epoch. In January 1810, Sweden officially joined the Continental System and formed an alliance with France in exchange for the return of Pomerania. But it was a half-hearted alliance because Sweden—and Russia—were the major victims of a blockade that crippled their profitable trade with Britain. The Continental System was bound to forge a Russo-Swedish alliance.

The dynastic question intervened to add to the rapidly changing situation. Charles XIII had no heir, and it was the Riksdag's responsibility to select an heir presumptive. The successful candidate was Jean Bernadotte, one of Napoleon's marshals, who gained popularity in Sweden not only because he was a Frenchman—memories of the prerevolutionary Franco-Swedish tie remained strong—but also because he had kindly treated Swedish prisoners of war during the operations of 1805–1807. But he also harbored a strong hidden resentment against Napoleon, and this would prove fatal to the new alliance. He arrived in Stockholm in October 1810 and was adopted by the king under the name of Charles John. He soon relegated the old king to the role of a figurehead and took to heart the interests of his new country. As relations with Napoleon began to sour, Alexander I sought a common ground with the future king. Bernadotte could not share the Swedes' resentment at losing Finland but could share their interest in Norway. The annexation of that Coastland country as compensation for the loss of Finland fitted in well with a

Russian strategy to turn Sweden outward, beyond the Kjølen, against the whole weight of its history that had always drawn the country eastward.

Napoleon, obsessed with mastering space and creating an autarkic system that could sustain French hegemony in Coastland and Heartland, was inexorably led to push the Continental System to the limits of the possible and to confront the Russian Empire as its rising gravitational pull in the Heartland threatened the viability of his own conquests. In December 1810, he annexed the entire northern coast of Europe from the estuary of the Rhine to Lübeck on the Baltic. The territory included the duchy of Oldenburg, ruled by a relative of the tsar, for which Alexander had secured Napoleon's guarantee at Tilsit. The move was taken as a breach of faith, and Alexander immediately wrote to Charles John expressing a desire for closer relations. The crown prince answered in January 1811 that Russia could count on Swedish help. Gustav Armfelt, who had returned to Sweden to become "war minister" but had gotten into trouble again, entered Russian service and became chairman of a Commission on Finnish Affairs.[1] He and other "men of power" in Finland became the brokers of a Russo-Swedish reconciliation—only then could Finland enjoy peace and stability. Secret talks began in the fall for an alliance directed against Denmark and France, paving the way for a radical shift in Swedish foreign policy the following year.

Napoleon's disregard of his allies' interests accelerated the shift. Angered by widespread smuggling in Swedish Pomerania, he ordered French troops to reoccupy the country in January 1812. The move forced Sweden into Russia's arms. In early February, the option of sending two Russian divisions to Sweden was discussed in Petersburg. They would combine with Swedish troops and land in Germany to threaten Napoleon's rear when the anticipated French invasion of Russia took place. The stumbling block was Swedish insistence that Russia accept the annexation of Norway before Sweden entered the war. The Russians kept hoping Denmark would join of its own free will the northern coalition against France, while the Swedes wanted to begin the war with an attack on Denmark and Norway. The Danes made it easier for their opponents to agree: they signed in March a military convention with France freeing them from the obligation to join the invasion but pledging them to guard the coast from the Rhine to the Oder against an enemy landing.

The Russo-Swedish alliance was signed in April. The two powers would commit 25,000 Swedes and 15,000 Russians under the command of the crown prince to make a diversion in northern Germany "to disturb the operations of the French army." To protect Sweden's rear, it was agreed that the annexation of Norway would precede a landing, and Denmark was promised compensations in Germany if it agreed to the loss of Norway without war. If it did not, the joint expeditionary force would land on Seeland (Sjelland), the large island containing Copenhagen. Such a plan was opposed by Britain because it threatened a long drawn-out war with Denmark and would establish a Russo-Swedish presence on the other shore of the Sound, with disturbing implications for the future.

Such was the situation in June, when Napoleon invaded Russia. The Russian withdrawal during the summer made it impossible to divert troops to support the Swedes against Denmark. Russian and Swedish interests began to diverge, the Russians concentrating on blocking a French advance on Petersburg. To iron out their differences, a meeting was arranged at Åbo between the crown prince and the tsar. They met in August, and the Swedes, sensing mistakenly that developments on the battlefield were working in their favor, offered to defend the Russian capital in exchange for the "temporary" return of Finland and recognition of Sweden's annexation of Seeland. Neither offer served Russian interests: a partition of Denmark would give Sweden control of the Sound. The convention that closed the meeting (attended by Armfelt) pledged Russia to increase its contribution to the expeditionary force to 35,000 men, to guarantee any agreement reached by Sweden with Britain over Seeland in exchange for a Swedish promise to recognize Russia's annexation of Poland to the Vistula—in short, a rather meaningless document, soon to be made irrelevant by the evolution of the war. Napoleon entered Moscow in September, and the Swedes were informed Russia could no longer afford to join the expedition against Denmark. Russian troops stationed in Finland were sent instead across the Gulf of Finland into Livonia, and after Napoleon abandoned Moscow in October and began his disastrous retreat, they were sent to Bielorussia, where they joined one of the Russian armies pursuing Napoleon.

The Russian determination to continue the war until the final defeat of Napoleon shifted the strategic emphasis from northern Germany and the Baltic to central Germany, along the Erzgebirge, in the direction of the Rhine. The great battles of Lützen, Bautzen, and Leipzig (May–October 1813) were fought between the Spree and the Saale, in the valley of the Elbe on the periphery of the Heartland. Denmark and the Baltic coast became a secondary theater and Swedish help expendable. Sweden had been but a pawn in the Russo-French conflict, and the conflict was about to be decided far from its shores. In January 1813, Britain, which had shown a passing interest in the annexation of Norway in 1807 because it could become a splendid workshop for its navy, pledged to guarantee its annexation by Sweden. Still, it was the Russians who liberated Hamburg in March. They continued their westward march, bypassing Denmark and its two duchies of Schleswig and Holstein. In May, the Swedes finally landed in Pomerania, but Denmark refused to be intimidated and renewed its alliance with Napoleon in July. Only after the "battle of nations" near Leipzig in October did the allies launch a mopping up operation against Denmark. The Danes, who had placed all their hopes in Napoleon, gambling they might be able to recreate a Scandinavian union for the first time since 1523, became the greatest losers of the war.

Sweden and Denmark made peace in January 1814, and the terms of their agreement were confirmed by Britain and Russia. Denmark joined the war against Napoleon and had to place a contingent of 10,000 men under Swedish command, but it was too late. It had to cede Norway, but retained the Faeroes Islands, Iceland, and Greenland. The cession was presented as an exchange—Sweden abandoned Swedish Pomerania and Rügen Island. The Danes would not even keep that modest compensation for long: the Congress of Vienna gave it to Prussia in 1815 in exchange for the small duchy of Lauenburg adjacent to Holstein.

The peace was a catastrophe for Denmark. The country lost 85 percent of its territory, including Finnmark that had blocked Swedish and Russian access to the North Atlantic, and 40 percent of its population. Moreover, it altered the environment in which Denmark would have to live. The Norwegians had reinforced the Nordic element against the German; the new Denmark was in danger of becoming a peripheral Germanic power. Holstein and Lauenburg were linguistically German. Even in Schleswig, the nobility and officials spoke German, the peasantry and townsmen Danish. Kiel had been an important German cultural center; it would now agitate for Holstein's independence. When the new Germanic Confederation was created in 1815, the Danish king as duke of Holstein and Lauenburg was given a seat in the Frankfort Diet. He hoped thereby to keep Holstein bound to Denmark, but he also became fated to be drawn into the coming struggles for German unification.

What of Sweden? Bernadotte's treason to Napoleon and to France had paid off handsomely for Sweden, but it was a victory without substance. The annexation of Norway would create no more than a political alliance; the Kjølen remained an insuperable barrier to Norway's integration into a Greater Sweden. Swedish Pomerania was gone and with it Sweden's last stronghold in northern Germany. Sweden became the dominant Scandinavian power, but at a price. Bernadotte declared after the peace with Denmark that he would follow the dictates of Russian policy. The loss of Finland put an end to revanchist dreams against Russia. Petersburg was secure, and the annexation of the Åland Islands gave Russia the ability to pursue a risk-free fortress-fleet strategy. But the annexation of Norway also restricted Sweden's freedom of action: Britain would never tolerate a projection of Russian influence across the Kjølen. Caught between Britain and Russia, Sweden's only solution was to withdraw into neutrality.

Russo-Polish Relations, 1796–1815

The third partition of Poland (1795) had ended more than two centuries of direct relations between the Russian and Polish core areas maintained ever since the Union of Lublin (1569) had incorporated the entire Russo-Polish frontier into the Polish Empire. The Polish core area had been apportioned between the Prussians and the Austrians; Lithuania (with Bielorussia) and the Right-Bank Ukraine had been absorbed into the

Russian Empire. Tsar Paul's affinity for Prussia and the conservative alliance against revolutionary France entailed the maintenance of the territorial status quo, despite such friendly gestures to the Polish cause as the liberation of Kościuszko.

Alexander I, however, was already swayed by the attraction of two seemingly irreconcilable policies. He was the heir to a tradition that viewed Poland as the hereditary enemy, a tradition that would not be fulfilled until both Poland and its frontier had been incorporated into the Russian Empire. He also harbored a feeling of guilt about the partitions and the ruthlessness of his grandmother, Catherine II. That feeling was nurtured by his association with Adam Czartoryski, deported to Petersburg in 1794 in order to be trained as a loyal subject of the empire. Czartoryski was 24, Alexander 17. The Russians had always sought to win over the men of power in one of two ways—by supporting their desire for emancipation from the political authority of a rival core area or, if they could lay their hands on them, by demanding that they send hostages to the capital, there to vouch for the good behavior of their relatives, to learn to appreciate Russian ways, and to respect Russian might. Later, at the propitious time, they would be sent back to work for the transformation of the frontier zones into an inner frontier of the Russian Empire. It was possible, of course, that men of power with enough charisma could convince the tsar-emperor of the rightfulness of their cause. That was the case with Alexander and some influential Polish families; it was also probably the case in Finland and Georgia. But such expectations were bound to create dangerous misunderstandings because they were founded on a test of unequal wills—the exclusionary will of the men of power in frontier and core area and the inclusionary policy of the Russian government.

Czartoryski convinced the future tsar of the need to atone for the injustice of the partitions by "restoring Poland," but this expression was a source of confusion. The Poles viewed Poland in historical and class terms—the nobility as the "Polish nation" from the Oder to the Dvina and the Dniepr. Russia saw it also in geopolitical terms—a Polish empire consisting of a core area and a frontier. Russia, acting alone, could only restore Lithuania and the Right-Bank Ukraine, the frontier, within the borders of 1772. The restoration of Poland, the core area, required a victorious war against the Prussians and the Austrians. The restoration of the Polish Empire required a cataclysmic upheaval beyond the grasp of any of the leaders of the three powers.

Alexander visited Lithuania after his accession, and charmed the inhabitants of Vilno with vague promises "to restore Poland." These promises found an echo in the nostalgia of some Lithuanian magnates, notably Mikhail Oginski, for the old principality that had been united with Poland for so long but had never quite merged with it. Later, after 1809, Oginski would be influenced by the creation of the Grand Duchy of Finland. He, like Armfelt, belonged to those men of power who believed that the support of Russian policy would not only confirm their "rights and privileges" but would also give their territorial base in the frontier a privileged status within the Russian Empire. Significantly, Oginski's views were anathema to Czartoryski: to "restore Poland" was incompatible with the detachment of the frontier from the Polish core area. The thought of "restoring Lithuania" was also anathema to most of the Russian ruling elite (and to foreigners of Germanic stock co-opted into it), because Lithuania was the ancestral land of some of Russia's oldest families and was considered part of the Romanov's inalienable patrimony. It was bound to arouse the most violent opposition. Likewise, the retrocession of the Right-Bank Ukraine was not negotiable—it had once belonged to Kievan Rus', to which the Muscovite core area claimed an exclusive right.

If it was beyond Alexander's political power to create an independent frontier, and beyond the realm of the possible for him to restore the Polish core area, it was not beyond Napoleon's power to break Prussia's and Austria's hold on the territory acquired through the Polish partitions. Austria was defeated in December 1805, Prussia in October 1806, Russia in June 1807. Poland, like Sweden, became a pawn in the Franco-Russian power game and, like Prussia, a frontier zone between the French and Russian empires. Napoleon assumed at first that his immediate influence would not go beyond the Elbe, the dividing line between Coastland and Heartland. The lands between the Elbe and the Niemen would form a "barrier" separating the two large empires, in fact, a frontier of historical and human zones where the French emperor would maintain an equilibrium serving both French and Russian interests. But frontier zones are not static constructs; they are living organisms with interests of their own, and the rivalry of their interests was fated to activate a forward policy that would eventually lead Napoleon to extend his immediate influence to the Niemen and strike at Russia itself.

Just before the two emperors met at Tilsit in June 1807, Napoleon had told a Russian representative that the Vistula should be the boundary between the possessions of France and those of Russia. Such a boundary would give East Prussia to Russia and satisfy an old ambition going back to the Seven Years War. But the annexation of East Prussia would create an implacable hatred of Russia in Berlin, and Prussia was needed as a potential ally. It was therefore quite logical that the tsar should be the one to propose the restoration of Poland by creating a Duchy of Warsaw consisting of almost all the Prussian share in the three partitions, while making it appear that it was Napoleon who did it. Prussian sensibilities would be spared and Polish expectations satisfied, as the tsar would show his determination to fulfill his promises. Nevertheless, the Tilsit agreement also gave Russia a small slice of the Prussian share: the Białystok district between the Bobr (Biebrza), the Narew, the Nurzeć, and the Bug—that wooded and swampy edge Prussia had not wanted in 1795.

The Duchy of Warsaw was a landlocked country: Prussia retained Pomerelia and the land east of the Vistula but lost the Poznan district, most of the Netze district including the military road linking Küstrin

(Kostrzyn) on the Oder with Thorn on the Vistula, and the Kulm district between Thorn and East Prussia. The annexation cut off Brandenburg's southern communications with Königsberg. Danzig was restored as a free city but under French protection, cutting off Brandenburg's northern link with the East Prussian capital. The duchy was placed under the king of Saxony in Dresden on the Elbe, while Saxony became part of the Confederation of the Rhine, the successor of the Holy Roman Empire abolished in 1806 and a French protectorate. Napoleon's decision suited the tsar well—it was a characteristic feature of Russian foreign policy to turn the rival core areas outward, toward the boundary of the Heartland. It was evident in Sweden and we shall see it again in Persia. Alexander made this very clear when he told the French ambassador in April 1809 that he considered the Duchy a province of the Saxon kingdom, not a restored Poland with its inevitable irredentism in the former Russo-Polish frontier. The tsar, however, was neither realistic nor logical. Poland had always faced east, and even the partial restoration of the core area outside the Russian Empire was bound to have a destabilizing effect in the inner frontier of the Empire.

It soon turned out that the creation of the Duchy served Napoleon's interests better than Alexander's. "Restored Poland" became the focus of French and Russian frustrations, as the two emperors proved unable to compose their increasingly bitter differences over the Continental System, the treatment of Prussia and Austria, and policy toward the Ottoman Empire. As early as 1808, Petersburg strongly suspected that the indemnity France had imposed on Prussia was an excuse to maintain troops there and in the Duchy until it had been paid, and it was feared the Duchy, far from facing west, would become France's forward outpost in the east. The Poles were actively restoring symbols of their former empire, including Lithuanian decorations, and Alexander resented Napoleon's unwillingness to quash this attempt to "bring the dead back to life."[2]

Resentment turned to anger when the Poles used Napoleon's determination to crush an Austrian challenge to "do a Tilsit" on Vienna. Austria had not conceded defeat in 1805 but had remained on the sidelines while Napoleon defeated Prussians and Russians. It was not bound by the Tilsit agreement and refused to accept the restoration of Poland. At Erfurt in October 1808, Napoleon had secured Alexander's reluctant promise to join forces against Austria, and Russian troops were moved to the Galician border at the end of the year. Austria had been re-arming, and invaded the Duchy in April 1809, calling on the Poles to rise up against the French. Instead, Polish troops from the Duchy crossed into Little Poland between the Pilica and the Vistula, annexed by Austria in 1795, and set up a temporary government. Local Poles set up a separate one in Lvóv (L'viv, Lemberg) in Galicia between the Carpathians, the Vistula and the Zbruch, annexed in 1772. Calls to arms were issued in Lithuania, and the Vilno Poles began to hope for Polish military support to liberate Lithuania. The restoration of the Polish Empire was in full swing, beyond

Napoleon's and Alexander's ability to check the groundswell of popular support. Meanwhile, Napoleon moved rapidly and crushed the Austrians in July.

The Russians had taken little part in the war. They managed to take Kraków in July, provoking Napoleon's anger at the Russian delay in reaching the Vistula from Volhynia while he had to cross the whole of Germany and most of Austria to beat the enemy at Wagram near Vienna. The Russians invoked their war with Sweden in Finland and with the Ottomans in Moldavia. In fact, they had more serious reasons. They had had to accept the partial dismemberment of Prussia but were not ready to tolerate the dismemberment of the sprawling Habsburg Empire, an ideal frontier of physical, cultural, and historical zones between the periphery of the Heartland and their possessions beyond the Bug and the Zbruch, and a "natural bulwark" between Russia and France. The crushing of Austria would raise the question of what to do with its share of the partitions of 1772 and 1795. Alexander warned in April that any enlargement of the Duchy of Warsaw would be a step toward the restoration of Poland. Another warning came in May—any "augmentation of the Polish domain"[3] would be a threat to Russia's vital interests. Therefore, Russia would oppose a second Tilsit not only for broad strategic reasons—to maintain the territorial integrity of the Habsburg Empire—but specifically because it would result in the enlargement of the Duchy to a size where population, resources, and the national revival would generate enough energy to create a gravitational pull in the inner frontier of the Russian Empire, in Lithuania and the Right-Bank Ukraine.

But how is one to reconcile this determination with Alexander's intention to restore Poland? An alternative was recommended by General Sergei Golitsyn, the commander of the army sent against the Austrians, who told the tsar he should simply annex Galicia and proclaim himself king of Poland. Golitsyn had good reasons for his opinion. He had been a close relative of Potemkin, had served under him, and no doubt shared his views on the incorporation of the Russo-Polish frontier into the Russian Empire. He was the brother-in-law of Ksaveri Branicki, one of the creators of the Confederation of Targowica, now a full general in the Russian army. Last but not least, he was also the scion of one of the great families of the empire that traced its origins to Lithuania.

Here, perhaps, was a way to reconcile the seemingly irreconcilable—the restoration of Poland but within the Russian Empire—before challenging Napoleon for the control of the Duchy of Warsaw. The annexation of eastern Galicia, between the Bug and the Zbruch, could be presented as the completion of the process of incorporation of the Russo-Polish frontier—its population was largely Ukrainian and Orthodox. Moreover, some of the men of power in the frontier were not exceedingly happy with the creation of the Duchy. The French commander in chief in northern Germany, Marshal Louis Davout, had reported in 1807 that "the great families looked with an unfriendly eye at Napoleon's measures to create a Polish people,"[4] because it would destroy the old equation between the nobility and the "Polish nation" and undermine their influence. Russia could thus count on a conservative party to oppose the "democratization" of Polish society under French influence. The proclamation of Alexander as king of Poland in Galicia would simply mark a return to the time-honored conservative alliance between Russia and the men of power for the purpose of destabilizing the government in Warsaw.

Alexander half-heartedly turned down Golitsyn's suggestion, referring prophetically to the cases of Hungary and Ireland—their annexations had become a source of instability in the Austrian dominions and the United Kingdom, respectively. And would not the restoration of Poland threaten to recreate a Polish empire within the Russian Empire with all its unfortunate consequences? He might have added that the destruction of Poland served Russia's interests by binding to it the Germanic powers in a lasting alliance. Nevertheless, he ordered Golitsyn to sound out the magnates on the possibility of uniting the Duchy with Galicia into a Polish kingdom under the Russian scepter. The tsar, however, was not yet master of the situation in the field. Tensions with Russian troops rose when the Warsaw government proclaimed the annexation of Galicia in its own name, but without the effective power to hold it. Franco-Austrian negotiations took place in Vienna without the participation of the Russians. They ended with the Peace of Schönbrunn in October. Austria lost 2.4 million subjects. Two million joined the Duchy from the Zamość district adjacent to western Galicia, between the San and the Bug, and a small district on the right bank of the Vistula facing Kraków; the other 400,000 in the Tarnopol district in eastern Galicia were assigned to the Russian Empire. Napoleon even insisted that Brody, the only important trade center in the area, must remain in Austrian hands. To make the pill even more bitter for the Russians, the Polish army was raised to 60,000 men. The Duchy now had a population of 4.3 million and an area of 155,430 square kilometers.

The Russians had no choice but to accept this new Tilsit despite their warnings that it threatened their vital interests. This defeat in 1809 was a major milestone on the road to the war of 1812. They propagated the fiction that Poland had not been restored, that it did not exist, that even the enlarged Duchy was merely a province of Saxony without any standing in international law. They induced the French ambassador to sign in January 1810 a convention pledging the two powers to agree that the Polish Kingdom would never be restored and that the words "Pole" and "Poland" would "disappear forever from every official and public act." In fact, the convention was nothing more than an attempt to force Napoleon to accept the settlement of January 1797, when Russia, Prussia, and Austria agreed to "blot out anything that may recall the existence of the Polish Kingdom."[5] The convention would also bind France to block any further aggrandizement of the Duchy of Warsaw. When Napoleon repudiated his ambassador's signature, he signaled to the Russians that his restoration of

Poland was a step toward the restoration of the Polish Empire to be completed by expelling them from their empire's inner frontier.

As Napoleon prepared for war, an intense competition began for the allegiance of the Duchy of Warsaw. Czartoryski was instructed by Alexander in December 1810 to sound out the leading political families in Poland, to offer to place their children in the exclusive Corps de Pages at the Russian Court, to accept Poles willing to serve in the Russian army and civil service. It was hoped that by drawing the men of power into the ruling elite and the managerial apparatus of the Empire and reminding Poles of the horrors of war from which they had already suffered so much since the beginning of the eighteenth century, they would reject Napoleon's blandishments and become channels of Russian influence, helping to bring a restored Poland into the Russian fold. Such a Poland, autonomous under the Russian crown, would fulfill the tsar's youthful ambitions and bring to an end the ageold enmity between Poland and Russia. These two policies—restoring Poland and eliminating it as a rival—might not be irreconcilable after all.

What was overlooked was that Poland was not a frontier but a core area—this alone renders inept the often made comparison between Finland and Poland in the Russian Empire. As a core area, Poland was an irreducible social, religious, and cultural complex possessing remarkable energy and restrainable only by the application of superior force. In propitious circumstances it would inevitably fight for the re-incorporation into the Polish Empire of its frontier with Russia. Czartoryski soon realized that every Pole in the Duchy wanted the restoration of the empire within the borders of 1772 and that this was more likely to be achieved in alliance with France against Russia than the reverse. The tsar's intentions, no matter how generous, had to be set against the traditional enmity of the Russian army toward Poland, used as it was to treat it as an occupied country and to see in it a potential ally of the Turks. The fact that Russia was at war with the Ottomans at the time, while the commander in chief of the Polish army, General Jozif Poniatowski, roused enthusiasm for the coming war, and Poles kept portraits of Napoleon in their homes, was not likely to convince the Russian high command of the strategic value of a restored Poland. Another development could only confirm the army's fears: in January 1812, Napoleon demanded from the Duchy a contribution of 65,000 recruits, raised to 97,000 in August.

The war began in June, when Napoleon crossed the Nieman into Lithuania. Poles and Lithuanians flocked to Napoleon's standards. A temporary government was set up in Vilno in July with jurisdiction over most of Lithuania and Bielorussia, and was placed with the government of the Duchy of Warsaw under Napoleon's minister of foreign affairs. A Polish empire was gradually being restored within a French empire. Not for long, of course. The retreat began in the fall, and by March 1813, not only Lithuania but the entire Duchy with the exception of some fortified places had been occupied by the Russian army. A provisional government was set up in Warsaw for civil affairs, and Polish troops were placed under Russian command. The coordination of Russia's Polish policy was vested in General Alexei Arakcheev, the tsar's closest deputy. Lithuania was reintegrated into the Russian Empire under the overall supervision of the military governor of Vilno.

The ultimate fate of Poland, however, depended on the outcome of the general offensive against Napoleon's hegemony, and the cooperation of Prussia and Austria was essential. At Reichenbach, south of Leipzig, the three powers agreed at the end of June to partition the Duchy among themselves in an "amicable settlement," without entering into specifics. The agreement was no more than a tactical move on Alexander's part to avoid controversy among the allies at a time when unity of action was essential on the battlefield. When a congress of European powers met at Vienna in September 1814, it quickly became obvious that the Polish question promised to be the most destructive of the general harmony among the victorious powers. The tsar was in the strongest position—his troops occupied the Duchy. He had the chance at last to fulfill his promise to restore Poland, but a Poland joined with Russia in an indissoluble union under the same crown—a Russian-inspired latter-day version of the Union of Lublin. The annexation would satisfy the Russian military, because Polish troops would be under Russian command. It would drive a wedge between Brandenburg-Prussia and Silesia and give Russia a strong territorial base from which to arbitrate Austro-Prussian differences. From a strategic point of view, it would place the two Germanic powers at Russia's mercy.

It was thus logical for Alexander I to repudiate the Reichenbach agreement and to announce the restoration of Poland. Prussia and Austria would receive compensations elsewhere—Austria in "Illyria" and northern Italy, Prussia in the Rhineland and Saxony. Saxony, like Denmark, had followed Napoleon to the bitter end and was made to pay the price. Its administration was turned over to Prussia in November 1814, and the final settlement in June 1815 gave its northern half to its powerful neighbor. Russia's ambitions in Poland and the transfer of Saxony to Prussia brought about the violent opposition of Austria, faced with the aggrandizement of its two rivals, Prussia and Russia. Metternich, the Austrian foreign minister, went as far as to threaten war, insisting on the retention of Kraków and the fortress of Zamość, essential to its security, and the salt mines of Wieliczka, profitable to its treasury. He was supported by Britain and France in the triple alliance signed in January 1815.

The tsar was forced to compromise, and a settlement was reached in May. Russia kept four-fifths of the Duchy of Warsaw under the new name of Polish Kingdom, also known as Congress Poland—the Poland created by the Congress of Vienna. It had a population of 3.3 million and an area of 128,500 square kilometers. Prussia recovered Danzig, the Netze and Kulm districts with the strategic fortress of Thorn, and the Poznan district. The new Prussian border ran from the Vistula above Thorn to the confluence of the Warta and the Prosna, and followed the Prosna past Kalisz to the Silesian border. Despite its strong stand, Austria did not recover the Zamość district, only the small enclave facing Kraków and the salt mines as well as the Tarnopol district ceded to Russia in 1809. Its boundary followed the Vistula to a point below the confluence of the San, thence, skirting the Zamość district to the Bug, merged with the old border from the Bug to the Zbruch. Kraków became a "free and independent city" under the protection of the three powers Russia, Austria, and Prussia. Poland had been partitioned once again.

Epilogue, 1815–1917

A truncated Polish core area and the entire Russo-Polish frontier had been incorporated into the Russian Empire to form an inner frontier of zones from the Dvina and the Dniepr to the Prosna. Russo-Polish relations ceased to be an object of Russia's foreign policy, to become instead part of an inner frontier policy shaping the creation of an empire. Alexander had declared in August 1814 that he did not want to be asked any questions at the Congress of Vienna about the internal affairs of the Duchy of Warsaw, and that would remain Russia's attitude until 1917. The tsar was proclaimed king of Poland in 1815, and he had been grand duke of Finland since 1809. In fact, Poland's status was lower than Finland's, because the Russians insisted on calling Poland a *tsarstvo,* and the official title of the Romanov emperors equated the Polish Kingdom with the former khanates of Astrakhan, Kazan, and Siberia. Nevertheless, the settlement of May 1815 was followed by granting a liberal constitution to the kingdom in November. Constitutions, especially one granted by the ruler of a powerful core-area government known for its policies of inclusion in the frontier zones, must remain pieces of paper if they are out of touch with political realities. The "Charter," as it was called, left two burning questions unanswered.

One question was the meaning of the term *restoration of Poland.* The Poles expected that the union of the two crowns would lead to the restoration of the Polish Empire of 1772 within the Russian Empire. The settlement of May 1815 contained a vague reference to the possibility of "internal aggrandizement" of the Polish Kingdom. That could be achieved only by re-incorporating at least part of Lithuania and the Right-Bank Ukraine. But to do so would recreate within the Russian Empire, between the Russian and Polish core areas, the old rivalry for the allegiance of what had become the inner frontier of the empire. It was bound to create a highly unstable situation, as the tsar had foreseen in 1809. The intractable dilemma reappeared between a generous promise to restore Poland and the impossibility of restoring its empire. The only realistic alternative would have been to give up in 1815 the idea of restoring Poland and to return to the situation of 1795, leaving the Polish core area partitioned among the Germanic powers. But in that case, Russia would have received little compensation for its war effort in the liberation of Germany.

The second question was the real structure of political and military power in Poland. The tsar, as king of Poland, needed a permanent representative in Warsaw. It was assumed by many Poles and by Czartoryski himself that he would be appointed viceroy, but his personality was too strong for Alexander, and his equivocal behavior in 1812 (when he adopted a wait-and-see attitude as long as the fate of the Napoleonic invasion remained uncertain) was unforgivable for a member of the Imperial ruling elite. The tsar appointed instead General Jozef Zajonczek, a Pole from the frontier (the Right Bank), whose disreputable political past included serving in Kościuszko's army and commanding a division during the invasion of Russia. The appointment was a model of perversity, as if the Russian government had been disposed to strike down with one hand what it was presumably building with the other. It certainly showed contempt for the post of viceroy. On the other hand, Alexander appointed his brother, Grand Duke Constantine, to command the Polish army of 25,000 men, and the grand duke established his headquarters in Warsaw. To make matters worse for the viceroy, an Imperial commissioner was given broad powers of supervision over civil affairs. Neither the post of commander in chief nor that of Imperial commissioner had been provided for in the Charter.

By 1825, the year of Alexander's death, these two questions were being settled in truly original fashion, showing that the tsar had pursued a consistent course for more than twenty-five years despite the occasional equivocations required by his tortuous relationships with Napoleon, the Prussians, and the Austrians. He had restored the Polish core area within the limits of the possible in 1815. He would also restore the Polish Empire, but in such a way that the opposition of his entourage would be deflected by his conservative approach. A so-called Lithuanian Corps had been created in 1817 under Constantine's command; its troops were stationed in Lithuania and the Right Bank. In 1822, the grand duke had been given the powers of a commander in chief in wartime over the Polish army and the Lithuanian Corps. These powers placed the provincial civil administration under the overall administrative authority of the grand duke and his Imperial commissioner. In practice, Constantine had become the de facto viceroy of a restored Polish empire within the Russian Empire; he would govern with the help of two "governors general," one in Warsaw (the viceroy), the other in Vilno (the military governor), and the two governors of Volhynia and Podolia. The two policies that had seemed irreconcilable for so long—the incorporation of the frontier together with the elimination of the Polish core area as an independent state, and the restoration of Poland—had become reconciled.

It is impossible to say whether the solution would have been a durable one had Alexander lived much longer. It certainly would have had to cope with the antagonism of the Poles toward the Zajonczek government and their hostility to the grand duke, whose good intentions were marred by brutality and the lack of sensitivity even toward the Polish officer corps. It would certainly have fallen victim to the rise of conservatism in Russia after 1815. The new tsar, Nicholas I (1825–1855), had no sympathy for administrative, let alone political, regionalism that smacked of federalism, but he kept Constantine in Warsaw out of respect for the memory of Alexander I. Russian conservative nationalism with its inclusionary tendencies to russify the frontier zones was incompatible with Polish resentment that fought to exclude "Muscovite" influences. They were bound to clash eventually, and they did in December 1830, when opposition to Russian rule exploded in Poland and spread to the frontier zones. The revolt was put down by force, and the Manifesto of March 1832 declared Poland an "indivisible part" of the Russian Empire and its inhabitants "a single people of likeminded brothers" (*edinyi narod soglasnykh bratii*).[6] The institutions created in 1815 were closed, and Poland was placed under a Russian viceroy with a Polish name (Paskievich), in command of both the military and civil administration, but without the authority of his predecessor, who had been the tsar's own brother. Thirty years later, another rebellion accelerated the process of unification, and after 1874, a systematic attempt was made to integrate the entire frontier into the Russian core area.

Russo-Baltic relations after 1815 followed a different course. Sweden withdrew from the international rivalries on the European mainland, and the long reign of Charles John (1818–1844) was marked by goodwill toward Russia and concentrations on relations, not always friendly, with Norway. Swedish energies turned outward, and Finland became a zone of peace, where the Russians kept but a token presence. Its capital was moved from Åbo to Helsingfors in 1821, and its governor general, who represented the tsar as grand duke of Finland, kept his residence in Petersburg after 1823. The Finnish men of power, still largely shaped by Swedish culture and by their marital ties with the elite in Stockholm, were able, like their Germanic cousins in Livonia, to establish a modus vivendi with the Russians that served both their interests and those of the ruling elite in Petersburg. It was a remarkable achievement, but one that depended on the maintenance of a certain geopolitical equilibrium in the eastern Baltic. An equilibrium, however, is always relative and seldom long lasting.

Russian policy was shaped increasingly by considerations of naval strategy, and it was probably no coincidence that the governor general of Finland between 1831 and 1855 was also chief of the Naval Staff (1828–1855). In the Gulf of Finland and the Gulf of Bothnia, a fortress-fleet strategy was best suited to the defense of Russian interests. Beginning in the early 1830s, the Russian navy established a naval base at Bomarsund on one of the Åland Islands, on the margin of the ice-free zone. It sealed the entrance into the Gulf of Bothnia, the maritime zone of the old Russo-Swedish frontier, and was Russia's most forward naval outpost in a network of four naval bases, with Reval, Sveaborg, and Kronshtadt. They barred access to Petersburg and created a defensive perimeter enclosing the entire frontier within the Russian Empire. But that perimeter could also be transformed into an offensive one against Stockholm, should Sweden depart from its neutral stance. In other words, it served to enforce Swedish neutrality. Palmerston expressed concern over the Russian buildup at Bomarsund in 1833, and Britain and France, despite their failure to bring Sweden into the Crimean conflict, insisted on including in the Treaty of Paris of March 1856 a convention for the demilitarization of the Åland Islands. This convention opened up the Gulf of Bothnia and removed the threat of a naval attack on their rear in the event of another war with Russia. In fact, demilitarization turned out to favor the Germans instead, during the First World War.

The allied decision, "senseless and unbelievable,"[7] must be understood in the context of a stubborn perception, at least in London, that Russia was working its way toward the development of a fleet-in-being strategy in Finnmark. The demarcation treaty of May 1826 established a "temporary" boundary along a line following the watershed between the basin of the Gulf of Bothnia and that of the Norwegian Sea, the Tana River, and a line of hills cutting off Russia from the Varangerfjord facing the Barents Sea. Most of the inhabitants of northern Scandinavia above the Arctic Circle were nomadic Lapps who roamed across international boundaries between the plain of the interior and the Finnmark upland. Finnmark had for three centuries gravitated toward its Finnish and Russian hinterland, beyond the Kola peninsula, all the way to Arkhangelsk, and suspicions developed in the 1830s that the Russians intended to use the Lapps to establish a claim to Finnmark and demand from Sweden-Norway the cession of a strip of land pushing their boundary to the Lyngenfjord only twenty miles away, and to the Varangerfjord at an even shorter distance.

The annexation of Finnmark would enable Russia to outflank the northern end of the Kjølen, reach the excellent harbors of the Lyngenfjord, and establish a naval base at the ice-free Hammerfest, a kind of Bomarsund of the north, from which its navy could pursue a fleet-in-being strategy along the Norwegian coast to the North Sea. In June 1851, the Russians did demand a tract of territory along the Varangerfjord to be set aside for the Lapps. The Norwegians refused, and Russia closed its border to the migrating Lapps, causing them considerable losses. Whether Russia did intend to resort to an offensive strategy is debatable, what with the logistical difficulties of outfitting and supporting a fleet at such latitudes, but the perception of a threat was enough for Britain and France to join Sweden-Norway in November 1855, when the Crimean War was approaching its decisive stage, and pledge that any Russian attempt to acquire territory or pasturage and fishing rights on the Norwegian coast would be met by joint naval action. It was a way of reminding Petersburg that the European Coastland must remain beyond Russia's limit of an optimum of conquest.

This decision by the Coastland powers to uphold their containment policy was made at a time when the equilibrium of the North established in 1815 was slowly being sapped within the Heartland. Danes and Swedes had been affected by the spread of nationalism. Such nationalism was not without danger, because it strengthened Norwegian resistance to Swedish policies. But nationalism also generated "Scandinavianism," a collective consciousness transcending separate nationalisms, the awareness of a common heritage different from that of the Germans on the mainland. In the 1830s and 1840s, it reawakened Swedish nostalgia for its vanished empire and hatred of Russia as the historical enemy. Nicholas I, there and elsewhere, was the champion of despotism and the oppressor of the Poles, the enemy of national aspirations everywhere. Russophobia grew apace, and the four successors of King Charles John were not immune to it. Scandinavianism was friendly to the democracies of the Coastland, but, as a development rooted in the basin of the Baltic, it was also pro-German.

The emergence of the German Empire in 1871 radically disturbed the equilibrium of the North. Germany left the Russian orbit in which Prussia had been forced to gravitate after 1815 and developed as a core area straddling the valley of the Elbe with a potential for destabilization in both Coastland and Heartland. Its tremendous energy fueled by the development of its exceptionally rich human and material resources created a gravitational pull in the entire basin of the Baltic, and threatened to transform the Baltic, Sweden, and Finland into a new Russo-German frontier. The rapid expansion of Sweden's economic relations with Germany, growing German influence in Swedish schools, and the admiration of Swedish officers for their German colleagues in the German army was likely to blend Germanophilism with Russophobia into a major threat to the Russian position in Finland and to the security of Petersburg itself, located since the return of Karelia (Vyborg province) to Finland in 1811, a mere twenty miles from the Finnish border.

By 1899, the Russian General Staff had assumed the probability of a German-Swedish offensive against Petersburg; the result was the integration of Finland for the first time into the defense system of the Empire. The Russians built a railroad from Uleåborg to Tornio to facilitate the transportation of troops to the Swedish border, and began a diplomatic campaign for the remilitarization of the Åland Islands. These moves were perceived as threats by the Swedes, who pointed out that the islands were only six hours away from Stockholm. But the First World War was not fought in the Baltic. Sweden remained neutral, but its restriction of the movement of arms and munitions across its territory had the paradoxical effect of forcing Russia to build a railroad linking Petersburg with Murmansk in order to receive supplies from the Coastland powers, thereby paving the way for the establishment of a naval base on the Barents Sea and the development of a fleet-in-being strategy fifty years later.

In December 1917, Finland declared its independence and signed a treaty of alliance with Germany in March 1918. But both Germany and

Russia had lost the war, and the Russo-Swedish frontier reappeared almost in its entirety for the first time since 1700.

Looking back on two centuries of Russia's relations with Poland and Sweden, we find four salient features. The first is a westward expansionist drive, an accumulation of energy generated by the establishment of a new dynasty and the emergence of a ruling class in the seventeenth century, a determination to exploit the country's material resources, and a willingness to learn from neighbors who had only recently taken advantage of Russia's political weakness to impose a humiliating withdrawal. These factors combined to propel Russia toward the Baltic and Poland, two worlds along which it had been but a marginal presence. A concentration on redirecting the trade routes of the North toward more accessible outlets in order to increase revenue from international trade, and the opening of channels to the technological resources of the Coastland and Germanic powers, fueled enmity toward Sweden and Poland—they had always been barriers keeping Russia out of the affairs of Europe.

The second feature is Russia's ability to turn in its favor the fragmentation of the frontier. A frontier possesses a certain unity by the very fact that it occupies a broad expanse of territory between two core areas and is the permanent object of their ambitions. Finland and Estland, Lithuania and the Right-Bank Ukraine, were neither Russian nor Swedish, neither Russian nor Polish. But a frontier is by definition a succession of zones—proximate zones of opposite core areas separated by intermediate zones—and each zone was susceptible to a greater or lesser extent to the conflicting gravitational pulls of rival core areas. The task of an expansionist Russia was to generate a force of attraction that would neutralize the preponderant influence of Poland and Sweden and then substitute its own, until the entire frontier was transformed into the inner frontier of an expanding empire. The superiority of military power was an essential element in the creation of such a centripetal orientation of the frontier toward Russia; so was the perception of a commonality of interests between a self-confident Russian ruling class and the men of power in the frontier zones calling for the guarantee of their "rights and privileges" and the maintenance of the social status quo based everywhere but in Finland on the enserfment of the population. The Russians expanded in the Western Frontier under the banner of social and political conservatism.

Livonia and the largely unpopulated Karelian isthmus were conquered in 1721, Finland in 1809. In both cases, victory on the battlefield was preceded by dissatisfaction among the local men of power with Sweden's policies toward them and took place when they were willing to switch allegiance in the defense of their interests. In Bielorussia, Lithuania, and the Right-Bank Ukraine, the ambitions of the men of power, Polish and Lithuanian, were inextricably intertwined with the religious question— the quarrels between Catholics, Uniates, and Orthodox. The Orthodox dissidents needed Russian support to force Warsaw to recognize their rights and privileges. The Catholic men of power needed it to carry out some day the fundamental reforms of the Polish government without which Poland was doomed to become the victim of Germanic and Russian ambitions, or to prevent those very reforms. Such a hopelessly confused political muddle bred an anarchy all the more dangerous because it invited Russian military power from its strongholds in Latvia, Smolensk, and Briansk into the frontier to support the partisans of Russia and restrain its enemies. It matters little who was "responsible" for starting the process that eventually destroyed Poland and its empire—the Russians, the Prussians, or the Austrians. The breakdown of order in the frontier, certainly encouraged by the Russians, had its own native causes. It also reflected the decline of Warsaw's gravitational pull and called for Russia to restore order at the propitious time. What a paradox that the Targowica confederates who "legalized" the Russian intervention were among those most responsible for perpetuating disorder in the frontier. If the conquest of Livonia and Karelia enabled Russia to "open a window" on the Coastland and channel its northern trade through the Sound to and from Petersburg, the incorporation of the Russo-Polish frontier gave Russia the valley of the Dniepr, the Dvina, and the Niemen, channels of the trade in grain, timber, and naval stores between the Baltic and the Black Sea.

A third feature of Russia's relations is the systematic policy to destabilize the Polish and Swedish core area governments. Such a policy could not have worked without the support and encouragement of the men of power. Russia's task was made easier by the internal weakness of Poland, never so much in evidence as under the Saxon kings after 1697, and in Sweden after 1720. Swedish and Polish "liberties" were the product of an ingrained distrust of a strong monarchy, but they degenerated into an anarchy that served everyone's interest, if not the country's common good. There were differences between the Swedish and Polish situations. The Swedish monarchy was stronger—it was not elective. The Riksdag was not paralyzed by the liberum veto. Confederations were not part of the Swedish political tradition. But in both countries, there were men of power willing to form parties that sold their allegiance to the Russian ambassador and united by a common determination to prevent the restoration of strong government. The defense of liberties was associated with a conservative defense of the status quo and, perversely, with the encouragement of anarchy.

That the interests of those men of power coincided with those of the Russian government was obvious enough. It is less clear what purpose was served by a destabilization policy. One may speculate that the Russians pursued at the same time a maximum and a minimum program. To encourage anarchy prevented the enemies of yesterday from restoring an offensive capability in the Western Frontier. It was a defensive policy, somewhat out of touch with political realities, because the growth of the Russian core area and its inherent dynamism had left Poland and Sweden by the 1720s far behind in the competition for supremacy in the frontier. But destabilization also served the larger purpose of softening up the core area for eventual annexation or at least partition. The annexation of Poland would have been blocked by the containment policy of the Germanic powers; that of Sweden, by Denmark and the Coastland powers. We know that Poland was eventually partitioned by Russia, Prussia, and Austria; it is very likely that, given the right circumstances, Sweden too would have been partitioned, the Russian share going perhaps as far as Karlskrona, while the Danes recovered Halland, Skåne, and Blekinge, lost to Sweden in 1645 and 1660.

Finally, Russia pursued in the Baltic an essentially defensive naval policy built around a network of naval bases barring the entrance to the Gulf of Bothnia and the Gulf of Finland. Karlskrona could have become its perfect key, but that was fated not to be. Without access to the Heartland's periphery, a fortress-fleet strategy was the only realistic policy.

II

RUSSIA AND ITS SOUTHERN FRONTIER

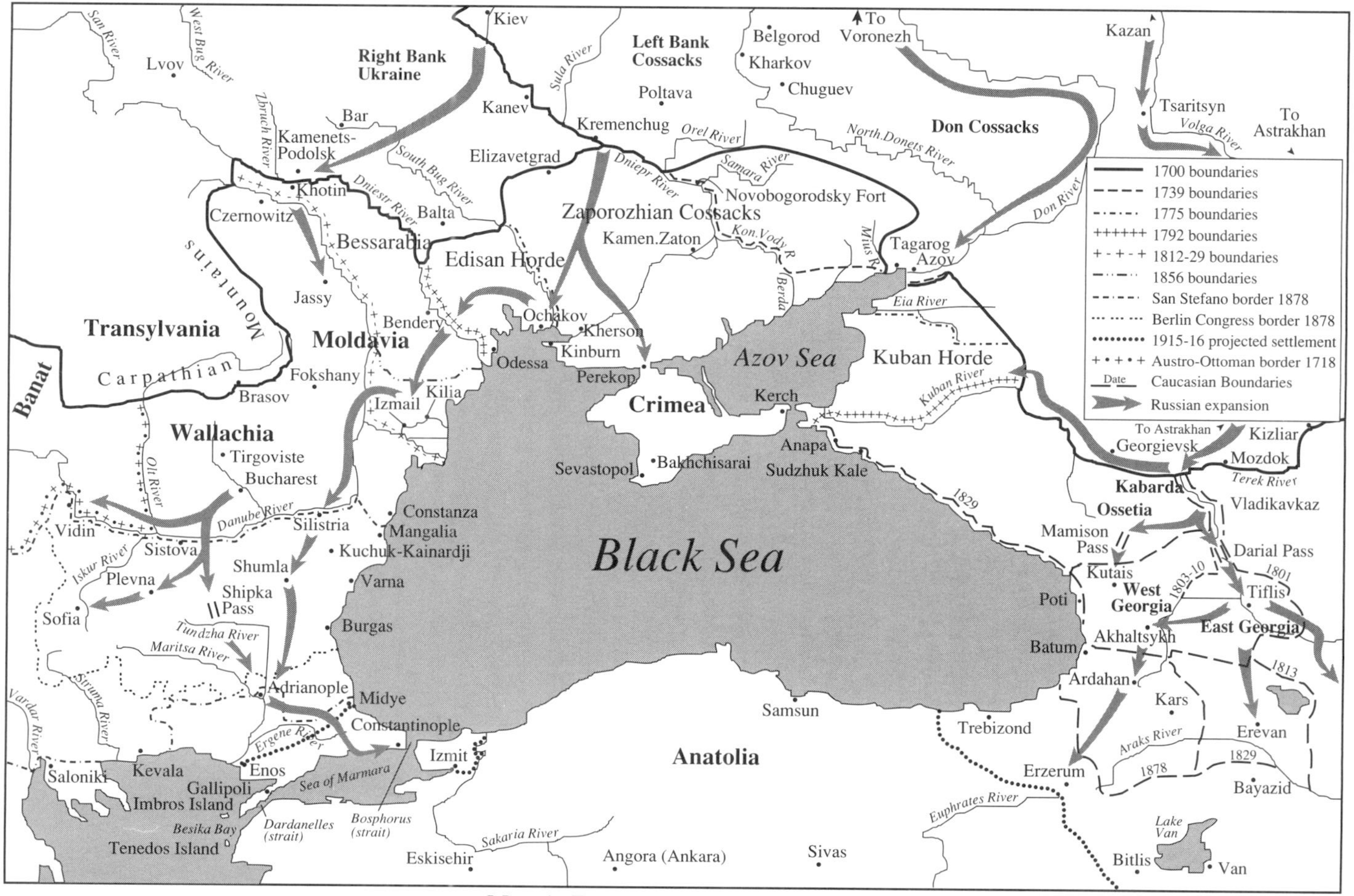

Map 4. The Russo-Turkish Frontier

Legend:
- 1700 boundaries
- 1739 boundaries
- 1775 boundaries
- 1792 boundaries
- 1812-29 boundaries
- 1856 boundaries
- San Stefano border 1878
- Berlin Congress border 1878
- 1915-16 projected settlement
- Austro-Ottoman border 1718
- Caucasian Boundaries
- Russian expansion
- Date

PIKE

4

The Advance into the Frontier, 1700–1791

The First Phase, 1700–1725

When Peter became tsar of all the Russias in 1682, much energy had already been spent to fuel the expansion of the Russian core area into the former territory of one parent culture—Byzantium-Kiev—and that of the other—the Turco-Mongol nomadic world of the steppe centered in the valley of the lower Volga. The incorporation in 1667 of Kiev—the "holy city" of the eastern Slavs—had been a major step. Much more energy would have to be spent before Russia could break the Ottoman hold on the Russo-Turkish frontier.

Several factors combined to create a Russian strategic interest in the basin of the Black Sea in the context of a slowly emerging change in the Russo-Turkish balance of power. One was the depredations of the Crimean Tatars in the frontier zones and the Russian core area itself—they called for counterthrusts until the khanate was subdued or destroyed, but that could not be done without a protracted conflict with the Ottomans, since the peninsula was their proximate zone. Another was the crusading spirit against the infidel; it had received a considerable boost when the Ottoman offensive was defeated before Vienna in 1683. That spirit would create a "natural" alliance between Russia and Austria for the purpose of eventually liberating the Christian populations in the Balkans and Transcaucasia and expelling the Turks from Europe—including Constantinople, the second "holy city" of both Orthodoxy and Latin Christendom. A third was the southward advance of Russian colonization toward the richer lands of the Ukraine, preceded by Cossack settlements looking outward to the sea. A fourth was the lure of the Levantine trade, the southern counterpart of the White Sea

and Baltic trade. Access to it would open a window to the Coastland powers, and commercial access was inextricably linked with the establishment of
a naval presence in the Mediterranean.

The failure of 1683 was the signal for a crusade to roll back Ottoman
power from the Austro-Turkish and Russo-Turkish frontier. The Crimean
expeditions of 1687 and 1689 had faced insuperable logistical problems
in the steppe. War was resumed with Peter's campaigns against Azov in
the summer of 1695 and 1696; they were attempts to reach the same
objective from another direction. Azov on the Don was one of the three
daunting fortresses marking out the forward defensive perimeter of the
Ottoman Empire in the north, with Ochakov in the estuary of the Dniepr
and Khotin on the Dniestr, near the confluence of the Zbruch. It surrendered in July 1696; Peter later built a port at Taganrog on the northern
coast of the Sea of Azov, Russia's first naval base in the Black Sea basin.
These gains were limited, however, as long as the fortress of Kerch controlling the channel between the Azov and Black Seas remained in
Ottoman hands. Only after its capture could an attack on the khanate
have any real chance of success. But Russia was not yet strong enough to
fight both the Tatars and the Ottomans. Such a conflict would set fire to
the entire frontier, where the allegiance of the Cossacks could never be
taken for granted. The tsar discovered during his grand tour of Europe in
1697–1698 that the interest in an anti-Ottoman crusade had waned; the
focus of interest was shifting to the Coastland, where the War of the
Spanish Succession was about to break out. The war had to end; negotiations began at Karlowitz in October 1698, and the Austrians made a separate peace in January 1699.

The Russians obtained only an armistice for two years; negotiations
continued in Constantinople, where peace was signed in 1700. Russia
gained Azov and retained Taganrog, but agreed to raze the forts it had
built on the lower course of the Dniepr between Ochakov and the
Zaporozhian Cossack zone and to leave deserted (*inculte et inhabité*) the
area between the Perekop isthmus and the Mius River, the approaches to
the Crimea. The Ottomans agreed to end the custom by which the tsar
was still paying tribute to the Crimean khan: it had been argued that the
payment of tribute to a vassal of the sultan made Russia a vassal state of
the Ottoman Empire, the successor of the Golden Horde. Thus by 1700,
Russia finally emancipated itself from its vassalage to the world of its other
parent culture, the Turco-Mongol oecumene, of which it had been a marginal phenomenon for so long.

The peace of 1700 was not destined to last, despite Peter's conviction
that a war with Sweden was likely to be much more profitable than an
endless one with the Turks. Russian forces were moved to the Western
Frontier; the object of Russo-Ottoman relations became the maintenance
of the status quo. The Ottomans had reluctantly conceded to Russia in
1700 the right to keep a permanent envoy in Constantinople. The choice
fell on Peter Tolstoi, one of the most capable members of the tsar's

entourage. He sounded out the Ottomans on letting Russia send mer-chantmen into the Black Sea. The Porte refused—only ships flying the Ottoman flag could navigate that sea. The Russians tested the Ottoman and Crimean resolve by building a fort at Kamennyi Zaton on the Dniepr, on the edge of the Zaporozhian zone, arousing fears about their inten-tions. But what shook the peace of the frontier was the revolt of the Don Cossacks in 1707–1708 and the southward advance of Charles XII, fol-lowed by the defection of Ivan Mazepa, the hetman of the Left-Bank Cossacks, to the Swedish cause. After his defeat at Poltava in July 1709, Charles fled into Ottoman territory and was given asylum at Bendery in Moldavia. He sought to involve the Ottomans in the war, uniting the Western and Southern Frontiers against the Russian core area. The tsar demanded Charles' extradition. The Ottomans refused, and declared war in November 1710.

The war did not go well for the Russians and only confirmed the wis-dom of concentrating energies on the Western Frontier. In this first attempt to carry the war around the Black Sea in the direction of the Danube, Peter I inaugurated a policy of appealing to the men of power in the Balkans, all the way to Montenegro, to ally with Russia against the enemy of Christendom. But it was a long way between appealing to Christian solidarity and transforming it into logistical support. The *hospo-dars* (governors) of Moldavia and Wallachia did not deliver the expected provisions, and the tsar found himself stranded with an army of 40,000 on the banks of the Prut River at the height of the summer heat in July 1711, without supplies and without cavalry. Only the Ottomans' reluc-tance to engage the Russians (strengthened by a hefty bribe) saved the tsar from complete disaster.

A temporary peace was negotiated on the spot. It canceled the gains made in 1700. The Russians had to abandon Azov and raze Taganrog and Kamennyi Zaton as well as Novobogoroditsky Fort at the mouth of the Samara River, a tributary of the Dniepr. They would no longer be permitted to keep a permanent representative in Constantinople. They had to promise not to obstruct Charles XII's return across Poland and to withdraw their troops from the Polish frontier: they would have to cross the Right-Bank Ukraine to reach Moldavia. And the Ottomans expected the tsar to ease his pressure on the Ottomans' ultimate zones—the Zaporozhian Cossacks and the Kuban Horde.

Once out of the trap, however, the tsar was in no hurry to fulfill his promises, at least not until the Swedish king had left the Ottoman Empire. During the ensuing negotiations in Constantinople, the Ottomans vainly sought to get the Russians to withdraw from the Left-Bank Cossack zone—it would roll back Russian power to the core area's periphery. Peace was finally made at Adrianople (Edirne) in June 1713. It confirmed the Prut settlement and established a demilitarized zone between the Orel and the Samara rivers to separate the Russian from the Ottoman empires. It also established the Dniepr as the boundary between the Cossacks under Russian and those under Crimean jurisdiction, thereby cutting the Zaporozhian zone into an eastern and western part. And the Swedish king was allowed to leave.

Russia's interest in its frontier with Persia had similar causes and similar objects, and was stimulated by the recognition that power relationships gave Russia the advantage against a Persian dynasty in the throes of a terminal disease. The traditional enmity between Turks and Persians strengthened that advantage, and enabled Russia to play off one core area against the other and prevent their united action in Transcaucasia. There, raids by mountain tribesmen were a constant source of insecurity for the settlers in the Kura valley and the Russians who traded with Persia. Dagestan played the same unsettling role as the Crimean khanate in the Russo-Turkish frontier. Men of power in Georgia and especially Armenia, torn between their Christian conscience and the necessity to convert to Islam to retain their position and even make brilliant careers at the shah's court, were seeking to involve Russia—their only choice—in rolling back the Persians from the frontier zones. The spirit of crusade was inseparable from commercial ambitions. Beyond the Caspian, the silk trade of Persia, the caravan trade of Central Asia, and the magic word "India" beckoned all traders, regardless of religious convictions. All these factors combined, as they did in the Russo-Turkish frontier, with Russia's expansionist energy to draw the core area into the frontier zones and to generate an irresistible advance that could stop only when it reached the periphery of the Heartland.

In June 1701, a well-connected Armenian merchant who had lived twenty years in Europe but kept his ties with the Armenian community in Persia submitted to the tsar in Smolensk a plan to liberate Armenia and Georgia from the Persian yoke. Cossacks would link up with local troops to take Shemakha, the entrepôt of the Persian trade and the key to Armenia; would move against Nakhichevan and Erevan; and finally would turn on Tabriz, the capital of Azerbaijan. The plan was ambitious but hardly realistic at the time—the tsar had barely begun to recover from his Narva defeat. Eleven years later, in 1712, news was received that the Lesgians, one of the most warlike tribes of Dagestan, had burned Shemakha and killed Russian and Armenian merchants. Russia could not retaliate because of the tensions with the Porte and the invasion of Finland. Yet there was considerable interest in the potential profits of an expanding Russo-Persian trade, what with canals being built to link the Volga with the Neva, the Baltic with the Caspian, Petersburg with Astrakhan. The tsar sent Artemii Volynsky, the courier who had brought the Adrianople treaty to the capital, to be Russia's permanent representative in Persia. His mission was to obtain compensation for the losses suffered at Shemakha, to negotiate a commercial treaty, and to conduct a broad survey of Persia's political condition, military capabilities, and economic resources. He was also to find out whether the Caspian was connected with India by water. Volynsky left Petersburg in July 1715 and reached Isfahan, the Persian capital, in March

1717. He signed a commercial treaty in July, giving Russian merchants the right to trade freely all over Persia and to buy as much silk as they wanted. But the shah refused to let him stay, and he had to leave in September; he was back in Petersburg in December 1718.

One reason for the Persian refusal to let Volynsky remain in Isfahan was the perception that his mission was part of a two-pronged offensive against "India." And indeed it was. From Kazan, the great hub of the Russian advance into the Persian frontier, one corridor of expansion followed the Volga to Astrakhan and entered Persia via Shemakha and Tabriz; the other went east to the Ural (Iaik) River, where Cossack settlements already stood guard on the edge of the Russo-Chinese frontier, crossed the Kazakh steppe in the direction of the Aral Sea and the valley of the Amu Darya and the Zeravshan, the ultimate zone of the Persian frontier in the northeast. The zone was one of transit between China and Persia; there were rumors that gold could be obtained from Yarkend (Yarkant, Shache) on the Silk Road, beyond the passes of the Sarikol Range, and Russia was deficient in precious metals. The zone also produced cotton, and the textile factories of the new Russia needed it.

The establishment of friendly relations with the khans of Khiva and Bukhara was high on Peter's agenda. In 1703, Khiva had invited the Russian advance by requesting military aid against its rivals. Political instability and succession crises offered rich possibilities for interference there and in Persia itself. There were good reasons to believe that a destabilization policy might be even more successful than in the Western Frontier. Early in 1716, the tsar sent Prince Alexander Cherkassky, from a family of men of power in Kabarda on the northern foothills of the Caucasus who had thrown in their lot with Russia, on a mission to Khiva. His instructions were to secure the khan's allegiance (*poddanstvo*) and to find the way to Yarkend. Engineers in his party had to determine whether the course of the Amu Darya could be rerouted toward the Caspian and whether the river led to India. But the khan was not eager to become a Russian subject and a pawn in Russia's Central Asian strategy; he induced Cherkassky to divide his force and massacred the entire party in August 1717. His reward was a gift of 20,000 rubles from the shah.

After his return to Petersburg, Volynsky submitted to the tsar an ambitious program of military and commercial expansion into Persia that overestimated the chances of success and overlooked logistical difficulties. He proposed no less than an all-out offensive to annex the northern provinces, Persia's richest lands between the Caspian and the Elburz Mountains, the center of silk production. The annexation would effectively make the Caspian into a Russian lake, a gigantic step in Russia's advance in the direction of India. The tsar showed interest and appointed Volynsky governor of Astrakhan with full military and diplomatic powers in the spring of 1719. Astrakhan would become for a century, until after the occupation of Tiflis, Russia's military, naval, and administrative headquarters for operations against Persia.

Volynsky used his extensive powers to negotiate with the tribesmen of Kabarda and Dagestan, with the Georgians and the Armenians. The Bagratid ruling house of Eastern Georgia invited the Russian advance. The Georgian nobility, like the Polish, was known for its fractious spirit and its hostility to a strong monarchy. The Georgian tsar requested Russian help against some members of his own nobility; in return, Georgia would overthrow Persian domination and join the war. Effective assistance depended, of course, on the ability to reach Georgia, and the tsar advised Volynsky to establish Russian bases in Derbent and Shemakha and build a fortress on the Terek River: it would dominate Kabarda and guard the mountain trail between the Cossack zone on the foothills of the eastern Caucasus and the Georgian capital via the Aragvi valley. Russia could thus count, if it remained determined and successful, on the support of the Georgian court in the Caucasian zones.

A war with Persia, however, had to wait until the conclusion of the Northern War, and a pretext had to be found. The pretext was another Lesgian attack on Shemakha in the summer of 1720 in which 300 Russian merchants were killed, and the shah's refusal to accept responsibility not only for the Sunni Lesgians but also for the Sunni Uzbeks of Khiva and Bukhara who raided the Russian caravans in Central Asia. The Northern War came to an end with the treaty of Nystad in August 1721. Russia would be ready for war the following year.

The year 1722 was a propitious time for an attack on Persia. Russo-Ottoman relations after 1713 had not been friendly, but the Porte was at war with Austria and had suffered a major defeat in the Balkans in 1718. The Ottomans and the Russians wanted peace, and the Treaty of Constantinople of November 1720 recognized once again Russia's right to maintain a permanent resident in the Ottoman capital. However, they could not control the turbulence in the frontier zones, and both were compelled to take sides in order for one to prevent the other from gaining a decisive advantage. The Kuban Horde was on the warpath, sending raiding parties into the Cossack zones along the core area and even into the core area itself, as far as Penza. Prince Cherkassky had been instructed to rouse the Kabardians against the Horde in 1711 and claimed to have won their allegiance to Russia; but the allegiance of frontier men of power must always remain fickle so long as no core area can establish its preponderant influence, and the Crimean khan was still considered more powerful than the Russian tsar. The Ottomans were also active in Dagestan, and sought to bring the Moslem population of the entire mountain zone to the Caspian under the sultan's suzerainty. Volynsky understood the danger and responded to the request of some Kabardian men of power to intervene in their perennial internecine conflicts. In December 1721, he claimed that the whole of Kabarda had taken the oath of allegiance to the tsar and given hostages—that general custom by which Russians, Turks, and Persians bound the frontier men of power to their oath.

Persia was facing disintegration. The Safavid dynasty had lost its energy, and centrifugal forces regained the upper hand. The greatest threat came from Persia's eastern frontier. The Ghilzais of Kandahar (Qandahar) rose against their provincial governor—he was a Bagratid in Persian service—and repelled Persian troops sent to put down the rebellion. Mir Vais, and after his death in 1715 his son Mahmud, resolved to overthrow the dynasty. Persia disintegrated, as the Afghans marched across the country to Isfahan, taking the city in October 1722. Shah Husayn, "the most incompetent ruler of Iran,"[1] abdicated in favor of Mahmud, but his son Tahmasp Mirza refused to recognize the Afghan shah and claimed to be the only legitimate ruler. The Afghan victory raised the possibility that the Turks might intervene and partition Persia by annexing eastern ("Persian") Georgia, Armenia, and Azerbaijan, the entire Transcaucasian zone where Russian, Turkish, and Persian interests interlocked.

The tsar left Moscow for Astrakhan in May 1722. The infantry boarded ship and cavalry—Cossacks, Kalmyks, and Tatars—took the long overland route along the Caspian coast. A new fort was erected on the estuary of the Sulak River (Sviatoi Krest) to keep an eye on the Tarki ruler who guarded the approaches to Dagestan from the sea. Derbent opened its doors in August, but disaster struck the expedition. As so often was the case in the Southern Frontier, oppressive heat and lack of forage decimated the horses. To make matters worse, the flour got wet when it was unloaded, depriving the army of its bread supply. The expedition returned to Astrakhan in October, but a detachment sailed on to Rasht to reconnoiter the southern coast of the Caspian. Meanwhile, the Ottomans, suspicious of Russian motives as the Russians were of theirs, had ordered the pasha of Erzerum to occupy Eastern Georgia and raised the Lesgian chief to a status equal to that of the Crimean khan. He used his new authority to annex Ganzha (Elizavetpol, Kirovabad), Nakhichevan, and Ardabil. Only Baku remained beyond the Ottomans' grasp.

Faced with this invasion of the interlocking frontier, Russia adopted a position that was both clear and consistent with its other ambitions in the Western Frontier. It could not accept the establishment of Ottoman power on the Caspian shore. That would deprive Russia of its strategic advantage in the Caucasus—its ability to use Georgia and Armenia as "proruptions" against both Turkey and Persia, with their men of power destabilizing the frontier in Russia's favor. Moreover, the transformation of Dagestan into another Crimean khanate and the consolidation of Ottoman rule among the Turkic populations of Azerbaijan would threaten Russia's influence north and south of the Caucasus and block any Russian advance into Persia. The Ottomans were willing to risk war, and so were the Russians because their vital interests were at stake, while those of the Ottomans were not. The Ottomans would have to yield, and they did, when a second expedition occupied Baku in the summer of 1723.

The disintegration of Persia also gave the Russians the opportunity to initiate a destabilization policy that would continue intermittently until

1917. They refused to recognize the Afghan shah and threw their support to Tahmasp, a fugitive but also a Safavid. Intervention in Persian affairs and territorial annexation were justified by a conservative appeal to the need to restore order and legitimacy. This goal was clearly stated in the treaty of alliance signed between Russia and Tahmasp in September 1723. Only he could renew "the old friendship" between the two countries, but he needed Russian support to restore his rule. To obtain that support, he agreed to cede to Russia "forever" Derbent and Baku and the three provinces of Ghilan (with Rasht), Mazandaran, and Astarabad (Gorgan) as supply bases for Russian military operations in Persia. In fact, Russia would gain control of Persia's silk and caviar industry and of the entire southern coast of the Caspian.

Having supported Tahmasp against the Ottomans, the Russians now sought an agreement with the Ottomans to consolidate their gains. The Russo-Ottoman treaty of June 1724 sanctified the partition of the Persian Empire and its core area. The Lesgian chief was recognized as khan of a demilitarized Shirvan khanate with its center in Shemakha, bounded by a line running from the vicinity of Derbent and west of Baku to the confluence of the Araks and the Kura. The whole of Transcaucasia except the Caspian coast was thus incorporated into the Ottoman Empire. The Ottomans also gained substantial Persian territory, west of a line drawn from the confluence of the two rivers past Ardabil to Hamadan and across the Zagros to Kermanshah (Bakhtaran). Should Tahmasp refuse to accept the partition, Russians and Ottomans would join forces to "pacify Persia" and impose "a Persian-born shah" in Isfahan.

Despite his gains, the tsar wanted more. Asserting that "Christians cannot refuse to protect Christians," he instructed General Alexander Rumiantsev, sent to demarcate the new boundary with Ottoman commissioners, to find out if there was a road from Baku to Tiflis and if the Kura was navigable in Georgian territory. The peace of 1724 was intended to be no more than the prelude to another war.

Standoff, 1725–1767

The tsar's death in January 1725 put a temporary stop to the expansionist impulse, but even without his death the Russians would have had to face the unpleasant fact that they had overreached the limit of an optimum of conquest. Russia, in possession of an army built in accordance with western models, could defeat the Swedes on land and at sea, and hold its conquests. If it could advance into the Southern Frontier, it still could not hold the frontier zones. Military conquest overpassed the line of effective administrative control. The population was sparse and Russian troops had difficulty adjusting to the alien climate; the frontier zones were strongly individualized, ensconced in mountain valleys of difficult access, governed by tribal leaders with religious beliefs antagonistic to the fundamentalist faith of the Russian ruling elite (except in Christian Georgia and Armenia) but receptive to the exhortations of their co-religionists in Turkey and Persia. Last but not least, Ottoman rule remained strong.

It was not enough to sign a treaty with a fugitive shah; the provinces—Baku and Derbent in the frontier—had to be held. Ghilan, Mazanderan, and Astarabad in the core area had first to be occupied and then held. The Russians encountered opposition to their advance, and as early as April 1725 the commander of the expeditionary force was ordered to put off the occupation of Mazanderan and Astarabad. Once in Ghilan they discovered the population had fled and there was no one to pay the taxes needed to support the troops. Russia's difficulties aroused the mountain tribes, and the Tarki chief's hostility threatened to cut off overland communications between Astrakhan and Rasht. Russian soldiers were dying from the heat and of a fever caused by the insalubrious Caspian coast; fresh recruits had to be sent repeatedly to replace the losses, and the Persian provinces were soon on the verge of becoming the "cemetery"[2] of the expeditionary force.

The domestic situation in Persia was not evolving in Russia's favor. Mahmud, the Afghan shah in Isfahan, was put to death and replaced by his cousin Ashraf, but the Afghans' nastiness and lack of administrative experience, added to the fact that they were Sunnis ruling over a Shi'ite society, strengthened the Persians' determination to reject their rule. The Ottomans saw an opportunity to improve their gains and marched on Isfahan, but Ashraf defeated them and compelled them to accept him as shah in December 1727. It was a Pyrrhic victory. Tahmasp, from his refuge in Rasht, was organizing Persian resistance to Afghan rule. His major support came from an adventurer with a following from Khorasan, on the very edge of the Persian core area. The price of his support was the unification of northern Persia, the crescent along the Caspian coast and the Kopet Dag flanking the Great Desert. That was achieved with the conquest of Meshed (Mashhad) in 1729, followed by a battle with the Afghans near Damghan. It was the beginning of the end. The Afghans were expelled from Isfahan and Shiraz in the spring of 1730 and returned to Kandahar. Ashraf was killed after escaping in the desert. The adventurer's reward was Tahmasp's daughter. Known as Tahmasp Kuli (Quli) Khan ("slave of Tahmasp"), he was soon to become one of Persia's great rulers.

The reunification of Persia placed Russia on the defensive and exposed the precariousness of its position beyond the limit of an optimum of conquest. In the fall of 1730, Anna's government informed Tahmasp of its readiness to negotiate the terms of a Russian withdrawal, which the reemergence of Persian military power rendered inevitable in any case. Negotiations began in April 1731 and ended with the treaty of Rasht in February 1732. Russia abandoned the three provinces of northern Persia and the Kura became the boundary between the two empires, leaving Baku and Derbent in Russian hands. The treaty confirmed the right of Russian subjects to trade freely everywhere in the Persian Empire without paying customs duties on Russian goods, even those in transit "to the

Indies or another country." The two empires agreed to be represented by ministers at each other's court and to allow the appointment of consuls, but Persia alone pledged to assume responsibility and pay compensation for losses caused by the shah's subjects—a clause that would allow Russia to pressure the shah whenever necessary.

Russia's withdrawal was followed by a Persian offensive in Transcaucasia. After Tahmasp's defeat in an engagement with the Ottomans, his slave removed him and had himself appointed regent for the former shah's infant son. Four years later, he removed the boy and was acclaimed ruler of Persia with the title of Nadir Shah. He recovered from the Ottomans the Shirvan khanate in 1734, Ganzha, Eastern Georgia, and Armenia in 1735. The Russians had to return Baku and Derbent in 1735, and in September 1736, the Ottomans abandoned the conquests they had gained under the 1724 treaty. Russia thus lost the two coastal cities that had served for more than a decade as landings for troops from Astrakhan and bases of operation in Transcaucasia. It also sacrificed the interests of the Georgians and Armenians, but it had no choice. On the other hand, supporting Nadir Shah blocked Ottoman attempts to unify the Caucasian segment of the frontier and threatened to open a second front against the Ottomans in the event of another war.

Russo-Ottoman relations had taken a turn for the worse after the treaty of 1724. Boundary disputes were magnified by mutual distrust and the Ottomans' irreducible hostility to the Russian advance toward the Black Sea and to the support given to a Shi'ite ruler in Persia. In September 1730, following one of Kuli Khan's local victories over the Ottomans, the sultan was overthrown in Constantinople and his successor gave the Crimean khan a privileged position in his government. The khan had always been the instrument of an Ottoman forward policy in the Southern Frontier between the Dniestr and the Caspian and in the Russian core area between the Dniepr and the Volga. His energies were now directed to the Caucasian zones between the Don and Christian Georgia and Armenia, for the purpose of bringing the Moslem men of power, largely Sunni, more closely under Ottoman control. The Ottomans also intended the khan to become the commander of a northern flanking attack against Persia through Kabarda and the Kura valley, while Ottoman forces would link up with their Azeri co-religionists between Eastern Georgia and the Caspian. The Cherkess (Circassians, Karachai) behind the Kuban, the Kabardians between the Kuban and the Terek, and the Kumyks of Dagestan were links in a vast chain linking the Black Sea with the Caspian. Once under Ottoman administrative control, they would form an impregnable barrier to Russian expansion and keep Georgia and Armenia out of Russia's reach.

Beginning in 1733, the entire Southern Frontier became the arena of an acute conflict for the mastery of space. The Ottomans were annoyed by Russia's military intervention against Stanislas Leszczynski in Poland. The Crimean khan sent parties into the demilitarized zone between the Orel and the Samara rivers, as if to remind the Russians they were vulnerable in the Ukraine. But in 1734, some 70,000 Tatars were sent across Kabarda and Dagestan to fight Tahmasp Kuli Khan; they and the Ottomans were beaten back. The Turko-Crimean concentration on the Caucasus gave the Russians a chance. The ruling elite resented its losses in the Russo-Persian frontier and recognized it could not recoup them. Flushed with its victory in Poland, it sought to find compensations in the valley of the Dniepr. Russia declared war on the Ottomans in May 1735, while Kuli Khan was winning victories in Transcaucasia. In October, the pasha of Ochakov reported to Constantinople that the Russians had reached the Perekop isthmus.

The war was costly and unsuccessful. Russia remained unable to conduct offensive warfare in the steppe, and nothing seemed to have changed since 1689. In fact, it had consistently pursued a close-border policy, as if unable to free itself from a fear of invasion across the boundless and mysterious steppe that went back to the great Mongol assault five centuries earlier. While its policy in the Western Frontier had been bold and clear-sighted, Russia had advanced in the "steppe-ocean"[3] by pursuing a fortress-fleet strategy on land, by building military "lines" across the steppe, defensive perimeters barring the way to Tatar raids into the core area. Projecting power by forceful thrusts across the steppe where an army could not feed itself required the preliminary establishment of supply bases and experience with the management of long-distance logistical operations. It would take another generation before the Russian high command could switch successfully to a forward strategy against the Ottomans and Tatars.

Russian forces were placed under the command of Marshal Burchard von Münnich (Minikh), born in Oldenburg, and a great believer in the overpowering force of heavy cavalry charges—while the Tatars' strength lay in their light cavalry. He inaugurated a two-pronged strategy that would be followed in every subsequent war with the Ottomans—to prevent the enemy from concentrating its forces and defeat it in separate encounters. One army would follow the Dniepr and move to the Crimea, the other would take Azov, and the two armies would eventually link up in the peninsula. Perekop on the isthmus was taken in May 1736; Bakhchisarai, the khan's capital, in July. Kinburn, facing Ochakov across the Dniepr's estuary, also fell in July. But the army had exhausted its provisions and had to return to the Cossack zones in September. Marshal Lacy, who had led Russian troops in Poland in 1733, took Azov in June, but went no farther. The Tatars countered with devastating raids during the winter, and it seemed the war had reached an impasse. The Russians returned in 1737, but Lacy's expedition from Azov to the Crimea failed in July and the storming of Ochakov in August settled nothing.

Negotiations began at Nemirov (east of Vinnitsa) in Podolia in August. Despite their lack of success, they deserve a brief mention, because the Russians put forward a comprehensive plan of territorial expansion so far-sighted that it would take a century to complete. The two negotiators were veteran diplomats: Peter Shafirov, who had been deputy minister of foreign affairs ("vice-chancellor") during Peter's reign (1709–1723), and Ivan Nepliuev, who had been resident in Constantinople for more than a decade (1721–1735). They claimed the Crimea, the Kuban steppe between the Don and the Kuban, and the entire coastline of the Black Sea from the Dniepr to the Danube. Moldavia and Wallachia between the Carpathians, the Danube, and the sea must become independent under Russian protection because their populations were Orthodox. These claims were fundamental for two reasons. The Russians aimed at the elimination of the Crimean khanate: it would give them control of the Ottomans' proximate zone, create a naval presence in the Black Sea, and break the chain of Moslem tribal zones barring access to the Caucasus. Russia also made for the first time a tangible and realistic claim to a zone of the Ottoman Empire on the ground of a common Christian religion. The Orthodox men of power in the Danube valley, like those of Lithuania and the other Christians in Georgia and Armenia, would form parties preparing the way for the Russian advance and giving it legitimacy. The Ottomans objected that such ambitions were not commensurate with Russia's successes on the battlefield. And indeed, a forward diplomacy could not succeed without a correspondingly successful forward strategy.

War was renewed in the spring of 1738. Münnich now directed his efforts toward Moldavia. He reached the Dniestr in August, but had to withdraw with enormous losses caused by disease and insufficient supplies. Lacy failed again against the Crimea. Even Ochakov and Kinburn had to be abandoned. The capture of Khotin in August 1739 and the occupation of Jassy in September came too late to overcome the general war weariness. Austria had been losing its war in the Balkans and was also ready for peace. It was signed at Belgrade in September, two weeks after the Russian occupation of Jassy. Russia retained Azov (but the fortress had to be razed) and annexed the Zaporozhian zone east of the Dniepr to a line following two steppe streams—Konskie Vody, flowing into the Dniepr, and the Berda, flowing into the Sea of Azov. Kabarda was declared a neutral zone ("barrier") between the Russian and Ottoman empires. Russian ships were again barred from the Azov and Black seas, and it was forbidden to rebuild Taganrog. What paltry gains from a war that had cost 100,000 casualties and enormous sums! In fact, the war was the Ottomans' last successful stand against the Russian advance.

Meanwhile, a new Persian empire had been taking shape in the Russo-Persian frontier. Nadir Shah had made peace with the Ottomans in September 1736, leaving the Russians to fight their war alone. He had gained his objectives in Georgia and Armenia. He then avenged the Afghan invasion of 1722 by taking Kandahar in March 1738. The expansionist impulse took him around the Hindu Kush to Kabul, then an Afghan province of Mughal India. The Mughal Empire, centered on the watershed between the Indus and Ganges rivers, was ruled by a dynasty descending from Chinggis Khan and Timur. The son of the dynasty's founder had found refuge in Persia and had invaded India through the

Hindu Kush passes as a vassal of Persia. This is a fact of the utmost importance, not so much because it would explain in part Nadir's own invasion of northern India and the capture of Delhi, the empire's capital, in March 1739, as because it would explain British India's pathological fear in the nineteenth century of a Russian-supported Persian attempt to reassert authority in Afghanistan and project Russian influence across the Hindu Kush. Nadir could not hold northern India, but, like all great conquerors of Persia and Central Asia, he took over the foothills of the Hindu Kush to the Indus River—they had been part of the Persian empire of antiquity.

Nadir's operations against the Afghans brought him into conflict with their ally, the Uzbek ruler of Balkh (near present-day Mazar-e Sharif) on the northern approaches of the Hindu Kush, but he was brought to heel in 1738. On his return from India Nadir proceeded to re-incorporate the Persian frontier zones north of the Kopet Dag into the Persian Empire. Like the Crimean khanate, the two Uzbek khanates of Khiva and Bukhara lived chiefly by rapine, including the slave trade; and their attacks on Russian caravans were matched by raids on Khorasan, Nadir's birthplace. From Balkh, the shah sailed down the Amu Darya to Charjui (Chardzhou) and crossed overland to Bukhara, whose khan promptly submitted in 1740. He agreed that the river should become Persia's boundary and he would supply a contingent of troops to the Persian army. The khan of Khiva, less inclined to compromise, was put to death, and thousands of Persian and Russian slaves were released, a gesture for which the Russians could only be grateful. While Persia was advancing into Central Asia, they had been moving across Bashkiria toward the Ural River. A new fort, Orenburg, was founded at the confluence of the Or in 1735, and would move to its present location in 1742. It would soon replace Kazan as Russia's administrative, military, and commercial headquarters for relations with Khiva and Bukhara.

Success began to spoil the shah, and his cruelty toward his subjects and members of his own family antagonized vital sources of support. When he invaded Dagestan in 1741, he found himself engaged with the Lesgians in a guerilla war he could not win. Defeats in the mountains provided a pretext, and the shah was killed by his own bodyguards in June 1747.

The death of Persia's last great shah took place at the beginning of a Russian revival following the somber years of the late 1720s and 1730s, when fiscal constraints and the limited abilities of the Empress Anna compelled a temporary retrenchment, notwithstanding the intervention in Poland and the war with the Ottomans. It was symptomatic of a period of stocktaking that the major figures in the high command were men of foreign origin; the ruling elite was passing through a phase of self-mutilation, when some of the major figures of Peter's reign were either banished or executed. The 1750s, however, would witness the recovery of the Russian economy and the development of an internal political consensus of exceptional strength under the leadership of the Empress Elizabeth who was, if not exceedingly capable, at least imbued with a strong sense of

Russia's destiny. The Seven Years War with Prussia (1756–1763) would produce a new crop of outstanding native military commanders, and by the mid-1760s Russia and its determined Empress Catherine would inaugurate both a forward policy and a forward strategy to begin a systematic rollback of the Turco-Tatars and Persians from the Southern Frontier.

Nadir Shah's empire had been held together by the strength of his personality and the swiftness of his retribution against offenders. Like most political formations in that part of the world from the Caucasus to India and in the steppe-ocean in the Russo-Chinese frontier, it had been a union of men of power negotiated for a transitory purpose and likely to fall apart when the shah was no longer able to impose his will. The men of power were the hereditary tribal chiefs with a strong local identification, despite their nomadic way of life; they contributed their cavalry to the shah's army. Persia was kept together by its distinctive ethnic and religious identity—it was surrounded by Sunni Turks, Arabs, Uzbeks, and Afghans. The shah was the first magistrate who enforced the common law, and the permanent centrifugal particularisms of the northern provinces, Fars, and Khorasan could be overcome only by a powerful ruler capable of winning and retaining the allegiance of their men of power—admittedly a rare occurrence.

One consequence of the disintegration of Nadir Shah's empire was the emergence of Afghanistan as a separate political identity with its own dynasty in the Sadozai family. Ahmad Shah Durrani, its founder, welded together the tribes of the Hindu Kush and built a kingdom stretching from the Indus River to Khorasan. In a striking reassertion of the frontier against the core area, he made Khorasan into a separate kingdom under Afghan protection and incorporated Seistan (Sistan), the upland on the periphery of the Heartland, which he then gave as a tributary to the ruler of Herat. Afghanistan, like Georgia-Armenia, would become in the nineteenth century one of those proruptions where the interests of powerful rivals must interlock, the focal point of a bitter rivalry between Russia, Persia, and British India. The emergence of Afghanistan coincided with the establishment of the East India Company in the Persian Gulf—from Bandar Abbas it moved its headquarters in 1763 to Bushire (Bushehr) in Fars province. Peripheral powers were establishing a foothold in the Persian core area at the very time Russia was about to resume its advance in the Caucasian zones. Beyond the Kopet Dag, Bukhara and Khiva regained their independence.

While maintaining relatively friendly relations with the Ottomans and the Persians, the Russians sought to detach tribal leaders of the Caucasian zones from their allegiance to the sultan and the shah and bring them into the Russian orbit. In 1742, Kabardian men of power had sent a deputation to Petersburg to congratulate Elizabeth on her accession and taken the opportunity to ask for Russian protection against the Crimean khan. Russia sent a military mission to mediate the disputes between the supporters of Turkey and those of Russia. To the south of Kabarda lay

Ossetia, straddling the great watershed between the valleys of the Kuban and the Terek and those of the Rioni and Kura in Transcaucasia. The Ossetes spoke a language related to Persian, but Georgia had converted them to Christianity in the twelfth century. They had ever since been a frontier zone of Greater Georgia. Russia's relations with Ossetia began in 1742, and an Ossetian embassy was in Petersburg in the early 1750s, offering to contribute 30,000 men to Russia's wars in the Southern Frontier in exchange for protection against Moslem raids. The importance of Ossetia, bounded in the east by the Terek, was its proximity to the Darial gorge through which a pass led to the Aragvi River and Tiflis, and its control of the Mamison pass leading to the valley of the Rioni and to Kutais, the major city of Western ("Turkish") Georgia. Ossetia was the key to influence in the central Caucasus.

Dagestan was the key to the eastern Caucasus. In the 1750s, some of its most important men of power gave their allegiance to Russia—a nominal allegiance to be sure, but it established a precedent to justify more insistent claims later on. The Crimean khan understood the implications of the Russian advance. When the Russians built a new fortress at Mozdok on the Terek in 1765, he aroused the Ottomans to protest this "dangerous and far-sighted move."[4] Short of war, the only possible response was to encourage the Lesgians to devastate Kakhetia between the Alazan and Kura rivers, while the Ottomans sought to extend their influence over Kartliia in order to block a possible Russian advance toward Tiflis. These moves and countermoves added to the endemic instability of the frontier into which Russia was bound to be drawn more and more deeply—to separate the Ottomans from the Persians and establish its own unchallengeable dominion.

There were other, more dangerous, grounds to fear the renewal of Russo-Ottoman hostilities. Relations with Poland had always been an integral part of Russia's relations with the Ottomans, because the Right-Bank Ukraine (together with the Tatar hordes west of the Dniepr) barred Russian expansion toward the Danubian Principalities. Petersburg's representative in the Turkish frontier was the governor general of Kiev, who corresponded with the Russian resident in Constantinople and the ministry (college) of foreign affairs on matters concerning Polish, Turkish, Tatar, and Cossack affairs. The intervention to impose a Russian-supported candidate on the Polish throne in 1733 had been a factor in the outbreak of the war in 1735. It was known through the governor general and other sources that the Ottomans, with the usual support of France, would oppose intervention when the king died. On his death in 1763, they had to swallow their pride, however; they accepted the election of Stanislas Poniatowski in August 1764. When the king's opponents formed the confederation of Bar in 1768 to overthrow him and Cossacks pursued confederates into Ottoman territory at Balta and Dubossary, killing some Turks and Moldavians, the Ottomans vented their resentment by arresting the Russian minister in Constantinople in September, after Russia rejected their ultimatum to withdraw its forces from Poland. The move was their usual method of declaring war.

Breakthrough, 1768–1791

The Russian plan of operations built upon the experience gained in 1711 and 1735–1739; it was also much more ambitious. Russia would seek the support of the men of power among the Balkan Slavs and the Greeks in a general crusade against Ottoman rule. To facilitate contact with them and improve the chances of success, it would for the first time send its Baltic fleet into the Mediterranean, with the additional mission to engage the Ottoman navy and keep it out of the Black Sea. The Ottomans would be attacked no longer from two, but from three, directions—in the valley of the Danube, in the Crimea, and in Western Georgia. Military reforms in the 1760s, including a reorganization of the supply administration, had considerably strengthened Russian striking power on the Left Bank, and the appointment in 1765 of General Peter Rumiantsev as governor general in Glukhov had placed the command of troops in the valley of the Dniepr in the hands of a commander soon to become one of the most famous figures in Russian military history.

In January 1769, the Crimean Tatars launched their last raid into the Ukraine, and failed. The Russians appealed to the Balkan Slavs, and revolts began in Montenegro, Bosnia, Herzegovina, Albania, and Macedonia. A First Army moved from Kiev across the Right Bank in the direction of Khotin. A Second Army marched from Kremenchug toward Elizavetgrad (Kirovograd) in order to split the Turkish counteroffensive. In June, the Ottomans crossed the Prut, and Bessarabia became the major theater of war. They were defeated on the Dniestr in August, and the First Army took Khotin and Jassy in September. An expedition against the Crimea failed, however. The following year was the year of great victories, even though the Russians remained unable to break the will of a stubborn enemy. In July 1770, the Baltic fleet destroyed most of the Ottoman navy at the battle of Cheshme (Çeşme) near Smyrna, but the Christian uprisings failed. On land, Rumiantsev inflicted three major defeats on Ottomans and Tatars in Bessarabia and went on to take key fortified positions on the Danube—Izmail, Kilia, and Braila. By the end of the year, Moldavia and Wallachia, including Bucharest, were in Russian hands.

Once the Russians had pinned down the Ottomans on the Danube, the diversion against the Crimea turned into a major offensive. Turmoil in the Crimean leadership gave them a long-awaited opportunity. A strengthened Second Army invaded the peninsula in June 1771 while the Azov flotilla landed troops and supplies in the east. The Russians withdrew, however, after signing an agreement with a new khan, Sahib Girei, that proclaimed the independence of the Crimea but also gave them Kerch and Enikale, the two fortresses guarding the exit from the Sea of Azov. Meanwhile, a small expeditionary force had crossed the Caucasus in 1769 and, with the help of Georgian troops, had taken Kutais. But it was too small to overwhelm the two Ottoman strongholds, Poti and especially Akhaltsykh, whose pasha was the most redoubtable embodiment of Ottoman power in Western Georgia. The expedition withdrew in 1772, but not without reviving Georgian and Armenian hopes and convincing the Kabardians of Russia's superiority over Ottomans and Tatars.

The time had come to talk peace. Russians and Ottomans met at Fokshany (Focşani) in Moldavia for three weeks in August 1772 and resumed negotiations at Bucharest in October. In each case, Russian arrogance and the Ottoman refusal to accept the secession of the Crimea, bolstered in the fall by the news of the Polish partition that seemed like a portent of things to come in the Ottomans' own empire, caused the negotiations to fail. War resumed in 1773 with disappointing results, but 1774 was the year of final victory. While the Second Army laid siege to Ochakov, Rumiantsev's First Army crossed the Danube, and the capitulation of Shumla (Shumen) decided the fate of the war. The Ottomans sued for peace in July at Kuchuk Kainardji (Küçük Kaynarca), a village near Silistria (Silistra) on the right bank of the Danube.

Peace was signed in July, sixty-five years to the day after the disastrous peace of the Prut, but the roles were now reversed. The treaty was a complex document, but it dealt with three major issues. It was first and foremost a political and territorial settlement affecting the Danubian Principalities, the Crimean and other Tatars, and the Caucasus—the zones of the Russo-Turkish frontier west, north, and east of the Black Sea. It was in a very real sense the first partition of the Ottoman Empire by the Russians. They retroceded Moldavia and Wallachia with Khotin, Bendery, Izmail, and other fortresses, but on condition that their populations suffer no Ottoman retaliation and be free to exercise their Orthodox religion, and that their hospodars be represented in Constantinople, where the Russian minister might "remonstrate" in their favor—a claim extending Russia's sphere of influence to the bank of the Danube even after the withdrawal of Russian troops.

The treaty proclaimed the existence of a "Tatar nation" consisting of the Crimean khanate; the Budzhak, Edisan, and other hordes between the Dniepr and the peninsula; and the Kuban Horde between the Eia and the Kuban. It would be governed by its own khan, "of the race of Chinggis Khan," to be elected by "all Tatar peoples." The Russians would then withdraw behind the 1739 boundary. They kept Kinburn, facing Ochakov that remained in the Ottoman Empire, Kerch, and Enikale. The Sea of Azov became a closed sea, and the Zaporozhian Cossack zone was integrated into the inner frontier of the Russian Empire. Russia acquired enough bases from which to apply decisive pressure on the Tatar nation whenever necessary. In the Caucasus, Kabarda was incorporated into the Russian Empire, subject to the consent of the Crimean khan and the "elders of the Tatar nation." Russia pledged to withdraw its troops from Western Georgia on condition that the Ottomans stop collecting taxes, including the tribute in children. Petersburg was obviously staking a claim to becoming the "protector" not only of the Danubian Principalities but of Western Georgia as well.

The treaty also took up the cause of the Orthodox subjects of the Ottoman Empire. This second issue later became a source of great controversy. Article 7 stated that the Porte "promises to protect constantly the Christian religion and its churches" and to give friendly consideration to the Russian minister's representation of a new church to be built in Constantinople. It has been claimed that the minister's representations were restricted to the protection of that particular church and that subsequent Russian claims to protect all the sultan's Orthodox subjects rested on a "generous (and questionable) interpretation"[5] of the article. There is no question that the text of the article was ambiguous, but it is also clear that it contained two clauses and that the first pledged the sultan to protect Christianity and *its churches*. It must also be noted that the Ottoman government had to promise not to oppress Christianity specifically in the Greek archipelago (Art. 17), in the Danubian Principalities (Art. 16), and in Western Georgia (Art. 23). The unchallengeable corollary was that if it did, an official representation would be in order. Moreover, whatever legal interpretation is given to Article 7, it is no stretch of the imagination to see that the Russians intended to use the "Christian question" in the Balkans, Greece, and Caucasus in the same way they had used the "dissident question" in Poland—indeed, the ambassador sent to Constantinople to exchange ratifications in 1775 was none other than Nikolai Repnin, who had used the dissident question so successfully in the Polish empire to destabilize the frontier and core area government.

Finally, the treaty opened up the question of Russian navigation in the Black Sea and passage through the straits. It ended the Ottoman monopoly and allowed merchantmen flying the Russian flag to carry goods across the Black Sea and to cross the straits into the Mediterranean. It allowed Russian subjects to trade in the Coastland regions of the Ottoman Empire and in its Balkan possessions along the Danube. Russia was permitted to appoint consuls wherever it considered expedient. Both powers gave each other the benefits of the most-favored-nation status. The treaty, however, ignored a fundamental question, largely because it was premature: would Russia be allowed to build warships in the Black Sea and cross the straits? As long as the Crimea remained independent, Russia could have no navy in the Black Sea—the Sea of Azov freezes over from November to April and its exit was too shallow for large warships. Russia's future as a naval power in the Black Sea thus depended on a settlement of the "Crimean question."

The Treaty of Kuchuk Kainardji could not create a durable peace because it symbolized a radical shift in the balance of power in the Russo-Turkish frontier. The Ottomans had grown used to being the masters there, with the help of the Crimean Tatars, but they were now faced with the ominous fact that Russia, rather than Austria, had become their major and implacable enemy. They could accept the treaty only as the first round of a struggle to be fought for supremacy in the frontier. But the Russians had gained the initiative and would never lose it for the remainder of the Imperial period, despite temporary setbacks. The strength of the core area and its growing industrial and military superiority—vis-à-vis the Turkish and Persian core areas entering a long period of inexorable decline bred self-confidence and ambition. For the Russians as well, the treaty was a first round, but one on the road to additional conquests, until they had brought the entire frontier into the Russian Empire.

These ambitions were embodied at an early stage in the new leaders of the foreign policy establishment. For Catherine II, of course, brilliant victories over the Ottomans secured the legitimacy of her rule and whetted her ambition for fame and power. For the upper strata of the ruling class, the annexation of the steppe promised rich rewards in the form of land grants and commercial opportunities in and beyond the Black Sea, just as the partitions of the Polish Empire promised to give Russia control of the entire Baltic trade in naval stores. It was therefore no coincidence that the two men who played decisive roles in the formation of Russian foreign policy after 1774 came from the valley of the Dniepr. One was Alexander Bezborodko, Catherine's principal secretary, recommended to her by Rumiantsev. He came from the Left Bank, and his father had worked with Rumiantsev's father in the 1730s. The other was Grigorii Potemkin, who became the empress's favorite, her war minister, and the governor general of the frontier zones conquered from the Ottomans. He came from the Smolensk region, on the watershed between the Dvina and the Dniepr, but he looked south, and the entire Southern Frontier became the field of his dreams and political ambitions. Like the Keyserlings and Stackelbergs in the Western Frontier, both men were men of the frontier.

As early as 1774 or 1775, Potemkin conceived an "eastern system."[6] It aimed at annexing the Crimea, destroying Ochakov, "the key to the Black Sea," and replacing it with a naval base from which Russia would gain supremacy in that sea and threaten Constantinople. In the Caucasus, it called for the building of a line of fortifications across the watershed between the Kuban and the Terek from which to launch expeditions into Western Georgia "to undermine Asiatic forces in Asia itself," and encourage local pashas to enlarge their autonomy from the Ottoman government. These successes would make "the Greeks and other co-religionists" "impatient" to raise arms against the Ottomans and expel them from the entire frontier. This essentially military program was vastly enlarged by Catherine II, who submitted a partition plan to Joseph II, the Holy Roman Emperor, in September 1782, the year Kherson was founded on the lower Dniepr and a Black Sea fleet was born. Russia wanted Ochakov (Potemkin also called it the Kronshtadt of the South), the Ochakov steppe between the Bug and the Dniestr, and one or two islands in the Aegean Sea "for security and facility of commerce." Such gains would render Constantinople vulnerable to attack from the north and the south.

The empress also refurbished old plans of 1711 and 1736 to transform
the Danubian Principalities into a Russian protectorate called Dacia under
an Orthodox prince—and Potemkin very much wanted to be that prince.
Catherine's plan was realistic and by then had a long tradition behind it,
but the same could not be said of her suggestion to reconstitute the core
of the Byzantine Empire on the ruin of the Ottoman as an "independent
state" under her second grandson born in March 1779 and appropriately
named Constantine. As Joseph II politely put it, "this would have to
depend on the outcome of war."[7]

Potemkin's eastern system was carried out to its successful conclusion.
Its first victim was the Crimea. Peninsular politics remained tense. A new
khan, Devlet Girei, was elected in March 1775, but his opposition to the
annexation made him unacceptable to the Russians, who supported Shagin Girei, the former khan's brother. Russian troops entered the Crimea
in November 1776, the khan fled to Turkey, and Shagin Girei was proclaimed khan of all the Tatars in the spring of 1777. He showed himself
unfit to rule, and had to put down a number of revolts with Russian support. Nevertheless, he was forced to flee in July 1782. Potemkin retaliated
by reoccupying the Crimea. In April 1783, Russia announced the annexation of the peninsula, of the Kuban steppe, and of the Taman peninsula.
The Ottomans had no choice but to accept it in December. Thus ended
the seven-year existence of the Tatar nation.

In the Caucasus, the fortified line was extended until it stretched all the
way from the Taman peninsula to the mouth of the Terek, blocking raids
by mountain tribes into the steppe and cutting off their access to vital
sources of salt. Russia's forward policy beyond that line depended for its
success on close ties with Eastern Georgia beyond the mountains. It was
an axiom of a forward policy that the control of the passes on the inner
side of a mountain chain creates a momentum to see what is on the other
side and control the entrances to the passes. Otherwise, a mountain frontier "is only a military mouse-trap."[8] The aim of that policy was to create
a Christian state "in Asia" capable of rallying the Georgians of Eastern
and Western Georgia and the Armenians under the Russian banner, that
is, one of those proruptions serving to relay and expand the core area's
striking power into the ultimate zones of the entire frontier.

Russian ambitions met Georgian desires halfway. Tsar Heraclius II
needed Russian support for his dynasty, threatened by bitter rivalries
among the children of his two wives, and for his country, against a
reassertion of Persian power by a strong shah seeking to rebuild the
empire of Nadir Shah. Mutual interest thus dictated the Russo-Georgian
treaty of July 1783, by which Eastern Georgia left the Persian and entered
the Russian orbit. The treaty made five major points. Georgia abjured any
form of dependence on Persia or another power, but would conduct its
foreign relations with the consent of the Russian commander in chief in
the Caucasus and the Russian minister in Tiflis. The Bagratid dynasty
remained hereditary "for ever," but every new tsar would require the

confirmation and investiture of the Russian government. He would continue to administer his kingdom without Russian interference. The Georgian nobility was granted the same rights and privileges as the Russian—it was integrated into the ruling class of the Russian Empire. In exchange, the Georgian tsar would consider Russia's enemies his own and would contribute troops to the common defense.

Russia's striking successes in 1774 and 1783 strengthened the advocates of a forward strategy, but Ottoman resistance soon created serious obstacles to the consolidation of Russian gains. The commitment to support the Bagratid dynasty in Tiflis was meaningful only so long as Russia could establish an unchallengeable military presence beyond the Caucasus, and this in turn required safe communications between Mozdok and Tiflis. It was for that purpose that a new fortress was built on the Terek in 1784 with the challenging name of Vladikavkaz, "Dominator of the Caucasus" (later Ordzhonokidze), from which the Russians expected to consolidate their rule in Kabarda and extend their influence in Ossetia. The Ottomans exploited local resentment against the growing Russian presence in the mountains and supported the revolt of Sheik Mansur in Dagestan who sought in 1785 to cut off communications with Tiflis and with Astrakhan. The revolt was crushed in 1786, but there would be others, and it would take three generations before Russian rule was secure in the mountain zones.

The Ottomans refused to recognize the treaty of 1783, even though Eastern Georgia had been a vassal of the shah. They did not need to know the term to understand the military significance of *proruptions*. The pasha of Akhaltsykh was ordered to launch devastating raids into Georgia, capturing slaves, driving away cattle, burning villages, and destroying silver mines, and to form alliances with the tribal principalities of Azerbaijan in a holy war against the Russians. Massive expeditions took place in 1785, no doubt coordinated with the Mansur uprising; the Russians could only oppose token resistance, to the great disappointment of Heraclius and of the Russians themselves, who had expected Georgia to stand up on its own. By 1787, however, Russia began to prepare for another showdown with the Ottomans.

Catherine II openly challenged them by undertaking a spectacular journey down the Dniepr and throughout the Crimea during the spring of 1787. She met Joseph II (and Stanislas, the Polish king) to discuss joint military action and an eventual partition of the Ottoman Empire. She was much impressed, and perhaps misled, by the existence of a Black Sea navy based in Sevastopol, at the southern end of the Crimea. Ochakov (with Khotin and Azov) had formed the Ottoman last line of defense against the Russian advance toward the Black Sea shores. Sevastopol symbolized Russia's offensive, fleet-in-being strategy against the Ottomans, aiming at no less than the transformation of that sea into a Russian sea, very much as Astrakhan had already eliminated Persian power from the Caspian. But it was still premature to claim superiority over the Ottomans.

When Catherine, flushed with the success of her trip, demanded the cessation of Ottoman hostilities in Georgia, the Porte answered with an ultimatum in July demanding the return of the Crimea; the recognition of Eastern Georgia as a vassal of the Ottoman Empire; the closing of the Russian consulates in Jassy, Bucharest, and Alexandria; and the right to search all Russian ships in the Black Sea, suspecting with good reason that the Russians had been sending warships through the straits disguised as merchantmen. When the Russians refused to yield, the Ottoman government declared war in August. For all its bluster, Russia was not yet ready for war. Personal rivalries in the high command, notably between Rumiantsev and Potemkin, did not bode well for the success of military planning. Sensing that the war would not be a repeat of the first Turkish War of her reign, Catherine cut her losses in Georgia by withdrawing the Russian detachment, sending home the Georgian representative in Petersburg, and even ordering the demolition of Vladikavkaz. Heraclius was abandoned to his fate.

The Russians attacked the Ottomans in a giant pincer movement, toward the Danube on one side of the Black Sea, toward Anapa and Sudzhuk Kale (Novorossiisk) on the other, with a major thrust against Ochakov in between. Ochakov was stormed in December 1788, but little progress was made elsewhere. British unfriendliness made it impossible to take the risk of sending the Baltic fleet again into the Mediterranean. The Balkan Christians did not revolt. Sweden went to war against Russia in June. And Potemkin's political vision and administrative talent were not matched by decisiveness on the battlefield. The following year, in 1789, the Russians were in Moldavia, where Suvorov distinguished himself, but that was not enough to force the Ottomans to make peace. In 1790, however, the tide began to turn. Fortresses on the delta of the Danube surrendered to a naval attack, Izmail was stormed in December. Another Ottoman defeat at Malchin on the right bank of the Danube, the surrender of Anapa, both in June 1791, together with a disaster at sea off Cape Kaliakra (near Varna) in August combined to break Ottoman resistance, and peace negotiations began at Jassy. They were delayed by the death of Potemkin in October, but peace was finally signed in January 1792.

The Treaty of Jassy bore some resemblance to the Treaty of Verele signed with Sweden less than two years earlier in that both restored the territorial status quo. The Russians had to retrocede the Ottoman fortresses guarding the approaches to the Danube (and Anapa) and abandon their goal of making the Danubian Principalities into a protectorate. There and in Eastern Georgia, political ambitions had exceeded military capabilities, at least for the time being. However, they retained Ochakov and acquired the Ochakov steppe, a small gain after such an expenditure of energy. Nevertheless, the new boundary along the Dniestr made the Russian Empire contiguous with Moldavia, and the Ottomans found their second defensive perimeter, along the Danube, directly threatened, even more so after the annexation of the Right-Bank Ukraine in 1793. They had to accept the annexation of the Crimea, recognize the Kuban as the new boundary of the Russian Empire in the Caucasus, and pledge to stop inciting the Akhaltsykh pasha against Eastern Georgia. The negotiations had been a sobering experience for Catherine's government, coming after some extravagant hopes to partition the Ottoman Empire with Austria, but the stark fact remained that the Ottomans had been defeated once again. A new spatial configuration was emerging in the basin of the Black Sea, as the Russians continued to show a relentless determination to incorporate the frontier zones on both sides of the sea. This Russo-Turkish war would also remain memorable for another reason: it awakened Britain to the danger of Russia's advance toward the southern periphery of the Heartland.

5

In Search of an Optimum of Conquest, 1792–1856

Consolidation, 1792–1813

A temporary peace had been achieved in the Russo-Turkish frontier, but Russia soon found itself at war with Persia for the first time since 1722. The long dynastic interlude following the death of Nadir Shah in 1747 came to an end with the rise of Aga Mohammed Khan, the chief of the Kajar (Qajar) tribe in northern Persia. After the defeat of his last rival at Kerman in southern Persia in August 1794, he moved his capital to Tehran. His dynasty would last until 1925. The reunification of the core area created its own logic of expansion to reoccupy the frontier zones. During the spring of 1795, he restored Persian authority over the khans of Shirvan, Derbent, and Baku, the last two promising to block Russian expeditions along the Caspian shore. The prize, however, was Eastern Georgia. After 1747, the Georgian tsars had taken advantage of their Persian vassalage and the internal disintegration of the Persian Empire to claim jurisdiction over the Armenian khanates between the Kura and the Araks Rivers. The shah now proposed that Heraclius return to the Persian fold (abandoned in 1783) in return for becoming the shah's surrogate in the Christian zones. Heraclius refused; the shah invaded Georgia and took Tiflis in September 1795. He then returned to Persia with some 30,000 captives, leaving behind a trail of desolation the Georgians would never forget. The Russian response was inadequate, but it announced a shift to an offensive strategy that would continue until 1828. Catherine declared war in March 1796, and Valerian Zubov, the favorite's brother, was given the command of an expedition of some 20,000 men to retrace Peter's steps and invade northern Persia. It failed. Zubov took Derbent in

May and Baku in July, and may have gone as far as the Araks. But the advance was eventually stalled by poor planning, late deliveries of supplies or none at all, Persian scorched earth policy, and the usual effect of the heat on the troops. One of the first acts of the new emperor, Paul I, was to cancel the expedition.

The new reign began with the withdrawal of Russian troops, but the rapidly changing international situation and the turbulent politics of the men of power in Georgia convinced Petersburg there was no alternative to a forward policy in Transcaucasia. The shah was assassinated in June 1797. He was succeeded by his nephew Fath Ali Shah (1797–1834), who was no less intent than his uncle on restoring Persian hegemony in Transcaucasia. Heraclius died in January 1798, but his son George XIII was not recognized by his half-brothers who, like the Polish magnates, did not hesitate to turn to outside help against their dynasty. Meanwhile, the Russians had become aware of Georgia's mineral wealth, and annexation became an attractive option. It would serve a triple strategic purpose: trap the mountain tribes between the Caucasian Line and a new military infrastructure south of the mountains; establish a new military headquarters with an adequate force and shorter logistical lines, without which any attack on Persia was likely to suffer the fate of the 1722 and 1796 expeditions; and project power from there against the Ottomans in Western Georgia and, beyond it, in Anatolia itself, while the Black Sea fleet threatened Constantinople. Following the death of George XIII in December 1800, Georgia was faced with civil war. In May 1801, Russia abandoned the Bagratid house and, in September, announced the annexation of Georgia into the inner frontier of the empire under the authority of the commander in chief of the Caucasian Line. From that time on, the Turco-Persian hegemony in Transcaucasia was doomed.

While Russia was taking the fateful step of establishing a proruption in Eastern Georgia, it was also turning to a forward strategy in the Black Sea. The creation of a Black Sea navy gave Russia two options. Hostility toward the Ottomans for the purpose of annexing additional frontier zones required the establishment of naval supremacy in the Black Sea by pursuing a fleet-in-being strategy that would also keep Russian ships in that sea out of the Mediterranean because of the impossibility of negotiating the narrow straits in the face of Ottoman opposition. Friendly relations with the Ottomans, on the other hand, would require the suspension, if not the abandonment, of the advance into the frontier, of a destabilization policy in the Balkans pursued in the name of Christian solidarity. It would also render possible an agreement with the Porte to let Russian ships cross the straits into the Coastland and back into the Black Sea, within the Heartland. These two options created the basic dilemma of Russo-Ottoman relations. A third option complicated it. A fleet-in-being strategy in the Mediterranean was certain to antagonize at least one of the Coastland powers. The opening of the straits to Russian warships was bound to be followed by the granting of a similar right to Britain and

France, traditionally friendly to the Ottoman government. As a result, the Coastland powers would be at liberty to pursue their own fleet-in-being strategy against the Russians in the Black Sea. It would then be in Russia's interest to keep the straits closed to all but Ottoman warships. These three options, all tempting and contradictory, constituted the essence of the "Eastern question," born in the late 1790s.

Bonaparte's expedition to Egypt during the summer of 1798 was a major turning point. The new France seemed to be turning away from its old alliance and preparing a partition of the Ottoman Empire by detaching Egypt before attacking Constantinople from the sea. The frightened Ottomans forgot their hatred and appealed to Russia for help. The appearance of Russian ships in the Bosphorus in September was followed by the Treaty of Alliance of January 1799. This crucial treaty made three points. It allowed Russian warships to cross the straits in both directions "after prior agreement" with the Porte for the purpose of defeating France's "naval and merchant navigation" in the Mediterranean, but only for the duration of the hostilities. It also provided for the future. Russia pledged not to consider the privilege of crossing the straits a pretext for claiming the free passage of its warships, but nevertheless understood that this passage was "solely reserved for the situation of a common war or the despatch of such aid"[1] the sultan might request. Finally, it pledged both powers to consider the Black Sea closed to the warships of any *other* powers. The treaty followed a joint Russo-Turkish naval expedition to expel the French from the seven Ionian Islands along the western coast of Greece. The islands were placed in April 1800 under the common jurisdiction of the two powers, with the right to maintain garrisons. Russia had gained the exclusive right to send its warships through the straits for the duration of the war and had established a naval base in the Mediterranean.

But the alliance was so unnatural that it could not last. France reasserted its influence in Constantinople, and a series of incidents capped by the unilateral dismissal of the two hospodars friendly to the Russian cause brought Russian troops into the Principalities. In December 1806, the Ottomans declared war once again. Russia was then at war with Napoleon and about to suffer severe defeats in East Prussia before making peace at Tilsit in June 1807. In March 1808, discussions were held with the French in Petersburg for a general partition (*grand partage*) of the Ottoman Empire. Russia demanded the Principalities and Bulgaria to the Maritsa River, almost expelling the Ottomans from Europe and drawing very close to Constantinople. This would remain Russia's maximum program until 1878. The Russian commander in chief, General Alexander Prozorovsky, also wanted the Morea—to gain influence in the Adriatic—and the islands of Lemnos (Limnos) and Tenedos (Bozcaada)—to control the entrance into the Dardanelles. The war took the Russians deeper into the Russo-Turkish frontier. They captured Izmail in September and Braila in November; crossed the Danube and took Silistria in August 1810, Rushchuk (Ruse) and Zhurzha (Giurgiu) in September; and moved upstream in the direction of Serbia, going as far as Vidin in August 1811. Meanwhile, faithful to their two-pronged strategy of fighting the Ottomans west and east of the Black Sea, they had taken Poti in November 1809 and Anapa in July. Growing tensions with France made continuation of the war impossible. The Russians decided to force the issue, and Kutuzov's victory at Slobodzia in October 1811 brought the Ottomans to the negotiating table. Peace was made at Bucharest in May 1812, just one month before Napoleon's invasion of Russia.

As at Jassy in 1792, Russia's gains were modest, but they represented one more step in its steady and relentless advance in the frontier zones. It could not keep the Principalities but annexed Bessarabia, the larger part of Moldavia between the Dniestr and the Prut, and gained a foothold on the northern arm of the Danube delta. There would be no more bloody battles over Khotin, Bendery, and Izmail. Russia also had to return Anapa and Poti, and the treaty, by ignoring Russian gains in Western Georgia, implicitly confirmed them. In February 1810 and April 1811, the leaders of Guria, Imeretia, and Abkhazia had pledged allegiance to Russia; Megrelia had already done so in December 1803. Most of Western Georgia had passed under Russian overlordship, and the commander in chief of Russian forces in the Caucasus had moved his headquarters to Tiflis.

An important casualty of the war of 1806–1812 was Russia's fleet-in-being strategy. The alliance of 1799 lost its raison d'être when the Ottomans made peace with France. In 1805, in violation of its own pledge of 1799, Russia sought to make it a permanent alliance based on the need to maintain communications between the Black Sea and the Ionian Islands. The September agreement declared the Black Sea a closed sea to all other warships and allowed the free passage of Russia's warships for as long as its troops would remain on the islands. But Russia's defeat at Austerlitz in December 1805, the retreat of 1806, the restoration of French influence at Constantinople, and the outbreak of war in 1806 doomed the agreement from the start. At Tilsit, Alexander I surrendered the islands to Napoleon, and they would become a British protectorate in 1815. Once again, only Ottoman warships could navigate the straits. One detects the emergence of an implicit consensus among the British and the Russians. Both agreed it would be in their interest to keep their warships out of the straits—British interests would be served by keeping Russian warships within the Heartland, Russian interests by keeping British warships out of it. But that consensus also freed Russia from its dilemma—if it no longer needed the Ottoman alliance, it could freely return to its traditional policy of destabilizing the Russo-Turkish frontier.

The establishment of direct rule in Tiflis was followed by an attempt to bring the men of power in the mountains into the Russian fold, but with little success. Persia had not recognized the annexation of Eastern Georgia and continued to use its own men of power to destabilize Russian rule. To bridge the gap between factions, Petersburg had replaced in September 1802 its Germanic commander in chief, Karl Knorring, with Pavel

Tsitsianov (Paata Tsitsishvili), whose grandfather had accompanied Tsar Vakhtang to Russia in 1725 and remained there to join the Imperial elite. He was related to George XIII, the last king of eastern Georgia. Tsitsianov was a perfect example of those men of power who entered the ruling elite and later became its agents in the expansion of Russian power when the ruling elite manage to fuse their interests with its own.

The general took a hard line against the Georgian opposition, but he also took up the banner of Georgian imperialism under Russian protection by reviving old Georgian claims to neighboring khanates, notably Gandzha, on the ground that its khans had once been the vassals of the Georgian tsars. The storm of its fortress in January 1804 catalyzed Persian resistance to Russo-Georgian expansion. A Persian army moved toward the Araks, but Tsitsianov blocked its advance by taking Erevan in July. Russia found itself at war with the shah. The Persians returned in 1805 but failed to take Gandzha; Tsitsianov occupied the Shirvan khanate (with Shemakha) but failed to take Baku; he was treacherously killed there in February 1806. Both Persia and the Ottomans were at war with the Russian Empire beginning in December, but Persian troops made little headway. After the Ottomans left the war in 1812, and, in spite of Napoleon's invasion of Russia, the Persians suffered decisive defeats at Aslanduz on the Araks in October and Lenkoran on the Caspian coast in December, and had to sue for peace. A settlement was signed at Gulistan (Golestan) in October 1813.

The peace terms were a disaster for Persia. They included a territorial settlement giving Russia the khanates of Gandzha and Karabakh (Shusha), Sheki, and Shirvan in the valley of the Kura; Kuba, Baku, and Talysh (in part) on the Caspian coast. They also established the Araks as the southern boundary of the Empire. In August 1808 and again in February 1809, Alexander I had told the French ambassador he wanted a major river (*un grand fleuve*) for a boundary.[2] There was none, but the Araks would be an acceptable substitute. It flowed across Armenia and descended from the Bingöl upland, the watershed between the Kara and the Murat, the two rivers that merge to form the Euphrates, the great highway to Syria and the Persian Gulf. And the advance to the headwaters of the Euphrates would give Russia control of the ancient and profitable caravan route from Trebizond (Trabzond) on the Black Sea to Tehran, via Erzerum and Tabriz.

The peace terms also confirmed the right of Russian merchantmen and warships to navigate the Caspian Sea, but with the additional provision that no other power might share that privilege, effectively shutting out Britain. This provision was later called "superfluous and absurd" and the manifestation of a "jealous spirit."[3] Superfluous it was, but not absurd. The Russians' geopolitical vision made them look at the Black Sea and the Caspian from the same perspective. The Turkish Straits were the gateway to the Coastland; at the southeastern end of the Caspian there began a corridor of expansion through Khorasan and Herat to the passes of the Hindu

Kush. Both seas had to be "closed" and their navigation by warships restricted to the riparian powers Russia and Turkey, Russia and Persia.

Finally, the terms provided that Russia would recognize the designated heir apparent and give him assistance against his opponents, but would not interfere in his "dissensions" unless the shah requested its help. This confused phraseology, so characteristic of Russia's treaties with the Ottomans and Persians, was nothing less than a disguised attempt to pursue a destabilization policy. To support a crown prince who usually resided at Tabriz, in Persia's Azerbaijani frontier zone, would serve the same purpose as the defense of Polish and Swedish "liberties" in the Western Frontier.

Probings, 1813–1833

The emergence of two global powers in the wake of Napoleon's defeat in 1814 had important consequences for Russia's relations with the Turkish and Persian core areas in the Southern Frontier. As the Russians drew closer to the core areas and the British extended their network of bases along the periphery of the Heartland and advanced from Calcutta deeper into India in the direction of the Indus River, the effect was to transform the Southern Frontier and the core areas themselves into frontier zones separating the Russian and the British empires. Every move by either one of the global powers triggered anxiety and called for a response in the other's capital, and both powers began to probe for a line of an optimum of conquest to demarcate the outer boundary of their respective possessions.

In February 1797, when Russia's commitments in the Black Sea and the Caucasus were about to increase dramatically, a separate department was created in the college (ministry) of foreign affairs to deal with the affairs of the "Asiatic peoples" already living in the Russian Empire and to conduct relations with those living outside. In April 1819, the department would become autonomous, a kind of miniministry of foreign affairs in charge of Russia's relations with frontier zones and core areas from the Balkans to the Pacific. Three years earlier, in April 1816, Karl Nesselrode, the state secretary (later minister) for foreign affairs, had written to the Russian ambassador in London that Russia's "Asiatic policy" was a separate domain governed by principles different from those regulating relations with the European powers: it would admit "no mediation, intervention, and even good offices" by any foreign court because Asiatic affairs were in fact Russia's "domestic affairs." Nesselrode claimed Russia was only imitating Britain, which accepted no outside interference in its relations with the Indian state.[4] If he had chosen to place Russia's relations in the context of Russian history, he could have added that Russia was only claiming the inheritance of its parent cultures, the legacy of Byzantium and Chinggis Khan.

The Treaty of Gulistan had cut off Persia from the mountain tribes of the Caucasus and nearly expelled it from the Kura-Araks mesopotamia.

There, Persia retained only the khanates of Nakhichevan and Erevan to the Arpa (Akhturian) River, its boundary with the Ottoman Empire. Beyond the river were the pashaliks of Turkish Armenia in Kars and Ardahan, and Akhaltsykh in Western Georgia. Persian resentment increased with the arrival in 1816 of General Alexei Ermolov, the new Russian proconsul in Tiflis. Ermolov believed, not without reason, that Russia must secure its dominion in the cruel world of "Asiatic" politics by a display of overwhelming might and by taking ferocious reprisals for every act of treachery. He dealt ruthlessly with the men of power who refused their unconditional allegiance, and pursued a close-border policy, drawing a political and military curtain between Persia and its old frontier zones. He broadened the road between Vladikavkaz and Tiflis—it became known as the Georgian Military Highway—and laid the groundwork for the conquest of the mountain zones where Russian authority was tenuous if not entirely rejected, as battalions of troops set about imposing the discipline of a sedentary people on the fiercely independent tribes.

The shah's government exploited the ensuing turmoil in the inner frontier of the Russian Empire in the continuing contest for supremacy in the Russo-Persian frontier; did not Britain, Persia's ally since 1814, claim that the shah's legitimate authority extended as far north as the Terek River? Russia countered the threat by supporting Abbas Mirza, one of the shah's younger sons, against the machinations of an older brother, but the latter's death in 1822 made the prince less dependent on Russia. When Ermolov seized a disputed area late in 1825, the shah went to war with the blessings of the Shi'ite clergy, calling for a holy war against the Russians in the entire frontier. Ermolov did not expect the powerful offensive launched by Abbas Mirza toward Tiflis in July 1826, but stopped it nevertheless. He was replaced in 1827 by General Ivan Paskievich, who moved to the offensive and took Nakhichevan in July and Erevan in October. The Russian counteroffensive continued beyond the Araks, captured Tabriz and Ardabil, and moved on toward Tehran, forcing the shah to make peace before the opening of new hostilities between Russia and the Ottomans. Peace was signed at Turkmanchai (Torkoman) in February 1828, after Russia rejected an offer of British mediation, claiming as a "general maxim" of its foreign policy that Persian affairs belonged to the sphere of its "exclusive interests."

The peace treaty was no longer one between equals—it granted Russian nationals extraterritorial rights. Litigation and criminal cases among them came under the jurisdiction of the Russian minister or consuls in conformity with the laws of the Russian Empire. Criminal cases between Russians and Persians were tried in Persian courts but in the presence of a Russian representative, and a Russian national found guilty was sent back to Russia to receive his punishment. Trade between the two countries was made subject to a single low duty of 5 percent ad valorem, collected at the point of entry or departure. Persia agreed to pay an indemnity of 20 million silver rubles—a sum it could not pay, but the provision was a means of continuing pressure. Russia agreed to recognize Abbas Mirza, selected by the shah as his heir apparent, gaining a pretext to support an increasingly weak dynasty in exchange for additional concessions. Russia pushed its boundary upstream along the Araks to the confluence of the Arpa by annexing Nakhichevan and Erevan, and completed the incorporation of the Talysh khanate by advancing to the Astara River, skirting the Talysh upland to the Caspian coast. Finally, the treaty went beyond Gulistan by forbidding Persia to keep warships in the Caspian.

This humiliating treaty was followed in Persia by the same policy pursued in Sweden after 1809—turning the defeated core area outward to stifle irredentist yearnings. Of its Caucasian holdings Persia retained only Azerbaijan south of the Araks, and Tabriz became dangerously close to the Russian border. Tehran's attention had to be directed toward Central Asia. There, the Russian caravan trade was growing, so much so that the East India Company in Calcutta drafted a "master plan" in January 1830 to increase British commercial presence in the Central Asian towns. In 1817, Ermolov had demanded that the shah send an expedition to the Amu Darya against the pirates of the desert who raided the Russian traders. His agents were already in Khorasan, seeking influence among the men of power who had never loved the Kajar shahs. Supporting the dynasty and inciting its opponents opened up remarkable possibilities to a power pursuing everywhere a consistent destabilization policy. And beyond Khorasan there was Herat, guarding the approaches to the Afghan tribes. In 1832, the Russian embassy in Tehran convinced the shah that it was necessary to reconquer Herat; Abbas Mirza was sent against the city. However, he died in the fall of 1833, forcing Persia to lift the siege. His father, Fath Ali Shah, died in 1834 (leaving fifty-seven sons and forty-four daughters), and the crown passed to Mohammed Shah (1834–1848), Abbas Mirza's oldest son.

While the Russians were breaking down the last Persian resistance to their occupation of nearly the entire Russo-Persian frontier west of the Caspian and seeking to transform Persia into a protectorate to expand their influence east of it, the Greek independence movement was drawing them southward toward the Aegean Sea. The Greeks had long been encouraged to revolt against Ottoman rule by Russia's policy of supporting the Christian population and creating "dissident" movements. Russian interest in Moldavia and Wallachia was not only strategic—the establishment of a new offensive perimeter along the Danube. It had a larger goal—to forge relationships with the Greek men of power within the enemy camp. These men consisted in large part of Phanariot Greeks, some fifty families from the Phanar, a suburb of Constantinople. Their wealth and power came from their position as tax farmers, governors, and grain traders for the Ottoman government; their usefulness to the Russians from their divided allegiance—to the Ottomans and to those other Greeks in the Morea and elsewhere who dreamt of restoring the independence of Greece. They and much of the political establishment in the Principalities had been drawn to

Russia since the Prut expedition of 1711. Russia was their only hope against Ottoman suspicions and arbitrary power.

A "Friendly Society" was organized in Odessa in 1814 by three Greek merchants. Odessa was slowly becoming the greatest commercial port of the Black Sea, from which Russia exported the grain of its inner frontier zones to the Mediterranean. The Society sought the support of Ioannis Capo d'Istrias, a Greek and second secretary of state for foreign affairs, but he refused to commit himself. It then turned to Alexander Ypsilanti, a general in the Russian army and aide de camp to the tsar; he was also the son of a Wallachian hospodar. He led the Society's supporters into Moldavia in March 1821, but the Ottomans took advantage of the dissentions between Rumanians and Greeks to crush the revolt. The tsar disavowed Ypsilanti, who fled to Austria.

The revolt placed the Russian government in a quandary. If the basic dilemma of Russo-Ottoman relations was between supporting the increasingly oppressive Ottoman government against its own mutinous Christian populations in order to obtain concessions in the straits on the one hand, and supporting the Christians in order to destabilize the frontier and facilitate the Russian advance on the other, the Greek question—the Orthodox question in general—created a dilemma within a dilemma. Alexander I, with Austria and Prussia in tow, had become the great defender of order and legitimacy after 1815, and military intervention was justified only to uphold the political status quo. The Greeks were co-religionists, but they were also the sultan's legitimate subjects. And since it was clearly apparent that Ottoman power was weakening, would not support for the Christians cause the empire to collapse, spreading chaos and revolution, and necessitate a partition that might bring about a head-on collision between Russia, Austria, and Britain?

The revolt in Moldavia was only the beginning. The Greeks revolted in the Morea the following month, in April 1822, and atrocities were committed by both sides. When the Ottomans failed to put down the revolt, the sultan took the momentous step of asking the help of Mehmet Ali, the pasha of Egypt, a man of the frontier (Albania) co-opted into the Ottoman ruling elite. In return, he was promised the Morea and Syria. The pasha sent his son, Ibrahim, who landed in February 1825 and proceeded to exterminate the Greeks systematically until Athens fell in June 1827. In the meantime, the Russians had used the Porte's difficulties to impose in October 1826 the convention of Akkerman (Belgorod Dniestrovsky) near Odessa, binding the Ottomans to recognize the autonomy of the Principalities, give the hospodars seven-year terms, and remove all Moslems except those stationed in fortresses.

By then, the new Russian tsar, Nicholas I, who had succeeded his brother in December 1825 and claimed to be the guardian of legitimacy everywhere, had decided to use the Greek question to extract maximum concessions from the Ottomans. In July 1827 and again in August, Russia, Britain, and France offered to mediate the "war of extermination" and sought the Porte's agreement to the creation of an autonomous Greece, its borders left undetermined. The Ottomans refused. In October, warships of the three powers cruising off Navarino Bay (near Pilos) engaged the Ottoman-Egyptian fleet and sank it, causing the sultan to denounce the Christian powers, reject the Akkerman Convention, and call for a holy war in December. While Britain and France insisted on maintaining the concert of the three powers, Nicholas decided to go it alone and declared war in April 1828, two months after signing the Treaty of Turkmanchai with Persia.

The war showed how far the balance of power in the Russo-Turkish frontier had shifted against the Ottomans since 1768. The now traditional pincer movement around the Black Sea was more successful than ever. The Russians crossed the Prut into Moldavia in April, the Danube into Bulgaria in June, and took Adrianople, the sultan's second capital, in August 1829. Across the sea, Anapa surrendered in June. Paskievich took Kars and Poti in July, Akhaltsykh and Ardahan in August. By the fall, he had reached the headwaters of the Euphrates and the Araks; in June 1829, he took Erzerum and moved on toward Trebizond. The fall of the Black Sea port and the occupation of Turkish Armenia with the caravan route to Tabriz was more than the Ottomans were willing to accept. Peace was made at Adrianople in September. The Russians refused to give Britain a copy of their peace conditions on the ground that they "did not accept foreign intervention in [their] differences with the Turks."[5]

The Treaty of Adrianople was an important treaty, not only for what it conceded to the Russians but for its implications as well. It contained, first of all, a territorial settlement in the Principalities and in the Caucasus. The Russians withdrew from Bulgaria, Wallachia, and Moldavia but kept Bessarabia, acquired in 1812, and incorporated the entire delta of the Danube. The marshy and sandy delta, inhospitable to commercial development (there is still no single important port on it) was nevertheless the only maritime exit within the Heartland for the entire basin of the Danube, including the Austrian core area and the Hungarian plain. The power that gained control of it would possess an important means of pressure on the economic life of the Russo-Austrian frontier. The delta had three channels—Kilia, Sulina, and St. George (Sfintu Gheorghe). The new boundary ran from the confluence of the Prut, the lower Danube, and the St. George channel to the sea. The lower Danube remained open to Russian and Ottoman merchantmen, but Russian warships were forbidden to sail upstream beyond the confluence of the Prut. The Principalities remained under the sultan's suzerainty, but Russia became their protector, guaranteeing all previous concessions made (and largely unobserved) by the Ottomans, with freedom of trade and an "independent national existence." It was implicitly assumed Russia gained the right to intervene, should these concessions be withdrawn. In the Caucasus, the gains were considerable. The Russians did retrocede Kars, Ardahan, Erzerum, and Bayazid (Dogubayazit) in Western Armenia, but gained most of Western Georgia with Akhaltsykh and Poti. Russia annexed the entire coast from Anapa to Poti, thereby cutting off the Ottomans from the Cherkess between the Kuban and the sea.

In the second place, Russia gained a potentially crucial means of pressure on the Ottomans. The Porte had to promise not to interfere with Russian trade in the Black Sea and in the straits and to protect it against "any violence or chicane"—an across-the-board commitment covering limitless possibilities. Should the Porte refuse to give "prompt and full satisfaction" to the Russian minister when an infraction had occurred, Russia was recognized the right "in advance" "to consider such infraction a hostile act and to use immediate reprisals against the Ottoman Empire." Russia had fought a successful war, had drawn close to the Ottoman capital, had retroceded a large part of its territorial gains, but had gained the right to threaten military intervention for a trifle. All this was part of a larger plan. "If we have allowed the Turkish government to continue to exist in Europe," wrote Nesselrode in 1830, "it is because that government, under the preponderant influence of our superiority, suits us better than any of those which could be set up on its ruins."[6]

The Ottoman defeat paved the way for the independence of Greece. In July, the Porte had accepted the creation of a small Greece, bounded in the north by a line running from the Gulf of Volos to the Gulf of Arta, still a vassal of the Ottomans but with an hereditary Christian dynasty, with religious and commercial freedom—in short, a status similar to that to be granted shortly to the Principalities. Greece in the Coastland would match the Principalities in the Heartland. But the extent of Russia's victory at Adrianople gave Britain and France reason to fear that less than total independence would give Russia ground to interfere in Greek affairs. In February 1830, Greece, within the same borders, was proclaimed an independent hereditary kingdom; its first king, a Bavarian prince, was installed three years later.

There remained a major question. Mehmet Ali and his son had taken no part in the Russo-Turkish war; they hoped for an Ottoman defeat that would give the pasha an opportunity to found a new dynasty in Constantinople. His hopes unfulfilled, the pasha declared war on the sultan in November 1831. Ibrahim invaded Syria and moved into Anatolia, where he defeated an Ottoman force at Konya, on the edge of the Taurus Mountains, in December 1832, 540 kilometers from Constantinople. The sultan, finding no support in Austria or Britain, turned to Russia in desperation—"a drowning man clings to a serpent,"[7] as he put it. The Russians had expected the request for aid: a military mission arrived in Constantinople on the day of the Konya defeat. The sultan requested 30,000 troops, four ships of the line, and four frigates in February 1833. Russian ships were in the Bosphorus before the end of the month, and troops landed north of Constantinople at the beginning of April. The Ottoman dynasty was saved; the Egyptian advance stopped 270 kilometers from the capital; the sultan and Ibrahim made peace in May. The new Russo-Ottoman alliance was sealed in the

Treaty of Unkiar Skelesi (Hünkar Iskelesi), a town facing Constantinople across the Bosphorus, in July.

This treaty is the shortest of all Russo-Ottoman treaties and has remained the most controversial. In any discussion of the Straits question it is necessary to remember that there were two straits—the Bosphorus, 29 kilometers long and on average 1.8 kilometers but in places less than 700 meters wide, with Constantinople on the western, European, side; and the Dardanelles, 45 kilometers long and wider, with sparsely populated shores. Between them was the Sea of Marmara, 306 kilometers long and, at most, 90 kilometers wide. The treaty aimed at securing the entire independence of the Ottoman government (the Porte); should that government need, once again, Russia's military and naval assistance, it would be placed at the Porte's disposal for defensive purposes. The controversy was in the secret article, introduced at Nicholas I's initiative. Should Russia need Ottoman aid—and the Porte was required to respond since the treaty was one of mutual defense—Russia would disclaim that aid and request instead that the Porte close the Dardanelles to the warships of any other power.

The treaty was Russia's second brilliant victory, resolving for the first and only time the central dilemma of Russo-Ottoman relations. Russia had used the Christian question to make war in 1828 and advance deeper into the frontier zones. In 1833, it used the Ottoman-Egyptian conflict to become the ally of the Ottomans and gain concessions in the straits. But what concessions? No one really knew. The Russians shared with the "Asiatic" Turks and Persians a love of ambiguity, but ambiguity is also a source of controversy, especially when powerful interests are involved. What is beyond doubt is that the treaty of Unkiar Skelesi was a worthy successor of the treaty of 1799 and was in fact inspired by it. Any Russo-Ottoman alliance opened the straits for operations in the Mediterranean in support of the Ottomans. Moreover, should Russia feel threatened by Britain and France and invoke the Treaty of Unkiar Skelesi, the Porte was bound to close the Dardanelles to their warships but was not bound to close the Bosphorus to Russian warships. *That* was the ominous novelty: the geographical unity of "the straits" was abandoned in favor of its constituent elements. Russia gained the right to penetrate the straits and sought to keep Britain out of them. The treaty was the embodiment of a fortress-fleet strategy, of a close-border policy, drawing the "red line" at the entrance of the Dardanelles and no longer at the Bosphorus, the entrance to the Black Sea. It was an attempt to transform the Turkish core area into a Russia protectorate and to advance the boundary of Russian influence to the periphery of the Heartland. That had been the purpose of the extravagant provision of the Treaty of Adrianople on treating trifling commercial disputes as "hostile acts": it was the hidden purpose of Unkiar Skelesi. The two treaties were complementary. How else could Nesselrode have written in July, two weeks after the treaty's signature, that "our armed intervention in Turkish affairs had just acquired a legal foundation"?[8]

Stalemate, 1833–1856

Success has its price. Beginning in 1832, when the military weakness of the Ottoman Empire became manifest in all its starkness, the Russian government adopted "a very precise program" of keeping the empire "utterly destabilized" (*complètement défaillant*).[9] Such a policy could not have been effective earlier, so long as the intermediate frontier continued to form a barrier of complexity and a succession of obstacles: it was well nigh impossible to project power into the core area itself. Military victories had now brought Russia to the Danube and the eastern shore of the Black Sea, and had shattered the Ottomans' self-confidence. Russia, probing for a line of an optimum of conquest, unwittingly crossed it. The consequence was a passionate reaction in Britain and a grim determination to call a halt to Russian expansion.

A hint of what at least some circles in the Russian government hoped to achieve with the Unkiar Skelesi treaty was given in 1838. In January, Alexander Menshikov, chief of the Naval Staff and governor general of Finland, obtained the tsar's approval to send two ships of the line from the Baltic fleet "under the pretext of maneuvers" into the Mediterranean, thence to proceed through the Dardanelles to the Black Sea. The purpose was to test the new Russo-Ottoman alliance, to stretch it to the point where the Porte would be convinced that maneuvers could replace a naval base in the Mediterranean to justify the maintenance of naval communications with the Black Sea. The parallel with the situation between 1799 and 1806 was quite obvious, and the still unsettled rivalry between the sultan and the pasha provided a clear and present danger of war when the Ottomans would again need Russian assistance. Nesselrode, however, took a different stand and argued eloquently that if the Porte allowed Russian warships to cross the straits, Britain and France would demand the same privilege, appear in the Black Sea, and seek a naval base there. Russia would be "destroying the political and moral barrier that the *Dardanelles* establish between us and the maritime Powers."[10] The tsar sided against Menshikov. The controversy exposed the treaty's ambiguity. Britain thought it allowed both a fleet-in-being strategy in the Mediterranean and a fortress-fleet strategy in the Black Sea. It could not do both without challenging Britain's determination to return a Russian challenge with a challenge of its own. This ambiguity had to poison Anglo-Russian relations until the Russians yielded.

The pasha did not abandon his ambitions and yield to the sultan until June 1841, closing at last the possibility of a Russian intervention on the Ottoman side. It was then possible to face the straits question with greater equanimity. Russia had to recognize that its alliance with the Ottomans was unacceptable to the Coastland powers because it contained an offensive component giving Russian warships the exclusive right to navigate the Bosphorus and the Dardanelles and the implicit right to project naval power from the Black Sea across the Heartland's periphery into the

Mediterranean. The Straits Convention of June 1841, signed by Russia, Britain, France, Austria, and Prussia, reaffirmed the "ancient rule" of the Ottoman Empire forbidding "at all times" foreign warships to enter the Dardanelles *and the Bosphorus,* and the sultan pledged not to admit foreign warships "in the straits" "as long as the Porte was at peace."[11] A certain ambiguity remained, but since that single clause repeated the British declaration of January 1809 almost verbatim, the convention was a victory for Britain and a defeat for Russia. If we remember the basic dilemma in Russo-Ottoman relations, however, thwarting the Russians in the straits gave them a free hand to exploit the "dissident question" elsewhere.

Meanwhile, the Danubian Principalities were being drawn closer into the Russian orbit. Russian troops remained after 1829, but an enlightened administrator, General Pavel Kiselev, was appointed to draw up an Organic Statute, promulgated in Wallachia in 1831 and in Moldavia the following year. The hospodars would be elected for life by a small group of ecclesiastical dignitaries and landed proprietors. The general favored annexation, in line with a tradition that considered "independence" in disputed frontier zones merely a step on the way to incorporation into the inner frontier of the Empire. The independence of the Tatar nation from the Ottomans in 1774 and of Eastern Georgia from the Persians in 1783 were cases in point. But at a time when Russia was pushing for maximum advantages in the straits, the annexation of the Principalities would almost certainly have precipitated a war with Britain and Austria. One senses in Russia's relations with Moldavia and Wallachia at the time a vague realization that a line of an optimum of conquest had been reached and that it must not be crossed. Russian troops withdrew in 1834, but the Principalities were fated to live under the menacing shadow of the Russian eagle for the next twenty years.

The decade between the Straits Convention and the Crimean War was a lull before the storm, Russia seeking by a studied resort to ambiguity a way to compensate for its defeat in 1841, Britain refusing any commitment that might give Russia an opening to pursue. In January 1844, conversations were held in London during a brief visit by the tsar, and their gist was recorded in a memorandum written by Nesselrode. The document shows how far the official position had moved since 1830, when the maintenance of the Ottoman Empire was accepted as being in Russia's best interest. It was now asserted that the empire contained numerous "elements of dissolution"; that the sultan's government was increasingly guilty of "flagrant vexations and religious intolerance"; that neither Russia nor Britain could remain indifferent, should "unforeseen circumstances hasten its fall"; and that Russia had a preponderance on land, Britain at sea. It was the duty of both powers to pursue in concert a policy toward "the new state of affairs."[12] Behind the circumspect language, it was clear that Russia was seeking an agreement to partition the Ottoman Empire.

The defense of Christian rights in the Holy Land, pursued by France for domestic political reasons and by Russia in the name of Kuchuk

Kainardji, provided an ideal opportunity to destabilize the Ottoman government. The tsar sounded out the British ambassador, George Seymour, in January and February 1853 about joint action in the event of a total collapse of the Ottoman Empire. As in 1844, he emphasized its advanced "state of decrepitude" and reasoned that "the bear was dying"—an expression that gave rise to the famous saying that Turkey had become "the sick man of Europe." Russia was duty bound to watch over several million Christians in Ottoman lands. An Ottoman collapse, no doubt assisted by a new Russian advance into Bulgaria, would give Russia "the temporary occupation of Constantinople." Seymour, on instructions from his government, merely countered that "countries do not die in such a hurry."[13] While ambiguity continued to dominate official conversations, candor was the striking feature of the tsar's correspondence with Marshal Paskievich, now the viceroy in Warsaw, and one of the tsar's closest confidants. The marshal knew what he wanted. The Principalities must be annexed to the Russian Empire, together with the northern part of Bulgaria, including the important port of Constanza (Constanta), the rest becoming "independent." Constantinople must be a free port; Russia would garrison the Bosphorus, Austria the Dardanelles. Britain would acquire Crete and Cyprus.

Even before his second conversation with Seymour, the tsar had sent Menshikov to Constantinople with an ultimatum demanding the maintenance of the status quo in the Holy Land and the sultan's recognition of Russia's right to protect all the Orthodox subjects of the Ottoman Empire. He was rebuffed and left in May. In June, Russian troops crossed into the Principalities in a final effort to compel the Ottomans to yield. The tsar had forgotten that Russo-Ottoman relations had become internationalized in 1840, that Nesselrode's assumption of 1816 that they were part of Russia's internal affairs was untenable. Despite Austria's attempts to find a compromise, events moved inexorably toward war. At the Porte's request, four British and French warships entered the straits in September. The Ottomans declared war in October and were joined by Britain and France in March 1854. Their goal was to take Sevastopol and destroy Russia's Black Sea fleet and naval installations. Once that was done, the "straits question" would disappear for a long time. The operations need not detain us. An Anglo-French expedition landed in the Crimea in September but could not take Sevastopol until September 1855. The Russians captured Kars in November. Austria played a decisive role: in December, it threatened to enter the war if Russia kept refusing to sue for peace. There was no choice: a coalition of containing powers had checkmated Russia in its inner frontier. Peace was signed in Paris in March 1856.

The treaty made two major points. Russia had to return Kars and retrocede the delta of the Danube, even the lowland of southern Bessarabia. It found itself cut off from the Danube. The regulation of navigation on the lower course of the river was internationalized—a seven-power commission took over the task of dredging the delta after the Russians deliberately allowed it to silt up to prevent competition to Odessa. The heart of the treaty, however, concerned the Black Sea. It was "neutralized"—an innovation in international law because the concept had hitherto been confined to land. Both Russia and Turkey were forbidden to maintain warships and rebuild arsenals on its shores. To render the humiliation more stinging, Britain insisted on the demilitarization of the Åland Islands in the Baltic as well. The treaty has rightly been called "a diplomatic blunder";[14] it would soon compel a radical reassessment of Russian policy toward the Germanic powers and unleash Russian expansion into Central Asia.

It is time to return to Russia's relations with Persia. Mohammed Shah was the first ruler to be mesmerized by Russia's overwhelming might; he became the willing tool of a policy so carefully crafted that Persian and Russian interests seemed to coincide. But Russia was clearly the dominant partner and was increasingly able to exercise a powerful influence in Tehran. With the growth of Russian power in Transcaucasia, the Tiflis headquarters developed into a powerful regional center, where the struggle in the mountains combined with the co-optation of the elites to generate a dynamic interest in the Orient south and beyond the Caspian Sea. Not only had Persia tasted defeat in 1813 and 1828; it was now forced to live with the threat of another Russian intervention, should it be so bold as to stand up on its own against Russian pressures. The stage was set for a successful destabilization policy.

Late in 1832, Russian troops set foot on the island of Ashuradeh, at the mouth of Astarabad Bay (where Bendar-Torkoman is now located) under the pretext of protecting Persian trade against Turkmen raiders. Russia was entering the Persian frontier from within, so to speak, in order to protect the weakening core area against depredations committed by tribesmen from its proximate frontier zone, over which it no longer had any control. A Russian base on Ashuradeh gave a triple advantage—it complemented the base in Baku and the consulate in Rasht to place the provinces between the sea and the Elburz Mountains (and Tehran on the other side) under a permanent Russian threat; it drew a wedge between the core area and its proximate zone and facilitated Russian expansion into the Turkmen tribal lands from the Caspian to the foothills of the Hindu Kush, complementing the Orenburg headquarters to form eventually a powerful vise against Khiva and Bukhara; and it opened Khorasan to Russian influence. By 1848, the Russians had built a naval arsenal on the island for the rendezvous and refitting of their Caspian flotilla and begun negotiations with Turkmen men of power. The new shah, Nasr ed-Din (1848-1896), only 18 years old at the time of his accession, had grown up in Tabriz where, according to custom, the crown prince was governor of Persian Azerbaijan. Russian influence was already strong there, and the shah, like his father, lived in fear of Russian power.

The insidious penetration of northern Persia was accompanied by a deliberate attempt to keep turning the core area outward toward Afghanistan, where a second proruption was taking shape in Persia's eastern frontier with India. There, Britain's advance toward the Indus River had matched Russia's advance toward the Hindu Kush, and both were transforming that frontier into a Russo-British Indian frontier. The Russian minister in Tehran, Ivan Simonich, had convinced the shah in 1837 to resume the attempt against Herat, abandoned in 1833, and the shah had laid siege to the city in November. At the same time, the Russians strengthened their influence in Kabul by obtaining from the emir the removal of a British emissary and the retention of a Russian one, who had been sent ostensibly to return the emir's visit to Petersburg. The combined Russo-Persian advance brought about a British reaction across the Hindu Kush, and the shah had been forced to lift the siege in June 1838. Russia's relations with Britain were tense that year, as the memory of Unkiar Skelesi still rankled in London and Russophobia dominated public opinion. Wisdom dictated a retreat. Simonich and the emissary were recalled.

But Russian policy did not change. Britain became involved at great cost in Afghan power struggles between the four major centers—Kabul and Kandahar, Herat and Balkh. A political crisis broke out in Herat in the fall of 1851 and brought to power "an imbecile youth"[15] who appealed for Persian support. The shah was willing, but British influence with the grand vizier dissuaded him in January 1853. However, Russia's preponderant influence soon reasserted itself and sought to bring Persia into the conflict with Britain in the Black Sea, with Dmitrii Dolgorukov, the Russian minister, even resorting to physical violence against the grand vizier. Diplomatic relations were broken in 1854, and the shah moved against Herat. When he succeeded in capturing the city in the spring of 1856, Britain declared war and forced the shah to abandon all his claims to Afghanistan.

Russian support of Persia's eastern policy was accompanied by a systematic advance into the northern zones of the Russo-Persian frontier. Russo-British trade rivalry in Central Asia precipitated and favored that advance because the Tiflis and Orenburg headquarters were already able to apply substantial pressure beyond the Caspian, whereas British India was too far removed to counter the growth of Russian influence in the valley of the Amu and Syr Darya. In 1834, an important foothold had been established on the eastern shore of the Caspian at Fort Alexandrovsk, opposite Astrakhan, facing toward the Aral Sea. By 1838, the Russians had built a line of forts some 720 kilometers south of the original Ural-Irtysh Line, from which they would steadily increase pressure on the khanates, despite the failure of General Vasilii Perovsky's expedition against Khiva in the winter of 1839–1840.

But the expedition also taught a lesson. Frontal attacks would not do until Russia could bring enough power to bear over shorter distances. This required building additional fortified lines closer to the khanates. Between 1845 and 1848, the Russians erected three important forts in the heart of the steppe—Karabutak and Uralsk (Irgiz) on the Irgiz River and Orenburg Fort (Turgai) on the Turgai River, where the caravan route from Bukhara bifurcated toward Orsk and the west Siberian plain. They also built Fort N. 1 (Aralsk) at the northern tip of the Aral Sea, the first of a line of forts along the Syr Darya. In July 1853, Perovsky captured the important Kokandi fort of Ak Mesjed and renamed it Perovsky (Kzyl-Orda), about 540 kilometers upstream from the Aral Sea. A small flotilla of troop-carrying steamers was already plying the river. The founding of Vernyi (Alma Ata) in 1854, followed by the extension of a line westward to the Uzbek fort of Pishpek (Frunze) in October 1862, brought Russian troops from the Irtysh Line to the very gates of the Kokand khanate. The khanates were now exposed to attack from three sides—the Caspian, Orenburg, and western Siberia.

6

Showdown, 1856–1917

Russia, Persia, and Central Asia, 1856–1906

Fortified lines across the Kazakh steppe, even along the Syr Darya, were fated to be no more permanent than those built in the seventeenth and eighteenth centuries in the Ukraine to stop Crimean Tatar raids, because they cut across the living organism of a frontier where the desert, the river, and the oasis formed a unified whole. Every zone and subzone was "an area inviting entrance,"[1] the entire frontier a network of geographic and social compatibilities drawing in the conqueror even against his will. The frontier facilitated an advance directed by its own dynamic logic and its own geopolitical goals—the annexation of space and the incorporation of natural resources into the autarkic economy of the Russian Empire. Alexander Gorchakov, the Russian foreign minister, spoke the language of the geopolitician in his famous declaration of November 1864, justifying the Russian advance by the turbulence of the frontier zones, the social unity of the Russo-Persian frontier, and the development of Russian trade.

The conquest of the frontier took place in four stages. The first aimed at linking the Syr Darya with the extension of the Irtysh Line, still separated by 900 kilometers of barren steppe. Converging columns took Turkestan and Aulietta (Dzhambul) and met in Chimkent in October 1864, completing the junction. The conquest gave the Russians the "granary of the entire country between the Chu River and the Syr Darya."[2] Tashkent, the Kokand khanate's second most important city, fell in June 1865, and Khodzhent (Leninabad), its last stronghold, a year later. The conquered territory was annexed as the province of Turkestan, under the

130

authority of a governor general in Tashkent. He and the viceroy in Tiflis became Russia's two proconsuls in the Southern Frontier. A new khan, appointed by the Russians, was installed in Kokand.

The second stage, from 1868 to 1873, was the occupation of Bukhara and Khiva. Bukhara fell in May 1868, soon after the occupation of Samarkand, the former capital of Tamerlane's empire that had once unified the Persian core area and the entire Central Asian frontier. There remained Khiva, more defiant than ever. In February 1865, Petersburg had ordered the occupation of Kislovodsk (Qizil-Su, Krasnovodsk) on the eastern shore of the Caspian, opposite Baku, now considered a more suitable location for operations against the Turkmens and Khiva; the Ashuradeh base was closed. Russian troops landed there in November 1869, the first operation east of the Caspian conducted from the Tiflis headquarters. Another base was established at Chikishlier further south, from which columns could follow the valley of the Atrek into Turkmen lands. It was decided to attack Khiva from three sides—Tashkent, Orenburg, and Kislovodsk. The khanate fell in June 1873, despite the desperate resistance of its Turkmen allies. General Konstantin Kaufman, the governor general, compelled the khan in August to cede all his lands on the right bank of the Amu Darya, to abolish slavery (the Russians found 30,000 slaves in the khanate), and to become the tsar's "obedient servant."

The third stage was the incorporation of the Turkmen zone, between the Karakum Desert and the Kopet Dag, Persia's proximate zone. The Turkmen, "the worst freebooters of Central Asia,"[3] had been alternately at war and in alliance for a century with Khiva, Persia, and the Afghans. Their very fickleness made them a source of discord on the frontier—and of attraction for the Russians. The military governor of Kislovodsk inflicted heavy losses on them in May 1877, when Russia was again at war with the Ottomans, but the tribesmen banded together and sent raiding parties as far as Chikishlier. An assault on their stronghold at Geok-Tepe failed in September 1879, but another succeeded in January 1881. In May 1884, the Turkmen zone became the province of Transcaspia, under the authority of the viceroy in Tiflis.

The logic of expansion across the Caspian into the Turkmen zone led the Russians on toward the Merv (Mary) oasis and the approaches to Afghanistan, in a semicircular movement around the Kopet Dag and Khorasan. The oasis had once been a commercial emporium, a center of learning, and the seat of a Christian (Nestorian) diocese. Its medieval glory came to an end when the Mongols demolished the great dam on the Murgab and transformed a flourishing oasis into a desert swamp. It recovered to become one of the frontier's foremost cultural centers and, under Persian rule, "a great and opulent country." After Bukhara sacked it in 1794, however, it never recovered. By the 1870s it had become a "den of (Turkmen) robbers."[4] Merv's strategic importance lay in the fact that for centuries it had been a resting place for conquerors on their way to Herat and the Hindu Kush passes.

The Russians followed in their footsteps. Turkmen men of power were invited to the coronation of Alexander III in May 1883, to impress them with Russian pomp and might. They promoted a pro-Russian party among the elders of Merv, who abandoned their resistance to the Russians and launched looting parties into Khorasan instead. In January 1884, they addressed to the tsar a petition for admission to the Russian Empire, and deputies from the oasis took the oath of allegiance in Ashkhabad in February. The entire Russo-Persian frontier had become part of the inner frontier of the Russian Empire. The Russians then proceeded to link their new possessions with a Transcaspian railway from Kislovodsk. It reached Merv in 1886 and Samarkand in 1888. A branch line would in 1898 connect Merv with Kushka, less than 200 kilometers from Herat.

The incorporation of Bukhara in 1868 gave the Afghan question a new urgency. No one really knew where the boundaries of the khanate ran. The khans had claimed jurisdiction beyond the Amu Darya on Balkh and Konduz to the foothills of the Hindu Kush; Russia inherited those claims and endorsed them, despite its predilection for "major rivers" as boundaries. The emirs' position in Kabul had never been secure, and Afghan refugees would flee to Bukhara in droves; some even joined the Russian army. The frontier zones created an irresistible movement toward the Hindu Kush, and the passes drew the invader across the chain to Kabul, the Khyber Pass, and the Indus beyond. The Turkmen zone led to Merv, Merv to Herat, Herat to Kandahar, the Bolan Pass, and the lower Indus. The annexation of the Kokand khanate in 1876 took the Russians to the Tien Shan Mountains and the Pamirs, wild and undemarcated lands, the periphery of the Heartland. There, a great arc from the Dorah Pass to the Karakoram Pass guarded the approaches to the headwaters of the Indus and linked Afghanistan with Chinese Turkestan. The very physical complexity of the Afghan "proruption" and its unchartered territory challenged the Russians to push for a line of an optimum of conquest. If Alexander the Great and Babur, Akbar's father, had once crossed the Hindu Kush and established their rule in the valley of the Indus, why should General Kaufman not also make a try?

The death of Ahmad Shah Durrani in 1773 had been followed by sixty years of civil war between the two powerful Afghan clans, the Sadozais and the Barakzais, until Dost Mohammed, a Barakzai, consolidated his power and assumed the title of emir in 1834. His fight with the Sikhs brought about the first British intervention, in 1839. He annexed Balkh in 1850, Kandahar in 1855, and Herat in 1863, a short time before his death. His son Shir Ali did not feel secure until 1869. He then sought to expand the northern boundary of his domain to the Amu Darya, including Badakshan along the great loop of the river, and Wakhan, east of the Dorah Pass. The Russians rejected his claim in November 1871, because the ambitious emir was certain to use the two territories as a springboard for intrigues in Bukhara, Kokand, and Kashgar. They also had their own claim to the major trade route between Bukhara and

Kashgar that ran along the Wakhan valley. Nevertheless, they had to accept in January 1873 Britain's virtual "ultimatum" of October 1872: it established the border of northern Afghanistan along the Pamir River from Lake Zorkul—the river then merges with the Murgab to form the Amu Darya—and along the Amu Darya to Kwaja Salar (Bosagit); from that point it would run to the Persian border. The Russians had been cut off from the passes, unless they could establish a protectorate over Afghanistan.

Anticipating Russian attempts to regain the initiative, Britain in 1875 sought the emir's approval to place residents in Kabul and Balkh, Herat and Kandahar. The emir refused. In August 1876, Kaufman sent an agent to Kabul to explain the annexation of the Kokand khanate, a precedent for involving Shir Ali in future negotiations with the frontier tribes. In April 1877, Russia went to war against the Ottomans, raising concern in London over the fate of the straits. It was then that the Russians resorted for the first time on the scale of the entire Southern Frontier to one of those pincer movements they have always favored: Britain's opposition to Russia's march on Constantinople would be neutralized by an attempt to bring Afghanistan into the Russian sphere of influence. Kaufman sent General Nikolai Stoletov to Kabul to exploit Shir Ali's distrust of Britain. A treaty of assistance was signed in August 1878—Russia offering military training and promising to come to the aid of Afghanistan in the event of an invasion by a "foreign power" whose identity was obvious. The emir agreed to send a mission to Tashkent.

News of the treaty brought about the second Afghan war. Kabul and Kandahar were occupied by British troops and Shir Ali was forced to flee to Turkestan. He later returned to Balkh, where he died in March 1879. The Russians did nothing to help him: the Congress of Berlin had brought the Russo-Ottoman war to an end. Afghanistan became a British, not a Russian, protectorate. Nevertheless, the Stoletov episode had two consequences. One was the realization that Afghanistan was the only place where Britain was vulnerable on land. The other was the decision to speed up the occupation of the Turkmen zone and the Merv oasis. If Kabul and Kandahar were within striking distance of British bases on the Indus, Herat was within striking distance of Merv.

The Russians annexed the Merv oasis in the spring of 1884. Their advance continued along the Murgab in the direction of Herat. They occupied the Pendjdeh oasis in March 1885, expelling the Afghans who had seized it in the hope the commission demarcating the boundary from Kwaja Salar would include it in Afghanistan. The Russian advance caused panic in London and Calcutta, and there was talk of war. No one wanted it, and a compromise was reached in May. Russia retained the oasis and the entire valley of the Murgab but gave up the Zulfikar Pass, the old plundering road of the Turkmen and the traditional "way out to Persia" from the east. Herat was saved. The demarcation of the Russo-Afghan boundary was almost complete; an agreement was reached in March 1895.

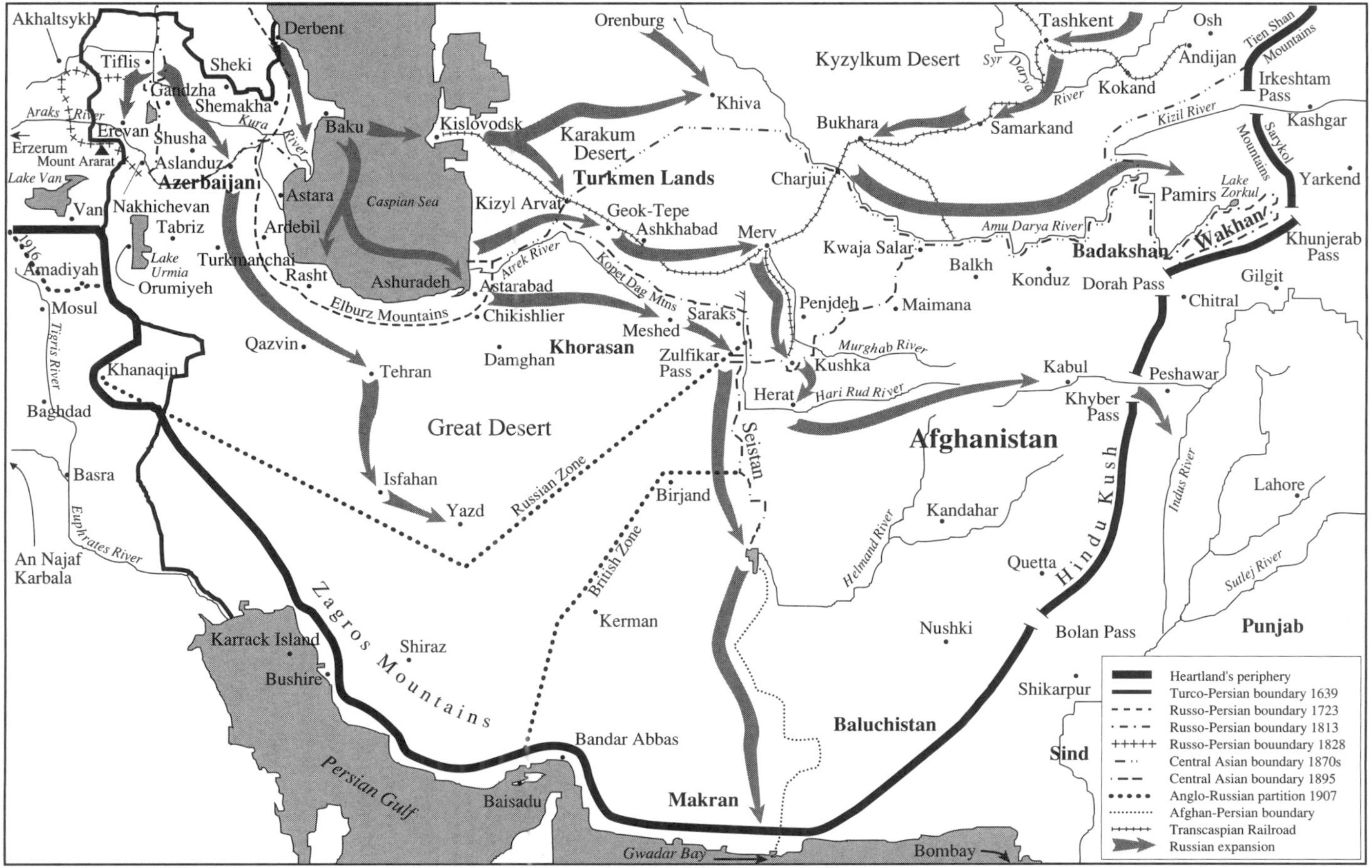

Map 5. The Russo-Persian Frontier

PIKE

Legend:
- Heartland's periphery
- Turco-Persian boundary 1639
- Russo-Persian boundary 1723
- Russo-Persian boundary 1813
- Russo-Persian boundary 1828
- Central Asian boundary 1870s
- Central Asian boundary 1895
- Anglo-Russian partition 1907
- Afghan-Persian boundary
- Transcaspian Railroad
- Russian expansion

Tien Shan Mountains
Irkeshtam Pass
Kashgar
Yarkend
Khunjerab Pass
Sarykol Mountains
Osh
Andijan
Kizil River
Pamirs
Lake Zorkul
Wakhan
Gilgit
Chitral
Tashkent
Kokand
Badakhshan
Dorah Pass
Peshawar
Samarkand
Syr Darya River
Amu Darya River
Konduz
Khyber Pass
Punjab
Lahore
Sutlej River
Indus River
Kyzylkum Desert
Bukhara
Balkh
Kabul
Hindu Kush
Bolan Pass
Charjui
Kwaja Salar
Maimana
Afghanistan
Quetta
Shikarpur
Sind
Orenburg
Karakum Desert
Turkmen Lands
Khiva
Merv
Penjdeh
Murghab River
Kushka
Kandahar
Nushki
Bombay
Geok-Tepe
Ashkhabad
Saraks
Hari Rud River
Herat
Baluchistan
Kopet Dag Mtns
Seistan
Zulfikar Pass
Birjand
Helmand River
Makran
Kizyl Arvat
Atrek River
Chikishlier
Meshed
Khorasan
British Zone
Gwadar Bay
Kislovodsk
Astarabad
Damghan
Kerman
Baisadu
Ashuradeh
Elburz Mountains
Great Desert
Russian Zone
Bandar Abbas
Caspian Sea
Tehran
Yazd
Baku
Rasht
Qazvin
Isfahan
Persian Gulf
Derbent
Astara
Ardebil
Shiraz
Zagros Mountains
Shemakha
Turkmanchai
Bushire
Gandzha
Kura River
Azerbaijan
Tabriz
Karrack Island
Sheki
Shusha
Nakhichevan
Lake Urmia
Orumiyeh
Akhaltsykh
Tiflis
Aslanduz
Van
Khanaqin
Erzerum
Mount Ararat
Lake Van
Araks River
Erevan
Amadiyah
Mosul
1916
Baghdad
Basra
Euphrates River
An Najaf
Karbala
Tigris River

Three areas remained of special interest to the Russians—Khorasan, Seistan, and Persian Azerbaijan. In 1886, the British legation in Tehran obtained secret documents showing Russia intended to obtain a substantial slice of Khorasan. That same year, the Tiflis "viceroy," Alexander Dondukov-Korsakov—he was, incidentally, of Kalmyk ancestry—sent his chief of staff to negotiate a secret convention in Tehran, giving Russia the right to use Khorasan as a base for operations against Afghanistan and India and binding the shah to give assistance, failing which Russia would annex Ghilan and Mazanderan provinces. The Russians' geopolitical vision had not changed since 1722; it retained that broad sweep only "space consciousness" can give. In 1888, Dondukov-Korsakov told the British minister visiting Tiflis on his way to Tehran that a partition was inevitable. The following year, the shah finally agreed to let Russia open a consulate in Meshed—but also asked Britain to open one, so that the Russian flag would not fly alone in one of Persia's most important religious centers. From then on the destabilization of Khorasan was in full swing. Russia supplied the tribes with rifles and incited them to rise against the shah, while the military governor of Transcaspia, General Alexei Kuropatkin, opened a correspondence with his counterpart in Herat (1891). It weakened the fiscal resources of the province by using force and the pretext of a nonexisting disease to divert the Herat trade to Merv (1896).

Khorasan led to Seistan and Scistan to the periphery of the Heartland, beyond which beckoned Gwadar Bay on the Gulf of Oman. The military importance of Seistan was in its abundant supply of camels, the possession of Baluchistan tribesmen who depended more on Afghanistan than on Persia, and the fact that a Russian establishment there would outflank the Hindu Kush, indeed the whole of Afghanistan. By 1897, the Russians had gained the ascendancy in Seistan, with doctors, scholars, newswriters, and other agents determined to establish a presence with small detachments of Cossacks. And that influence was clearly subversive, siding with the population against corrupt officials to win popularity and influence. The approach to the Heartland's periphery from within was accompanied by an attempt to establish a similar presence on the Persian Gulf, with doctors studying local diseases and artillery officers surveying sites for coaling stations.

Like Khorasan, Persian Azerbaijan just across the Araks River was a porous march—its population was largely Turkic but its history had made it an intrinsic part of the core area. Destabilization there would be achieved by descending into Persia's "heart of darkness," the corrupt politics of the court, and by sabotaging its economic development in order to facilitate the "rotting process"[5] propagated by the ambitious men in the Tiflis and Tashkent headquarters and in the Asiatic Department—two of three directors between 1875 and 1897 also served as ambassadors in Tehran. The British ambassador in Petersburg wrote to London in October 1889 that Russia wanted to recreate a *Pax Romana* "within the ring fence" of its dominions, but kept pushing the fence forward by fostering chaos on the other side. "The worse the condition of these neighbors, therefore, the more helpless their squalor and decadence, the nearer she is to the attainment of her goal."[6]

The Persian foreign minister was devoted to the advancement of the Russian cause. Russia used him to overthrow the grand vizier. It then gained a following among the shah's wives and even the clerics opposed to the extension of British influence, after a British subject, Julius Reuter, won an exceptionally generous financial and industrial concession in July 1872. When the shah traveled to Europe in 1878, he was much impressed by the Cossack escort the Tiflis viceroy had placed at his disposal. A so-called Cossack Brigade was sent to him in 1879, eventually growing to 1500 men, a small force no doubt, but in a country without an army, large enough to assume control of Tehran and to send small parties as far as Shiraz and Seistan to accompany the flag bearers of Russian imperialism. Russian influence became so strong in Tehran that when the new ambassador, Nikolai Dolgorukov, arrived in 1887 he made a display of arrogance and disdain reminiscent of the behavior of Repnin, Keyserling, and Stackelberg in Warsaw a century earlier.

Russia sought to delay the development of Persian railroads, partly to stymie British plans to open up the country, partly to nurture the rotting process. In September 1887, Dolgorukov obtained the shah's pledge not to allow foreign companies to build railroads or waterways without first "consulting" the Russian government. The pledge was renewed in 1890 and again in 1899, and would last until 1910. Russia aimed at integrating Azerbaijan into the economic and transportation network of Transcaucasia; the Baku oil fields, for example, could and did supply the whole of northern Persia with cheap kerosene. Russia had built an economic ring fence by terminating free transit across Transcaucasia in 1883 to keep German and Austrian goods out and by raising prohibitive tariffs against the import of British Indian goods through Khorasan in 1895. Thus autarky boosted Russian trade across the Caspian. The opening of the Discount and Loan Bank of Persia in 1890 gave Russia a powerful instrument to buy off the ruling elite with loans on easy terms to princes, selected clergymen, and landowners.

But the rotting process could only go so far in the core area where a sense of a common destiny had always overcome structural weaknesses and centrifugal forces. The new shah, Mozaffara ed-Din (1896–1906), was a good-natured but sickly and uneducated man. His incompetence and the influence of the Court camarilla led Persia to bankruptcy. The shah borrowed from Russia first in 1900, again in 1901, a third time in 1905; the money was wasted on favorites and trips to Europe. The rotting process had a logical end: chaos and revolution. When riots broke out in Tabriz in April 1897 with anti-Armenian overtones, the Russian consul warned the shah that 5000 troops were ready to cross the border "to protect the Christians." The clergy went on the offensive against both the shah and the Russians in 1902. The shah was forced to agree to the election of a national assembly; it met in October 1906, two months before his death.

Russo-Ottoman Relations, 1856–1906

The advance into the Russo-Persian frontier after 1856 had met little resistance and had even received subtle encouragement in the interplay of physical geography with the greed and ambitions of men of power. In the Russo-Turkish frontier, however, it was fated to generate growing resistance. Russian expansion had its own dynamic; a persistent shifting of the balance of power had created a favorable wind. But the frontier zones south of the Prut were so many skerries and shoals against which the force of Russian expansion would have to spend itself and, when faced with a contrary tide, to retreat. This would be true in the Danubian Principalities, in Greece, and in Bulgaria.

The Treaty of Paris, in March 1856, had kept the Principalities under Ottoman "suzerainty," but the defense of their privileges, including the right to an "independent and national administration," had been internationalized. The Porte would restore order in the event of an internal threat only after securing the prior agreement of the five powers Russia, Prussia and Austria, Britain and France. Events soon took an unexpected turn. The election of Alexander Cuza as hospodar of Moldavia in January 1859 and of Wallachia the following month unified for the first time the principalities under a single ruler—and Rumania was born. The Russians had to accept the fait accompli. With the support of Britain and France, Cuza and the men of power who supported him stood up to Russian pressure and drew up for the Russians a line of an optimum of conquest along the Prut. Cuza's nationalization of the "dedicated monasteries"[7] in December 1863 outraged the Russians and the Greek Orthodox establishment in Rumania and was a factor in his overthrow in February 1886. But his elected successor would no more than Cuza be a channel of Russian influence. He was Charles of Hohenzollern-Sigmaringen, a former prime minister of Prussia, a relative of its king, and a Catholic. Charles sent an emissary to Vienna and Petersburg in 1869, inaugurating Rumania's foreign relations, over Ottoman objections. Independence was the next step, but both Russia and the Ottomans opposed it, Russia even threatening to go to war over it. And yet, Russia, caught in the cross currents of international obligations, had to recognize implicitly that Rumania had slipped out of its orbit and that its territorial ambitions no longer went beyond the recovery of southern Bessarabia.

The Russians were even less successful in Greece, where the determination of the Coastland powers to prevent any accretion of Russian influence was understandably stronger. The settlement of 1830 had created a Greece eager to complete the work of unification by annexing Thessaly and Epirus; the Crimean War (1854–1856) saw Greece on Russia's side—until Britain and France enforced a neutral stand. After the war, the Bavarian king squandered his popularity and was forced to flee in October 1862. The national assembly elected a new king in March 1863—Prince William of Denmark, who converted to Orthodoxy and ruled as

George I (1863–1924). His marriage in 1867 to the niece of Alexander II did not alter his strongly pro-British orientation. The Cretan uprising in the summer of 1866 gave Russia a chance to win popularity in Greece. Gorchakov urged the Porte to transfer the island to Greece, and Russian warships (from the Baltic fleet) ferried Greek volunteers to support the islanders. But after the Ottomans crushed the revolt with their usual ferocity, an international conference urged the king to accept their terms—Crete to become autonomous, with a Christian governor.

These setbacks seemed to confirm a loss of energy in the Russian core area government. In August 1856, Gorchakov made his most famous statement in a circular despatch to Russian missions abroad: "Russia sulks, they say? Russia does not sulk. Russia meditates."[8] Meditation restores energy and a sense of purpose after painful reverses. It came to an end when the conquest of the Russo-Persian frontier was launched in 1864 and with the decision to keep a benevolent neutrality when Prussia expelled Austria from German affairs in 1866 and 1870. This revolutionary and misguided decision had a decisive bearing on the straits question. At the end of October 1870, three days after France's capitulation at Metz, Gorchakov announced that Russia was regaining its freedom of action. The Treaty of Paris, he claimed, had been violated by the Coastland powers' naval incursions in the Black Sea and by their support of Rumanian developments. Russia had been disarmed and rendered defenseless while the Ottomans kept warships in the straits and the Aegean Sea and the Coastland powers kept them in the Mediterranean, within striking distance of Russian shores. Nevertheless, the repudiation provoked a major diplomatic crisis, the Coastland powers insisting that an international treaty could not be declared void by a party when it no longer suited its convenience; the Russians invoking the no less valid doctrine of *rebus sic stantibus*—that treaties were valid only so long as circumstances remained substantially unchanged. To defuse the crisis and restore the consensus that Russo-Ottoman relations could not be bilateral but must be "guaranteed" by an international concert of containing powers, an international conference met in London in January 1871. The Russians won their point, and the Black Sea was "deneutralized." They restored their dignity, but Russian warships would not reappear in the Black Sea until 1883.

Bitter disappointments lay ahead in Bulgaria despite a promising beginning. Russian policy toward the Balkan frontier was affected by spontaneous developments in the frontier zones. Until 1856, Russia had pursued a "Pan-Christian" destabilization policy of supporting the Orthodox Christians against Ottoman oppression, not without some occasional bad conscience about siding with subjects against their legitimate rulers. In practice, however, Russia had been able to project little effective power on a permanent basis because the intermediate Balkan zones remained too far removed from its military bases. Its efforts had been limited to courting local men of power whose support might be crucial in some future contingencies. But these men of power had been largely Greeks because the Orthodox Church, the only organized force in the zones, was staffed with Greek clergy. And the Greeks had been a disappointment in the principalities and in Greece itself; their eyes and their interests were turned toward the Coastland. After 1856, Russian policy moved hesitatingly toward the defense of "Slavdom"; the Slavs' rallying point was the struggle not only against the Ottomans but also against the international and notoriously corrupt Phanariot Greeks. Their aim was to create a new generation of men of power dedicated to the task of national revival. Here was the rub. A "Pan-Slav" policy contained the seeds of failure, for the men of power engaged in the process of building a power base with expanding interests did not pursue Slav but national policies. Much as they might welcome the Russian advance against the Ottomans, they were certain to block Russian attempts to incorporate their zones into the inner frontier of the Empire after the war of liberation. The case of Rumania, although not a Slav country, was a serious warning. It was not heeded.

A new Russian ambassador, Nikolai Ignatev, arrived in Constantinople in 1864. "Original, aggressive, and independent,"[9] he believed that the support of the Pan-Slav cause was the most effective way to expel the Ottomans from Europe and that sponsoring the creation of separate states in the frontier zones was the most promising policy to advance Russian interests. The best place to begin was Bulgaria: it had been conquered by Russian arms in 1828; it was on the way to Constantinople; Russia and Austria were not yet rivals there; and a strong movement was agitating for the creation of a national Bulgarian church. For Ignatev, Russia's "meditation" was over, and the time had come for the systematic destruction of the Ottoman Empire.

In March 1870, the sultan, for reasons of his own and with Ignatev's encouragement, created a Bulgarian exarchate, independent of the Orthodox patriarch in Constantinople. The move strengthened the re-emerging national consciousness of the Bulgarians. It also had subversive implications—any district could join the exarchate if two-thirds of its population so desired. The first exarch was excommunicated by the Greek patriarch in February 1872. Support for the Bulgarian church did not mean a relaxation of Ottoman rule, however. When the Bulgarians joined in April 1876 a revolt that had begun in Bosnia-Herzegovina the previous year, Ottoman troops crushed it with more than their usual ferocity. The "Bulgarian atrocities" caused revulsion in Britain and Russia, leaving the Porte isolated. The accession of a new hard-line sultan, Abd ul-Hamid II (1876–1909), made compromise difficult.

In the Crimea, where Alexander II was spending the fall of 1876, the mood was bellicose. Here at last was an opportunity to combine a Pan-Christian, Pan-Slav, and national policy in a grandiose maneuver to reach Constantinople, cut off the retreat of the Ottomans from the Balkans, and complete the unification of Georgia and Armenia. The success of the Central Asian conquest might be duplicated in the Balkans; the nearly completed military reforms gave hope Russia would be able to apply overwhelming power on land to reach its goals. By the convention of

Reichstadt in June, Russia obtained Austrian agreement to the "independence" of Bulgaria and Rumelia (between the Balkan and Rhodope Mountains); to the Greek annexation of Thessaly and Epirus; and to Constantinople becoming a "free city." Independence, however, always meant for the Russians an intermediate stage between the liberation of a frontier zone from the domination of a rival core area and its incorporation into the inner frontier of the Russian Empire. The appointment of Prince Vladimir Cherkassky on the staff of the commander in chief to become governor of Bulgaria after its occupation was ominous—he had acquired a sinister reputation as the "russificator" of Poland after the 1863 revolt.[10] In January 1877, the Russian headquarters moved to Kishinev in Bessarabia. In April, Rumania agreed to the passage of Russian troops and Russia declared war on the Porte. In May, Rumania proclaimed its independence.

The war of 1877–1878 was a repeat of the war of 1826–1828. It was even more successful, despite the fact that the Russians had no navy and the Ottomans had iron-clad warships to ferry troops and supplies to their fortresses defending the approaches to the Balkan Mountains. By May, the Russians had bypassed the Rushchuk-Silistria-Shumla-Varna quadrilateral and were approaching the Shipka Pass into Rumelia, where the valley of the Maritsa offered adequate supplies to support an advance to Constantinople. But they were unexpectedly delayed by the strong resistance of Plevna (Pleven); the fortress was taken at great cost only in December. The advance resumed, and the Russians reached Adrianople in January 1878. Negotiations were moved to San Stefano, only ten kilometers from Constantinople, and peace was signed in March. The Russians were under the walls of the Ottoman capital, but disease, exhaustion, and the presence of a British squadron in the straits compelled them to desist from fighting the mother of all Russian battles—the storm and occupation of the holy city of Greek Orthodoxy. In Transcaucasia, Ardahan had fallen in May 1877, Kars in November, Erzerum in February 1878.

The Treaty of San Stefano, negotiated by Ignatev, was the most far-reaching Russo-Ottoman territorial settlement since the Treaty of Kuchuk-Kainardji. In 1774, Russia had occupied the Ottomans' ultimate zone in the valley of the Dniepr and won "independence" for the Crimean khanate. At San Stefano, they won "autonomy" for Bulgaria, the Ottomans' proximate zone. It was as if the entire Russo-Turkish frontier had fallen out of Ottoman control—the zones to the Prut forming the inner frontier of the Russian Empire, those south of the river an outer frontier about to succumb to the Russian advance.

In Transcaucasia, Russia gained Batum on the Black Sea and Kars, Ardahan, and Bayazid in Armenia, but returned Erzerum. It secured an Ottoman pledge to introduce reforms in the remaining Armenian provinces, opening the way for using the Armenian question to destabilize the eastern margin of the Anatolian core area. The treaty discreetly avoided the straits question, because Ignatev wanted to emphasize the bilateral nature of the negotiations and Russia's role as protector of the Armenians and Bulgarians. The treaty's most controversial part concerned Bulgaria. The country was declared an "autonomous principality." It would have a Christian government headed by an elected prince confirmed in office by the Porte with the agreement of the five powers; a national militia would maintain order; and Ottoman troops would leave the country and their fortifications would be razed (leaving Bulgaria defenseless). The surprise was in Bulgaria's territorial configuration. The boundary began just north of Mangalia on the Black Sea, followed the Danube to the confluence of the Timok, ran past Vranje to the Korab chain, included Lake Ohrid, turned sharply east to follow the divide between Mediterranean and continental climate, avoided Salonika but included the Gulf of Kevala (Kavalla), curled around the Rhodope chain, skirted Adrianople but ran along the middle course of the Ergene (a tributary of the Maritsa), and reached the Black Sea near Midye. Finally, Russia regained part of the territory lost in 1856—southern Bessarabia to the Kilia channel of the Danube, but not the entire delta—and the Ottomans pledged to give Thessaly and Epirus the same autonomy they had granted Crete in 1868. The Greeks had reason to be dissatisfied with the Russians. The inclusion of Macedonia and the Gulf of Kevala into Bulgaria and the failure to acquire Thessaly and Epirus were blows to their irredentist hopes.

The Treaty of San Stefano created a storm, and it is easy to understand why. The storm was not over Great Bulgaria, as is often claimed; it was over Russia's access to the Coastland. It was assumed that Bulgaria's autonomy would become a fiction; that the removal of the Ottoman fortresses would gradually transform Constantinople into a free city at the mercy of a Russian *Blitzkrieg* across Bulgaria. There was no doubt that Russia's ultimate objective was a special status for the Ottoman capital and a Russian presence on the Bosphorus. Much has been made of Alexander II's pledge to the British ambassador in November 1876 that he would not go to Constantinople and would occupy "part of Bulgaria" only "temporarily." The pledge was worthless. In January 1873, Alexander had told London Russia had no intention of taking possession of Khiva; in August, the city was taken and given special status within the Russian Empire. And the Russians reached Constantinople in January 1878.

There were other, even more serious, implications. If Bulgaria entered the Russian orbit, Kevala was certain to become a Russian naval base. Kuchuk Kainardji had paved the way for the establishment of a naval base on the Black Sea; San Stefano would give one on the Mediterranean, supplied overland across Rumania and Bulgaria. The eastern and southern borders of Great Bulgaria happened to coincide with the Heartland's boundary. With a base in Kevala, Russia would cross that boundary and establish itself in the Coastland. Thus, at San Stefano Russia had taken full revenge for the humiliation of 1856.

Russia had won the war, but was about to lose the peace. The combined opposition of the containing powers, Britain and Austria (a Great

Bulgaria would kill Austrian hopes of ever reaching Salonika) led to the convocation of an international congress in Berlin, where Bismarck had to play the difficult role of balancing conflicting ambitions. Once again, Russia had to recognize that its relations with the Ottomans on the western shores of the Black Sea could not be bilateral, let alone form part of its "domestic affairs." It belonged to a larger regional framework in which the Heartland's boundary defined the vital interests of the Coastland and Germanic powers. The Congress met from mid-June to mid-July 1878. Few changes were made in Transcaucasia. Russia had to give up Bayazid and the valley of the Alashkert (Eleşkirt), losing the chance of retaining access to the Trebizond-Tabriz caravan route, still the major commercial route for the Germanic powers from the valley of the Danube to Persia. Batum was declared a free port, essentially commercial.

The congress forced Russia to abandon its project to create a Great Bulgaria. The new Bulgaria lost Macedonia and its window on the Gulf of Kevala. It was also divided into two zones—Bulgaria proper, with Sofia as its capital, north of the Balkan Mountains; and Eastern Rumelia, between the crestline of the Balkan and Rhodope mountains, its capital in Philippopolis (Plovdiv) on the Maritsa. The valley of the Maritsa belonged to the basin of the Aegean Sea; Bulgaria was contained within the valley of the Danube. Bulgaria became "autonomous" under the sultan's suzerainty, with its assembly and its elected prince. Eastern Rumelia received only "administrative autonomy" under the political and military authority of the Porte. Russian agencies created at San Stefano to administer Bulgaria were largely neutralized by a maze of European commissions. The Russian imperial commissioner, however, remained responsible for drawing up a new constitution. Cherkassky had died in February 1878; he was succeeded by General Dondukov-Korsakov, who withdrew with Russian troops in September 1879 and became "viceroy" in Tiflis three years later. A Russian general remained in Sofia to become war minister of the new Bulgaria. Finally, Rumania won recognition of its independence and gained Dobrudja (Dobrogea) with Constanza, a wedge of land between the lower Danube and the sea, the Kilia channel, and the Bulgarian border.

The Russians' troubles were only beginning. Bulgaria's assembly elected its prince, Alexander of Battenberg, a dashing 22-year-old Prussian officer and the nephew of the Russian empress. He would rule with a liberal constitution drawn up by Dondukov-Korsakov. The Russians left a legacy of goodwill because they had won for Bulgaria its emancipation from Ottoman rule and were expected to encourage rebellion in Eastern Rumelia and its annexation by Bulgaria. Relations soured very quickly, however, exposing the incompatibility between Pan-Slav solidarity and the ambitions of local men of power. The Russians showed a lack of tolerance for political pluralism except when it served their interests; the heavy-handedness of Russian officers left in charge of building up a Bulgarian army, together with Prince Alexander's dictatorial and pro-Russian proclivities, antagonized the men of power. In May 1881, the prince pressured the assembly to give him dictatorial powers; in July 1882, he appointed three Russian generals in his government, including one, Leonid Sobolev, as minister-president. The dictatorship proved unworkable. Bulgarian nationalism turned anti-Russian, and a coalition forced Alexander in September 1883 to restore the constitution and expel the Russian officers. To save his own position, the prince sided with Bulgarian nationalism, thereby incurring Russia's hatred. When Bulgaria invaded Eastern Rumelia in September 1885, Russia opposed the move and forced Alexander to abdicate the following year. His successor was not recognized until 1896. Russian influence then once again became predominant and a secret military convention was signed in December 1902. In the meantime, Rumania had thrown in its lot with the Germanic powers; it had signed an alliance with Austria-Hungary and Germany in October 1883, at the height of the Russo-Bulgarian crisis.

Russia's inability to incorporate the frontier zones between the Prut and the valley of the Ergene—its only failure in the Southern Frontier— were matched by a renewed insistence on "solving" the straits question in its favor. On the eve of his appointment to Constantinople in 1882, Alexander Nelidov had reminded the tsar that Russian control of the straits was an "historical necessity,"[11] and that Constantinople must become a free city. That had been the program of Alexander I and Nicholas I. But there were now additional reasons for Russia's concern over the straits—the growing economic role of the Germanic powers in the valley of the Danube and the Black Sea, their rising political influence in Constantinople, and the development of Russian grain exportation from Odessa. By the first decade of the twentieth century, 37 percent of all Russian exports passed through the straits. Russia could no longer afford the risk of the Porte's closing the straits to commercial shipping in alliance with any other power, let alone a power hostile to Russia.

But the Russians had to face a new, troublesome, and fundamental fact—for the first time since the 1780s, the military balance of power in the Russo-Turkish frontier was beginning to shift back in the Ottomans' favor. The Russian navy had gained superiority over the Ottoman navy in the Black Sea in the 1820s; defeat in the Crimea had crippled it in 1856; its reappearance in the 1880s was no threat to the Ottomans, who would soon be able to buy warships from the Germans, while the Russians, who could not bring warships through the straits into the Black Sea, would have to build them in their notoriously inefficient shipyards. When Nelidov proposed in late 1896 a landing in the Bosphorus to take advantage of Ottoman difficulties in Crete and of the backlash against the massacre of Armenians, the navy opposed it on the ground it did not have enough transport ships. Diplomacy was running ahead of naval capabilities, a secret unknown to everyone but the highest circles of the Russian government. The alliance between Rumania and the Germanic powers had made a military advance into the liberated zones of the Russo-Turkish frontier impossible; a fleet-in-being strategy was not an option as long as the straits were closed; and closer ties between the Porte and the Germanic powers were testing the validity of a fortress-fleet strategy in the Black Sea and threatening vital commercial interests.

A Pyrrhic Victory, 1907–1917

Russian diplomacy continued to press for a revision of the international status of the straits. Conversations were held in 1907 and 1908, Russia seeking an exclusive right of passage for its warships to protect its merchant trade. But no agreement was reached. In November 1911, Nikolai Charykov, the Russian ambassador in Constantinople—he had been envoy to Bukhara (1886–1890), Bulgaria (1896–1897), and Serbia (1900–1905), and deputy minister of foreign affairs (1908–1909)—presented to the Porte a draft agreement reminiscent of the Treaty of Unkiar Skelesi: in the event of an attack on the Porte, Russia would be given the right to send its warships into the Aegean Sea to protect the straits. The casus belli was not some hypothetical contingency: in September, Italy, seeking to obtain Tripoli, had declared war on the Porte, and the war of 1911–1912 would bring about the closing of the straits to merchant shipping and cause considerable losses to Russia and other powers. But the specter of Unkiar Skelesi continued to haunt the straits question. Charykov was disavowed and recalled in March 1912.

Russian ambitions did not change, however. A year later, in November 1913, Foreign Minister Sergei Sazonov declared that Russia's control of the straits was essential not only for a fleet-in-being strategy in the Mediterranean but also for offensive operations in Anatolia and for hegemony in the Balkans. The statement was remarkable for its geopolitical vision—once in possession of the straits, the Russians would be in the same position as the Ottoman Turks in the fourteenth century. From that strategic channel, the very core of the Turkish core area, they could expand east and west and claim the legacy of the Ottomans within the Heartland from Bosnia-Herzegovina to the Persian border, and across the Heartland, in the eastern Mediterranean. Anatolia was also vulnerable from the east. At the end of 1912, the Russian embassy had drawn up a plan for the reform of Turkish Armenia—it would become a single province (instead of six) under a Christian governor general, appointed by the sultan with the approval of the powers. The parallel with Eastern Rumelia in 1878 was striking.

In the Balkans, the Russian ambassadors in Belgrade and Sofia encouraged in 1909 negotiations to form a Balkan League, overlooking the bitter rivalry between its prospective two members over Macedonia. The Balkan wars of 1912–1913 exposed that policy as totally unrealistic. Turkey, it is true, lost all its possessions west of the Enos (Enez)-Midye line; the defeat marked the end of the Ottoman Empire in Europe. But the victorious allies could not agree on the division of the spoils. In the end, Bulgaria did not regain Macedonia, lost to Rumania the southern part of Dobrudja, but gained a new foothold on the Aegean Sea, between Enos and the Gulf of Kevala. Times had changed since 1878, and there was nothing the powers could do. Were not the Coastland powers and Russia now in the same camp? However, Bulgaria's resentment at losing its bid for Macedonia focused on Serbia and led to a reorientation of Bulgarian policy toward the Germanic powers. When the First World War broke out, both Rumania and Bulgaria, and Turkey, had entered the orbit of the Germanic powers.

The war began in August 1914. German influence in Turkey had become so strong—in military reform, railroad building, and commercial expansion—that the Entente powers could not expect the Young Turk government, installed in 1908 to stop the catastrophic disintegration of the sultanate under Abd ul-Hamid, to open the straits to their warships. Turkey was at first neutral, but closed the straits to merchant shipping in September, cutting off Russia's lifeline with the Coastland powers in the Mediterranean. In October, Turkish ships under German command attacked Russian ships and ports in the Black Sea; Russia, Britain, and France declared war in November, but the straits would remain closed for the duration of the war. The failure of Britain's expedition against Gallipoli in February 1915, together with Russia's retreat in Galicia and Poland, convinced Bulgaria to join the Germanic powers in October. Rumania remained neutral until 1916, both because of irritation at Austrian support of Bulgaria and a growing ambition to incorporate Transylvania, a goal that could not be reached without Russian support and the defeat of Austria-Hungary. Following the successful Brusilov offensive in the spring of 1916, Rumania declared war on the Germanic powers in August. In Greece, the strong pro-German sympathies of the king delayed the country's entrance into the war on the Entente side until June 1917.

The fickleness of the men of power in the old frontier zones and the seemingly inevitable consolidation of the Austro-German-Turkish alliance induced Britain and France on the one hand, Russia on the other, as "flanking powers," to settle among themselves the two basic disputes making up the Eastern question—the partition of the Ottoman Empire and the straits question. An exchange of notes between Sazonov and the British and French ambassadors in March 1915 conceded to Russia at the end of the war Constantinople, the European side of the Bosphorus with the Sea of Marmara and its islands, and so-called Southern (or Western) Thrace from that sea to the Enos-Midye line; on the eastern ("Asiatic") side of the Bosphorus the entire peninsula to a line following the Sakaria River to a point on the Gulf of Izmit; and finally, the islands of Imbros (Gökçeada) and Tenedos, guarding the approaches to the Dardanelles, considered as far back as 1808 essential to Russia's domination of the Straits. The cession was made conditional on the prosecution of the war by the three powers until victory and the realization of Anglo-French ambitions in the Near East. Sazonov expressed his "profound gratitude" and promised Russia would not interfere in merchant shipping; Constantinople would become a free port for goods in transit to and from non-Russian territory.[12] Nothing was said about warships, but with such an impregnable position on both sides of the Bosphorus, the least said the better.

Russia had finally reached its goal in the straits, although they still had to be conquered from the Turks, and the issue was uncertain. Russia also reached its goal in Armenia. In April and May 1916, the three powers agreed on a partition of the Ottoman Empire, Russia annexing Trebizond, Erzerum, Bitlis, and Van. The new boundary brought virtually the whole of Western Armenia into the Russian Empire, included the headwaters of the Euphrates and the Tigris, and ran past Amadiyah to the Persian border. In the event of victory, the Turkish core area, deprived of all its frontier zones, would be caught in a Russian vise. The Russian acquisitions would march on northern Persia, now part of the Russian Empire, to form a continuous belt from the Black Sea to Afghanistan.

The Anglo-Russian rapprochement also favored Russian interests in Persia. Russo-Persian trade more than doubled between 1901 and 1907 and amounted to more than twice the value of British trade by 1907. There were Russian banks and consuls in Isfahan, Hamadan, Kerman, and Seistan and, in the Gulf, in Bender Abbas and Bushire. There were plans to link Tehran with the Transcaucasian railway, Meshed with the Transcaspian. The rotting process was proceeding apace, and Lord Curzon, the viceroy of India, declared in September 1899 that "Russia is interested not in the reform of Persia, but in its decay"; and that "in the background of her ambitions is the vision of a country and a people falling from inherent debility into her grasp."[13] Frederick II could have written the same thing about Russia and Poland in the 1770s and 1780s: only a partition could keep the entire country from becoming a Russian protectorate.

In 1904, when there was yet no evidence that Russia was interested, the War Office discussed a project to partition Persia. The dividing line between the Russian and British shares would run from Kermanshah past Isfahan, Yazd, and Kerman to the Afghan border. The line ran along the northern skirt of the Zagros Mountains and included Seistan in the Russian sphere. It clearly assumed that Russia must not cross the periphery of the Heartland and must stay out of the Persian Gulf and the Monsoon Coastland. The project was not acted upon, but the mutual desire to eliminate sources of tension after the Russian defeat in the Russo-Japanese war, Britain's determination to reduce its commitments in the Southern Frontier for budgetary reasons, and the Russians' conviction that the acceptance of a partition might convince Britain to be more amenable in the straits question—all these factors led to the agreement of August 1907 on Persia and Afghanistan.

In Afghanistan, Russia recognized the status quo. The country was outside the Russian sphere of influence and its foreign relations were conducted through the intermediary of the British government. But the agreement also paved the way for Russian penetration by recognizing the principle of equality of commercial opportunity and the possibility of appointing commercial agents—a distinct, but for the time being meaningless, concession, since the Afghan market remained closed to Russian traders as late as 1916, when Kuropatkin, by then governor general in Tashkent, called for territorial readjustments, the development of trade, and the construction of a railroad across the Hindu Kush to link the Transcaspian with the Indus River. The agreement partitioned Persia into three zones. The Russian share was the largest, with eleven of the twelve major cities and with the trade routes from the Black Sea to Central Asia and India. It included Persian Azerbaijan, most of Khorasan, and the three provinces first annexed in 1723. Its boundary began at Qasr-e-Shirin, facing Khanaqin in Turkey, ran past Kermanshah, Isfahan, and Yazd (as in the 1904 project), but then turned sharply north till it reached the Zulfikar Pass. The British zone included Seistan and Baluchistan and was bounded by a line running from the Persian Gulf near Bandar Abbas past Kerman and Birjand to the Afghan border. The intermediate zone was declared a neutral zone, where neither power would seek political or commercial concessions. The major difference between the agreement and the 1904 project was that the Russian zone was no longer contiguous with Afghanistan; even the Zulfikar Pass was in the intermediate zone.

The agreement came just in time. A new shah, Muhammed Ali, was crowned in January 1907. Called "perhaps the most perverse, cowardly, and vice-sodden monster on the throne of Persia,"[14] he became Russia's ideal tool to expand the rotting process. He was determined to destroy the constitutionalist and nationalist movement. The Cossack Brigade surrounded and fired on the National Assembly (Majlis) building in June 1908, and its commander, a Russian colonel, was made military governor of Tehran. The shah's rule by martial law only whipped up opposition, until he was forced to take refuge in the Russian embassy in July 1909. He was then deposed, but his successor was his 12-year-old son, whose tutor and physician were Russian. Russian troops occupied Tabriz, Qazvin, and Tehran to block the election of a new Majlis in the spring and summer, but failed. By 1911, however, some 12,000 troops were deployed in northern Persia. The second Majlis was expelled in December, and Russian military commanders and consuls took over the administration of much of their zone under the guidance of the Tiflis headquarters. The rotting process, despite the nationalist revival, seemed to have reached its logical end.

Despite its location, Persia did not escape the consequences of the First World War. Turkish troops entered the country in September 1914 on their way to Tabriz; the Turkic population of Azerbaijan was expected to welcome them. Russia used the invasion as another pretext to declare war on Turkey in October. A rump Persian government continued to operate; it declared Persia neutral in November. The third Majlis, fiercely anti-

British and anti-Russian, met in Tehran in January 1915. It began to flirt with the Germans, a foolish decision because the Germans could offer no effective assistance; their allies, the Turks, had all too often been Persia's enemies; and Britain and Russia remained the dominant powers in the country. A consequence was that the March 1915 agreement on the straits also dealt with Persia. In exchange for Russia's agreeing to make Constantinople a free commercial port, Britain granted Russia a free hand in its zone, effectively recognizing its annexation to the Russian Empire. The Russians gained some additional territory near Isfahan and Yazd and a wedge along the Afghan border to include the Zulfikar Pass. The remainder of the neutral zone was added to the British zone, bringing the oil fields and the entire coast of the Persian Gulf under British juris-diction. In February 1913, the Russians had been granted a concession to link Julfa with Tabriz by rail, with a branch to Orumiyeh, and the right to exploit the coal and oil resources in a zone 108 kilometers wide on each side of the line. In March 1916, they gained the exclusive right to exploit the oil and gas reserves of the three northern provinces (Ghilan, Mazanderan, Asterabad) for seventy years. Russia's ring fence had reached the Zagros Mountains and the Great Desert. The Persian core area had seemingly ceased to exist; its most populous provinces were being inte-grated into the inner frontier of the Russian Empire. To discuss what hap-pened after the Bolshevik Revolution brought (temporarily) Russia's "historical mission" to a halt in the Southern Frontier is beyond the scope of this book. To imagine what might have happened if it had not taken place would be pure speculation.

But it will be helpful to recapitulate. The same expenditure of energy that propelled Russia to expand into the Western Frontier drove the Russians into the Southern Frontier. In fact, that drive was much older, more deliberate, and more persistent. The core area's "logic of expansion" from the margin of two empires with a universal mission urged the Russians into the territory of their parent cultures, that of Byzantium and that of the Turco-Mongol world, to claim their legacy and develop a universal mission of their own. This primal urge took Russia from its forested core area across the "steppe-ocean" toward the Ottoman core area in the direction of Byzantium-Constantinople; toward the Persian core area in the direction of Isfahan and Samarkand. In that expansion the search for advanced technology was not a factor, as it was in the Western Frontier. The Ottomans, Safavids, and Kajars no longer had anything to offer; their ancestors had already taught the Russians the source, the purpose, and the modalities of political power. Colonization, that slow but irresistible movement of peasants escaping from the forest and from an oppressive political system with limited economic resources, drove settlers toward the Black Sea and the Caucasus. The insecurity of the frontier, caused in large part by the traumatic incursions of the Crimean Tatars, delayed the expansion, but also led to the creation of Cossack zones to defend the pioneer fringe. The Cossacks also relayed that expansion and gave it new vigor. And the ruling elite, its space consciousness sharpened by a physical universe without boundaries but with large rivers forming so many corridors of expansion toward the Black Sea, the Caucasus, and the Caspian, was resolved to wage with the Ottoman and the Persian core areas a struggle for the redistribution of space, until the core areas were partitioned and Russia reached the boundary of the Heartland, the only truly insuperable physical barrier to its further expansion.

This determination was strengthened by the conviction that the Russian core area's energy was stronger and more concentrated and that, as a result, the balance of power in the Southern Frontier was shifting in Russia's favor. Not without some considerable effort, however. There were only four Russo-Persian wars, the last one in 1828, but it took ten Russo-Ottoman wars between 1696 and 1917 to remove the Ottomans from the entire frontier, and in only one (in 1711) did Russia suffer a defeat. Ottoman fortresses and desperate courage could not stop the Russians' superior organization and fire power. And so it happened that one zone after another was occupied. The Cossack zones were integrated into the empire's inner frontier in the 1770s; the Crimea in the 1780s; the Ochakov steppe in the 1790s; the Caucasus, north and south, from the 1770s to the 1810s, although the unification of Armenia was not completed for another century; the Persian frontier, in the 1870s and 1880s. Almost everywhere, the Russians could count on the support of many, if not all, men of power. Religion and the defense of a social order based on serfdom played an important role in the early years, ethnicity at other times. And emancipation from the Ottoman yoke left no choice but to accept the lesser Russian yoke.

There was a conspicuous exception, however. The Balkans formed an interlocking frontier between the Russian, Austrian, and Turkish core areas and even, within a larger framework, between Russia and the Coastland powers. There, emancipation did not lead into Russia's embrace, and local men of power, their roots in sedentary and better structured societies, were more likely to turn to the containing powers—Austria and Germany, Britain and France. There *was* an alternative, and that explains Russia's failure in the Principalities and Bulgaria. Everywhere else, Russia built a ring fence and pursued a policy of inclusion, of political, economic, and social autarky.

The advance into the frontier was accompanied by a destabilization policy no less consistent than in the Western Frontier. There were differences, however. The "dissident" issue was of little value in Persia; there were no Christians; supporting the Sunni against the Shi'ite Moslems served only short-term purposes, the Russians being infidels. But the structural weaknesses of the Persian core area offered rich possibilities;

political fragmentation grew on physical multiformity. If the capital was in Isfahan or Tehran, there were strong autonomous centers in Tabriz and Ardabil, Shiraz and Meshed—and Herat. In a devilish mix of conservatism and subversion, Petersburg and its regional headquarters in Astrakhan, Tiflis, and Tashkent incited local chieftains against the shah and supported the shah against them, all the while smothering a disintegrating dynasty under the trappings of pomp and power.

In their Ottoman policy, the Russians could never reconcile their two options. The Orthodox Christian population beginning at the Prut was an ideal "dissident" party, not in the sense of its seeking equality of rights and privileges with the Ottoman ruling class, but in the sense of its forming a local party receptive to Russian influence. Indeed, the championship of Orthodoxy had been one of the major ingredients in the combustible mixture generating Russia's expansionist energy since at least the seventeenth century. But a Pan-Christian policy of destabilizing the frontier zones guarding the approaches to Constantinople could only stiffen Ottoman resistance and render impossible the attainment of another cherished goal—the opening of the straits to Russian warships. In both cases, however, Russia's actions were certain to bring about, throughout the nineteenth century, an overwhelming British reaction and a de facto Anglo-Ottoman alliance. The Ottoman dynasty's remarkable tenacity in resisting the Russian advance was strengthened by Britain's preponderant influence in Constantinople, following that of France in the eighteenth century. It left no opening for a policy of subversion in the sultan's government.

The Russians also had to formulate a naval strategy in the Black Sea, following the buildup of a navy in the 1780s. Its purpose was defensive: to erect a naval "ring fence" to defend their coastline, as in the Baltic. The Sound, despite occasional proclamations to the contrary, could not "close" the Baltic Sea; its shores were controlled by two powers. A Russian alliance with both Denmark and Sweden, traditional enemies, was unlikely. The volume of trade between the Baltic and the Coastland powers and their strategic interests in that sea were so great that closing the Baltic would have been an immediate cause of war.

But the Black Sea *was* a closed sea, the Ottomans controlling both shores of the straits. Russia had an interest in keeping it closed, and there were three incompatible ways of reaching that objective. Russia had to gain naval superiority over the Ottoman navy by pursuing a fleet-in-being strategy to destroy Turkish ships in wartime—a successful policy until 1853, a failure by the 1910s. That sea must remain closed to other than Ottoman warships to remove any threat to Russian security between the delta of the Danube and the boundary of eastern Anatolia. This could not be done if Russia and the Porte were at war: hence the basic dilemma between a Pan-Christian or Pan-Slav policy and friendship with the Ottomans. Finally, to prevent those enemy warships from entering the Black Sea in the event of a war with the Coastland powers, Russia needed to navigate the straits and close the Dardanelles from its naval bases on the Aegean islands. Such a strategy had to assume either an Ottoman alliance or an Ottoman defeat; it could also easily turn into a fleet-in-being strategy in the eastern Mediterranean. That is why the ghost of Unkiar Skelesi never ceased to haunt the straits question, until the Coastland powers surrendered in 1915 and gave Russia what it had wanted for five generations.

III

RUSSIA AND ITS EASTERN FRONTIER

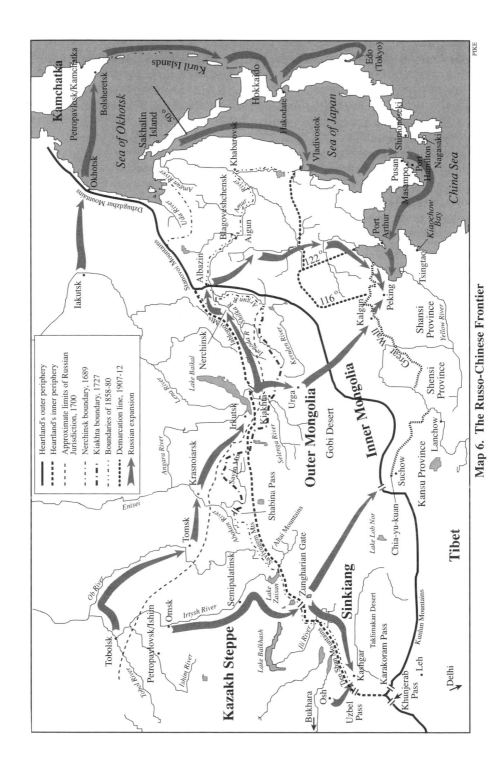

Map 6. The Russo-Chinese Frontier

154

7

Early Relations, 1689–1848

The Setting, 1689–1759

The search for fur-bearing animals—the "colonial" product of a land locked core area—propelled Russian expansion across the vast expanse of Siberia. The great rivers of Arctic drainage and their numerous tributaries were separated by portages presenting no serious obstacles to a hardy race of Cossack *coureurs de bois* in quest of profits and adventure. They founded Iakutsk on the Lena in 1632; Okhotsk on the bleak and near polar Sea of Okhotsk in 1647; Irkutsk, where the Angara flows into Lake Baikal, in 1651; Selenginsk in 1666 and Verkhneudinsk (Ulan Ude) two years later, in the valley of the Selenga between Lake Baikal and the Iablonoi chain. Twelve years earlier, in 1656, they had founded Nerchinsk: the valley of the Khilok, a tributary of the Selenga, led across the periphery of the Heartland to the Ingoda, the Ingoda to the Shilka, and the Shilka to the Amur. In only two places on the entire periphery of the Heartland from the Scandinavian Kjølen to the Dzhugdzhur range was Russia able to cross into the Coastland with impunity. Okhotsk was inhospitable and hard to reach. It would nevertheless become the starting point for the exploration of the northern Pacific, the Aleutian Islands, and Alaska. The valley of the Amur—broad, rich, and beckoning—strengthened the logic of Russian expansion in the direction of the Sea of Japan and the China Sea.

The building of a fort at Albazin on the Amur in 1651 had created alarm in Peking, where the Manchus had just founded a new dynasty destined to create the largest empire China had ever known. The Russians saw in China a great market for Siberian furs. The Manchus showed little interest in trade but considerable concern over the geopolitical implications

155

of the Russian advance; they were determined to force the Russians to abandon Albazin and Nerchinsk and roll them back behind the Iablonoi and Stanovoi ranges. Disputes over these incompatible goals and the Russians' inevitable involvement in the Manchus' disputes with the Mongols, including giving asylum to the Manchus' opponents, convinced Moscow to send a high-level embassy to negotiate these festering differences. Fedor Golovin arrived in Selenginsk in 1687, two years after the Manchus had destroyed Albazin. A Zunghar attack forced a postponement of the negotiations; they were renewed in Nerchinsk, where the first Russo-Chinese treaty was signed in August 1689.

The Russians were at a disadvantage. Golovin had an escort of a few thousand men, isolated in none too friendly Buriat territory. The Manchu delegation was accompanied by 10,000 men with artillery, and incited the Buriats to keep the Russians in a state of uncertainty. The negotiations lasted more than two weeks, the Manchus insisting at first that all land east of Lake Baikal was part of the Chinese Empire, the Russians demanding that the Amur and the Zeia become Siberia's boundary with the Manchu homeland. These were extreme positions, exacerbated by a misunderstanding: the Russians rightly pointed out that the Amur was the main river from the confluence of the Shilka and the Argun to the sea, while the Manchus were convinced the Sungari was the main river and the Amur its tributary. This misunderstanding remained a sore point through the end of the Manchu dynasty.

Despite their military superiority, the Manchus had worries of their own. Galdan Boshughtu (1671–1697), the Zunghar leader, had been building a powerful empire among the Western Mongols. In 1688, he had invaded Mongolia, advancing as far as the Kerulen River, seizing immense amounts of livestock and forcing thousands of Eastern Mongols to flee to Manchu-ruled areas. The emergence of the Zunghar empire, no less than an attempt to unify most of the Russo-Chinese frontier, was bound to complicate relations between the two core areas. The Manchus viewed the Zunghars as their main enemy between the Irtysh and Manchuria, a threat to Mongolia and through Mongolia to Peking, and they would not rest until that threat had been eradicated. On the other hand, they also had to consider the possibility of a Russo-Zunghar alliance as an additional factor in the destabilization of the frontier zones. To use force to roll back the Russians behind the Heartland's periphery might incite them from their base in Tomsk to support Zunghar ambitions and prevent the Manchus from asserting their authority in the frontier.

A compromise was in order. It was brokered by the Jesuits, then in high favor at the Peking Court, and the Treaty of Nerchinsk, the first treaty to be signed not only between China and Russia but also between China and a European power, was written in Latin. The Latin and Russian versions do not coincide, and there has been some controversy over the meaning of the treaty's provisions, much of it due to the fact that the region was little known and no maps existed. Suffice it to say that the treaty was essentially a boundary treaty. The boundary began at Abagaytuy on the Argun River, followed the river close to its confluence with the Shilka where the two rivers merge to form the Amur, and ran along the Shilka upstream to the Little Gorbitsa River, an ecological boundary. Then it followed the watershed between the basin of the Lena and that of the Amur, curled southward to follow the watershed between the valley of the Uda and that of the Amur, and finally ran to the Sea of Okhotsk between the Uda and the Amgun rivers. The treaty thus conceded to the Russians access to the Coastland between the Iablonoi range and the Argun River with Nerchinsk, the silver mine, and the salt lake, but barred access to the Amur; north of it, the boundary followed the Stanovoi range, the Heartland's periphery. Albazin was razed and its population removed to the Russian side. Fugitives would have to be returned, but merchants with official passports were allowed to cross the border to trade. The prospects for commercial penetration of the Amur valley were weak, however. After Nerchinsk, the Manchus forbade both Chinese and Manchus to settle in the territories north of the Amur; natives were evacuated. By creating a no-man's land, the Manchus hoped to forestall a new Russian advance. They also created a secure frontier zone that served both Russian and Manchu interests: neither side would have an interest in modifying the status quo. Nevertheless, Nerchinsk was a great Russian victory. Once established in the Coastland, the Russians would patiently wait until the weakening of Manchu power opened the road to the Sea of Japan.

The expansionist impulse, fed by the hunter's and the trader's greed for peltry but checked at the gate of the Amur valley, found an outlet around the Sea of Okhotsk. Kamchatka was discovered in 1697 and Bolsheretsk founded in 1700. That giant step around the Heartland's periphery was momentous. It gave the Russians an inkling of Japan's existence and a foothold on the Kuril Islands; in short, it created a Russo-Japanese frontier, an additional zone within the Pacific frontier.

Japanese fishermen and merchants engaged in the intensive coastal trade between western Japan and Edo (Tokyo), the capital, were often caught in dangerous storms and became castaways as far north as the coast of Kamchatka. One of them, Dembei, landed there and was sent to Moscow, where he was received by Peter I in January 1702. He gave valuable if at times inaccurate information about Japan's location, economy, society, and government. His accounts created among the Russians a passion not unlike their obsession with reaching India. The quality of Japanese goods, shipwrecked here and there, attracted their attention; so did the prospects of trade with a country presumably rich in precious metals. Japan already harbored some 30 million inhabitants, and Edo, with possibly a million people, was the most populous city in the world. It was then that an awareness was born that the economy of eastern Siberia, poor in agricultural resources to sustain a sedentary population but rich in furs, and that of Japan, based on trade and sophisticated crafts, might be complementary. That awareness became a crucial factor in the advance into the Russo-Japanese frontier. By the end of Peter's reign, however, Moscow had learned from Lorents (Ivan) Lange, a Swede and Russia's first commercial agent in Peking for three short years (1719–1722), of Japan's exclusion policy: the shogunal government had banned since 1636 all contacts with foreigners and did not engage in foreign trade.

But reaching Japan was not easy without a merchant marine. The difficulties attending the shipment of tribute in furs collected from the natives overland from Kamchatka prompted the development of Okhotsk as both a commercial and a naval port. The first ship built there made the trip to Bolsheretsk and back in 1716. Meanwhile, the Russians had discovered that Cape Lopatka, the tip of Kamchatka, pointed to an island, the first in the Kuril archipelago stretching over 1200 kilometers to Hokkaido. The native Ainus were willing to barter their beaver pelts for cloth and iron. The actual exploration of the archipelago began in 1711. By 1713, the Russians had claimed the two northernmost islands. In 1716, Cossacks visited the Shantar Islands facing the mouth of the Uda, the terminal point of the Russo-Chinese boundary established at Nerchinsk. An exploration reached the southernmost Kurils in 1721–1722, and by 1769 the Russians had counted twenty-three islands, including Hokkaido and "Japan." The outline of a fortress-fleet strategy was about to take shape, even though its realization would remain in the distant future; the archipelago was destined to become an outer naval perimeter to defend Russian possessions in the Sea of Okhotsk.

Japan was far away and perhaps unlikely to rescind its exclusion policy in Russia's favor. Peking could be reached overland, and the treaty of Nerchinsk allowed trade across the border. In accordance with China's traditional view of itself as the Middle Kingdom surrounded by barbarians, trade was a form of tribute, and tribute bearers who sought admittance before the emperor had to perform the kowtow—three kneelings and nine prostrations—a rite recognizing him as the suzerain of the world. But trade was also conducted in the marketplace without the offering of tribute and served to satisfy the more mundane interests of Chinese and barbarians alike. Goods were transported in caravans, and the Chinese government assumed their protection and upkeep as long as they remained within the empire. Ten government-run Russian caravans traveled to Peking between 1693 and 1717, and there were many more private ones until Moscow forbade private trade with China in 1706. They reached the Chinese capital via the valleys of the Nonni and the Liao; the trip took about 150 days.

The Russo-Chinese trade was always based on a misunderstanding. The Russians viewed it as a profitable undertaking to obtain precious metals and expensive cloth, the Manchus as a means to keep the Russians away from a dangerous alliance with the Zunghars and to force them to make concessions in contentious border issues. The first official Russian caravan was that of Izbrant Ides, a merchant born in Denmark, who sought permission to trade with the "khan of China."[1] He arrived in Peking in

November 1692 and performed the kowtow. Both sides already showed an interest in keeping a close watch on the caravan trade, Moscow demanding that the gold and silver acquired by private merchants be turned over to the Treasury (by sale or in the form of customs duties paid in Irkutsk), the Manchus restricting the frequency of caravans to one every three years and the number of merchants in each to 200. Private merchants continued to come, however, either on their own account or on that of the Siberian *voevody*, who cared little about the Treasury's interest and traded on their own, until Siberian furs so glutted the market that prices fell disastrously and ruined the official trade. The government's concern explains the prohibition of private trade in 1706. Two years earlier, the Manchus had allowed the official caravans to use the shorter route via the Selenga valley, Urga and Kalgan, reducing the Journey's length to seventy days. The last caravan was admitted in the wake of the Izmailov mission in 1720, an attempt to gain for the Russians freedom of trade in the entire Manchu Empire. The Manchus, however, showed greater interest in revising the 1689 boundary and demanded vainly the return of Mongol deserters. By then, the progress of their campaign against the Zunghars had killed the political importance of the Russian trade. In May 1722, Lange was ordered out of Peking and all Russians were later expelled from Mongolia.

The Manchus' major concern in the Russo Chinese frontier during the reign of the K'ang-hsi (Kangxi) emperor (1662–1722) had been to eliminate the Zunghar threat. A Manchu counterattack rolled back the Zunghar invasion of Mongolia after the conclusion of the Treaty of Nerchinsk. Galdan sought Russian support, but Russia could not afford to support the Zunghars without jeopardizing its newly won position in the Coastland. Hunted out of Mongolia in 1696, Galdan finally committed suicide in May 1697. His nephew and successor: Tsewang Rabtan (1697–1727), however, was no less ambitious in his attempt to unify the Mongol tribes, a move the Manchus viewed as a vital threat to their dynasty.

The new Zunghar chieftain had to face the threat to his rear from the Kazakhs, a large confederation of nomads who had been part of the Golden Horde. Their khan resided in Turkestan, a city seized from the Uzbeks. They wandered all over the "steppe-ocean" between the Volga and Zungharia, gave their allegiance and paid tribute to the Manchu emperor. Their internal struggles revolved around the rivalries of powerful chieftains and the control of abundant pastures; their conflict with the Zunghars focused on the approaches to the Heartland's periphery. The Zunghar theater of operation was the vast frontier zone between the inner and outer boundary of the Heartland—between the Sayan range and the Kunlun Mountains. It included the Zungharian Gate, the valley of the upper Irtysh and Lake Zaisan, and the great pass of Inner Asia comparable in importance to the Khyber Pass: both gave access to the Monsoon Coastland, one in China, the other in India. The struggle with the Kazakhs centered on the control of the basin of Lake Balkhash and the upper

Irtysh. It also involved the Russian advance across the mountains from
their base in Tomsk. The Zunghars had sought Russian support against
the Manchus; the Kazakhs sought Russian support against the Zunghars;
and the destabilization of the entire westernmost segment of the Russo-
Chinese frontier compelled the Russians to lay the foundation of a close-
border policy along the great arc around the Kazakh upland from
the Caspian shores to Lake Zaisan. The first step was the expedition of
Colonel Ivan Buchholz in 1714. One of its goals was to find gold;
another, to build a fort controlling access to Lake Iamyshevo along the
Irtysh, a vital source of salt for the steppe nomads. The expedition failed,
but it was followed by the founding of Omsk in 1717, Zhelezinsk and
Semipalatinsk in 1718, and Ust-Kamenogorsk in 1720—all major outposts
on what would later be called the Irtysh Line, the embodiment of a close-
border policy.

The death of the K'ang-hsi emperor at the end of 1722 brought the
war against the Zunghars to a temporary halt. Hostilities resumed in
1729 after the new Zunghar chief, Galdan Tsering (1727–1745), refused
to submit to China. A Manchu embassy proceeded to Petersburg, where
it was received in 1732, but the Russians turned down an offer of alliance
against the nomads. Zunghar ambitions served Russia's purpose well:
they maintained a buffer zone between western Siberia and the Manchu
Empire and they kept the Kazakhs at peace with the Russians in the still
undemarcated boundary between Russian settlements east of the Ural
River and in the Kurgan steppe. In fact, they imperceptibly pushed the
Kazakhs into the Russian orbit. The war was prosecuted with new vigor
by the Ch'ien-lung (Qianlong) emperor, the second great ruler of the
Manchu dynasty (1736–1796). In 1739, an agreement was reached set-
ting the Altai Mountain as the boundary between the Zunghars and the
Eastern Mongols, thereby expelling the Zunghars from the basin of Lake
Baikal and most of Outer Mongolia.

But the Manchus had not abandoned their goal of destroying the
Zunghars. Tribal confederations were always loose arrangements, and
their strength rested on that of the ruling clan. Internal dissensions that
weakened the leadership induced tribal leaders to go their own way. This
is what happened after Galdan Tsering's death in 1745. Not all tribal
leaders recognized the new chieftain, and one of them, Amursana,
became a bitter rival. His example was followed by other tribal chiefs,
some turning to the Russians for support, others to the Manchus. In
1754, Amursana defected to the Manchus. They used him to capture the
last Zunghar chieftain in 1755, but refused to recognize him as successor.
Amursana raised the banner of revolt once again, this time against the
Manchus. By then, Manchu power had become overwhelming in the
frontier. A large-scale offensive occupied Zungharia between the Altai
and the Tien Shan Mountains in 1756. Amursana fled to the Kazakhs and
was given asylum by the Russians. He died of smallpox the following year.
The epidemic killed large numbers of Zunghars, and the Ch'ien-lung

emperor ordered the systematic destruction of the others. The last steppe empire in the Russo-Chinese frontier had ceased to exist. In Kashgaria, south of the Tien Shan, where the religious leaders (*khojas*) installed by the Manchus in 1755 had massacred a Manchu mission in charge of collecting the tribute, Peking restored its authority in 1759.

The long struggle with the Zunghars had serious repercussions in Russia's frontier policy. The turbulence of the frontier was intensified by the division of the Kazakh world in three formations, the Little, Middle, and Great Hordes. The Little Horde roamed between the Caspian and the Tobol River; warfare with the Zunghars induced these Kazakhs to move farther west and give their allegiance to Russia in 1731. The Zunghar offensive of 1741–1742 caused mass migrations and frightened the sultans (horde leaders) of the Middle Horde into dividing their allegiance between the Russians and the Zunghars. Faced with so much uncertainty, the Russians pursued in part the close-border policy they had initiated in the 1710s. A fortified line of Cossack outposts was built along the Ural River in the 1730s, and a governor was appointed with extensive powers in Orenburg in 1744. The line was extended along the Ui River to Zverino-golovskoe on the Tobol River in the 1730s and 1740s; the Irtysh Line was completed between Omsk and Ust-Kamenogorsk. In the early 1750s, during the Zunghar civil war, Zverinogolovskoe was linked with Omsk via Petropavlovsk on the Ishim River, founded in 1752. A strategic boundary had been created, a line of an optimum of conquest, but a temporary one; the gravitation of the Kazakh hordes toward the lines would gradually bring about a switch to a forward policy a generation later.

Both the Russians and the Manchus had been pursuing a similar close-border policy in the Mongolian segment of the frontier. During the lull in the war with the Zunghars, the Russians made an attempt to restore relations interrupted in 1722. Savva Vladislavich, a Bosnian Serb from Ragusa with considerable diplomatic experience in Russian service, was appointed in August 1725 to head an embassy to Peking with instructions to discuss three major questions: boundary disputes, commercial relations, and the establishment of an ecclesiastical mission in Peking. Among those in his suite were Lange and Colonel Buchholz, by then quite familiar with the situation in the frontier. The embassy reached Peking in October 1726 and remained there until May 1727. Negotiations continued at Kiakhta, on a small tributary of the Selenga, where a number of agreements were signed in August and October, known collectively as the Treaty of Kiakhta.

The Treaty of Nerchinsk had ignored the Russo-Mongolian boundary. The Manchus knew the Russians had been seeking to push the line of their Cossack settlements upstream in the valley of the Selenga and along the caravan route to Peking, the periphery of the Heartland. The turbulence in Mongolia induced Mongol tribesmen and deserters from the banners (the Manchu military units) to seek refuge with the Russians, but the lack of a boundary agreement made it impossible to determine beyond what point a demand for extradition was justified. The Treaty of Kiakhta divided the boundary into two sectors. The eastern sector, 1046 kilometers long, began at Kiakhta, followed the Chikoi River, crossed over to the middle course of the Onon River, then followed the ecological boundary of the Daurian steppe to Abagaytuy on the Argun, where the Manchurian boundary established at Nerchinsk began. The western sector, 1664 kilometers long, followed the crest of the Dzhida chain past Lake Hobsogol (Hövsgol Nuur), swerved north to follow the Sayan chain, and continued to the Shabina Pass overlooking the Abakan valley. The western boundary kept Russia away from the Heartland's periphery—north of the Sayan Mountains and the sources of the Enisei. The eastern boundary confirmed Russia's establishment in the Coastland, beyond the Iablonoi range.

Commercial relations were placed on a new footing. Both Manchu and Chinese had been unhappy with the Russian official and private caravans and, in general, with the presence of the Russian merchants. Elsewhere in China, the Manchus had restricted foreign trade with British and other merchants to Canton, where the customs commissioner had access to the emperor and dealt with a guild of foreign merchants held responsible for the foreigners' behavior and financial solvency. The treaty extended this so-called Canton system to Russo-Chinese commercial relations. It allowed the Russians to run an official caravan every three years, but the Manchus later set so many restrictions that the caravan trade eventually came to an end. All other commercial transactions were restricted to two border points, Kiakhta and Tsurukhait (Priargunsk) on the Argun. The boundary settlement embodied a close-border policy pursued by both sides. The commercial settlement included a Manchu close-border policy, striking at the heart of Russia's intentions in the Eastern Frontier: the development of trade for fiscal reasons and ultimately, to reach political objectives.

Paradoxically, the Manchus recognized at the same time the existence of a Russian "ecclesiastical and diplomatic mission" of four young Orthodox priests. The model, of course, was the Jesuit mission that had made such a good impression at the Peking Court. The Russians were allowed to send four more youths, who knew Latin, to learn Chinese. It became a practice to send a mission every ten years, and thirteen would go to China between 1729 and 1859. A language school for Russians was inaugurated in 1728; students received a Chinese subsidy during their ten-year stay, and they had to wear Chinese dress.

Russia's Flanking Advance, 1759–1848

The energy fueling Russia's expansion across Siberia had been generated by an insatiable passion for the furs of beavers, sables, and foxes. It was hardly a coincidence that the Manchus should have brought that expansion to a halt at the entrance of Manchuria and at the gates of Mongolia, where it was well known that the quality of the fur was inferior to that expected among the animals of the Siberian forests. An economic impulse had been stopped by a combination of ecological change and political will backed by superior Manchu power. However, on the flanks of the Mongolian and Manchurian segments, in the Kazakh steppe-ocean and Zungharia on the one hand, and in the Russo-Japanese zone on the other, the frontier remained an "organic" frontier, in which every zone and subzone was part of a larger organism kept alive by the diversified ecology of the steppe and the sea and by the wanderings of their nomads, hunters, and fishermen. It has been said of the British that the frontier was the area in which their empire must expand[2]; so it was with the Russians. The geography of the Eastern Frontier facilitated the execution of one of those pincer movements to which the Russians resorted whenever faced with an obstacle to their advance into the frontier zones: a movement on a continental scale, one prong directed first from Orenburg, later from Omsk; the other from Irkutsk.

The lack of unity among the Kazakhs and their inability to form a powerful, even if temporary, confederation; the attraction of commerce along the military lines, and especially at Petropavlovsk, Omsk, and Orenburg; the nomads' need of access to the salt lakes, increasingly controlled by the Russians; disputes among tribal leaders into which the Russians were drawn willy-nilly; Kazakh depredations against Russian caravans crossing the steppe in the direction of Khiva and Bukhara and widespread horse rustling on both sides—all these factors made it impossible to pursue a rigid close-border policy. There were additional reasons why such a policy of exclusion was difficult to maintain. The Ural and Irtysh rivers were not ecological boundaries or physical obstacles, like the Sayan Mountains along the Mongolian boundary. Pastures extended beyond the Ural to the Volga and beyond the Irtysh to the Altai and Sayan; and beyond the artificial boundary created by the fortified line between the Ural and the Irtysh, into the Kurgan steppe as far north as Tiumen. Moreover, the Cossack way of life was a transitional form between the sedentary life of the settled peasant and the wandering life of the nomad; extensive agriculture and extensive livestock breeding had something in common. The Russian peasant had always been a nomad of sorts. The evolution of Kazakh society, caught between the Russian advance beyond the Ural Mountains and the Caspian and the transformation of the Chinese core area into a Manchu Empire following the incorporation of Mongolia, Zungharia, and Kashgaria, was slowly pushing the nomad into a more sedentary way of life, at least along the fortified line.

The three Kazakh hordes formed so many subzones, their gradual inclusion into the Russian orbit so many stages in the Russian advance. The Little Horde had given its allegiance to Russia in 1731. Separated from its bitter enemies, the Bashkirs and the Kalmyks (a tribe of Zunghars who had migrated to the shores of the Volga in the 1630s and returned to Zungharia in 1771), by the Ural River and the fortified line, its independence was gradually restricted as it passed under the jurisdiction of the Orenburg governor. Its khan, Abdulkhair, had been murdered in

August 1748 by a sultan leaning toward the Zunghars. His son, Nur Ali, was elected khan with the help of the governor. He proved to be a weak leader, unable to cope with the challenges to his authority and the increasing conflicts with the Cossacks. A harsh winter and large-scale seizures of Kazakh horses precipitated an uprising in 1783. It was crushed by the Russians, but Nur Ali was forced to flee; Catherine II deposed him in 1786. The Russians wanted to replace him with a mixed border authority representing Kazakh and Russian officials. The Kazakh elders wanted a new khan; they had to accept a Russian candidate. A border authority was finally created in March 1799, subordinated to the Orenburg governor. Some of these Kazakhs were allowed to cross the Ural River in 1801 to occupy the lands left vacant by the Kalmyks' departure. They were incorporated into the inner frontier of the empire and became known as the Internal Horde. The others remained outside the empire and retained their khan until 1824, when their pastures were divided into three districts: one between the Ilek and Temir rivers and the Aral Sea; a second between the upper Tobol, the Toguzak, and the Ayat; a third near the Syr Darya. Each district was headed by elders and sultans devoted to Russia. The reform created an extensive fringe of "nomadic settlement" beyond the fortified line, the official boundary of the empire, to the Syr Darya and the Kazakh upland, with an infrastructure of native men of power preparing the way for the Russian advance. Russian policy in the steppe-ocean recognized no permanent boundaries and accepted the truth of Friedrich Ratzel's famous statement that "the seemingly rigid border is but the temporary stop of a movement."[3] A close-border policy was slowly developing into a forward policy.

The Middle Horde, some 20,000 strong, roamed between the Tobol, the Irgiz, and the Irtysh and as far south as the middle course of the Syr Darya. These Kazakhs became known as the Siberian Kazakhs ("Kirgiz") because their relations with Russia depended on the Tobolsk governor and later, after 1822, on the governor general of western Siberia in Omsk. The Horde's chief leader, beginning in the 1750s until his death in 1781, was sultan Ablai, who did not become khan until 1771. The Great Horde, with about 54,000 nomads, migrated between the Talas and Ili Rivers as far away as the Zungharian Gate. The success of the Manchu offensive against the Zunghars brought Manchu troops into the grazing lands of both hordes and caused mass migrations toward the fortified line and a Russian military buildup in western Siberia. However, Ablai was recognized by the Manchus, who forbade the Middle Horde to graze east of the Ayaguz River that flows into the eastern end of Lake Balkhash. The Manchus were creating their own fringe of "nomadic settlement," the Great Horde forming the proximate zone between the boundary of their empire and the Russian lines. Ablai was required to pay tribute in children and horses.

But the Middle Horde continued to be racked by internal dissensions, the inevitable fate of the men of power in an intermediate frontier zone.

Some sultans, influenced by their neighbors in the Great Horde, remained faithful to the Manchus; others, influenced by the example of the Little Horde, leaned toward Russia. After Ablai's death, Petersburg and Peking backed two different khans. In 1805, Vali Khan sought to take the Middle Horde to Zungharia but failed. When he died in 1819, the Russians refused to recognize a new khan, and the Statute on the Administration of the Siberian Kazakhs of July 1822 abolished the office. It divided the horde's grazing lands into eight districts, including Akmolinsk (Tselinograd) on the Ishim, Sergiopol (Ayaguz) on the Ayaguz, and Kokpekty on the approaches to Lake Zaisan. The creation of the districts was not completed until 1844. It was followed by the construction of advanced fortified positions at Fort Uralsk (Irgiz) in 1845 and Fort Orenburg (Turgai) in 1848.

A small pincer movement within a larger one had slowly been taking place. Trade along the Irtysh Line, the growing settlement of the Altai region, and conflicts with the Cossacks reproduced the conditions found along the Orenburg Line. Other developments encouraged the pursuance of a forward policy. The sudden emergence of a powerful khanate in Kokand destabilized the Manchus' proximate zone in the Ili valley. In 1819, large numbers of men of power in the Great Horde, disturbed by Kokandi incursions, sought Russian support. A military settlement was built on the Karatal River in 1826, but Manchu objections forced its abandonment. By 1842, when Manchu power was in full decline, the Russians were established in the Ili valley. In 1847, following the assassination of the last khan, the entire horde entered the fringe of nomadic settlement. From then on, the Russians were ready to begin the conquest of the Persian frontier from their bases north of the Aral Sea and south of Lake Balkhash and to continue with the penetration of Zungharia in the Manchu Empire.

The Kazakh steppe, like the Ukrainian steppe in the Russo-Turkish frontier, had been "an area inviting entrance." The accumulated energy created by the industrial development of the Ural region, the crushing of Bashkir resistance to Russian colonization, and, beyond the Irtysh, the buildup of a military-economic base in the Altai Mountains, had propelled Russian power into the steppe-ocean and carried Russian influence from clan to clan and from horde to horde until that influence reached the Zungharian Gate, on the boundary between the Kazakh and Zunghar zones. The Manchus maintained a military presence in Zungharia and Kashgaria, separated by the easily crossed Tien Shan Mountains. They called these two zones their Western Region; others called them Eastern or Chinese Turkestan. A Manchu military governor was appointed in Hui-yuan (Huocheng), and commandants were assigned to the major cities including Urumchi (Ürümqi), Kulja (Gulja, Ili, Yining), and Tarbagatai-Chuguchak (Tacheng) in the north, and Kashgar in the south, from which trade routes led into Kashmir and Central Asia. The sway of the Manchus extended as far as the Fergana valley and Kokand, linked with Kashgar via Osh by a caravan route across the Alai range.

But the Manchus' position was weak, despite the remarkable projection of their power so deep into the frontier. By the end of the eighteenth century, the Russians had the advantage of greater accessibility to Zungharia. The extension of the Irtysh Line to the mouth of the Bukhtarma in the 1760s created a nexus of commercial interests in the valley of Lake Zaisan. A journey by camel from Semipalatinsk to Tarbagatai and Kulja took only two months one way, but it took from six to twelve months to go from the Chinese core area to Kulja. And the growth of Russian power began to coincide with the gradual weakening of the Manchu dynasty after the death of the Ch' ien-lung emperor in 1796. There were reports in 1812 that the Russians were seeking a share in the caravan trade between Kokand and Kashgar in order to reach the Chinese market at the western extremity of the Great Wall. The Manchus resisted, but Russian probings continued. In 1813 or 1814, a Russian detachment crossed Manchu picket lines near Tarbagatai. An aggressive Kokand khanate had come into being in 1808, and the grandsons of the Kashgar *khojas* who had fled the Manchus in 1759 were plotting to restore their family's rule in Kashgar. In 1820, one of them began to harry the border of the Manchu Empire in alliance with the freebooting Kirgiz. The climax came in 1830, when the Manchus sealed the border to Kokandi commerce, provoking a Moslem holy war and a successful invasion of Kashgaria that exposed their military weakness. And the Manchu weakness invited the Russian advance, for it is an axiom of frontier politics that "zones between two comparatively powerful states must be under the influence of one or the other of these states."[4] Internal disorders in the Chinese core area, the inability of the Manchus to cope with the British challenge to their exclusion policy, and their overextension in the wake of diminished resources and energy were creating a new situation in the frontier zones.

One prong of the giant pincer movement had taken the Russians across the Kazakh steppe-ocean to the edge of Chinese Turkestan; the other had taken them island-hopping from Kamchatka to northern Japan, even as far as Nagasaki, at the entrance of the Yellow Sea. Trade and the exceptionally rich marine ecology were the chief factors behind the advance into the Russo-Japanese frontier. That advance was nothing more than the continuation of the conquest of Siberia. Islands replaced the river valleys of the Great Lowland and the Lena upland within the Heartland as so many stepping stones into the unknown; and the expansion could not stop until Russia had occupied the entire frontier or had been contained within it.

The government-sponsored expeditions of Captain Vitus Bering of 1725–1730 and 1738–1741 had for their primary purpose the exploration of the northern Pacific and the survey of the Alaskan coast, but they could not leave out of account relations with the mysterious power beyond the Kuril archipelago. Indeed, the more distant the projection of Russian power, the greater the need to establish supply bases for the outfitting of ships and the provisioning of their crews in a favorable environment, far from the barren shores of the Sea of Okhotsk and the coast of Kamchatka. Bering was also fully aware that Japanese trade with the Ainu in the archipelago was an invitation to share in it, because the Russians, like the Ainus, had furs to barter; the Japanese had tools, food, and cloth. He recommended in April 1730 that an effort be made to open trade relations with Japan. The occasion came with his second expedition, "one of the most elaborate, thorough, and expensive expeditions ever sent out by any government at the time."[5] One of its members, Martin Spanberg, a Dane like Bering, was given a mission to survey the archipelago and establish friendly relations with Japan. He started out in June 1739, landed on the eastern coast of Honshu, and discovered an eagerness to deal with foreigners that sharply contrasted with the official insistence on maintaining the exclusion policy. The expedition had no immediate results. Bering was more successful: he founded Petropavlovsk on the eastern coast of Kamchatka in 1740, later to replace Okhotsk as Russia's naval headquarters in the Pacific, and he landed on the Alaskan coast.

There were two ways to seek trade relations with the Japanese. One was to follow the archipelago to Hokkaido, still sparsely populated—27,000 Japanese and 30,000 Ainus in 1765—but very dependent on trade; the other to send an expedition to Nagasaki, where some trade was conducted through the Dutch, sequestered on Deshima Island, off the waterfront. Both ways were tested, with few results. The Russians moved on from island to island, cutting into the hunting fields of the Ainus, in search of beavers and sea otters. An expedition led by the Cossack Chernyi took them across the broad central strait south of Simushir Island in the 1760s, a major step that had deterred his predecessors. Beyond the strait were the three large Islands of Urup (Uruppu), Iturup (Etorofu), and Kunashir(i) and beyond them Hokkaido, where the town of Akkeshi had been the entrepôt of Japanese-Ainu trade since the 1620s. The Russians had acted as if the smaller islands were already part of the Russian Empire, dutifully recording the allegiance of Ainu tribesmen who had no concept of it. But once they crossed into Urup, they encountered Ainu resistance to the collection of tribute and became conscious of the proximity of the Japanese. Nevertheless, they were ready to move on. Dmitrii Shabalin landed on Hokkaido and reached Akkeshi, where he was told in September 1779 not to come again. Japanese resistance encouraged the Ainus; earthquakes did the rest; and the Russians gave up hope of establishing a foothold on Hokkaido for the next decade.

The last quarter of the eighteenth century was the age of exploration in the northern Pacific. James Cook surveyed the North American coast to the Bering Strait in 1778 and twice visited Kamchatka; Jean-François La Perouse did much the same thing, but also crossed the Kuril archipelago and gave his name to the strait separating Sakhalin from Hokkaido, also called the Soya Strait; and George Vancouver explored the Alaskan coast and the Aleutian islands in 1793–1794. These explorations paved the way for the subsequent penetration of the northern Pacific by audacious

American whalers, who became a threat to Russia's exclusive control of the Alaskan panhandle. In 1785, the merchants Grigorii Shelikhov and the Golikov brothers, Ivan and Mikhail, formed a company with government support to coordinate mercantile activities and organize expeditions to establish trade relations with Japan, China, and Korea, and even the Philippines; they would exchange Siberian furs and fish for rice and salt. Trade inevitably carried the flag with it, and Alexander Vorontsov, the minister of commerce, advised the empress in 1786 to create a Pacific squadron to defend Russian possessions and back Russian demands for the opening of Japan to Russian trade. The difficulty was in finding a suitable port in the maritime frontier closer to Japan than distant Petropavlovsk.

Meanwhile, a number of castaways shipwrecked in 1783 on one of the Aleutian Islands had been sent to Irkutsk, where they arrived in February 1789. They aroused great curiosity, and one of them accompanied to Petersburg Eric Laxman, a Finnish-born naturalist who had been engaged in research in Eastern Siberia. Returning the castaways would provide a pretext for sending another expedition to Japan. In September 1791, Catherine II, convinced by Laxman's arguments, ordered the governor general of Irkutsk to prepare such an expedition under the command of Adam Laxman, Eric's son, a military officer. The expedition landed at Nemuro on Hokkaido in October 1792 and created a stir. The lord of Matsumae—the governor of Hokkaido—was informed and asked for instructions from Edo. The expedition was ordered to proceed to Hakodate, where Laxman was told in July 1793 that the exclusion policy still stood and that Japan would not open its doors. Laxman was back in Irkutsk in January 1794, but not without some hope the Japanese would receive a Russian ship in Nagasaki. The western port had lost some of its importance, however. The discovery of Hakodate's splendid bay raised hopes that the port might become a trade outlet and perhaps a naval base; such a development would revolutionize the geopolitics of the Russo-Japanese frontier. The expedition had created a precedent; an official exchange had taken place on the outer fringe of the Japanese core area between a Russian expedition and the Tokugawa government in Edo. Laxman had indeed been Russia's first envoy to Japan.

The company founded in 1785 had failed to prosper, in large part because this first Russian commercial enterprise on the very edge of the Coastland lacked a prosperous hinterland in the Heartland, while the great companies created by the maritime powers always had the advantage of being part of a vibrant and interdependent Coastland economy, slowly developing into the global economy that would form the foundation of British power. Owing to the influence of Nikolai Rezanov, Shelikhov's son-in-law and a high official in the Imperial government, the company was reorganized into the Russian-American Company in 1799, modeled after the British and Dutch East India companies. It would be no more successful than its predecessor, but the change of status marked a new stage in the history of the Russo-Japanese frontier: the government assumed the leadership of the Russian advance, and an essentially commercial venture was transformed into a strategic interest, raising military and naval considerations of the highest order.

There was a third way to reach Japan, no longer from Kamchatka to Hokkaido, considered by the Russians to be the last of the Kuril Islands, or from Kamchatka to Nagasaki directly, but from Kronshtadt, the headquarters of the Baltic fleet, around the Cape of Good Hope or Cape Horn. The distances were enormous, but the steamship remained until the laying of railroads the fastest and most capacious means of transport. Long before the opening of the Suez Canal, the sea route from the European to the Monsoon Coastland would become the lifeline of the British Empire.

A proposal by the Russian American Company in July 1802 to test the feasibility of supplying its outposts in the northern Pacific from the Imperial capital was accepted, and Captain Adam Krusenstern was appointed in August to command an expedition to circumnavigate the globe. Six months later, in February 1803, Nikolai Rumiantsev, the minister of commerce, recommended to Alexander I the sending of an embassy to Japan to establish friendly relations and open up the country to Russian trade. The tsar accepted the proposal and appointed Rezanov head of the mission. He and Krusenstern were to travel together and then go their separate ways as they approached Japan, Rezanov proceeding to Nagasaki, Krusenstern to the Aleutians. Krusenstern's ambitions were larger than Rezanov's; to establish regular communications between Kronshtadt and Alaska via Canton and, if possible, Japan. Russian furs would be sold in Canton for provisions destined to support the Pacific outposts, while cordage, sails, and anchors would be transported from Kronshtadt around the globe. The embassy left Petersburg in August 1803, rounding Cape Horn in March 1804. Rezanov reached Nagasaki in October, was allowed ashore, but had to wait until April 1805 to receive from Edo the usual answer: the shogunal government would not relax its exclusion policy.

Rezanov had failed, but he took his revenge. He encouraged two naval officers, Gavril Davydov and Nikolai Khvostov, to lead raiding parties along the Japanese coast. They left Petropavlovsk in May 1807, burned the Japanese settlement on Iturup, seized booty there and on Urup, and returned to Okhotsk in July after sinking a number of Japanese boats on the way. The Japanese had every reason to believe Russia had embarked on a new course to impose its rule by force on the Kuril Islands. Four years later, in 1811, when a Russian warship commanded by Vasilii Golovnin sent to survey the southern Kurils dropped anchor in July on the coast of Kunashir to seek fresh supplies, Golovnin and part of the crew were taken prisoner. He was able to convince the Japanese the two adventurers had acted on their own and was released in October 1813.

But Russian policy may have been taking a new course. Rivalry with the United States in the northeastern Pacific led the Imperial government to announce in September 1821 that Russian subjects had an exclusive right

to hunt and fish north of the fifty-first parallel (the northern end of Vancouver Island) and within 100 miles of the Alaskan coast, the Aleutian
Islands, and the Kuril chain to the southern end of Urup Island (lat.
45°50').[6] Russian warships were given orders to seize foreign ships found
within the new perimeter. The decision to erect a ring fence along the
Kuril chain showed a determination to pursue a fortress-fleet strategy and
protect Russian interests behind a "red line," the first stage of a policy of
autarkic seclusion. It stopped short of "closing" the Sea of Okhotsk, however, and implicitly recognized Japanese jurisdiction over Iturup and
Kunashir, the last and largest islands of the chain.

The Mongolian and Manchurian Frontier, 1759–1848

Russia's energies had focused after 1759 on the patient elaboration of a
forward strategy in the Kazakh steppe-ocean and the Kuril archipelago. Its
ultimate objective was to reach a line of an optimum of conquest deep into
the Eastern Frontier vis-à-vis both China and Japan, two powers in the
Monsoon Coastland determined to bar exchanges with other core areas or
restrict them to the barest minimum. Between the Kazakh steppe and the
Pacific, the Russian advance remained at a standstill after 1727; both the
Russians and the Manchus pursued a close-border policy serving a common interest. Nevertheless, the Russians kept trying to expand relations
with the Manchu dynasty and find a way to reach the Amur River. Indeed,
the "Amur question" was fated to become the dominant issue in the relations between the two core areas, because it was inextricably linked with
the broader issues of Russia's access to the Pacific, the destabilization of
the Manchurian frontier, and the fate of the Manchu dynasty itself.

The Kiakhta trade was an important part of Russia's total foreign trade.
In 1760, it contributed 20 percent of the customs revenue; in 1775, some
38 percent. The last government-sponsored caravan reached Peking in April
1763: Catherine II's government frowned on monopolies of any kind and
favored free trade, secure in its conviction that Russia had more to export
than it needed to buy. Prohibitions imposed in the 1730s and in 1752 on
the export of certain Siberian furs like Kamchatka and Iakut beavers and
sables, Nerchinsk and Iakut squirrels and foxes, were lifted. Russia imported
chiefly rhubarb, considered a medicinal plant at the time, and tea.

But the Kiakhta trade faced two obstacles. One was the Manchu government's refusal to look on trade as a purely commercial activity. Trade
was instead a political weapon to be used against the Russians whenever
disputes flared up over the flight of criminals into Russian territory. The
Manchus closed the Kiakhta trade on three occasions between 1762 and
1792. The other was the increasing competition of the Canton trade.
Goods reached Canton by sea from the Indian Ocean and the Pacific. The
Russians were barred from that trade: Kiakhta was the only border outpost where the Russo-Chinese trade was permitted, once the official caravan trade was abandoned. Russian traders—even those from the Kurils,

the Aleutians, and Alaska—had to take their furs to Okhotsk, cross into the Heartland to Iakutsk, navigate the Lena upstream and move on to
Irkutsk, then across Lake Baikal and Buriat country to Kiakhta. A ship
from the North American coast could transport more furs faster to Canton than several parties of Russian traders. The customs revenue fell dramatically; in 1785 it was half of what it had been four years earlier. The
explorations of the northern Pacific in the 1780s and 1790s were bound
to increase the competition to Russia's disadvantage. The Kiakhta trade
was reopened in February 1792, following negotiations between Ludwig
von Nagel, the governor of Irkutsk, and Chinese delegates. The official
protocol pointedly remarked that trade was a favor granted to the Russians as a reward for good behavior, as long as they were willing to "treat
our officials politely and deferentially."[7]

These developments explain the growing interest in Russian naval circles
and in the ministry of commerce in gaining access to the Canton trade and
to open up Japanese ports. Much more was involved than the need to supply Russian settlements in the northern Pacific. Russia, the dominant
power in the Heartland, was staking a claim to become a major player in
the Monsoon Coastland, using its raw-material base in Siberia and its
Pacific possessions to create a regional market gravitating toward the Kurils
and the Sea of Okhotsk. The vision was broad and daring, but flawed.
Despite the development of Irkutsk as a major administrative and military
center, East Siberia remained hampered by its sparse population, its climate, its distances and difficult terrain; it could not build an economic base
from which to compete with the British East India Company and the
United States across the Pacific. The importance of the Russian core area
vis-à-vis a declining China was growing, and the energy accumulated in
Irkutsk from those persistent probings in the northern Pacific was only
waiting to be harnessed by a vigorous proconsul and flung against China.
But Russia's position in what might be called a Russo-American frontier
across the Pacific was declining, and Russia's attempt to become a maritime power from its only foothold in the Coastland was destined to fail.

There was more. Russian foreign policy took for granted a number of
geopolitical assumptions—that space is power; that autarky is the highest
goal because it guarantees the security of a supposedly immutable political
order; that a continental economy (*Grossraumwirtschaft*) must be protected
by a ring fence, a red line to keep foreigners out, even though the red line
kept advancing. An exclusion policy was always a built-in component of the
Russian outlook. But not all space is power; autarky and economic leadership are incompatible; and the exclusion of outsiders maintains backwardness and defeats political ambitions. This dilemma between political
ambitions and an exclusion policy would continue to plague the Russian
advance into the Eastern Frontier and in the end would defeat it.

The Manchu government showed no inclination to admit Russia to the
Canton trade. In January 1806, Peking asked the Russian Senate whether
Krusenstern's trip to Canton with a cargo of furs had been authorized by

Petersburg and represented Russia's intention to abandon the Kiakhta trade. Without waiting for an answer, Peking ordered the governor general responsible for Canton to expel Krusenstern and refuse admittance to any Russian ship in the future. But China was increasingly on the defensive. The development of its economy left Russia behind the European Coastland powers and the German states, but pushed it far ahead of China and shifted the balance of power in the frontier against China. Siberia's population was growing—it doubled from 1.5 million to 2.9 million between 1815 and 1854, although it was chiefly concentrated in western Siberia. By contrast, that of Mongolia may have declined and that of northern Manchuria remained insignificant. China became the only market for Russian manufactures: they could not compete on the European markets. Russian exports via Kiakhta rose sixfold from 1825 to 1859, imports sevenfold, but the share of the China trade in Russia's total foreign trade declined to between 15 and 20 percent.

The Opium War and the Anglo-Chinese Treaty of Nanking in August 1842 dealt a mortal blow to the Kiakhta trade. The treaty opened five ports in southern China to foreign trade, abolished the monopoly in Canton, and gave extraterritorial rights to foreigners. Britain did not pursue an exclusive policy. Still secure in its position as the leader of the world's economy, it did not create ring fences but broke them down and extended far and wide the networks of economic exchanges because they also strengthened the sinews of British power. The treaty contained a most-favored-nation clause: Russia and other nations were invited to join it. There was no time to lose. Britain quickly gained a dominant share of China's trade—68 percent of its imports, 60 percent of its exports in 1844. Russia ranked second with 19 and 16 percent, respectively. The overland Kiakhta trade had become anachronistic; the future continued to belong to seaborne trade.

In the Chinese world order, the Russians were "barbarians," the Cossacks were no different from the nomads who had kept the frontier insecure for centuries, and the Russian Empire was another of those political confederations that had no choice but to gravitate around the Middle Kingdom, the center of the universe, and its emperor, who had the Mandate of Heaven. These assumptions underlay the paternalistic attitude of the Peking government toward the "tributary states," despite the fact that they were not all of a kind and that it was known in Peking that the Cossack nomads were backed by a powerful government with a developed military infrastructure in Siberia, along the frontier's edge. But the vast expanse of the frontier and the multiplicity of zones operating as so many buffers between Russians and Chinese meant the two peoples were seldom in direct contact except in Kiakhta, and in fact often had a similar interest—to put an end to tribal conflicts and reduce the turbulence in the zones in order to secure their respective authority and control.

Both Russians and Chinese sought to obviate potential conflicts. Even before their conquest of China in 1644, the Manchus had reorganized an already existing Mongolian Office into the Li-fan Yüan, the Board of Colonial Affairs, a kind of "barbarian control office"[8] to manage relations with the Mongols and, later, the Tibetans and the Uighurs of Turkestan. During the Kiakhta negotiations in 1727, the Russians requested that their relations with Peking be included in the Li-fan Yüan's jurisdiction, thereby accepting their place in the "barbarian" community. There was a simple reason for the request. Direct correspondence between the Manchu office and the Russian Senate would leave the two emperors out, and the Russian tsar-emperor would no longer be subjected to the condescending and offensive communications of the Manchu emperor to his vassal, the "White [western] Khan" in Petersburg.[9] But one detects a more subtle reasoning as well. By accepting, or pretending to accept, its place, Russia entered the Chinese world order and, like other barbarians in China's long history, might some day want to claim the inheritance of the Chinese core area. Were not the Manchus themselves a barbarian people? Once inside the system, frontier relations and even relations with the core area became "internal affairs" to be decided between Petersburg and Peking, without the interference and even the good offices of foreign governments. It is clear that the Russians adopted a unified ideological approach to their relations with the Turkish, Persian, and Chinese core areas; it was no coincidence that they were combined after 1797 and especially after 1819 under the jurisdiction of the Asiatic Department.

For their part, the Manchus sought to prevent conflicts by pursuing one of the most systematic close-border policies ever attempted. After the Treaty of Nerchinsk, many natives had been removed from the vicinity of the new Russo-Chinese border. A century later, in 1776, the Ch'ien-lung emperor, faced with Chinese population pressures, forbade Chinese immigration in two of the three provinces of Manchuria, Kirin and Heilungkiang. The effect was to leave Manchuria a virtual desert, the hunting preserve of the dynasty and the depository of its memories. A similar policy was pursued in Mongolia. In addition, there and in Tibet, the Manchus supported Lamaism, a strict form of Buddhism emphasizing celibacy. Such a systematic depopulation policy created a vacuum in both Mongolia and Manchuria, reducing the possibility of Russo-Chinese conflicts but also paradoxically challenging the Russians to lay claim to these two segments of the frontier as soon as the balance of forces began to tilt in their favor.

The first attempt to challenge the status quo took place in the early years of the nineteenth century. In 1803, Nikolai Rumiantsev had won the tsar's approval to send an expedition to Japan. The minister of commerce was the son of Marshal Rumiantsev, who had broken the Ottoman hold on the Russo-Turkish frontier in the 1770s. He was the strong supporter of a policy to continue his father's work in fostering the Russian advance in the Southern Frontier; he was determined to challenge Japan in the Pacific segment of the Eastern Frontier and ready to assert Russia's authority in the entire overland frontier from the Kazakh steppe to the

Pacific. In January 1805, he advised Alexander I to broaden the scope of an expedition to Peking, originally intended to announce the tsar's accession, into a "grandiose enterprise."[10] The embassy would seek China's agreement to open up both Canton and Nanking to Russian trade, to allow that trade not only on the tiny Bukhtarma but also along the entire Irtysh Line, and to let Russian caravans cross Chinese Turkestan on their way to India through the Karakoram Pass.

The choice of an ambassador fell on Count Iurii Golovkin, a "vain, haughty, and superficial"[11] individual, ill-suited for such a delicate mission. His instructions incorporated several of Rumiantsev's proposals. They also called for the opening of trade at Ili and Tarbagatai, the opening of the Amur to Russian shipping and the appointment of a consul at the river's mouth, the establishment of diplomatic relations with Peking with an ambassador in the Chinese capital, and the sending of "supervisors" with Kalmyk pilgrims going to Lhasa in Tibet, the center of Lamaism. The Russians were exploiting for the first time the religious unity of the Buddhist frontier zones in Mongolia and Tibet in order to send their Lamaist subjects to penetrate the frontier. The rivalry between Chinese Buddhism and Lamaism promised to create a "dissident" movement, a destabilizing factor in the frontier, which the Russians had already used to their advantage in the Western and Southern frontiers.

The Golovkin embassy was a head-on challenge to the Chinese concept of the world order, but it was premature. The Manchus were still strong in Turkestan and on the Amur, and Russia, engaged at the time in the great struggle with Napoleon for supremacy in the Prussian and Austrian core areas, could not spare the troops to back up its political and commercial ambitions with the threat of force. The time had not yet come to claim the Manchu inheritance in the frontier. Golovkin arrived in Kiakhta in October 1805 and discovered that the Manchus would treat him as a "tribute-bearing envoy" and expect him to perform the kowtow. They demanded the reduction of his impressive suite to sixty or seventy persons. He was then allowed to proceed to Urga, and reached Kalgan on the Great Wall in January 1806. There he refused to perform the kowtow before a silk screen concealing a tablet representing the emperor, whereupon the embassy was summarily dismissed in February for being "ignorant of our ceremonials."[12] It had not even reached Peking.

This dismal failure seems to have left no rancor, however. Russia abandoned its ambitious goals in favor of returning to its more traditional policy of pretending to accept its position among the "barbarians." Four years later, the Manchus accepted a Russian offer to discuss relations, and the Irkutsk governor, Nikolai Treskin, traveled to the Mongolian border for an exchange of views with the two governors of Urga in March 1810. The kowtow was not required, but Treskin conformed to Chinese etiquette and won the friendship of the governors. The Manchus asked for another Russian embassy; Treskin would not consent unless they agreed to send an embassy to Petersburg. The Manchus were not ready to accept

Russia's equality, and the talks had no immediate results. Nevertheless, they proved to be another stage in the cultivation of Mongol men of power that would later prove so useful in the extension of Russian influence in the frontier zone. After 1810, Russia no longer pressed Peking to change course; it focused its energies on the Kazakh steppe, where prospects were bright.

Stalled in the Mongolian and Manchurian segments of the frontier by Manchu power and resistance, Russian energies found an outlet in a flanking advance into the Kazakh steppe and the Pacific frontier. But this change of course did not end the pressure to gain access to the Amur River. The logic of Russian expansion since the sixteenth century had been to advance in the direction of the Pacific; the simplest and more profitable way to it always remained the Amur valley.

The Russians intended to prepare for the day when the Manchus might be induced or forced to let them use the mighty river. In December 1753, a so-called Nerchinsk Secret Expedition (office) was created under the jurisdiction of the governor of Siberia in Tobolsk with the mission to open a navigation school and build boats on the rivers converging to form the Amur, to survey the approaches to the river, and in general to lay the foundations of a communications network linking Irkutsk with the Manchurian border. Two schools were created, one in Irkutsk, the other in Nerchinsk, where a shipyard built river boats to transport provisions from Irkutsk across Lake Baikal on the Khilok and the Ingoda to the Shilka. A separate governor was appointed in Irkutsk in 1764, to emphasize Russia's determination to assert its authority in eastern Siberia. But the Manchus were no less determined to bar Russian access to the river and were as strong in the 1760s as they had been at Nerchinsk in 1689. They regularly patrolled the border regions, "terribly cold and without water, grass, beast or bird,"[13] and could count on reinforcements should the Russians try a *coup de main* on the Amur. Their decision to close the Kiakhta trade for long periods clearly showed they had the upper hand. Russia was in no position to pursue a forward policy, and the Nerchinsk Expedition was closed in January 1765.

The exploration of the Pacific frontier gave the Amur question a new twist. Okhotsk was not a suitable location for the headquarters of Russian activities in the Coastland, both naval and commercial. Petropavlovsk in Avacha Bay faced the Pacific but had no hinterland and had to be supplied from Okhotsk. The numerous parties sent to explore the Okhotsk coast discovered not a single suitable location for a port. A half-hearted attempt was made at the mouth of the Aldoma, but was quickly abandoned. Attention began to turn to the mouth of the Amur. If the river could be reached from its source in the west, a port might be built at its mouth in the east. Such a port would cut distances to the Kuril archipelago; but its real value would be to provide an outlet to the Tatar Strait and the Sea of Japan. One could not be sure, however, until it was determined that Sakhalin was an island. La Perouse had entered the strait in 1787 but concluded that the narrow passage between the modern settlements of Lazarev and Pogibi was a sand bar connecting Sakhalin with the mainland.

Laxman's expedition to Japan in 1792 reflected a renewed determination, for the first time since the 1760s, to reach a settlement with China in the Amur question. Laxman himself was in favor of using the Amur as the shortest way to the Pacific and Japan. He had the support of Ivan Iakobi, the enterprising former governor general of Irkutsk, whose father had been commandant in Selenginsk for twenty-eight years (1740–1768). The governor general had been recalled in 1789 on trumped-up charges that he planned to embroil Russia in a war with China. Back in Petersburg, he recommended the annexation of the Amur and the creation of a port at its mouth to trade with Korea and Japan. In 1801, Gustav Strandmann, the former commanding general of Russian garrisons in Siberia (1789–1798), recommended the annexation of the Amur's left bank to open up trade with Japan, North America, and India, and to supply Okhotsk and Kamchatka by sea instead of overland from Iakutsk. If China refused to concede the left bank, force should be used. Strandmann added the revealing comment that Russia would then be in a position "to force China to trade with us, even to the exclusion of other people, and in places (we) considered most advantageous."[14] Here was the clear expression of an autarkic policy seeking not the opening of Manchuria to the world economy but its inclusion behind a ring fence excluding other trading nations. It is doubtful such a policy would raise Russia's "fame and greatness to the highest level," but the goal of autarky can create a seductive mirage for those willing to be deceived.

Rumiantsev's proposals and Golovkin's instructions were more modest in scope: China should grant the right of passage to several Russian ships a year loaded with grain and other provisions destined for settlements on the Sea of Okhotsk and on Kamchatka. There were no more than 1600 troops in the entire region at the time, but more than 14,000 horses were required to supply them from Iakutsk, a heavy burden on the natives. In the meantime, Krusenstern had tried to discover a passage between Sakhalin and the mainland, but ice and fogs had foiled his attempt. The next forty years were spent collecting information, sometimes from fugitive convicts seeking redemption. Two of them told local authorities in 1828 that the Amur was navigable, without rapids, that its mouth was thirty kilometers wide, and, not far off, there was a big island. But Petersburg rejected recommendations to send an expedition down the river.

Two important developments followed the Opium War. One was the Middendorf expedition of 1844–1845. It explored the valleys of the Bureia and the Zeia, and discovered Chinese markers well south of the Nerchinsk supposed boundary, implicitly conceding to Russia an additional 54,000 square miles. The expedition also discovered that some of the tribes that had been paying the fur tribute to Russia had migrated eastward because no more animals could be found in the old hunting grounds; however, they had continued to bring their tribute to the same Russian authorities near the Amur boundary. In other words, the tribes' migration had extended the fringe of Russian authority deeper into the frontier. These discoveries, made at a time when the Manchu dynasty was losing its grip on the frontier, raised hopes that the time might have finally come to resume the advance into the Manchurian frontier. On the other hand, a Captain Gavrilov, sent by the Russo-American Company to try to find a passage between Sakhalin and the mainland, concluded in July 1846 that there was none. Nicholas I declared the Amur to be "a useless river."[15] The Amur question seemed to have reached a dead end.

8

On the Offensive, 1848–1894

The Manchurian Frontier

The appointment of General Nikolai Muravev at the age of 39 as governor general of Eastern Siberia in 1847 was a decisive event in the history of Russia's frontier policy. But his success would not have been possible without the disintegration of Manchu power in the valley of the Amur, the weakening of the Chinese core area, and the increasingly forceful intervention of the maritime powers. The balance of power that had favored China in the Eastern Frontier since the seventeenth century was shifting dramatically in Russia's favor. The time had finally come to claim the Manchus' inheritance.

The solution of the Amur question could not proceed until it had been determined beyond any doubt whether Sakhalin was an island. Gavrilov's conclusions were not found convincing everywhere, and a naval officer, Gennadii Nevelskoi, decided to make another try on his own. Appointed to command a ship transporting supplies from Kronshtadt to Okhotsk and Petropavlovsk, he left the capital in August 1848 and reached Petropavlovsk in May 1849. There, much to his satisfaction, he found a draft of Muravev's instructions (not yet confirmed by Nicholas I) to explore the mouth of the Amur and the Sakhalin coast. In June, he sailed around the northern end of Sakhalin, entered the estuary of the Amur, and discovered a "canal," 7.5 kilometers wide, with a strong current that took him into the Tatar Strait to the latitude reached by La Perouse in 1787. The canal is now known as the Nevelskoi (Mamiya) Strait.[1] It was the mouth of the river; the river led to the Sea of Japan; Sakhalin was an island.

When the news reached Petersburg, Nevelskoi was severely criticized for exceeding his original instructions, but Muravev's support saved him from punishment. In July 1850, he sailed up the Amur, a short distance from its mouth, and founded Fort Nikolaevsk. The tsar supported the move, saying that "when the Russian flag has been raised, it must not be lowered."[2] The fear of an armed conflict with China and the unwillingness to cause tension with Britain during the 1840s that marked a lull in the Russo-British antagonism had not been the only reasons for the long reluctance to force the issue. There were ideological reasons as well. Among those opposed to Nevelskoi was the governor general of western Siberia, Petr Gorchakov, who wrote to the war minister that Russia did not need the Amur, that the desolate basin of the Sea of Okhotsk was an adequate frontier for Siberia to protect its inhabitants against contact with foreigners with their dreadful propaganda and their encouragement of disorders. Gorchakov was calling for Russia's self-containment behind the Heartland's boundary, with only a foothold in the Coastland between the Iablonoi and the Argun, a policy of economic and political autarky.

But Muravev was committed to a forward policy and was supported by his government. In February 1851, the Li-fan Yüan was informed that since the Amur began at the Russo-Chinese border and the frontier was inadequately demarcated, the river was the common possession of both powers and that no other power must be allowed to navigate it or establish a settlement at its mouth. Peking did not answer this overt claim to treat the Amur question as part of Russia's and China's internal affairs, but Muravev was determined to proceed as if it were. The appearance of American whalers in the Tatar Strait caused anxiety in Irkutsk, and the discovery of coal deposits on Sakhalin in 1852—at a time when the maritime powers were searching for coaling stations to supply their steamers on long-distance voyages—convinced Muravev a race was on for the control of the Tatar Strait. Two more forts were built on the strait in 1853, in De Kastri Bay and "Imperial Harbor" (Imperatorskaia-Sovetskaia Gavan), a third on Lake Kizi (Mariinskoe), an offshoot of the Amur.

An additional impetus to the Russian advance was the Crimean War. Britain and France declared war on Russia in March 1854, raising the possibility of a naval attack on Petropavlovsk. It actually took place in August, but failed. Muravev was now determined to risk a conflict with China. In January, he had been empowered by the tsar to negotiate territorial questions. A Transbaikal Cossack Host was created to man the future settlements. In May, Muravev sailed down the river for the first time, and sent reinforcements to Petropavlovsk. The Manchus did not move. Now confident that time was on his side, he informed Peking in May 1855 of his intention to send down a second party and offered to meet Chinese negotiators at the confluence of the Sungari. At a brief meeting in September, they were told Russia wanted the right to navigate the Amur and the removal of tribal settlements under Manchu jurisdiction on the river's left bank. The second expedition left 7000 Russian settlers to winter in the new settlements, and Fort Nikolaevsk became the administrative and military center for the lower Amur. Both expeditions exposed the now hopeless state of Manchu defenses. A third expedition in May 1856 deposited more settlers, and its leader told the Manchus there were 10,000 Russians at the river's mouth and another 5000 were expected. The Manchus could no longer dislodge the Russians; by the end of 1856, the annexation of the Amur valley north of the river had become a fait accompli.

At the very time Muravev was celebrating his triumph, Manchu China, weakened by the Taiping Rebellion that had begun in the Yangtse valley in 1850 and would not end until 1864, found itself embroiled in a second war with Britain, the so-called Arrow War. Military operations did not go into high gear until after the crushing of the Sepoy Mutiny in India in 1857. When it became known that the British, supported by the French, were prepared to send a substantial force to negotiate a new agreement with China to open ten new treaty ports, keep a legation in Peking, and travel without restrictions in China's interior, the Russians were for the first time faced with a choice between supporting the Anglo-French undertaking to pressure China and posing as the Manchu dynasty's defender in its time of trial in order to obtain as a reward territorial and other concessions. Egor Kovalevsky, the director of the Asiatic Department, recommended the second option, arguing that Britain could not be allowed to take Peking, any more than Herat; that the establishment of British power in Herat would draw Central Asia into Britain's orbit; and that the control of the Manchu dynasty would "paralyze all our beginnings on the shores of the Pacific and on the Amur."[3]

Kovalevsky's position was traditional. It had always been the Russian government's assumption, in Sweden, in Poland, in Persia, and even in Turkey, that Russia's interest was to encourage the rotting process in the surrounding core areas in the name of legitimism, in order to obtain maximum advantages from weak rulers, governments, and dynasties willing to "cling to a serpent"[4] to save their power. Subversion in the name of conservatism was always the hallmark of Russian foreign policy. Convinced by Kovalevsky's arguments, Petersburg appointed Admiral Evfim Putiatin, a naval officer hostile to Britain, minister to China in February 1857. The admiral was no stranger to frontier politics. In 1842, he had been sent on a diplomatic mission to Persia and was a believer in a strong naval presence in the Caspian in order to extend Russia's influence from its foothold in Asterabad. In 1855, he had finally opened Japan to Russia.

Putiatin was instructed to give the British and French no material aid but to offer instead to defend Manchuria for the dynasty. Unaware of this, the Manchus first refused him admittance through Mongolia and Manchuria. Undeterred, he sailed down the Amur and reached Tientsin (Tianjin), Peking's port, at the beginning of August. He was again refused admittance. He returned in April 1858, when the war was about to reach a decisive stage, and was finally given a hearing. He offered military assistance and convinced the Manchus he could influence the allies to moderate their demands. This illusion explains why the Manchu government signed a treaty with Putiatin in June, only two weeks before the British and French signed their own Treaty of Tientsin at the end of the month.

Meanwhile, Muravev had conducted separate negotiations with Manchu authorities in northern Manchuria. The Treaty of Aigun, signed in May, was a boundary treaty, negotiated from a position of strength. The *rapport de forces* that had prevailed at Nerchinsk in 1689 had been exactly reversed in Russia's favor. The treaty conceded to Russia the entire left bank of the Amur, but it turned out that Fort Nikolaevsk was an icebound port, largely useless: the Amur's estuary and most of the Tatar Strait froze in winter because the enormous outflow of the river reduced everywhere the salinity of seawater, as far away as the southern Kurils. But the Russian advance to the river's mouth had already created its own expansionist momentum, its own logic of expansion. The energy accumulated during decades of patient waiting for the collapse of Manchu power had to continue beyond the left bank until the entire valley had been occupied, just as an advance to the foothills of a mountain range must continue until it incorporates the passes and the foothills on the other side.

Moreover, Muravev and others were all too aware of the growth of American power in the northern Pacific. American whalers had ignored the ring fence from the Aleutians to the Kurils. Commodore Perry had opened Japan ahead of the Russians. Americans looked to the Pacific as their Mediterranean and on the rivers flowing into it as their trade routes into the interior. Russia could not accept the creation of "a new California on the Amur."[5] An American presence there backed by American economic power would generate a gravitational pull toward the Pacific in Russia's foothold in the Coastland, beyond the Iablonoi and Stanovoi ranges; it would spread republican ideas into Siberia and create dangerous centrifugal forces in the basin of Lake Baikal. The Amur question kept raising a larger issue—the consolidation of Russia's position in the Coastland. To achieve that goal, Russia could not resort to a forward policy, a fleet-in-being strategy, in the Pacific, because Siberia did not provide a sufficiently strong population and economic base to support such a policy. Its only option was to protect its foothold behind a close-border policy and a fortress-fleet strategy. The question facing Russian policymakers was to determine where a line of an optimum of conquest lay.

These considerations explain the other provisions of the Treaty of Aigun. Muravev obtained the recognition of a joint Russo-Chinese dominion in the so-called Maritime Province between the right bank of the Amur, the Ussuri River to Lake Hanka, and the Sea of Japan. The coast of that sea was almost as barren as that of the Sea of Okhotsk, seemingly without any bay suitable for a major port—until Muravev discovered one, south of Lake Hanka, where he would found Vladivostok in 1860. That the port would "dominate the east," as its name proclaimed, was far from certain; that it would be a major link in the ring fence protecting the valley of the Amur was all too obvious. The treaty also gave Russia joint navigation rights on the Sungari River (as well as on the Amur and the Ussuri), to the exclusion of other powers. There was no question there of promising most-favored-nation privileges to other powers. The treaty was a family affair. The Sungari watered the Manchurian plain; it was the hydrographic axis of Manchuria. Access to it could some day extend Russian influence up the Nonni and, beyond the Changchun hills, to the Liao valley. Muravev's was a daring geopolitical vision of Russia's future in the Coastland. It contained the program of Russia's expansion for the next half century.

The Treaty of Tientsin did not deal with boundary questions—Putiatin had been forbidden in January to discuss them. He obtained for Russia the same privileges granted by the Treaty of Nanking first to Britain, then to France and the United States. Russo-Chinese relations were placed on a footing of equality; correspondence would henceforth be conducted between the Russian ministry of foreign affairs and the Manchu head of government. Peking was not yet open to foreigners, and the Russian representative would have to reside in one of the treaty ports. Missionaries were allowed to travel in China's interior. The exclusive Kiakhta trade was abolished, but no mention was made of navigation rights on the Sungari. Regular postal communications were established between Kiakhta and Peking, but the Manchus refused to let the Russians lay a telegraph line between the two cities. Not included in the treaty was an informal acceptance of Russian military assistance, including instructors, in July.

The two treaties had been signed but were not ratified, nor was the treaty signed by China with Britain and France. When the Manchu emperor was persuaded to reject it, war resumed in June 1859 and did not end until after the occupation of Peking in October 1860. The Anglo-French decision to take the war to the capital compelled the Manchus to withdraw their limited forces from Manchuria, leaving the region totally defenseless and the Manchu government at the mercy of the Russians. In January 1859, Petersburg had appointed General Nikolai Ignatev its political agent in China; his mission was to secure the ratification of the two complementary treaties. Ignatev was only 27, but, like Putiatin, no stranger to frontier politics. He had played a role in the Paris negotiations following the Crimean War, and had just returned from a trade mission to Khiva and Bukhara; he would later make a controversial career in the Balkans. Ignatev went to China with a "huge convoy"[6] of arms, but left them in Urga before continuing to Peking. They could also be used to finance Mongol "dissidents" against Manchu rule.

Ignatev encountered resistance in Peking. The Manchus refused to ratify the Aigun treaty, claiming that their local commander who had signed it did not have the authority to do so. They insisted that the Nerchinsk treaty was still valid, and that the left bank had only been loaned to the Russians to help them protect it against a British attack. But Ignatev wanted not only the treaty's ratification, he had additional claims: the cession of the Maritime Province in Russia's full possession and the appointment of consuls in several towns of Chinese Turkestan. While he was negotiating in Peking, Muravev was continuing his explorations of the coast of the Maritime Province. He discovered Posiet Bay, another attractive site, and reached the mouth of the Tumen in June. The river, with the Yalu flowing in the opposite direction, formed the historical boundary of Korea. Muravev sailed on and reached Tientsin in July, convinced that the entire coastline from the Amur's mouth to Posiet Bay, if not to the mouth of the Tumen, must belong to Russia. The organic unity of the Pacific frontier was such that Russia's access to the mouth of the Amur triggered a chain reaction across the entire frontier. The Amur question raised the Sakhalin question and the Korean question and the Japan question, making it well-nigh impossible to agree on a line of an optimum of conquest.

Muravev kept Ignatev informed of his latest explorations. The envoy played a subtle game. In total secrecy from the other side, he encouraged the British and French to use force and raise their demands, while encouraging the Manchus to resist, but was unable to convince Peking to accept his arms and the instructors left behind in Urga. After Lord Elgin, the British commander, ordered the burning of the Summer Palace to compel the Manchus to open the gates of Peking and capitulate, Ignatev worked to moderate the allied demands and posed as the dynasty's savior. His reward was the Treaty of Peking in November 1860, negotiated in such secrecy that the allies remained in total ignorance. That Ignatev followed a pattern of deception there is no doubt, but his behavior was already part of a characteristic pattern. The Russians would avoid using force and causing a showdown with unpredictable repercussions that would reverberate across the entire land frontier from the Zungharian Gate to the Pacific; they would seek whenever possible to avoid being identified with the maritime powers eager to use force and to show their contempt for the Chinese. After all, was not the settlement of frontier issues—the only issues affecting Russo-Chinese relations while the maritime powers were trampling on the integrity of the core area—part and parcel of the "internal affairs" of the Russian Empire and the Manchu dynasty?

The treaty took up three major questions. It ceded the Maritime Province to Russia and abandoned the fiction of joint dominion. The land boundary followed the Amur, the Ussuri, and the Sangacha rivers to Lake Khanka, and then, beyond the lake, the Tur and Khubtu rivers, finally crossing overland to the coast, twenty Chinese miles east of the Tumen's mouth. It confirmed the Treaty of Tientsin but also "supplemented" it with new provisions governing the passage of Russian merchant caravans through Kiakhta, and allowed Russia to open a consulate in Urga but not in Kalgan on the Great Wall. Russian merchants were given extraterritorial status and placed under the "special protection" of both the Russian and Chinese governments. Finally, the treaty established procedures for communications between border authorities on the basis of "perfect equality"—the governor general of Eastern Siberia and the military governor of the new Amur province in Blagoveshchensk on the Russian side, the military governors of Heilungkiang in Aigun and of Kirin on the Manchu side. The following year, in 1861, Russia, together with Britain and France, opened a permanent legation in Peking, and an additional convention was signed in March 1862 regulating the overland trade.

The next three decades following the Treaty of Peking marked a lull in the Russian advance in the Manchurian frontier; it was a period of stocktaking. The energy of the Russian core area, intensified by the Great Reforms that created new demands in all spheres of public and private life, focused on the rounding out of Russia's possessions in the Pacific frontier and the conquest of Central Asia. We witness a new flanking advance similar to the one that had taken place before Muravev's arrival in Irkutsk. The advance into the Russo-Japanese frontier, in a persistent attempt to find adequate resources to support Russia's forward positions in the Coastland, not from a hopelessly undeveloped hinterland but from more favorable locations in the Coastland, antagonized Japan; the conquest of Central Asia developed its own logic of expansion and took the Russians beyond the Zungharian Gate to the headwaters of the Ili and the Tien Shan passes, almost provoking a war with China.

The willingness to risk a military conflict with China and Japan was an intrinsic factor in any policy groping to find a line of an optimum of conquest. As the Russians surveyed their position in the Manchurian frontier, they discovered their prospects were not bright. In 1872, they moved their naval headquarters from Nikolaevsk, icebound for six months and fogbound for several months more, to Vladivostok. Twelve years later, the Irkutsk Military District was split in two, with the creation of a new one for the Amur region in Khabarovsk, thereby completing the strategic encirclement of Manchuria. But Russia had only 15,000 troops in eastern Siberia in 1883 and 30,000 in 1895, facing an indeterminate number of Chinese. By 1890, Manchu China had built the largest navy in the northern Pacific; it was anchored at Port Arthur. Vladivostok's position as the "dominator of the east" was being threatened from Kirin and Port Arthur, all the more so since the provisioning of the Maritime Province depended on imports from Kronshtadt.

The recognition of Russia's vulnerability in the Manchurian and Pacific frontiers exposed the fundamental dilemma in its Coastland policy. An internal memorandum written in 1881 by the former secretary of the commander in chief of Russian naval forces in the Pacific declared that "in 1860 we obtained from China a luxuriant region. In 20 years, we made absolutely nothing out of it. On the contrary, we ourselves are promoting its impoverishment and ultimate ruin, while obtaining from all its riches not a single kopeck of profit."[7] But there could be no sustained development of the Russian Far East without a willingness to create "a new California," and that could not be done by building a ring fence but only by opening up the frontier to foreign capital and its nefarious influences on a conservative political order. The Russians had entered the Coastland but refused to enter the global economy. Their highly developed geopolitical sense should have taught them that the destiny of the Coastland regions was with the great oceans and not with the Heartland.

There was still a promising way out. Connecting Irkutsk and Vladivostok with European Russia by means of a railroad would facilitate the provisioning of the Coastland, accelerate the deployment of troops, and inaugurate the resettlement of peasants from the overpopulated Black Earth provinces to the Amur valley. The railroad promised to reorient the destiny of the Coastland regions by making them face the Heartland. That it was a hopeless dream could not yet be known. The decision was made in February 1891 to build a line across Siberia beginning at Cheliabinsk in the southern Urals and ending at Vladivostok. The new Russian finance minister, Sergei Witte, told the tsar in November 1892 that the new line would be a "weapon" to strengthen the Russian navy in the Pacific and give Russia "control of the entire movement of international commerce" in Pacific waters. Russia needed to be at peace with China in order eventually to bring the economy of northern China into the Russian orbit and cause a "reversal in the direction of communications between Europe and the Asiatic East."[8] Witte's position came close to a statement of an autarkic policy; as such, it was fatally flawed.

Witte's program was clear, his imagination contagious. A certain Petr Badmaev, converted Buriat, Slavophile physician, and cattleman-politician, proposed in February 1893 the expansion of the Siberian railroad from Lake Baikal not only to Vladivostok but also southward to Lanchow, at the strategic crossing of the routes linking Mongolia, Turkestan, and Tibet with China. From here Russia could incite the local men of power in the frontier zones to rise up against the Chinese and the Manchus. Witte was impressed, and commented that if the project could be carried out, "from the shores of the Pacific and the heights of the Himalayas Russia could dominate not only the affairs of Asia but those of Europe as well."[9] More modestly, the project's completion would mean the incorporation of the entire Russo-Chinese frontier into the Russian Empire.

The Turkestan Frontier

While Muravev, Putiatin, and Ignatev were spearheading the Russian advance into the Manchurian and Russo-Japanese frontiers, the Russians had not been inactive in the vast upland between the Irtysh and the Syr Darya. The incorporation of the Kazakh frontier had taken them into the basin of Lake Balkhash and the conquest of Central Asia to the foothills of the Tien Shan Mountains south of Lake Issyk Kul. The energy spent in the conquest of the Russo-Persian frontier did not stop until it encountered the countervailing power of Britain, forcing Russia and its Coastland rival to agree on a line of an optimum of conquest. The drive to incorporate the Kazakh frontier was irresistibly funneled into Zungharia and was bound to

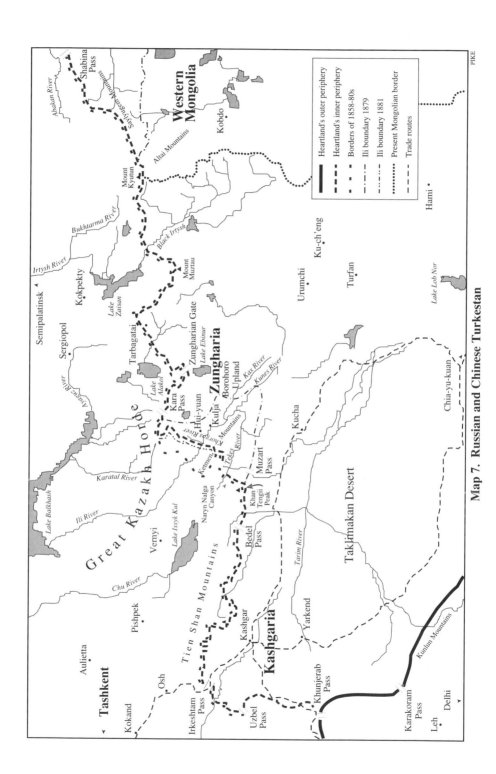

Map 7. Russian and Chinese Turkestan

Heartland's outer periphery
Heartland's inner periphery
Borders of 1858-80s
Ili boundary 1879
Ili boundary 1881
Present Mongolian border
Trade routes

Western Mongolia

Kobdo

Aksan River

Shabina Pass

Saylyugem Mountains

Altai Mountains

Mount Kyutun

Bukhtarma River

Black Irtysh

Irtysh River

Mount Muztau

Semipalatinsk

Kokpekty

Lake Zaisan

Zungharian Gate

Lake Ebinur

Hami

Ku-ch'eng

Urumchi

Turfan

Lake Lob Nor

Sergiopol

Tarbagatai

Lake Alakol

Kara Pass

Zungharia

Borohoro Upland

Kax River

Kunes River

Hui-yuan

Kulja

Ayaguz River

Kara Pass

Khorgos River

Kemen

Tekes River

Muzart Pass

Kucha

Great Kazakh Horde

Karatal River

Naryn Nalga Canyon

Khan Tengri Peak

Chia-yu-kuan

Lake Balkhash

Ili River

Vernyi

Lake Issyk Kul

Tien Shan Mountains

Bedel Pass

Tarim River

Taklimakan Desert

Chu River

Pishpek

Aulietta

Tashkent

Osh

Irkeshtam Pass

Kashgar

Kashgaria

Yarkend

Kokand

Uzbel Pass

Khunjerab Pass

Karakoram Pass

Kunlun Mountains

Leh

Delhi

PIKE

186

keep propelling the Russian advance until Peking could gather up the strength to bring it to a halt.

Trade led the Russian advance. The Manchus, who had steadily refused to allow the Russians to trade in Turkestan—because trade was restricted to Kiakhta—finally agreed to negotiate in March 1850, following disorders in the valley of the upper Irtysh and the strong stand taken by Governor General Gorchakov. In July 1851, they agreed to let the Russians open consulates in Kulja and Tarbagatai, but not in Kashgar. Caravans had to arrive between March and December and would receive a Chinese escort; trade was duty-free; judicial matters, including extradition, would follow the rules established at Kiakhta. Eastern Turkestan's population was unknown at the time—figures ranged from 100,000 to 300,000. The Ili valley was its richest region, producing grain and cotton. Coal, iron, copper, oil, and gold deposits were known to exist. Its exports to Russia grew rapidly with the establishment of trade relations; they doubled between 1852 and 1856. Hopes ran high.

The Ili valley also led to Kashgaria through the Muzart Pass on the watershed with the Tarim River along the northern skirt of the Taklimakan Desert. The pass led the traveler to the northern segment of the Silk Road, the great overland commercial highway since antiquity between Lanchow on the fringe of the Chinese core area and the Mediterranean via Kashgar, Samarkand, and Aleppo (Halab). Captain Chokan Valikhanov, whose family belonged to those Kazakh men of power who had joined the Imperial elite and were now turned outward to pave the way for the Russian advance deeper into the frontier, visited Kashgar in 1858. He became convinced that Russian trade would encounter no serious obstacles south of the Tien Shan because the Silk Road was cut off from northern India by the nearly impassable Kunlun Mountains. Indeed, the Yarkend-Leh route, 720 kilometers long and with eleven major passes, only two of them lower than Mont Blanc, was "probably the highest and most difficult trade route of any size in the world."[10] The Kunlun Mountains seemed to be an ideal line of an optimum of conquest; Valikhanov urged the transformation of Kashgaria into a Russian protectorate independent of China. The southern segment of the Silk Road would pass under Russian control, and Russia would reach the outer periphery of the Heartland. The structural alignment of the Kunlun Mountains is with the Gobi Desert and the watershed between the valley of the Sungari and that of the Liao to Vladivostok. A protectorate in Chinese Turkestan would be an important step toward the incorporation of the Russo-Chinese frontier into the empire. The Treaty of Peking, in November 1860, allowed the Russians to trade in Kashgar on the same basis as in Kulja and Tarbagatai and to open a consulate there, but an upsurge of Russo-Chinese hostility following the Moslem uprising delayed the arrival of the first Russian consul until November 1882.

The Moslem uprising against Chinese rule began in Kucha (Kuqa) in June 1864, the thirteenth since the beginning of the century, but the most serious. In May, the Russians had launched a pincer attack against

Kokand. The resulting turbulence convinced Petersburg and Peking that it was in their mutual interest to supplement the Treaty of Peking with another boundary treaty to delimit their respective possessions in that indeterminate zone between the Turkestan and Kazakh frontier and the basin of Lake Balkhash. Their agreement was contained in the Protocol of Chuguchak (Tarbagatai) in October 1864, delimiting 2080 kilometers of boundary between the Shabina Pass and the Kokand border, as far as the Uzbel Pass, and giving Lake Zaisan to Russia.

The revolt spread to Kashgaria, where a certain Yakub Beg, who had fought the Russians in Tashkent, proclaimed himself leader against the infidel in 1866. A Chinese reaction was inevitable, and the Russians could not but be aware that a new Moslem state was likely to become a pole of attraction for the Moslems of Central Asia recently incorporated into the Russian Empire, or about to be. The Russians thus faced a dilemma. Yakub Beg harbored hostile feelings and was a danger to Russian political and commercial interests. But the rebellion had taken place in the Manchu Empire, beyond the recently delimited boundary, against Manchu and Chinese rule. To interfere militarily might bring about a war with China with repercussions in the Amur valley and a British response, at a time when the Black Sea was still neutralized and the Russian coast defenseless. In 1869, General Kaufman, the governor general of Western Turkestan in Tashkent, was instructed to establish the same relations with Kashgar as those existing with Kokand: Russia would not interfere in its internal administration but insisted on safety of passage for Russian caravans. But Kashgar was far away and Kaufman could not back up his demands with the threat of force. Yakub Beg's power was growing in Zungharia and his progress was supported by the governor general of British India, who saw the new Moslem state as a barrier between Russia and India, not unlike Afghanistan. The possibility of Yakub Beg's invasion of the Ili valley under British sponsorship triggered Kaufman's preventive strike. In August 1870, Russian troops occupied the descent of the Muzart Pass, making Zungharia indefensible from Kashgaria. The so-called Ili crisis had begun; it would last a decade.

The preventive strike soon developed its own momentum. Justified officially as a last resort to stop the disorders in Zungharia, including the destruction of Russian property and the flight of tribesmen into the Russian Empire, it was but a dramatic episode in the Russian advance into the basin of Lake Balkhash in search of a line of an optimum of conquest. The Ili and its tributaries, the Tekes, the Kunes, and the Kax, were so many nerves of an organic triangular zone formed by the Tien Shan range and the Borohoro upland. It was the land of the Kirgiz, whose transhumance carried them from Western to Eastern Turkestan and back in complete disregard of the artificial 1864 boundary. The Russian advance thus marked the completion of the broad sweep from the Kazakh upland to the Tien Shan; it carried out the unification of the basin of Lake Balkhash and could also mark the beginning of the encirclement of Mongolia from the east.

These considerations help us understand Kaufman's decision in June 1871 to occupy Kulja and annex most of the Ili valley to the Russian Empire "in perpetuity." When Peking demanded the territory's return, the Russian minister, Alexander Vlangali, pledged Russia would return it if the Chinese could hold it and give assurances against future border disturbances.

Once a connection was established between Russia's presence in the valley and the restoration of security, it became Russia's interest to support Yakub Beg and the Moslem rebellion against China, even at the cost of souring Sino-Russian relations. Russia was then fully committed to a forward policy in Central Asia, and the recognition of its vulnerability in the Amur valley made it very tempting to make a stand in the Turkestan frontier where Russia was, or thought it was, in a strong position. Kaufman sent an agent in June 1872 to negotiate a treaty of peace and friendship with the Moslem chieftain. It gave Russian merchants the right to trade wherever Yakub Beg's authority was recognized, subject to a 2.5 percent ad valorem duty, and to build warehouses. Yakub Beg's nephew traveled to Tashkent and Petersburg, where he was received by the tsar, a gesture that came close to a recognition of his uncle's independence from China. But Yakub Beg also negotiated a similar treaty with British India, with an additional provision for a permanent representative with ambassadorial status. He looked to Turkey as the leader of the Moslem world, and Constantinople sent him 3000 rifles, thirty guns, and instructors to drill his troops; he flew the Ottoman flag beside his own. However, the isolation of Kashgaria and the control of the Muzart Pass gave the Russians the military advantage. They could look forward to the eventual transformation of Kashgaria into a Russian protectorate, as Valikhanov had proposed fifteen years earlier.

That it did not take place was due to China's decision to counter the Russian challenge with a challenge of its own. Kaufman soon discovered that he had a patient and determined enemy in General Tso Tsung-t'ang, the apostle of China's resistance to the Russian advance. China was then recovering from the great Taiping Rebellion and was in the midst of a "restoration" to carry out a conservative program of reforms with a view to overcoming the humiliation of the "unequal treaties" with the "barbarian" world. Tso could count on the support of his government. The Moslem rebellion had spread beyond Turkestan as far as Kansu (Gansu) province south of the Great Wall. Tso was made governor general of Shensi (Shaanxi) and Kansu provinces in 1866, and went about crushing the rebels systematically, until the capture of Suchow (Suzhou) in 1873. He was then ready to move into Turkestan. He was given full powers to proceed in April 1875, and struck the following year. Urumchi fell in August 1876, Kashgar in December 1877. Yakub Beg had died in May, perhaps by his own hand. Eastern Turkestan, except the Ili valley, was again in Chinese hands.

The Russians' dilemma reappeared. Once order was restored, they had to return the valley. However, the annexation of Kokand in February 1876 had given them full control of the caravan route between Kokand and

Kashgar and placed the latter at the mercy of a military expedition across the Alai range via the Irkeshtam Pass and the Kizil River. With Kokand went a vague title to Kashgaria that would legitimate Russian intervention. On the other hand, a decision to retain the valley and raise a claim on Kashgaria was certain to bring about an armed conflict with General Tso, more than ever determined not merely to reintegrate Turkestan into the inner frontier of the empire but to make it an integral part of the Chinese core area. Kaufman and his protégé, Alexei Kuropatkin, the chief of the Asiatic Section of the General Staff, began to have second thoughts about keeping the valley. They were supported by the tsar and the foreign and navy ministers against their own superior, War Minister Dmitrii Miliutin. But there was a price: the valley must be exchanged for an enormous "indemnity" of 120 million rubles to be used to finance the construction of a railroad across Siberia. In other words, Russia would trade its withdrawal from the Turkestan frontier for an increase in striking power in the Manchurian frontier.

While the Russians were groping for a diplomatic solution, Peking decided to send the military governor of Mukden, Ch'ung-hou, on a diplomatic mission to Petersburg. The controversy over the choice of the envoy, his qualifications, and his behavior in the Russian capital need not concern us. He arrived at the very end of 1878 and was received by Alexander II, who then left with the foreign minister for Livadia in the Crimea. The Russians decided to confront the envoy with a maximum program: retention of the valley, an indemnity for Russian losses during the disorders, a revision of the boundary protocol of 1864, amnesty for the Moslem rebels to stop their flights into Russian territory, and navigation rights on the Sungari to Petuna, 640 kilometers upstream from its mouth, near the confluence of the Nonni. Such a concession would allow the Russians to establish a presence in the very heart of the Manchurian Plain. The harsh Russian stand may have been motivated in part by resentment in the wake of the Congress of Berlin, in part by an irresistible urge to take advantage of a gullible envoy, but it also showed Russia's determination to complete the unification of the basin of Lake Balkhash and prevent China from consolidating its victory in Turkestan. Most of the Russian demands were included in the Treaty of Livadia, signed in October 1879. China ceded nearly the entire valley, the indemnity was fixed at 5 million rubles, and the rebels were pardoned. The treaty also represented a vast commercial offensive in Turkestan, Mongolia, and Manchuria. Not only did Russia obtain navigation rights to Petuna; it also gained the right to open seven consulates at Urumchi, Turfan, Hami, and Ku-ch'eng (Jimsar) in Turkestan; Ch'iayukuan at the extremity of the Great Wall in Kansu province; Kobdo (Hovd) and Uliasutai (Uliastay) in Western Mongolia.

Ch'ung-hou left Petersburg nine days after signing the treaty, apparently unaware of what he had done. The treaty caused an uproar in Chinese officialdom. General Tso was outraged—"when the Russians are given an inch, they want a foot"[11]—and prepared for war. Ch'ung-hou was sentenced to death, but was saved by the intervention of foreign ministers. How to repair the damage? The Manchu Court was aware of the possibly disastrous consequences of a military defeat. The Russians began to feel they had gone too far, despite Kaufman's readiness to meet the Chinese on the battlefield. They accepted China's offer to renegotiate the treaty. The new envoy, Tseng Chi-tse, who had been minister to Britain and France, arrived in Petersburg in July 1880, when the best season for war on land or at sea was passing, and time was beginning to work in China's favor. He refused to grant navigation rights on the Sungari and permission to open the seven consulates. A settlement was reached in the Treaty of Petersburg, in February 1881. Russia abandoned most of its gains in the Ili valley, including the Muzart Pass; obtained an indemnity of 9 million rubles to cover the costs of the occupation since 1871 and compensate Russian subjects for their losses during the rebellion; and gained the right to open only two consulates, in Turfan and Suchow (near Chia-yukuan), with another five to be opened "gradually." Russians in the Ili valley retained their property and were allowed to trade duty-free in Turkestan, at least until the establishment of a tariff between the two empires. The Russians, recognizing that they had more to gain from a friendly policy toward China, retreated. Their change of course convinced some of the leaders, notably Grand Secretary Li Hung-chang, that the major threat to China came from the maritime powers, and especially Japan.

Peking's victory was followed by the full integration of Eastern Turkestan into the Manchu Empire. The Manchus had traditionally relied on local men of power, the begs, to whom they had delegated authority. The system had made it possible to keep Chinese troops at such great distances from the core area to a minimum—Urumchi was 4116 kilometers from Peking, Kashgar, 5360. The rebellion had shown that the local elites could not be trusted and that the Russians could also use them to stir up opposition against Manchu rule. General Tso wanted to establish direct Chinese rule, settle Chinese peasants, and build a sufficiently strong military infrastructure to counter the Russian presence in Central Asia and facilitate immediate intervention against internal threats. In November 1884, Peking took the unprecedented step of transforming Turkestan into a Chinese province to be known as Sinkiang or the New Dominion. A Chinese governor was immediately appointed in Urumchi. The effect was to transform a frontier into a part of the core area. China advanced to the inner periphery of the Heartland, and the fate of Turkestan became a vital interest. But the Russians were not willing to concede defeat, and Turkestan remained for them a frontier to be penetrated and eventually detached by nonviolent means. Before the reform, the first Russian consul had already established himself as the "virtual ruler of Kashgar,"[12] domineering toward the Chinese, quick to intrigue against British India. Russian trade began to eclipse the Indian Kashgar trade, and Russian goods filtered across the mountains into Kashmir and Chitral province, in British India's Northwest Frontier.

Another consequence of the Petersburg treaty was the demarcation of the boundary between the two empires. It began with the middle section. The protocol of October 1882 established boundary markers from the Kara Pass in the Alatau Range, the watershed between the basin of Lake Balkhash and that of Lake Ebinur, to the Naryn Nalga canyon. North of the Kara Pass, the protocol of July 1883 demarcated the boundary between the Tarbagatai Range and Mount Kuytun on the Saylyugem Range and the Mongolian border. The southern section was first demarcated in November 1882, along a line from the Naryn Khalga canyon, past Mount Khan Tengri, to the Bedel Pass across the Tien Shan Mountains. The remainder, from the Bedel to the Uz Bel Pass, was demarcated in May 1884. There, the passes were numerous—twenty-eight in all—separating the lands of the old Kokand khanate from Kashgaria. Those were the passes that had so facilitated political and commercial relations between Kokand and Kashgaria, that had taken the *khojas* into Kashgaria and the Manchus to Kokand. Beyond the Uzbel Pass there remained 307 kilometers to the Russo-Chinese-Afghan trijunction that would not be demarcated before 1917. In 1893, China claimed the Pamirs as far as a line from the pass to Lake Zorkul and nearly brought about an armed conflict with Russia. Sino-Russian negotiations were abandoned with the outbreak of the Sino-Japanese war, but a de facto settlement was achieved when the Russians gave assurances they would not cross beyond the Sarykol watershed into the Tarim basin. By the 1890s, then, the Russian advance had been stopped behind the inner periphery of the Heartland by China's containment policy. Russia would never be able to cross into the intermediate zone between the Heartland's inner and outer periphery and would never succeed in incorporating the entire Sino-Russian frontier into the Russian Empire.

The Russo-Japanese Frontier

Russia first gained access to the Pacific frontier when it crossed the Heartland's periphery at Nerchinsk and Okhotsk. The annexation of the left bank of the Amur was a giant step toward claiming hegemony in the narrow seas between the continental coast and the continuous archipelago from Kamchatka to Korea—the Sea of Okhotsk and the Sea of Japan. Like the Balkans, Transcaucasia, and Afghanistan, the Pacific frontier was an interlocking frontier, between the East Siberian upland of the Russian core area on the one hand and the Chinese and Japanese core areas on the other. Russia and Japan were rivals for preponderance in the narrow seas; Russia and China for supremacy in the valley of the Amur; Russia, Japan, and China for the mastery of Korea and the Liao valley. Korea, like Georgia and Afghanistan, was a "proruption," a forward position from which power could be projected in several directions; whoever established hegemony in the peninsula would dominate the Sea of Japan, the Yellow Sea, and the Liao valley; and the control of Sakhalin determined the fate of the Sea of Okhotsk. The history of the Russian advance into the Pacific frontier after 1848 is thus the history of a struggle for the redistribution of space among a dynamic Russia, a China determined to resist despite its growing weakness, and a vigorous Japan bent on building an empire to the detriment of both.

But Japan first had to be "opened"—in some perverse way brought into the frontier as an active partner. There were already signs that the energy accumulated during 200 years of isolation was being released, and it was stimulated by a growing debate within Japan over the validity of the policy of exclusion, the ominous appearance of foreign ships off the Japanese shores, and the news of China's defeat in the Opium War. In 1849, some sixty-four foreign ships, chiefly from the United States, were sighted in the Korean Strait. In March 1852, the U.S. Congress voted to send an expedition to Japan commanded by Commodore Matthew Perry. In April, a special committee discussed Russia's options toward Japan and recommended the despatch of a Russian expedition to China and Japan. It was commanded by Putiatin, who left Kronshtadt on the frigate Pallada in October, rounded the Cape of Good Hope, and arrived off Nagasaki in August 1853. Perry had reached Edo Bay in July. Putiatin was instructed to negotiate a clarification of boundaries in the Kuril archipelago and on Sakhalin Island, and an opening of Japanese ports to Russian trade. The Russians continued to look on Japan as a source of provisions and equipment for their Coastland settlements, still ignorant of the fact that the staples of the Siberian trade, timber and furs, were not in demand in Japan and that the Japanese were not yet eager to enter the world economy after living in a perfect state of autarky for several generations.

Negotiations began in January 1854. Putiatin was refused permission to travel to Edo and received no answer to his demands; the Japanese preferred to deal with one "barbarian" at a time. As it was too late to sail on to the Sea of Okhotsk, he left Nagasaki for the Philippines in February. On his return in October 1854, he learned that Perry had been successful in opening two Japanese ports, Shimoda and Hakodate, in March. He reached Shimoda in December and signed the first Russo-Japanese treaty in February 1855. The treaty opened three ports to Russian ships—Shimoda, Nagasaki, and Hakodate—and the Russians were allowed to buy provisions and coal. Japan pledged to give Russia the same privileges as those granted to other friendly nations; and the Kuril archipelago was divided, the boundary running through the Friza Strait, leaving Iturup and Kunashir to Japan, Urup and the other islands to Russia. Sakhalin remained "undivided." The Treaty of Shimoda was supplemented by a commercial treaty signed in Nagasaki in October 1857, regulating commercial transactions in Hakodate and Nagasaki. Shimoda, considered an unsafe harbor, was left out. Trade in the two ports was free but subject to a 35 percent duty. More important, restrictions were imposed on the export of rice and barley—those very items the Russians had been counting on—and even on the delivery of coal.

The opening of Japan continued under pressure from the Americans, the British, and the French, and despite the increasingly tense atmosphere of Japanese politics. The presence of foreigners was becoming a rallying issue for all those in the military elite dissatisfied with the Tokugawa government and resentful of the Western barbarians' arrogance that did not shrink from the use of force. As in China, the Russians dissociated themselves from the maritime powers. Putiatin even gave assurances that Russia would side with the Japanese government if other countries "caused disturbances."[13] The maritime powers took for granted the demise of the Tokugawa shogunate; the Russians, faithful to their diplomatic tradition, preferred to encourage the rotting process, hoping to benefit from it in additional commercial and territorial concessions.

Putiatin's reward for siding with the Manchus was the Treaty of Tientsin in June 1858. He then returned to Japan and signed in Edo a treaty of friendship and commerce in August. It gave Russia the right to appoint a diplomatic agent and consuls in the open ports. Three more ports were opened. Russians were allowed to reside there, rent land, and buy houses. A tariff schedule was appended with a scale of duties on exports and imports. But Russian trade made no headway. Until the appointment of a diplomatic agent in 1871, Hakodate remained the center of Russia's representation in Japan. From that important location, the Russian consul should have been able to broker the development of Russo-Japanese trade. Yet the Russian share of Japanese foreign trade remained insignificant between 1854 and 1868: 0.5 percent of exports, 3 percent of imports. The absence of a Pacific merchant marine and of convenient roads across the Heartland's periphery blocked the development of a regular flow of goods between the two core areas in the Pacific frontier. If the Russian settlements could not become a powerhouse in the frontier, they were bound to become Japan's backyard as soon as the Japanese economy entered the world economy, dominated, in the Pacific, by Britain and the United States. Moreover, it is well known that the existence of a merchant marine is a prerequisite to the development of naval power. The Russians could build an impressive Pacific squadron for an occasional demonstration of power against China and a Japan not yet committed to the radical restructuring of its government and economy on the western model, but it could not sustain it over a long period without an economic base solidly anchored in the Coastland. The Russian advance continued to be paved with disappointments—Okhotsk, Petropavlovsk, the mouth of the Amur. . . .

The founding of Vladivostok in 1860 awakened new hopes. Two years later, a Japanese mission visited London, Paris, and Berlin, and reached Petersburg in August, where negotiations with Ignatev, by then director of the Asiatic Department, focused on Sakhalin. The Japanese, who had been charmed by Putiatin's manner, encountered the hard line of the geopoliticians already committed to the expulsion of the Japanese from the island and the building of a powerful naval base on the coast of the Sea of Japan opposite Hakodate and Niigata, the latter to be opened to foreigners. As the political crisis worsened in Japan, the British minister, Sir Harry Parkes, played an increasing role in the destabilization of the shogunal government. When it finally fell and was succeeded in January 1868 by a government committed to the full opening of the country, the Russians had been robbed of their hope to benefit from the rotting process. They would have to live with their defeat until 1905.

The Russians had "lost" Japan not only because the course of internal Japanese politics rapidly put an end to the rotting process from which they had most to gain, but also, and chiefly, because their advance into the Russo-Japanese frontier took a hostile turn under Muravev's leadership. Nowhere was this more clear than in the Sakhalin question. At the governor general's urging, Nicholas I ordered the Russian-American Company in April 1853 to "occupy" the island, an enormous strip of land stretching over 1000 kilometers to La Perouse Strait facing Hokkaido. The Company was told to appoint its own governor, to forbid any foreign settlement on the island, to protect its harbors "against the intrusion of foreigners,"[14] and to develop its coal resources. An expedition landed and raised the Russian flag at Tomari in Aniwa Bay in October. The coast was studded with Japanese settlements, established there for generations to take advantage of the rich fishing grounds between the Sea of Japan and the Sea of Okhotsk.

Muravev was working at cross purposes with Putiatin, who was engaged at the time in sensitive negotiations to open up Japanese ports, but the expedition was recalled on account of the Crimean War. The Russians left in June 1854, and the Treaty of Shimoda avoided the Sakhalin issue. But it was clear to some of the Russians at least that the occupation of Aniwa Bay was an aggressive act, part of "a military plan of action against Japan." The annexation of the bay and of the island would deprive the Japanese of one of their major sources of nourishment and "the loss of the shores of Aniwa is more important for Japan than the loss of the whole Amur region adjoining the Amur is for China."[15] The establishment of a naval base in the bay would pose a threat to Iturup and Kunashir islands of the Kuril chain; it would indeed be the decisive act in the elaboration of a fortress-fleet strategy to close the Sea of Okhotsk, a strategy that, in propitious circumstances, could also be directed against the coast of Hokkaido itself. In November 1854, the Japanese had been willing to compromise—they would accept a partition of Sakhalin along the fiftieth parallel, leaving the island's two large bays, Aniwa and Terpenie in Japan's inner frontier. But the Russians had shown no interest.

Muravev was in no mood to accept a setback. His dynamism and the logic of Russia's expansion into an organic frontier, in search of a line of an optimum of conquest, revived the determination to annex Sakhalin. Hakodate (and its bay) was becoming the headquarters of the Russian presence. A Dutch observer noted in 1859 that "from the beginning [the Russians] have conducted a sturdy and consequential policy of state. True, they do not bother with trade . . . and even assume the appearance of unselfishness.

They have stationed in Hakodate a very competent diplomat as political agent and maybe just there because [Hokkaido] is of the utmost importance to them. Moreover, for several years they have had a powerful fleet in these waters, on an average of about twenty ships."[16] In November 1858, Muravev had written to the Asiatic Department that Russia must have the entire island in its possession, to prevent the British from taking it. But his concern with British designs on the perimeter of Russia's possessions in the Coastland only served to hide the pursuit of a strategic interest. The following year, in August 1859, during a trip to Japan with a "formidable squadron" of seven ships, he declared that Russia must have Sakhalin because the island was "homogeneous"[17] with the Amur, had been Russian before 1689—the Treaty of Nerchinsk—and was Russian once again. His declaration angered the Japanese. Clearly, Muravev had overplayed his hand. His founding of Vladivostok on his return trip to the Amur, placed in the context of his recent declaration and of Russian activities in Hakodate, amounted to a challenge to Japan's vital interests.

Muravev failed to take into account a number of factors. Naval strength could not be built in a barren Coastland; Russian strength on land was insignificant and scattered over enormous distances; there was no convict labor at the time to mine the coal fields of Sakhalin; and a penal colony cannot create the flourishing economy needed to sustain a naval and military position. Last but not least, Muravev and others, influenced by reports that the Japanese were not to be taken seriously, underestimated Japan's determination to resist. The Pacific frontier zones gave Russia a unique opportunity to break through the isolation imposed by the refractory physical barrier of the Heartland's periphery, enter the world economy, and become one of the Pacific's great powers. Yet it was there that Russia failed to develop a suitable economic base and encountered the insuperable active resistance of the Coastland powers.

The diplomatic mission sent to Russia in 1862 could reach no agreement on the partition of Sakhalin. A second mission arrived in Petersburg in January 1867, but Petr Stremoukhov, the new director of the Asiatic Department who had succeeded Ignatev in 1864, was no more conciliatory than his predecessor, despite the willingness of the Japanese to partition the island along the forty-eighth parallel, giving Terpenie Bay to Russia, the Japanese retaining Aniwa Bay. Both sides agreed to disagree, leaving the island in the common possession of both. But the two governments were moving toward a showdown. The Russians raised their force on Sakhalin to 300 men, a Fort Muravev was built on Aniwa Bay, and regular communications were established between the island and the mainland. In November 1868, Gorchakov, the foreign minister, asked the navy to transport some 400 hard-labor convicts to Sakhalin. The government maintained its monopoly of coal mining in order to keep foreign enterprise out of the island.

The new Japanese government did not shrink from facing down the Russians, but also recognized that its major policy thrust would be directed against China, be it in Formosa or Korea, and that, consequently, it had to reach an agreement with the Russians so that Japanese vital interests would be protected. Following the arrival of the first Russian envoy, Eugen Bützow, in 1871 (he later served in China and Persia), negotiations resumed in June 1872. They did not go well, and were marked by mutual recriminations. The Japanese understood that the Sakhalin question would soon be followed by the Hokkaido question unless they could develop an impregnable position on the island; that could be done only by a policy of rapid settlement of peasants from the core area. On the other hand, the Sakhalin question had acquired such importance for the Russians that they were now willing to consider an exchange: they would gain the whole of Sakhalin but would have to lose some of the Kurils.

Negotiations moved to Petersburg after Bützow's departure in 1873, but it was not until February 1875 that Stremoukhov was allowed to surrender most of the archipelago. The agreement was formalized in the treaty of May 1875. Japan recognized Russia's full sovereignty over the whole of Sakhalin, and the boundary was made to run through La Pérouse Strait. In exchange, Russia surrendered to Japan eighteen islands, or the *entire* archipelago; the boundary ran between Cape Lopatka and Shumshu, the first Kuril island. Japanese ships were allowed to trade duty-free in the port of Kusun-Kotan, now called Korsakov, in Aniwa Bay, but the Japanese did not gain the "opening" of Vladivostok and Petropavlovsk to Japanese trade—the treaty only promised to give them most-favored-nation status in the ports of the Sea of Okhotsk and Kamchatka. Supplementary articles signed in August recognized the reciprocal rights of Russians and Japanese to fish, hunt, and keep their properties in the territories ceded to the other power.

The treaty marked Russia's second defeat since the appearance of Putiatin in Japanese waters twenty-two years earlier. It had been Russia's implicit policy, ever since the hardy days of island-hopping in the eighteenth century, to acquire the archipelago; the declaration of September 1821 had formalized that policy, although the Russians had already been forced to recognize Japanese jurisdiction over Kunashir and Iturup. The acquisition of the archipelago would have enabled Russia to pursue the same fortress-fleet strategy that had been the hallmark of its naval policy in the Baltic and Black seas, while a partition of Sakhalin would have accommodated Japanese interests and created a solid basis for cooperation within a closed or nearly closed Sea of Okhotsk. After 1875, that sea was effectively closed, but by Japan, and the Sakhalin question continued to fester—over fishing rights and the belief that the islands contained more mineral riches. Russia did gain Sakhalin but at the cost of being shut off from the northern Pacific. Instead of making Japan dependent on Russian goodwill within a ring fence patroled by the Russian navy, Russia was made dependent on Japanese goodwill. But that was not the end. Russia had "lost" Japan and lost the archipelago; Vladivostok faced south and led to Korea. The organic unity of the Pacific frontier, like that of the steppe-ocean in the Kazakh frontier, kept drawing Russia deeper into the frontier, as if possessed by the mirage of a line of an optimum of conquest, ever shimmering in the distance but nowhere yet to be found.

The Russian geopolitician surveying the Pacific frontier in the 1850s would have inevitably become attracted by the perspective of a defensive perimeter stretching from Kamchatka along the Kuril archipelago and the Japanese islands and across the Yellow Sea to the Shantung Peninsula, behind which to pursue a fortress-fleet strategy for the in-depth defense of Russian possessions in the Coastland, including the Amur valley, the object of Russia's immediate ambitions. Such a strategy would fortify the Kurils and build naval strongholds on the continental coast of the Sea of Japan, while the rotting process would keep Japan suitably weak. Its maximum goal would be to "close" the Korea Strait by establishing such naval preponderance in it that Russian ships could freely leave the Sea of Japan and enter the Pacific, while the entrance of foreign ships into that sea would depend on Russia's assent. The establishment of a base on Shantung Peninsula would complete the eastern prong of a giant pincer movement against northern China; the anticipated advance beyond the Kazakh steppe-ocean would threaten the Chinese core area from the east. The point is often made that the Russian advance was motivated by the search for warm-water ports, but that search was not an end in itself. It would be more accurate to say that Russia, as the largest land power in the Heartland, inward-looking and marked by a vision of political and economic autarky, was seeking to create a string of naval bases, including some in warm-water ports, that gave greater operational freedom, as so many links in a ring fence behind which to secure its continental possessions against the malignant influences of the maritime powers of the Coastland and the United States.

In March 1861, a Russian naval party landed on Tsushima Island in the Korea Strait, about midway between Korea and Japan, and hoisted the Russian flag. The move may have been generated by a fear that the British would annex the island first and bottle up the Russians in the Sea of Japan. As in the Turkish Straits, it was in Britain's interest to control the exit from a narrow sea, and in Russia's interest to keep foreign ships out of it. If the Russians had agreed to draw a line of an optimum of conquest across the Sea of Japan from Vladivostok to Hakodate, a certain balance of power might have been achieved between the two powers. But Vladivostok was icebound for about a third of the year, and Korea was certain to remain Russia's land bridge to northern China and Peking for as long as Manchuria was beyond Russia's control. The strong British response and the willingness of the maritime powers to use force—as they would against Japan in 1863 and 1864—forced the Russians to withdraw in the fall of 1861, one of them bemoaning the fact that "we had not looked before we leaped."[18]

The opening of Japan, the overthrow of the shogunate, and the establishment of a new government radically altered the geopolitical situation in the Sea of Japan and the Korea Strait. For the first time since the arrival of Muravev in Irkutsk in 1848, Russia was thrown on the defensive; the treaty of May 1875 confirmed the appearance of a redoubtable enemy in the Pacific frontier. The energies of the new Japanese government focused not only on the internal transformation of the country but also on the establishment of hegemony in Korea. After 1868, Korea's position as proruption became clear—the most sensitive zone in the Sino-Japanese and Russo-Japanese frontier.

Korea, a tributary state of China, remained closed to the outside world beyond the Sinocentric universe, but the Manchu government, only recently compelled to open more ports and even its capital to the barbarian invaders, was pressing Korea to do likewise. It was also determined to retain Chinese preponderance in Korea. Li Hung-chang sent a resident to Seoul, who took with him a German citizen, Paul von Möllendorf, a former employee of the Chinese customs service, as customs commissioner and foreign affairs adviser. Their policy was to use the Russians against the Japanese—asking Russia to send officers to train Korean troops in exchange for the use of the ice-free port of Lazarev (Gensan, Wonsan) on the northeastern coast of Korea. The violent opposition of both Britain and Japan doomed that policy. Möllendorf was recalled, but the Russians had been drawn for the first time into the vortex of Korean politics. The Korean king, caught between the radically divergent ambitions of the queen and his father, the regent, began to yearn for Russian support. The growing turbulence in such a sensitive frontier zone eventually caused the Japanese to strike against the Manchus and cut the secular link binding Korea to China. War broke out in August 1894, and China suffered an ignominious defeat. Japan was left to face Russia; the Korean question was born.

9

War and Peace,
1895–1917

Squaring Off, 1895–1898

Peace was made at Shimonoseki in April 1895. China recognized the complete independence of Korea and ceded to Japan in full and perpetual sovereignty the Liaotung peninsula from the mouth of the Liao to that of the Yalu. Since the independence of Korea meant no more for Japan than the independence of the "Tatar nation" had meant for the Russians in the 1770s, Japan's victory had the effect of smashing the eastern prong of the Russian advance, nearly fifteen years after the Russians had been forced to retract their western prong in the Ili valley, and of checkmating the naval buildup in Vladivostok. Moreover, the temporary occupation of Weihaiwei on the northern shore of the Shantung Peninsula had established a Japanese naval preponderance against the Russians in Korea Bay and the Gulf of Chihli.

Only the recognition of the geopolitical implications of the Japanese victory can explain the strong Russian reaction. Petersburg enlisted the support of France and Germany and delivered an ultimatum to Japan barely a week after the treaty's signature. Witte was ready to go to war if the Japanese refused to yield, but it is not clear what kind of war it would have been; the Russians had no substantial land forces in the frontier and their navy was dependent on the berthing facilities of still friendly Nagasaki harbor. In fact, the ultimatum served a dual purpose—to appear as the "savior of China," and to force Japan to give up the peninsula. The same principle continued to inspire Russian policy, whether in Sweden and Poland in the eighteenth century, or in Turkey and Persia in the nineteenth, in Ignatev's relations with China and Putiatin's with Japan—to support the rotting

200

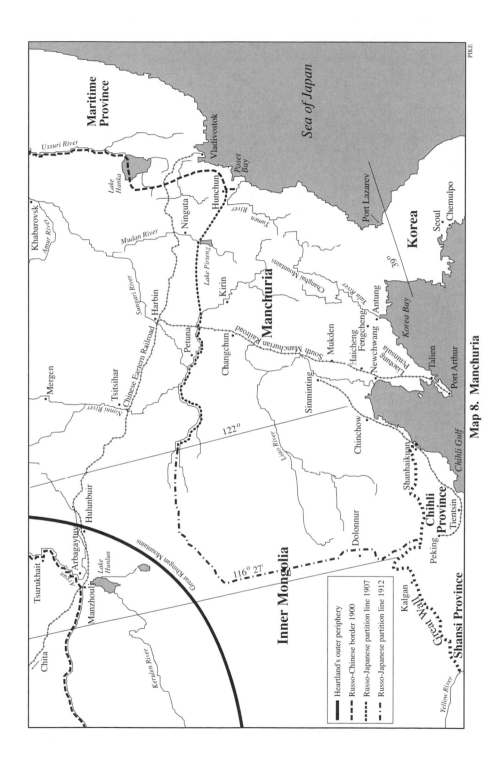

Map 8. Manchuria

Maritime Province

Sea of Japan

Korea

Seoul
Chemulpo

Port Lazarev

Korea Bay

36°

Antung

Yalu River

Fengcheng
Haicheng
Newchwang
Liaotung Peninsula
Talien
Port Arthur

Mukden

Changbai Mountains

Manchuria

Kirin

Lake Pirenz

Ninguta

Hunchun

Tumen River

Poset Bay

Vladivostok

Lake Hanka

Ussuri River

Khabarovsk
Amur River

Mudan River

Sungari River

Harbin

Chinese Eastern Railroad

Petuna

Changchun

South Manchurian Railroad

Simminting

Chinchow

Liao River

Dolonnur

Shanhaikuan

Chihli Province

Tientsin
Peking

Kalgan

Great Wall

Shansi Province

Yellow River

Inner Mongolia

Nonni River
Tsitsihar

Mergen

116° 27'

122°

Great Khingan Mountains

Hulunbuir

Arbagayuu
Lake Hunlun

Manzhouli

Kerulen River

Tsurukhait

Chita

Heartland's outer periphery
Russo-Chinese border 1900
Russo-Japanese partition line 1907
Russo-Japanese partition line 1912

Chihli Gulf

PIKE

process in the name of dynastic legitimism in order to obtain territorial and other concessions. The Japanese, encouraged by the British, accepted the ultimatum and retroceded the Liaotung Peninsula in November, after evacuating Weihaiwei. But the settlement created rancor in Japan, and independent Korea became the theater of a bitter rivalry with Russia.

The time had now come for China to pay the price of its salvation, and Russian moves disclosed a daring geopolitical vision. The treaty had imposed a heavy indemnity that China could not pay without a foreign loan. The Russians offered better terms than their competitors and, with the help of French capital, granted China a 100-million gold ruble loan in July. They also proposed the creation of a bank to operate under the auspices of the Russian government to finance commercial transactions and "counterbalance the enormous importance" of Britain in China. The charter of the so-called Russo-Chinese Bank was ratified in December. The loan contract guaranteed Russian participation in any future international agency set up to supervise China's finances.

The second price China had to pay was a military alliance with Russia, in which it was certain to remain the junior partner for some time. Grateful for the Russian loan, Peking sent Li Hung-chang to attend the coronation of Nicholas II. He traveled via the Suez Canal and Odessa and arrived in Petersburg in April 1896, with full powers to negotiate a wide-ranging settlement. One result of the negotiations was the treaty of alliance signed in June, providing that any Japanese aggression against Russian, Chinese, or Korean territory would be met by the combined forces of Russia and China and that all Chinese ports would be opened to Russian warships for the duration of the war. Nothing was said about granting Russia the lease of an ice-free port, and it is not certain Witte made the request at the time. He may have been waiting for an opportunity that was not long delayed.

In November 1897, Germany, eager to establish a foothold on the Yellow Sea, used the murder of two of its missionaries by a Chinese mob to claim Kiaochow (Jiaozhou) Bay on the southern coast of Shantung peninsula. By then, the penetration of China by the maritime powers had reached such a stage that the German move became the signal for a scramble to partition the Manchu Empire. After China's failure to borrow on the world markets, Li Hung-chang approached Witte with an urgent request for a new loan. The finance minister expressed interest if Peking would give Russia a monopoly of the construction of railroads and industrial enterprises in all three provinces of Manchuria and in Mongolia. Li received Witte's offer together with the news that Russian warships had anchored at Port Arthur (Lushun), from which they could watch German activities in Shantung, a barely concealed attempt to broaden the scope of the 1896 alliance to include other powers beside Japan in the list of potential aggressors. Li was also notified that Russia expected to obtain an anchorage on the Gulf of Chihli or in Korea Bay as an alternative to Nagasaki harbor, which was no longer friendly. Terms for the loan were agreed on in December. Russia dropped its demand for an anchorage, but gained the monopoly it had bargained for, and the loan was secured by the customs revenue of Manchuria and the salt revenue of the empire.

The Germans kept pressing Peking for a lease and were granted one for ninety-nine years in March 1898. The lease applied to Tsingtao (Qingdao), but the entire Kiaochow Bay was included in Germany's sphere of influence. As compensation, the Russians now demanded a lease on the Liaotung Peninsula, with Port Arthur, the ice-free naval port, and Talienwan (Dalny, Darien, Dalian), the commercial port. The agreement, reached three weeks after Germany's success, created two zones on the peninsula. The peninsula's end was reserved for the "exclusive use" of the Russian government in order "to secure for Russian naval forces a fully reliable foothold on the coast of Northern China"[1]; a neutral zone remained under Chinese civil administration, but Chinese troops were barred from it without Russian preliminary consent. Port Arthur was closed to all but Russian and Chinese warships; Talienwan remained open to commercial shipping. The lease was valid for twenty-five years.

One can argue the merits of the decision to annex part of the Liaotung Peninsula from which Russia had unceremoniously evicted Japan three years earlier. It certainly was not an act of "reactive desperation."[2] It marked another step in the advance into the Pacific frontier that had begun with the Nevelskoi expedition to the Amur mouth in 1849 and had continued with the founding of Vladivostok in 1860 and the attempt to seize Tsushima Island in 1861. It was as much a part of Russia's hostile policy toward Japan as it was part of Russia's friendly policy toward China. While the lease violated the territorial integrity of China, it did not mean the end of Russia's friendly policy. It is true that the peninsula, facing as it did the eastern terminus of the Great Wall, stood on the fringe of the Chinese core area, was even part of it on account of its location south of the so-called Willow Palisade, the northeastern extension of the Great Wall past Mukden (Shenyang) and Kirin (Jilin) to the Mudan River, a tributary of the Sungari. Russia, still unable to find a line of an optimum of conquest, was beginning to tread on the threshold of the core area, the most dangerous stage in its imperial expansion, but also the logical outcome of a consistent advance into an organic frontier. Russia's friendly policy toward a decaying core area government had never been disinterested; it had always been subversive. Territorial compensation would be its reward.

It was disingenuous of Witte to claim that the lease was an act of "unexampled treachery" committed at the urging of the tsar and Foreign Minister Mikhail Muravev. Had he not told the British ambassador in January 1898 that "Russia's geographical position must sooner or later assure her political predominance in the north of China" and that Russia would eventually "absorb" the northern provinces south of the Great Wall in the core area itself, of Kansu, Shensi, Shansi (Shanxi), and even Chihli (Hebei) with Peking as the prize?[3] Such an advance would surround Mongolia and place Chinese Turkestan in a vise from which it could not escape. But Witte also remained hostage to a very traditional dilemma among Russian policymakers, one we encountered in their dealings with Poland and Persia. He added in the same conversation that Russia's "true policy is to keep China intact." The dilemma vis-à-vis these three core areas was between a policy that would encourage the rotting process until the entire core area was ready to fall under Russian domination, and a policy accepting partition. In Poland and Persia, the Russians had to settle for partition; in China, there could be no alternative to it. The true importance of the lease was that it amounted to a declaration of cold war against the Japanese in a renewed determination to complete the ring fence around the valley of the Amur and the Maritime Province. Japan, with the instinct of a sea power, was ready to adapt, compromise, and concede. It would do so in Manchuria, but would draw the line in Korea.

China had to pay a third price for being "saved" by Russia in 1895. The construction of the Trans-Siberian railroad had begun in May 1891 from both ends, and the first train would reach Irkutsk from Cheliabinsk and Khabarovsk from Vladivostok in 1898. It was already known in 1895 that the sector from Lake Baikal across the Heartland's periphery to Khabarovsk would be the most difficult to build on account of the mountainous terrain and the need to cut a large number of tunnels. Moreover, the Russo-Chinese boundary along the Amur and around the Great and Lesser Khingan required an additional 700 kilometers of track. A shortcut had to be found to build a nearly straight line, and it had to be across Manchuria. However, the very size of the enterprise—the line would be between 1500 and 2000 kilometers long, by far the longest built in the Manchu Empire by foreign enterprise—and the exact location of the track caused controversy in Russian government circles.

Witte, former minister of communications and, since August 1892, minister of finance, was well equipped to understand the implications of railroad building. A railroad would move people and goods (and troops) from the core area into the frontier zones, disperse power and influence across the zones, concentrate military power at specific points for maximum effect, and, conversely, integrate frontier zones into the continental economy and military infrastructure of the core area. The railroad, and in that part of the world the railroad alone, would substantiate the claim that space is power and autarky a valid policy to reverse the currents of trade in the Heartland's favor. Witte had been in sympathy with Badmaev's projects to build lines to draw the Turkestan and Mongolian frontiers, even those provinces of China which he felt Russia would eventually "absorb," into the Russian orbit, but the on-going construction of the Trans-Siberian and the emergence of Japan created more pressing problems. After surveys between Sretensk, just east of Nerchinsk, and Khabarovsk disclosed in the summer of 1894 the full extent of the technical difficulties in completing the Trans-Siberian, Witte became convinced of the need to give priority to a line across Manchuria. In February 1895, a month before the treaty of Shimonoseki, he asked the foreign ministry to obtain China's assent to a line from Tsurukhait to Blagoveshchensk via Mergen (Nenjiang) on the Nonni. From Blagoveshchensk the line would follow the valley of the Amur to Khabarovsk. This early and relatively modest project had a clear objective—to integrate northern Manchuria between the line and the Amur into Siberia and to "rectify" the Amur boundary.

By May 1895, however, when it appeared that Japan could not afford to resist the three-power ultimatum without British support, the project was "metamorphosed" into a line from Chita to Vladivostok across the Manchurian plain between the Nonni and the Sungari. The opposition of shipowners who wanted the line as far as possible from the Amur may have been a factor in the transformation. In fact, the new project was the expression of an unfolding vision of Russia's role in the Pacific frontier. At long last, after so many disappointments, the Russians were gaining access to a Coastland region with good land and excellent resources; moreover, it was a center of hydrographic divergence toward the Amur and the Yellow Sea. The fact that the metamorphosis took place at the very time they were forcing the Japanese out of the Liaotung Peninsula is evidence that a connection had already been made in Petersburg between building a west-east line across Manchuria and a north-south branch to the peninsula. The line would become the axis of the Manchurian economy. It would supply Russian settlements in the Pacific frontier, a goal the Russians had vainly sought to achieve since the early eighteenth century. It would staff and provision the Vladivostok naval headquarters, even Port Arthur if it could eventually be "leased." It would accelerate the rotting process in Peking by placing the capital at Russia's mercy. Last but not least, it would pave the way for the elaboration of a pincer movement against Korea to turn the tables on Japan, Russia's enemy in the Pacific frontier. The vision was daring but flawed, and for the same reasons Russia's vision of its destiny in the Pacific frontier had been flawed in the past. Siberia remained sparsely populated, its economy undeveloped, its roads in a primitive state. It could never create a gravitational pull on a Coastland region and, to make matters worse, an autarkic policy could never build a "new California" in Manchuria. And the Russians did not anticipate the rapid colonization of the frontier by Chinese peasants. The vision had to remain a mirage, hovering over a harsh and unreceptive reality.

When Li Hung-chang was in Petersburg in the spring of 1896, Witte pressed him to grant a concession for the Chita-Vladivostok line with the help of an enormous bribe that Li would never collect in full. The alliance, signed in May, presented the concession as a means to enable Russia to fulfill its obligations—"in order to facilitate access by Russian land forces to threatened points." The line was called the Chinese Eastern Railroad; the concession was granted to the Russo-Chinese Bank for eighty years. A crucial piece of evidence showing Russian intentions was the requirement that the line must use the five-foot gauge of the Russian network instead of the narrower gauge in use elsewhere in China. The

Russian gauge was intended to be the chief tool to coordinate the Manchurian with the Siberian network. Witte also raised the question of building a branch to Port Arthur, the point most likely to be threatened in the event of a Japanese attack on Manchuria or China. Li agreed, but refused to accept the broader gauge, hoping the Chinese would eventually link southern Manchuria, already in the core area, with the Great Wall and Peking. Witte dropped the matter. The Chinese Eastern Railroad was completed in 1903.

The pressure on China to grant a second concession for a branch to Port Arthur became irresistible after Russia staked a claim to the Liaotung Peninsula in the fall of 1897. The March 1898 convention coupled the lease with China's agreement to let Russia build the so-called South Manchurian Railroad and, "if necessary," another branch to a point closer to the mouth of the Yalu River on the Korean border. The branch would use the five-foot gauge and begin at Harbin on the Sungari, a sleepy village that soon became a booming commercial and administrative center. It put Port Arthur within a fifteen-day journey from Petersburg and connected the port with Vladivostok, Khabarovsk, and Irkutsk. The prospect of shorter branches to Petuna, Ninguta, and Kirin, criss-crossing the Manchurian plain, was discussed. Russia's intentions were becoming increasingly clear to contemporaries. Count Hatzfeldt, the German ambassador, reported from London that Britain understood Russia's chief concern to be not Port Arthur and the Trans-Siberian, but "getting hold of a very considerable part of the Chinese Empire and cutting it off altogether from world trade."[4] In other words, the construction of a rail network in Manchuria was the first manifestation of a policy of autarky, to build a ring fence between the Great Wall and the mouth of the Yalu, the extension of the already existing ring fence from Sakhalin to Vladivostok. The next and final stage was to close the Korean gap between Vladivostok and the mouth of the Yalu.

Like Russia, the new Japan had been looking for a line of an optimum of conquest, and it was becoming clear in the early 1890s that such a line should follow the valley of the Yalu and the Tumen rivers, south of the watershed formed by the Changbai Mountains between Korea and Manchuria. The effect of the Treaty of Shimonoseki was to expel the Chinese from the Korean proruption to establish Japan's preponderant influence in the peninsula, and to "close" the Sea of Japan to the Russians. It also created an uneasy triangular relationship between China, Russia, and Japan with unclear implications but disturbing possibilities. Six months after the treaty was signed, in October 1895, the Japanese minister in Seoul engineered the murder of the Korean queen, who had been pro-Chinese. The king became a de facto prisoner of his pro-Japanese cabinet, and Korea was on its way to become a Japanese protectorate.

But the Russians' success in forcing the evacuation of the Liaotung Peninsula convinced them that they would be equally successful in the Korean peninsula, and that if Sakhalin had been "homogeneous" with

the mainland there were even better reasons to consider Korea homogeneous with Manchuria and China itself. History was on the side of the
Russians, now determined to collect the Manchu inheritance wherever
the dynasty had established a claim. The year 1895 witnessed the beginning of a Russian offensive to bring the advance into the Coastland to its
logical completion. The following year, in February 1896, the king fled to
the Russian legation, where he would remain for more than a year. In
April, he granted Russia a mining concession on the Tumen River, and
in September immense timber rights in the valley of the Yalu. On June 3,
Russia and China signed a military alliance, considered with good reason "an anti-Japanese secret alliance."[5] Six days later, the Russian foreign
minister, Alexei Lobanov-Rostovsky, signed with Marshal Yamagata
Aritomo—who, like Li Hung-chang, had come to Russia for the coronation—a protocol on Korea, creating a condominium to manage Korean
finances, communications, and even the maintenance of order in a number of cities. The Russians supported the king as the bearer of legitimacy
but were working against him at the same time. They were determined to
fight the Japanese with a comprehensive program of political, military,
and financial assistance. "Joint administration" had worked well for the
Russians in the Maritime Province; it should advance Russian interests in
Korea as well.

The anti-Japanese offensive continued in 1897, in full awareness but
total dismissal of the fact that the huge Japanese military buildup was
directed against it. Russian instructors were appointed to train Korean
troops; Russian vice-consuls became customs commissioners, and an
unsuccessful attempt was made to appoint a Russian head of the customs
service; the Korean foreign minister was pro-Russian. The king returned
to his palace near the Russian legation to discover that he had become an
agent of Russian expansion. He may have been told of Russian intentions
by the Japanese, but he had lost his freedom of maneuver, what with the
Russians and the Japanese having the same objective in Korea. In March,
the executive officer of the Russian finance ministry wrote that Korea was
of "paramount importance" to Russia, and that Russian ambitions might
receive Chinese support. A branch of the Chinese Eastern Railroad via
Kirin to a Korean port might facilitate the consolidation of Russian influence against Japan, now considered the main enemy since the Russian
decision to reach a peaceful settlement in the Ili valley in 1881. But playing off one core area against another in a strategic frontier was a dangerous game to play, and beyond the ability of the decaying Manchu
dynasty. On the other hand, their own success created a dilemma for the
Russians—should they advance in Manchuria and Korea at the same time
at the risk of antagonizing both China and Japan? Or should they give
priority to Korea or Manchuria? Their inability to choose would prove
fatal to the Russian advance in both areas.

The decision to gain a lease on Port Arthur committed Russia to seek
hegemony in Manchuria. It also antagonized the Japanese. Irresponsible

interests close to Nicholas II now convinced him that Russia could continue to challenge Japan with impunity. At the urging of two well-connected retired guard officers, the Cabinet—the agency managing the properties of the Romanov house—took over the timber concession granted by the king the previous year and turned it into a vehicle of Russian expansionism in northern Korea. The concession—5700 square kilometers along the entire Manchurian-Korean border—was made public in May 1898, three months after the lease on Port Arthur. It would provide cover for 20,000 troops disguised as lumberjacks and become the nucleus of an East Asia Company, subordinated directly to the tsar and not accountable to the ministries of finance and foreign affairs.

It was a paradox that this "unofficial" offensive should take place at a time when those two ministries were willing to reduce their commitments in Korea. In April, the Russian envoy, Roman Rosen, had signed an "arrangement" with the Japanese, pledging both powers to refrain from "direct" interference in Korean internal affairs while promising not to offer military or financial assistance without mutual consent. The Russians promised not to hinder the development of Korea's commercial and industrial relations with Japan. The Japanese were seeking an agreement on a line of an optimum of conquest satisfactory to both powers—if Russia would entrust Korea to Japan, Japan would consider Manchuria outside the Japanese orbit. But the Russians had not given up their goal of drawing a ring fence around the peninsula. The conviction was widespread in Korea that Russia continued to pursue a policy of autarky seeking "the effective exclusion of the remaining foreigners from participation in the economic exploitation of the country."[6] This view was not unfounded.

Confrontation, 1899–1905

In May 1899, after the Russians had gained their first objective in Manchuria—concessions to build an infrastructure of railroads to facilitate the assertion of Russian power—the new envoy to Seoul, Alexander Pavlov, who had just been transferred from Peking, met the commander of the Russian Far Eastern squadron, Admiral Makarov, at Masampo (Masan), one of the finest harbors in the Far East, facing Koje Island on the Tsushima Strait. The meeting was intended as a demonstration of force. The Russians were seeking a site for a coaling station and hospital intended to serve the steamship company that would maintain regular communications between Port Arthur and Vladivostok. A naval base, to be built later, would complete the ring fence around Korea and challenge Japan's decision to "close" the Sea of Japan. There was no room for compromise, but conflict was avoided: the Russians discovered the Japanese had already bought the site and would make sure no equivalent site was available in the area.

While the Russians kept probing in Korea against increasing Japanese resistance and refused to accept a line of an optimum of conquest along the Yalu and the Tumen rivers, the advance into the Russo-Chinese frontier continued. In April, Russia and Britain, "taking into consideration the economic and geographical gravitation of certain parts of the Chinese Empire," agreed on the empire's partition—Britain would not seek railroad concessions north of the Great Wall; Russia waived them in the valley of the Yangtse. The agreement was the equivalent of a partition into three zones, with a neutral zone between the Great Wall and the Yangtse, the very zone Witte had felt in 1898 that Russia would eventually "absorb." Britain thus abandoned Mongolia and Manchuria to Russia. Since Japan would be satisfied with Korea, all the elements of a grandiose compromise were in place, with Russia gaining a free hand in the entire frontier. Wisdom dictated that the Russians ought to accept it, but the Korean "proruption" had become a destabilizing factor, and a lack of coordination at the highest levels of the Russian government added to the confusion.

A possible compromise was also threatened by the Boxer Rebellion. The weakness of the Manchu dynasty had been increasingly evident since the 1870s when a former imperial concubine, Tz'u-hsi, later known as the empress dowager, placed her infant nephew on the throne. She intended to rule even beyond the boy's majority, and blocked his dramatic attempt to reform dynasty and government during the so-called Hundred Days in 1898. Her limited vision and her tenacity, together with the conservatism of Chinese officialdom, prevented the dynasty from rising to the challenge provided by the maritime powers and doomed the dynasty to rot from within. The only recourse of the dynasty was to take advantage of Chinese xenophobia exacerbated by "haughty foreign ministers and consuls and aggressive missionaries and traders"[7] treading on the dignity of a proud nation. Famines, economic dislocation, and official powerlessness contributed to the formation of secret societies motivated not by a program of modernization but by a nostalgic yearning for a happier past. The rotting process was at work, and it could only favor the Russians.

One of those secret societies was known to foreigners as the Boxers, after the old-style calisthenics practiced by its members. Their superstitions included a belief in immunity from bullets and the leadership of divine generals in battle. Their goals varied, but they were united in a determination to expel foreigners. Some members of Tz'u-hsi's entourage convinced her the Boxers were a winning cause, and the movement grew in intensity as official support increased. The Boxers became prominent in Peking in May 1900, burned the British summer legation, and murdered the chancellor of the Japanese legation and the German minister in June. The empress broke off diplomatic relations, and a siege began of the foreign legations. The response of the powers took the form of an international relief operation, consisting of 8000 Japanese, 4800 Russians, and 3000 British, among others. In August, Tz'u-hsi and the Court fled Peking, and Li Hung-chang was called upon to reach a settlement. In December, the eleven powers imposed an indemnity for the loss of life and property, Russia receiving 29 percent of the total. Their troops left Peking in September 1901, but Tz'u-hsi's Court did not return until January 1902.

The uprising gave Russia a golden opportunity to stake a claim on Manchuria. The demolition of over 200 kilometers of track on the South Manchurian Railroad and the attack on Blagoveshchensk across the Amur were used to justify sending 200,000 Russian troops into the country. Tsitsihar was occupied in August 1900, Mukden in October. By the fall, the whole of Manchuria was under Russian occupation. Cossack troops even entered Mongolia and advanced as far as Urga, in order to strengthen the position of the Russian consul. Once in Manchuria, the Russians proceeded to consolidate their position. The frontier was divided at the time into three provinces, each under a Manchu military governor residing in Aigun, Kirin, and Mukden, respectively. The territory leased to the Russians on the Liaoting Peninsula had become Kwantung province, under a de facto governor general, Admiral Evgenii Alekseev, residing in Port Arthur. The war minister, Kuropatkin, who had served under Kaufman during the Ili crisis, urged his government to negotiate a new status for Manchuria, not with the Manchu dynasty but with the three governors separately.

Only one such agreement was negotiated, by Alekseev with the Mukden governor in November. Russia agreed to withdraw most of its forces from the province. The governor assumed responsibility for the maintenance of order along the segment of the Chinese Eastern Railroad in his province, with the help of Russian troops remaining in Mukden and in several points along the line. Should the local police be unable to maintain order, the governor would call on them for help. A Russian commissioner was assigned to him for liaison with the "central authority" in Port Arthur. All Chinese troops would withdraw from the province. In other words, the governor of a province over which the Russians had just ceased to exercise direct control continued to be treated as an agent of the Russian military command. In the other two provinces, Russian authority remained absolute. Witte expected the occupation to last "for many years," and wanted to place Manchuria under Alekseev, thereby extending the lease all the way to the Amur River.

A few days after the agreement with the Mukden governor, a conference of three ministers—Kuropatkin for war, Witte for finance, and Lambsdorf for foreign affairs—outlined the "fundamentals" of Russian policy in Manchuria. The occupation would be "temporary," a favorite term in the Russian political vocabulary to conceal a commitment to a long-term policy. Its purpose was to guarantee China's ability to fulfill its obligations toward the construction and security of the Chinese Eastern Railroad. Then, in blatant disregard of any logic, China would have to withdraw all its troops from Manchuria, and the governors, stripped of their military duties, would be appointed with the agreement of the Russian minister in Peking. Russia clearly aimed at the incorporation of the Manchurian frontier into the Russian Empire, and the approach resembled that followed in the Ili valley in 1871. To bring the rotting process to a successful completion, the Russians had offered the Manchu Court asylum in Mukden, its own birthplace, in October, but Li Hung-chang had declined. Even he, who had been so consistently pro-Russian, could not bear to see his empress reduced to the level of a Korean king.

The occupation of Manchuria, however, created sufficient concern to force the Russians to pause. Geopoliticians consider a boundary a "political isobar"[8] along which the competing pressures of political rivals reach a temporary balance. The comparison applies even more accurately to a line of an optimum of conquest. If such a balance cannot be achieved in a peaceful manner, then force must be used to reduce the stronger pressure to a satisfactory level and give the isobar its appropriate contour. The Russians began to feel an external resistance to their determination to push the isobar out to sea along a line from Port Arthur to Vladivostok, and an internal resistance as well, that contributed to a reassessment of their goals, at least in Manchuria. Geopolitical visions are expensive. They can determine the greatness of states, if they are based on a sound assessment of political and economic strength; they can also lead to disaster if they lack such an assessment. The costs of maintaining the Chinese Eastern Railroad and keeping troops in Manchuria was staggering, and the continued inability to develop an industrial base in eastern Siberia threatened to destroy all prospects of ever carrying out an autarkic policy.

The full extent of Russian ambitions became apparent in January 1901, when another conference of the three ministers agreed on the draft of a treaty to be submitted to China. It contained the same contradictions as the "fundamentals" of the previous October. The draft agreed to the restoration of Chinese authority in Manchuria but forbade China to keep troops there, at least until the completion of the Chinese Eastern Railroad. Russia would have the right to demand the dismissal of governors and other officials whose activities "would not be in harmony with the established friendly relations between the two empires." The principle of an indemnity to compensate for damages caused by the Boxers was accepted, but China would have the option of paying it in the form of new privileges and concessions. What they must be, as a beginning, was made clear. China would grant a concession to build a line from a point on the Chinese Eastern Railroad or the South Manchurian Railroad to the Great Wall, "in the direction of Peking." China would give Russia veto power over the grant to foreigners of concessions for railroads, mining, and industrial enterprises, not only in Manchuria but also in Mongolia and Sinkiang. The draft went far beyond the partition agreement with Britain in 1899, and probably represented Russia's maximum program of establishing a line of an optimum of conquest along the outer periphery of the Heartland.

Negotiations began in February but were broken off in March by the Chinese, encouraged in their resistance by Britain, France, and Germany. Unknown to the Russians, a triple coalition was forming to force them to abandon their "independent and aggressive policy"[9] in China. The Japanese were particularly concerned over Russia's refusal to accept their own independent and aggressive policy in Korea, and were beginning to accept the inevitability of war to force the Russians to negotiate a settlement of the Korean question. Li Hung-chang died in November, a crippling blow to Russia's influence in Peking. When Japan made clear that it would support a strong Chinese policy to force the Russians to withdraw—one not unlike General Tso's strong stand in Turkestan in the 1870s—Lambsdorf and Witte became alarmed at the prospect of a Sino-Japanese alliance backed by Britain and perhaps even Germany.

As if to confirm their fears, Britain and Japan formed an alliance in January 1902, Britain pledging neutrality in the event of a Russo-Japanese war but virtually giving Japan a free hand to safeguard its "special interests" in Korea. The warning was taken seriously, and Russia decided to cut its losses in Manchuria. The Russo-Chinese agreement signed in Peking in April preserved almost nothing of the draft treaty of January 1901. It reestablished Chinese authority in Manchuria, "an integral part" of the empire, and pledged Russia to withdraw its troops in three stages— from the southwestern part of Mukden province to the Liao River within six months (by October 1902); from the remainder of the province and from Kirin province within twelve months (by April 1903); and from Heilungkiang (Aigun) province within eighteen months (by October 1903). Chinese troops would return to Manchuria, but not in "excessive numbers." And Russia returned to China the so-called Imperial Railroad from Shanhaikuan on the Great Wall to Sinminting (Xinmin) near the Liao River, a short distance from Mukden on the South Manchurian Railroad. In so doing, Russia abandoned its goal to build or control a railroad "in the direction of Peking," since Shanhaikuan was already linked with Peking by rail.

One suspects, however, that these concessions to China represented but a temporary retrenchment rendered necessary by the need to concentrate resources on the anti-Japanese offensive. At a series of conferences held between November 1902 and April 1903, Witte was sharply criticized for the priority given to Manchuria, and he would be forced to resign from the finance ministry in August 1903. Much more was involved than personal rivalries and the tsar's uneasiness with the powerful personality of his finance minister. The Russian advance, it bears repeating, possessed its own inner logic and could not stop until it had reached a line of an optimum of conquest linking Vladivostok and Port Arthur around the Korean peninsula. Korea was part of an organic frontier stretching from Kamchatka to the strait separating the Liaotung and Shantung peninsulas, the gateway to Peking, and the Russian advance could no more stop short of Korea than it could have stopped short of Sakhalin. There could be no peace until Russia *or* Japan had imposed its hegemony in the narrow seas. Japan's hegemony in Korea threatened Russia's hegemony in the Liaotung Peninsula and destroyed the usefulness of Vladivostok, "the dominator of the east." Russia was building a continental railroad to Vladivostok and Port Arthur; Japan was threatening to turn these two terminal bases into dead ends.

In June 1902, Itō Hirobumi, one of Japan's leading statesmen and a supporter of friendly relations with Russia, was still convinced that peace was possible if Russia would recognize Korea as part of Japan's exclusive sphere of influence, but Witte still insisted on acquiring a naval base on the Tsushima Strait. In January 1903, Nicholas II ordered Witte to transfer two million rubles from the treasury to the Yalu enterprise, and suggested that the "appearance" of the Japanese on the banks of the Yalu would justify a suspension of the withdrawal from Manchuria. In July, two months before the term set for the final evacuation and just before Witte's dismissal, the tsar raised Alekseev to the post of viceroy and ordered him "to propose a new course" that included keeping foreign influence out of Manchuria and placing Russian fighting power "in perfect equipoise with (Russian) political and economic tasks."[10] In January 1904, Alekseev was made commander in chief of Russian land and naval forces on the Pacific frontier. The post of viceroy was an exceptional one in the history of Russian administration—there had been only two, in Poland and the Caucasus. Its distinguishing feature was the viceroy's direct subordination to the tsar and his full authority over the ministries' local agents. The appointment brought the Liaotung peninsula into the inner frontier of the empire; it was a direct challenge to Japan. On February 7, the Japanese struck at Port Arthur and crippled the Russian squadron. Three days later, the two powers went to war, a war to determine the extent of a Heartland power's ability to consolidate its position in the Monsoon Coastland.

The personal and structural problems encountered during the war reflected the discrepancy between the Russians' traditional close-border policy and fortress-fleet strategy on the one hand, and the forward policy and fleet-in-being strategy on the other, imposed by the tsar's impetuous actions and the underestimation of Japan's military and naval strength. The indecisiveness of Kuropatkin, who left the war ministry to assume command of the field army in Manchuria, and his unfriendly relations with Alekseev, his nominal superior; the downgrading of the Pacific theater's importance and the resulting poor quality of the commanders and their staffs; the general state of unpreparedness; the still inadequate carrying capacity of the Trans-Siberian Railroad, and the shortage of equipment and ammunition—all these factors were characteristic more of an essentially defensive posture suited to the jealous maintenance of a ring fence than of an offensive strategy against the Japanese that sought to expel them from Korea and even to land on the Japanese islands, as some of the more exhuberant Russians hoped to do before coming face to face with reality on the battlefield.

The Far Eastern squadron had seven battleships, seventeen cruisers, twenty-five destroyers, and a large number of auxiliary ships. Most were anchored at Port Arthur, one cruiser was at Chemulpo (Inchon), four were at Vladivostok. The initial attack was followed by the siege of Port Arthur, and the ships that were not crippled remained out of action until they decided to sortie in August and were sunk. The squadron had pursued a fortress-fleet strategy and had to pay the price; its opponent, a fleet-in-being strategy, was the only proper one for an island core area. The Japanese landed at Chemulpo, the port of Seoul, and moved on toward the Yalu, crossing it at Antung (Dandong) in April. A light railroad was later built, linking the port with Mukden on the South Manchurian Railroad, and the Japanese used it to move toward the city in expectation of a gigantic battle of encirclement that would annihilate the Russian army. Meanwhile, Japanese troops had also landed on the Liaotung Peninsula and besieged Port Arthur from the landward side, but the base resisted several assaults until it was forced to capitulate in January 1905. Its brave resistance tied down a substantial number of troops led by one of Japans' most forceful commanders. Their use with the main army might have given the Japanese a decisive victory.

Russians and Japanese moved toward Liaoyang as if in accordance with a preordained plan. Kuropatkin was forced to give battle against his better judgment, when 158,000 Russians met 125,000 Japanese in August. The Russians had to retreat, but Liaoyang was not a decisive Japanese victory. A Russian attack along the Sha-ho River in September left both sides exhausted. The third great battle was fought near Mukden in February 1905, pitting 276,000 Russians against 270,000 Japanese. At no time since Borodino in 1812 and Plevna in 1877 had the Russians faced such a stubborn enemy. They lost, and Kuropatkin was relieved of his command in March.

In earlier and happier days, when Russia had been seeking the opening of Japan to Russian trade, the Russians had discovered that Japan could be reached from the north, from Kamchatka and the Kurils, and from the south, by sailing around the "World Island,"[11] from the Baltic via the Cape of Good Hope and the Strait of Malacca. Their strategy in the war adopted a similar approach. In October 1904, they had decided to commit their Baltic navy to the defense of their Far Eastern possessions. It was an all-or-nothing gamble, for if they lost, they would have no navy left, what with the insignificant Black Sea squadron bottled up in a closed sea. The Baltic fleet—eight battleships, twelve cruisers, nine destroyers, and auxiliary craft—reached Madagascar in December, when Port Arthur was about to surrender. Its mission canceled by circumstances, it sailed on toward the Strait of Tsushima, there to be wiped out in a few hours at the end of May. The Japanese then drove the Russians out of their Korean concessions, made threatening moves against Vladivostok, occupied Sakhalin, and even landed a small force at the mouth of the Amur.

But both sides recognized they could not fight a decisive battle and that a stalemate had been reached. Russia was in the throes of a revolution and its ally, France, refused to finance a continuation of the war after granting a last loan in April 1904. By the summer of 1905, Russia had no more financial resources beyond the issue of its own banks. The Japanese counted on the mediation of the United States, and the tsar decided to invoke it, despite the assurances of General Nikolai Linevich, Kuropatkin's successor, that the army was ready to go on the offensive. The Japanese had not yet won the war; they were physically and financially exhausted. The Russians were morally spent. Even with a revolution threatening the stability of the core area, a more decisive leadership in Manchuria might have restored morale. But Japan won the peace at Portsmouth in September 1905, three weeks after Britain recognized Japan's "paramount interests" in Korea.

The Treaty of Portsmouth dealt with three major issues. It was a territorial settlement. Russia ceded to Japan its lease on Port Arthur and the adjacent territory. Russia and Japan pledged to withdraw their forces from Manchuria, and a subsequent convention, in October, bound them to complete the withdrawal by April 1907. Russia had to agree to the partition of Sakhalin along the fiftieth parallel, an old Japanese objective that kept the Russians out of the two large bays. The island was neutralized, and both powers agreed not to obstruct navigation in the Tatar and La Perouse straits. The treaty was the logical successor of the 1875 agreement on the Kurils. It destroyed Russia's ability to pursue a fortress-fleet strategy from Kamchatka to Port Arthur designed not only to encircle Manchuria but also to deny Japan access to it as well as a dominant influence in Korea. Without that ability, the Russian presence in the narrow seas of Okhotsk and Japan was at the mercy of a Japanese forward policy there and in Manchuria.

The treaty also dealt with the rail network. Russia ceded to Japan most of the South Manchurian Railroad, from Kuen-cheng (near Changchun) to Port Arthur, and had to recognize that its exploitation of the Chinese Eastern Railroad to Vladivostok must serve "no strategic purpose." These concessions announced the partition of Manchuria. Finally, it forced Russia to concede Japan's "paramount political, military, and economic interests" in Korea and to pledge not to oppose any measures Japan might consider necessary to take in the peninsula. Russia would have no "exclusive concessions" in Manchuria, but would grant Japanese subjects fishing rights along the Russian coast of the seas of Japan, Okhotsk, and Bering. Russia was conceding the economic exploitation of its resources in the entire basin of the Amur and the Pacific frontier to Japan, now the dominant power in the Monsoon Coastland.

Accommodation, 1906–1917

The peace settlement pushed the "political isobar" inland, but how far was not immediately apparent. The Russian General Staff worked out a plan in December 1906 for a resumption of the war; Kuropatkin and other "westerners" who had given priority to operations against the Germanic powers now called for a reorientation toward the Pacific. Others saw a future war through a glass darkly, convinced that Japan had the power to force Russia to abandon the Coastland altogether and withdraw behind the Heartland's periphery. However, the debate was soon rendered irrelevant by a realignment of the Coastland powers and the United States following the Portsmouth negotiations. China and the United States recognized that Japan had become the most dynamic power in the Pacific frontier and sought to "internationalize" Manchuria in order to keep it open to international financial capital seeking investments in mining and commercial enterprises as well as railroad building. This common threat to the interests of both Russia and Japan led to a rapprochement of the two recent enemies, who discovered a common prey in China, where the Manchu dynasty was nearing its end. A common threat and a common interest brought about a radical transformation in Russo-Japanese relations.

The first manifestation of the new spirit was the conventions of July 1907. One was public and sought to assuage Chinese and American concerns by proclaiming the independence and territorial integrity of the Manchu Empire. The other, kept secret, effectively partitioned Manchuria "to avoid complications arising from competition." The partition line, the new political isobar, began at the junction of the Russo-Korean-Manchurian boundary near Hunchun; ran past the northern end of Lake Pirteng (Jingpo) to the elbow of the Sungari River, halfway between Harbin and Changchun (leaving a section of the South Manchurian Railroad in the Russian sphere); and followed the course of the river to the confluence of the Nunkiang, this river to its tributary, the Tola, and the Tola to its intersection with the 122nd meridian in the foothills of the Great Khingan. The line divided the Manchurian plain between the two powers, but gave Russia the greater part of Manchuria and the valley of the Sungari, while the Liao valley with the coal, iron, tin, and lead mines remained in the Japanese sphere. Moreover, the Japanese remained within striking distance of the Chinese Eastern Railroad.

The recognition of a new line of an optimum of conquest raised the question of what Russia should do with its share of the Manchurian frontier. To build a ring fence around Manchuria and Korea had been impossible without a commitment of resources Siberia did not have, but the integration of northern Manchuria seemed to have greater chances of success. A consensus was developing in the Russian government for giving priority to building up economic and military strength in eastern Siberia, completing the Trans-Siberian railroad along the loop of the Amur, and giving up any ambitions in the Pacific frontier. The Chinese Eastern Railroad administration, supported by some 30,000 railroad guards, began to develop a political jurisdiction, creating municipalities in the railroad zone and taxing Chinese residing in them. But a new danger appeared. The opening of Heilungkiang province, fronting Siberia over 2000 kilometers, to Chinese colonization reinforced the natural gravitation of Transbaikalia toward China. As early as 1907, the province had a population of

2.5 million, or five times the population of the Russian Far East, and the influx of Chinese settlers who, paradoxically, used the South Manchurian and Chinese Eastern railroads to penetrate Manchuria, was expected to exceed the Russian influx fifteen times. Yet the same Russians who recognized a clear and present danger in Chinese immigration kept thinking that Harbin, at the junction of the railroads and the Sungari, could become the great economic hub of the Amur valley, overlooking the fact that Harbin did not gravitate toward Siberia, but Siberia toward Harbin. Economics and geography were bound to defeat Russia's inclusive policy, while favoring Japan's.

The sphere of influence was also threatened by the Sino-American offensive to internationalize future railroad construction and by China's intention to buy back the Chinese Eastern Railroad. When Peking first proposed the redemption in January 1909, the Russian envoy was "astonished"[12]; Petersburg could not countenance the surrender of its lifeline with Vladivostok. The danger strengthened the Russo-Japanese rapprochement, and both powers signed another two conventions in July 1910. The public one ignored the territorial integrity of the Manchu Empire but pledged to maintain "the status quo resulting from all existing treaties"; the secret one brought the two closer to a formal alliance by calling for "common action or support" to defend their interests in their respective spheres. By December, the Russian ministers of finance and foreign affairs were in agreement that "the annexation of North Manchuria was for [the Russian government] an imperative necessity" and that Russia was only waiting for a favorable time.[13]

The retrenchment behind the Manchurian isobar equalized the pressure between Russian and Japanese ambitions. It also channeled the energy that had been expended in vain in the conquest of the entire Manchurian frontier toward Mongolia. The windswept Mongolian upland was the basin of the Selenga from Lake Hövsgöl in the west to the watershed with the valley of the Amur east of Urga, on the Heartland's periphery. Bound in the south by the Gobi Desert, it had always gravitated toward Lake Baikal. The Kiakhta customs house had been since 1727 the symbol of a close-border policy pursued by both Russians and Manchus, although the Mongol men of power had given their personal allegiance to the Manchu dynasty since its beginning. Peking's policy of keeping the Chinese out of Mongolia and supporting Lamaism was seeking to create a no-man's land between the Sayan Mountains and the Great Wall.

The Russians' lack of interest in Mongolia had begun to change when they sought to open the Manchurian frontier. The Mongol men of power (princes and lamas) with whom Muravev had been able to establish personal contacts were told of the supposedly impending demise of the Manchu dynasty and advised to switch their allegiance to the Russian emperor. In 1854, the proconsul even advised Petersburg to claim Mongolia as a protectorate, but the government continued to feel the time was premature to claim the Manchu inheritance. Russia was granted the right to open consulates at Uliasutai and Kobdo in 1881, but the first consuls were not appointed there until 1905 and 1911, respectively. Little obvious progress had been made in fifty years. However, the opening of the frontier to Chinese immigration in 1906 and the introduction of a Chinese administrative and military infrastructure in 1910 coincided with the renewed activity of Russian agents seeking to convince the Mongols they could count on Russian support if they broke away from the dynasty. In August 1911, an interministerial conference in Petersburg concluded that "it would be desirable to intervene actively in Mongolian affairs";[14] in October, large numbers of Russian troops arrived in Urga under the pretext of protecting the consulate. Then in October, a revolution broke out in China, and the Manchu dynasty collapsed.

The last Manchu emperor abdicated in February 1912, and China became a republic. Its president until 1916 was Yüan Shih-k'ai, who had been Li Hung-chang's representative in Korea in the 1880s and had later built a following among military commanders in northern China. Outer Mongolia, between the Gobi and the Sayan Mountains, had already declared its independence, and the Hutukhtu (Living Buddha) in Urga had been proclaimed Great Khan of a new Mongolian empire in December 1911. The Russians had actively supported the move, but hesitated before a choice of policies. One was to claim the Manchu inheritance and simply incorporate Mongolia into the inner frontier of the empire. The other was to recognize the new China's interests and even sovereignty but to obtain for Russia at the same time the role of "mediator" between China and Mongolia. As in the Maritime Province, joint administration would be a stage on the way of annexation. It would keep Mongolia within the internal affairs of Russia and China—if Mongolia remained under Chinese sovereignty, it would have no right to conduct foreign relations.

In March 1912, the Russians undertook to create a Mongolian army and pledged in November to help Mongolia maintain its "autonomous" regime. Russian subjects were given extensive and exclusive commercial privileges, and the Mongols agreed that Chinese troops must not be allowed into Mongolia and that Chinese colonization must cease. Mongolia was suffering the fate of every frontier—it had "liberated itself from Chinese colonization to become a colony of Russia." Sazonov went so far as to declare in December that the deployments of Chinese troops in Mongolia would be "an act of war."[15] The Russians' preference for the words *Mongolia* and *Mongolian people* left open the question of Mongolia's boundaries. Inner Mongolia, between the Gobi, the Great Wall, and the Manchurian plain, also belonged to the Mongolian people, and there were Mongols in Manchuria, the so-called Barguts, in the basin of Lake Hunlun fed by the Kerulen descending from the Heartland's outer periphery. The region was rich in coal and iron ore, lead and silver ore, but was better known for its gold mines. Its two major centers were Manzhouli and Hulunbuir (Hailer). The Russians had failed to obtain it at Nerchinsk in

1689; their advance into Mongolia now made it possible to support, within limits, the liberation of the Mongolian people. In January 1912, the Barguts revolted with Russian support and seceded from China.

The spread of Russian influence in Mongolia necessitated a new agreement with Japan to demarcate the spheres of influence beyond the Great Khingan. In July 1912, the two powers signed a third secret convention reaffirming those of 1907 and 1910 and partitioning Inner Mongolia. The partition line of 1907 was extended from the intersection of the Tola River with the 122nd meridian across the Great Khingan along steppe streams and watersheds to the Peking meridian (116°27') and followed it southward to the mountains of Jehol, the watershed between Inner Mongolia and the Chinese core area, just east of Dolonnur (Duolun). Russia thus gained Japan's recognition of its preponderant influence in the entire frontier zone between the Great wall and the Sayan Mountains, between the inner and outer periphery of the Heartland. The objective was part of a broader vision seeking to incorporate almost the entire Russo-Chinese frontier—Russia would resume activities in Turkestan; incorporate at least Zungharia and draw a line of an optimum of conquest along the Tien Shan Mountains, the Great Wall, and the new Russo-Japanese isobar, all the way to the Sea of Japan; and keep the Chinese out "by means of various restrictions."[16]

Russian influence continued to grow in 1913. The Russians trained a Mongolian Brigade and equipped it with guns and machine guns. Like the Cossack Brigade in Persia, it was commanded by a Russian officer appointed by the war ministry. A Mongolian mission arrived in Petersburg at the end of the year to obtain more arms in return for a pledge not to buy weapons from other foreign sources. It also sought Russian cooperation for the incorporation of Inner Mongolia into a greater Mongolia. By then, however, the Russians had committed themselves to the partition of Inner Mongolia and could no longer openly support the liberation of the Mongolian people. The Russians were now ready to reach an agreement with China to sanction the legitimacy of their activities. In November, while the Mongolian mission was in Petersburg, the Russian envoy to China, Vasilii Krupensky (who later served in Tokyo), signed a declaration recognizing Chinese suzerainty over Outer Mongolia, defined as the territory (still undelimited) that had been until 1911 under the administration of Peking's agents in Urga, Uliasutai, and Kobdo, that is, the Mongolian upland and the lake region to the Saylyugem Range. Both powers agreed to keep their troops out of the country—but the Mongolian army was Russian trained. China recognized the "autonomy" of Outer Mongolia, confirmed the commercial privileges granted to the Russians in 1913, and accepted Russian good offices to help restore relations with Mongolia.

The declaration was a significant achievement. The next step, taken in September 1914, was a decision to discuss the feasibility of building a railroad in Mongolia and connecting it with the Trans-Siberian, and to give the Russians a concession to build a telegraph line linking Kiakhta with

Urga and Uliasutai. No wonder that an author, closely connected with the Russian war ministry could write of Russia's "fervent hopes for the incorporation of Mongolia," a rich land "suitable for our settlers . . . a source abundant with raw materials not only for Siberia but for European Russia as well."[17] The outbreak of the First World War did not reduce Russian pressure. A tripartite conference held in Kiakhta from September 1914 to June 1915, with Russia as the "mediator," concluded with an agreement that Outer Mongolia was a part of China, under Chinese suzerainty and thus unable to negotiate political treaties; and that its ruler must be invested by the president of the Chinese Republic. The agreement created a legal fiction behind which Russia's economic penetration continued. Outer Mongolia had already received four loans in 1913 and 1914. The official of the Russian finance ministry appointed in 1914 remained Mongolia's fiscal adviser until 1917. A state treasury was created to facilitate Russian control of revenues and expenditures; a Mongolian Bank began to issue Mongolian and Russian monetary units; new taxes were introduced; a survey of Mongolia's economic resources was carried out. The country was truly becoming a Russian protectorate under Chinese suzerainty. A similar status was created for the land of the Barguts, the so-called Hulunbuir district in November 1915.

The war gave Japan unprecedented opportunities to expand its activities in China. It also transformed the post-1905 rapprochement into a formal alliance, signed in March 1916. The alliance confirmed the three secret conventions giving Russia a free hand in its sphere of influence. Russia had just negotiated a partition of the Turkish (and Persian) core area with Britain and France, and some military men felt the time was approaching when Russia must also round out its possessions in the Eastern Frontier. One was Kuropatkin, now governor general of Turkestan, who submitted to the tsar in 1916 that the potential danger represented by an empire of 400 million people made it "absolutely imperative" to rectify the Russo-Chinese boundary. To protect Turkestan against China, the boundary should be moved to the Tien Shan Mountains; from there it would run straight toward Vladivostok, shortening the distance by over 4000 kilometers. Kuropatkin was only advocating a partition with the Monsoon Coastland powers of the frontier between the Heartland's inner and outer periphery—with China in the Turkestan and Mongolian segments, with Japan in the Manchurian segment. The Revolution brought these ambitions to a temporary halt.

The Eastern Frontier was the only one of the three where Russia was able to gain a foothold in the Coastland—Sweden escaped Russia's embrace, and the partition of Turkey remained on paper. Yet it was in the Eastern Frontier that Russia was most vulnerable and its hold most tenuous. Clearly, Russia's eastward advance possessed certain features and took place within a specific context that explains its successes and failures, and raises the question whether its half-hearted determination to play the role of a Coastland power did not endanger its ability to complete the incorporation of the Russo-Chinese frontier and consolidate its position in it. If that were the case, then it might as well be asked whether Russia's persistent resolve to break through the Heartland's periphery in the Southern Frontier would not endanger its hold on the Ukraine, Transcaucasia, and Central Asia. To this question also there can be no definite answer, but the question belongs to the discussion of whether the Heartland's periphery was not fated to remain Russia's line of ultimate conquest.

If we reduce an infinitely complex development to a few simple propositions, it can be said that the Russian advance into the Eastern Frontier was guided by three principal motives. Up to the nineteenth century, fur-bearing animals kept luring trappers and Cossacks across Siberia beyond the Sea of Okhotsk to the northern Pacific; gold deposits in the Altai and lead and silver ore in Transbaikalia induced them to stay; and permanent settlements challenged the core area government to build forward positions to relay energy toward the periphery, creating a logic of expansion deeper into the frontier zones. The advance was also at the heart of an immense endeavor to incorporate the successor khanates of the Mongol oecumene into a Russian empire. The tsars had claimed the inheritance of the Chingissids before asserting their parentage with Byzantium; in the nineteenth century, the Russian advance was motivated, politically and ideologically, by the ambition to collect the inheritance of the Manchus, a tribe on the margin of the Mongol world that had conquered China in 1644. And finally, Russian expansion had an ultimate, strategic, objective—to draw somewhere a line of an optimum of conquest behind which to pursue a fortress-fleet strategy to defend that inheritance against the maritime powers of the Coastland.

Vast river basins created natural corridors of expansion: the Irtysh in the Kazakh steppe-ocean toward Chinese Turkestan, the Selenga into Mongolia, the Amur into Manchuria. The Kazakh steppe did not attract the hunter, but it stretched as far north as Tobolsk, and Tobolsk was the capital of Siberia. An organic frontier of river valleys, watersheds, and salt lakes was an "area inviting entrance" from the north and the south; the turbulence of the frontier zone in the basin of Lake Balkhash kept pushing the Kazakh toward the Russian and drawing the Russian into the steppe, until the great Manchu thrust into Turkestan imposed a permanent political isobar across the Zungharian Gate. In Mongolia and Transbaikalia, not only Manchu strength imposed a line of an optimum of conquest; the trapper's lack of interest in the less valuable furs deflected the Russian advance toward the Sea of Okhotsk. Only when it became obvious that their presence beyond the Iablonoi Mountains would remain a dead end as long as they had no access to the Amur did the Russians show a new determination, for the first time since Nerchinsk in 1689, to seize control of the valley. Their resolve also coincided with the decline of the Manchu dynasty. The dynasty's eventual collapse opened the door to

Mongolia and raised new hopes to extend influence into Turkestan. Russia's maximum program was to incorporate the entire Russo-Chinese frontier including the immense zone between the inner and the outer periphery of the Heartland; it might have succeeded without the Revolution of 1917 and China's increasing determination, despite its political weakness, to counter Russia's penetration with the mass emigration of its peasant settlers. And if it had, Russia would indeed have collected the inheritance of the Chingissids everywhere (except in China itself), as it was expecting to do in the Southern Frontier.

The expansion into the Eastern Frontier followed, by and large, the same methods as in the Western and Southern frontiers—the creation of a common interest with the men of power, the destabilization of the frontier zones, and the encouragement of the rotting process in the core area. However, some restrictions in the Russians' ability to duplicate the same successes were specific to the Eastern Frontier—the near impossibility of finding "dissidents"; the barrier imposed by Islam and Buddhism; the sparse population and vast distances; the inability to find men of power in Peking willing to cooperate in the destabilization of their core area. Russia could only watch in expectation the natural evolution of a process governed by its own dynamic. In the Pacific segment, however, Russia had to deal with a unique situation.

The creation of a string of settlements on the barren coast of the Sea of Okhotsk, on the Kuril islands, and later on the left bank of the Amur and in the Maritime Province, raised two fundamental problems: how to support their continued growth, and how to defend them. It appeared very early that the Kiakhta trade was unsuited to the supporting task and that Russia needed to open relations with Japan, from which adequate food supplies and the necessary equipment would presumably be imported. The Russians thus implicitly recognized that their possessions in the Pacific frontier would gravitate toward Japan and not toward the Heartland. Their advance, to be successful, had to overcome a contradiction— the more settlements there were, the more they would have to depend on outside support, if not on the sea route from the Baltic. However, that contradiction reflected an incontrovertible fact—that the Pacific frontier, an integral part of the Coastland, did not have a hinterland in the Heartland but would derive its potential wealth from integration into the Coastland economy. The uncomfortable recognition of that contradiction was a major factor in the advance into Manchuria, where good land and mineral resources could create at long last the foundation of a regional economy capable of supporting a growing Russian presence in the frontier. There was nothing "adventurist" in the attempt to annex Manchuria—it would have marked the logical completion of an advance that could not have stopped in the middle of nowhere in the search for regional self-sufficiency.

To defend these possessions, at least until the construction of the Trans-Siberian railroad, required the elaboration of a fortress-fleet strategy drawing a "red line" from Kamchatka to the Liaotung Peninsula. The attempt began in 1821 and ended in 1898. But that strategy was realistic only as long as Japan was in the throes of the rotting process that eventually brought down the Tokugawa shogunate. The rapid and unexpected rise of Imperial Japan dashed all hopes of ever being able to count on such a strategy. The only way to restore those hopes was to resort to an offensive strategy against Japan. This unwise, "adventurist," policy explains the depth of Russia's antagonism toward Japan, in many ways similar to its antagonism toward Prussia in the eighteenth century and after 1870. Defeat in 1905 resolved the contradiction between military policy and economic realities. It also shook the Russian position in the Far East to its foundations. It encouraged China's colonization policy and threatened Russian gains in Manchuria and even in Mongolia. Finally, it doomed the Russian Far East to remain an economic backwater from which the core area could never again hope to project sufficient power in the Coastland.

IV

THE CONTAINMENT
OF RUSSIAN
EXPANSION

The Germanic Powers

10

The First Phase, 1700–1796

The Northern War, 1700–1721

The containment of Russian expansion by the Germanic powers is a complex matter. It is easy to detect a pattern of constant hostility toward the Ottomans and the Poles and, to a lesser extent, the Swedes and the Persians. Russia's relations with Austria and Prussia oscillated between hostility and friendliness, depending on the times and circumstances. In every frontier, the Russians had the good fortune of facing pairs of rivals— Poland and Sweden, Turkey and Persia, China and Japan—but nowhere was the antagonism so great as between Prussia and Austria from the beginning of the eighteenth century to 1879. That antagonism facilitated the Russian advance and undermined the formation of a joint containment policy. Moreover, the Germanic powers had their own agenda, and a Russian alliance would come in handy for advancing specific goals, even if that alliance had the effect of neutralizing a containment policy. But consciously or not, during much of the Russian Imperial period, Prussia and Austria were united in a joint effort to contain Russian expansion. Both were dynamic core areas, and both were bound at various times by their alliances with the core areas of the European Coastland to become part of a concert of powers bent on keeping Russia from ever reaching the Heartland's periphery.

The long war with Sweden caused severe disturbances in northern Germany and awakened Prussia and Austria to the existence of a new danger from the east. Fought as it was in the basin of the Baltic, it affected Prussian interests more directly. It also gave the determined Prussian kings opportunities to use the strategic position of Brandenburg, between

Swedish Pomerania and Poland, to extort concessions from Russia as they went about building up a core area government that would soon be perceived by Russia as a mortal threat to its interests in the German lands.

On his way to Europe in 1697, Peter I stopped at Königsberg, where he was met by the Great Elector (there was no Prussian king until 1701) who was then eager to join a defensive and offensive alliance against Sweden. The two rulers swore in June a "stable and eternal friendship" and opened their possessions to trade "without restrictions," and the Elector agreed to receive the tsar's envoys on the same footing as those of the Holy Roman Emperor in Vienna. However, when the Northern War broke out in 1700, the Elector refused to honor his promises, even to consider a new alliance, to the tsar's great anger. His position established a pattern—Prussia would take no active part in the war, but would use favorable circumstances to gain territorial concessions from a hardpressed Russia, as when he first proposed a partition of Poland in 1703. In the meantime, Russians, Poles, and Swedes had shown little respect for Prussia's neutrality. After Charles XII forced Poland out of the war in 1705, Frederick I, the Prussian king, now certain of Sweden's eventual success, formed an alliance with Charles XII, but one directed against Austria rather than Russia. After Sweden's defeat at Poltava in July 1709, he joined Poland and Denmark the same month in a pact to defend their possessions against a Swedish attack; Russia became a fourth member in November. Prussia agreed to block the passage of troops from Swedish Pomerania to Poland and Russia pledged to occupy Elbing, the important Polish fortress near the Baltic coast guarding the approach to Königsberg, and cede it to Prussia.

After gaining an important strategic stronghold at little cost to himself (should the Swedes abandon offensive operations in northern Germany), Frederick I refused to accept additional commitments. The tsar persuaded the king's envoy to Moscow to sign in March 1711 a new treaty pledging Prussia to enter the war on Russia's side in the event of a Swedish invasion of Poland. He placed 10,000 men at the king's disposal to strike at Swedish Pomerania (*Vorpommern*) and agreed not to make peace until it was ceded to Prussia. A secret article presented Prussia's entry into the war as "a great service" to Poland that would require the usual compensation. The tsar would use his good offices to convince Warsaw to cede a corridor linking Prussian Pomerania (*Hinterpommern*) with the Vistula and presumably with Elbing as well. This concession was the first version of the partition of 1772. The days of containment had not yet come; it was Russia that favored Prussia's eastward expansion at the time.

Despite these tempting offers, Frederick I refused to ratify the draft treaty because he would not commit himself to enter the war openly until he was certain that Sweden's misfortunes had passed the point of no return. He had reasons to be cautious. In July, the tsar suffered a humiliating defeat on the Prut and had to agree to let Charles XII return to Sweden. The war continued with an invasion of Swedish Pomerania, and

Peter I, eager to complete his anti-Swedish coalition, went so far as to promise at Greifswald in September 1712 that the Russians would besiege the key fortress and port of Stettin on the Oder and would then let the Prussians negotiate its surrender. Frederick I still refused to enter the war against Sweden.

The king's jealously guarded neutrality paid off handsomely the following year, when the regent for the young duke of Holstein, who was seeking to arrange the duke's marriage to one of the tsar's daughters, put forward a plan intended to win over Prussia to support the duke's claims to the Swedish throne. The plan, supported by the tsar, led to the Treaty of Schwedt (on the Oder, south of Stettin), negotiated in October 1713 by Marshal Menshikov, the Russian commander in chief in northern Germany. The treaty was not a formal alliance; it only took note that the king accepted the offer, as "a mark of trust," to take over and hold ("sequester") the remaining Swedish fortresses in Pomerania—once they had been occupied by the Russians—including Stettin, Stralsund, and Wismar, as well as Rügen Island, until the end of the war. This substantial "gift" would eventually transfer the whole of Swedish Pomerania to Prussia, a stiff price to pay not even for Prussia's entry into the war but for its continued neutrality and support of the Holstein claims.

The new king, Frederick William I, who had succeeded his father in February, understood that an open commitment to the Russian cause had become in Prussia's interest after Denmark's victory over Sweden in May followed by the annexation of Schleswig. Prussia needed to be on the winner's side in order to gain a share of the spoils. King and tsar agreed on a partition of the Swedish Empire in June 1714, just one month before Russia's decisive naval victory at Hangö. Swedish Pomerania was divided along the Peene River, Prussia gaining the eastern half with Stettin and the islands of Usedom and Wolin controlling access to the Oder's mouth. The remainder would remain a Swedish possession until 1815. In return, Prussia recognized Russia's annexation of Estonia, Ingria, and Karelia. The king joined the anti-Swedish coalition and even agreed to take part in the preparation of a common plan of operations against Sweden (one that was never carried out, however).

The opening of Russo-Swedish negotiations in May 1718 caused great concern in Berlin, where the king feared a separate peace would deprive him of the gains made four years earlier. However, the tsar guaranteed Prussia's acquisitions in August and pledged to use force against Britain and Denmark should they side with Sweden against Prussia. The negotiations failed and did not resume until April 1721. Meanwhile, Prussia had made its own separate peace with Sweden in January 1720, the Swedes recognizing the Russo-Prussian agreement of 1714, the Prussians promising they would give Russia no help until the end of the war. The tsar had reason to view Prussia's decision as a breach of faith and a hostile act.

Nevertheless, tsar and king still found a common ground in their relations with Poland. They agreed in February that "Polish liberties" must be maintained and that the Saxon dynasty must not be allowed to make itself hereditary in Warsaw. The foundation of a Russo-Prussian alliance against Poland had been laid; it would also support Prussia's containment policy until the final partition in 1795. A first, hesitant, step was taken in the Kurland question. We remember that Anna Ivanovna, the tsar's niece, had married the duke of Kurland shortly before his death in 1711. Frederick William advanced the candidacy of his cousin for Anna's hand in the spring of 1718—Brandenburg that had incorporated Prussia continued to lay claim to the inheritance of the Teutonic Order. An eventual annexation of Kurland would strengthen Germanic influence in Riga and bar the way to Russian expansion into Samogitia, the barrier guarding the approaches to East Prussia from the north. The king's bid failed, in part because the prospective groom showed little interest, in part because the tsar refused to pay the considerable dowry requested by the king. But one could also detect larger apprehensions, still too vague to be officially declared. The war with Sweden was drawing to an end and a new, powerful, and triumphant Russia no longer needed Prussia. On the other hand, Frederick William, one of Prussia's greatest kings, was a determined practitioner of *Wehr-Geopolitik*—geopolitics focused on preparation for war—long before the term became popular 200 years later. Drastic domestic reforms would rapidly transform a small and poorly endowed core area into a powerful military state, and its king understood that Prussia's future would depend on the issue of a struggle for space, not only against Austria, but also against Russia, a struggle for hegemony in the Polish core area between the Oder and the Niemen. By 1725, Russo-Prussian relations had cooled considerably. Both powers had discovered that they were potential enemies. If Russia refused to be contained, it would have to destroy Prussian power.

Russian activities in northern Germany during the war had given the Prussian king ample opportunities to be wary and apprehensive. Peter I inaugurated a policy of negotiating dynastic marriages with ruling houses in the German states of the Holy Roman Empire. In October 1711, he married off his son Alexei to a princess of Brunswick-Wolfenbüttel, adjoining the western end of Brandenburg. He then gained a foothold in Mecklenburg, a duchy on the Baltic coast between Holstein and Swedish Pomerania.

The settlement with the Ottomans on the Prut released Russian troops for operations along the Baltic littoral in preparation for an allied landing in Sweden. The road to Sweden ran through Prussia and Mecklenburg; both had declared their neutrality and had to be won over. We saw how difficult it was to obtain Prussia's cooperation. Negotiations with Mecklenburg were less tortuous. A Russian envoy appeared at the ducal court in September 1712 asking for the right of passage and for provisions in return for a Russian promise to keep the Swedes out of Mecklenburg and help the duke obtain Warnemünde at the peace settlement. Since

Prussia insisted on remaining neutral, Russian troops in the duchy would have to come by sea in order to attack Swedish Pomerania from the west.

The Russians, however, soon became embroiled in a bitter dispute between the duke and his nobility, who accused him of violating their rights guaranteed by the Holy Roman Emperor in Vienna. To strengthen his hand, the duke asked for the hand of one of Peter's nieces, Ekaterina Ivanovna, despite the fact that he had not yet been granted a divorce from his first wife. The tsar agreed, and the marriage contract signed in February 1716 contained a Russian promise to help the duke obtain not only Warnemünde but also Wismar. The Prussian king to whom Wismar had been promised in 1713 agreed to relinquish it. The wedding took place in Danzig in April and was followed by a treaty of alliance pledging the tsar to defend the duke against "internal and external disturbances" and to use force against the nobility, should they seek foreign support. The treaty transformed Mecklenburg into a Russian protectorate.

A Russian foothold in Mecklenburg was worrisome enough; the great commercial cities of Lübeck, Hamburg, and Danzig were also caught in the vortex of Russo-Swedish hostility. After Lübeck bowed to Swedish demands not to send artisans and sell munitions to Russia, Russian troops occupied the city in the spring of 1713. It imposed a contribution on its inhabitants, but withdrew after it was paid, promising not to interfere with its Baltic trade. Hamburg suffered the same fate for refusing to crack down on authors of libelous pamphlets against the tsar. Danzig was briefly occupied in the fall of 1717 for refusing to stop trade and correspondence with Sweden. Russia's sway extended as far as Hanover, where the Elector—who became king of England in 1714—wanted to expel the Swedes from the "European continent," hoping to benefit from their expulsion.

It is easy to understand that this immense projection of Russian power along the entire Baltic coast all the way to the Heartland's periphery, the destruction of Polish independence, and the unequal alliance with the elector of Saxony whose heart and residence were in Dresden on the Elbe, were sufficient to create a siege mentality in Berlin and to strengthen the king's determination to expel the Russians from northern Germany once the war was over. On the eve of his death, Frederick I was already seeking allies in the Coastland to contain "the vast and ambitious designs of the eastern barbarian."[1] Russia's treatment of Danzig served as a reminder of what the Russians could do to Königsberg if they were not contained beyond the Niemen.

Relations with Austria followed a different course during Peter's reign. Austria played a major role in the War of the Spanish Succession fought with Britain against France for the inheritance of the Spanish king, while Prussia's contribution was insignificant. It was not until peace was made with France in March 1714 that Austria could return to its traditional mission as the leading state in the Holy Roman Empire and the valley of the Danube.

Austrian interests were not directly threatened during the Northern War, but Russian activities in northern Germany, the Protestant zone of the empire, created apprehensions in Vienna. Austria's natural alliance with Russia, born spontaneously after 1683 when the two powers discovered they had a common enemy in the Ottoman Empire, had fallen on hard times after the peace of Karlowitz, when Austria, encouraged by the mediation of the British and Dutch eager to draw it into their conflict with France, had signed a separate peace and left the Russians in the lurch. Russia's early defeats in the Northern War earned it Austrian contempt, at least until the battle of Poltava suddenly awakened Vienna to the existence of a powerful Russia. Rumors spread by the Swedes that the tsar intended to place his son or Menshikov, his favorite, on the Polish throne were disquieting. The Mecklenburg affair offended the dignity of the Hapsburgs. The rise of Prussia and Hanover, leaders of the Protestant cause, was irritating. The expulsion of Sweden from the continent could only result in the aggrandizement of Prussia, but a Swedish victory would establish the preponderant influence of another Protestant power in Poland, the Holy Roman Empire's eastern neighbor. Austria's policy was thus forced to remain ambiguous and very much aware of its inability to influence events taking place on the Baltic littoral. Tensions with Russia did not prevent the empire from accepting the marriage of the princess of Brunswick to Alexei, Peter's son, in October 1711; she was also the emperor's sister-in-law. The family tie had its tragic side, however. When Alexei ran away from Moscow in October 1716, he received asylum in the empire, a gesture that did not endear Charles VI to the Russian tsar.

Nevertheless, the Austro-Russian natural alliance remained tacitly in being because it was rooted in geopolitics. By the very fact of its existence and the ambitions of its ruling elite to continue its own *Drang nach Osten* along the Danube, Austria increased the risk for the Ottomans of an attack in the Russo-Turkish frontier: the Ottomans might be faced with a two-front war. But the natural alliance was full of contradictions because a community of interests against the Ottomans concealed an Austrian determination to contain Russian expansion in the direction of the Danube.

The peace of Karlowitz in January 1699 had been the first stage in the Austrian conquest from the Ottomans of the kingdom of Hungary-Croatia that had once stretched from the Kvarner Gulf on the Adriatic to the Carpathian Mountains and from Bratislava to the Iron Gate of the Danube. The new boundary followed the Transylvanian Alps in the east, swerved north to the Mures River, and followed it to the Tisza (Theiss) at Szeged. It then ran along the Tisza to the Danube north of Belgrade, crossed the Danube-Sava mesopotamia to the mouth of the Bosut, followed the Sava to the confluence of the Una and the Una to its source in the Dinaric Alps, the Heartland's periphery. The Austrian advance created considerable turbulence in the Hungarian plain. Hungarian nobles revolted both against the considerable influx of Slavs in the so-called Vojvodina and against Vienna's centralizing policies. From their bases in

Poland, the Russians supported the rebellion of Ferenc Rákóczi, the last independent prince of Transylvania until a settlement was reached in April 1711, and gave refuge to other rebels. The rebellion was barely over when the tsar had to face the Ottoman challenge in Moldavia. We know that the expedition failed on the Prut in July, but Vienna had to be seriously concerned by Russian attempts to establish an influence in Transylvania and Moldavia, even in Wallachia, where the hospodar was known to be devoted to Russia. The Austrian and Russian advance created an interlocking frontier with the Ottomans where Vienna and Petersburg were fated to fight a long struggle for preponderance until 1914.

The steady stream of Serbian, Moldavian, and Wallachian officers entering Russian service and the trip of the Montenegrin *vladika* to Petersburg in 1711 were among the factors that determined Austria to resume the advance into the frontier. War was renewed with the Ottomans in 1716, and the peace of Passarowitz (Požarevac) in July 1718 near the confluence of the Morava and the Danube completed the second stage. The new boundary ran from the Transylvanian Alps along the Olt (Oltul) River to the Danube, along the Danube past the Iron Gate to the confluence of the Timok. It then ascended the Timok's lower course and crossed over to the Drina past Paraćin, and followed the Drina to the Sava. In addition, the Austrians incorporated the Ottoman forts on the right bank of the Sava between the Drina and the Una. Their move challenged the Russians in two areas: in Wallachia, now truncated with the loss of Little Wallachia (Oltenia, west of the Olt River), and in Serbia, where the metropolitan of Karlowitz was becoming an agent of russification of the Serbian educational and ecclesiastical institutions.

Shifting Alliances and War, 1725–1762

The Austro-Russo-Ottoman frontier was still vast enough, however, and studded with enough Ottoman fortresses to justify the restoration of the Austro-Russian alliance. That its architect was Andrei Osterman, the vicechancellor and a leading figure in the Russian government after Peter's death, was a fortuitous circumstance. Interests determine the guidelines of a country's foreign policy; statesmen formulate those guidelines and provide the operational leadership to carry them out. The end of the Northern War and the development of peaceful relations with Sweden restored the pre-eminence of Russian interests in the Russo-Turkish frontier, and those interests were inextricably linked with the Austrian alliance.

The alliance was embodied in the treaty of August 1726. Austria adhered to the Treaty of Nystad and guaranteed all Russian possessions "in Europe." The two powers pledged 30,000 troops to a war against either party, and Austria, together with Spain, its ally, agreed to open its ports in the Mediterranean and the Atlantic to Russian warships in wartime. A "most secret clause" somewhat enlarged the treaty's scope by pledging Austria to commit the same number of troops in the event

"Russian provinces in Europe outside Persia" should come under attack following a Russian decision to prevent the Ottomans to extend their sway over the whole of Persia. Both powers were still seeking each other's aid against their current enemies—Russia against the Ottomans, Austria against Prussia and France—and the alliance committed Austria to fight the Ottomans on Russia's side, Russia to fight Prussia on Austria's side.

The treaty was first tested in Poland, however. When the death of Augustus II became imminent, both powers agreed that Stanislas Leszczynski was unacceptable and that the next king of Poland would have to accept the Pragmatic Sanction—a declaration of Charles VI, published in various versions between 1713 and 1724, seeking international recognition for the rights of his daughter Maria Theresa to succeed him in the absence of a male heir. Russian troops imposed the son of Augustus on the Polish throne in 1733. Austria did not take part in the operation, but its open support of the Saxon candidate brought about a war with France, Leszczynski's chief supporter. When Austrian troops suffered reverses in 1734, Austria invoked the 1726 alliance, asserting it would support Russia "in any war" if only Russia would send troops into Germany to fight on Austria's side. Russian troops moved on from Poland across Saxony and linked up with the Austrians near Heidelberg in April 1735. Only a quickly arranged armistice stopped their progress to the Rhine, and the Russian contingent was withdrawn in November.

But Russian ambitions beyond the Dniepr were bound to test the alliance in the Russo-Turkish frontier as well. When it happened, Austria resolved for the first time to pursue a containment policy designed to block Russia's access to the Danube. The secret of Austria's—and Prussia's—containment policy in the eighteenth century was that it served the Germanic powers' policy of territorial aggrandizement as well, so that it is often impossible to separate the ultimate objectives of both policies. The inner contradictions of the Russo-Austrian alliance first appeared in the 1730s—Russia and Austria had a common enemy in the Ottoman Empire, but were bound to become rivals for the distribution of the spoils.

Russia declared war in May 1735, forced its way into the Crimea, and reached the khan's capital in July 1736. Austria showed no eagerness to enter the conflict as long as the Russian thrust was directed against the Crimea. The prospect of the war's extension into the Danubian Principalities prompted the Austrian high command to draw up in August a plan of operations against the Ottomans seeking to obtain Bosnia between the Sava and the Adriatic and Albania and Montenegro to the headwaters of the Drina, and to complete the annexation of Wallachia and extend the Austrian Empire to the Prut by annexing most of Moldavia. The plan was bold, and drew for Austria a line of an optimum of conquest that would bar a Russian advance to the Carpathians and give Austria complete control of the river traffic on the Danube. The string of Ottoman fortresses between Brăila and the Black Sea coast would supplement the Austrian defense perimeter and block a Russian advance to the lower Danube.

The Austrians did not enter the field until after the fall of Ochakov in August 1737. By then, however, the Ottomans had concentrated enough forces against both their opponents to bring operations to a standstill. The Nemirov negotiations brought into the open the certainty of an Austro-Russian rivalry in the Principalities—the Russians wanted their independence, the Austrians opposed it, although they were forced to reduce their claims, seeking only an extension of their boundary beyond the Olt to the Dimbovița River that flows through Bucharest on its way to the Danube. In Bosnia, they would be satisfied with the foothills of the Dinaric Alps (with Bihac), but they sought the aggrandizement of Serbia by claiming the valley of the Danube from the Timok to Lom, with the key fortress of Vidin.

These claims became castles in the sand when the Ottomans regained the initiative. Reverses during the 1738 campaign placed Austria in the humiliating position of having to request for its own defense the 30,000 troops promised by the 1726 alliance. Russia's refusal may have been a factor in the Austrian defeat following an Ottoman thrust on Belgrade in the summer of 1739. As in 1699, Austria sued for a separate peace, forcing Russia to leave the war. Its containment policy had failed piteously: the Russians had reached Jassy, but the Austrians had fallen back on Belgrade. When peace was signed in September, Austria lost Belgrade and all the territory south of the Sava and the Danube gained at Passarowitz in 1718. Its half-hearted participation in the war, as if expecting a war of attrition between the Russians and the Ottomans, and the suspicion of Austrian motives in Petersburg left a long legacy of mistrust. But the natural alliance continued to hold: the empress Anna Ivanovna agreed to give her niece Anna Leopoldovna in marriage to a nephew of the Austrian empress and pledged to defend the Pragmatic Sanction.

The year 1740 witnessed the death of the three protagonists—Frederick William, the Prussian king, in May: Charles VI and Anna Ivanovna in October. The Pragmatic Sanction, over which so much diplomatic effort had been spent, proved unenforceable, and Maria Theresa (1740–1780) was immediately faced with Prussian and Bavarian claims on her inheritance. The new Prussian king, Frederick II (1740–1786), invaded Silesia, one of the richest of Austria's nuclear lands, but Austria's request for military assistance was met with Russian equivocation. The imminence of a new war with Sweden and the memories of Austria's behavior in the recent war with the Ottomans had much to do with it. Nevertheless, the reign of Elizabeth (1741–1762) was marked by a consolidation of the Austro-Russian alliance, despite an inauspicious start. The empress remained for some time suspicious of Austrian policy because of her personal antipathy toward Maria Theresa, suspected of sympathy for her deposed relative, Anna Leopoldovna, who was fated to die a slow death in the wastelands of northern Russia in March 1746. And the implication of the Austrian ambassador in a scandal at the Russian court poisoned relations until 1744.

However, Elizabeth's relative neglect of Polish and Ottoman affairs removed geopolitical conflicts from the Austro-Russian alliance, and Frederick II's invasion of Bohemia in August 1744 created a common interest in resisting Prussian ambitions. The two powers renewed the 1726 alliance in June 1746, and pledged in June 1753 to declare war on the Ottomans "immediately" in the event of a violation of the treaty of Belgrade. Russia committed itself to support Austria against Prussia and France, and the immediate consequence of the alliance's renewal was the dispatch in January 1748 of a Russian corps of 30,000 across the Holy Roman Empire in the direction of the Rhine to assist the Austrians against the French. Paradoxically, however, the alliance of 1746 that promised such close collaboration in the Balkans was soon undermined by a conflict over religion. Toward the end of 1749, Elizabeth, a strong supporter of the Orthodox Church, made known her opposition to the Austrian persecution of the Orthodox in Croatia, Transylvania, and other parts of the Austrian Empire. Some of the persecuted Slavs decided to leave for Russia (they were later resettled in the Ukrainian steppe) but Maria Theresa's refusal to give them passports angered the Russian government. Differences were ironed out in the fall of 1752, but an issue of potentially devastating importance had been raised for the first time.

The Russians' return to their natural alliance with Austria in 1726 was bound to bring about a long cold war with Prussia. The Prussian king's unswerving policy of territorial aggrandizement was certain to threaten Austrian and Russian interests. It threatened Austrian interests because Berlin would no longer take for granted Vienna's primacy in German affairs and any territorial acquisitions upset the delicate balance of power in German Imperial politics. It antagonized Russia because territorial acquisitions in Poland ran counter to Russia's policy of encouraging the rotting process in the Polish core area, in preparation for its transformation into a Russian protectorate that would bring Russian influence to bear directly and permanently on the Oder. Moreover, Prussia was not alone but was linked with France and had influence in Sweden.

Russo-Prussian relations began auspiciously when the two powers signed a defensive alliance in August 1726, four days after Russia signed a similar alliance with Austria. They guaranteed each other's possessions and pledged to commit 5000 troops to each other's defense. The true purpose of the alliance was in the secret articles. Berlin agreed to support Russia's policy in the Schleswig-Holstein question; gave up its claim on Kurland and agreed the duchy must remain independent of Poland, in effect a Russian protectorate under Anna Ivanovna, soon to become empress of Russia; and readily concurred that "Polish liberties" must be maintained. The Polish question brought about the fateful alliance of September 1730. Both powers were moved by "compassion" at the sight of Polish persecutions of their co-religionists, Protestant and Orthodox "dissidents," and agreed to make "the strongest representations" in Warsaw to protect them until the advent of "better times." The joint intervention in Polish religious affairs, an all too evident cloak to conceal political and territorial objectives, had logic on its side, but its effect was to favor Prussian interests—Warsaw, Danzig, the Vistula, and the heart of the Polish core area in the Poznan region were within striking distance of Prussian bases on the Oder.

Despite the agreement on the need to maintain "Polish liberties" and protect dissidents, the Polish question was certain to exacerbate Russo-Prussian relations. Poland's disintegration combined with geography to create an insoluble double dilemma. Prussia could not extend its power in Poland without Russia's consent and without accepting the principle of territorial compensation. Its territorial ambitions thus worked against its containment policy, despite the fact that they would also serve to contain Russian expansion behind the Niemen. Prussia could not intervene in Poland without bringing about a Russian intervention, and the ghost of Peter I was still haunting the Prussians. On the other hand, Russia could not keep Prussia out of Poland in the long run, but Prussia's aggrandizement meant an accretion of Prussian power. Russia's military intervention in the succession crisis of 1733 may have had as its other and no less important purpose to show that Petersburg could impose its will in Warsaw and Danzig, even without Prussia's participation and even against Berlin's will. There were good reasons for the resulting chill in Russo-Prussian relations.

It grew worse following the accession of Frederick II in March 1740. The young king made war on Austria, forcing it to cede Silesia in June 1742, but Empress Elizabeth refused to recognize the annexation until November 1743. Meanwhile, his strong-willed sister, Luise Ulrike, had married Adolf Frederick, chosen as heir to the Swedish throne in June 1743, who would become king in March 1751. The rapid emergence of the Prussian core area, straddling the Elbe and the Oder; endowed with rich natural resources after the incorporation of Silesia; led by a political elite imbued with a dynamic Protestant faith and a military elite shaped by memories of the Teutonic Knights; and allied with France, Russia's natural enemy, could not but create the gravest misgivings in Petersburg. The consequence was a revolution in geopolitical perceptions within the Heartland. The two core areas that had been Russia's rivals in the Western Frontier, Sweden and Poland, were in full decline, while Russia's power was on the rise, giving hope that some day Russia might once again, as it almost had in the 1710s, extend its influence to the Kjølen and the Elbe. But the emergence of an aggressive Prussia created a new "super-core area" and a new frontier with Russia in which Sweden, Finland, and Poland would become mere zones. The Russians quickly understood, as they would 150 years later when Japan emerged on the international scene, that they were faced with a dangerous enemy: only those two powers would at a later stage of their development generate enough energy not only to contain Russian expansion but to roll back the Russian advance. Frederick had defeated Russia's two diplomatic allies,

Austria and Saxony, and his undisguised contempt for Empress Elizabeth seemed to announce a Prussian forward policy. Osterman's successor as the leading figure in the formulation of Russia's foreign policy, Alexei Bestuzhev-Riumin, saw clearly as early as 1744 that "our dangers grow with Prussian power."[2] In June 1746, the Prussian ambassador was declared persona non grata; in December, Russia withdrew its recognition of the annexation of Silesia. Four years later, in October 1750, both powers broke diplomatic relations, and Petersburg resolved in May 1753 to block by force of arms any further expansion of Prussia.

The "diplomatic revolution" of 1756—in which Prussia deserted France in January to form an alliance with Britain, and France abandoned its traditional anti-Habsburg policy to join Austria in an alliance for the recovery of Silesia in May—did not affect Russia's determination to crush Prussia in alliance with Austria. In fact, the newly established "Conference" in Petersburg adopted a militant anti-Prussian policy in March and urged Vienna to take drastic action. Frederick II, convinced that a pre-emptive strike might destroy the coalition being forced against him before France and Russia gained enough time to move decisively, invaded Saxony at the end of August, bringing about the so-called Seven Years War (1756–1762).

The Russians entered the war in the spring of 1757, a few months after renewing the alliance of 1746. Austria pledged in addition to pay a subsidy of one million rubles to facilitate the movement of Russian troops "as deep and as soon as possible into Prussia."[3] The war was a series of bloody encounters, but the Prussians succeeded in stopping the Russian advance on the Oder in August 1758. The usual disagreement with Austria prevented the coordination of operations. The Russians' brief occupation of Berlin in October 1760 was a coup de main that could not be sustained: the king rallied his people for the desperate defense of the core area. Nevertheless, the Russian elite began to discuss ambitious plans to dispose of a defeated Prussia. Russia might annex not only East Prussia but Pomerania as well. The territory would pay for itself and might even contribute additional revenue to the Imperial treasury; Russia would reach the Oder; with its food stores and artillery left permanently in Prussia-Pomerania, it would be able to pursue a forward policy to the Elbe at any time; with a foothold in the Holy Roman Empire, it would become a guarantor of the Treaty of Westphalia and have a voice in the settlement of all German affairs. And as a consequence, the Polish Empire would become the inner frontier of the Russian Empire. These goals were not realistic at the time. Both Prussia and Russia were exhausted and had to accept the limits of the possible. Their inability to win a decisive victory, the devastation of Prussia by Kalmyks and Cossacks, and the resignation in October of William Pitt, who had been the Prussian king's major supporter, forced them to make peace. But the decisive event was the death of Elizabeth in January 1762. The new emperor, Peter III, bluntly told Vienna in February that Russia was withdrawing from the war, and concluded an armistice in March. Austria and France followed suit in November.

Prussia had nearly lost the war, and the king expected to lose some of his possessions. Instead, he merely had to promise to contract no alliance contrary to Russian interests and those of the Holy Roman Empire. Russia pledged to return all land, towns, and fortresses captured during the war, including, of course, East Prussia. The Austrians were unable to obtain the restitution of Silesia when they made peace the following year. Peter III betrayed the hopes of his aunt Elizabeth, the interests of his dynasty, the honor of his generals, and the blood of his soldiers. But he was a "German" by birth, by upbringing, and by conviction. By withdrawing Russian troops to Livonia and the Russian core area and canceling the Russian advance, he served Prussia's containment policy better than Frederick could have done.

Strains and Stresses, 1763–1796

Russia's intervention in Poland in 1733 and its battlefield victories during the Seven Years War asserted its preponderant power in the Western Frontier, and the advance into the Western and Southern frontiers during the reign of Catherine II marked a new stage in the empire's transformation into a global power. Catherine II was another German on the Imperial throne, but she was Russian by much of her upbringing and certainly by conviction. One of her major contributions would be to establish Russia's leading role as a mediator between the two Germanic powers by a mixture of cajolery and threats backed by what increasingly became a Germanic perception of invincible military power. In these circumstances, it seemed that a containment policy could have no chance of success. But that was not the case.

Frederick II had been chastened and made to see that his uncompromising anti-Austrian policy entailed unbearable risks, because Russia could not accept the humbling, let alone the destruction, of the Habsburg Empire and the creation of a single Germanic core area. A direct confrontation had become unthinkable, but geopolitical realities continued to assert themselves, even if the king had become more cautious. The retention of Silesia gave Prussia the industrial base necessary to sustain the growth of the core area. As the core area grew in fame and power, it created a dynamic frontier with rival core areas. Between Prussia and Austria there remained only Saxony, but a new frontier developed between Prussia and France, now enemies, in the confused and checkered Holy Roman Empire between the Elbe and the Moselle, and the accelerating distintegration of Poland continued to transform its empire into a Russo-Prussian frontier. Almost independent of the king's rule, the emergence of Prussia as a major player straddling the Heartland's periphery created an expansionist urge to seek a dominant position in both frontiers; the logic of that urge was to contain a corresponding urge in the rival core areas.

Similar forces were at work in the Austrian core area and the Austro-French and Austro-Russian frontiers under the forceful leadership of Maria Theresa, her chancellor Wenzel von Kaunitz, and her son Joseph II (1780–1790). However, the rivalry of Prussia and Austria in their ambition to achieve similar objectives gave Catherine II the opportunity to balance one against the other and to make significant gains against both. The victims of their rivalry were the Polish and Ottoman empires and, to a lesser extent, the Holy Roman Empire, subjected for the first time to the conflicting destabilization policies of Russia and the Germanic powers.

Catherine II felt a natural affinity for Prussia—her father was a general in Prussian service and Frederick II had arranged her marriage—and Prussia's envoy, Count Viktor Solms, sent to Petersburg in November, was admitted to her inner circle. She had no intention of renewing the war. The death of the Polish king in October 1763 and her powerful intervention in favor of Stanislas Poniatowski received the support of Prussia, eager to break out of its isolation, and led to the alliance of April 1764 pledging both powers to contribute 12,000 troops each to the common defense and to work together in support of the "dissidents" in Poland and the Constitution of 1720 in Sweden. In the event Prussia became engaged (against France or Austria) in the Coastland west of the Weser and Russia in the Russo-Ottoman frontier, the other would contribute, instead of troops, a subsidy of 400,000 rubles a year. Frederick also supported Catherine's plan for a Northern Accord of "active" and "passive" powers, although his "sane and practical mind"[4] did not, or chose not to, understand what it was all about.

Frederick II needed the Russian alliance because, as he put it in November 1765, "no one" (meaning Austria above all) "will dare attack me,"[5] but his memories of the Seven Years War and his observations of Repnin's high-handedness in Warsaw convinced him of the necessity to roll back Russian influence in Poland. The permanent stationing of Russian troops in the Polish capital and the implicit Russian claim that the Vistula had become a forward perimeter from which troops, supplied from stores strung along the river and filled by the inexhaustible Polish grain trade, could move to the Oder at a moment's notice, were keeping a sword of Damocles over the Prussian kingdom. Frederick's acute geopolitical sense warned him against letting Poland become "a Russian borderland and the permanent camping ground of the Russian army" (*ein russisches Nebenland und der ständige Lagerplatz russischer Heere*).[6] Had it not been for Russia's undisguised attempt to transform the Polish Empire into a protectorate, it might have served Prussian interests better to preserve Poland as a buffer to block the Russian advance, but Russia's forward policy matched Prussia's urge for aggrandizement. When Russian troops finally broke the Ottoman resistance in the Russo-Turkish frontier and Berlin had to face the possibility of an Austro-Russian war, the necessity of reaching a settlement with Russia at Poland's expense became imperative; an agreement on territorial "compensations" would defuse the tension. When Russia annexed eastern Bielorussia, it withdrew from Pomerelia and Galicia, the Prussian and Austrian shares. The territorial aggrandizement of the Germanic powers also served to roll back the Russian presence in Poland.

The first partition had unexpected consequences, however. One year after the Polish Diet ratified it, the Russians made peace with the Ottomans at Kuchuk-Kainardji in July 1774. There followed a major change in the direction of Russian foreign policy, away from the Baltic and Poland toward the Black Sea, not unlike the reorientation that had taken place after the Northern War. The consolidation of Russian gains in the Russo-Turkish frontier required Austrian cooperation, and the Prussian alliance became expendable. Friendly relations turned into calculated coldness, both powers using the Danzig question to fight a war of nerves. Frederick was forced to lift the blockade of the city at the end of 1783, despite his conviction that "in order to gain the most from Russia one must pursue a harsh and inflexible policy,"[7] but war became a distinct possibility in 1785 following Joseph II's attempt to acquire Bavaria. When Frederick died in August 1786, he had become convinced that a Russo-Austrian coalition was bent on making war on Prussia once again.

The great king was succeeded by his nephew, Frederick William II (1786–1797), less capable but more relaxed than his austere uncle. He had to guide Prussia during the difficult early years of the French Revolution, when France destroyed until 1815 Prussia's hopes of establishing its preponderance in the Franco-Prussian frontier. By way of compensation he inaugurated an anti-Russian containment policy on all fronts, maximizing to an unprecedented extent Prussia's determination to replace France as the great containing power, and by the same methods. He supported Sweden during its war with Russia (1788–1790) and signed an offensive alliance with the Ottomans in January 1790, when they were still at war with Russia, and an alliance with Poland in March. The following year, the king was ready to go to war against Catherine, and only the withdrawal of British support kept the peace. The second partition of the Polish Empire in 1793 forced Russia to withdraw from the valley of the Warta and the middle Vistula, and the third, in 1795 and in alliance with Austria, gave Warsaw to Prussia and rolled back Russia behind the Niemen and the Bug. The partitions gave Russia the Russo-Polish frontier but expelled it from the Polish core area.

The Austro-Russian alliance had failed during the Seven Years War—Russia had not destroyed Prussia and Austria did not recover Silesia. Russia's alliance with Prussia in 1764 was bound to create resentment in Vienna, not only because it precluded another Austrian war of revenge against Prussia, but also because it checked Austria's resolve to oppose Russian expansion in the Austro-Russian-Ottoman frontier: a decision to oppose the Russian advance by force would be met by a Prussian attack on Austria from Silesia across the Moravian Gate. This combination of circumstances created a dilemma in the Austrian government. Kaunitz believed that the containment of Russian expansion in the direction of the Black Sea and the Danube was possible either by securing a peaceful agreement that would concede Russia's aggrandizement in exchange for its acceptance of a line of an optimum of conquest, or by resorting to force, or at least the threat of it, to impose a barrier (*ein Damm*) to Russian expansion.[8] However, the second option required Prussia's cooperation, an impossible achievement in the climate of mutual distrust and even hatred pervading Austro-Prussian relations. In other words, a successful containment policy demanded an Austro-Prussian alliance or at least a temporary agreement on a specific issue—the partition of Poland, for example. Elsewhere, Austria had little choice beyond a negotiated settlement.

The Russo-Turkish war of 1768–1774 was not welcome in Austria: Austro-Russian relations were unfriendly. Russia was going it alone, and Austria would have no share of the spoils. In May 1769, Vienna declared that its pledge of 1753 to support Russia "immediately" had been canceled by Russia's withdrawal from the Seven Years War in 1762. At the end of the year, Austria concentrated troops in Transylvania to threaten a Russian advance toward the Danube, but the move did not deter the Russians, who won striking victories during the summer of 1770 and then occupied Moldavia and Wallachia. In October, it sought compensations by annexing the county of Spisz, the first step toward the partition of Poland. Convinced that the "autonomy" of the Danubian Principalities under Russian protection and the "independence" of the Crimean Tatars would result in "a dangerous change in the balance of power,"[9] Kaunitz forged an alliance with the Ottomans in July 1771, exchanging military assistance for a subsidy and territorial concessions. There was talk of war in the event the Russians crossed the Danube in an attempt to reach Constantinople.

But the opposition of military men to an Austro-Ottoman war against Russia and the general distaste for a war with the infidel against another Christian power stalled the chancellor's determination. As long as Prussia remained Austria's most dangerous enemy, Austria could not afford to go to war against Russia. When the Russians and the Ottomans met to discuss a peace settlement in the summer of 1772, Vienna announced it would support Russia's position. Negotiations with Russia appeared much more rewarding. Austrian and Prussian views began to converge on the attractive possibility of combining territorial aggrandizement with the rollback of Russia's presence in Poland. The first partition removed the Russians from the approaches to the Carpathians and confined them behind the Bug and the Zbruch. An ambitious plan to partition the Ottoman Empire in Europe also reconciled aggrandizement with containment and removed whatever reticence remained against Austro-Russian cooperation. The plan rested on an overoptimistic assumption that the Russians could reach Constantinople in one campaign from their bases on the Danube and that the Ottoman Empire had reached the same stage of decomposition as the Polish Empire.

The Austrian partition line would run along the Olt River to the Danube, include Nikopol, and then follow the Iskur River to Sofia and the Struma (Strimon) River to the Aegean Sea. Austrian appetites had grown considerably since 1699 and 1718. Bosnia-Herzegovina, Serbia, Albania, Montenegro, Macedonia, and Greece would join the Austrian Empire; the Russians would gain the Danubian Principalities (less Little Wallachia) and most of Bulgaria. Austria's intentions were clear: the partition would block a Russian advance toward Serbia—the soft underbelly of the Austrian Empire on both banks of the Danube—and the Heartland's periphery, save in the south between the Strimon and the straits. However, no partition plan could prevent the Russians from using their subversive weapon against Austria: the support of the Orthodox population against their Ottoman—and Catholic—oppressors. Austria's containment policy, pursued in self-defense, contained the seeds of its own destruction.

Even if their assumptions were totally wrong, the Austrians could look forward to making substantial gains in alliance with Russia. Maria Theresa's death in November 1780 facilitated a rapprochement with Russia, and the two powers signed a new alliance in May 1781. Each pledged 12,000 troops "to maintain peace in Europe," or an annual subsidy of 400,000 rubles, provisions identical with those of the Russo-Prussian alliance of 1764. The heart of the agreement was an Austrian guarantee of the treaty of Kuchuk-Kainarji and a promise to commit the same number of troops as Russia against the Ottomans should they violate the treaty, and to declare war on any power that might attack Russia while it was at war with the Ottomans. The agreement dealt a mortal blow to the Russo-Prussian alliance and confirmed the new orientation of Russian foreign policy.

Joseph II was playing a dangerous game, however, ignoring the advice of his brother Leopold that Austria should seek the support of France and Prussia to contain Russian expansion rather than an alliance of the flanking powers to expel the Ottomans from the Balkans. And indeed, it turned out the Russians had all the cards. Catherine II annexed the Crimea in April 1783 and extended Russia's protection to Georgia in July, but showed little interest in the Austrian emperor's intentions to carry out even a part of the partition plan. Russian ambitions compelled the Ottomans to declare war in August 1787, forcing the Austrians in turn to go to war on Russia's side in April 1788. This was a bad time for Joseph II, in poor health and facing growing opposition to his reforms. The war was moderately successful for the Russians—they advanced to the Dniestr—but it was a disaster for the Austrians. The Ottomans crossed the Danube and overran the Banat and inflicted a decisive defeat on the Austrians at Zhurzha in June 1790, four months after the emperor's death. The Prussian king used their predicament to arrange a meeting at Reichenbach, south of Leipzig, in July, where he induced Leopold, the new emperor, to seek an armistice and abandon the Russians.

Peace was not made at Sistova (Svishtov) on the Danube, between Nikopol and Zhurzha, for another year, in August 1791. It confirmed the disastrous peace of Belgrade (1739), but the Austrians held on to Buko-vina, obtained in May 1775—a strategically located strip of land centered in Czernowitz (Chernovtsy), along the eastern foothills of the Car-pathians. It extended the Austrian share in the first partition of Poland and served the same purpose: to keep the Russians away from the moun-tains and the passes into Hungary. Austria had entered the war not so much because of its treaty obligations, and certainly not to please Russia (*pour les beaux yeux de la Russie*),[10] but to block a Russian expansion sim-ilar to that carried out at the time of Kuchuk-Kainardji. In 1791, its con-tainment policy was a dismal failure. The third partition of Poland in 1795 was a poor substitute for the grandiose projects of the 1770s.

The awakening of Prussia and Austria to the emergence of a powerful Russia forced them to recognize that Russian expansion must be con-tained in their own self-interest. For Prussia the options were limited, and containment meant essentially a trade-off between Prussia's conceding Russian expansion into the Russo-Polish frontier and Russia's accepting to withdraw from the Polish core area, to be partitioned with Austria. For Austria, the Polish option was supplemented by the Balkan option—conceding Russian expansion into the Russo-Turkish frontier provided it stopped at the Danube (one variant) or along a line defending the approaches to Greater Serbia between the Struma, the Timok, the Dan-ube, and the Una (a second variant). But a containment policy was cer-tain to bring about a Russian response. Since the containment of Russia was inextricably linked with the territorial aggrandizement of the two Germanic powers in the frontier zones, it was to be expected that the Russians would pursue their own containment policy toward Prussia and Austria; toward Prussia they would go so far as to make war; toward Aus-tria they would take advantage of the country's military weakness and of the "dissident" issue to slow down expansion into what Kaunitz called in 1777 "unhealthy, backward (*kulturlose*), and depopulated provinces with unreliable Greeks."[11] Last but not least, Russia would seek to destabilize any attempt by Prussia and Austria to join forces, and this could best be achieved by playing on their rivalries in the Holy Roman Empire.

To establish a base in the empire, Catherine II returned to Peter I's policy of marital alliances with princely families. Her only son, the future Paul I, married a princess of Hesse-Darmstadt in 1773, and after her death three years later, a princess of Württemberg. Seven of his ten children by his second wife would marry into families of the empire, one into the House of Austria, another into the House of Prussia. In addition, Russia was repre-sented in Dresden (Saxony), Münich (Bavaria), Hamburg, and Lübeck; at the Imperial Diet in Regensburg on the Danube; and, beginning in 1781, in Frankfurt-on-Main. Ever since the annexation of Silesia, the empire had become the battleground between Prussia and Austria for dominance in German affairs. Russia, faithful to its traditional policy, would invoke the increasingly anachronistic "constitution" of the empire. There, as in

Sweden, Poland, and later in Persia, the support of the rotting process in a legitimate but paralyzed political system favored Russian interests.

The first serious Austro-Prussian clash took place in 1778. The elector of Bavaria died at the end of 1777, leaving no heirs. Vienna declared the throne vacant and began preparations for the annexation of the duchy, a handsome compensation for the loss of Silesia. Berlin supported the candidacy of the count palatine and his heir, the duke of Zweibrücken, between the Rhine and the Moselle, and declared war on Austria in July. No significant military operations took place, however. Frederick II claimed the high ground in defending the Imperial constitution against Austrian encroachments and counted on Russian military assistance, but Petersburg offered to mediate the dispute, seizing a golden opportunity to strengthen its influence in German affairs, in the Franco-Prussian-Austrian frontier, and in the Coastland.

Catherine II's choice of mediator fell on Nikolai Repnin, the empire's great troubleshooter during her reign, a consummate diplomat and forceful military commander, but also an arrogant proconsul who brooked no resistance to his imperious demands. When he arrived in Breslau (Wroclaw) to meet the king of Prussia and behaved like a minister who had come "to dictate the laws to Germany in the name of his Court," Frederick was strengthened in his conviction that "friendship was only a way for Russia to interfere in German affairs and in those of all Europe as well."[12] Negotiations began at Teschen (Cieszyn) in March 1779, and an agreement was reached in May. It was a compromise, but also a victory for Prussia. It guaranteed once again Prussia's possession of Silesia and recognized the count palatine's right to the Bavarian succession in exchange for the cession to Austria of the small Burghausen district between the Inn and the Salza rivers. The agreement's true importance was in the precedent it created—Russia's right to mediate disputes in the Holy Roman Empire. Russia joined France as the guarantor of the settlement of Westphalia that had created the empire in its modern form in 1648. German affairs acquired an autonomous importance, and Petersburg compelled Berlin and Vienna to place their relations with Russia at the center of their foreign policy.

Vienna did not give up its ambitions to annex Bavaria, and Joseph II proposed at the end of 1783 to exchange it for the Austrian Netherlands—much of present-day Belgium and Luxemburg—"a sick place in the Habsburg economy."[13] Bavaria promised to yield a much larger revenue. Frederick II called the emperor "a public thief,"[14] but Catherine supported Austria to repay its friendly gesture in welcoming Russia's annexation of the Crimea. She instructed her envoy to Frankfurt, Nikolai Rumiantsev, the marshal's second son, to convince the count palatine to accept the exchange, but Joseph II dropped the plan in 1785, in part because of difficulties with the Dutch, but chiefly because of French opposition and the Prussian counteroffensive.

The king took advantage of the opposition generated among the German princes by the exchange project to make a dramatic gesture, of little immediate import but of enormous long-term significance. In July 1785, he signed in Berlin with the envoys of Saxony and Hanover an agreement to form a League of Princes directed against Austrian policies in the empire. The League was a peaceful successor to the war with Austria for the possession of Silesia forty-five years earlier; its aim was to increase Prussian power. Formally, the League's purpose was to defend the constitution, but the union of the three largest states in northern Germany was certain to upset the balance of power in the empire, very much in the same way that the annexation of Bavaria was designed to give Austria a decisive edge against Prussia. The agreement was not a military alliance; it only pledged the three powers to keep in friendly touch, to agree on a candidate at the election of a new emperor, and to respect the treaties of Westphalia and Teschen.

No increase of Prussian power could be welcome in Petersburg, and the move created "a funereal atmosphere" at the Russian Court. The Russian envoy to Berlin, Sergei Rumiantsev (Nikolai's brother), was instructed in February 1786 to point out that Russia's friendship could not be taken for granted (*n'est pas fondée sur la nature des choses*) and to make the king "understand that the strength of the Prussian monarchy has been carried by him beyond the limits acceptable to his neighbors."[15] Russia refused to recognize Prussia as a great power and would destroy it at the first opportunity. Rumors of war began to circulate, but they did not deter other German princes from joining the League, even after the king's death in August 1786 and Rumiantsev's ostentatious gesture of refusing to attend his funeral. By the summer of 1789, it seemed that most of the German states north of the Main River had agreed to form a coalition against the Russo-Austrian alliance, two years before Frederick William became determined to go to war. However, the outbreak of the French Revolution created radically new dangers and opportunities in the rapidly disintegrating Holy Roman Empire.

11

Interlude,
1797–1870

A Common Enemy, 1797–1815

Two events dramatically altered the nature of Russia's relations with the
Germanic powers—the partitions of Poland and the French Revolution.
The three partitions did indeed confine Russia behind the Niemen and
the Bug, but they also created a gravitational pull that gradually
brought Prussia and Austria into the Russian orbit. Russia's interven-
tions in the affairs of the Holy Roman Empire, in the European Coastland, had the effect of creating a line of an optimum of influence along
the Heartland's periphery from Hamburg to the Dinaric Alps, behind
which Prussia and Austria found themselves as if caught in a net under
the vigilant and potentially devastating supervision of Petersburg. The
third partition established a common boundary between the three powers and ipso facto brought a Germanic containment policy to an end.
Henceforth, Russia could be contained only in the interlocking frontier
between the Austrian, Russian, and Turkish core areas. The French
Revolution and the rise of Napoleon had two consequences. One was to
spread the principles of a new political and social order throughout the
European Coastland and to prepare a conservative reaction within the
Heartland that would bring Russia, Prussia, and Austria together in an
ideological alliance in defence of the old order. The other was to
weaken Prussia and Austria and to stimulate a tremendous increase in
Russian power. Their combined effect was to reduce the Germanic
powers to the status of vassals of the Russian Empire, transformed by its
vast exertions during the Napoleonic conflict into a global power and
the only superpower in the Heartland.

Paul I (1796–1801) vainly insisted that Prussia and Austria compose their differences in the face of a common danger, and sent Repnin to Berlin in April 1797 to induce the king to join Russia and Austria in an offensive alliance against France. Repnin encountered duplicity at the Prussian Court led by a new, weak, and vacillating young king, Frederick William III (1797–1840), and a leading minister, Count Christian Haugwitz, who leaned toward the French and "whom no one could trust."[1] If Repnin knew his history, he must have anticipated that Prussia would behave exactly as it had during the Northern War—it would not commit itself until the issue had become clear. This time, however, it would become the major loser. Repnin was unable to convince Berlin to re-enter the war (Prussia had left it in April 1795) and was recalled in June 1798. Napoleon appeared to be the winner, and there was hope that an agreement might be reached with France to restore "the system of Frederick"— Prussia's annexation of the most important states in northern Germany. Relations with Austria were no more satisfactory, despite the tsar's preference for Vienna. A joint expedition was launched in the spring of 1799 to take the war into France itself, but the Austrians' usual ambivalence between the need for Russian assistance and the determination to contain Russian expansion poisoned the alliance, and Paul broke off diplomatic relations in April 1800.

Alexander I (1801–1825) was no less insistent than his father on creating a tripartite alliance to harness the two Germanic powers behind Russia's leadership in order to create "a system of general opposition against the declared enemy of the rights and property of mankind,"[2] but Prussia's reticence remained the stumbling block. The occupation of the left bank of the Rhine and the revolution's subversive impact in the German states between the Rhine and the Elbe convinced Berlin that France, no more than Russia, would accept the "system of Frederick," and that in the end, the Prussians might be "the last ones to be eaten,"[3] as Haugwitz put it in the spring of 1803. But the king, mesmerized by Napoleon, refused to take sides until the execution of the duke d'Enghien in March 1804 convinced him that a Russian alliance had its virtues. Haugwitz was replaced by Karl von Hardenberg, a partisan of a close Russo-Prussian relationship to ensure "the tranquillity and security of the North, and consequently, that of all Europe."[4] Meanwhile, Alexander had restored diplomatic relations with Austria in April 1801 and appointed his first ambassador, Andrei Razumovsky, with the cryptic statement that it was his fundamental policy to use all means at his disposal "for the preservation of a state whose weakness and poor administration are precious guarantees of security."[5] But a Russian alliance with the Germanic powers still stood no chance against Napoleon's forward policy. Austrian and Russian troops were crushed at Austerlitz (Slavkov) in Moravia in December 1805; the French entered Berlin in October 1806, forty-six years after its brief occupation by Russian troops in 1760. Russia alone remained in the war, but was forced to make peace at Tilsit in June 1807.

At first glance, these developments were a disaster for the Russians. In retrospect, it is clear they represented a victory for them in their relationship with Prussia. By destroying Prussian power and pursuing a systematic anti-Prussian policy, Napoleon was working to Russia's advantage, for it had been Russian policy since 1740, sometimes muted, sometimes more openly stated, that a dynamic Prussian core area was a threat to Russia's vital interests. After 1807, Russia was certain to wield overwhelming power; the Prussian danger had disappeared.

The Russians also pursued an anti-Austrian policy despite their recognition that the existence of the Austrian Empire was a necessity, at least as long as it remained weak and poorly managed. Disorders in the Ottoman administration of Serbia caused an outbreak of revolution in February 1804. The Serbs wanted autonomy and an end to direct Ottoman rule. They sought Vienna's support, but Austria was at war with Napoleon and had no power to spare beyond the Danube. They then turned to Petersburg, where their delegation was told in February 1806 that Russia could not remain indifferent to the fate of Serbia because of "the similarity of origin and of religion."[6] They entered the war on Russia's side against the Ottomans at the end of the year, and signed a convention in June 1807 placing Serbia under direct Russian protection, with a governor appointed in Petersburg. Defeat and the peace of Tilsit stalled Russia's ambitions, but its attempt to create a chain of three "autonomous" territories in Moldavia, Wallachia, and Serbia from the Prut to the Una threatened Austria's interests along the Carpathians and the Danube, where its containment policy had been directed since the 1760s. By 1807, the shadow of the Russian eagle had spread far and wide over the containing powers.

The king did not take part in the Tilsit negotiations; he was only the passive observer of his country's humiliation by a triumphant Napoleon. He had to accept the Confederation of the Rhine and the loss of Prussian possessions west of the Elbe and the creation of the Duchy of Warsaw in July that deprived Prussia of about half its territory and population. Most galling of all, perhaps, was the Russian annexation of the Bialystok district, a first step toward the encirclement of East Prussia. These changes in the relative positions of Russia and Prussia were accompanied by a change of tone on Russia's part. Elizabeth had never made a secret of her hatred of Frederick II; Catherine II never trusted him; Paul may have revered his memory but was impatient with Prussia's dilatoriness; Alexander I and Frederick William III exchanged vows of eternal friendship; and beautiful Queen Louise (from Mecklenburg) added a romantic touch to the fraternal union of Romanovs and Hohenzollerns. The effusive exchange of expressions of mutual admiration and respect would continue until the unification of Germany.

But we should not be misled to the point of forgetting that geopolitical realities and not rulers determined the course of Russo-Prussian relations. As in Sweden and Poland, one detects a consistent Russian policy of turning Prussia outward in order to deflect its energies beyond the

Heartland's periphery. Little could be done between 1807 and 1812, but it was never too early to plan for the future. The humiliation of Prussia generated a powerful national revival; it was bound to be directed against France and ought to be encouraged. Napoleon's brusque interference in Prussian domestic affairs led to the dismissal in September 1808 of Karl vom Stein, one of the leading figures of the Prussian revival; he moved to Russia and entered Russian service in March 1812, with the privilege of direct access to the tsar. He advocated an uprising in the Rhine Confederation and the reorganization of "Germany" under Russian protection in such a way that it could resist French ambitions. His ideas were considered revolutionary in ever-cautious Berlin and even in Petersburg, but they served Russia's short-term interests.

Alexander insisted on keeping the peace with Napoleon after 1807, convinced that neither Prussia nor Austria could yet afford to challenge Napoleon at the height of his power. Prussia and the Duchy of Warsaw must remain proximate zones in the new Franco-Russian frontier. The Russians insisted that France withdraw its troops from Prussia in 1808 and keep them out of the Heartland altogether, thereby conceding Russia's hegemony in Berlin and Vienna. But the new frontier was unstable, and there was no hope of creating a permanent political isobar as long as Russia, by its position, power, and ambitions, continued to challenge Napoleon's claim to continental hegemony. Moreover, the Continental System designed to keep British trade out of Europe was sapping the economy of both Prussia and Russia and fueled discontent in their political and military establishments. It rendered inevitable a new European war between Napoleon, the Germanic powers, and Russia.

In June 1811, when French power still seemed invincible, the king signed a convention giving France access to all military roads within Prussia in preparation for an invasion of Russia. He rightly claimed he had no choice. Moreover, his government was divided and included partisans of a Franco-Prussian alliance that would restore Prussia's containment policy. In February 1812, he agreed to the incorporation of half the Prussian army into Napoleon's Grand Army, despite his acceptance the previous October of a convention of military cooperation between a Prussian army corps commanded by General Johann Yorck and the right wing of the Russian army. Faithful to a tradition that Prussia must always be on the winner's side, the king made ready for all contingencies. In December, when Napoleon was in full retreat but not yet defeated, Yorck took a neutral stand.

Meanwhile, Russia's relations with Austria had been less than friendly, if only because it was much more difficult to establish Russia's uncontested hegemony in Vienna. When the Holy Roman Empire was abolished, the Habsburg emperor became simply emperor of Austria, while retaining his titles of king of Bohemia and Hungary. Francis I (+1835) was a narrow-minded and repressive ruler who believed in the French alliance and the containment of Russia. His aunt, Marie Antoinette, had been the last queen of France before the revolution; his daughter, Marie Louise, would marry Napoleon in 1810. Despite the vicissitudes of revolution and war and despite mutual misgivings and suspicions, the Franco-Austrian alliance, created in 1756, was always ready to reassert itself because the two powers had a common objective: the containment of Prussia and Russia.

Austria was not ready to accept defeat in 1807 and was left out of the Tilsit negotiations altogether. Archduke Charles, the emperor's brother and the most capable Austrian commander, carried out military reforms in 1807–1808 intended to give Austria another chance to challenge Napoleon. The tsar opposed Vienna's policy because an Austrian defeat, which he considered inevitable, might be followed by a partition of the Austrian Empire, and that was unacceptable. When Alexander Kurakin, the Russian ambassador, wrote in July 1808 that the Austrian Empire was "a useful and necessary barrier" (*une digue utile et nécessaire*), he was thinking of a frontier, not so much as a line but as a succession of zones, buffers necessary to keep French power out of the Heartland. The empire was "necessary to civilization"; Russia and France needed "a third party independent of both."[7] But Russian policy was not without ambivalence. If Austria went to war against Russia's advice and was defeated, would not a humbling of Austria draw it closer to Russia?

Austria declared war in April 1809, but was forced to make peace in October; the price was the loss of its possessions in Poland, Croatia, and Dalmatia. France reached the Heartland's periphery, but did not cross it. The Russians entered the war, bound as they were by their alliance with France, but took their time and contributed nothing to Austria's defeat. However, they made the cardinal error of annexing the Tarnopol district of eastern Galicia and aroused such intense resentment in Vienna that Austria, rather than drawing closer to Russia, returned to the French alliance. The symbol of the new orientation was the appointment of Clemens von Metternich, the former ambassador to France, to head the Austrian foreign ministry in the fall of 1809; he would soon become the tsar's bitter antagonist. In March 1812, Austria agreed to contribute a corps of 30,000 to the Grand Army. It would operate in Galicia; its objective would be to recover the Tarnopol district. And the Russians discovered in June, on the eve of the French invasion, that the Austrian ambassador in Stockholm was working to break the Russo-Swedish alliance.

Despite the fact that the Napoleonic empire threatened both Russia and Austria, the Austrians did not forget that their strategic interest after the Russians reached the Dniestr in 1792 was to contain their expansion toward the Danube and beyond. General Staff studies made after 1807 agreed that Austria must recover Serbia between the Drina and the Timok—gained in 1718, lost in 1739—in order to gain control, south of the Danube, of the first stages of a direct route to Constantinople and prevent the Russians' getting there first. The Austrian foreign minister, Johann Stadion, revived in February 1809 the old objective of annexing Serbia, Bosnia-Herzegovina, and western Bulgaria to the Iskur, with a southern boundary running, no longer along the Struma, but along the Vardar to Saloniki. No wonder that at the very time Petersburg was voicing apprehension about the purpose of the Austrian rearmament, Archduke Charles, who was known to be anti-Russian, planned to advance into the Balkans. The Serbs were at war with the Russians against the Ottomans and had ambitious goals: to recognize the tsar's sovereignty in return for joint operations to annex Bosnia-Herzegovina and reconstitute a Greater Serbia under Russian protection. The possibility of a first Austro-Russian war for the control of the Balkan frontier could not be discounted.

Austria's defeat in October 1809 did not dampen its determination to contain the Russian advance. General Joseph Radetzky, a supporter of the archduke and a future famous field marshal, declared in March 1810 that the Danube was the lifeline (*die grosse Pulsader*)[8] of the Austrian Empire and that the defense perimeter of the monarchy ran along the Carpathians (Galicia was expendable) and included the Danubian principalities, Serbia and Bosnia, those very frontier zones to which the Russians, on their own or in alliance with the Serbs, were about to lay claim. He was supported by Francis I and Metternich, who were ready to go to war to block Russia's establishment on the Danube. In February 1811, the Russians occupied Belgrade and went as far as Šabac on the Sava. A showdown was approaching. But Napoleon's preparations for the invasion of Russia diverted attention from the Balkans. The Russians made peace with the Ottomans in March 1812. They reached the Prut and the Kilia channel of the Danube delta, gained autonomy for Serbia, but had to withdraw their forces from the country and the Principalities. The showdown had been postponed.

Faced with the hesitancy of Prussia and Austria (and of his own high command) after the Grand Army was expelled from Russia, the tsar took an uncompromising stand: Napoleon and the French Empire must be destroyed and the Germanic powers must be harnessed to the Russian chariot. Thus the tsar would impose his will in Paris. The Russian thrust into the Coastland was accompanied by a firm reminder that any postwar settlement and territorial readjustments in both Heartland and Coastland would require Russia's consent, and that consent was predicated on a reorientation of the Germanic powers' ambitions and the abandonment of whatever hopes they retained to contain Russian expansion.

Prussia entered the war on Russia's side in February 1813, Austria in August. The Allies marched into Paris in March 1814, and a congress met in Vienna to reorganize the political and territorial map of Europe. When David Alopäus, a Finn, was appointed Russian envoy to Berlin in March 1813, he was instructed never to forget that Prussia must be used as "Russia's avant-garde" to protect the security of northern Europe in the new balance of power; and Alopäus was convinced that Russia must use the ineradicable Austro-Prussian antagonism to give its "advice and opinion"[9] in the affairs of the new Germany. This new Germany, created at the Congress of Vienna, was the so-called German Confederation of thirty-five monarchies and four free cities, dominated by Austria and

Prussia. Its Diet would meet in Frankfurt-on-Main, and the Austrian emperor would preside over it. Prussia was enlarged considerably, gaining a compact territory between the Weser and the French border, where it would stand guard against French revanchism. Prussia would then become Russia's surrogate on the Rhine.

Austria too was turned outward. Not only did it regain its possessions in Croatia and Dalmatia looking westward toward Italy; it also gained Lombardy and Venetia between the Po River and the Alps—and the burden of a commitment to defend conservatism along the southern approaches to the Heartland. As compensation for their gains in the Coastland, both Germanic powers had to concede Russia's advance into the Polish core area and the Austro-Russian frontier in the Balkans. The tsar's declared intention in the spring of 1814 to annex the entire Duchy of Warsaw aroused the violent opposition of Austria and was a decisive factor in the triple alliance with France and Britain against Russia and Prussia in January 1815. Napoleon's return from Elba restored unity against the common enemy, and Russia had to accept the retrocession of about one-fifth of the Duchy in May; but almost all of it went to Prussia, to Austria's discomfiture.

In Serbia, moreover, the Russians had to settle for modest gains. Their withdrawal in 1812, and the concentration of both Austria and Russia on expelling Napoleon from the Heartland, gave the Ottomans a free hand. The rebellion's leader, Karadjordje Petrović, found himself in a desperate situation; when it was all over by October 1813, he was forced to flee into Habsburg territory. But the Serbs, determined to attain the independence that was denied in March 1812, raised the standard of revolt once again in the spring of 1815 under a new leader, Miloš Obrenović, who cleared Serbia of Ottoman troops by the summer and got himself recognized by the Porte as "supreme prince" two years later, with the right to collect taxes and keep troops, but under the Ottomans' continued suzerainty. He also had Karadjordje assassinated when he returned from exile. Necessity, conviction, and religion made him look east for Russian support.

Serbia was sacrificed at the Congress of Vienna because the antagonism between Alexander I and Metternich precluded joint action against the Ottomans at the time and because Metternich preferred to see the Serbs return to the Ottoman yoke to their falling under Russian control. But traditional Russian policy reasserted itself with a new urgency. In a circular note of February 1815, the tsar announced that Russia was the "natural protector" of the Orthodox Christians in the Ottoman Empire, in the same way Austria and France were the natural defenders of Catholic interests. Russia was obviously staking a religious claim to the entire Balkan frontier from the Una to the Black Sea in direct opposition to Austria.

Russia's Hegemony, 1816–1849

Once the dust had settled on the Napoleonic epic that had convulsed Coastland and Heartland from the Atlantic to the Volga, a stark fact dominated the international scene: Britain and Russia had become global powers, one imposing its hegemony in the Coastland, the other in the Heartland. The Germanic powers, prisoners of their ambitions, mutual antagonism, and geographic position, were being forced to continue to recognize Russia's leadership. Russia's immense power was felt in every corner of the Heartland, Britain's in every bay, estuary, and narrow sea of the Coastlands. Henry Adams would later write that in those decades Russia's influence was felt even more powerfully than France's had been until 1815 in the great plain of northern Europe and in the valley of the Danube. The Russians had finally reached their objective: any settlement within the heartland would have to require their participation and consent.

Grand Duke Nicholas, the future tsar, married Frederick William's daughter Charlotte in July 1817, and the occasion provided another opportunity to exchange letters of gratitude and friendship. But it was also well known in Berlin that Prussia "remained under a kind of Russian control"[10] and that Petersburg still refused to concede to Prussia the status of a great power. Prussia remained in Russian eyes a dissatisfied power—dissatisfied with its insufficiently large share of Saxony partitioned in 1815 in a Prussian attempt to complete the encirclement of Bohemia, and with Russia's advance into the Polish core area that created a salient placing Silesia and East Prussia at Russia's mercy. Moreover, sharp differences between Brandenburg's conservative traditions and the more liberal temper of Rhineland politics created a risk of political destabilization in Prussia and required constant vigilance in Petersburg, more set than ever in its determination to freeze the conservative status quo sanctified by the victory over Napoleon. The Russians were aware that some members of the Prussian political and military establishment were anti-Russian, and were already complaining in 1823 against the violent criticism of their policies in Prussian newspapers. And there was something slightly ominous in Tsar Nicholas' letter to the king, three weeks after his inauguration in December 1825, that while he treasured his family ties, Russia's interests would tell him where his duty lay.

The crushing in 1831 of the Polish uprising, of revolution within the Heartland, gave Petersburg the opportunity to insist on closer military cooperation between Russia and Prussia to face the subversive threat to order and institutions emanating from London and Paris. The result of Russia's encouragement of the Germanic powers' expansion into the Coastland now became manifest: that expansion contributed to the destabilization of the Germanic powers by exposing their westernmost possessions to the winds of radical change. Destabilization gave Russia a lever in German affairs. Conservatism and subversion remained the hallmark of Russia's policy.

The Prussian core area was unlike the Swedish, Polish, Turkish, and Persian core areas over which Russia had been seeking to establish its hegemony or had already imposed it. Prussia was a growing core area; defeat and humiliation had generated tremendous energy, and it understood that economic growth was the foundation of military power. Prussia expanded its economic base by building a customs union in Germany, north of the Main. It began officially in 1834, but Prussia had inaugurated a free-trade policy with its smaller neighbors as far back as 1818. Such a policy—and only an economically confident power can afford free trade—was bound to have repercussions in Russo-Prussian relations. One of its consequences was the creation of a containment policy in economic garb.

Russia's treaties with Prussia and Austria of May 1815 established freedom of navigation on all rivers and canals of the former Polish empire in its 1772 borders and imposed a single duty on river boats to eliminate obstacles to the free transit and export of goods between the various parts of the old empire, now partitioned between Russia and the Germanic powers. With the growth of the Prussian economy after the annexation of Silesia in 1740, the Polish Empire had become a profitable market for Prussian industry and trade, and Prussia sought to monopolize Russia's overland imports of manufactured goods. The establishment of the Russians in Warsaw and the creation of Congress Poland imposed upon them the burden of protecting Polish industry in addition to their own, which was beginning to show potentially dangerous signs of backwardness vis-à-vis the economy of Prussia and the Coastland powers. Free navigation and trade threatened to maintain the economic unity of the Polish Empire but within Prussia's orbit. In addition, the fact that Congress Poland was landlocked placed its export trade toward the Baltic under Prussian control: Danzig, Königsberg, and Memel were all in Prussia.

The Russians understood very quickly the Prussians' intensions of making up for their territorial losses by strengthening their commercial position not only to the Niemen and the Bug but beyond, to the Dvina and the Dniepr. A convention was negotiated in 1816 to develop the summary provisions of the 1815 treaty, but the tsar refused to ratify it; he would not concede Prussia's economic preponderance in the old Russo-Polish frontier. Lithuania and Bielorussia were placed behind Russia's protective tariff of 1816. To pacify the king, Prussia was given transit rights to export its cloth and leather goods across Russia to China. Berlin continued to apply pressure, and Russia yielded in December 1818. The new tariff of 1819 was motivated in part by the desire to conciliate Prussian public opinion and business circles. Three years later, however, it was discovered that free trade with Prussia and the rest of Europe was undermining the Russian and Polish economies. The tsar was forced to write the king in February 1822 that the flood of Prussian goods with which no one could compete was destroying even trading houses with a solid reputation, and that self-interest required a return to protectionism.

Faced with the inevitable, the Prussians disclosed their real objective when their foreign minister suggested that Russia, in order to limit the damage, should close its ports and borders to British, French, and Austrian manufacturers but keep them open to Prussia's. The move would effectively establish a Prussian monopoly in the old Russo-Polish frontier and in Russia's largest cities. But the Russians had made up their mind, and the highly protective tariff of 1822 created anger in Berlin. It did not apply to Congress Poland, however. With characteristic tenacity Prussia continued negotiations to settle various commercial matters, including transit rights across Polish territory. In 1834, Berlin even brought up the question of Congress Poland's joining the North German customs union! In 1840, it refused to quote the stock of a company the Russians had formed to build a railroad from the Niemen to Libava (Libau, Liepaja) to divert the trade of the frontier from Königsberg to a port in the Russian Empire, claiming it would destroy the East Prussian trade. Nicholas, however, took a strong stand. Not only would Russia not return to the 1819 tariff; it extended the Imperial tariff to Congress Poland in 1847. Prussia's policy of economic containment had failed.

Metternich's conviction that Austria must continue to contain Russian ambitions—in alliance with Britain, which had replaced France as the great containing power in the Coastland—was counterbalanced by the realization that Austria needed Russia's assistance to maintain the conservative order in the German Confederation and that Austria no longer had sufficient power to compel the Russians to retreat against their will. There had always been a certain lack of correlation between Austrian ambitions and capabilities. After 1815, Russia's overwhelming military superiority exposed Austrian weakness for all to see.

Russia's envoy to Vienna, Gustav von Stackelberg, the son of Otto, who had been Catherine's hard-line envoy to Warsaw and Stockholm, was certain Metternich wanted to create an alliance of German-speaking states to damage Russian interests wherever possible. He had to be recalled in 1817. His successor, Iurii Golovkin, became convinced of Austrian duplicity and hostility toward Russia; he too had to be recalled. Metternich was better disposed toward the third envoy, Dmitrii Tatishchev, who remained in Vienna for nearly twenty years (1822–1841) and was more willing to take Austrian official declarations at their face value. Russia's interest in the southern German states (Alexander's mother was from Württemberg, his wife from Baden), and above all in Bavaria, created concern in Vienna: Austria considered the states south of the Main River to be in its exclusive sphere of influence. Vienna could easily detect a Russian policy to create a political base in the southern states from which to balance Prussian and Austrian interests. After all, that had been Catherine II's policy in the 1780s.

The revolutions of 1848 that spread across the German Confederation showed how far the Germanic powers had become dependent on their powerful neighbor. When the Prussian king, upset at the liberal turn of events in Berlin, begged the tsar in September 1848 to support "good, old, and loyal Prussia" against revolution, he was told Prussia had first to be restored to the condition "in which your Papa transmitted it to you."[11] In Vienna, the revolution's first casualty was Metternich, who fled to Britain. The multinational empire was in much greater danger, and

Petersburg made it clear from the beginning that the integrity of the Danubian monarchy was a vital interest. The reaction came swiftly. Marshal Radetzky crushed the revolution in Italy in July 1848; order was restored in Vienna in October and a new emperor, Francis Joseph (1848–1916), began his reign with Russia's blessing. The tsar had insisted that the Austrians must restore order on their own, but they were not confident enough to scatter their forces across the vast expanse of their empire. The new Austrian government appealed to Nicholas in March 1849 to put down the revolution in Hungary. The Russians crossed the Carpathian passes from Galicia and Moldavia in June and made short shrift of the rebels. The revolution was over by August. The Austrian Empire had been saved by Russia. Not only did Russia intervene in Hungary, it also refused to take advantage of the Austrian Slavs' yearning for independence to weaken the monarchy. True, the denial was motivated by self-interest, but it was clear that Russia's hegemony over the Austrian Empire never appeared so unchallengeable as in 1850.

In the Balkans, Russia had taken a hard line against Austria. Conservatism, subversion, and the striving for hegemony were closely intertwined. Russia's war preparations against the Ottomans had placed Vienna in a quandary. If the Russians were successful, they were certain to take the war south of the Danube and perhaps move against Constantinople. Should Austria use its strategic option of crossing the Carpathians from Transylvania into Moldavia and Wallachia to block the Russians' advance or even cut off their retreat? Tatishchev reported in November 1827 that Austria had mobilized its armed forces, concentrated troops in Transylvania, and hinted it might occupy the Principalities. But Nicholas was not to be deterred. If Moldavia and Wallachia were a vital interest to both Russian and Austria, the issue would have to be settled by force of arms. In December, the Russian commander in chief was given orders to consider an Austrian use of force as a declaration of war. In that event, three army corps would be directed against Austria from Congress Poland: one would occupy Galicia and another enter Moravia and stop at Olmütz (Olomouc), to provide a reserve for the third and strongest corps marching on Vienna. The Austrians backed down and did not oppose the Russians when they crossed the Danube in June 1828.

But the peace of Adrianople provoked an angry memorandum from Marshal Radetzky. By failing to stand up to the Russians, Austria (and Europe) had conceded Russia's hegemony (*Übergewicht*)[12] in the Balkans. It was Russia's intention to create a system of four dependent states—Moldavia, Wallachia, Serbia, and Greece—that would effectively shut out Austria from the Black Sea. The system's keystone was the delta of the Danube; it was now in Russian hands. Since the economic development of the Hungarian plain and Transylvania depended on access to the Black Sea and the straits, the future of the Austrian monarchy had become dependent on Russia. Radetzky was thinking in geopolitical terms. Greece and the Danubian Principalities formed a vise around Bulgaria; Serbia led to

Bosnia. Russia was seeking no less than a line of an optimum of conquest along the periphery of the Heartland.

Subsequent events would show the future was not so dark as the Austrian commander saw it. Greece never fell under Russian control; the Russians never could annex the other three territories in the valley of the Danube; Bulgaria would become an apple of discord. But the Russian show of force had destroyed the credibility of Austria's containment policy. Reconciliation was now in order. When Nicholas and Francis I met at Münchengrätz in September 1833, two months after Unkiar-Skelesi, they agreed in vague terms on a partition of the Balkan frontier in the event the pasha of Egypt should overthrow the sultan (he never did).

That same year, Miloš was able to obtain from the Ottomans an additional slice of territory between the Drina and the Timok that included the valley of the Western Morava and stretched just north of Nish (Niš). Only six Ottoman garrisons remained in Serbia, but there was still one in Belgrade. In 1836, Vienna and Petersburg appointed their first consuls; they would fight their respective country's battle for preponderance. Miloš, who had become increasingly authoritarian, was forced to abdicate three years later, and his son and successor was forced into exile in 1842. The Karadjordje family returned to power in 1843, when Prince Alexander was elected in June over Russia's protests. He would rule until December 1858 and lean toward Austria, especially after Vienna granted autonomy to Vojvodina in 1849. Russia's influence remained preponderant in the Danubian Principalities; it was slowly being undermined in Serbia.

Austria's and Russia's Revenge, 1850–1870

Hegemony has its price. It creates hubris in the hegemonic power and resentment in proud but subservient states. The humiliation of Austria during much of Nicholas' long reign fed a desire for revenge at the first opportunity. It would come during the Crimean War when Austria, by its belated intervention, forced Russia to capitulate. And the humiliation of Russia by a coalition of Austria, Britain, and France caused the Russians to remain indifferent to Austria's fate when Prussia forced a final showdown for the unification of Germany. The end result was the emergence of a powerful and dynamic new core area that would eventually roll back Russia to its 1650 borders and destroy the peace in both Heartland and Coastland.

The revolution of 1848–1849 brought to center stage the issue of German unification that had agitated the more far-sighted Germans, especially after the Vienna settlement of 1815. But there could be no unification without deciding whether Austria belonged to the new Germany. The Austrian Habsburgs had inherited a dual mission: to maintain the unity of the German-speaking lands and to expel the Ottomans from the valley of the Danube and the Balkans. It was becoming painfully obvious that Austria could not be both a Coastland and a Heartland monarchy, a Rhineland

and a Danubian empire: one rested on the glorification of nationalism, the other on its suppression. Prussia became the beneficiary of the yearning for unification. From Cologne to Königsberg, and from the Rhine to the Bohemian Mountains, the German nation was fragmented into three dozen states and divided between Catholics and Protestants, but it spoke one language. In the age of nationalism, that was the decisive factor.

But the Russians would not accept a unification of Germany that would expel Austria from German affairs and immeasurably strengthen the power of Prussia. Perhaps some statesmen in Petersburg still remembered Bestuzhev-Riumin's warning that Russia's "dangers grow with Prussian power." Moreover, a Germany born of a revolutionary upheaval was unacceptable to the guardian of the conservative order. The Russian envoy to Berlin, Peter von Meyendorff, made no bones about it. He directed violent attacks against the foreign minister, General Joseph von Radowitz (of Hungarian origin), who supported a German union without Austria, and even went so far as to warn Berlin that Russia might intervene militarily in Prussia "as it had in Hungary."[13] The king gave in, Radowitz was forced to resign, and Prussia capitulated at the Olmütz meeting in November 1850. A wave of indignation swept over the country, and Nicholas emerged as the chief obstacle to the realization of Prussia's most cherished ambitions. The conservative alliance forged in the exalted atmosphere of 1813–1815 was slowly breaking down.

It received its deathblow when Nicholas decided to use the "dissident" issue in the Balkans to destabilize the Austro-Russian-Ottoman frontier and gain a preponderant influence in Constantinople. Following the return of Menshikov, who had failed to gain his objective in the Ottoman capital, the tsar ordered the occupation of the Principalities in June 1853. Backed by Britain and France, determined to call a halt to Russia's global expansion, the Ottomans declared war in October; Britain and France followed suit in March 1854.

Both Germanic powers had a vital interest in the outcome of the crisis. Nicholas I had every reason to expect the support of his relatives, the king of Prussia and the Austrian emperor, but relations between states are governed by the pursuit of interests, and one of the chief interests of the Germanic powers was the containment of Russia. Both protested the invasion of the Principalities and felt uneasy about the partition of the Balkan frontier that it seemed to portend. Some people in the Austrian government saw that geography placed Austria at a disadvantage and no longer felt the blissful excitement of their predecessors at the thought of aggrandizing Austria and containing Russia in the Balkans. In any deal, Austria would gain "raw Bosnia, arid Herzegovina, desolate and mountainous Albania," while Russia occupied the lower valley of the Danube, "the granary of Europe," and the Constantinople bridgehead linking Europe with "Asia."[14] Austria should insist on the territorial status quo and the substitution of a European for a Russian guarantee of Serbia and the Principalities, freedom of navigation in the delta of the Danube, and the rights of the Christians.

Such was the essence of the Vienna Note of August 1853. The Russians accepted it, but events moved irrevocably toward war because the Austrians, despite their apprehensions, were determined to achieve what they had failed to carry out in 1828. Nicholas and the Russian high command were equally determined to force the issue once again against both the Austrians and the Ottomans. By November 1853, Nicholas had embraced a Pan-Christian position: Russia would work for the "independence" of Moldavia, Wallachia, Serbia, Bosnia, and Bulgaria; the aggrandizement of Greece; and an uprising of *all* Christians under Moslem domination. His generals planned for an offensive across the Danube at Vidin into Serbia supported by calls to revolt in Montenegro, Epirus, and Thessaly. The road to Constantinople ran through Vienna, and the dismemberment of the Austrian Empire had to precede that of the Ottoman Empire. The Russians kept looking for a line of an optimum of conquest along the Heartland's periphery, but the hubris of a conservative global power had finally blinded them to a realistic assessment of the existing balance of power between Heartland and Coastland.

The Russians crossed the Danube in March 1854, activating the trip wire of Austrian vital interests. In April, Vienna and Berlin signed a treaty of defensive and offensive alliance: the two Germanic powers guaranteed each other's "German and non-German" possessions and pledged that an attack on one would be tantamount to a declaration of war on the other. A Russian advance beyond the Danube toward the Balkan Mountains would bring the offensive alliance into operation. A military convention committed Prussia to raise 200,000 men by June, Austria 250,000 by July in Hungary, Transylvania, and Galicia. By the summer, Austria had decided to obtain the evacuation of the Principalities "at any price." This time, it was the Russians who blinked. They withdrew in August, and the Austrians moved in to garrison the Principalities. The Russians had been contained behind the Prut for the first time since 1815, and the Prut was Austria's line of an optimum of conquest. Its strong stand guaranteed that the war would be fought not in the Balkans but in the Crimea, where the British and French landed in September. In December, Austria joined the Anglo-French alliance but did not enter the war. It would only stand guard on the Prut and the delta of the Danube to prevent a return of the Russians, while giving the Allies the necessary facilities for crossing the Principalities.

Once the immediate danger of an Austro-Russian war had passed, Prussia, true to tradition, adopted a neutral stance. The king even wrote Nicholas in June that Austria was "a sick man who must be kept from becoming rabid."[15] Commercial exchanges continued, and Prussia contributed to the Russian war effort while standing by Austria. The Russians would be grateful at their hour of defeat; they were already pleased to watch the rise of Otto von Bismark at the Frankfurt Diet and appreciated his "implacable hatred of Austria."[16] But the war had first to end before Bismark could use his talents to win over the Russians to the cause of

German unification without Austria. After the fall of Sevastopol in September 1855 and the Russians' continued refusal to accept the Allied terms, Vienna served an ultimatum to accept the Vienna Note with an additional concession: a withdrawal from the Danube delta. Prussia urged the new tsar, Alexander II, to make peace, and the Russians, unwilling to accept an extension of the war, capitulated in January 1856. The Treaty of Paris, in March, recognized the full autonomy of Serbia under Ottoman suzerainty, but placed it under the guarantee, no longer of Russia alone, but of the five European powers: Britain and France, Austria and Prussia, and Russia. Austria had taken its revenge for the humiliation of 1829.

The Austro-Russian struggle for the control of the Balkan frontier increased political turbulence in the zones. What had been a rivalry for a strategic objective—the valley of the lower Danube from the Iron Gate to the delta—was transformed and enlarged into an increasingly bitter competition for the political allegiance of the men of power in the frontier zones and a race to block Russia's advance toward the Heartland's periphery between the valley of the Vardar and Constantinople.

After the humiliation of the Treaty of Paris, Russia's Balkan frontier policy turned aggressively against Austria in a clear attempt to destabilize the region, expel the Ottomans, and keep the Austrians out. Its most articulate champion was Nikolai Ignatev, who became the director of the Asiatic Department (it had jurisdiction over the Balkans) after his return from China in 1861 and later represented his country in Constantinople (1864–1877). He would later write that he had been inspired by the "view that Russia alone could rule in the Balkan peninsula and the Black Sea so that Austria-Hungary's expansion would be halted and the Balkan peoples, especially the Slavs, would direct their gaze exclusively to Russia and make their future dependent on her." He did not even shrink from destabilizing the Austrian Empire, calling not only the Slavs in the frontier but also those in the inner frontier of the empire, "our allies, the weapons of our policy against the Germans."[17] By contrast, Vienna was clearly on the defensive. Faced with a dynamic Russian policy combining "Pan-Christian" with "Pan-Slav" elements, Austria found itself in the uncomfortable position of helping the Ottomans maintain the status quo, the very denial of its historical mission. The containment of Russia ceased to be a forward policy to become a close-border policy, and for a good reason: Austria needed to secure its rear in anticipation of the showdown with Prussia in German affairs.

There was much discontent in the Balkan frontier, fed by land hunger, the oppressive fiscal policies of the Ottomans, and their mistreatment of the Christians. Montenegro sought additional territory, and found itself at war with the Ottomans who suspected it of supporting the revolt that broke out in Herzegovina in January 1858. Vienna offered to let the Ottomans land at Ragusa to facilitate their reconquest of the Neretva valley. In December, Alexander Karadjordje was deposed in Serbia and

Miloš Obrenovič returned to power. Riots and disturbances caused anxiety in Belgrade's Ottoman garrison, and Vienna promised military assistance should its commander ask for it. Gorchakov, on the other hand, insisted on joint support of the Christian population. Miloš died in September 1860 and was succeeded by his son, Michael, Serbia's ablest modern ruler. The Russians began to look at Serbia as their most strategic zone, from which they could support insurrectionary movements everywhere else in the Balkans. The lines were being drawn. In Montenegro, Vienna supported the Ottoman trade embargo designed to starve the Christians into submission, claiming an Ottoman failure would destabilize the Porte; and in November 1861, a small Austrian force entered Herzegovina from Dalmatia to show support for the infidel.

The climax came in 1862. Riots between Christians and Moslems caused the Ottoman garrison to bombard Belgrade. The demonstration gave Gorchakov the initiative. An international conference met in Constantinople. The Ottomans and the Austrians were pitted against the Russians, but finally agreed in September that the last Ottoman garrisons in Serbia must withdraw and that the Moslem population must emigrate. The evacuation was completed in 1867. Prince Michael's victory was also Gorchakov's. Serbia was recognized as having the same autonomy as Rumania and Montenegro; all three remained under nominal Ottoman suzerainty. The prince had little time to enjoy his victory, however: he was murdered in June 1868 by supporters of the Karadjordje family.

Three further developments gave Russia opportunities to show its displeasure with Austria; one of them eventually gave it a chance to take its revenge. In Italy, the king of Piedmont and his minister, Camillo Cavour, were determined to unify the peninsula under their leadership, and the major obstacle was Austria in possession of Lombardy and Venetia. Events were leading to war, and Austria invoked conservative solidarity against revolution in an effort to enlist Russian support. The Russians declined, and Alexander II even spoke of concentrating a force on the Austrian border large enough to tie down 150,000 Austrian troops. France supported Piedmont; war broke out in April 1859; Austria was defeated three months later and had to abandon Lombardy. Conservative solidarity reasserted itself in 1860, but the Polish uprising upset a possible Austro-Russian rapprochement. While Berlin dramatized its support of Russian policy, authorizing Russian troops to cross into Prussian territory in pursuit of insurgents, Austria joined Britain and France in April 1863 in remonstrating with the Russian government, even after the tsar had granted an amnesty. To the Russians this was evidence Austria had returned to the alliance of the Crimean War. Russification and the dissolution of the Catholic convents could not but create rancor in Catholic Vienna, already upset by Russia's support of Serbia and Montenegro. Austro-Russian relations were heading for a showdown.

Next came the unification of northern Germany, the decisive blow to Austria's prestige. It had long been in the making. After 1856, there could be no room in the future Germany for both Prussia and Austria. Prussia's neutrality during the Crimean War and Austria's engagement on the side of Russia's enemies made the Russians supportive of Prussian ambitions, and the emergence of Bismark gave Prussia the statesman it needed to carry out the unification in the teeth of Austria's opposition. Tensions rose beginning in 1864, when Bismark used a revival of the Schleswig-Holstein question to entangle Austria in a web of political contradictions from which it could not escape. Defeat in July 1866 forced Austria out of Venetia and transformed northern Germany into a federal state under Prussian leadership.

The war of 1866 was only the first round. The Compromise of March 1867 giving Hungary full autonomy in the Austrian Empire, henceforth to be called Austria-Hungary, exposed Austria's defensiveness before the rise of nationalism and weakened its ability to resist further Prussian ambitions. The Russian government, faced with the certainty of another war, now decided to take its revenge. In February 1868, six months after Prince Michael signed an agreement with Greece providing for the eventual annexation of Bosnia-Herzegovina by Serbia—a step also contemplated by Austria despite Russia's warning that it would be a casus belli—Alexander II offered to mass 100,000 men on the border to keep Austria in check in the event of a war with Prussia. Bismark declined the offer, but the tsar may have renewed it in May 1870, even proposing to occupy Galicia should Prussia become involved in a war with France and Austria-Hungary simultaneously. No alliance was concluded, largely because Bismark looked beyond the final exclusion of Austria from German affairs to a reconciliation with Austria to face "the hostility of the Muscovite party towards Germany and (the) dislike of the tsarevich [the future Alexander III] to everything German."[18] The war for the completion of Germany's unification was fought with France. France was defeated in the fall of 1870; the German states south of the Main were incorporated into the German Empire proclaimed in January 1871. The king of Prussia became the emperor of the new Germany. By supporting Germany's unification, Russia destroyed the great power status of two containing powers—France in the Coastland, Austria in the Heartland. But it was left alone to face a new and immeasurably strengthened Prussia that would eventually destroy the Russian Empire.

12

The Second Phase, 1871–1917

Bismarck and Containment, 1871–1890

The momentous events of 1866–1870 forced Russia and the Germanic powers to pause for an assessment of the new situation and of its implications for the future. Bismarck had achieved his objective of uniting the German nation but was now haunted by the specter of an alliance of the flanking powers, Russia and France, and even Austria-Hungary. His ability to prevent it was a tribute to his diplomatic skill, but no one, not even Bismarck, could resist in the long run the dynamism of the new core area, a compact mass straddling for the first time the Heartland's periphery. That dynamism—the product of geographic location; of Prussia's long frustrated ambition to become a great power; of the German nation's yearning to overcome the particularism of its petty kingdoms, duchies, and Imperial cities; and finally, of Germany's extraordinary economic transformation—released enough energy to destabilize Heartland and Coastland.

The historical mission of old Prussia and Austria had channeled their energy across the north European plain toward the Gulf of Finland, into the valley of the Danube toward the Black Sea. Germany alone, despite Bismarck's fears, was bound to return to Prussia's containment policy that had been an essential component of its historical mission. In alliance with Austria it would create a single Germanic core area that would inherit Prussia's and Austria's containment policies and fuse them into a powerful thrust directed against the Russia core area. The days of Russia's hegemony over the Germanic powers were gone. Germany's transformation into the dominant economic power in Coastland and Heartland recreated a situation analogous to the balance of power that followed the emergence of the Napoleonic Empire. From a geopolitical point of view, Germany would more than match Russia's economic and military power. The consequence was the transformation of the Russian Empire's inner frontier from Finland to the Carpathians, of Hungary, Rumania, Bulgaria, and even the Ottoman core area into a Russo-German frontier over which the two superpowers would fight an increasingly determined struggle for hegemony. And, as in the days of Napoleon, Russia's only recourse would be to make peace with the maritime powers in the Coastland, its traditional rivals, in order to join in the containment of Germany's dynamism in both Heartland and Coastland.

William I and Francis Joseph met at Bad-Ischl near Salzburg in August 1871, and Bismarck assured the Austrians that Germany had no territorial designs on Austria-Hungary. In November, the conduct of Austrian foreign affairs passed to Julius Andrássy (1823–1890), a Hungarian count who had taken part in the Hungarian uprising of 1848–1849 and had been forced to remain in exile until 1858. "Expansionist and Slavophobe Hungarians"[1] were coming into prominence after the Compromise of 1867. Andrássy supported a dynamic containment policy in the Balkans, but its success depended on Germany's support. The tsar's warm reception of Milan Obrenović, Michael's cousin and successor, in October was a reminder that Russia continued to consider Serbia its political base in the Balkan frontier. Andrássy felt compelled to warn Gorchakov in August 1872 that Vienna would not tolerate a Greater Serbia.

Bismarck, however, wanted a reconciliation between Austria and Russia. It would enable Germany to mediate Austro-Russian disputes, thereby reversing the roles played between 1779 and 1850 when Russia had mediated Austro-Prussian differences. The Russians now had to face the possibility of an Austro-German alliance if they refused to play Bismarck's game. The rapprochement was sealed in September 1872, when the three emperors met in Berlin for the first time. No agreement was made, but the meeting had symbolic importance. William I returned Alexander II's visit in May 1873 and even signed a military convention pledging mutual assistance in the event of war. Bismarck convinced his emperor to repudiate it: his priority was friendly relations with Austria. The tsar then traveled to Vienna where he agreed in writing with Francis Joseph in June 1873 that Russia and Austria would exchange views when necessary "to prevent divergences on special questions from prevailing over consideration of a higher order" and even consider a military convention. These exchanges "masqueraded under the rather pretentious title of the Three Emperors' League."[2] Their purpose was to calm the atmosphere and lay the foundations of future collaboration. In fact, divergent interests were pulling apart Russia and the Germanic powers. When rumors circulated in the spring of 1875 that Germany was planning a preventive war against France, Alexander II intervened personally to let Gorchakov assume the part of champion of France and defender of European peace. Bismarck would never forgive Russia's intervention and Gorchakov's self-righteous proclamation that he had kept the peace.

That same year, in the summer of 1875, a revolt broke out in Bosnia-Herzegovina, between the Una and the Drina. These two Ottoman provinces were ethnically Slav, Serb by language, Orthodox in religion, but with a strong Catholic, mostly Croat, minority looking to Austria across the Sava. There were also large pockets of Moslem population, including the more substantial landowners. Restless Montenegrins joined the revolt, and Serbia saw an opportunity to assume the leadership of the opposition to Ottoman rule, despite opposition in Vienna and Petersburg to accepting developments over which they might have no control. In December, Andrássy proposed a solution: the granting of complete religious liberty to the two provinces, the abolition of tax-farming, the end of the Ottoman practice of syphoning off the revenue from direct taxation, and the improvement of the condition of the peasantry. The Porte accepted it, but showed no intention to implement it.

These developments reached a climax in 1876. The Bulgarians revolted in April, the sultan was murdered in May, Serbia and Montenegro formed an alliance in June and declared war on the Ottomans in July, despite Russian entreaties to maintain the peace. Clearly, events were getting out of control. The ambitions of the men of power in Serbia and Bulgaria; a maturing ethnic consciousness in the face of continuing Ottoman oppression; the rise of nationalism and Pan-Slavism in Russia, encouraged by the tsarevich; the recognition in Austria that instability along what had once been called the Croatian-Slavonian military border had the potential of destabilizing Austria-Hungary—all these factors finally merged to cause an explosion on the Balkan frontier and a radical change in its geopolitical physiognomy. Russian volunteers flocked to Serbia, including General Michael Cherniaev, who had made a name for himself in the conquest of Central Asia and assumed the command of the Serbian army. Nevertheless, the Ottomans crushed Serbia in September, and only Alexander II's ultimatum kept them from carrying out a war of extermination. Unfortunately, the mobilization it necessitated made another Russo-Ottoman war inevitable.

In fact, Russia and Austria had already joined the conflict by agreeing at Reichstadt in July on what they would do in the event of an Ottoman defeat. The crucial issue was whether the Balkan frontier should be transformed into a single Slav state, the product of a Serbo-Bulgarian alliance that would unite all the Slav lands between the Heartland's periphery and the Danube, or simply a latter-day variant of the fourteenth-century Serbian empire with its axis in the basin of the Morava and the valley of the Vardar. Whether the Russian government subscribed to Pan-Slav ideas is less important than the fact that it had an interest in the creation of a large Slav state as long as Petersburg remained convinced such a state would eventually become a Russian protectorate. Austria's interest was to oppose the political unification of the Balkan frontier. The position of the protagonists was very similar to what it had been in Poland during the

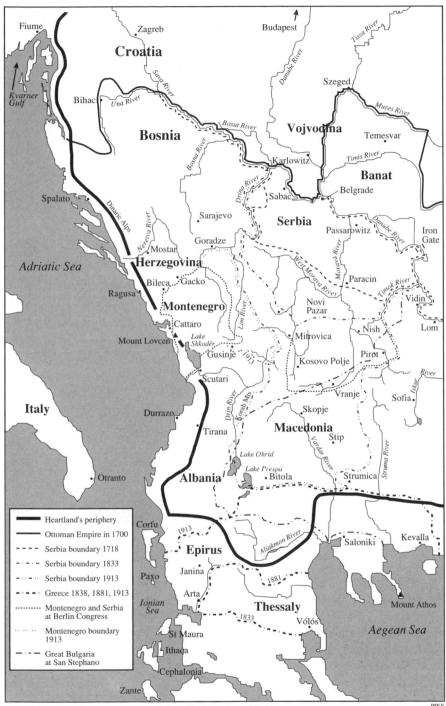

Fiume

Zagreb

Budapest

Croatia

Tisza River

Kvarner Gulf

Szeged

Bihac

Una River

Sava River

Mures River

Bosnia

Bosut River

Vojvodina

Temesvar

Bosna River

Drina River

Karlowitz

Banat

Spalato

Dinaric Alps

Nerevta River

Sabac

Belgrade

Sarajevo

Serbia

Passarowitz

Danube River

Iron Gate

Goradze

Mostar

West Morava River

Morava River

Paracin

Timok River

Vidin

Herzegovina

Bileca

Gacko

Montenegro

Novi Pazar

Lim River

Nish

Lom

Ragusa

Adriatic Sea

Cattaro

Mount Lovcen

Lake Shkodër

Gusinje

1913

Mitrovica

Kosovo Polje

Pirot

Iskur River

Scutari

Vranje

Sofia

Drin River

Korab Mts

Italy

Durrazo

Skopje

Tirana

Macedonia

Stip

Otranto

Lake Ohrid

Lake Prespa

Vardar River

Struma River

Albania

Bitola

Strumica

Corfu

1913

Aliakmon River

Saloniki

Kevalla

Epirus

Janina

Paxo

1881

Arta

Ionian Sea

Mount Athos

Thessaly

1833

Vólós

Aegean Sea

St Maura

Ithaca

Cephalonia

Zante

	Legend
━━━	Heartland's periphery
────	Ottoman Empire in 1700
- - - -	Serbia boundary 1718
-·-·-	Serbia boundary 1833
-··-··	Serbia boundary 1913
-··-··	Greece 1838, 1881, 1913
········	Montenegro and Serbia at Berlin Congress
·· ·· ··	Montenegro boundary 1913
-·-·-	Great Bulgaria at San Stephano

Map 9. Western Balkans

PIKE

267

reign of Catherine II, even if the situation in the field was somewhat different. It had not been in Russia's interest to partition the Polish Empire and for the same reason; partition had been in the interest of the Germanic powers, to roll back the Russian presence behind a more acceptable "political isobar," a line of contact of territorial power structures in relative equilibrium.

Austria-Hungary could not accept the creation of a large Slav state— a Serbo-Bulgarian state, a Greater Bulgaria, or a Greater Serbia—and this was made clear at Reichstadt. Bulgaria between the Danube and the Balkan Mountains would become an autonomous state; so would Rumelia—the valley of the Maritsa and the Tundzha, and Bulgaria's richer part. Austria-Hungary "could not permit"[3] Serbia to occupy Bosnia-Herzegovina, but would allow its aggrandizement in Bosnia along the Drina, in the direction of Niš toward the watershed with Bulgaria, and in the *sanjak* of Novi Pazar. The "Black Mountain" state would be enlarged by the annexation of the southeastern corner of Herzegovina and, beyond the headwaters of the Drina, of another part of the *sanjak*, west of the Lim River. What was left of it would continue to form a corridor separating Serbia from Montenegro. Austria-Hungary would then annex the remainder of Bosnia-Herzegovina, and Russia would return to its "natural boundary" on the southern channel of the Danube delta. One is reminded of Prussia's annexation of Pomerelia and Russia's advance to the Dvina and the Dniepr in 1772. Austria-Hungary would round out its possessions between Slovenia and Dalmatia, and Russia would regain control of the delta. Neither Kaunitz nor Radetzky would have approved such an unequal partition.

Serbia's defeat convinced Petersburg that Prince Milan's government was not a dependable base for the extension of Russian influence. The deterioration of Russo-Ottoman relations after the tsar's ultimatum led to the Ottoman declaration of war in April 1877. The Russians crossed the Balkan Mountains and imposed on the Porte the Peace of San Stefano in March 1878. The war focused their attention on Bulgaria, and the tsar, once he reached headquarters, abandoned the implicit promise he had made at Reichstadt to create on the ruin of the Ottoman Empire in Europe a collection of states that would roughly match the zonal divisions of the frontier. Gorchakov had to yield precedence to other civilian and military leaders, including Ignatev, and the tsar committed himself to the creation of a Greater Bulgaria. Its fate has been examined in Part II.

Austria did not enter the war, but could not remain indifferent to its outcome. Petersburg had to consider the possibility of war: it had been an Austrian concern for a century that Russia must not be allowed to reach Constantinople ahead of Austria. After Serbia's defeat, Alexander II inquired in Berlin whether Germany would support Russia in the event of a war with Austria. Bismarck had refused to commit himself and disclosed the question to Andrássy, whose suspicions of Russian ambitions needed no encouragement. Russo-German economic relations were taking a turn for the worse at the time, and an Austro-German bloc was slowly taking shape. The Russians knew it, and there was widespread talk in the high command that an eventual war with Germany should be taken for granted.

On the eve of the Russo-Ottoman war, in January 1877, Andrássy negotiated with Evgenii Novikov, the ambassador in Vienna, the terms of a settlement that confirmed the Reichstadt agreement but also made changes in tone and substance. It pledged Russia explicitly to recognize that "the establishment of a great compact Slav or other State is excluded." And Andrássy shrank from his determination to annex Bosnia-Herzegovina, convinced that "the Christian and Moslem populations are too much intermingled for it to be permissible to expect from a mere autonomous organization a real amelioration of their lot." In fact, he proposed to retain the Ottoman jurisdiction, and announced that the "occupation" (no longer the annexation) of Bosnia-Herzegovina by Austrian troops would not "assume a character of solidarity with the occupation of Bulgaria by the Russian Army"; Austria-Hungary reserved to itself "the choice of the moment and the mode of occupation" and it was understood that such an occupation would not "present a character of hostility towards Russia."[4] Andrássy's commitment would assume fundamental importance in the later history of the Bosnian question, but it also represented a stark withdrawal before the growing power of Russia in the Balkan frontier.

The San Stefano settlement came as a shock to Vienna. The creation of a Greater Bulgaria was a clear violation of the understanding that no large Slav state would be formed in the Balkan frontier. Moreover, by annexing most of the Ottoman provinces of Skopje, Bitola, and Saloniki, Bulgaria appropriated territory the Serbs claimed as their own, including the capital of their medieval empire and the hallowed ground of Kosovo Polje. Nevertheless, Serbia, kept out of the war by its own weakness and at Russia's insistence, received additional territory in the valley of the Morava. Montenegro was the great winner after Bulgaria: its territory was considerably enlarged in the north and west. Not much remained of the *sanjak*, and Serbia's merger with Montenegro into a Greater Serbia appeared to be only a matter of time. The creation of two large Slav states under Russian protection in the Balkan frontier would shut Austria-Hungary out of the Black Sea, confine it behind the Una and the Sava, and prepare the ground for an Austro-Serbian conflict over Bosnia-Herzegovina.

Such a revolutionary change in the geopolitics of the frontier was unacceptable to the containing powers in Heartland and Coastland. Britain and Austria joined hands to defeat Russian ambitions, and Bismarck used the opportunity to offer Germany's mediation. At the Congress of Berlin in the summer of 1878, Montenegro, Serbia, and Rumania finally won their independence, but all three lost some territory. Rumania lost southern Passarabia; Serbia and Montenegro what they had gained in the *sanjak*, including Novi Pazar. That vital corridor between Bosnia-Herzegovina and the valley of the Vardar leading to Saloniki was retroceded to the Porte.

The Berlin settlement was a Russian defeat and an Austro-Hungarian strategic victory. The tsar made no secret of his "outright loathing"[5] of Bismarck. Perhaps he understood, a little late, that Russia's danger did indeed grow with Prussia's power. Austria-Hungary took immediate advantage of the concessions obtained at the Berlin Congress. Its forces "occupied" Bosnia-Herzegovina in the summer of 1878, not without encountering strong resistance, and the territory was placed under a governor in Sarajevo responsible to the Austro-Hungarian finance minister. Vienna's policy would be to build an administrative and economic infrastructure in the desperately poor country while creating dissensions between Serbs and Croats, Orthodox, Catholics, and Moslems. Austria-Hungary also gained the right to keep garrisons and maintain military and commercial roads in the *sanjak* as far as Mitrovica on the Sitnitsa: Serbia was surrounded in the north, west, and south. The offensive move against a principality the Russians had considered their protégé for three generations was the initial step in Austria's return to a containment policy. But Austria-Hungary needed German support. Had not the German ambassador told Novikov in Vienna in August 1871 that its existence would henceforth depend on German goodwill?

The atmosphere of violent mutual recrimination between Petersburg and Berlin played into Bismarck's and Andrássy's hands. The Hungarian minister knew Russia was Austria-Hungary's archenemy, and Bismarck wanted a rapprochement with Vienna. A mutual objective led to the Austro-German alliance signed in September 1879, while the *sanjak* was being garrisoned. Despite protestations of friendship for Russia by both sides, the alliance was presented as a defensive one against Russia, pledging that a Russian attack on one would be met by "the whole war strength of both empires."[6] However, the line between a defensive and an offensive alliance is often a thin one, and the Russians were justified in viewing it as an offensive alliance as well. If they had any doubts, the Austrian advance in the Balkans must have disillusioned them. In June 1881, three months after the assassination of Alexander II and the accession of his son, the tsarevich (whom Bismarck had good reasons to consider anti-German), Vienna signed a treaty of alliance with Serbia. Its two key provisions bound Serbia not to tolerate "any political, religious or other intrigues" on its soil directed against the Habsburg monarchy, Bosnia-Herzegovina, and the *sanjak*, and not to negotiate any political treaty without Vienna's consent if it contained anything "contrary to the spirit and tenor" of the alliance.[7] In fact, the treaty did not create an alliance but an Austrian protectorate over Serbia. There was something unreal about the Three Emperors' League renewed in Berlin at the same time, a pathetic yearning to maintain conservative solidarity and an attempt to reconcile the irreconcilable. One can see in retrospect that the die had been cast by 1881. As an Austrian diplomat wrote after the Berlin Congress, "the Serbian people belongs in our sphere of power . . . Serbia under us, Greece with us, and Romania not opposed to us—with these elements . . . , we have little to fear from Russian encroachments in the Balkans or from Panslavism with Bulgaria as its center."[8]

Prince Milan, disappointed by the lack of Russian support in 1878, had moved Serbia into Austria's orbit, where it would remain until 1903, in return for the recognition of Serbia as a kingdom—Milan proclaimed himself king in March 1882—and of its aspirations for "Old Serbia" (Kosovo and the valley of the upper Vardar). The Germanic offensive continued along the Danube into Rumania: Vienna signed a treaty of alliance with Bucharest in October 1883. The Rumanian king already belonged to the ruling house of Prussia-Germany, and his prime minister, Ionel Bratianu, bitter at the Russian annexation of southern Bessarabia in 1878, looked to the Central Powers, as Germany and Austria-Hungary were beginning to be known. Each promised to enter into no commitments against the other and to enter a defensive war fought by the other. Germany joined the alliance, thereby guaranteeing that Russia must be contained behind the Prut, Austria's old line of an optimum of conquest. In March, Berlin and Vienna had renewed the alliance of 1879 for another five years.

There was more to come. The growth of anti-Russian feelings in Bulgaria culminated in the break of September 1885. King Milan saw an opportunity and declared war on Bulgaria in November. His troops made it as far as Slivnitsa, but Serbian military incompetence became obvious once again. A Bulgarian counteroffensive might have reached Belgrade, had not Vienna intervened and imposed a restoration of the status quo in March 1886. Serbia moved more deeply into Vienna's orbit, while Bulgaria was decidedly moving out of Petersburg's. The merger of Bulgaria with Rumelia was followed by the choice of another German prince as king of Rumania; Russia refused to recognize him. That same year, in August 1885, there were disturbing reports that William I of Germany might soon die (he was 88) and that his death would "change things very much, for the next people are very anti-Russian"; and that Alexander III, in the face of Russia's expulsion from the Balkans, had declared "the Slavs must now serve us, and not we them."[9] All the elements of the future confrontation were already in place.

The unsteady structure built by Bismarck quickly began to totter. Vienna's aggressive stance and "extraordinary military preparations" in Galicia caused a war scare in Berlin and Petersburg in 1887, and the Franco-Russian rapprochement created concern in Berlin. Bismarck's caution induced him to negotiate a "reinsurance treaty" for three years in June. It finally abandoned the fiction of the Three Emperors' League, but reaffirmed the Austro-German alliance of 1879. It also recognized the "legitimacy" of Russia's "preponderant and decisive"[10] influence in Bulgaria. The treaty did not stop the deterioration of Russo-German relations. William I died in March 1888. After a three months' interval, his grandson succeeded him as William II; he had made an unfavorable impression on Alexander III during a recent visit to Petersburg. Bismarck was forced to resign in March 1890, and William II decided not to renew the reinsurance treaty. Russia and the Central Powers finally acknowledged they had few interests in common.

The Germanic Offensive, 1891–1907

The growing Russo-German antagonism was not only fanned by the turbulence that had to follow the creation of a new balance of power between core areas, by conflicting strategic interests, and by the Germans' return to their historical mission of containing Russian expansion, with its highly charged ideological baggage of memories going back to the Teutonic Knights. Russian Germanophobia was beating the drums of frustrated nationalism to stir up resistance against the German threat. It also had a solid economic foundation. The trade rivalry that would continue until 1914 was no more than a continuation of the wranglings we encountered after 1815. Competition between irreconcilable economic interests was built into the Russo-German relationship; it aggravated divergences in other areas.

At first glance there seemed to be a perfect economic symmetry: Germany was an industrial power, Russia an agrarian economy; Germany had capital to export, Russia was starved of capital. Germany became Russia's largest creditor when Petersburg embarked on an ambitious program of railroad building. Germany's manufactured goods were ready to conquer the Russian market, and its rapidly growing population made it the best customer of Russian grain. Tensions with Britain, beginning in the 1870s, closed the London capital market and reinforced a relationship seemingly based on mutual economic interests. But at the very same time, both countries turned to protective measures for a variety of reasons, including two simple ones. Russia's protectionism during the days of its hegemony in the Heartland had aggravated its economic backwardness and reduced its relative economic power to a level from which it might never return to the ranks of the great economic powers. A temporary willingness to open up its markets so threatened the position of the Moscow-based industrialists that a return to protectionism became a political and economic necessity and its support an essential ingredient of Germanophobia. On the other hand, the unification of Germany exposed the country's division between the industrialized regions in the Coastland and the agrarian interests beyond the Elbe, in Brandenburg and East Prussia. An integrated economy and the political survival of the government required the conciliation of industrial and agrarian interests, and East Elbian interests were bitterly opposed to imports of cheap Russian grain. Thus it happened that both powers completed the transition to protective tariffs between 1877 and 1879 while Bismarck was mediating Austro-Russian differences and then signed the fateful alliance with Austria-Hungary.

The economic depression of the second half of the 1880s brought about a tariff war. Petersburg raised tariff rates in April, Berlin in May,

1885; and again in May and December 1887, respectively. A campaign began against Russian funds in German banks. In the fall of 1888, they refused to negotiate a Russian loan. Bismarck was set on a collision course; so were the chiefs of the General Staff, Helmut von Moltke and his successor, Alfred von Waldersee, who were planning a preventive war against Russia. The Russians escalated the war with the "ultraprotectionist" tariff of June 1891, raising rates by 20 to 30 percent. At the end of the year, Berlin signed several commercial treaties, including one with Austria-Hungary, that reduced rates on agricultural imports by more than 30 percent. The concession was not extended to Russia on the ground that no treaty with it included the most-favored-nation clause. Witte, the finance minister, pronounced the action unfriendly and discriminatory, pointing out that the German lower rates applied to grain exports from the United States with which Germany had no such treaty. Two months later, German imports were hit with another increase of 50 percent; Berlin retaliated with a similar increase. The Russian action practically stopped imports of German machinery, iron, and hardware, but the industrial recession in Germany limited the damage and Russia's poor harvests reduced grain exports. Both sides, having made their point, agreed to negotiate a commercial treaty.

The treaty of March 1894 was signed for ten years. It contained a most-favored-nation clause, prohibited discrimination in tariff and railway rates, and reduced rates across the board. It may have been more advantageous to Germany, however, although Russian exports to Germany continued to exceed imports from Germany until 1904. By 1902, Germany took 41 percent of Russia's exports against 24 percent in 1892, and shipped back 35 percent of Russia's imports against 25 percent in 1892. The treaty was not simply renewed but renegotiated in July 1904. It raised rates significantly and consolidated Germany's position in what was becoming an increasingly unequal relationship. An exchange of notes enabled Russia to raise a loan on the Berlin market during its disastrous war with Japan.

Ten years later, as the First World War was about to break out, a disturbing development had become noticeable. Not only had Germany remained the leading supplier of manufactured goods to the Russian Empire; it had also become an exporter of grain, competing successfully in Russia's traditional markets. East Prussian grain was taking over the Scandinavian market and even evicting Russian grain from the inner frontier of the empire, in Russian Poland and in Finland, prompting Petersburg to introduce the Russian protectionist tariff in 1914, as it had in Poland in 1847. Germany's superior economic power was felt far beyond its borders—in the Balkans, in Anatolia, in the Caucasus, and in Persia, placing Russia at a constant disadvantage. The German trade offensive had left Russia on the defensive. Russia's economic relationship with Germany was one of colony with metropolis: exports of agricultural products and raw materials in exchange for imports of manufactured goods were typical of colonial relationships. Russia may have been the fourth largest industrial power in 1913, and its growth may have caused concern "from Galicia to Persia to Peking,"[11] but it was a great economic power on the Southern and Eastern Frontiers, not on the Western Frontier. Moreover, the legitimacy of its political system had been challenged since the emancipation of the serfs in 1861. Aggravated by the war with Japan, unrest was spreading in town and countryside and caused a revolution in 1905.

Germany found itself in the happy situation that had so favored the Russian advance into the three frontiers: it would watch and, when necessary, encourage the rotting process in order to weaken the core area, contain its expansion in the Southern Frontier, and loosen its grip in the inner frontier of the empire. For the result of Germany's rising economic might was the transformation of the inner frontier—the old Russo-Swedish, Russo-Polish, and Russo-Turkish frontiers—into an economic hinterland of East Prussia, Silesia, and even the Rhineland. Germany came too late to find colonies beyond the great oceans, but the challenge was there to transform the inner frontier (and, for the more ambitious among the Pan-Germans, even European Russia) into a colony of the German Empire. Success in such a long-term endeavor would go beyond containment; it would roll back Russia to the boundary of its core area, from Lake Peipus around the Central Upland to the Volga. But could such a concerted attempt against Russia's vital interests be successfully carried out without war?

The seemingly irreversible change in the balance of economic power, with its ominous implications of a redistribution of territorial space within the western segment of the Heartland, caused enough unease in both Germany and Russia to raise the question whether the old alliance could not be restored. The tradition of conservative solidarity to resist the subversive influences emanating from the Coastland was still strong; business ties and intellectual exchanges going back to the 1720s had created a reservoir of goodwill, despite the ideological antagonism between Teuton and Slav, German *Kultur* and "eastern barbarism." But alliances must have a common enemy and serve the interests of the parties. After 1890, Germany's transformation had so upset the political equilibrium created in 1815 that an alliance of the flanking powers naturally reasserted itself. The Franco-Russian rapprochement of 1891–1894 coincided with the Russo-German tariff war. After 1894, the alliance of the flanking powers became a crucial factor in Russo-German relations.

To the Russians, an alliance with Germany would encourage expansion into Persia and China and facilitate a redeployment of troops against the Japanese. That Witte, the architect of Russia's eastward expansion, also supported at least a settlement of Russo-German differences was no coincidence. Such an alliance would have the additional advantage of combining Russia's favorable geopolitical location in the Heartland with Germany's economic power in order to launch an offensive against Britain, Russia's enemy and, increasingly, Germany's. It would be in accord with Russia's traditional policy of turning rival core areas outward.

But it was not a realistic option unless Russia was willing to accept the crippling of France by Germany, and in 1875, Petersburg had made clear it would not acquiesce in its further diminution (*Verkleinerung*). Neither would Britain, and it followed that a victorious Germany in the continental Coastland would threaten both British and Russian vital interests. Finally, such an alliance could not have reversed the disparity between a self-confident Germany and a Russia in the throes of a rotting process that became increasingly evident after the accession of Nicholas II in November 1894. That disparity drew Germany eastward; it aggravated rather than restrained the ideological antagonism; and it confirmed the wisdom of Russia's alliance with a Coastland power.

A Russo-German alliance was much more attractive to the Germans. It would destroy the Franco-Russian alliance and break Germany's encirclement, give Germany a free hand in the Coastland, and, by crippling France, magnify Germany's economic and military power against Britain and Russia. It would also encourage Russia to become embroiled in the politics of destabilized Persia and China and face Japanese ambitions in the Monsoon Coastland, thereby worsening the rotting process at home, at least as long as it did not topple the Romanov dynasty (it was not yet in Germany's interest to welcome chaos in Petersburg and Moscow).

In the spring of 1895, Germany gave Russia its unconditional support to force the Japanese to relinquish the Liaotung Peninsula and contributed its share to the assets of the Russo-Chinese Bank. It did not oppose Russia's lease on the peninsula three years later. By 1902, Berlin had realized that the Far East was becoming "Russia's Achilles heel,"[12] and refused to join Petersburg in protesting the formation of the Anglo-Japanese alliance. Germany remained neutral during the Russo-Japanese War, hoping for a war of attrition that would substantially weaken Russia's military standing and financial stability. Military weakness could only favor the German economic offensive and undermine the Franco-Russian alliance. The tsar saw in the war a justification of his ingrained Anglophobia; William II took advantage of it and proposed in October 1904 a Russo-German defensive alliance directed against Britain. France might be invited to join it later.

The tsar wavered, but did not yield. The Kaiser resubmitted his proposal when the two rulers met in the seclusion of the Imperial yachts at Björkö in July 1905, but without any reference to France. The tsar finally agreed. In its new form, the proposal was no less than a global alliance of the Heartland powers against the powers of the European and Monsoon Coastland. No wonder it appealed to Witte, who praised "the wise principles enunciated at Björkö."[13] But it did not please the tsar's foreign minister, who was not present at the encounter and was shocked by his master's implicit rejection of the French alliance. In the end, no action was taken. Wiser counsels prevailed, including that of Alexander Nelidov, the ambassador to France, who concluded in October that "to be on genuinely good terms with Germany an alliance with France is necessary.

Otherwise, we will lose our independence and I know nothing more painful that the German yoke."[14] Indeed, France soon became instrumental in bringing about the Anglo-Russian settlement of August 1907 that completed the alliance of the flanking powers and left Germany isolated and more unstable than ever.

The growth of Germany's economic and military power threatened Russia's position not only in Poland and the old Russo-Polish frontier, but also in Scandinavia and Turkey. The geographic imperative reasserted itself, as it always does when large territorial masses seek to create a new political isobar: Germany adopted a containment policy based on support for the Swedish and Turkish core areas. Britain had done the same thing in the nineteenth century, France in the eighteenth. Space in the emerging Russo-German frontier was indeed loaded with political and military power that needed to be harnessed in the process of creating a continental economic and military bloc capable of surviving on its own resources and eventually rolling back Russia to its 1650 borders.

A German military mission first appeared in Constantinople in 1883, the year Berlin formed an alliance with Bucharest and renewed its alliance with Vienna. Its chief, General Colmar von der Goltz, was instructed to reorganize the Ottoman army and to place military orders with German industry. William II visited the sultan in 1889 and again in 1898. The Germans began to cut into Britain's privileged position. The share of German capital in banking enterprises operating in Turkey reached one-fifth of total investments by the beginning of the twentieth century. German exports to Turkey increased seventeen times between 1894 and 1912, even though trade with Turkey remained a fraction of Germany's foreign trade. In 1908, on the eve of the Young Turk revolution, Germany's and Austria-Hungary's influence in Constantinople was "unlimited."[15] Many of the Young Turks had been educated in Germany, including one of their leading figures, Enver Pasha, the future war minister. Germany was replacing Britain (which had replaced France) in Turkey's partnership with the European Coastland to contain the Russian advance toward the straits.

The consolidation of Germany's influence in the Turkish core area and its extension into Persia in the direction of the Indian Ocean required the development of a rail link. In the eyes of contemporaries, railroads were revolutionizing geopolitical relationships by shortening "interior lines"[16] that had been such an obstacle to territorial integration in the age of the horse, the camel, and the riverboat. The Trans-Siberian, begun in 1891, was Russia's ambitious attempt to transform its immense interior line into a strategic advantage and a factor of integration in the tenuous connection with the Persian and Sino-Japanese frontier. The Suez Canal shortened the interior lines of the British Empire between the European and the Monsoon Coastland; the so-called Berlin-Baghdad Railroad was Germany's attempt to create an overland link between the western periphery of the Heartland and the Monsoon Coastland.

Constantinople was linked with Berlin and Vienna in 1888. The following year, a German group obtained a concession for a German Anatolian Railroad Company to build a first segment from Haydar Pasha on the Bosphorus to Ismit and another from Ismit to Angora (Ankara) via Eskişehir. Angora was reached in 1892. In 1893, in return for another loan, the company obtained a second concession to extend the line from Eskişehir to Konya; the task was completed in 1896. In December 1899, a third concession was granted to build the Konya-Baghdad segment and extend it to the Persian Gulf; Basra later became its terminus. The construction of the trunk line aroused fears in Russia (and Britain) that branch lines would later bring German influence and industrial goods into Transcaucasia and Persia. As a result, the company had to agree in March 1900 not to build tracks north of a line Angora-Sivas-Diyarbakir-Van, implicitly recognizing Russia's preponderant influence in Western Armenia and on the southern shore of the Black Sea. The agreement of March 1903 reorganized the company into the Imperial Ottoman Baghdad Railroad Company, fixing its route via Konya, Ardana, and Mosul with a branch from Baghdad to Khanaqin, arousing again Russian fears that the railroad would monopolize the transportation of Persian Shi'ite pilgrims to the holy cities of Karbala and An Najaf and the shipment of German goods into northern Persia. A Turko-German alliance was certain to threaten the Russian hold on the northern provinces, which the Anglo-Russian partition of August 1907 would assign to Russia's exclusive commercial and political influence. In fact, the Baghdad Railroad was not completed until 1940. By 1918, it had reached Nisibis (Nusaybin) from the west and a station on the Tigris north of Baghdad, leaving a 480-kilometer gap in between.

While the German diplomatic and economic offensive was unfolding with the self-confidence that only the certainty of success can give, Austria-Hungary and Russia agreed they should suspend their active rivalry in the Balkan frontier. Russian influence was restored in Bulgaria in the 1890s, but Rumania remained allied with the Danubian monarchy and Serbia continued to be an Austrian protectorate. Vienna had important differences with its Czech and Hungarian subjects; Petersburg's attention was focused on the Far East. In May 1897, the two powers agreed to maintain the status quo, but also looked to the future. In the event of another destabilization of the frontier, Vienna claimed the right to "annex" Bosnia-Herzegovina and the *sanjak* at the opportune moment, to create an independent Albania on the Heartland's periphery between Lake Shkodër and Janina (Ioannina), and to impose, in agreement with Russia, "an equitable partition" of the remainder among the existing Balkan states. The Russians only objected that the transition from "occupation" to "annexation" of Bosnia-Herzegovina would require "special scrutiny at the proper time and place."[17]

They had not given up the hope of restoring their influence in Serbia. A new envoy, Nikolai Charykov, arrived in Belgrade in the spring of 1901; he would later write that he never worked so hard as he did in the

Serbian capital. His instructions were to create friendly relations between Serbia and Bulgaria and prepare for the construction of an "Adriatic Railway"[18] to link the Danube with the Adriatic across Serbia and Montenegro. Two years later, in June 1903, King Alexander was murdered, the Obrenovič regime came to an end, and Prince Peter Karadjordje succeeded to the Serbian throne. He was pro-Russian, a leader of the Greater Serbia movement, and believed in closer relations with Bulgaria. Vienna's answer was to force a cancellation in 1906 of a proposed Serbo-Bulgarian customs union and to launch a tariff war against Serbia, the so-called Pig War, an embargo on Serbian pork products. It did not achieve its purpose of forcing Belgrade to change course. Then, three appointments in 1906 announced a major change in Vienna's policy. Aloys von Aerenthal became Austro-Hungarian foreign minister, and Conrad von Hötzendorf became chief of the Austro-Hungarian General Staff. Both believed in a forward policy in the Balkan frontier. The third appointment was that of Helmut von Moltke, son of the Moltke of the 1880s, to the post of chief of staff of the German General Staff. The new German emphasis on an offensive war against France and a defensive posture in the east necessitated a switch to an offensive strategy by Vienna; it transformed the alliance of 1879 into an offensive combination against Russia. All three appointments had a common background: a conviction that the rotting process in the wake of the 1905 revolution had rendered the Russian Empire unable to resist an active containment policy.

The Triumph of Containment, 1908–1917

Beginning in 1908, the situation in the Balkan frontier disintegrated at an increasing speed, until a war, welcomed by some, dreaded by others, finally destroyed the three monarchies—but not before the Central Powers succeeded in occupying the entire frontier separating them from the Russian core area. In January, Aerenthal announced he had obtained the sultan's agreement to survey a route through the *sanjak* for a railroad linking Sarajevo with the Turkish line from Saloniki to Mitrovica. Sarajevo was already connected with Budapest, and Budapest was on the Berlin-Vienna-Belgrade-Sofia-Constantinople trunk line. The announcement was not well received in Belgrade, Sofia, and Petersburg; it signaled an Austrian forward policy in "Old Serbia" and Macedonia, and struck at Serbian and Bulgarian aspirations. On his way to Paris in September, the Russian foreign minister, Alexander Izvolsky, met Aerenthal at Buchlau in Moravia. Instead of focusing on containing Austria's ambitions in the Balkans, he showed a willingness to trade Russia's acceptance of Vienna's "annexation" of Bosnia-Herzegovina for its support of a Russian proposal to renegotiate the status of the straits with the Coastland powers. In so doing, he betrayed Serbia's interests, at the very time Aerenthal and Hötzendorf had already decided that the time had come not only to annex the province but to partition Serbia as well.

Vienna had followed a consistent policy since 1876. It had been agreed at Reichstadt and again in Berlin in July 1878, and in Petersburg in May 1897, that Austria would determine the opportunity of the "annexation" and that it would not be regarded as a move directed against Russia (despite the latter's reservation in 1897). But the growth of nationalism everywhere and Russia's feeling of humiliation after 1905 transformed the annexation, announced in October, into a blow directed against its interests in the Balkans. Little could be done to challenge Vienna's fait accompli. There was talk of war, but Russia was not ready to answer Austrian military preparations against Serbia, and Germany stepped in to guarantee there would be no war. In March 1909, Berlin sent an ultimatum demanding a Russian and Serbian unconditional acceptance of the annexation. The crisis was over, but it intensified the Austro-Russian rivalry, and the object of that rivalry became Serbia once again. In the fall, Nikolai Hartwig, the former director of the Asiatic (now called First) Department and envoy to Persia, arrived in Belgrade to carry out, sometimes beyond his instructions, a Pan-Slav and anti-Habsburg policy. He would remain until 1914. The issue was joined.

That same year, in the spring, General von der Golz returned to Constantinople with a second German military mission. The Young Turks were now serious about reorganizing the army, and the general, while remaining directly subordinated to the German foreign ministry, was made vice president of the Turkish Military Council. Turkey was divided into military districts, and some twenty-five German instructors were appointed to guide the modernization of the command structure. More orders were placed with German industry, and the new Turkey, with its remaining possessions in the Balkans, joined with the Central Powers to complete their pincer movement from the Baltic to the Caucasus. Von der Goltz returned to Germany in 1912, followed by General Liman von Sanders, who arrived in December 1913. The new mission was larger and of a different kind. Sanders was given the command of the First Corps stationed in and around Constantinople. This, the Russians objected, was tantamount to establishing a German garrison on the Bosphorus. His position as corps commander and chief of mission gave him the opportunity to influence decisively Turkish military planning from Adrianople to the Caucasian border.

The appointment naturally created strong opposition in London and Petersburg, and William II and the sultan were forced to compromise. Soon after his arrival, in January 1914, the sultan promoted Sanders to field marshal and made him inspector general of the Turkish army. The promotion deprived him of his command, but he gained a broader jurisdiction over the Second Corps stationed in Adrianople and the Third in Erzerum. The objectives of Germany's containment policy were clear: to achieve full control of the Turkish war ministry and a dominant influence in the foreign ministry, and to stiffen Turkey's resistance to Russian pressures. Some Germans even wanted a resettlement of the Armenians, to be replaced by Turco-Mongol tribesmen, in order to create "a steel barrier against Russia."[19] In August, the defense of the straits, fortified by heavy guns bought from Krupp, was placed under German command.

While the Germans were consolidating their position in Constantinople and the Austrians plotting to undermine the revival of Serbia encouraged by Russia, the poor showing of the Porte in the war with Italy (1911–1912) convinced Serbs, Bulgarians, and Greeks that the time had finally come to expel the Ottomans from Europe. The Russians remained faithful to their old objective, first made clear in 1877, of creating if not a single large Slav state, at least two—in Serbia and Bulgaria—that might perhaps later form a customs and even a political union. The convention of December 1910 bound Montenegro not to take military action without their consent. Montenegro was considered at the time a Serbian land, and its union with Serbia had long been a cherished objective of the Greater Serbia nationalists. In October 1911, Serbia began negotiations with Bulgaria, already bound to Russia by the military agreement of December 1909, and signed with Sofia a treaty of alliance in March 1912, to which Montenegro later adhered. It pledged the parties to take concerted action against the Ottomans and recognized Russia's role as the arbiter of future disputes over an "equitable partition" of their last possessions in Europe. In October, Montenegro declared war on the Porte with Russia's tacit approval, and was joined by Serbia and Bulgaria (and Greece).

The Balkan war was a disaster for the Young Turk government and an embarrassment for the German military mission. Serbian troops reached the Adriatic and seized Durrazo (Durrës), their hope for a port to link Belgrade with the sea. The Montenegrins seized Scutari (Shkodër)—it would give them full control of the lake and enlarge the kingdom to the east. In November, Albania declared its independence from the Porte. However, unable to agree on an equitable partition at a conference held in London in May 1913, Serbia and Bulgaria went to war to partition Macedonia among themselves. Bulgaria lost, and the Treaty of Bucharest in August confirmed Serbia as the winner of the war, even though it took an Austrian ultimatum to compel Belgrade to evacuate the corridor to the Adriatic across Albania. Indeed, Austria's support for Albanian independence was motivated by a determination to keep Serbia landlocked. The *sanjak* was abolished and divided between Serbia and Montenegro. They became neighbors, but Montenegro had to abandon Scutari. Serbia was considerably enlarged to the south by the annexation of Old Serbia and the valley of the Vardar (the greater part of Macedonia) to a line running from the Korab Mountains through lakes Ohrid and Prespa along the watershed with the basin of the Aliakmon in Greek Thessaly and continuing between Štip and Strumica to the watershed with the Struma in Bulgaria. A new Greater Serbia had appeared in the Balkan frontier. General von Hötzendorf had his reasons for believing it must be destroyed and incorporated into the Austro-Hungarian Empire.

The emergence of Serbia must be placed against the background of a rapidly changing geopolitical situation in the Balkan frontier. The Turkish core area being increasingly dominated by Germany, the Balkans were becoming an interlocking frontier between Austria-Hungary, Germany, and Russia. After the incorporation of Bosnia-Herzegovina into the inner frontier of the Austro-Hungarian Empire, Serbia and Bulgaria were being turned into outer frontier zones between Austria-Hungary on the Drina and Germany on the Bosphorus. This alone can explain the otherwise incomprehensible fact that, when the final crisis came in 1914, Vienna acted "as if Russia did not exist."[20] Despite Russia's mediation during the Balkan war of 1912–1913 and the activities of Hartwig and his colleague, Anatolii Nekliudov, in Sofia, who were supporting Serbian and Bulgarian aspirations (thereby canceling each other's efforts!), Serbia had become a problem for the Central Powers to settle among themselves. During the war, Germany had remained aloof, refusing to accept Vienna's fears that Serbia must become the Piedmont of the Balkans. In 1914, it would give Austria its full support in order to complete the assertion of Germanic influence in the entire frontier and keep Russia contained behind the Prut.

The crisis began with the assassination of Francis Ferdinand, the heir to the Austro-Hungarian throne, during a state visit to Sarajevo in June. The assassin was a Bosnian student connected with Serbian nationalist and terrorist organizations, some of whose members were army officers and police officials. The Austro-Hungarian foreign minister, Leopold Berchtold (Aerenthal had died in February 1912) convinced William II that Serbia must be eliminated as a political factor in the Balkans. Encouraged by Germany's support, he demanded in mid-July that Serbia demobilize its army, suppress anti-Habsburg propaganda, remove officers and officials known for their hostility to Vienna, and prosecute all persons involved in the assassination. Serbia, given forty-eight hours to reply, accepted the ultimatum except its last provision—that Austrians take part in the inquiry and in political repression. Vienna did not expect Serbia to comply and used its only reservation to break off diplomatic relations.

But Russia could not be ignored, because there existed in Petersburg "a rooted conviction that a favorable moment was approaching for settling with Austria-Hungary for the sins of the Aerenthal policy," and there was such sympathy among the public for Serbian aspirations that the government was in danger of losing control.[21] Russia decreed partial mobilization; so did Austria, which declared war on Serbia at the end of July. Russia then ordered a general mobilization, a step interpreted by Berlin as an act of war. Both Austria-Hungary and Germany declared general mobilization; Germany declared war on Russia on August 1, followed by Austria-Hungary six days later. The great war for the control of the Russo-Germanic frontier had begun.

The war did not begin well for the Central Powers. Geography dictated there would be three fronts—one between Austria-Hungary and Russia, beyond the Carpathians, for the control of Galicia, Bessarabia, and eventually the whole of Ukraine; another between Germany and Russia, for the control of Poland and the old Russo-Polish frontier; a third in Serbia. The Austro-Hungarians failed in their attack to "eliminate" Serbia despite the capture of Belgrade in December, and were driven back across the Drina. A massive Russian offensive in East Prussia was stopped in August at Tannenberg, where the Slavs had been on the winning side in 1410 when the Poles had defeated the Teutonic Order. But the Russians were successful in Galicia, capturing L'vov (L'viv) in September and besieging the fortress of Przemysl, which surrendered in March 1915. A German relief force failed to reach the Austro-Hungarians, who were forced to withdraw across the Carpathians into Transylvania. Rumania refused to honor its obligations under the 1883 treaty and remained neutral; so did Bulgaria.

The Central Powers went on the offensive in 1915. On the northern front, the Germans occupied Warsaw and Brest-Litovsk in August and took Vilno and Grodno in September. They mobilized sufficient power to help their allies in the south; Przemysl and L'vov fell in September. By the end of the year they had invaded Kurland and Lithuania, and the Austrians had recovered their losses of 1914. Now convinced that the Central Powers would win the war, Bulgaria saw its chance to wipe out the humiliation of 1913 and declared war on Serbia in October. Exposed to attacks from west and east, Serbia quickly collapsed. The Central Powers occupied Belgrade and the Bulgarians occupied Pirot, Niš, Skopje, and Bitola, recreating much of the Greater Bulgaria of 1878. In January 1916, the Austrians invaded Montenegro and Albania. The entire Balkan frontier was now in the camp of the Central Powers. The Russians tried to break the Germanic advance with an offensive of their own, led by General Brusilov in the summer of 1916. Its thrust was directed against the southern front, considered the weaker one. It succeeded in rolling back the Austro-Hungarians from eastern Galicia and even beyond the southern Carpathians as far as Sibiu and Brasov. The success of the offensive required Rumanian cooperation, but it could not be obtained until Bucharest was certain of Russia's success and secured promises of territorial aggrandizement in Transylvania to the Tisza River and in the Banat, with their large Rumanian population. When Rumania finally entered the war in August 1916, it was too late to help the crippled Russian offensive. The Germans retaliated by invading Rumania and capturing Bucharest in December, while Bulgaria invaded the Dobruja and took Constanza. At the end of the year the stalemate remained unbroken.

In the euphoria of what appeared to be certain victory, German war aims became more specific. One of the major figures of the Pan-German movement, Paul Rohrbach, called for the exclusion of Russia from European affairs and echoed Frederick I of Prussia 200 years earlier in demanding the rollback of the "eastern barbarian." Rohrbach and his friends in the high command, notably General Erich Ludendorff, wanted Russia rolled back behind the Narova River and Lake Peipus, the Dvina and Berezina marshes to Kiev. West of that natural and strategic zone lay the old Russo-Polish and Russo-Swedish frontier, still sparsely populated. It would be settled with German peasants, thoroughly Germanized, and transformed into an agricultural and livestock base for the continental economy of an industrialized Germanic core area. The frontier and Russia itself would become the hinterland of that economy, as in the days of the Hanseatic League and the Teutonic Order, "when the entire Russian commerce to the Urals was brought to Germany in German ships."[22] And the Ukraine was to be detached from Russia, presumably for the same purpose. Rohrbach was advocating no less than the expulsion of the Russians from the entire Western and Russo-Turkish frontier and its incorporation into the German Empire, a complete reversal of the respective positions of Germans and Russians since 1815.

The stalemate was broken by the Bolshevik Revolution that brought the rotting process to a successful completion. The Peace of Brest-Litovsk in February 1918 recognized the independence of the Baltic provinces, Lithuania, and the Ukraine, before their transformation, like Poland, into German satellites. For a brief moment, between February and November, not only the containment but the rollback of Russia succeeded beyond the wildest aspirations. But Germany was fated to lose the war at the hands of the maritime powers, and the rotting process was at work in Berlin and Vienna as well. Their historical mission accomplished, the Hohenzollern and Habsburg monarchies collapsed, recreating for another brief moment the medieval frontier between Slav and Teuton.

The Prussian and Austrian core areas had been born in medieval times on the margin of the Coastland facing the western and eastern Slavs. Geography had determined the direction of their expansion—across the northern European plain to the Gulf of Finland and the Niemen; down the Danube to the Black Sea. The Germans had been driven by the inner logic of their expansion to occupy the river mouths, behaving very much like a sea power, as we shall see presently. But the mouths of the Oder, the Vistula, the Niemen, and the Dvina were but the exits for the outflow of trade from vast hinterlands, and the starting points for missionaries and conquerors. The struggle for the hinterlands brought the Germans into conflict with the Poles and then the Russians, the latter to be contained as much as possible behind the watersheds demarcating the river basins. By contrast, the Austrians began in the hinterland of the Danube, and the logic of their expansion took them toward the delta. It also conditioned them to seek control of the entire basin of the Danube, watered by its tributaries on the left bank from the Tisza to the Prut, and those on the right bank: the Sava first of all, fed by the Una, the Drina, and the Morava; and, beyond the Iron Gate, the Timok and the Iskur. The Austrian southeastward drive complemented the German eastward push; its ultimate justification was the expulsion of the Ottomans from the delta of the Danube and keeping the Russians away from the great river, Constantinople, and the straits.

Geography gave Prussia and Austria a common geopolitical interest, but their bitter rivalry for dominance in the Germanic coastland of their common origin weakened their effectiveness and left them exposed to the divisive tactics of the Russians, who sought eventually a line of an optimum of conquest along the Heartland's periphery, incorporating into their empire the continental hinterlands of the Baltic and Black seas. Prussia was still weak during the Northern War, fought by Russia with Sweden for the inheritance of the Teutonic Order, and its kings had to witness, following the occupation of Riga, a Russian presence in Danzig, Stettin, Stralsund, and Wismar. The Russians were first in Kurland, and Königsberg was threatened. A consequence of the war was the Prussian military buildup to escape the bondage of clientage to the Coastland powers for which Prussia had been but a pawn. In 1740, military power was used to impose a territorial settlement on Austria that would enlarge Prussia and give it the economic base and the fiscal resources to transform the northern kingdom into a first class military power. After 1740, Prussia's mission became the weakening and, eventually, the destruction of Poland. But the destruction of Poland also involved a containment policy designed to keep Russia out of it, behind the Niemen and the Bug. Austria had a similar objective: the annexation of Poland between the Vistula and the Bug kept Russia out of Galicia and away from the approaches to the Carpathians.

The Austrians were less successful in the valley of the Danube. Austria and Russia had to advance far enough into the inhospitable zones of an extended frontier before Vienna could embark on an effective containment policy, but the vision was there all along: the Russians must be kept away from the Danube delta. It was not until the Russian strategic breakthrough during the war of 1768–1774 that Vienna faced the necessity of having to threaten war to attain its objective. The Russians kept advancing until they reached the Dniestr in 1792. By then it had become clear that Austria did not have the military power both to advance into the frontier against the Ottomans and to force the Russians to withdraw. Moreover, its rivalry with Prussia over the management of German affairs made it a certainty that an Austro-Russian war would be accompanied by a Prussian attack on Austria; and any additional advance into the Balkan frontier would bring more Slavs into the Austrian Empire, weakening the core area and exposing the empire to Russian-led subversion in the name of ethnic and religious solidarity.

It was a paradox that France, which traditionally had been the chief containing power in the eighteenth century, should have weakened, during the Napoleonic wars, Austria's and Prussia's ability to remain a barrier to Russian expansion. The reconstitution of a small Poland drove a wedge into Prussian territory and took Russia in the end beyond the Vistula, giving it a strategic advantage against Brandenburg and Hungary. The wars also strengthened Russia, and for the next thirty years it exercised an undisputed hegemony as far as the Elbe and the Moravian corridor. Its forceful intervention in Prussia in 1848 and in Hungary in 1849 marked the two high points of that hegemony. The result was Austria's withdrawal before the growth of Russian influence in Serbia and the abandonment of its strategic goal of keeping the Russians from the delta of the Danube: all three channels were in Russian hands by 1829.

Russia used its superior power to turn Prussia and Austria outward, to redefine their mission as containing powers. They would have to become a barrier against the subversive influences from the Coastland powers, France and Britain. To reassert their traditional mission, the Germanic powers had two options: overcome their rivalry for the leadership of Germany; form an alliance with the Coastland powers. An alliance with the Ottomans, the linchpin of French and British policy in the Southern Frontier, was not available to Austria—it would have been a betrayal of Vienna's historical mission, would have caused strong opposition among the southern Slavs of its empire, and would have facilitated Russian subversion. The option of reconciliation was still too premature to be realistic; it would have to wait until a Prussian victory in Germany. Austria sided with the Coastland powers in 1854. The result was the greatest success of containment before 1918. And indeed, only a permanent alliance between the Coastland and Germanic powers could impose an insuperable barrier to the Russian advance. Conflicting interests made such an alliance impossible.

Berlin and Vienna finally made peace in 1879, and their alliance had the effect of creating a single Germanic core area welding together German power and Austrian ambitions. The focus of Germanic containment policy had been the Polish Empire in the eighteenth century; it would be the Ottoman Empire in the late nineteenth, chiefly the Balkan frontier and the Turkish core area. The Central Powers' superior economic and military power seemed to promise an eventual success. But the old balance between Heartland and Coastland reasserted itself. The emergence of a Germanic core area brought about an alliance of the flanking powers, Russia in the Heartland, Britain and France in the Coastland; and it was certain to cancel out Germanic superiority. For if space is power, Russia and the Coastland powers had more space and more resources, especially after America's intervention. The singular political ineptitude of the Germans gave that alliance an additional advantage. Containment by the German powers won its greatest victory at Brest-Litovsk. Whether that victory could have been sustained is highly doubtful, what with the disintegration of the three monarchies and the explosion of nationalism in the Russo-Germanic frontier. Anyway, no matter how successful, Germanic containment was bound to remain regional in scope. Only the Coastland powers could oppose a continuous barrier to Russia's global ambitions.

V

THE CONTAINMENT
OF RUSSIAN
EXPANSION

The Coastland Powers

13

A Basic Alternative, 1700–1815

Containment or Flanking Alliance? 1700–1762

A certain equilibrium between Heartland and Coastland, at times unstable but always permanent, has been a central feature of international
relations since the beginning of the eighteenth century. Russian expansion into the three great frontiers aimed at establishing hegemony in the
Heartland. The internal disintegration of the Swedish, Polish, Ottoman,
and Persian empires seemed to render that hegemony inevitable. But the
timely emergence of Prussia-Germany and the considerable staying power
of the Austrian Empire obstructed the path to Russia's eventual victory.
Russia thus had to deal with three sets of powers—Sweden-Poland,
Turkey-Persia, Prussia-Austria. The first two sets could only slow down
Russian expansion toward the Heartland's periphery, the last could effectively contain it. But Russia's relations were not limited to these six
powers. The Coastland powers—France and Britain in the European
Coastland, British India, China, and Japan in the Monsoon Coastland—
had a no less substantial interest, not only in opposing Russia's claim to
hegemony in the Heartland, but also in preventing it from occupying a
number of strategic straits through which it would gain unrestricted
access to the great oceans. That access would not turn Russia into a great
sea power, but would enable the Russians to apply enough pressure to
transform the narrow seas—the Baltic, the Black Sea, the Sea of Okhotsk,
and even the Sea of Japan—into closed seas. They could then build a
defense perimeter capable of cutting off the Coastland powers' access to
the core areas within the Heartland, placing these at Russia's mercy and
consolidating its hegemony within the Heartland. Thus Russia's relations

with those ten powers (counting Britain and British India as one) must be placed within the global configuration of two balancing games— one within the Heartland where the Russians and the Germanic powers became the two dominant players, the other between the Heartland and the Coastlands, where Britain and much later Japan became the major opponents of Russian expansion.

The opposition between Heartland and Coastland was never a pure one, if only because relationships among the Coastland powers were seldom friendly and were fueled by economic and strategic interests unrelated to the containment of Russian expansion. And it happened that a Coastland power, forgetting that containment was its true geopolitical mission in the end, would seek a Russian alliance against another Coastland power. In so doing, that power abandoned containment in favor of inviting the Russian advance toward the Heartland's periphery. Examples of such alliances of "flanking powers" were those between Britain and Russia against France; between Britain, France, and Russia against Germany, when Germany began to stake a claim to hegemony in the European Coastland; between Britain and Russia in Persia; between Japan and Russia in northern China. But such alliances were as a rule of short duration. By their very nature, they suspended the operation of a containment policy and their certain consequence was to encourage the establishment of Russia's hegemony in the Heartland. We must now turn to an examination of the policy of global containment pursued successfully for a long time by the Coastland powers, not in concert, because there could be no coordination of their policies until late in the nineteenth century, but separately, whenever geography, circumstances, and opportunities determined that it should be pursued in their own interest.

And yet, we must begin with a failure, the greatest and the most irreparable in the history of containment. China, with its long seaboard and mighty rivers draining into the Pacific, always had the potential of becoming a sea power of the first rank, but the permanent threat from the nomads and the location of the capital in the north, far from the country's most productive regions, had focused the strategic concerns of one dynasty after another on the necessity to repel invasions. The threats had come from the great arc stretching from the Kunlun Mountains to the Great Khingan, that broad swath of semiarid and windswept steppe between the inner and outer peripheries of the Heartland. And in 1644 the Manchus had come from the north, from the valley of the Amur in the Coastland populated by Tungus tribes, among which they were the most prominent. By the mid-seventeenth century the Manchus claimed jurisdiction over the entire Amur basin to the Iablonoi and Stanovoi ranges, the Heartland's periphery, and had appointed "defense commissioners," in effect military governors, one in Kirin on the Sungari in 1676, the other at Aigun at the confluence of the Zeia with the Amur in 1683. As a result, the appearance of new nomadic intruders, the Cossacks, in the valley of the Amur, with their firearms and collection of in-kind tribute, was a threat to both

Chinese and Manchu interests. By 1685, the forward Cossack settlement at Albazin had been destroyed and the Amur cleared of Cossacks.

The Manchus had a keen sense of geopolitical realities. In 1689 they demanded the surrender of Nerchinsk and of Selenginsk, in effect expelling the Russians from the valley of the Selenga that led into Mongolia and claiming that the boundary must run from Lake Baikal along the Iablonoi and Stanovoi ranges. Such a boundary would keep the Russians away from the pass in the Khilok valley that led to Nerchinsk and the valley of the Amur. In other words, the Manchus sought to confine the Russians within the Heartland. Moreover, they possessed a military preponderance in the area, while the Russians were isolated in unfriendly territory. It is therefore all the more surprising that the final settlement was a geopolitical disaster for them. Three factors may have played a role in their abandonment of their maximum program: their concern over the Mongol threat; the unsettled situation in southern China, where Manchu rule was still insecure; and the activities of the Jesuits, who served as interpreters and may have favored the Russians in the hope they might be allowed to travel overland to Europe. Whatever the reason, the Manchu failure of nerve invited the Russians to entrench themselves in the Coastland until more favorable circumstances would enable them to resume their advance.

Despite their failure, the Manchus understood that Russia had become a threat. The K'ang-hsi emperor declared in November 1693 that "the Kingdom of Russia has many able men, but they are narrow-minded, obstinate, and their argument is slow. . . . After many generations, Russia might cause trouble," and "therefore, building up our strength is a matter of fundamental importance."[1] Manchu China was then a confident and expanding core area, and powerful thrusts would soon take its armies into Turkestan and Tibet. In 1720, during the Izmailov mission, as if aware of its excessive concessions at Nerchinsk, China claimed not only Lake Baikal but the Angara River as its western boundary and declared its intention to build a fortress on the upper Irtysh as an advanced outpost against the Western Mongols—and the Russians. And the Treaty of Kiakhta (1727) confined Russo-Chinese trade to Kiakhta on the Mongolian border, save for the occasional caravan Russia kept sending to Peking with the Li-fan Yüan's permission.

A very different situation developed in the European Coastland. By the time the War of the Spanish Succession ended in 1714 Britain had emerged as the undisputed sea power. Its own strivings for hegemony in the long struggle with France that went back to the Hundred Years War had given it a sense of purpose and a concentrated energy based on the newly acquired awareness of its unchallengeable power at sea. The acquisition of Gibraltar and Port Mahon on Minorca Island established a British presence in the western Mediterranean, and the destruction of the Dunkirk fortifications removed the last threat to British power in the North Sea. It was thus inevitable that Britain's determination to brook no rival at sea would clash with Russia's ambitions to become a new sea power in the Baltic and use that power to destroy the independence of Sweden, that strong bastion guarding the Sound and the egress to the North Sea. Britain's naval policy in the Baltic was thus clear: Russia must not be allowed to dominate that narrow sea, and if it persisted in pursuing a policy that could be construed as seeking to "close" that sea, its navy must be destroyed.

But Britain's commercial policy was no less clear. The building of a new port in Petersburg and the annexation of Riga not only rerouted but vastly expanded British trade with Russia. That trade made British security dependent on Russia because naval stores—timber, hemp, potash, and tar—were a vital necessity for the Royal Navy, still unable to find substitutes in North America. And the considerable trade balance in Russia's favor created a cash nexus binding Russia to Britain. As a result, Britain's naval determination was undermined by its dependence on naval stores until 1815, and, in times of crisis, it was the commercial lobby in London that would determine Britain's overall policy toward Russia in the Baltic.

The emergence of Russian power was perceived as a threat not only to British naval security but to its interests on land as well. A new dynasty came to power in 1714 when George I succeeded Queen Anne. The king came from Hanover, between the Weser and the Elbe, on the very periphery of the Heartland, and any increase in Russian power in northern Germany was perceived as a threat to Hanover. Thus it happened that in the last decade of Peter I's reign the perception of a double threat to British interests brought about a response of exceptional strength. When Russian troops were stationed in Mecklenburg, George I declared that their presence would make Peter his enemy for life, and Admiral Norris, the commander of the Baltic squadron, was ordered to move against Russian ships and even capture the tsar himself. This was easier said than done, however, as British ships could not engage the Russian ships and galleys that easily concealed themselves behind the innumerable skerries forming a protective barrier off the Finnish coast and even continued to harry the Swedish coast. A strong protest in October 1720 by the Russian resident in London, Mikhail Bestuzhev-Riumin, that it was unforgivable for Britain to join with Sweden against Russia, "an old ally from which you have derived immense benefits,"[2] was met with the expulsion of the resident and a break in diplomatic relations that would last until 1728.

The restoration of ties was due in large part to the growth of the Anglo-Russian trade and to Britain's ambition to secure the right of passage across Russian territory to Persia and India. Negotiations led to the commercial treaty of December 1734, "one of the foundation stones of the Anglo-Russian connection in the eighteenth century."[3] But it was no small paradox that the rights of transit to Persia resulted in the establishment of a commercial base on the Caspian coast from which an enterprising Englishman, promoted to admiral by the shah, laid the foundations of a Persian navy. It was as if the containment impulse could never be repressed, even in the friendliest atmosphere.

But the Anglo-Prussian rivalry brought about even closer ties. The Austro-French antagonism remained at the heart of continental politics from the mid-seventeenth to the mid-eighteenth century, and the permanent Anglo-French antagonism dictated that the enemies of France were the friends of Britain. Austria and Russia being allies since 1726, Britain was Russia's putative ally. When the War of the Austrian Succession broke out, Britain supported Austria with subsidies. An Anglo-Russian alliance was signed in April 1741 and confirmed in December 1742, providing for a Russian contribution of 12,000 troops and a British one of twelve ships of the line carrying 700 guns or for subsidies, if no military assistance was requested. The alliance was limited to a European war; it did not apply to Russia's wars with the Ottomans, Persians, and "Oriental peoples" or to Britain's wars outside Europe, in North America for example. After the war, Britain forged a diplomatic coalition with Austria and Russia against France and Prussia. This alliance of the flanking powers against France (and Prussia) resulted in the dispatch in 1748 of a Russian expeditionary force of 30,000 under General Vasilii Repnin from Kurland via Kraków and Olmütz in Moravia to the Rhine for operations against the French. This unprecedented projection of Russian power beyond the Heartland was intended to realize the grandiose vision of the Russian chancellor, Alexei Bestuzhev-Riumin, of a Russo-Austro-British alliance to destroy Prussia, remove France's influence in northern Germany, and substitute Russia's. Commercial interests and hostility to France led Britain to abandon its containment policy in favor of propitiating Russia—for the destruction of Prussia could only encourage the Russian advance into the Polish Empire and the eventual transformation of the Polish core area to the Oder into a Russian protectorate.

France's containment policy remained much more consistent than Britain's throughout the eighteenth century. Britain's overall policy in northern Europe was strongly influenced by considerations of naval strategy. As long as Sweden could continue to resist Russian pressures, and the Russian navy—much neglected after Peter's death—had no chance of establishing a naval hegemony in the Baltic and close the Sound, British statesmen could accept the pre-eminence of commercial interests. A Russian advance on land would affect territories in which Britain had no substantial interests. France's trade in the Baltic was of secondary importance and was chiefly carried on in British and Dutch bottoms, but France, always torn between its ambitions at sea and the attraction of expansion on land, had clearly opted for a program of continental expansion since the end of the seventeenth century. Since the chief enemy was Austria, France formed a natural alliance with Sweden, Prussia, and Turkey to surround the Habsburg monarchy, and each of these powers was also Russia's enemy. Therefore it was in the nature of things that France's policy toward Russia should be one of dynamic containment. It should not be satisfied with a relatively static concept of perimeter defense, but should seek to strengthen the core areas within the Heartland to resist the Russian advance. None of the French kings was so anti-Russian as Louis XV (1715–1774), and his declaration that "the sole object of my policy toward Russia is to keep it as far as possible from the affairs of Europe"[4] summed up the essential purpose of that policy.

But France's containment policy was undermined by three unfavorable circumstances. Subsidizing Sweden, Poland, and the Ottomans was a poor substitute for the inability to project military power so far away across the Germanies, and subsidizing core areas in decline was counterproductive. France itself was suffering from the strains imposed on its economy by the long wars of Louis XIV. And Britain's hostility to France and friendliness toward Russia combined to oppose a policy of dynamic containment. In effect, Britain's willingness to invite Russia to take part in "the affairs of Europe," in preparation for the second great round in the Anglo-French struggle for hegemony in the Coastland, canceled out France's containment policy. And so it happened that the attempt to impose Stanislas Leszczynski, whose daughter was the Queen of France, in the teeth of Austro-Russian opposition failed ignominiously when 20,000 French troops sent to Warsaw to support Stanislas were forced to surrender at Danzig in June 1734. Subsidies fanned the flames of Swedish revanchism until the Swedes went to war in July 1741, but they lost, and so did France. And the Diplomatic Revolution of 1756 that brought about a Franco-Austrian alliance against a Prussia that felt its interests would be better protected by Britain placed France in the uncomfortable position of supporting Russian participation in "the affairs of Europe" in order to crush Prussia. But this second alliance of the flanking powers had the same effect of destroying the containment policy and inviting the Russian advance into East Prussia and Poland all the way to the Oder. The Seven Years War exposed the stark fact that the only alternative to a containment policy was an alliance with Russia against one of the Germanic powers or against France, and such an alliance could only benefit Russian interests and encourage the Russian advance toward the Heartland's periphery.

There was no serious Anglo-French rivalry in the eastern Mediterranean until the end of the eighteenth century, and France was in much the same strong position there as Britain was in the Baltic. The old alliance with the Ottomans, directed against the Habsburgs, was also directed against Russian expansion toward the Black Sea. France had been the chief beneficiary of trading privileges known as "capitulations," and as late as 1789, it controlled three-fifths of the entire European trade with Turkey; Britain controlled one-fifth. Turkey, it has been said, was "a virtual colony of France in the commercial field."[5] But although Russia was already firmly established on the Dniepr, it was a long way to the Black Sea, what with the Crimean khanate still able to launch devastating raids into the Ukraine. And the failure of Peter's Moldavian campaign in 1711 had shown that the Ottomans remained strong enough to resist the Russian advance. The Treaty of Belgrade (1739), brokered by the French ambassador in Constantinople, reiterated that Russia could not send merchantmen into the

Black Sea. Nevertheless, French policy in the region, like Britain's in the Baltic, was ambivalent at times. The Russian occupation of Azov, recognized in 1739, might be advantageous to French trade because it would open up the Russian market and give access to the overland route to Persia. Even a Russian naval presence in the Black Sea might serve French interests, and there were recurrent speculations that a Franco-Russian naval alliance in the Mediterranean would enable France to redeploy its warships against Britain in the Atlantic and the Channel. They would continue until the conclusion of the Franco-Russian alliance of 1894.

Britain had been seeking an overland route across Russia to India, but the experiment made after 1734 came to an end in 1746, when the Russians became aware that a British presence in Persia did not serve their interests. The only other way to enter Persia was from the east. Bombay became the starting point for the economic penetration of the Persian Gulf, where Bander Abbas, and later Bushire, on the desolate Persian coast became the centers of the entrepôt trade with Baghdad and Alexandretta (Iskanderun). British expansion in "Arabia"—defined by Mackinder as the land bridge linking the European with the Monsoon Coastland—was motivated by various considerations, some of them unrelated to the containment of Russian expansion. To be sure, there had been concern over Russian intentions in northern Persia between 1722 and 1735, but that expansion was also motivated by the need to cut off sea and land communications between France and its possessions in India and, in a larger sense, by Britain's determination to develop its commerce, broaden the network of naval bases supporting it, and control the entrance to all the narrow seas, including the Persian Gulf. The struggle with France was uppermost in the minds of the British establishment. Even in Constantinople, the chief function of the British ambassador was to counter the dominant influence of France, and Britain continued to treat Turkey and Russia as "unrelated states operating in watertight compartments."[6]

Squaring Off, 1762–1796

A containment policy is a means to a larger end, and that larger end was (and remains) to prevent Russia from establishing its hegemony in the Heartland. The acceleration of Russian expansion during Catherine's reign in both the Western and Southern frontiers raised for the first time, at least in London if not in Paris, the question of coordinating policy on both frontiers. In consequence Britain lengthened considerably the perimeter of its forward deployment along the Heartland's periphery, from the Scandinavian Sound to the Caspian Sea. Questions were now raised: what specifically had to be contained? where was the decisive point? It would take more than a generation, however, before the new geopolitical relationships became clear and the appropriate conclusions could be drawn.

The major event was Russia's war with the Ottomans, which began in September 1768 and ended with the peace of Kuchuk-Kainardji in July

1774. Russia for the first time deployed its naval power beyond the Heartland's periphery and sent its fleet from the Baltic around France and Spain to the Greek Archipelago, where it defeated the Turks at Cheshme in July 1770. Here was an opportunity for France, always the containing power, in alliance with Spain to destroy Russia's naval power, but Britain's support for the expedition stymied French intentions. Britain, where hostility to France was "a deeply ingrained and essentially irrational tradition,"[7] continued to view its relations with Russia beyond the narrow Baltic theater as part of the larger framework of its relations with France, as long as the struggle for hegemony in the Coastland remained undecided. In addition, there existed a certain condescending assumption, but one fully justified, that Russia could not truly become a sea power, let alone one that could threaten Britain. In March 1770, the British ambassador in Petersburg declared that it was "impossible" that Russia could "ever [become] a rival capable of giving us jealousy either as a commercial or as a warlike maritime power."[8] In September, the foreign secretary informed him that Britain supported Russia's conquests and its demands for free navigation in the Black Sea, and that the British squadron in the Archipelago would be superior to that of France. He also proposed "perfecting the natural alliance" with Russia to counter a possible Franco-Austrian combination. The same alliance of the flanking powers with Russia that was the cornerstone of British policy in the Western Frontier was being extended to the Southern Frontier, but the possibility begged a disturbing question: would the alliance be also directed against the Ottomans? And if it was, was it truly in Britain's interest?

While the Russians were consolidating their gains on the Danube, they also became a party to the first partition of Poland in 1772. The partition was a blow to French interests and "as such it was welcome to almost every Englishman,"[9] but the Swedish coup in August created apprehension in London because France was wrongly suspected of having instigated it in order to threaten the communications between Petersburg and its fleet in the Archipelago. Britain's obsession with France had warped its perception of the Russian threat, and its encouragement of Russian expansion kept destroying whatever ability France retained to contain that expansion. Petersburg had no illusion about France, Panin blaming it in August 1773 for its persistent attempt "to reduce Russia to the rank of a secondary power" and "to strip us, one way or another, of our freedom of action in the affairs of Europe."[10]

Britain was not only willing to forgo its containment policy so forcefully asserted between 1716 and 1720; it was also willing to invite Russia to play a military role on a global scale far beyond the Heartland's periphery. When the American colonists revolted, George III asked the empress in September 1775 to supply 20,000 Russian troops for service in Canada under British command. The request had no legal foundation. The treaty of 1742 had lapsed with the Seven Years War, and had specifically excluded Russian assistance in North America. Its only justification was a moral one—to press Russia to repay its debt of 1769 when, as the British ambassador pointed out, only the threat of British intervention had prevented the Franco-Spanish fleet from sinking the Russian expeditionary squadron in the Mediterranean. It embarrassed Petersburg, and the empress firmly refused to accommodate George III, not without causing considerable resentment.

There would soon be a price to pay for encouraging Russian expansion. The American war lasted until the Paris settlement of September 1783. It was marked by a ruthless campaign of commerce raiding in which British warships and privateers seized neutral ships at sea and blockaded French and Spanish ports. International law had never been altogether clear on the rights of neutral shipping, but it had become a general principle that the neutral flag protected enemy cargo, except war contraband occasionally defined in commercial treaties. Or, as the saying went, "free ships, free goods, unfree ships, unfree goods." In enforcing its claim to naval supremacy in the narrow seas and in the Atlantic, Britain was claiming that might made right, at least so long as its demands never met with superior force, but it had logic on its side. As Pitt later declared, Britain had never acknowledged "that a friendly ship could protect the property of the enemy."[11] Its policy was in fact a policy of total war against France, the hereditary enemy.

But Catherine II took up the British challenge. When two Russian ships belonging to Vyborg merchants were seized in the fall of 1778, she demanded their release, but in vain. She then informed London in March 1779 that a Russian squadron would cruise in the North Sea to protect the trade of Russia, Sweden, and Denmark. A year later, in March 1780, she issued a Declaration of Armed Neutrality, reasserting the right of neutral ships to trade with belligerent powers—the old principle that the neutral flag protected all cargo except war contraband, and that a blockaded port was one only when a belligerent power could effectively blockade it. The Russian move gained support in Sweden, Denmark, Prussia, and Holland, but the Dutch had to pay for their audacity with a British declaration of war. Britain, however, was not in a position to oppose the Russian move by force because of its overseas commitments in the Americas and its own dependence on naval stores. By a twist of logic, Catherine's Declaration "legalized" the neutral trade in naval stores with a nation that considered it a hostile act. But logic was not the issue. The issue was Britain's assumption that any challenge to its naval supremacy was intolerable.

The shocks administered to London in 1775 and 1780 by an increasingly confident Russia transformed what had been a largely commercial alliance into a political relationship and reawakened the sense of a larger purpose: that naval supremacy was not only a means to gain hegemony in the Coastland but also a weapon to contain Russia within the Heartland. Some concern was already apparent about the consequences of Kuchuk-Kainardji, and some farsighted Englishmen had warned that "even the powers of Europe most friendly to Russia must be utterly averse to Russia's possessing an island in the Archipelago."[12] And it was assumed that the opening of the Black Sea to Russian commerce in Russian bottoms, while the trade of the Coastland powers would have to continue to be carried in ships bearing the Ottoman flag, would benefit Russia and damage British commercial interests in the Baltic, since "both the northern and the southern trade cannot exist in equal vigor."[13] Britain continued to support Russian interests in Constantinople, but refused to bind itself with Russia against the Ottomans in the event of a new Russo-Turkish war. The annexation of the Crimea in April 1783 and the building of a naval base in Sevastopol raised apprehension in a power so prone to equate the naval ambitions of other powers with threats to its own security.

The gradual reassertion of a British containment policy was accompanied, naturally enough, by a French willingness to let Russia participate in "the affairs of Europe." The Franco-Russian rapprochement became apparent at the Teschen Congress in May 1779, when the two powers joined hands to mediate the Austro-Prussian dispute. France let Russia become for the first time a guarantor of the Treaty of Westphalia (1648), the constitutional charter of German politics, thereby atoning for its brusque rejection of Russia's participation at Aix la Chapelle in 1748. The Declaration of Armed Neutrality elated the French, and the Russians mediated the Anglo-French settlement of 1783. The arrival of a new French ambassador, the Count of Ségur, in March 1785 inaugurated a brief period of friendly ties before the French Revolution broke out. He convinced Potemkin that direct trade relations with France, without Dutch intermediaries, would serve the interests of Russian, Greek, and Armenian merchants in his new bailiwick of New Russia. Russia refused to renew its commercial treaty with Britain but signed one with France in January 1787, giving a monopoly of French trade to Marseilles and Toulon.

Nothing was better designed to increase the hostility of the British government led between 1784 and 1801 by William Pitt the Younger. He was the son of the great Pitt who had destroyed French power in Canada, the West Indies, and India during the Seven Years War, and who had won for Britain a position of near hegemony in the European Coastland. When Russia went to war with the Ottomans in August 1787 and sought to repeat its strategy of 1769 by sending the Baltic fleet via the Sound and Gibraltar into the Mediterranean, Pitt refused to let Russia rent transport ships in Britain and, in May 1788, recalled British sailors in Russian service. The move effectively denied Russia's ability to conduct naval operations in the Coastland without Britain's consent. But Pitt was willing to go much further. He formed an alliance with Prussia in August, struck by the realization that a Russian victory against the Ottomans would make the Russians the masters of the Black Sea and that the growth of Russian influence in Lithuania and on the Right-Bank Ukraine would eventually enable Russia to divert the trade in naval stores from the basin of the Baltic to that of the Black Sea and favor France's dominant commercial position in the Mediterranean. He may have hoped to include Poland as well to form a barrier to Russian expansion. Britain would seek to reduce its excessive dependence on the Russian trade by developing exchanges with Poland and transforming Memel (Klaipeda) into a rival of Riga. Britain's determination was expressed, somewhat fatuously, by the ambassador to Petersburg, who wrote in November 1790 that "if our friendship has made [the Russians] what they are, our enmity can as easily reduce them to what they ought to be."[14]

In March 1791, the Cabinet resolved to go to war. Thirty-five warships were to be sent to the Baltic, another dozen kept in reserve for operations in the Black Sea, if the Ottomans allowed them to cross the straits. But the expedition never took place, Pitt had to back down, and Petersburg's contemptuous treatment of the British envoy sent to explain Britain's position could only stiffen Britain's hostility to the growth of Russian power. The attempt failed for a number of reasons. Pitt was ahead of public opinion and did not prepare it for what would have been a drastic reversal of British policy—or a drastic return to the position taken in 1716–1720. And the "vociferous mercantile lobby"[15] refused to take chances: the dependence on naval stores was still too great. Pitt's decision had been much influenced by a memorandum written by Sir Joseph Ewart, the British ambassador in Berlin, calling for a combination of Turkey, Poland, and "one of the inferior Baltic powers"[16] against Russia. Geography did indeed determine the setting of a containment policy, for Ewart was advocating no less than the assumption by Britain of France's traditional role as a containing power in alliance with Sweden, Prussia, Poland, and the Ottomans.

The attempt also failed because it demonstrated how difficult it was for a sea power to exert direct military pressure on a land power of Russia's size. It has been said that "landpower and seapower cannot easily engage each other"[17] because their strategic orientations are fundamentally different, and the crisis of 1791 was the first to show the truth of that dictum. To put it in contemporary language, it was discovered that "we could bombard Riga but could not pluck a single grey hair from the old Lady's head" (Catherine's).[18] Sending such a squadron would be very expensive, and Russia would confiscate British property and immobilize half a million tons of British shipping. And there were dangers in naval warfare in the Baltic, with its shoals, currents, islands, and rocks, and a navy that had just fought with distinction against the Swedes in those very same waters.

It seemed the "Ochakov crisis" had been nothing but an embarrassment for Britain. It had important consequences, however. The British establishment, or at least some segments of it, became aware of a strategic link between the Western and Southern frontiers and of the fact that the containment of Russian expansion could no longer be limited to the Baltic sector alone. The capture of Ochakov, in itself of insignificant importance and quite incapable of firing the sultry jealousy of a people used to taking victory for granted, directed British eyes toward the Cau-

casus, where the implications of the treaty with Georgia (1783) threatened to upset geopolitical relationships by opening the way to Persia and
across Persia to the gates of India, while French activities in "Arabia"
raised similar fears. The extension of the perimeter of containment and
the realization that Britain could not apply overwhelming force in the
Baltic, within the Heartland—any more than Russia could apply such
force in the Coastland—showed that Britain's essential role was to deny
Russia uncontrolled egress from the "choke points,"[19] of which there
were now two—-the Scandinavian Sound and the Turkish Straits; and
that the decisive area where naval power must be concentrated was the
eastern Mediterranean.

The early years of the French Revolution confirmed the validity of this
assessment, but they also raised fundamental questions about where the
decisive point truly was by complicating the containment policy to an
unprecedented extent. Catherine wrote at the end of 1791: "I am wrack-
ing my brains to find ways of maneuvering the courts of Vienna and
Berlin more deeply into French affairs,"[20] and both her concerns and the
threat to their interests led Prussia and Austria into war with France in the
spring of 1792. In other words, the empress sought to redirect the containment policy of the Germanic powers of the Heartland against France
in the Coastland, and French victories recreated the alliance of the flanking powers of the 1740s. In February 1795, eight months before the final
partition of Poland, Britain and Russia renewed the alliance of 1742. It
contained a new article (15), however, that symbolized their emergence
as global powers: each would support the other in the event of an attack
by a European power against their possessions "anywhere in the world,"
and, for the first time, Britain pledged to support Russia in the event of
an Ottoman attack. The treaty also implicitly recognized the Baltic to be
in the Russian sphere of naval influence by providing that British ships
would enter it to support Russia only if the Russian Baltic fleet was inadequate to cope with an enemy force, while Russian ships were invited to
cruise in the North Sea in the defense of British interests. In spite of the
treaty, however, Catherine continued to refuse to commit Russian troops
until the collapse of the Austrian position in northern Italy in July 1796.
In August, she pledged 60,000 men, to Britain's immense satisfaction,
but she died in November before they could leave. Thus, by the end of
Catherine's reign, Britain's containment policy suffered from a fundamental flaw—the expansion of revolutionary France compelled Britain to
support a Russian alliance, while Russian activities in the Black Sea and
the Caucasus (the Persian campaign was then in progress) were creating a
potential threat to Britain's naval position in the eastern Mediterranean.

Early Strains, 1796–1815

The story of Russia's expansion cannot be separated from the story of its
containment. Containment served to define the limits of expansion, the

political isobar that kept moving west, south, and east until Russia encountered the superior force of the containing powers. The containment of Russian expansion by the European Coastland powers also shows the extent to which that expansion was facilitated until 1815 by the unending Anglo-French antagonism, one power encouraging it to damage the interests of the other. Only after 1815, when Britain established its uncontested hegemony in the Coastland, did it become possible to pursue a consistent policy. Britain would replace France with a policy resting on the same geographic foundations, but with greater power and on a global scale.

The expansion of revolutionary France recreated the alliance of the flanking powers. Britain invited Russia in December 1798 to join a British expeditionary force sent to restore the independence of Holland, and even to defend Britain in the event of a French invasion attempt. The expedition was a disaster, the Russians blaming the British, and the troops were taken prisoner in October 1799. Britain welcomed Suvorov's expedition to northern Italy and even dictated its plan of operation in Switzerland, where Russian troops suffered reverses and were forced to withdraw. Resentment at British ineptitude and the coup of November (18 Brumaire) 1799 that created a consulate with Bonaparte as its first consul seemed to bring the revolution to an end. The state was set for a reversal of alliances in 1800.

The flanking alliance extended to the Southern Frontier as well. A truly revolutionary situation had been created in the eastern Mediterranean by Bonaparte's expedition to Egypt. The French had taken Malta in June 1798, then Alexandria on the delta of the Nile, but the French squadron was destroyed by Nelson at Aboukir Bay in August. The expedition had two consequences. It confirmed British apprehensions that the eastern Mediterranean had become since the 1780s a strategic sector of primary importance, as the French were certain to seek to recoup their losses in India by reaching the subcontinent across "Arabia" and the Persian Gulf. Britain's naval presence had to be reinforced in the Archipelago and on the Egyptian coast. And the expedition frightened the sultan into the arms of Russia: the Russo-Turkish alliance of January 1799 allowed Russia to send its warships from their Crimean base across the straits straddling the Heartland's periphery. Russia's naval ambitions were shaking off their dependence on British consent. The move drew Britain into the Russo-Ottoman alliance in order "to render abortive the pernicious designs"[21] of France. As had been the case in previous conflicts, Britain set about destroying France's trade, here its Levantine trade, by keeping its merchantmen out of Ottoman ports. As a reward, Britain obtained from the Porte the same rights as Russia had gained in 1774—free commercial navigation in the Black Sea. In the fall and winter of 1798–1799 a joint Russo-Turkish naval campaign drove French forces out of the Ionian Islands, and Russia acquired for the first time naval bases in the Ionian Sea. Russia had willy-nilly been welcomed into the Coastland.

But another development warned Britain that a Russian naval presence in the Mediterranean was a threat to its supremacy, and the Anglo-Russian flanking alliance foundered on the realization that it no longer served Britain's interests, at least in the Mediterranean. The decisive point was Malta. The island had been since 1530 the property of the Knights Hospitalers of St. John of Jerusalem, but the knights, caught in the turmoil of the revolution, had persuaded the tsar to accept the title of protector of their order in November 1797. The island had a strong fortress and capacious port (Valetta) controlling traffic between the eastern and western Mediterranean and guarding the security of southern Italy. Britain had seized the island from France in September 1800 but refused to return it to the knights and their Russian protector. The acquisition of Malta gave Britain a forward position in the Mediterranean from which it could watch Russian naval movements in the Archipelago and threaten the Russian presence on the Ionian Islands.

The refusal fueled Russian resentment, and in November 1800 Paul placed an embargo on British shipping in Russian ports and ordered the internment of more than 1000 sailors. His next move was to recreate the armed neutrality league of the 1780s with Sweden and Denmark. But circumstances had changed, and Britain was not engaged in an overseas war. In March 1801, when the Russian fleet was still icebound and the Swedish fleet remained idle in Karlskrona, a powerful British squadron bombarded Copenhagen and forced Denmark to leave the league. Only the tsar's early death forestalled a naval demonstration before Reval and Kronshtadt. The flanking alliance had collapsed in both the Western and Southern frontiers, and Russia had been warned, as it had in 1716-1720, that Britain would not tolerate a Russian threat to British naval interests. The Anglo-Russian break brought about a Franco-Russian rapprochement; its fruit was the extravagant attempt to invade India overland. Some 70,000 French and Russian troops were to land at Astrabad on the Caspian and march toward India via Herat and Kandahar. The impatient tsar decided to act alone, and in January 1801 ordered 22,000 Don Cossacks to march via Orenburg, Bukhara, and the Khyber Pass to the valley of the Ganges, there to destroy British factories and perhaps stir up an uprising against British rule. Such an expedition had no chance of succeeding because distances, the climate, anarchy, and the hostility of the khanates were certain to decimate the troops long before they could reach the Hindu Kush. Alexander I canceled it immediately after his accession. Nevertheless, the expedition showed how closely bound Russian expansion was at certain times with the conflicting policies of the containing powers. Britain was willing to encourage Russian expansion into the Mediterranean if it damaged French interests; France was ready to encourage it into Persia and Central Asia to undermine Britain's position in India.

Britain, France, and Russia were at peace in 1802 and 1803, but it became obvious that Russia intended to exploit its new position in the

Mediterranean to obtain additional gains on the coast of the Adriatic and in the Morea. Its request to be allowed to station troops on Malta and the declaration of the Russian ambassador in London, Simon Vorontsov, that the Black Sea was a closed sea inaccessible to British warships and that British commerce-destroyers would be treated as pirates, seemed to disclose a vast and threatening enterprise to establish Russia in the Coastland and keep Britain out of the Heartland, an attack on the unwritten assumption that Russia must not be allowed to establish a permanent position in the Mediterranean. But the war resumed with a British declaration of war on France in May 1803, and the alliance of the flanking powers was automatically restored, despite British misgivings about Russian intentions. France returned to its traditional role as containing power but on a much larger scale and much more openly than under the monarchy. Napoleon's ambassador to Constantinople, Horace Sebastiani, incited the Ottomans against the Russians. War resumed in December 1806, automatically cutting off the lifeline of the Russian Mediterranean squadron and leaving it vulnerable to attack. One month earlier, Napoleon had entered Berlin and inaugurated the Continental System, a commercial blockade of the British Isles. French troops advanced as far as East Prussia where they defeated the Russians at Eylau and Friedland. At Tilsit, in July 1807, Napoleon forced the tsar to give up the Ionian Islands, gaining control of the entire coast of the Adriatic and the Ionian Sea.

Napoleon followed his victory by pursuing a containment policy that clearly aimed at keeping Russia out of "the affairs of Europe." The tsar agreed to join the Continental System in return for Napoleon's acquiescence in the annexation of Finland. The election of a French marshal as heir to the Swedish throne in August 1810 seemed to restore the traditionally predominant influence of France in Stockholm. Prussia was devastated by the loss of Polish lands acquired at the three partitions, and of its enclaves in the Rhineland. It was rolled back beyond the Elbe. The Holy Roman Empire ceased to exist. Some of its lands were annexed from France, others went to form the Confederation of the Rhine. The Austrian Habsburgs lost their Polish lands and their possessions on the Adriatic coast and in northern Italy. France was substantially enlarged by the annexation of Holland and now bordered on Denmark in Holstein. And the creation of the Duchy of Warsaw promised to sow seeds of discord between Russia, Prussia, and Austria.

Napoleon thus aimed at no less than the transformation of the continental coastland and the old core areas of Sweden, Poland, Prussia, and Austria into a structure of zones separating the two super-core areas of Napoleonic France and Russia. He told the tsar at Tilsit that the "influence" of France would stop at the Elbe and that the territories between the Elbe and the Niemen, the natural border of eastern Poland, would form a barrier between the two empires "to cushion the pinpricks that precede the cannon shots."[22] They would in fact become satellites of France to keep Russia out of "the affairs of Europe," and if need be, staging areas for an attack on Russia itself. And the Continental System would create an immense autarkic empire that would bring Britain to its knees in due time.

This grandiose scheme, elaborated between 1803 and 1810, failed for a variety of reasons. For one thing, its geopolitical foundations were unnatural. It ignored the fundamental dichotomy between Heartland and Coastland, and sought to harness the energies of the Heartland against France's sister power and hereditary enemy in the Coastland. Napoleon forgot his own belief that an alliance was solid only when founded on political relations deriving from trade and geography. Geography bound France and Britain, but trade bound Britain to the Heartland: the Continental System contained the seeds of its own destruction. Napoleon's containment policy was not limited to northern Europe. It encouraged the Ottomans to remain at war with Russia, and the alliance with Persia of May 1807 was not only designed to investigate the possibility of another expedition to India but also to keep Persia at war with Russia among the khanates of Azerbaijan. And there were (fantastic) rumors of a Franco-Chinese alliance to complete the ring of alliances along the entire periphery of the Heartland.

Despite the restoration of the alliance of the flanking powers, Britain's position was much more ambivalent. A year before the creation of the Third Coalition against Napoleon, in September 1804, the tsar had sent one of the comrades of his youth, Nikolai Novosiltsev, to London on a secret mission to discuss his own vision of the future world order. Novosiltsev and Pitt—he was again prime minister from May 1804 to his death in January 1806—saw themselves as the representatives of two flanking and global powers balancing each other, as Pitt put it in January 1805, in a system in which "the insular situation and extensive resources of England, aided by its military exertions and naval superiority," matched "the immense power, the established continental ascendancy and remote distance of Russia."[23] The two powers would reduce France to its former limits, reestablish a general system of public law in Europe, and bring Prussia across the Elbe back into the Coastland with the annexation of the Rhineland in order to forestall French expansionism. When Magnus Alopäus, the Russian envoy, left London in April 1806, the king told him there could not be an alliance more natural and solid in the world than that between Britain and Russia, and "since the geographical position that forms the foundation of their union cannot change, their union must be eternal."[24]

But nothing is eternal, and strains soon appeared in the alliance. Britain's refusal to guarantee a Russian loan on the London market and to send more troops to the continent while Russian troops were driven back to the Niemen, the changed mood after Tilsit, and Napoleon's demand that Russia joined the Continental System resulted in a break in relations in November 1807. Russia declared war in January 1808, but how was a large land power the size of Russia to strike at Britain? Rather, it was the British navy that blockaded the Russians in Baltic Port in September and demanded the surrender of half the fleet in return for letting the other half leave port, that threatened Arkhangelsk in June 1809 (but could do nothing against its defenses), that burned fishing boats and buildings in Kola, and that intercepted Russian ships in the gulf of Finland and the Gulf of Bothnia. Britain, however, refrained from an all-out bombardment of Russian naval installations, operating, in Mahan's brilliant phrase, "with a slightness of exertion which calls to mind the stories of the tap of a tiger's paw."[25] Russian trade was ruined, while Britain's continued to expand in the Atlantic. Steps were taken to find new sources of naval stores, and great pressure was put on the tsar to return to the alliance of the flanking powers.

While the Anglo-French struggle was heating up in northern Europe and Napoleon resorted to a policy of all-out containment, even rollback, of Russia's positions in the Heartland, Britain and France found themselves in agreement to expel the Russians from the Coastland in the Mediterranean. Napoleon reached that goal in 1807. Britain was in a quandary because the need to maintain the alliance of the flanking powers against France required the elaboration of a definite policy toward the Ottomans that went beyond keeping an eye on the French and would integrate that policy into the larger framework of Britain's relations with Russia. The Ottomans were at war with Russia; supporting the Russians meant showing hostility to the Porte. But how was Russia to be contained behind the Heartland's periphery without Ottoman support? Tensions with Russia in northern Europe facilitated the new orientation of British policy. In January 1809, Britain signed a commercial treaty and a secret alliance with the Porte recognizing "the ancient Ottoman regulation" that the straits must be closed to the warships of all nations in peacetime, thereby shutting off the Russians from the eastern Mediterranean. Only warships from the Baltic fleet could henceforth ply its waters, and the British navy could easily intercept them in the Sound, the Channel, at Gibraltar, and at Malta. It was more than a coincidence that Britain and France, locked in the last round of the fight for supremacy, had connived to keep Russia behind the Heartland's periphery—it was a natural reaction by the Coastland powers to maintain the inviolability of a natural barrier.

And yet, even the supporters of naval supremacy were not free from some ambivalence. Bottling up Russia in the Black Sea was the embodiment of a close-border policy, a policy based on a static concept of linear perimeter defense. Such a policy was certain to deprive Britain of effective means to pressure the Russians whenever differences arose in the uneven course of their relationships. It did serve Russian interests, but did it serve Britain's? A pamphlet published in 1807 asserted that it did not. Russian forward positions in the Dardanelles and even in Greece, like the extended horns of a snail, would render Russia vulnerable, and Britain, secure in its naval supremacy from its base on Malta, could use them as bargaining chips in negotiating Russian concessions elsewhere. This view was not without its risks, of course, and it was found safer to draw a red line that Russia would not be allowed to cross.

Britain and Russia restored diplomatic relations at the same time, in January 1809, in preparation for the gigantic conflict that was about to pit France against Russia. It was a coincidence, but one that exposed the ambivalence of British attitudes toward Russia, that the British ambassador in Constantinople, Robert Adair, was replaced as chargé in June 1810 by his young secretary, Stratford Canning, soon to become Russia's most redoubtable enemy in the containment of Russia in the Russo-Turkish frontier. The Anglo-French rivalry was heating up in Persia as well. There were fears, all unrealistic, lest France send an expedition across "Arabia" to the Persian Gulf and India. The "rampant gallophobia"[26] of the British establishment had already sent a Captain John Malcolm to Muscat (Masqat) in October 1799 and on to Tehran to negotiate the political and commercial treaties of January 1801, pledging the shah "to extirpate" the French should they ever enter Persia. In January 1809, on order from the governor general of India, Lord Minto, the first formal Anglo-Afghan agreement was signed in Calcutta pledging Kabul to prevent the "confederacy of French and Persians" crossing into India. It was quite obvious that the containment of France would easily merge into the containment of Russia as soon as the French danger was past. It is worth noting once again that it was the global Anglo-French conflict that both facilitated the Russian advance and compelled the British to establish or strengthen their presence in the core areas within the Heartland, a presence that enabled them to move rapidly to contain Russian expansion after 1815.

The French retreat from Russia in 1813 brought about a coalition of Britain, Russia, and the Germanic powers to crush Napoleon once and for all. Britain became the paymaster of the coalition, and the Allies entered Paris in March 1814. Joy at the French defeat was tempered by apprehension at the tremendous growth of Russian power and the total collapse of containment. As if to guard against the new danger, the Anglo-Persian treaty of November 1814, when the French danger was past, pledged Persia not to allow any "European" troops to enter the country and proceed to India. Moreover, Britain pledged to strengthen Persia's influence in the frontier zones of the Russo-Persian frontier by helping the shah's efforts to induce the rulers of Khiva, Bukhara, and Samarkand to oppose such an invasion. But in Europe, the Congress of Vienna, which ended in June 1815, gave Russia the fruits of Napoleon's failed containment policy and of Britain's "natural alliance" with Russia. Russia had annexed Finland and restored Poland—that "Muscovite promontory [jutting] into the center of civilization"—from which it would exercise a "pernicious influence" over Prussia and Austria,[27] and through them, over the Germanic Confederation. The Vienna settlement had turned the Napoleonic system on its head in Russia's favor.

While the Coastland powers were struggling for hegemony and working sometimes in tandem, sometimes at cross-purposes, to contain Russian expansion, China's ability to continue its role as containing power was weakening. The eighteenth century had seen the greatest extension of Chinese power; the longest struggle had been with the Zunghars, who were defeated in 1757. There was no alliance of the flanking powers— Russia and China—but the geopolitical situation in the steppe frontier was bound to impose one in all but name, for both powers had a common interest in putting an end to the threat of nomadic raids from which they had suffered for so long. And such a common interest meant that, as the Chinese advanced into the frontier, so did the Russians, but from the other side. This differed from the containment policy of the Germanic powers, which compelled Russia to withdraw as they advanced into Poland or the Balkan zones. The Manchus' imperial policy showed vividly how the alliance of the flanking powers, even one that did not formally, or perhaps even consciously, exist, always served Russia's interests in the end by inviting its penetration deeper into the frontier zones. Moreover, the death of the Ch'ien-lung emperor in 1796—the same year as Catherine's—marked the beginning of Manchu China's decline, caused by a loss of energy in the imperial house and the military establishment, the ossification of the political apparatus, and economic stagnation brought about by an enormous increase in population. While Britain emerged as the global containing power with a unified policy from the Scandinavian Sound to the Hindu Kush, China's containment policy was certain to suffer considerable strain.

14

Hegemony and Containment, 1815–1879

The Rise of Russophobia, 1815–1830

The defeat of France created a radically new situation. Britain's hegemony was now secure both at sea and in the European Coastland, and London needed to work out three sets of policies. One was designed to develop a global economy inspired by free-trade principles to open up markets to British manufactures. An aggressive policy of economic imperialism would seek to integrate not only both Coastlands, "Arabia," and the Americas into a world market dominated by Britain, but also Turkey, Persia, and Central Asia, and if possible, even Russia itself. In the late 1820s, 40 percent of Russia's imports came from Britain and 48 percent of its exports went to the island empire. This trade was five times that of the leading competitor, the Hanseatic towns. The second set of policies aimed at expelling Russia from the affairs of the European Coastland, the third at creating distractions for Russia within the Heartland to slow down its expansion toward the Heartland's periphery. The decisive point where British power must be concentrated was the Turkish Straits.

The stationing of Russian troops in France until a satisfactory settlement of claims to compensate the victors for the losses suffered from the French wars was tolerated as a temporary pis aller. But the Russians also intended to use their position as members of the four-power alliance of November 1815 to enforce conservative principles in the Coastland, where the French Revolution, even if it had caused an upsurge of nationalism, had also left a legacy of libertarian principles in harmony with Britain's own constitutional principles. And the line between military intervention "in the name of Europe" and the establishment of a military presence for ulterior motives was an easy one to cross. The Russians sensed very early that the British government "cannot get used to tolerating the slightest participation on our part in any affair taking place beyond the European coast," and that in fact it was determined that "the influence of the continental powers must cease where the sea begins."[1] But even in the Coastland itself, Russia's participation in "the affairs of Europe" was unwelcome. The British foreign secretary, Robert Castlereagh, refused to accept the decision of the Congress of Troppau in the fall of 1820 to put down insurrections in Spain and in the Kingdom of the Two Sicilies (Naples), declaring that the alliance "was not intended for the government of the world."[2] He rejected the principle put forth at the Laibach (Llubljana) Congress in the spring of 1821 that the powers had a responsibility to restore the status quo in the affairs of the Coastland states. His successor, George Canning, disliked entangling alliances, and the Congress of Verona in the fall of 1822 was the last international congress of its kind.

The Anglo-Russian alliance had been "natural" only so long as the two flanking powers needed each other to counter French expansionism. The British had not overcome their initial impression, dating back to the days of Queen Elizabeth, that Russia was a great and cold land of "barbarous manners, ignorance, and arbitrary violence."[3] The sudden collapse of the eighteenth-century international order; the annexation of Poland, for which the British discovered a sudden affinity; Russia's hegemony in the European plain within the Heartland and its ambitions in the Coastland, created a powerful sense of insecurity. These factors transformed a useful ally into "this monster of an empire"[4] and released a dormant Russophobia, an affliction to which Anglo-Saxon nations are singularly prone in their hour of triumph. As early as 1817, when it was discovered that Russia had sold eight ships to Spain (they proved to be unseaworthy) and rumors began to circulate that Spain might have given away Minorca, a *Morning Chronicle* editorial, mistaking the beam in British eyes for the mote in Russian eyes, declared in October that Russians believed they were destined to be the rulers of the world. Colonel Robert Wilson, who had been stationed at the tsar's headquarters in 1813, published at the same time an alarmist *Sketch of the Power of Russia,* and warned Britain to negotiate "with a trident in her hand."[5]

There were other reasons for the spread of Russophobia, including the fear of Russian ambitions in the Mediterranean and a religious revival that exposed the inequities of slavery and, by extension, of serfdom, the foundation of Russia's social order. Commercial expansion generated a vast romanticized travel literature that, unfortunately, left its readers prone to hysteria because it did not teach "that the barren steppes and rugged mountains . . . formed a natural barrier [to Russian expansion] more formidable than an opposing army."[6] Pride in Britain's constitutional system matched Russia's pride in autocracy, both sanctified by victory over Napoleonic France. Last but not least, Russian protectionism was resented as an offense against the new doctrine of free trade, and the reduced dependence on Russian naval stores meant that the mercantile lobby no longer identified its well-being with the Russian trade as in the days of Pitt. Emotionally, Russia replaced France as the bugbear of British statesmen of all stripes.

But there were sound strategic reasons for British alarm. Friendly relations with Sweden and the transformation of Prussia into a quasi-protectorate had brought Russia's influence to bear permanently for the first time on the Heartland's periphery. In the south, despite the acquisition by Britain of the Ionian Islands in November 1815, the Greek crisis raised British concern, as it was expected to bring Russia into "the affairs of Europe" and result in a permanent Russian presence in the eastern Mediterranean. Russian warships (from the Baltic fleet) were showing the flag in Ottoman ports, and, in the Archipelago, they threatened the Dardanelles while their sister ships in the Black Sea threatened the Bosphorus. And the effect of their activities was to create those very forward commitments the pamphleteer had welcomed in 1807 because they would be at Britain's mercy in a showdown. But they also complicated the neat picture of a Russia that must be confined behind the Heartland's periphery.

Both Russia and Britain were placed in a quandary by the Greek revolt that began in March 1821. Castlereagh and Canning, no less than the tsar, believed in legitimism, and the Greeks were rebels, but rebels against an oppressive "Asiatic" government for which there was little sympathy in Britain. Greece was the fountainhead of Western civilization and its oppression aroused pro-Hellenic sentiment everywhere in the Coastland. Ideology did not point the way to a simple solution. An Anglo-Turkish rapprochement had taken place after 1815 because the containment of Russian expansion required that Britain become the "natural" ally of the Ottomans, that Britain find an ally among at least one of the Heartland powers, both to strengthen that power's resistance to Russian expansion and to keep Russia distracted. Such another power was Austria, and the geopolitical strains attending the pursuance of a policy of dynamic containment restored the natural alliance between Britain and Austria that had been an article of faith in London before 1756.

The Greeks knew that they could not rely on Britain's official support, at least until March 1823, when London finally recognized the rebels as belligerents, that is, it "legalized" the rebellion. But that was done in order to steal the initiative from the Russians rather than out of conviction. For the Russians, despite their own qualms about supporting rebels against their legitimate government, could not ignore the exciting opportunity of becoming the patrons of a Greek autonomous movement. Their proposal of January 1824 to create three Greek principalities represented in Constantinople by the Patriarch, who was looked upon by the Porte not only as the ecclesiastical head of the Greek nation but as its temporal leader as well, was an undisguised attempt to establish a new foothold in the Coastland. London had already refused to accept Russia's claim to protect the Christians in Greece: it would "constitute Russia a co-state in a part of (Turkey's) domain," give it "shared sovereignty,"[7] and effectively create a Russian protectorate.

But London did not have full control over its agents in the field. Sir Thomas Maitland, the British commissioner on the Ionian Islands, felt the time had come to extend British protection to the Morea. He had to be disavowed, but the islands remained a base of support for the rebellion. And in the spring of 1826, Stratford Canning became ambassador in Constantinople; he would proceed with determination and a clear view that Russia must be contained in the Black Sea to establish Britain's authority in the councils of the Porte to an extent unseen since the days in the eighteenth century when the French ambassadors had sought to keep Russia distracted in the Heartland. British and Russian attitudes toward the Ottoman Empire began to change radically. The Russians would seek to encourage the rotting process in the empire by destabilizing one zone after another, here establishing a protectorate, there annexing a zone outright as in Transcaucasia. Britain would seek to arrest the rotting process and strengthen the empire, so that it would continue to block access to the straits and stand guard over the Heartland's periphery and protect the overland route to India. For India was beginning to loom large in Britain's imperial calculations, and concern would soon become an obsession no less irrational than the perception of a French threat in the eighteenth century.

The accidental sinking of the Ottoman fleet at Navarino in October 1827, the choice of the Duke of Wellington to become prime minister in January 1828, and the Russian declaration of war on Turkey in April combined to clarify British policy. The Duke reversed a policy of cooperation with the Russians and referred to Turkey as "an ancient ally."[8] The war was a worthy successor to that of 1768–1774, and it struck a blow in the Principalities and Transcaucasia from which the Ottomans would never recover. The combined land and sea operations were clearly aimed at gaining a strategic victory that would finally place Constantinople at Russia's mercy. The war was a direct attack on Britain's containment policy, and it released another wave of Russophobia, especially after it became known that the admiral of the Russian squadron in the Mediterranean had announced a blockade of the city and insisted on visiting neutral ships to keep war contraband and food from reaching it. Such a step was a slap at Britain's naval hegemony. A Colonel Evans published a brochure, *On the Designs of Russia*, claiming that with Constantinople as a base, "universal domination was within Russia's easy reach," and calling for naval attacks on Russian coasts to drive back the tsar "into the steppes of Asia"—a latter-day British version of Louis XV's determination to exclude Russia from "the affairs of Europe." A second brochure published in 1829 explored the "practicability of an invasion of India."[9] Cooler heads prevailed in the British government, if only because Lord Heytesbury, the British ambassador in Petersburg, had a spy who gave him copies of the most confidential documents. Nevertheless, Russia dictated the peace of Adrianople in September 1829, and the presence of a Russian army within striking distance of Constantinople was a frightening development. On the other hand, the creation of an independent Greece in February 1830—and not one simply autonomous under Ottoman suzerainty and under the protection of the powers, including Russia—was a decisive blow to Russian ambitions in the Coastland: there were to be no naval bases in the Ionian Sea after 1815 and there would be none in the Archipelago after 1830.

One decisive point in Britain's containment policy was the Turkish Straits; the Khyber Pass, the land "strait," was becoming another. From the perspective of British India, the Afghan and Persian questions were one, because invasions of the valley of the Ganges had come in the past across Afghanistan and chiefly from Persia. The Treaty of Gulistan (1813) had brought Russian power to the Araks River and transformed the Caspian into a Russian lake. Britain's response had been the treaty of November 1814. But it was all too obvious that proconsuls of Ermolov's mettle would not be satisfied with the administration of restless khanates, and that the Russian advance from Tiflis and Orenburg, whether political, military, or commercial, was designed to establish a strong presence in Tehran and beyond Tehran, in Herat, the gateway to Afghanistan. Both Britain and France were allies now in Persia and cooperated on the establishment of a rudimentary infrastructure from which they could seek to arrest the rotting process. The Russian chargé in Tehran, Simon Mazarovich, was aware that a counteroffensive of the Coastland powers was in progress, but Nesselrode, his chief in Petersburg, refused in 1823 to believe in "the gigantic system supposedly being organized against us."[10] He was wrong.

As Britain's hegemony in the European Coastland gradually led to the establishment of a similar hegemony in the Monsoon Coastland, its strategic position began to suffer from internal strains. A strong sea power, even with a healthy commerce and a powerful navy as its foundation, must have the strategic advantage of a central position in order to shorten its "interior lines"[11] and be able to concentrate its naval forces in the shortest possible time. The dispersion of British power from the North Sea to the eastern Mediterranean was not without creating some problems already, even if it was agreed that the decisive point was the Turkish Straits. But "Arabia" and the entire African continent before the opening of the Suez canal in 1869 constituted a massive obstacle to the coordination of British strategy in both Coastlands, all the more so since the headquarters of British India was not in Bombay but in Calcutta, at the far end of the Indian subcontinent. The existence of two Coastlands, even linked by a land bridge, created two separate sets of strategic responsibilities, sometimes complementing each other, but at other times threatening to pull apart London's effort to maintain a unified containment policy. Geography dictated there must be two containment policies focusing on two decisive points and managed from two political centers.

London decided in 1824 that the British mission in Tehran would be officered and directed from Calcutta, where the governor general reported to the Secretary of State for India in London and not to the Foreign Office. In effect, the decision integrated Persia politically into a Greater India under the joint management of the East India Company and the governor general, who would deal with the shah as he had been dealing with the potentates of Indian states. It removed Persia from the sphere of European politics and shifted it to the larger framework of "Asiatic" politics. But it also helped magnify the Russian danger to India as Persia became the ultimate zone of a new British India-Russian frontier. Ultimate zones were the most sensitive to external threats, because these threats reverberated throughout the web of frontier interests and were amplified by those who, out of ignorance or in pursuance of their own interests, would want to commit Calcutta to a policy of dynamic containment within the Heartland. That same year, it was discovered that an agreement had been made in London to establish an Anglo-German colony in (Persian) Azerbaijan to develop agriculture, trade, and industry as well as to improve sanitation to encourage the growth of population. That company was set up as a barrier against the Turks "*and other people*,"[12] who could be only the Russians. Persian reverses during the 1826–1828 war only increased anxiety in Calcutta, although Britain refused to send troops to the shah's defense. The combination of self-righteousness and impotence was not conducive to the pursuit of a policy free from exaggerated fears. The Treaty of Turkmanchai (1828) allowed Russia to establish a permanent mission in Tehran, next to Britain's, the only other foreign mission at the time. Russia's victory was Britain's defeat, and an effort was made in London to "disencumber itself" from an ally that could not pass the test of resistance to Russian expansion. Nevertheless, the battle was joined in Tehran—there was no way to avoid it—a battle for Persia's allegiance, because that allegiance would determine whether Russia could be contained beyond Herat.

A policy of containment seeking to establish a political isobar along the inner boundary of the Persian core area was a difficult undertaking. More ambitious and more certain to fail was the attempt to keep the Russians out of the basin of the Aral Sea, the region of continental drainage that led to Herat from the north. The advance into the Kazakh steppe, the organization of commercial caravans to Khiva and Bukhara, various scientific and topographical expeditions, were so many Russian probings into the Russo-Persian frontier. A containment policy as it was understood in Calcutta sought not only to stymie the Russians in Persia but also to checkmate their moves in Central Asia. In British India's mind, Afghanistan, Persia, and Central Asia formed a single complex of interdependent parts, and a containment policy had to remain indivisible.

In January 1830, the East India Company Board of Control and its president, Lord Ellenborough, the future governor general, instructed the then governor general to carry out a "master plan" to contain the

Russian advance. The Board sought to dispel the fear of an invasion of India via the Khyber Pass on the ground that a Russian army would arrive at Kabul "diminished in real force" and would be wiped out before it could cross into India. But the Board pointed out with great foresight that the real fear in Calcutta was not an invasion but of "the moral effect produced among our subjects in India by the continued apprehension of that event."[13] Moreover, British India did not mean at the time the entire Indian subcontinent but only Bengal and the Deccan, leaving out the large internal provinces of Sind and Punjab and the motley of tribal lands beyond the Indus River. Khiva and Bukhara must be integrated into a regional market—"our first object is to introduce English goods and not Englishmen into Kabul and Central Asia"—and that market would become a part of Britain's global economy, while the Russians would be shut out of the khanates. But Britain's containment policy also possessed its inner perverse logic: to make it effective required the completion of the conquest of India. A mind attracted by the paradoxes of great power politics might suspect the unconscious existence of an Anglo-Russian alliance of the flanking powers to divide the great "Asiatic" space between the Aral Sea and central India among themselves until they established a political isobar along the Hindu Kush, the Heartland's periphery. Such an alliance would expose the weakness of a containment policy pursued within the Heartland. For if it was assumed that Russia must not be allowed to establish a strategic presence in the Coastlands, it also had to be assumed that Russia would not allow Britain to establish a strategic presence within the Heartland—unless Russia fell victim to the rotting process it had found so useful in other core areas, and unless Britain acquired such overwhelming power that it could impose its will in the frontiers, a prospect that neither geography nor the transport revolution still to come promised to make realistic. Mackinder's vision had been stark and clear: "The Heartland," he wrote in 1919, "is the region to which, under modern conditions, seapower can be refused access."[14]

Britain on the Offensive, 1830–1848

The 1830s and 1840s were a time of intense "cold war" in Anglo-Russian relations, as if the two powers had decided to test the limits of acceptable activity. In fact, that cold war had become inevitable, because expansion was bringing the Russians dangerously close to the establishment of their hegemony in the Heartland. Much of the invective directed against Nicholas I and the arrogance displayed against his policies proceeded from an awareness that it was so difficult to engage the Russians on land. A feeling of insecurity and impotence pervaded British attitudes, as if the unavoidable necessity of containing Russia kept reminding London, and especially Calcutta, that international relations had become bipolar on a global scale, and that France had been replaced by a much more dangerous rival, permanent, self-righteous, and irreducible.

In 1831, Lord Durham was sent to become ambassador in Petersburg without London even asking the Russians whether he was acceptable, as was normal diplomatic usage. The repression of the Polish revolt and the activities of the Polish associations in Britain popularized the stereotype of Nicholas I as "the oppressor of Poland, master of noble slaves, the ravisher of women, and assassin of children."[15] The hysteria had barely died down when news reached London in July 1833 that the Russians had signed a treaty of alliance with the sultan at Unkiar-Skelesi. The British had good reason to be concerned about the real meaning of the famous secret clause, and the suspicion was strong that Russia had gained the right to send its warships into the Mediterranean while the Royal Navy would have no access to the Black Sea. In other words, Russia had violated the unwritten rule that the Heartland's periphery must be the political isobar separating the spheres of British and Russian interests in Turkey. But the ensuing crisis had been caused in part by Britain's overcommitment. The French Revolution of 1830 had refurbished the old image of France as the hereditary enemy, and British squadrons had been assigned to the Dutch and Portuguese coasts. When the sultan asked for help against Mehmet Ali, Britain had no commanding force to impose a settlement in the eastern Mediterranean. The discrepancy between the assumption that Britain's role was to rule the waves if not the world and its inability to concentrate a naval force at the decisive point in one of the Coastlands prompted wild calls for damming up the Baltic and Black seas, destroying the Russian navy, and annihilating Russian commerce.

The official incarnation of Russophobia was Lord Palmerston, the foreign secretary between November 1830 and August 1841 and again from July 1846 to December 1851, and prime minister from February 1855 to his death in October 1865. He declared in March 1835 that "Russia is a great humbug" and that Britain could "throw it back half a century" out of the affairs of Europe.[16] His great fear would remain an alliance between France and Russia, "these two ambitious and aggressive powers,"[17] and his prescription was a strong Germany under Prussian leadership and supported by Britain. Supremacy, it has been said, is not conducive to hard thinking.[18] The unofficial embodiment of Russophobia was David Urquart, "passionate and mystical,"[19] the founder of the domino theory of Russian expansion. Russia wanted Constantinople and the straits, would then transform the Ottoman Empire into a protectorate, and would finally turn to Persia to establish an advanced base at Herat for the conquest of India. Such were indeed Russia's goals, save for the conquest of India, but Urquart's writings had the effect of transforming Russia's long-range goals into immediate prospects. The more Urquart pressed his views the more he wandered into a world of fancy, until he became convinced by 1837 that even Palmerston was a traitor in the pay of the Russian government.

The crisis was not resolved until July 1841, when it was agreed that the straits must remain closed in peacetime to the warships of all nations.

Palmerston recognized that Russia's influence in Turkey was "natural and legitimate" because it rested on Russia's "geographical location," and that Britain had no more reason to send warships into the Black Sea than Russia had to send its own into the Mediterranean. London thus assumed at the time that the isobar had to include the Sea of Marmora, the Dardanelles, and the Bosphorus, and if Petersburg agreed, "we could be snarling at each other, hating each other, but neither wishing for war."[20] The height of the anti-Russian campaign had been reached in 1837, when the Russians seized and confiscated the Vixen, a merchantman sent by Urquart to the Caucasian coast with a cargo of powder and munitions. Palmerston, forgetting his own geopolitical vision, challenged Russia's suzerainty on the Caucasian coast, but overplayed his hand. He vented his frustration on the Russian ambassador, Pozzo di Borgo, with a violent philippic that Pozzo called "extraordinary and quite incredible."[21]

It was of little help that Lord Durham had reported from Petersburg in March 1836 that Russian power, however impressive, was of a defensive kind, "When Russia steps out into the open plain, (it) is then assailable in front and rear and flank, the most exposed from her gigantic bulk and unwieldy proportions; exhibiting as in Poland and Turkey the total want of that concentrated energy and efficient organization which renders invincible smaller but more civilized bodies."[22] Or perhaps the ambassador's words justified Palmerston in believing that the "gigantic bulk" could be challenged within the Heartland. An extraordinary campaign was launched to magnify Russian naval power in the Baltic despite the tsar's reassurance that the size of the Russian navy there had not changed since the days of Catherine II and Alexander I. Palmerston accused Russia in December 1833 of "violating British rights" by fortifying the Åland Islands. Located as they were at the mouth of the Gulf of Bothnia where the sea almost never freezes over, they would enable the Russian fleet to begin early in a campaign against Britain in the North Sea, a claim Martens called "almost insane."[23] It was at this time that the vice consul in Hammerfest stirred up the Varangerfjord issue, concluding that Russia was "maturing for a great war"[24] in order to gain full access to the Atlantic and the Mediterranean, and the "ordinarily sane" Duke of Wellington took seriously a rumor that Russia was about to despatch an armada from the Baltic against India in March 1839.

Palmerston thus assumed that a close-border policy, a policy of static defense along the Heartland's periphery at the Turkish Straits, did not apply in Scandinavia, where the British felt free to project power within the Heartland, and where the isobar had to run from Åbo to Riga. But these two approaches to containment were in fact complementary—if the Russian's decided to apply pressure in the straits, they exposed themselves to British naval attacks in the Baltic. But what could such attacks achieve against Russia's fortress-fleet strategy in the Gulf of Finland? A whale would always have a problem grappling with an elephant, as Bismarck once put it, and what an Anglo-Russian war would have brought about was never clear. Moreover, was the Royal Navy truly able to apply commanding force at two decisive points, even in the same Coastland? The precedent of 1833 was not encouraging. Only such doubts, born of the frustration of not being able to "solve" the Russian problem, could explain a public mood in which "almost everyone is animated with hatred of Russia" (1835) and "Russia was almost universally repugnant to Englishmen" (1840).[25]

The cold war was not limited to the European Coastland. It was even colder in the Monsoon Coastland and almost brought about a shooting war between Englishmen and Russians. "The Russian shadow (had been) darkening over the Persian land" since Turkmanchai.[26] The resident minister in Tehran was pursuing a systematic policy of turning the Persian core area outward toward Herat and Afghanistan. Some Englishmen in India believed Britain should abandon the hope of gaining influence in Tehran and concentrate on establishing a strong position in Afghanistan, still a loose political configuration resting on four cities: Herat and Balkh, Kandahar and Kabul. A strong presence in Kabul and Kandahar would draw a defense perimeter along the western slopes of the Hindu Kush, a red line defending the valley of the Indus. Others continued to feel that the defense of Persia, Central Asia, and Afghanistan remained indivisible. In 1834, Palmerston still wanted to believe that Britain and Persia were acting in the same spirit in Persia: both wanted to maintain the country's internal tranquillity, integrity, and independence.

But as long as the pressure remained unequal no political isobar could be drawn across Persia and the Russo-Persian frontier, and as long as the isobar refused to materialize British India had to face the near certainty of losing ground. Even in Kabul, the British managed to be outmaneuvered by the Russians in 1835. In March 1836, a new governor general of India, Lord Auckland, arrived in Calcutta with instructions to "raise a timely barrier against the encroachments of Russian influence."[27] A new British minister, John McNeill, as militant a Russophobe as Stratford had been in Constantinople, arrived in Tehran the same year with the task of preventing the establishment of a Russian protectorate over Persia and to thwart Persian ambitions in Afghanistan. But the Russians clearly had the upper hand, and they encouraged the shah to move against Herat in November 1837. The world was then treated to the "strange spectacle"[28] of Russian officers and a Russian battalion serving with the Persian army facing the defenders of Herat commanded by British officers.

Lord Auckland was a firm believer in a forward policy and, at McNeill's urgings, despatched a force of 500 to Karrack (Kharg) Island deep into the Persian Gulf in the spring of 1838 as a demonstration against the shah's pro-Russian sympathies. The move was instrumental in getting the shah to lift the siege of Herat. Auckland, however, not content with this local success, then proceeded, in a dramatic challenge to Russia, to make "gigantic preparations" to bring the entire massif of the Hindu Kush between Herat and the Indus River under British control in order to integrate the Khyber and other passes into the Indian defense perimeter. His challenge brought British India in conflict with some of the Afghan tribes leaning toward Russia and compelled him to launch the disastrous first Afghan War in the spring of 1839. Nevertheless, British troops demonstrated their control of the Khyber Pass and withdrew in December 1842. In both Constantinople and Kabul, Britain had blocked the exits across the Heartland.

But Britain was losing Persia and Central Asia. In a revealing conversation with Pozzo di Borgo in 1838, a former governor general of India, Lord Wellesley, expressed his disapproval of British India's strategy. "The worst we could do," he said, "is to throw the shah into [Russia's] arms." It should not be British policy to give you a pretext "to cross your boundary," that is, to establish a Russian hegemony in Persia, yet Calcutta was doing just that (*"On veut vous y forcer"*). "We cannot resist Russia in Persia, and the evidence of our inferiority will turn the heads of all the natives" all the way to the Ganges.[29] Lord Wellesley thus insisted on the unity of the strategic theater between the Caspian and the Ganges. Palmerston had a similar vision when he declared in 1840 that Khiva should be "a non-conducting body between Russia and British India, and separated from both by a considerable interval of space."[30] However, these perspectives were no longer realistic in the face of Russia's determination. British India's government kept its nose closer to the ground and was already preparing for the crucial battle over Afghanistan. Perovsky's expedition against Khiva in December 1839 was Russia's answer to the British victory in Herat and to the Afghan expedition. Although it failed, it was Russia's first move in the war for Central Asia, which Russia would eventually win.

Both powers were clearly engaged in a race for the Heartland's periphery. The British advance both matched Russia's moves and caused Russia to advance further toward the Syr Darya. Lord Auckland would countenance no further resistance to Britain's expansion in the subcontinent in the pursuit of its strategic interest. Sind was annexed in 1843 and Punjab in 1849 after a long and bloody uprising. The annexation gave Britain a strong power base in Peshawar and Shikarpur, one giving control to the approaches to the Khyber Pass and Kabul, the other to the Bolan Pass leading to Kandahar, the second major exit across the Heartland from Persia and Central Asia. The 1840s witnessed the systematic annexation of territories in northern India by invoking the doctrine of lapse, according to which Britain inherited any state whose ruler did not have a legitimate successor.

While British India was vainly seeking to stop the Russian advance toward the Heartland's periphery and was preparing for a last-ditch defense of the Afghan passes, other developments in the Monsoon Coastland were about to stretch Britain's strategic responsibilities to a dangerous point. The East India Company lost its monopoly of the China trade in 1834, and that trade was opened to all British subjects. A chief superintendent of British trade in China was appointed to Canton, who soon became unhappy with the Manchu commissioner's unwillingness to accept more opium from Bengal into China and his refusal to see the benefits of opening China to free trade. Tensions between the two sides led to the Opium War of 1839–1842 and a Chinese defeat. Five ports were opened to foreign trade, and China had to recognize the most-favored-nation principle according to which any concession granted to one power was automatically extended to other signatories, including Russians.

The "opening" of China was unrelated to the containment of Russian expansion, but it had one important consequence: it exposed China's weakness. The Russians had lived in the Eastern Frontier in the shadow of Nerchinsk since 1689: China was a powerful state that could not be trifled with. It now turned out that a few gunboats could force that powerful state to make major concessions. The appointment of Muravev as governor general of Irkutsk in 1847 was a result of this new awareness of a changing geopolitical situation. Geography, as well as political and economic ambitions, was certain to create a spontaneous alliance of the flanking powers against China. Britain's determination to gain a dominant economic position in southern China and the valley of the Yangtse River was bound to be matched by a Russian determination to gain a commanding presence in northern China to the Yellow River. And such a flanking alliance, which invited the Russian advance, was also certain to bring about in the long run the elaboration of a British policy to keep Russia contained, not within the Heartland—since Russian had already crossed its periphery in 1689—but within a safe distance of the Yellow Sea, another narrow sea leading to the Pacific. Anglo-Russian relations were becoming truly global, from the Scandinavian Sound to the Korea Strait.

Showdown, 1848–1879

The highlights of the next thirty years from the late 1840s to 1878 were the Crimean War, the Russo-Turkish War, and the second Afghan War. All three conflicts were about the control of the two decisive points, the Turkish Straits and the Khyber Pass. They appeared at first glance as major successes of Britain's containment policy. Paradoxically, however, the crisis of 1878 marked the climax of a policy to block Russia's egress to the Mediterranean; it would also mark the beginning of a gradual abandonment of that policy. And the Afghan War, if it did keep Russia out of Afghanistan, also revealed the collapse of British attempts to keep Russia out of Central Asia and to stem the growing Russian influence in Persia.

Anglo-Russian relations had greatly improved after the Straits Convention of July 1841. Palmerston was out of office; Nicholas I visited London in 1844. Britain invoked free trade, the weapon of the strong, to open up new markets everywhere, including Turkey; Central Asia, where Russian exporters faced stiff competition; and even Russia. An Anglo-Russian commercial treaty was signed in January 1843 that did not quite satisfy British interests. The prime minister, Robert Peel, had insisted that

Russia was and must remain an agricultural country; it should not even try to protect its manufactures. Even the revolutions of 1848 did not damage relations despite Britain's support of the Frankfurt Parliament and northern Italian ambitions; Palmerston, back in office, supported the crushing of the Hungarian uprising.

But other developments were leading to a showdown. Britain had two proconsuls in the east—its governor general in Calcutta and its ambassador in Constantinople. Stratford Canning, created viscount de Redcliffe in 1852, had acquired such a reputation for Russophobia that when it was suggested in 1843 that he be sent to the Petersburg embassy, Nicholas I declared he would never receive him. As the Ottoman Empire became virtually an open market for British manufactures and the British share of all Danube shipping reached one-third by 1853, British economic interests penetrated into the Heartland, and Palmerston and Stratford declared their readiness to challenge any Russian move. The security of grain exports from the Danubian Principalities together with the Austrian strategic interest in keeping Russia contained behind the Prut combined to check Russian intentions on the Danube and beyond. Palmerston's and Stratford's imperious manner showed itself once again when they supported the Porte's refusal to extradite the Hungarian rebels in 1849. Palmerston objected to the Russians' legitimate extradition request, made in accordance with Article 2 of the Treaty of Kuchuk-Kainardji, by saying that "Russia may state claims but the sultan does not have to execute them."[31] At the height of the crisis, in November 1849, Stratford ordered Admiral Parker of the Mediterranean squadron to cross the Dardanelles to the entrance of the Sea of Marmora, a clear violation of the Straits Convention and an unwise one, because Russia could then claim the right to enter the Bosphorus to the northern entrance—Constantinople. Palmerston had to back down.

In the confused sequence of events leading to the Crimean War, one thing stands out. The British government, with unprecedented hubris, decided at last to incorporate the Black Sea into the Coastland and claim control over the mouths of the Danube, the Dniepr, and the Don. In January 1853, it drew a line along the right bank of the Danube beyond which a Russian advance would be met with a declaration of war. And it pledged to defend any Turkish port in the Black Sea against a Russian attack. Such was the official position. But Palmerston, who was then out of office, had a much larger view. In the 1830's, in the wake of Unkiar Skelesi, he had drawn a distinction between the Black Sea and the Baltic. For strategic reasons, he had insisted that the Baltic belonged to the Coastland, the Black Sea to the Heartland. He now dropped that distinction. A victorious war with Russia would restore Finland and the Åland Islands to Sweden, Prussia might gain some of Russia's Baltic provinces, and "a substantive Kingdom of Poland" must be restored between Prussia and Russia, that is, Russia must be rolled back behind the Niemen and the Bug. In the basin of the Black Sea, Moldavia-Wallachia and the delta of the Danube must be given to Austria, the Crimea and Georgia must be restored to the Ottomans, and the eastern coast of the Black Sea (Circassia) must become either independent or a vassal of the Porte.

Such an ambitious program sought to restore some of the frontier zones to Sweden and Turkey. The ultimate goal was to cripple Russian sea power in both narrow seas and push back the political isobar to Kotlin Island and into the Ukrainian steppe. It also required a massive victory over Russia, but avoided the question of how the whale would grapple with the elephant. And it was by no means certain that the Swedes and the Ottomans were eager to recover the zones. The Swedes certainly were not. Weaker core areas could not risk recovering lost territory in the face of Russian opposition only to be exposed much later, when British support could no longer be taken for granted, to the full force of a Russian revenge.

In fact, the war turned into a series of far-flung naval operations unlikely to settle anything. In July 1854, a British squadron occupied the Åland Islands and bombarded the Solovetsky monastery in the White Sea, and in August an Anglo-French force attached Petropavlovsk in distant Kamchatka, but could not take the port. Only in the Crimea did a large allied force launch a major operation, but the siege of Sevastopol would last until September 1855. In December 1854, when the siege was tightening, Lord Clarendon, the foreign secretary (1853–58), set forth Britain's goal—the demolition of Sevastopol and other Russian fortresses on the eastern coast of the Black Sea to shake Russia's hold on the Caucasus, the elimination of Russia's naval installations in that sea, the reduction of its navy to four ships, and a revision of the Straits Convention to allow Britain and France to maintain the same number of warships in the Black Sea. The Treaty of Paris of March 1856 moderated these radical demands by reasserting the "ancient rule" that British and French warships would not be allowed into the Black Sea in peacetime, but it neutralized the Black Sea by ordering the closure of Russia's naval installations and pledging Russia to keep no warships in the Black Sea. The friendship between a grateful Porte and the two maritime powers guaranteed that in the event of the war the sultan would allow their warships to cross into the Black Sea, there to attack a defenseless Russia.

The Paris settlement was a great geopolitical victory, but it was also unwise because it humiliated a great power, and a great power always possesses the potential to take its revenge. Moreover, British policy began, hesitatingly, to ponder whether the straits were truly the decisive point over which London must be ready to go to war. There was dissatisfaction with the Ottoman performance during the war, with the Porte's inability to reform the Imperial administration and finances to become the bulwark of a British containment policy. Besides, the neutralization of the Black Sea removed the naval threat. France had been active in Egypt, and Britain could not prevent the digging of the Suez Canal, which opened in November 1869. The canal shortened sea communications between the Atlantic and the Indian Ocean and made Egypt a new prize that downgraded the importance of the straits. And not only Egypt, but the Arab states of "Arabia" linking the two Coastlands. The release of Russian energies with the completion of the pacification of the Caucasus in 1865 raised the possibility that Russia might want to cross the Heartland's periphery toward Baghdad and Aleppo. Disraeli, the future prime minister (1868, 1874–1880), declared in 1866 that Britain was no longer a European but had become an imperial power and should cease to interfere in European affairs. A year before, shortly before his death, Palmerston had expressed his conviction that "Germany" must be strong enough to contain Russian aggression and that a dynamic Prussia was essential to German strength. One begins to detect an attempt to devolve the containment of Russia in the European Coastland to Germany while reassessing where the decisive point truly lay in the eastern Mediterranean. And when Prussia went to war in 1870, the London *Times* exulted in France's defeat. While France was being defeated, however, Russia denounced the Black Sea clauses of the 1856 settlement and regained its freedom of action. But there was the hope that a new Anglo-German alliance would contain a possible resurgence of Russian expansionism.

These hopes were soon disappointed. The new Germany had no intention of becoming Britain's surrogate in both Coastland and Heartland (containing France and Russia), but showed a disquieting tendency to link its future with Austro-Hungary and Russia, and London worried lest the new Austro-German bloc would impose its will on Russia. During the war scare of 1875, when Petersburg opposed Bismarck's policy, Disraeli supported the Russians against Berlin. The move had no immediate consequence but was significant: the rise of a strong Germany upset British calculations, and its effect was to restore for a fleeting moment the alliance of the flanking powers. It was the first breach in Britain's containment policy since 1815.

While Britain scored a major success in 1856 by destroying Russian naval power in the Black Sea, its position was deteriorating in what some contemporaries called the "debatable land"[32] between the Caspian and the Kindu Kush. The shah had been compelled in January 1853 to desist from taking advantage of the imminent Crimean conflict to move against Herat, but the old antagonism between Persia and Afghanistan, fanned by the Russians, reasserted itself, and the shah occupied Herat in October 1856, prompting a war with Britain. Units from British India landed on Karrack Island once again, and the Anglo-Persian treaty of March 1857 bound the shah to abandon Herat and his claims on Afghanistan. It is tempting to use this episode as an illustration of the "pendulum movement" in Russian foreign policy—increasing pressure in one geostrategic theater after suffering reverses in another—but that would be very misleading. Until Turkmanchai (1828), British influence in Persia had been paramount. Thereafter, it was supplanted by Russian influence, until Persia became the avant-garde of the Russian advance toward the Hindu Kush. Britain could no longer use Persia to contain Russia; it had to contain Persia to contain Russia. To contain Persia it had become necessary to go to war, and Persia's defeat could only keep the country more firmly in the Russian embrace. The Russian advance had acquired its own momentum, irrespective of developments in other theaters.

Britain's military victory in 1857 was a strategic defeat. There were more to come. The East India Company was closed in 1859, and the British minister in Tehran ceased to be responsible to the British Indian government and was subordinated directly to the Secretary of State for India in London. The move marked a recognition of the fact that, as British responsibilities for the containment of Russia became global, policymaking must be centralized. London also recognized that it had become impossible to continue to assert the indivisibility of the strategic theater from the Caspian to the Indus River, and that the jurisdiction of British India must be restricted to the defense of the approaches to the Hindu Kush on the Heartland's periphery.

The Russian conquest of Central Asia, long in preparation and certainly no reaction to the Crimean defeat, destroyed the British position in the valleys of the Amu and Syr Darya. A debate had been taking place in British India between a "forward school" and a "buffer school," the former calling for a forward policy to integrate Afghanistan into British India and establish the Amu Darya as the boundary with the Russian Empire, in order to keep Russia "penned back"[33] in Central Asia. Even the forward school had abandoned Khiva, Bukhara, and Kokand to the Russians. The "master plan" of 1830 was but a sweet memory of past illusions. The buffer school wanted British India to stop at the Indus River and Afghanistan to become an independent state and a buffer with Russia. The question, of course, was whether Britain would be willing to risk war to preserve the independence of Afghanistan.

The viceroy of India, Sir John Lawrence (1863–1868), instituted a policy of "masterly inactivity," reminiscent of Lord Wellesley's view that challenging the Russians was not to Britain's advantage. But the Russians did not need the challenge. In 1868, the entry of European goods into Central Asia had been prohibited. By 1873, Khiva, Bukhara, and Kokand had been occupied, and General Kaufman had invaded the Ili valley. The Amu Darya was becoming the de facto boundary of the Russian Empire. Fear now gripped the Indian government lest an "Asiatic Russia" emerge in Central Asia that would rival the British Empire in India and even undermine it: had not past invasions of northern India come from Persia and Central Asia? The forward school triumphed with the election of Disraeli in 1874 and the arrival of Lord Salisbury at the India Office (1874–1878). In February 1876, Salisbury gave Lord Lytton, the new viceroy (1876–1880), instructions to strengthen British influence in Afghanistan because the rapid Russian advance in Central Asia "will influence an oriental chief with ill-defined dominions."[34] That influence could be strengthened only by placing agents in Kabul and elsewhere who would report to Calcutta, and to block any Russian attempt to do the same. A red line had been drawn through Herat, Kandahar, and Kabul. Britain had to accept that India could not be defended within the Heartland and that the Russian advance could be stopped only on its periphery, on the western slopes of the Hindu Kush guarding the approaches to the passes that led into the Monsoon Coastland.

While the Russians were consolidating their position in Central Asia and keeping the British "penned back" beyond the Hindu Kush, developments in the Balkans were leading to yet another Russo-Turkish war. It broke out in April 1877, and immediately raised the possibility that the Russians might reach Constantinople and invade western Armenia. In May, Lord Derby, the foreign secretary (1874–1878), warned the Russian ambassador that Britain considered that its vital interests included not only the straits and Constantinople but also Egypt, the Suez Canal, and the Persian Gulf. Gone were the days when Palmerston dreamt of rolling back the political isobar into the Ukrainian steppe. There was concern that a successful war might so destabilize the Ottoman Empire that the Russian advance would become irresistible. Even Disraeli, who entertained the idea of sending troops via Batum into Armenia and even occupying Tiflis, considered the possibility of a Russian advance through Syria to the delta of the Nile. Such a perspective was the brainchild of a statesman on the defensive, despite all the bluster: while Palmerston had wanted to integrate the Black Sea into the Coastland, his successors were warning the Russians against gaining a foothold in "Arabia."

In February 1878, when the Russians were almost under the walls of Constantinople, a British squadron dropped anchor off Princes' Islands, facing the Russians "in majestic impotence."[35] But when the news of the Treaty of San Stefano reached London in March, the Cabinet called up the reserves and ordered Indian troops to the Near East, while an outburst of Russophobia swept the country and Queen Victoria called for war against the "great barbarians."[36] In June, Britain and Turkey signed a defensive alliance to stop the Russian advance toward Anatolia. Should Russia retain Batum, Kars, and Ardahan, Britain would support Turkish attempts to recover them, demanding in return the right to "occupy and administer" Cyprus. After the cession of the Ionian Islands to Greece in July 1863, Britain had been without a forward naval base in the eastern Mediterranean. Cyprus was intended to become a staging area for landings at Alexandria, from which British troops would counter a Russian advance toward the valley of the Tigris and the Euphrates.

The Congress of Berlin (1878) is usually seen as a defeat of Russian ambitions in the Balkans. It also exposed Disraeli's "gigantic piece of bluff."[37] The British squadron had been sent to Constantinople over Turkey's opposition, and only the exhaustion of the Russian army prevented the occupation of the city. The cession of Cyprus in June 1878 antagonized the Ottomans, without whose support a containment policy was meaningless. The threat of a British expeditionary force facing the Russian army on the desolate plateaus of Armenia was not credible. Only the support of a rejuvenated Turkey could stave off the collapse of Britain's containment policy, and it was not forthcoming.

No wonder, then, that a "hawk" like Salisbury saw the future through a glass darkly. In May 1878, he had declared to the British ambassador in Constantinople his conviction that the Ottoman Empire in the Balkans was doomed and that the "Asiatic Christians," that is, the Armenians, might well pass under Russian rule. And how could Turkey maintain itself "in Asia" at a time when "the Arabs and the Asiatics generally will look to the Russian as the coming man?" He had no answer, except to say that Russian influence in Syria and Mesopotamia would be "a serious embarrassment."[38] Salisbury's position was symptomatic of an imperceptible shift taking place in Britain's containment policy. Britain would seek a strong base in "Arabia" and especially Egypt to defend the sea lancs to India, but the center of gravity would move to the Suez Canal and the straits would become an expendable asset. But Britain's retrenchment in the Greek Archipelago and the eventual abandonment of the old strategic objective in the straits would match the eventual restoration of an alliance of the flanking powers directed no longer against France, but against Germany. A new geopolitical configuration began to take shape after 1878; it would force a radical reorientation of British policy toward Russia. And in both cases, the new policy would invite the Russians' advance toward the Heartland's periphery and even accept the possibility of their crossing into the European Coastland.

Salisbury was much more secure in his conviction that British India could stop the Russian advance toward Afghanistan. His program was a preparation for an offensive war, with rail links from Shikarpur to Quetta and Nushki to facilitate the transport of troops deep inland to Kandahar and Herat. Lytton forced the issue by insisting that the emir receive a British mission. The emir refused but incautiously received General Stoletov in June 1878 and even signed a treaty with him. This was a direct challenge to the forward school. An expeditionary force was assembled, and the viceroy struck in November. Kandahar was taken in January, Kabul in October 1879. The Treaty of Gandamak (on the road to Kabul) compelled the emir in May to accept a British mission in Kabul and agents elsewhere "as occasion might require," and to conduct his foreign policy in accordance with Britain's wishes. This second Afghan War transformed Afghanistan into a British protectorate, "impenetrable" to Russian influence.

There were more good news from the Far East. The second Anglo-Chinese War, known as the Arrow War (1858–1860), was intended by Palmerston "to teach the Chinese a lesson."[39] The most important provision of the Peking settlement of October 1860 was the opening of ten more ports on the China coast and on the Yangtse River. One of them was Newchang (Yinkou) on the estuary of the Liao river. A British commercial presence at the mouth of a river giving access to the central plain of Manchuria and the Sungari River was a challenge to the Russian advance in the Amur valley; Palmerston may have wanted to teach a lesson not only to the Chinese. The Tsushima affair (1861) activated the reflex of a sea power bent on controlling the exits of all the narrow seas, and it was Britain that compelled the Russians to withdraw from the island. Britain then became an active participant in the struggle to overthrow the Tokugawa shogunate, and a new Japanese government took office January 1868.

The Meiji Restoration released enormous pent-up forces in Japanese society; they were quickly channeled into social reconstruction, rapid economic development, a military and naval buildup, and territorial expansion. These developments favored British interests, at least in the short run. One sea power understood another and knew instinctively that the Japanese would seek to bottle up the Russians in the Sea of Okhotsk, neutralize the naval base in Vladivostok, and eventually close the Sea of Japan. Japan was a natural ally to block Russian expansion in distant North Pacific waters where Britain had few commercial interests. And indeed, the Japanese pressured the Russians to abandon the entire Kuril archipelago in May 1875, closing the Sea of Okhotsk. In February 1876, they negotiated a treaty with Korea, opening two commercial ports in addition to Pusan, where the lord of Tsushima had kept a representative for generations. This was a first step toward closing the Sea of Japan. A new chapter began in Japanese-Korean relationships, tortuous and cruel. It would end with the destruction of Russian power in the Far East thirty years later.

15

Triumph and Collapse, 1879–1917

Doubts, 1879–1895

The containment of Russian expansion now became a truly global enterprise, but the more responsibilities Britain had to assume, the more contradictions began to afflict its containment policy. The main question was no longer to determine where the decisive point was: paradoxically, the decisive point had become the Khyber Pass, the only place on the entire Heartland's periphery where Britain could not use its greatest asset, its navy. Far more important was the growing overcommitment of British naval resources—in the Mediterranean, the Persian Gulf, the Indian Ocean, and the China Sea. And finally, new concerns in domestic politics demanded that more attention be given to social questions, forcing the Exchequer to establish priorities inimical to the maintenance of the country's global position.

Lord Lytton had reached his goal. "If we resolve," he had said in 1879, "that no foreign interference can be permitted on this side of the mountains, or within the drainage system of the Indus, we shall have laid down a natural line of frontier which is distinct, intelligible, and likely to be respected."[1] A proponent of the forward school had come to speak the language of the buffer school. Britain's victory was not quite complete, however, and the "arrangement" of August 1880 established a "preclusive protectorate" in which the emir's only relations would be with the British Indian government. However, Calcutta would not insist on the appointment of a British resident in Kabul, let alone elsewhere, and would have to be satisfied with a "Moslem agent." Nevertheless, the main objective had been achieved: there would be no Russian presence in Afghanistan.

The success of a containment policy depended in large part on the ability of the containing power to keep Russia distracted within the Heartland. There were fewer opportunities in the 1880s. The Russians were now able to distract the British by coordinating their moves in Central Asia and in the basin of the Black Sea. Britain could no longer pursue a similar policy: if the Russians decided to upset the political isobar along the Hindu Kush, Britain could not resort to a forward strategy in the Black Sea. Although the Russians had repudiated the Black Sea clauses of the 1856 treaty in 1870, the London treaty of March 1871 stipulated that, while the straits remained closed in peacetime, the sultan "might open" them to the warships of friendly powers, should he find it necessary to safeguard the execution of the other clauses of the 1856 treaty. But the sultan was no longer friendly after 1878, and the first German mission arrived in Constantinople in 1883, the year Egypt became a British protectorate. Britain had lost not only its option of distracting Russia in the valley of the Amu Darya, it had also lost its complementary option of striking at Russian naval installations and cities on the Black Sea coast. The Indian government was increasingly insecure despite its victory in Afghanistan which, also paradoxically, gave Russia a free hand in the Turkmen steppe all the way to Merv and the approaches to Herat. When Calcutta called in 1887 for "making war with Russia all over the world,"[2] Lord Salisbury, now prime minister (1885–1892 and 1895–1902), tartly commented this was an empty phrase unless Britain commanded the Turkish army, and that it never could hope to do. The appearance of Russia on the eastern coast of Korea had prompted a swift British response in April 1885—the occupation of Port Hamilton on an islet facing the southern coast. The islet turned out to be unsuited to becoming another Malta, and Britain withdrew in February 1887 after receiving a Russian promise not to occupy Korean territory. Britain's response had been a typical one for a sea power obsessed with the control of the narrow seas, but such a projection of power so far north could not be sustained, and "the spirit of Port Hamilton never returned."[3]

Dissonant voices were now heard in the British political establishment on how to cope with Russian expansionism, reflecting in part well-established different perspectives in London and Calcutta. The British ambassador to Petersburg, Sir Robert Morier, could still declare in 1888 that a Russian move against Herat would be a casus belli, and one of the delegates of British India who had negotiated with the Afghan emir in 1880 could still state in 1889 that "England is as much bound in honor to defend Herat, Maimana, Balkh or any portion of Afghanistan against Russia as she is to defend the Isle of Wight against France."[4] Such brave words were beginning to ring hollow. The consolidation of a German-Austrian bloc in Central Europe, the growth of German economic and military power, Bismarck's inability to give a durable geopolitical foundation to an empire based in Heartland and Coastland and therefore unable to determine where its destiny lay, the death of William I in 1888 and concern over his grandson's lack of restraint, were so many reminders that Germany had become Britain's rival for hegemony in the European Coastland. And as had always happened in the past when France sought hegemony, the need for an alliance of the flanking powers reasserted itself. But the Anglo-Russian mistrust had been so great since 1815 and had been fed by so many irrational fears, especially from the perspective of British India, that some time was needed before the two powers could agree that the German danger to both transcended their differences. Just as the containment of Russia in the eighteenth century had fallen victim to the Anglo-French antagonism, it would fall victim in the twentieth to the antagonism between Germany and both Britain and France.

In October 1887, Lord Randolph Churchill traveled to Russia to conduct extensive discussions of Anglo-Russian differences, and ended by proclaiming an identity of interests between the two powers. In Persia, now drawn into the vortex of European rather than Indian politics, the British ambassador, Sir Henry Drummond Wolff, proposed a partition to the Russian ambassador in 1888. An Anglo-Russian rapprochement was premature, however, but it was encouraged by similar attempts in France, although these were directed as much against Britain as against Germany. Lord Kimberley, the secretary of state for India, had declared in 1886 that France's hostility to Britain played everywhere in Russia's hands, and the director of military intelligence echoed the Wellington of 1829 by saying in 1887 that "the worst combination we have any reason to dread is an alliance of France and Russia against us."[5] By 1888, rumors were circulating of a Franco-Russian alliance to expel the British from the Mediterranean. France's resentment of the annexation of Alsace-Lorraine and of its reduced status in Europe called for revenge, while Russia's growing apprehension of the power and ambitions of Germany demanded a new alliance of the flanking powers to contain German expansion. At the time, the other power could only be France. But France had always been a containing power and, since 1789, a hotbed of revolutionary ideas. Its consistency and revolutionary legacy had left deep rancor among the Russian elite.

However, circumstances and geography were much stronger than men, and a common hostility to Britain and Germany compelled a rapprochement. Germany's irresponsibility facilitated it. In the fall of 1888, the refusal of German banks to negotiate a Russian loan took the Russians to Paris, and a substantial order for army rifles was placed in Russia at the end of the year. By early 1891, Russia had received six large loans from French sources. Bismarck had been forced to resign in March 1890. German policy was becoming more forceful in the pursuit of its ambitions, and the new chief of the General Staff, Alfred von Schlieffen, already believed it might be possible for Germany to achieve total victory in war with both France and Russia.

In March 1891, in a major departure from traditional policy, the Russian foreign minister, Nikolai Giers, informed the French government, much to its surprise, that the "entente cordiale happily established between France and Russia . . . assures the most favorable balance of forces for the creation of a certain counterweight to the influence"[6] of the Triple Alliance of Germany, Austria, and Italy. In July, a French squadron visited Kronshtadt, and Europe was treated to the spectacle of a bareheaded tsar standing while the orchestra played the "Marseillaise." Negotiations began to draft a military convention, and the two governments exchanged notes in August, formalizing the existence of an entente cordiale, pledging to confer on "all questions" threatening the peace, and to agree, in the event of such a threat, on measures requiring an "immediate and simultaneous" adoption.

Despite the fact that the Russians had in fact taken the initiative, they were reluctant to commit themselves to a binding alliance and to specific military commitments beyond a simple exchange of views. Such commitments were of two kinds. Russian strategy placed a primary emphasis on the destruction of Austro-Hungarian forces to be followed by an offensive or defensive war against Germany. France's only concern was with a devastating German offensive. The other issue revolved around the implication of mobilization: was it a preliminary step, or was it war itself? How should the French and Russian general staffs coordinate their mobilization plans? The Military Convention of August 1892 sought answers to these questions, and called for periodic conferences between the two staffs to exchange information and prepare contingency plans. It was agreed that a German or Austrian attack on Russia or a German attack on France would commit the other party to use "all its available forces" against Germany. Moreover, the term *attack* was stretched to include mobilization. The chief of the Russian General Staff had written in May that mobilization signifies "the inauguration of military operations themselves," indeed that "it represents the most decisive act of war." In the event that any member of the Triple Alliance should mobilize, France and Russia would "mobilize immediately and simultaneously the totality of their forces."[7]

The convention, signed only by the two chiefs of staff, was not yet a binding document. The following year, however, in July 1893, the Reichstag voted to increase the size of the German army to give greater offensive power to the Schlieffen Plan, which called for an initial and massive offensive against France. The Russians did not know this, and interpreted the vote as the fulfillment of an earlier strategic plan focused on the destruction of the Russian army. This interpretation was decisive in overcoming Alexander III's resistance, and a new exchange of notes between Giers and the French ambassador in December and January 1894 constituted the official ratification of the convention. Nicholas II's visit to Paris in October 1896 and President Faure's return visit to Petersburg in August 1897 made the alliance public, although the text of the convention remained secret until 1918.

Against whom was the Franco-Russian alliance directed? The official texts made it clear it was directed against the Germanic powers, but a cryptic statement by General Nikolai Obruchev, the chief of the Russian General Staff, raised a tantalizing question. His memorandum of May 1892 asked the rhetorical question "Whom should we regard as our most dangerous enemy—the one who fights us directly or the one who waits for our weakening and then dictates the terms of peace?"[8] His reference to the Congress of Berlin certainly pointed to Germany, but did it not refer to Britain as well? Indeed, the first manifestation of the Franco-Russian entente cordiale had an anti-British hue. A Russian squadron visited Toulon in October 1893 to return the French visit of 1891, causing apprehension in the Admiralty at the prospect of a Franco-Russian combination in the Mediterranean. In 1894, France had serious quarrels with Britain in Newfoundland, North Africa, and Burma and on the Indo-Chinese border—Russia, in Central Asia and the Far East. If Central Asia was the only place on the continent where Russia could pressure Britain, the Mediterranean was the only naval theater where Britain felt directly threatened. As late as 1900, the two general staffs were considering ways to coordinate a Russian attack on Afghanistan with a French invasion of Britain.

It seemed at first that the Franco-Russian rapprochement, understood in a narrow sense, was a threat to Britain, but it was not if it is placed in a larger context. A Franco-Russian alliance directed against Britain—like the alliances of the Seven Years War, of 1800, and of 1807—would have been an aberration. Neither power had an interest in supporting the other's distant commitments at a time when a powerful Germany was becoming a danger to both. The alliance, in fact, served a dual purpose: to restrain German expansionism and to force Britain to abandon its policy of splendid isolation proclaimed by Disraeli in 1866. The threat of a Franco-Russian combination served to remind Britain that it was also a European power and that the German danger required a reconciliation of the two Coastland powers and their joint flanking alliance with Russia. A reminder was necessary because a reactivation of the Anglo-Russian conflict along the Hindu Kush was likely to keep the center of gravity of British policy in northwest India while events were forcing it to shift to the European Coastland. What purpose would be served by holding the line on the Khyber Pass if Britain became mortally threatened in Flanders and the North Sea?

During the three Pamir crises (1891–1895) Russia sought to reach the Hindu Kush and outflank the British position in Afghanistan to gain access to the northern passes and reach the tribes of Kashmir, there to stir up unrest against British rule. The commander in chief in India, Frederick Roberts, was ready "to go for the Russians" in 1891, and in April 1893 a "council of war" representing the Foreign Office, the War Office, and the India Office resolved to go to war to keep the Russians out of the northern slopes of the Hindu Kush.[9] Here, as in previous cases, war was avoided, and a compromise boundary settlement was reached in November 1895. British India's strong stand was not caused by strategic considerations alone. An 1891 survey of Britain's global strategic posture stated that British rule in India was made possible by the manipulation of the ethnic diversity of the Indian subcontinent, the old and well-tested principle of divide in order to rule. "But report has gone forth in India that there is another race, Russian, which faces British audacity with an audacity of its own,"[10] and Britain could not afford to appear weak lest it lose face before its colonial subjects. The Indian national congresses that began to meet annually in 1885 showed Britain the precariousness of its rule. It was thus necessary to stand up to Russia not in order to affirm Britain's might, but to cover up its weakness. That weakness was all the greater because a successful containment policy in Afghanistan depended on a secure position in Persia and Turkey; and in both core areas, Britain's position was beginning to disintegrate.

There was hope in the Far East, however. China, it is true, exhibited all the symptoms of the rotting process, but Japan was showing a willingness to stand up to the Russians. Geography dictated that the new sea power, located vis-à-vis the Chinese world very much as was Britain vis-à-vis the European continent, would show the same urge to control the exits of the narrow seas and the mouths of the rivers emptying into those seas. The mouth of the Amur was already part of the Russian Empire. That of the Tumen was within striking distance from Vladivostok. A struggle was inevitable for the control of the mouths of the Yalu and the Liao. The struggle would have to be fought in Korea and the Liaotung peninsula in order to close the Sea of Japan and the Gulf of Chihli. The 1880s was a time of political reform in Japan, culminating in the constitution of 1889 and the creation of a political machine operated by the two great clans of Chōshu and Satsuma, one dominant in the army, the other in the navy, both bent on expansion in the Pacific frontier. The new geopolitical situation generated a permanent Russo-Japanese antagonism, no less natural and ingrained than the Russo-Prussian and the Russo-British antagonism.

But Russia and Japan could not square off in Korea and on the Liaotung peninsula until China had been eliminated: the peninsula was part of Manchu China and Korea was a vassal state. Japan's interference in Korean affairs, facilitated by the bitter factional rivalry at the Court, eventually led to the Sino-Japanese War of 1894–1895. It was a coincidence, but a symbolic one, that the antiforeign revolt that was the immediate cause of the war began in southern Korea on the same day (May 15) the Siberian Committee in Petersburg resolved to speed up the construction of the Trans-Siberian railroad and to complete it by 1899, save for the Amur section. Japan sent troops to put down the revolt, and China declared war in August 1894. Its navy was sunk; Port Arthur, its naval headquarters, surrendered in November; and China's last hope, the fortified position at Weihaiwei on the Shantung Peninsula facing Port Arthur, fell in February 1895.

The Treaty of Shimonoseki in April forced China to recognize the independence of Korea and to cede the Liaotung Peninsula, including the mouths of the Yalu and Liao rivers. The treaty also bound China to pay a large indemnity—it would later be used to finance the Japanese naval buildup—and to let Japan remain in occupation of Weihaiwei while it was being paid. The "independence" of Korea was but the result of an implicit Japanese determination that the entire coastline from Pos'et Bay to Port Arthur had to be off limits to Russian naval power. Japan had replaced China as the main containing power in the Eastern Frontier. But that determination was not without some ambivalence. Lord Salisbury perceived an emerging trilateral relationship when he wrote in August that "Japan may be of use in hindering Russia from getting an ice-free port . . . (but) the shrewder Japanese ministers will not be sorry to see enough Russian power in these latitudes to counterbalance the powers of England."[11]

Contradictions, 1895–1905

The next decade, from 1895 to 1905, witnessed the collapse of Britain's policy in the European Coastland, the consolidation of an uneasy modus vivendi on the Afghan border, and the triumph of Japan's containment policy in the Monsoon Coastland. In fact, it began with a Japanese defeat. Russia opposed the annexation of the Liaotung Peninsula and enlisted the support of France and Germany. Faced with the possibility of war, the Japanese retreated, retroceded the peninsula in October 1895, and promised to evacuate Weihaiwei within three months. The strategic withdrawal forced Japan to abandon an ambitious plan to project power deep into Manchuria and establish advanced positions ahead of the Russians. The plan included the construction of a railroad from Pusan to the mouth of the Yalu followed by another from Newchang to Chinchow (Jinzhou) with an extension northward to Mukden and another southward to Shanhaikuan on the Great Wall. Newchang, already Manchuria's main port, would become a strategic base from which to threaten Peking and to strike at a Russian advance from the north. The plan presented an uncanny resemblance to Salisbury's own blueprint twenty years earlier to build rail lines toward the Afghan passes and across Persia. Admiral Mahan would note that navies have a "limited capacity to extend coercive force inland"[12]; both Britain and Japan sought to remedy this fundamental strategic disadvantage by using "rail power"[13] to push the perimeter of effective military action as close as possible to the Heartland's periphery.

On the other hand, the reassessment of British policy in the European Coastland was accelerating. It was the "favorite thesis"[14] of the colonial secretary, Joseph Chamberlain, that Britain and Russia had to find a way to reconcile their divergent interests. The tsar's visit to London and Paris in the fall of 1896 was an important step in that direction, with Germany lending a helping hand. The Kiel Canal, linking the Baltic with the North Sea, was opened in 1895, increasing the perception of a threat. William II's famous telegram of January 1896 to Paul Kruger, the president of the Transvaal Republic, was an open defiance of British supremacy in the area. From its headquarters in Toulon, the French navy had begun to use the Tunisian port of Bizerte in 1895, positioning the French to pincer the British squadron in Malta and cutting off British communications between Egypt and the Dardanelles. Lord Rosebery, the foreign secretary, acknowledged that the Franco-Russian alliance was creating a "critical" situation for Britain.[15] And in 1897, Alfred von Tirpitz was appointed secretary of the navy; he would become the architect of Germany's naval expansion, a development Britain was bound to consider a threat to its vital interests. Britain's splendid isolation had become an untenable situation, and the time was approaching when a new diplomatic revolution would become inevitable.

The first casualty of an Anglo-Russian rapprochement that would pave the way for the restoration of an alliance of the flanking powers had to be the Turkish Straits. German influence was growing in Turkey, and heavy guns manufactured by Krupp would soon make a crossing a hazardous operation. By January 1897, Salisbury had to accept the fact that Britain could not assist "the sultan to an independence which he did not desire, against an invader whom he himself had welcomed," and that the defense of Constantinople had become "an antiquated standpoint."[16] As if the abandonment of the straits were not enough, the prime minister instructed his ambassador in Petersburg in January 1898 to seek an understanding with Russia on a "partition of preponderance" in the Ottoman Empire—Anatolia and the valley of the Euphrates and Tigris with Baghdad to become part of the Russian sphere of "preponderance." Salisbury had quietly forgotten the "serious embarrassment" he had felt in 1878. Disraeli's forward policy of 1878 had been turned on its head. Salisbury envisaged a similar partition of China—Russia gaining a preponderance north of the Yellow River, Britain in the Yangtse valley. And the abandonment of Anatolia and northern China to the Russians was coupled with a willingness to abandon the containment of Russia in Manchuria and Korea to the Japanese. How to keep the Russians both preponderant and contained at the same time required a more subtle hand than either Russia or Japan would be willing to play.

Salisbury's efforts were rebuffed. In November 1897, the Germans seized Kiaochow Bay on Shantung Peninsula, "the deepest and best harbor on the China coast."[17] While Chamberlain was in Tokyo discussing the possibility of an Anglo-Japanese alliance, the Russians retaliated against the German move by obtaining a lease on Port Arthur and the right to build the South Manchurian Railroad. Britain retaliated in turn by negotiating a lease on Weihaiwei "for so long a period as Port Arthur shall remain in the occupation of Russia." If that was Britain's "strategic reply to Russia's strategic action in seizing Port Arthur,"[18] it could not conceal the fact that Britain was on the defensive before a spectacular Russian advance that knocked every prop from under any effective containment policy. And indeed, Salisbury's proposal of January 1898 turned in April 1899 into a formal agreement to partition China, Britain renouncing railroad concessions north of the Great Wall in exchange for

Russia's doing the same in the Yangtse valley, the area in between forming a neutral zone. Left alone to face the Russians, the Japanese, still unable to apply brute force to contain their seemingly irresistible advance, sought to create a political isobar along an artificial boundary. In 1896, they entertained the idea of partitioning Korea along the thirty-eighth parallel. By March 1898, however, they were no longer willing to accept a Russian influence in Korea. Both powers were set on a collision course, and Korea became the decisive point.

Partition was in the air everywhere, but partition implied the existence of an understanding among the flanking powers directed against a core area that had been the mainstay of a British presence in the Heartland: an understanding between Britain and Russia against Turkey and Persia. In the Far East, it meant the betrayal of a Coastland containing power (China) by Britain and even Japan. And everywhere partition encouraged the Russian advance and gave it the sanction of legitimacy. In Persia, as in Turkey, Britain had come to realize that the country could not be reformed against the will of its rulers. Even Lord Curzon, the hard-line viceroy of India (1899–1905), agreed in 1899 with a report by the ambassador to Tehran that there was no alternative to a partition of Persia along a line from Khanikin (Khaneqin) on the Turkish border along the northern foothills of the Zagros Mountains through Kermanshah, Hamadan, Isfahan, Yezd, and Kerman to the Afghan border in Seistan. Britain was ready to abandon its long-standing insistence on the territorial integrity of Persia and fall back to the Zagros Mountains on the Heartlands periphery.

The Boer War (1899–1902), Russia's hard line in Manchuria during the Boxer Rebellion (1900–1901), and the German naval program administered rude shocks to Britain's containment policy. The Boer War stretched British capabilities to the limit and exposed political restrictions beyond which no government could afford to go. Rising levels of social spending resulting from the urbanization and democratization of British society and the refusal to increase taxation to levels approaching those on the continent placed a severe strain on the national budget. The dilemma was a simple one—either reduce global responsibilities or increase defense outlays at the expense of social services. Since neither policy was politically palatable, Britain embarked during the financial crisis of 1901–1905 on a third course: "through a combination of treaties, appeasement, and wishful thinking, the threats to which the empire was exposed were deemed to have been miraculously reduced."[19]

The Boxer Rebellion brought about a massive Russian intervention in Manchuria and created the prospect that the Manchurian plan, linking the Chinese Eastern Railroad with the Liaotung Peninsula, would eventually be annexed. This was unacceptable to Japan, if only because the annexation of Manchuria would put unbearable pressure on Korea, where Russian ambitions remained unchecked. In August 1900, Aritomo Yamagata, the most influential member of the military establishment, wrote that "we could no longer sleep undisturbed" if Korea fell under Russian control, and that the time had come to occupy it "to put a stop to Russia's southward movements in advance."[20] In October, a new cabinet was formed including as foreign minister, Takaaki Kato, an "avowed enemy of Russia."[21] From that day began an explicit mutual understanding that the two "island empires"[22] had a common interest in containing Russian expansion. The realization in London and Tokyo that this understanding should be formalized in an alliance would represent a fundamental departure in both British and Japanese foreign policy. It was truly paradoxical that at the very time it became possible for the first time to contain Russian expansion on a truly global scale from the Scandinavian Sound to the Korea Strait, Britain was about to abandon containment for an alliance of the flanking powers directed against Germany.

A containment policy is never free from some ambiguity. Britain looked to Japan to form in Manchuria an indestructible barrier to Russian expansion, because it was impossible for Britain to project decisive power so far north without a native population to form a local army, as in India. But Britain also had an interest in letting Russia apply continued pressure in the Pacific frontier. The statement by Arthur Balfour, the deputy prime minister in Salisbury's cabinet, in February 1896 that Britain would welcome a commercial outlet for Russia on the Pacific that would not be ice-bound half the year may not have been a lapse in geopolitical judgment. Russian expansion in Manchuria and its ambitions in Korea committed Japan to oppose them and created an additional theater for a containment policy, as if to bear out Admiral Mahan's advice that such a theater would force "Russia to engage herself so deeply in Manchuria that she would have neither the time nor money to spend on Constantinople or the Persian Gulf."[23] Russian expansion helped create a distraction, no longer within the Heartland to be sure, but already in the Coastland; Russian commitments there might be expected to reduce Russian pressure in other strategic theaters. No one could anticipate the future, of course, but some British statesmen may have remembered the pamphlet of 1807 that had suggested that Russia's commitments in the Coastlands in fact weakened its overall strategic posture because they exposed Russia's forward positions to devastating naval attacks, and, if they were close enough to a maritime core area, to a counter offensive on land as well.

As the Boer War went on, as overextension and inadequate resources imposed financial retrenchment, and as the rise of peripheral navies brought home the unpleasant fact that Britain would cease to be the balancer in a global international system and would have to become an equal partner, cultivating the friendship of a dynamic naval power was becoming the only way to reconcile a policy of economy with a policy of resistance to Russia. It would also allow Britain to redeploy its naval force from the China Sea to the Atlantic and the Channel to face the growing German threat. In July 1901, Francis Bertie, the head of the Asiatic Department of the Foreign Office (1898–1902), floated the idea that

Britain might give Japan naval assistance to resist a Russian occupation of Korea in exchange for Japanese *military and naval aid*[24] to resist foreign aggression in the Yangtse valley and South China. The idea of an Anglo-Japanese alliance was born.

It remained Japan's official position that an agreement with Russia was possible only if the Japanese were given a free hand in Korea. The peninsula was for Japan what Belgium was for Britain—one of those vital interests over which no compromise was possible: its occupation would give Russia an advanced position, a "proruption," from which to threaten the Japanese archipelago. In view of Russia's own unwillingness to compromise, there was no alternative to an alliance with Britain. That same month, in July 1901, General Katsura, the prime minister, stated his conviction that Russia would not stop with the occupation of Manchuria but would extend its influence into Korea "until there is no room left for us," and that it was Britain's policy to let Japan resist Russian expansion while its hands were tied in South Africa. In December, the head of political affairs in the Foreign Ministry declared that "the fate of Korea is a matter of life and death for us," and that Japan must not shrink from war. But it also needed an alliance with Britain to help contain the Russian advance into China, an alliance in which Japan would not be a junior partner, "since there are grounds for believing that Britain had already passed her zenith and will to some extent tend to decline."[25]

The Anglo-Japanese alliance was signed in January 1902, the only long-term alliance entered into by Britain between 1815 and 1914. It pledged both powers to take indispensable measures to strengthen their special interests, Britain's in China, Japan's in Korea. In the event either power was at war with Russia, the other would remain neutral and would enter the war only if Russia was joined by another power. In essence, the alliance was directed against Russia and France. It also contained a secret clause providing mutual facilities for the docking and coaling of warships and for the maintenance by each power, "so far as may be possible," of a naval force for concentration in Far Eastern waters superior to that of any third power. In May, the Japanese acquired a preponderant position at Masampo, "the Gibraltar of the Korea Strait."[26] By 1903, when their naval program reached completion, they held the balance between the Russo-French and British squadrons and were in a position to dominate naval politics in the region. It was a striking victory in the history of containment, but the true victor was not Britain, it was Japan.

These developments were in sharp contrast to the conviction in British India that the Russians would take advantage of Britain's overcommitments to move against Afghanistan. In March 1898, General (now Lord) Roberts had declared Russia could enter Afghanistan whenever it wished, and "the chance of her attacking us is being discussed in every bazaar in India."[27] In December 1901, Balfour, now the leader of the House of Commons, said that "a quarrel with Russia anywhere, about anything, means the invasion of India,"[28] an extraordinary confession of insecurity coupled with a totally unjustified overestimation of Russian power and capabilities. But even the War Office accepted in 1902 the principle that "in fighting for India, England will be fighting for her Imperial existence."[29]

And yet, while British India was seeking to overcome its own deep-seated insecurity by drawing up plans for a counteroffensive in Afghanistan, the new foreign secretary, Lord Lansdowne, was preparing the ground for the abandonment of northern Persia to the Russians. In a memorandum sent to Sir Arthur Hardinge, the minister in Tehran, reminiscent of Salisbury's statement concerning Turkey in 1897, he noted that "if Persia should elect to encourage the advance of Russian political influence and intervention," Britain would have to reconsider its policy of maintaining the independence and integrity of Persia. The new policy would give formal recognition to the fact that Russia possessed "a superior interest" in northern Persia while Britain had built "a substantial and preeminent mercantile position"[30] in the south. Britain was about to abandon its containment policy in Persia in favor of an alliance with Russia, and this new alliance of the flanking powers would impose a partition on Persia similar to the one they had imposed on China in 1899.

By 1903, the British government was beginning to acquire "a fuller sense of Britain's liability in the event of war with Russia and the magnitude of the military assistance which India would undoubtedly require."[31] The straits had ceased to be a decisive point in the containment of Russia. In February, the Committee on Imperial Defense concluded that in the present situation, when France and Russia were allies, it would make no difference if Russia gained possession of Constantinople and free egress from the Black Sea: "the maintenance of the status quo as regards Constantinople is not one of [Britain's] primary interests."[32] If northern Persia was also going to be abandoned to the Russians, there was a risk that Britain's entire strategic position along the Heartland's periphery from the straits to the Hindu Kush would collapse. The only alternative capable of staving off this dismal prospect was to join the Franco-Russian alliance.

The transition was facilitated by a shift in French policy. The foreign minister, Théophile Delcassé, was an ardent Anglophile, convinced that an "adroit flirtation"[33] with Britain would be more profitable to French interests than continued hostility. His judgment showed a solid understanding of geopolitical realities. An agreement with Britain, which Italy might be induced to join, would unify most of the European Coastland to form a single flanking power in alliance with Russia. Anglo-French negotiations were in full swing in the spring of 1903 to settle a broad range of colonial questions. An exchange of visits between Edward VII and President Loubet in May and August sealed the reconciliation. But the Russians still had to be brought into it, and the outlook was not promising at first. The Russo-Japanese war that began in February 1904 created considerable strains, the Russians blaming the British alliance with Japan for Japan's dynamic containment of the Russian advance into Manchuria. And the entente cordiale was almost a hostile act by France against its Russian partner, which found itself, in the midst of an unpopular war, without allies (unless one counts Germany, but its friendship was poisonous).

But events were taking their appointed course, despite anxiety in some quarters about the implications of the diplomatic revolution. The Coastland powers' containment policy had always been hostage to attempts by a continental power to establish hegemony. When the danger had come from France, Britain and Russia had discovered that geography created a "natural and eternal alliance" between them. The danger now came from Germany, whose restlessness across the Heartland's periphery created the greatest threat to the affairs of Europe since Napoleon's invasion of the Heartland 100 years earlier. Projections of a Russo-German alliance, even if entertained at the highest levels, did not make any sense: such an alliance would create a mortal danger for France, and that was not in Russia's interest. An Anglo-German alliance made no more sense: it might help contain Russia, but it would also destroy France, and that was not in Britain's interest. Pitt's and Palmerston's vision was no longer realistic after Germany's unification. Even the opponents of geographic determinism must concede that the emergence of a powerful and dynamic Germany had created by 1905 a natural alliance between Russia and the Coastland powers and that its prerequisite was an Anglo-French reconciliation.

Epilogue, 1905–1917

The decisive event of 1905 was, of course, the September Treaty of Portsmouth that brought an end to the Russo-Japanese war and gave Japan military and naval hegemony in the Pacific frontier. From then on, the containment of Russia in that strategic theater became independent of British wishes. Thus it happened that soon after it became a global enterprise under British leadership, the containment of Russia broke up, under the impact of conflicting interests, into three policies, in three separate theaters, managed from three headquarters: Tokyo, Calcutta, and London.

In London, the emphasis was on the redeployment of the Royal Navy in the Channel to cope with the increasing German threat. Britain was adopting the most concentrated form of fleet-in-being strategy, designed not only to keep the new German navy confined to the North Sea, but, if possible, to destroy it there. This required closing the China station and curtailing the Mediterranean fleet, but tripling the navy's strength in the Channel, the North Sea, and the Atlantic. The destruction of the Russian fleet at Tsushima in May 1905 had eliminated Russian naval power in the Far East; the entente cordiale had ended the Anglo-French rivalry in the Mediterranean. The decisive point had shifted to the North Sea, but the enemy was no longer Russia. It was Germany.

In Calcutta, the perpetual anxiety of the British Indian establishment was aroused to new heights by developments in Afghanistan. A younger emir, who had come to power in 1901, refused to collect the subsidy and declined to visit the viceroy. An envoy was sent to him when the Russo-Japanese war broke out, and "all Kabul knew that the Amir had declined to visit India and that India had visited him."[34] British India pledged in March 1905 to defend the Afghan borders against Russia, but left unresolved the question of how precisely to defend them. Lord Kitchener, the commander in chief in India, drafted a program requiring reinforcements from Britain and the stationing of five divisions in the Kabul area in the event of a Russian invasion. London had its doubts about the logistics of the enterprise, but could not ignore the eventuality of renewed Russian pressures after the completion in October 1904 of the Orenburg-Tashkent railroad, which could bring large numbers of troops within 400 miles of Kabul.

An exaggerated fear that containment might collapse on the Hindu Kush prompted new negotiations with the Japanese to strengthen the alliance of 1902. In March 1905, a Conservative member of the House of Commons, Claude Lowther, called for a renewal "on a stronger basis," a euphemism in those days of illusion for a policy of retrenchment bent on entrusting the defense of British interests to newly emerging peripheral powers. Sending British troops to India was unacceptable because it would require the introduction of "conscription, a system which would never be tolerated in this country, because it was wholly alien to the British character."[35] The only way out of the impasse was to ask Japan to send an army of perhaps 150,000 to India to deter the Russian threat. The director of naval intelligence gave his support, and the Foreign Office was even ready to seek Japanese military support in Persia, but Calcutta felt that sending Japanese troops to India would not be "consistent with our dignity or self-respect."[36]

Tokyo had no interests in Persia and declined the offer, but formally agreed in August to join Britain in a defensive war against Russia in India in return for Britain's pledge to side with Japan in a similar war against Russia in "East Asia" and to recognize Japan's "paramount political, military, and economic interests in Korea." Since Russia had just been eliminated as a naval power in Asia, the Japanese navy had become the strongest navy in the region, and the Japanese army had made a strong showing against the Russians, the alliance in fact abandoned the containment of Russia and the protection of British trade in the China Sea to the Japanese military establishment. The consequences of the agreement were immediately felt. By the end of 1905, the China station had been closed, its five battleships withdrawn to reinforce the Channel fleet, and the Japanese ministry of foreign affairs had assumed the "control and direction" of Korea's external relations. The Japanese assumed the leadership of Russia's containment, but the Chinese, in their slow-moving way and despite the worsening of the rotting process, were not far behind. The whole of Kirin province had been opened to Chinese colonization in 1902, to be followed by the northernmost province of Heilungkiang in 1906, the year when a special office for the colonization of Mongolia was created in Peking. China adopted its own form of containment by flooding the Russo-Chinese frontier in Manchuria with Chinese settlers and enterprising merchants who slowly but inexorably threatened to keep the Russians "penned back" behind the Amur.

A curious situation was beginning to emerge: Calcutta and Tokyo were determined to keep Russia contained in the Monsoon Coastland, one behind the Hindu Kush, the other out of the China Sea, while London was ready to abandon containment in the European Coastland in favor of an alliance of the flanking powers. In the fall of 1905, France took the lead in negotiating a large international loan to cover the Russian deficit, and Britain joined the effort in April 1906. The alliance was never formalized but had become a fact. The following year witnessed the final abandonment of containment in the European Coastland. Containment, it is true, never had a linear objective, except for the Heartland's periphery, beyond which the Russian advance would be met with a declaration of war. But where was Russia to be contained within the Heartland? Containment had depended everywhere on an alliance between Britain and the core areas, Sweden, Turkey, and Persia, as well as Austria, capable of maintaining a relatively permanent political isobar on Russia's frontiers with those core areas. Seen from this perspective, containment had been losing ground for a long time. More realistically, containment could also try to keep the isobar along the inner boundary of the core areas, thereby maintaining their territorial integrity and formal independence. Such a policy had been successful in the Baltic and in the basin of the Black Sea, in the latter case largely because the frontier was so complex and Ottoman resistance had been so stubborn. But as the Russians threatened to penetrate Anatolia, and German influence, unfriendly to both Britain and Russia, became dominant at Constantinople, the old containment policy was losing its purpose. And in Persia, it had been a failure for nearly a century, as Russia kept using Persia to contain Britain behind the Hindu Kush.

The acceleration of the Anglo-German naval race—after the launching of the Dreadnought caused an outpouring of Anglophobia in Germany and increased British perceptions of an imminent danger sufficient to override sentimental reservations about Russian domestic behavior—was the catalyst that compelled London to jettison the foundations of its Russian policy followed since 1815. In August 1907, the two powers settled their differences. Russia recognized Britain's protectorate in Afghanistan, but Persia was partitioned, very much as China had been in 1899, into three zones, with the middle (neutral) zone containing the Gulf coast and the oil fields. The partition was severely criticized by Lord Curzon, who had accepted it in principle in 1899, because the Russian zone was much larger than the one he had proposed. It gave Russia control of all but one of the Persian trade routes with Central Asia and India and extended its

influence quite close to the great Zagros chain from Suleimanieh (Sulay-
maniyah) to Kerman, "where each separate mountain group (is) another
Caucasus."[37] That same year, Lord Grey, the new foreign secretary, told
the Russian ambassador that "England must no longer make it a settled
object of policy to maintain the existing arrangement with regard to the
passage of the Dardanelles."[38] Britain's conviction that the North Sea was
the decisive point had resulted in a drastic reassessment of its global
responsibilities. The Russians understood the importance of that decisive
point for London and how they could use it to extort further concessions:
three years later, in October 1910, Foreign Minister Sergei Sazonov
would declare that "the English, pursuing as they do vital aims in Europe,
will if necessary sacrifice certain interests in Asia in order to maintain the
Convention [of 1907] with us."[39]

Similar developments were taking place in the Far East. Reconciliation
with the Russians in the European Coastland left the Japanese alone to
face the Russians in the Russo-Chinese frontier. The Japanese had a
geopolitical choice, the same choice Britain had had in its long relationship with Russia. They could band with China in an attempt to unify the
sinocentric universe of the Monsoon Coastland in order to contain Russia along the Altai and the Sayan Mountains, and eventually even the
Iablonoi and Stanovoi ranges; or they could seek an alliance of the flanking powers—Japan and Russia—against China. The first option was premature—China was about to disintegrate, its standing among the
imperialist powers from the European Coastland gave it little freedom of
action, and Japanese exclusiveness could not overcome the powerful current of sinocentrism in the Monsoon Coastland east of the Himalayas.
China's disintegration had the same effect on Japanese policy as Ottoman
and Persian disintegration had had on British policy, and if there was no
equivalent of the German danger as a catalyst, there was the lurking possibility that China's eventual renewal would challenge Japan's claims on
Manchuria and Korea. Moreover, the Anglo-Russian rapprochement canceled out the need for the Anglo-Japanese alliance.

In July 1907, Tokyo and Petersburg signed their first secret convention
for the partition of Manchuria recognizing "the natural gravitation of
interests and of political and economic activity" in the region. Japan
asserted its dominant interests in the Liao valley to the watershed with the
valley of the Amur and its exclusive interests in Korea in return for giving
Russia a free hand beyond the watershed and in Outer Mongolia. The
convention contained Russia within the basin of the Amur, from which the
only exit was now Vladivostok on the "closed" Sea of Japan. The Japanese
then proceeded to transform Korea—annexed to the Japanese Empire in
August 1910—into "a solid ammunition dump and camp, for the prompt
reception and outfitting of an army of one million, shuttled over from the
Japanese islands."[40] The ultimate purpose of this strategic offensive was, in
the words of the Russian commander of the Amur military district in
October 1909, to establish an hegemony over the eastern shore of the Asi-

atic mainland, "to paralyze any development by us of the lands lying east of Lake Baikal and to reduce them to a colonial position."[41]

Japan's policy of dynamic containment also sought to bring about a rapprochement with Russia. Both powers felt threatened by American ambitions in Manchuria—the "open door" policy and the attempt to internationalize railroad building—and they signed a second convention in July 1910 to defend their "special interests." It created an informal alliance of the flanking powers against China. After the Manchu dynasty collapsed in the fall of 1911, a long struggle began between Russia and China for the control of Outer Mongolia. Russia's gains gave it access to Inner Mongolia, the proximate zone of the Russo-Chinese frontier along the Great Wall, but the Japanese determination to contain the Russian advance was incorporated into the third convention of July 1912. It effectively blocked a possible Russian move toward Peking via Urga and Kalgan, and implicitly asserted a Japanese claim to protect the Chinese capital.

There now existed a tacit agreement between Japan and Russia to divide the Russo-Chinese frontier among themselves. There, as elsewhere, an alliance of the flanking powers invited the Russian advance, and the Russians took full advantage of their opportunities in Outer Mongolia. The outbreak of the First World War gave Japan the opportunity to seize Germany's possessions in China and to impose its famous Twenty-One Demands on China in January 1915. Britain's retrenchment accelerated, and the world was treated to an unprecedented spectacle—but it was the logical outcome of developments in the Monsoon Coastland for the past twenty years—as Britain requested the Japanese navy first to assume the protection of its maritime trade east of Singapore and, later, to provide additional assistance to patrol the seas in the Indian Ocean and the South Atlantic. Russia too became dependent on Japan. When the war broke out, only some 90,000 Russian troops were stationed along the Chinese Eastern Railroad, and some had to be withdrawn, thereby weakening Russia's entire strategic position in Manchuria. Russia asked for three Japanese army corps to be sent to the European theater. But the Japanese refused to commit ground troops. They would agree only to sell rifles and ammunition, and here their contribution to the Russian war effort was substantial. Russia also needed to be reassured that its Far Eastern possessions were secure against the possibility of a Sino-Japanese combination that would doom its presence in the Amur basin. Such was the purpose of the proposed Russo-Japanese alliance of August 1914 confirming previous conventions and providing for Japanese assistance in the event of a Chinese attack on Russian possessions. The Japanese demurred and also refused a Russian offer of a quadruple alliance against Germany. As long as the issue of the European war remained in doubt, they were obviously hedging their bets.

By late 1915, German successes followed by the stabilization of the western front led some Japanese leaders, including the powerful Yamagata, to fear that a European settlement might bring about an anti-Japanese coalition in alliance with China, which Japan had insistently kept out of the war. Such a coalition might also work against Russian interests, and the two powers joined hands in the alliance of July 1916. The Japanese wanted a strong defensive-offensive arrangement binding each party to come to the aid of the other, but the Russians agreed only on condition that they receive the support of their other allies. Deep suspicions of each other's motives remained ineradicable, because both sides recognized that the political isobar established by the three conventions would remain but a temporary accommodation until both governments could afford to resume their struggle for hegemony. On the eve of the Russian Revolution, Russia had been both contained and invited to expand, an unstable situation that was bound not to last. With the disintegration of the Russian state, the Japanese proceeded to fulfill the true mission of a sea power in the Pacific frontier. They intervened in Siberia in August 1918, rolling back Russian power as far as Lake Baikal, behind the Heartland's periphery. Unlike the great K'ang-hsi emperor, who had missed the chance in 1689, the Japanese did not miss theirs.

While the "natural" Russo-Japanese antagonism, rooted in solid and unchanging geopolitical foundations, was mitigated in part by a temporary alliance of the flanking powers, the Anglo-French containment policy in the European Coastland, pursued at various times for 200 years at cross-purposes and seldom in unison, was collapsing. The sultan closed the straits in September 1914, a month after signing a defensive alliance with Germany. Russia, Britain, and France declared war on Turkey in November, and Russia seized the opportunity to press the Coastland powers for the straits as spoils of war. By then, Britain was ready to oblige: George V told Count Benckendorf, the Russian ambassador, immediately after the declaration of war that "Constantinople should be yours."[42] In March 1915, Britain and France agreed to the cession at the peace settlement of Constantinople, the Bosphorus, and the western coast of the Dardanelles. In exchange, Russia agreed to the incorporation of the neutral zone in Persia into Britain's sphere of influence. No one seems to have asked whether the Turks and the Persians would accept the partition of their ancestral lands, and much was taken for granted. Nevertheless, both Coastland powers had agreed to let Russia establish itself at the most sensitive exit from the Heartland and along the Heartland's periphery in Persia. Containment had ended in failure.

Containment in the north European plain was expected to suffer the same fate. In the event of a successful war against Germany, Britain would destroy its navy and cripple its industry, France would reassert its influence in the continental Coastland. Russian expectations were far ranging. As far back as 1892, Giers had asked Alexander III what Russia would gain by helping the French to destroy Germany. The tsar had answered that Germany as such would cease to exist and would be broken up into small states, "the way it used to be." The breakup of Germany would bring Russian influence to the Elbe in a defeated Prussia. Giers mused that the tsar believed he would then become "the master of the world."[43] What a striking convergence of minds, that of Alexander III in 1892 and that of Mackinder in 1904, sharing the same geopolitical vision of the future—the unification of the Heartland under Russian leadership facing a Britain in full retrenchment. We know that a Russian "grand design" included the restoration of Poland to the Oder; the breakup of Hungary, its northern provinces annexed to Russia; and the creation of a kingdom of the Czechs under a Russian prince. No wonder that the *Manchester Guardian* could editorialize on August 1, 1914, "if Russia wins" the coming war, "there will be the greatest disturbance of the Balance of Power that the world has ever seen."[44]

Containment had been a policy designed first and foremost to prevent a Russian hegemony in the Heartland. Its practitioners were several, both in the Heartland and in the Coastlands flanking it. Carried out across enormous distances, containment could not be physically coordinated until after the 1870s, when internal strains caused it to fall apart. It fell apart where it had begun, in the Monsoon Coastland in the 1860s and then in the European Coastland fifty years later, although the Austro-German alliance succeeded in containing Russia in the Balkans and Japan contained it in the Amur basin. The First World War brought about the disintegration of the Russian core area, the Second the quasi-unification of the Heartland under Soviet leadership, challenging the United States to assume with its overwhelming power what had been the mission of France and China, Britain and Japan, and to maintain the age-old balance between Heartland and Coastlands.

Conclusion

Expansion, 1700–1796

In 1700, Russia was not a threatened state. Sweden was blocking access to the Baltic by occupying the mouths of the Neva, the Narova, and the Dvina, but had traced a line of an optimum of conquest from Lake Peipus to Lake Ladoga, leaving the Novgorod depression in Russian hands. The Saxon dynasty, recently established in Warsaw, could not help Poland recover from the disasters of 1660 and 1667. Only in the south was the proximate frontier zone of the Russian core area kept in a state of permanent insecurity by the incursions of the Crimean Tatars backed by the power of the Ottoman Porte, but the Tatars could no longer hope to destabilize the core area. Safavid Persia was in full disintegration and in no position to threaten the Russian stronghold in Astrakhan. And the Manchu dynasty was occupied with the governing of China; its only interest in the north was to keep the Russians from the Amur and the Zunghars from the Great Wall.

The sources of Russian expansion must be sought instead in the internal dynamism of the core area—in a dew dynasty that inherited the ambitions of its predecessor and claimed the inheritance of the Teutonic Order in the west, the Byzantine Empire in the valley of the Dniepr, and the Chingissid dynasty in the steppe from the Crimea to Mongolia; in the formation of a strong ruling class and the consolidation of serfdom; in a political-religious ideology strengthened by the Schism that sanctified the secular power; in a yearning for contacts with the world of the European Coastland that promised to give Russia the tools of modernization, blocked but also filtered by the Poles and the Swedes; and in a commitment to economic

347

Conclusion

development and military reforms in order to gain a strategic superiority over the enemies of yesterday on the Western and Southern frontiers. All these factors combined to create a core area of exceptional strength, possessing enough energy to create a slow but irresistible expansionist urge that would remain unabated until 1917. The expansion did not follow a pendulum movement as it is often alleged—shifting from one frontier to another when it encountered the insuperable resistance of another core area—unless we look only at the more dramatic events. The pressure was permanent and general, patiently creating a "fringe of settlement" or a political fringe that kept driving outward the "temporary stop of a movement"; and the forward movement was encouraged by the receding power and influence of the rival core areas.

Peter I's foreign policy was dominated by fiscal considerations. A powerful state could not be built without fiscal resources, and money was the sinew of war. Only trade could give Russia the precious metals and precious stones in which it was still deficient, and fiscal considerations had to shape a forward policy toward Sweden, the Ottomans, Persia, and China. The urge toward a warm-water port and the pursuit of "strategic interests" were subordinated to the need to tap the resources of international trade. Russia had a strategic interest in the Gulf of Finland chiefly because access to it would allow a diversion of the commercial traffic with Britain and Holland from distant and inhospitable Arkhangelsk to a closer and more accessible location. And the escape from the old capital to a new one on the Gulf marked a commitment to modernization and eventual integration into the Coastland economy.

The thrust of Russian expansion in the seventeenth century had focused on the Southern and Eastern frontiers. But the Ottomans remained too strong. Azov gave access to a shallow sea, the Crimea was impregnable, and Moldavia was an abyss. The Russians made no headway in the Russo-Turkish frontier. Their first great success was the Treaty of Nerchinsk. They had crossed the Heartland's periphery and retained a base in it, the more valuable because the approaches to the Amur contained lead and silver mines. The caravan trade pursued clearly fiscal interests: Siberian furs would be exchanged for bullion and costly silks. And the Orthodox Church gained a foothold in Peking, there to minister to the spiritual needs of the traders and gather political intelligence. The Manchus had imposed a settlement that would keep Russia away from the Amur for 170 years, but it would not prevent the Russians from following up their establishment in the Coastland with building a naval presence. On the contrary, it encouraged maritime expansion by deflecting their thrust from the southeast to the northeast.

The concerted assault on Sweden was intended to take advantage of a favorable situation—the accession of a young and inexperienced king. Instead, it turned into a long drawn-out war that would occupy most of Peter's reign. The war became Russia's baptism of fire in the struggle for breaking out of a landlocked core area into the basin of the Baltic and reaching the periphery of the Heartland. The long effort spurred industrial development and an unprecedented military and naval buildup that eventually forced Sweden to negotiate to avoid surrender. The occupation of the Baltic provinces was the first and decisive step in wresting the Baltic frontier from Swedish control. Trade with the Coastland powers was rerouted through the Sound to Petersburg and substantially increased. Poland was an even greater loser, its economy left in shambles and its dynasty discredited.

The war also created unease in northern Germany, where a Prussian core area had been emerging between the Elbe and the Oder. No other power in the northern German plain could challenge Russian ambitions to project power and influence to the valley of the Elbe, and the specter of Russian troops in Stralsund, Lübeck, and Hamburg seemed to portend the continuation of a forward policy toward the Heartland's periphery. Prussia was still weak, and deception became the hallmark of its policy in a frantic attempt to avoid allying itself with a power that might end up on the losing side. Britain, however, despite its dependence on Russian naval stores, which contributed substantial revenues to the Russian treasury, was already determined to block Russia's access to the periphery, whether in Sweden, in the Sound, or in the valley of the Elbe. Its strong stand and the superiority of its navy forced Russia to desist from any ambitions to turn the Baltic into a closed sea and the riparian powers into satellites of the new Russian Empire.

The war with Sweden was barely over when Peter turned against Persia to take advantage of another favorable situation—the Afghan invasion and the overthrow of the Safavid dynasty. This was no eastward shift of the pendulum. An attempt had already been made against Khiva five years earlier; there had been recurrent conflicts between Russian traders and the shah's Caucasian subjects; Georgian and Armenian "men of power" were reassessing the value of their allegiance to their overlords in Isfahan. The war's objective was commercial—to capture Persia's silk and caviar trade. Success was temporary, however: climatic conditions, logistical difficulties, and Peter's death would soon force the Russians to withdraw. They would not reoccupy Persia's northern provinces until the beginning of the twentieth century. By 1725, then, an extraordinary expenditure of energy had enabled Russia to establish its superiority on the Western Frontier and the Russo-Persian segment of the Southern Frontier. But Russia's very success also compelled Prussia and the Coastland powers, chiefly Britain, to grope for the outline of a containment policy that would keep Russia at a safe distance from the Heartland's' periphery.

One would expect the decade that followed Peter's death to have been a time of retrenchment, what with the struggle for power among the ruling elite and an economic crisis caused by heavy expenditures during Peter's campaigns. The Treaty of Kiakhta (1727) confirmed Russia's retrenchment in the Monsoon Coastland and its recognition of China's superior power, but the first Bering expedition (1725–1730) opened up new possibilities in the northern Pacific. The Austrian alliance of 1726 looked to the past and to the future—it restored a natural alliance against the infidel and laid the ground for joint operations, the Russians advancing along the Dniepr, the Austrians along the Danube. And in Poland and Sweden, the elements of a destabilization policy were being worked out— the defense of "liberties" to encourage the rotting process, the opposition to the establishment of a strong and hereditary dynasty, the systematic bribery to encourage men of power to pursue a pro-Russian policy and, in the Polish Empire at least, to win over the leaders of large clans and patronage networks in Lithuania and the Right-Bank Ukraine. Across the entire frontier from Sweden to China a patient effort was at work to probe for soft spots where the receding influence of rival core areas invited a Russian entrance. Nowhere was this more in evidence than in the Kazakh steppe, where the elaboration of a system of defensive military lines was preparing the way for a forward policy in the frontier.

The decade was barely over when the Polish succession crisis compelled Russia to reactivate a forceful policy against the rival core areas. The crisis also provided an opportunity to strike a blow against France's containment policy. In the eighteenth century, France pursued a consistent containment of the Russian advance, although its major enemy was Austria, at least until 1756. The containment of Austria was also the containment of Russia, and the Austro-Russian alliance was not directed against the Ottomans alone. Having chosen to solve its strategic dilemma by opting to become a chiefly continental power, France could contain Russia only by diplomatic means—by forging alliances with Sweden, Poland, Prussia, and the Ottomans. But such a system contained the seeds of its own destruction because it purported to reconcile irreconcilable interests, notably in Poland. A Polish king with strong support in France and Sweden was unacceptable to Petersburg and Berlin. The Russians intervened to maintain the bankrupt Saxon dynasty and consolidate their influence in an increasingly destabilized Polish Empire. A preponderant Russian influence in Stockholm and Warsaw would knock out two of the four props of France's containment policy.

The Polish question was inextricably linked with the future of Russo-Ottoman relations. The Ottomans wanted the Russians out of the Polish Empire because the Right-Bank Ukraine was the invasion route from Kiev to Moldavia, the Prut, and the Danube. But their determination to resist a reviving Persia, from which the Russians safely withdrew in 1735 on the eve of Nadir Shah's victory, committed large forces to their eastern front, and they were unable to intervene in the Polish crisis of 1733–1734. It also gave the Russians a unique opportunity to attack them on their western front with a reasonable chance of success. The Ottoman Empire retained much of its old strength, however, and even a joint Austro-Russian offensive could not break their hold on the Russo-Turkish frontier. The Crimea, like Moldavia, was an abyss from which the Russian army might never return. The Peace of Belgrade (1739) was a disappointment.

Nevertheless, it confirmed Russia's growing power. Peter had not been able to hold Azov and had suffered a humiliating defeat on the Prut, but the army of the Empress Anna had occupied the Crimea, returned to Moldavia and taken Russia deeper into the frontier, to the borders of the Crimean khanate. Military lines and Cossack settlements there and in the Kazakh steppe created a fringe of settlement that turned the frontier zones outward and drew Russian power toward the opposite core areas in search of a line of an optimum of conquest. These projections of power into the Russo-Polish and Russo-Turkish frontier were the first steps in the realization of a vast design aiming at the incorporation of the entire frontier into the Russian Empire, and it was already clear that the Russians had allies who would facilitate their advance, if only because this served their interests—the Orthodox in Bielorussia, Lithuania, and the Right-Bank Ukraine, and the Greek clergy in Moldavia and Wallachia. There is much truth in the characterization of Russian foreign policy as one exhibiting a "matchless simplicity of conception and persistence of effort."[1] Geography created definite corridors of expansion; a particular structure of human zones shaped by ecology predetermined the stages of the Russian advance; and the immense energy of a core area in the fullness of youth kept challenging the resistance of core areas that had passed their prime.

The 1740s witnessed ominous developments. The destabilization of Sweden had not prevented the war party, supported by France, from taking advantage of the difficult transition from Anna's to Elizabeth's reign to make war on Russia in the vain hope of regaining what had been lost at Nystad. The attempt failed, but exposed the vulnerability of Petersburg and resulted in Russia's advance to the lake district of Finland. At the other end of the empire, the disintegration of the Zunghar confederation prompted Peking to destroy its nomadic enemy in the west. Two decades of widespread turbulence in the Russo-Chinese frontier caused Russia to reinforce its military presence in western Siberia, at the very time the acquisition of the Altai gold mines by the government created a powerful interest for the maintenance of peace. The completion of the Siberian lines from the mouth of the Ural River to the confluence of the Bukhtarma with the Irtysh caught the Kazakh hordes in a pincer movement that pushed them toward the Russian settlements behind the lines, and announced the creation of fringes of settlement drawing the Russians into the Kazakh steppe-ocean.

As if the war on the Western Frontier and the threat of war in the Eastern Frontier were not enough, developments in the valley of the Oder, between Poland and the Heartland's periphery, were causing growing concern in Petersburg. Frederick II was set on transforming Prussia into a dynamic core area, the only one of its kind on Russia's continental horizon. The strength and consistency of their reaction to the rise of Prussia testified to the Russians' innate geopolitical sense. The alliance with Austria and the protectorate over Poland and Saxony gave them the hope of extending their influence to the valley of the Elbe. A dynamic and expansionist Prussia bent on containing Russian expansion destroyed that hope. And even if it cooperated in the destabilization of the Polish Empire, its location and ambitions made Prussia into a potential rival. It was then that Russia's deep-seated hostility to Prussia began, and no subsequent dynastic marriages and expressions of eternal friendship could alter that fundamental fact. The Prussian danger grew worse following the diplomatic revolution of 1756, when Britain replaced France as Prussia's protector and source of subsidies. For an alliance of two dynamic and expansionist core areas, one in the Heartland, the other in the Coastland, magnified the ability of each to contain Russian expansion. The Seven Years War failed to destroy Prussia, but the failure could not conceal the fact that the energy that had propelled Russia's advance so consistently and so successfully in the direction of the Heartland's periphery since 1700 had run against the countervailing energy of two core areas bound in an unwritten alliance against France and Russia.

The reign of Catherine II witnessed a major breakthrough in Russia's advance into the Western and Southern frontiers. There was little apparent movement in the east, where Russian energies were directed toward the creation of an economic, military, and administrative infrastructure without which the return to a forward policy against China would have been doomed from the start. The appointment in Irkutsk of a separate governor, later a governor general, with jurisdiction over the entire Mongolian segment of the frontier; the growth of Omsk as a military headquarters; the effort to develop the Ural, Altai, and Nerchinsk mines; the surveying of the frontier districts; and the occasional projections of power into the Kazakh steppe, not only engaged the energies of the managing elite but stored additional energy for use at a later time, when the countervailing power of the Chinese core area would begin to show the first signs of weakness.

In the Western and Southern frontiers, the ruling elite, flushed by its successful performance against a European power for the first time since the Northern War, returned to the offensive. It was encouraged by an ambitious empress, eager to establish her legitimacy, and by the continuing economic development that placed Russia among the leading economic powers of the day and made it the unchallenged leader in the Heartland. There was little originality in Catherine's foreign policy. Like that of ancient Rome, its chief features were "secular tenacity and feeble creativity."[2] Geography had predetermined the directions of the Russian advance. There remained to be exploited a shifting balance of power to force the rival core areas to retreat until a new political isobar was established, a new and temporary equipoise across the frontiers.

The flight of Russian peasants across the Dvina and the Dniepr had created a fringe of settlement. Chernyshev advocated in 1763 the stationing of Russian troops in it, while disclaiming any intention of annexing additional territory. Russia's second intervention in 1764 placed a Polish-born puppet on the Polish throne, and the appointment of hard-line proconsuls in Warsaw made it clear that Russia was claiming the entire Polish Empire as a protectorate. A forward policy in Poland had, once again, repercussions in the Southern Frontier, and brought about an Ottoman declaration of war. The Turkish War of 1768–1774 resulted in a dramatic transformation of the Russian position. For the first time, the Ottomans suffered a string of defeats despite their stubborn resistance, and even Austria had to abandon its cherished goal of keeping the Russians away from the Danube: the Austro-Prussian antagonism and the Russo-Prussian alliance made a concerted Germanic action impossible and gave Petersburg the opportunity to checkmate both Berlin and Vienna. The war was successful not only on land but at sea. Russia inaugurated a fleet-in-being strategy to project naval power from the Baltic across the Coastland to the Aegean Sea. Britain had perceived the Russian danger in the 1710s and 1750s. It now chose to ignore it and even welcomed Russian victories: deeply sunk as it was in Francophobia, anything that would knock out the Ottoman prop of France's containment policy would also contribute to the weakening of Britain's old enemy.

The Treaty of Kuchuk Kainardji (1774) was a great Russian victory. The first partition of Poland (1772) had been a recognition of Russia's inability to exploit a favorable geopolitical situation to maximum advantage. Access to the northern shores of the Black Sea opened up the empty steppe to colonization, but the annexation of the valley of the Dniepr north of Kiev and of the middle Dvina conceded Prussia's and Austria's right to demand a partial Russian withdrawal from Poland. Geography created a perverse logic for the Russians: the more they advanced into the Russo-Polish frontier, the more they would have to withdraw from the Polish core area. This unpleasant discovery was partly offset by the Teschen agreement (1779) establishing Russia's right to mediate disputes between Austria and Prussia. Their re-emergence as containing powers was accompanied by a cooling off of Anglo-Russian relations: Russia's refusal to help Britain in North America meant a death sentence for its fleet-in-being strategy. There would be no more projections of Russian naval power on the high seas until the disastrous expedition of 1905.

The offensive begun in the 1760s continued in the 1780s. The annexation of the Crimea (1783) gave a suitable location for the building of a Black Sea navy and opened up the Kuban steppe to colonization. The alliance with Georgia that same year and the founding of Vladikavkaz in 1784 advanced a claim to a preponderant influence in the Transcaucasian proruption from which Petersburg could checkmate Constantinople and Tehran. But Russia's rapid approach to the Heartland's periphery finally evoked in Britain a reaction similar to its determination to prevent the destruction of Sweden during the Northern War and the transformation of the Baltic Sea into a closed sea. The development of Russian trade in the Levant, where France was still strong, and the commercial treaty with France in 1783, the year the American frontier freed itself from the dominion of the English core area, forced Britain to face additional losses in its trade with Russia and to give a new priority to the Black Sea theater. The Turkish war of 1787–1792 was therefore unwelcome, and the prospect of another Russian victory on the scale of Kuchuk Kainardji more than alarming—it might have to be opposed by force. Another such victory would go far toward uniting the basin of the Black Sea under Russian suzerainty. Potemkin's ambitions in Moldavia and the Right-Bank Ukraine were well known. These lands contained the valleys of the Prut, the Dniestr, and the Southern Bug. If they could be wrested from the Poles and the Ottomans, Russia's sway would extend from the Danube to the Kura, and warships from Sevastopol would patrol the Black Sea and threaten Constantinople. These factors gave Ochakov an exceptional strategic importance.

The war ended in a modest victory. Ochakov was annexed, but not without Russia finding itself on the brink of a war with Britain and Prussia. The siege of Ochakov re-invigorated the Anglo-Prussian alliance and strengthened Frederick William II's determination to oppose Russia by force. Domestic opposition in Britain and awareness of Catherine's willingness to take up the challenge preserved the peace, but Russia had to withdraw from the Polish core area once again, while advancing into the frontier. The second and third partitions gave it the entire frontier, the core area to Prussia and Austria. Meanwhile, the Swedes, who had avoided a similar partition by restoring the effective power of their monarchy in 1772 and had taken advantage of the Turkish war to attack the Russians in 1788, discovered that Finland was slipping out of their control. Men of power there, as in Lithuania and the Right-Bank Ukraine, were beginning to look to the east to safeguard their interests.

The extraordinary energy generated by the Russian core area during the last decade of Catherine's reign was felt along the entire frontier. The destruction of the Polish Empire was barely completed when the empress contemplated another war with the Ottomans and launched an expedition against Persia reminiscent of Peter's campaign in 1722. As far away as the Monsoon Coastland, Shelikhov and his company were dreaming of a commercial empire, and Laxman visited Hokkaido on the first official mission to establish relations with Japan. Catherine and the Ch'ien-lung emperor died the same year (1796); Imperial Russia was about to become a global power while Manchu China entered a long period of decline.

Consolidation, 1797–1879

By destroying the international status quo, the expansion of revolutionary France created additional scope for the expenditure of Russian energies, and as the Russians continued to advance into the frontier zones they had to consider new strategies to deal with the core areas in both Heartland and Coastland.

It had been Catherine's intention to turn Prussia and Austria outward and transform them into Russia's agent for the restoration of order and the territorial status quo in the Coastland, but the Germanic powers were unable to cope with the French Revolution's improvised armies. Russia then entered the fray in alliance with Britain, but neither naval operations in Holland nor the ambitious attempt to invade France in 1799—reminiscent of the 1748 expedition—could break France's growing strength. The Second Coalition broke up in disarray at the end of 1800. Meanwhile, the French expedition to Egypt, a part of the Ottoman Empire which was France's traditional ally against Austria and Russia, seemed to signal a dramatic reversal of French policy, and a fearful Porte sought an ally in Russia. The result was the agreement of 1799 giving Russia the right to send warships from the Black Sea through the straits and, by extension, to maintain a naval presence in the eastern Mediterranean. A naval presence required bases: the Ionian Islands were placed under joint Russo-Ottoman jurisdiction in 1800. In addition, the Russians staked a claim to Malta, controlling the passage from the eastern to the western Mediterranean. Elsewhere in the Southern Frontier, the Russians first declared Eastern Georgia to be in their exclusive sphere of influence (1799), then annexed it two years later. And in the Far East, the creation of the Russian-American Company (1799) gave the government the leading role in the shaping of a commercial and naval policy in the northern Pacific from the Kuriles to Alaska. In both the Southern and Eastern frontiers, the Russians were breaking through the constraints of the Heartland's periphery and projecting power in the Coastlands for the first time in their history.

But a strategic advance also created dilemmas, and nowhere more clearly than in Russia's relations with the Ottomans. The Black Sea was a "closed sea" because the Ottomans controlled both shores of the straits. Sending warships into the Mediterranean required their agreement. They could not be expected to give it if the Russians continued to advance into the Russo-Turkish frontier, either in Western Georgia or in the Danubian Principalities. Moreover, the pursuit of a fleet-in-being strategy was certain to be countered by a similar strategy in France and Britain. It was not in Russia's interest to let the Coastland powers penetrate the Black Sea and thereby expose Russian ports to attack. Nor was it in Russia's interest to permit them to build bases in the remaining frontier zones. The situation was different in the Sound: the Baltic could not be a closed sea, even if the Russians wanted to think it was, because Sweden and Denmark shared the control of the shores and they were hardly on friendly terms. In addition, Petersburg was well defended against a naval attack by a fortress-fleet strategy in the Gulf of Finland. Therefore, Russia's fleet-in-being strategy on the Southern Frontier was doomed from the start. The straits would continue to bar Russia's access to the Mediterranean in Russia's own interest.

While Russia was at peace with France Between 1801 and 1805 and tried to consolidate its newly won position in the Mediterranean, expansion proceeded apace in Transcaucasia from the Georgian proruption, causing anxiety in Constantinople, Tehran, and London. The Russians circumnavigated the globe in 1803–1804, and another mission sought to open up Japan, again in vain. The Kiakhta trade was revived after a long interruption during Catherine's reign, but a formal embassy sent to Peking in 1805 failed against China's insistence that Russia was not an equal but a tributary state. Another dilemma was creeping up in Russia's relations with the Monsoon Coastland. Crossing the Heartland's periphery had been a great success, but Russia's possessions could not be supplied from Siberia. Their location in the Coastland made them dependent on the Chinese and Japanese economy. But China had been a containing power since the 1680s, and Japan was potentially an even greater one because its destiny was at sea. The determination to open Japan and China to Russian trade was bound to be counterproductive; the stronger the Russians became in the valley of the Amur and on the Pacific rim, the greater the resistance of at least one of the Coastland powers was certain to be and, paradoxically, the greater the exposure of those settlements to the currents of economic, political, and cultural exchanges in the Pacific, with their subversive influence on Russia's fundamentalist conservatism. As in the straits, retrenchment rather than continuous expansion might be the lesser evil.

War with France was renewed in 1805, this time for the control of the German lands. Two years later, Russia, Austria, and Prussia had been defeated and French troops had reached the Niemen. The aggrandizement of the French core area to the Rhine and of the French Empire to the Elbe and the Dinaric Alps created a new frontier between an expansionist France and an expansionist Russia, and required the establishment of a political isobar along the zones of maximum pressure on each side. To create a neutral zone between the Elbe and the Niemen would have been the safest solution, but one incompatible with the dynamism of the two empires. Napoleon took the offensive and claimed for France a dominant role in the western segment of the Heartland between the Baltic and the Adriatic, thereby upsetting the natural balance between Heartland and Coastland. The conquest of Finland (1809) served Russia's interests well; it had long been planned to guarantee the security of Petersburg from the landward. And a new "equilibrium of the North" seemed to be in the making with the election of a French marshal to the Swedish throne (1810). But the partial dismemberment of Prussia and the partial restoration of the Polish core area shifted the isobar dramatically to the east and threatened Russia's vital interests. Russia's response was to prepare for a showdown to roll back the French behind the Elbe and establish Russian hegemony on the frontier.

Defeat on the battlefield did not slow the continuous and relentless expenditure of energy from the core area, but helped Russia solve one of its dilemmas. The French had been active in Constantinople and Tehran, and Russia was again at war with the Ottomans in 1806. The war and the peace of Tilsit with Napoleon (1807) eliminated Russia as a serious Mediterranean power, leaving it free to resume the advance into the frontier. The

Russians reached the Prut in 1812 and made progress in Serbia and inroads into Western Georgia. They also fought the Persians at the same time, reaching the Araks in 1813, in the direction of the old and profitable caravan route from Trebizond to Tabriz across Western Armenia. The impending conflict with Napoleon restored the alliance of the flanking powers, Russia and Britain, and when Napoleon forced the issue and lost, Russia assumed the leadership of a coalition of Heartland powers, including Sweden, to destroy the Napoleonic Empire. It all ended with the Allies' entry into Paris in 1814.

But Russia's advance into the Coastland was no more acceptable to Britain than France's advance into the Heartland had been acceptable to Russia, and the natural balance of Heartland and Coastland reasserted itself. France became a satellite of Britain, Prussia a satellite of Russia. A truncated Polish core area was incorporated into the Russian Empire, projecting Russian power to within striking distance of the Oder and placing East Prussia, Silesia, and Hungary at Russia's mercy, while Austria sought to hide its dependence on Russia by assuming the leadership of a reactionary crusade against all manifestations of revolutionary spirit. Russia turned Sweden, Prussia, and Austria outward. It did so by granting Norway to Sweden; by letting Prussia establish a strong base in the Rhineland; and by supporting Austria's Italian ambitions. Russia's influence, if not power, reached the Heartland's periphery from the Kjølen to the Dinaric Alps.

If the Russians had reason to be satisfied in the west, where the new political isobar followed the Heartland's periphery and was maintained by British power, their energy continued to manifest itself on the Southern Frontier—where the Greek question was about to open a Pandora's box of geopolitical challenges—as well as on the Eastern Frontier. The proclamation of a fortress-fleet strategy along the Kurils in 1821 was an important step toward closing the Sea of Okhotsk. The Caspian Sea, closed by nature but not to British ambitions, was likewise declared closed in 1813, and the Russians had tacitly acknowledged in 1809 that the Black Sea was indeed closed. The elaboration of a global defensive strategy was obviously in the making, but such a defensive close-border policy did not preclude the pursuit of a forward policy on land. The division of the Kazakh steppe into districts beginning in 1822 created forward positions as far south as the Aral Sea and Lake Balkhash on which an infrastructure of military forts would later be built. The Russian advance was about to slow down, after the extraordinary expenditure of energy that had begun in the 1760s, but it would not stop. It would continue to probe along lines of least resistance from the Barents Sea to the Sea of Japan.

There is no greater misreading of Nicholas I's foreign policy than to see it dominated by the pursuit of "honor," by respect for treaties and the determination to maintain the status quo. His reign was no doubt a conservative age, if only because the victories of 1814–1815 had created a new balance between the two global powers, Britain in the Coastland,

Russia in the Heartland, and within both Coastland and Heartland steady enough to last for two generations. But the determination to conserve what had been acquired did not stop the continuing expenditure of energy that had brought the Russians to a new political isobar. That energy simply focused on other areas where a distinction had not yet been clearly made between an ideal and a realistic line of an optimum of conquest.

Rivalry over the Danubian Principalities and the Greek question invited the Russian advance into the Southern Frontier, despite the fact that the tsar, who made so much of the defense of legitimism, found himself supporting subjects who were rebelling against the sultan, their legitimate ruler. He was no natural friend of national movements—there were too many "red bonnets"[3] among them—but they destabilized the frontier and might even shake the foundations of a rival core area. His championing of the Principalities and Serbia served the goal of Russian expansion to the Heartland's periphery and resulted in another war with the Ottomans. In 1768, 1787, and 1806, they were the one who had declared war; the Russians now took the initiative. They occupied Adrianople and Erzerum, and Russian troops stood for a brief moment on the threshold of the Turkish core area. The Treaty of Adrianople (1829) gave them the delta of the Danube, Akhaltsykh, and the Black Sea coast to Poti. They were even ready to strike at the Austrian core area, should Vienna decide to block their crossing of the Danube. The Tiflis headquarters was already flexing its muscles; there were Russian agents in Khorasan seeking out men of power willing to destabilize the Kajar dynasty. And when that dynasty went to war, it suffered a crushing defeat at Turkmanchai (1828). The Russians gained Erevan, incorporated de facto the Caspian Sea into the Russian Empire, and imposed an extraterritorial regime on Tehran. So much for the maintenance of the status quo.

The 1830s witnessed Russia's attempts to consolidate its hegemony in the Southern Frontier, as it already had in the Western Frontier after 1815. There, the crushing of the Polish rebellion, caused in large part by the bullying tactics of a grand duke impervious to notions of honor, let alone of Polish self-respect; the fortification of the Åland Islands and the probings in Finnmark; and the new power relationship with Prussia and Austria, removed any doubt that Russia's position was unchallengeable, at least for a time. When the pasha of Egypt threatened the sultan's throne, the Porte's reaction was the same as in 1799. Unkiar Skelesi (1833) promised to recreate the old dilemma between supporting the Porte and continuing the advance into the frontier. But for the time being, the treaties of Adrianople and Unkiar Skelesi—for the two formed a whole—gave Russia one of its most brilliant victories. Its agility in the choice of methods and disregard of "honor" —its support of rebels against the sultan in Serbia, the Principalities, and Greece in order to gain territorial concessions, and then the support of legitimism against a rebellious pasha—made it clear that Russia's energies had not abated and that it would go on pursuing relentlessly its long-held geopolitical objectives—

reaching the Heartland's periphery. No wonder a French admiral stationed in the Levant could write in 1839 that "Muscovite diplomacy in general makes few mistakes; no other has such clear objectives and embraces a vaster horizon." The Russians are both "artful and strong" (*caressants et forts*).[4]

Russian energies were not directed against the Ottomans alone. Persia, like Sweden, Prussia, and Austria, had to be turned outward to serve Russian interests and directed against the other "strait," the Khyber Pass of the Hindu Kush. The founding of the Asheradeh station in 1837, the incitement of Persian ambitions against Herat in 1838 and again in 1854, the Khiva expedition of 1839—these were only the major signposts of a forward policy in "Asia" that had little to do with the maintenance of the status quo but undermined it systematically, until frontier and core area had been so destabilized that they would invite the Russian advance. By the mid-1850s, the great enveloping movement facing Central Asia was completed, with Russian forts on the Syr Darya and the approaches to the Tien Shan Mountains. Russia was even beginning to probe the weaknesses of Manchu China, already exposed by the Opium War (1839–1842). Explorations were preparing the way for the advance into the Amur valley. The appointment of Muravev (1847) was designed to take advantage of a rapidly changing situation on the Eastern Frontier.

Faced with such manifestations of overwhelming power and seemingly irresistible energy, the Germanic powers could do little to resume their historic mission—the containment of Russian expansion. The 1848 revolutions showed that Russian hegemony was not to be trifled with. The ultimatums to Berlin in 1848 and 1850 and the invasion of Hungary in 1849 (even at Austria's request) demonstrated that Petersburg could make its will felt all the way to the Heartland's periphery. But the very success of Russia's foreign policy within the Heartland strengthened Britain's determination to draw a line along the periphery that the Russians could cross only at the risk of war. Its most sensitive spot was the Turkish Straits, because their control determined the fate of the Balkan frontier, the Turkish core area, and the geopolitics of the Eastern Mediterranean. From a geopolitical point of view, the Crimean War was no accident. Had it not been for Russia's relentless pressure on the Southern Frontier and its hegemony on the Western Frontier, which created a potential threat against Sweden, it is unlikely that an Anglo-French-Ottoman-Austrian coalition would have been possible. And only a massive backlash against Russian ambitions could have resulted in the punitive terms of the Peace of Paris in 1856.

The Russians had to accept the demilitarization of the Åland Islands and the neutralization of the Black Sea; they had to withdraw from the delta of the Danube; and they paused to take stock of their losses and nurse the wound inflicted by an Austria determined after twenty-five years of humiliation to resume its mission to contain Russia behind the Prut. But as the intensity of the Russian presence abated in the Western and

Southern frontiers, the destabilization of the Eastern Frontier following the Opium War drew the Russians to the mouth of the Amur, into the Coastland north of the river, and along the Sea of Japan. Putiatin finally opened up Japan (1855) and negotiated Russia's adherence to China's treaties with Britain and France that gave foreigners access to more ports and to the interior. Muravev obtained the cession of the left bank of the Amur and the Maritime Province (1858–1860). This immense expansion of Russian power in the Pacific Coastland was more than enough compensation for the losses in the Southern Frontier. And the Russians could rejoice as early as 1859 at Austria's defeat in northern Italy.

The advance to the mouth of the Amur was almost an anticlimax—it had been frustrated for so long. So was the conquest of Central Asia, meaning essentially the Tien Shan massif with its spurs surrounding Kokand and the headwaters of the Syr Darya, the valley of the Amu Darya to the approaches of the Hindu Kush, and the Karakum Desert to the Kopet Dag. Geopolitically, the Russians were consolidating their position by occupying the hinterland of the Aral and Caspian seas in Central Asia, as well as the hinterland of the Sea of Okhotsk they had dominated for so long. Preparations had been made in the 1850s for a concerted attack from the Orenburg and Irtysh lines. The new exuberance of the Tiflis headquarters following the crushing of Shamil's resistance in the Caucasus added a third thrust along the Kopet Dag in the direction of Merv and the Afghan border. It is remarkable that the entire domestic reforms of the 1860s and the new commitment to industrialization did not absorb Russia's energies but instead continued to channel those energies outward. Indeed, that commitment was certain to intensify the expansionist urge. With the need for Central Asian cotton, for the export of grain through the Turkish Straits in order to pay for imports of manufactured goods and rolling stock through the Sound and the Gulf of Finland, a secure access to the Coastland became increasingly important. Moreover, the need to supplement the scarce resources of eastern Siberia in manpower and food required an extension of Russia's possessions in the Pacific Coastland and a diversion of their trade patterns toward the Heartland.

Tashkent fell in 1865, Kokand and Bukhara in 1868. The Russians reached the approaches to the Pamirs, the "roof of the world." An uprising broke out in Chinese Turkestan (1864), prompting a Russian decision to round out the conquest of Central Asia by annexing the entire basin of Lake Balkhash along the northern slopes of the Tien Shan range. By so doing, Russia invaded the sensitive frontier between the inner and outer periphery of the Heartland, where a political isobar would have to be created with China. This was no less the case in the Far East as well. The founding of Vladivostok (1860), the Tsushima incident (1861), and the hope the Russians might benefit from the "rotting process" in Japan were so many signs that they were pursuing a fortress-fleet strategy along the Kuril and Japanese archipelago, behind which they would then seek to extend their control over the entire valley of the Amur, including the still sparsely populated but rich Manchurian plain. However, the collapse of the Tokugawa government and the emergence of a new Japanese government in 1868 promised to revolutionize the geopolitics of the Monsoon Coastland.

Russian energies were simultaneously exerting pressure in the Balkan frontier, but with less success. The transfer of Ignatev from Peking to Constantinople in 1864 was a measure of Russia's ambitions. He would pursue a Pan-Christian and Pan-Slav policy seeking to bring all Slavs (or at least the southern Slavs, because the Poles, if not the Czechs, were resistant to Russian blandishments), Catholic and Orthodox, under the protection of the Russian eagle, thereby destabilizing not only the Ottoman Empire but the Austrian Empire as well. Austria's defeat in 1866 and Hungary's victory in 1867 were signs the Austrian Empire was affected by the rotting process; this needed to be encouraged. But there were difficulties on the path of Russia's expansion. A Pan-Slav policy made sense only as long as it remained destructive—it could not build anything because there was no Slav common interest. The Russian economy and that of the Balkan frontier were not complementary; they were even competitive, as in the case of Ukrainian and Rumanian grain. And most important, the men of power in the Balkans, despite their profession of the Orthodox faith, looked to Russia only to expel the Ottomans. For the future of their frontier zones they turned to Austria, France, and the new Germany rising on the horizon. Such a state of affairs would favor a containment policy and guarantee that the Balkan frontier would never become the inner frontier of the Russian Empire.

Darker clouds gathered in the 1870s. The Russian offensive began with the official rejection of the Black Sea's neutralization and the support for a Bulgarian exarchate (1870) that first exposed the inner contradictions of a Pan-Slav policy. Khiva was conquered in 1873, but under British pressure that same year the Russians had to accept the Amu Darya as Afghanistan's northern border. The Japanese penetration of Korea began, and Russia had to surrender the Kuril archipelago (1875) in exchange for the occupation of the whole of Sakhalin. Its fortress-fleet strategy along the outer perimeter of the Coastland had been destroyed; Japan controlled the exits from the "narrow seas" and placed Vladivostok in jeopardy. Japanese economic power was certain to redress the balance between Coastland and Heartland and maintain the outward orientation of Manchuria, in direct opposition to Russian ambitions. A Chinese counteroffensive was on the way to Turkestan, and Russia had to surrender in 1881 most of what it had occupied in the Ili valley in 1870.

And in 1875 Bosnia-Herzegovina exploded in the Balkans, leading by stages to the Russo-Ottoman war of 1877–1878. Russia won the war but lost the peace, largely as a result of an informal coalition of Britain, Austria, and Germany, transformed in 1871 into a powerful core area destined to generate an immense energy of its own. Russia's new geopolitical situation in Central Asia enabled it to test the political isobar with British

India between the Zulfikar Pass and the Amu Darya, in preparation for an eventual gigantic pincer movement against Britain's positions in the straits and India. But Britain's reaction kept the Russians out of Afghanistan, and the Congress of Berlin (1878) kept them out of the Aegean Sea. And in 1879, Germany and Austria formed their fateful alliance, creating a single Germanic core area facing the Russian Empire across the Balkan frontier. Russian expansion encountered for the first time a global containment policy pursued in tacit alliance by a reinvigorated Germanic core area, a Britain at the height of its power, and a Japan in the full vigor of a new youth.

Renewed Pressures, 1879–1917

Expansion had created uneasiness in the eighteenth century, both among the Germanic and Coastland powers, as the Russians advanced methodically into the frontier zones and staked a claim to join the concert of European core areas represented by France and Britain, Prussia and Austria. But vital interests were not yet threatened. Peter's formidable Baltic navy began to rot away after his death, and Russia never developed a merchant marine. The Heartland's periphery was safe in the north. Expansion went hand in hand with the aggrandizement of Prussia and Austria; the valley of the Elbe remained beyond Russia's reach. The Russo-Turkish frontier was vast and complex and studded with Ottoman fortresses; it was a long way to the straits. And the Russian eastern push was still beyond the ken of the containing powers. Uneasiness turned to anxiety in the early nineteenth century after a successful coalition of flanking powers—Russia, Prussia, and Austria on the one hand, Britain on the other—destroyed the power of France and gave Russia a preponderant influence in Sweden and hegemony over Prussia and Austria. Russia's formidable power was reaching the Heartland's periphery in the Baltic, the valley of the Elbe, and the corridor to the Dinaric Alps. Anxiety turned to fear when the Russians, under the cover of ambiguous declarations, sought to cross the Heartland's periphery in the Southern Frontier.

The Crimean War and the Congress of Berlin were milestones in a new containment policy to oppose an insuperable barrier to the continuing expenditure of Russian energies in the persistent effort to reach the periphery. Germany would become the dominant power in the Baltic, Turkey in the Black Sea. Rumania bound itself to the Central Powers (1883) and the Russians lost their bid for hegemony in Bulgaria (1885). Austria occupied Bosnia-Herzegovina, and Serbia moved into Vienna's orbit. Germanic influence advanced toward Salonika and Constantinople, dashing Russia's hopes. And Britain began to move the center of gravity of its eastern Mediterranean policy from the Straits to Egypt and the Suez Canal. Russia had to recognize a realistic line of an optimum of conquest that fell far short of its original goal.

But its energies continued to press in the direction of the Heartland's periphery elsewhere, until a definite political isobar could be created by the countervailing force of a containing power. A Cossack Brigade was sent to Tehran in 1879 and became the only organized military force to support the shah, who had to pledge in 1887 not to build railroads in Persia without Russian permission. The Pendjdeh crisis (1885) almost caused a war with Britain, but resulted instead in the demarcation of Afghanistan. Following this and the demarcation agreements with China (1882–1884) Russia's energies lapped against the foothills of the Hindu Kush, stopped at the Zungharian Gate, and remained safely behind the inner periphery in Mongolia. But the Tiflis headquarters, which had just obtained Kars and Ardahan from the Ottomans, had vast ambitions to destabilize British India by raising the banner of anticolonialism and stirring up the murky politics of the Northwest Frontier. And in Siberia, pressure was mounting for shortening the interior lines of the Heartland and building a railway to the periphery and even beyond, to the Sea of Japan. Without it, Russian possessions in the Coastland were certain to enter the Japanese orbit. In the Far East, a political isobar was nowhere in sight.

Such is the explanation for the concentration of Russian energies on the Manchurian and Pacific segments of the Eastern Frontier during the last decade of the nineteenth century. The decision to build a Trans-Siberian railway (1891) not only channeled those energies eastward but provoked Japan to work out a containment policy to block Russia from building a self-supporting position in the Coastland and, failing this, to checkmate the Russians by neutralizing their fortress-fleet strategy. The Russians knew the consequences of their decision; their geopolitical sense already told them Russia's danger would grow with Japanese power. Russo-Japanese relations after 1868 were fated to be marked by an enmity as persistent as that which characterized Russia's relations with Prussia-Germany after 1740.

Japan's elimination of China as a military and naval power in Korea and Manchuria during the war of 1894–1895 caused a strong reaction in Petersburg and strengthened the conviction that Japan was out to keep the Russians from the Yellow Sea and the approaches to Peking. Russia's energies had always been focused on gaining a preponderant influence in the core area's capital—to defend legitimism and encourage the rotting process it was necessary to have the ear of the dynasty and those men of power with a vested interest in shoring it up. They used diplomatic pressure to force the Japanese to abandon the Liaotung Peninsula and presented themselves as the saviors of China. They then formed an alliance with the dynasty against Japan and gained a lease to build a railroad linking Chita on the very periphery of the Heartland to Vladivostok (1896), with a branch to Port Arthur on which they gained the same lease (1898) they had forced the Japanese to give up in 1895. The two lines were intended to form the communication infrastructure of Manchuria and to turn the rich Coastland zone inward as a source of food and raw materials for the Siberian Heartland. The logic of Russian expansion transformed Korea into the strategic prize, not so much for the pursuit of a fleet-in-being strategy against Japan as for the completion of a new fortress-fleet strategy, no longer along the Kuril-Japan archipelago, but along the Vladivostok-Port Arthur supply line. The Russians needed a base in southern Korea, and we find them exploring the possibility of establishing one at Masampo (1899). The last year of the century also witnessed the Anglo-Russian partition of China, Britain recognizing Russia's predominant influence north of the Great Wall, in Inner and Outer Mongolia and the whole of Manchuria.

Russian energies were actively at work in the Southern Frontier as well. The rotting process was slowly destroying the Kajar dynasty, and British India was contemplating in 1899 a partition of Persia along a line that would equalize the pressure between Russian ambitions and British resistance. The Russians were penetrating Seistan and appearing on the Persian Gulf. The nationalist movement then threw the shah in Russia's arms. Even in its relations with the European Coastland, Petersburg was finding enough energy to use the rising threat of Germany to strike a blow against the containment policy of Britain and the Central Powers. The rapprochement with France was but another manifestation of Russia's natural tendency to form with a Coastland power an alliance of flanking powers against a continental power threatening both. It was the first stage in the encirclement of Germany that would save the Russian core area during the First World War.

But it was in the Far East that competing energies had to clash before a new political isobar could be created. The Japanese insisted that Korea was a vital interest; the Russians refused to concede the point and accept a compromise recognizing their preponderant influence in Manchuria in exchange for abandoning Korea. Their obstinacy was unwise but understandable. Only a protectorate over Korea could guarantee the security of their protectorate over Manchuria. The rivalry was settled by war, and a political isobar was finally achieved across Manchuria, separating the valley of the Sungari and Amur from that of the Liao, giving Korea and the southern half of Sakhalin to Japan. Russian energies had run up against a wall of resistance they could not overcome.

There remained the need to give the new political isobar formal recognition in bilateral agreements. The Russian high command had not given up the hope of engaging the Japanese in a second round for hegemony in Manchuria, but more pressing events in the Balkans compelled Petersburg to give priority to relations with the Central and Coastland powers. Russia and Japan partitioned Manchuria in 1907. The Chinese Eastern Railway and northern Manchuria remained in Russian hands, but the strong Japanese presence in the south and the annexation of Korea three years later checkmated the Russian advance toward Peking. The Russians also faced a more insidious danger. Northern Manchuria was opened to

Chinese colonization in 1906, the same year an office for the colonization of Mongolia was established in Peking. The Japanese were not yet seen as a colonial power; the Russians were, and Japan's victory in 1905 showed the white man's power had passed its zenith. From that time on, Russian possessions in the Far East were at the mercy of the powers of the Monsoon Coastland, whose mission was to support the natural affinity of the valley of the Amur with the Pacific. Russia's refusal, for sound political reasons, to let the maritime powers turn them into a new California doomed its future in the Pacific basin.

The year 1907 was also the year of Persia's partition with Britain. That partition was a victory for Russia because it forced Britain to abandon its insistence on Persia's territorial integrity. It also compelled Russia to abandon its attempts to establish a presence on the Persian Gulf and left the oil fields in the neutral zone, later incorporated into the British zone (1915). But the partition recognized the existence of a political isobar running along the approaches to the Zagros Mountains and confirmed the permanence of the isobar created twenty years earlier along the approaches to the Hindu Kush. Russia had reached the ideal line of an optimum of conquest along the Heartland's periphery. The two partitions—of Manchuria and of Persia—had global geopolitical repercussions. The rapprochement with Britain destroyed Britain's containment policy and completed the alliance of the flanking powers against Germany, pooling the resources of global empires—the Russian Empire on the one hand, the European Coastland powers and their overseas colonies on the other—against a destabilizing Germany unable to escape its destiny to remain a regional power despite its immense economic resources. It also destroyed the original Anglo-Japanese alliance, designed to contain Russia's expansion into frontier zones where Britain could project little power, and paved the way for a Russo-Japanese alliance directed not only against China but also against Germany.

Turbulence in the Balkan frontier kept calling into question the permanence of the isobar established in the 1880s. Austrian and German policy took an aggressive turn in 1906, on the eve of the Persian and Manchurian partitions. Austria annexed Bosnia-Herzegovina to block the creation of a Greater Serbia (1908). The Young Turk revolution (1909) sought to revitalize the Ottoman Empire and welcomed German influence, already paramount in Constantinople. The growth of German economic power in Anatolia gave a new urgency to the Straits question and threatened Russia's possessions in Transcaucasia, where the Armenian question kept drawing Russian energies toward Erzerum and the watershed with the Euphrates. Germany's willingness to risk war in 1909 to support Austria's forward policy in the Balkans challenged Russian energies to renew the pressure in the direction of the Dinaric Alps and the Straits, the Heartland's periphery.

Two events became catalysts in that renewal—the Tripolitan war with Italy and the collapse of the Manchu dynasty (1911). The Porte closed the straits to Russian commercial shipping, exposing a major weakness in Russia's economic position in the Black Sea, a weakness no great power could accept because its vital interests were at stake. But the Turks' poor showing against the Italians convinced Serbia and Bulgaria the time had finally come to expel them from the Balkans. The Revolution of 1905, despite the severe blow it dealt to the Romanov house, had not slowed the expenditure of energy. The dynasty was, after all, only one element in the mix that had released an expansionist impulse for so long. It seemed the Russians might even duplicate the success of 1828–1833: do a second Unkiar Skelesi by supporting the sultan against the Italians, then support Bulgaria and Serbia against him—that was the hidden purpose of Charykov's program. But history never quite repeats itself. The straits and Balkan questions had become so internationalized that a daring Russian move would have provoked a general war. The Balkan war did expel the Turks from the frontier and strengthened the Russo-Serbian rapprochement that had begun in 1903. It also released new energy in the Tiflis headquarters, where the prospect of the unification of Armenia under Russian leadership began to gain increasing attention. The rivalry to create a durable political isobar between Russia, the Central Powers, and the Turks was taking an ominous turn. And in distant Mongolia, the sudden disappearance of the Manchus invited Russian penetration of the Selenga basin to the Gobi Desert, the Heartland's outer periphery. On the eve of the First World War, the Russian advance had resumed.

It has been claimed that Germany's growing economic and military might was putting Russia on the defensive to such an extent that it would be unable to regain the initiative, its energies stalemated in Europe and Asia. Such a view reflects the pessimistic attitude of the Russian high command after the war against Japan and disregards the strength, persistence, and resilience of the energy that had propelled the Russian advance in the direction of the Heartland for two centuries. When statesmanship was still an art and a noble profession, Lord Salisbury had written to a viceroy of India, "You listen too much to the soldiers. . . . You should never trust experts. If you believe the doctors, nothing is wholesome; if you believe the theologians, nothing is innocent; if you believe the soldiers, nothing is safe."[5] The Russians, it is true, suffered defeat in Poland, Lithuania, and Kurland, but after three years of war, the Central Powers had not even reached Minsk and remained behind the Zbruch. Charles XII had made it to Poltava, Napoleon to Moscow, and Hitler would approach Petersburg and Moscow and take Kiev and Rostov after six months of war. It was by no means certain at the beginning of 1917 that the Russians would lose the war.

Despite their reverses at the beginning of the war, the Russians were preparing to consolidate their position on the Heartland's periphery. A railroad to Murmansk would allow them to outflank the Kjølen. The entire Polish core area would be incorporated into the empire. The agreement with Britain and France (1915) conceded the Straits, with Constantinople a free city; the partition of Anatolia (1916), Western Armenia. And a broad offensive was in progress to expel the Germans from the Baltic provinces and the old Russo-Polish frontier and resettle there masses of Russian peasants from the overpopulated provinces and, at the end of the war, demobilized soldiers. And not only there. It was discovered that local conditions would favor a similar resettlement along the Anatolian coast as far west as Samsun and in Western Armenia around Erzerum, Bitlis, and Van, while the Cossacks of the Kuban and Don would find a new home on the headwaters of the Euphrates. The Russians incorporated their Persian zone into the empire (1915) and obtained the inclusion of the Zulfikar Pass leading to Seistan and western Afghanistan. The Russo-Japanese alliance (1916) contributed military assistance to the war effort and gave Russia a free hand in Outer Mongolia and Turkestan, where Kuropatkin, whose interest went back to the 1860s, spoke of "rectifying" the boundaries to advance them to the Heartland's outer periphery. These were not the goals of a political establishment that had lost its nerve and was mesmerized by the German danger. Only the Bolshevik Revolution brought about the collapse of the Russian core area and the drastic retrenchment of 1918 that also marked the victory of a containment policy in all three frontiers. The greatest threat to Russian foreign policy in 1917 was in its exceeding a line of an optimum of conquest.

Where was such a line to be found? A difficult question to answer, but one the Russians had to face when the First World War broke out.

The Russians were a people of the plain, who built on the margin of the Byzantine and Mongol civilizations a core area straddling a center of hydrographic divergence. Rivers created a logic of westward, southward, and eastward expansion in search of furs, salt, metals, and better land. Beginning in the eighteenth century, the dynasty and its ruling elite, aware of the decline of Sweden, Poland, Turkey, and Persia, began to stake a claim to the inheritance of those once powerful political and military entities. The resulting shift in the balance of power throughout the Eurasian continent encouraged the Russian advance. Russian expansion was no sudden and forceful *Griff nach der Weltmacht*, but the slow advance of fringes of peasant, Cossack, and military settlement across an open plain until it encountered mountains and the sea, resistance, and the countervailing power of those and other core areas. Mountains were the great obstacle for a people of the plain, not only physical but economic and psychological as well. They discouraged extensive agriculture and favored pastoralism; confined movement and narrowed the horizon. The great, almost continuous, chain stretching from the Dinaric Alps to the northern shores of the Sea of Okhotsk created a nearly impassable barrier. It could easily be crossed in only four places: the Turkish Straits, the Khyber Pass, the Zungharian Gate, and the Khilok valley.

The great trek across the open plain also led to the sea, but the sea was not welcome. It was an even greater obstacle to continued expansion. The sea separates, while the land binds. It carried the voyager toward alien shores, where the transition would work toward dissolving the allegiance to the fundamentalist conservatism that is both the great strength and the great weakness of the Russians. The sea also brought subversive influences into the core area, dangerous to the stability of the political order—unless the sea could be "closed." The Russians tried to close the narrow seas along the Heartland's periphery—the Baltic, the Black Sea, and the Sea of Okhotsk—and create a ring fence to support a fortress-fleet strategy capable of protecting their shores, not only against a naval attack, but against a political presence by maritime powers that would inevitably carry subversive ideas. The narrow seas and the mountains thus created a drag toward the core area similar to the undertow formed by a wave crashing against a physical barrier.

As the Russians advanced into the frontier zones, they sought to control those relatively rare locations in an otherwise undistinguished landscape suitable for the creation of power bases around which to build an administrative, political, and military infrastructure that would protect their gains while they continued their advance into a great plain that kept inviting them. The tension between the compulsion to advance created by relentless native energies, an open plain, and the slowly shifting balance of power on the one hand, and Russian caution on the other, was partially caught by Palmerston, who declared in 1860 that "the Russian government perpetually declares that Russia wants no increases of territory, that the Russian dominions are already too large. But while making these declarations in the most solemn manner, (it) every year adds large tracts of territory to the Russian dominions . . . not for the purpose of adding territory but carefully directed to occupation of certain strategical points, as starting points for further encroachments or as posts from whence some neighboring states may be kept under control or may be threatened with invasion."[6]

In their advance, the Russians pursued an inclusive policy, reflecting confidence in their own strength and the certainty of their success. They formed alliances with the men of power in the frontier zones, whose allegiance was shifting with the balance of power, and made them part of the ruling elite. These men, in turn, like the lowly Cossacks who were always the pathfinders of Russian expansion, relayed Russian energies deeper into the frontier. There inevitably had to come a time when the advance would reach the threshold of the Heartland core areas. Only then did the question arise of where to establish a line of an optimum conquest. The Russians alone were not free to define where it lay. The Heartland's periphery imposed an ultimate physical limit to Russian expansion, because it was the great divide between continental and maritime civilizations. The Russians had no chance to establish a successful presence in the Coastlands, not only because the values of maritime civilizations, for all their diversity, were antithetical to their own, but also because such a presence was certain to be seen as a vital threat to the Coastland powers.

A line of an optimum of conquest had to run within the Heartland along a political isobar equalizing the pressure of Russian energies with the resistance of core areas guarding the landward approaches to the periphery, supported by the Coastland powers guarding those on the seaward. Such an isobar had been created in the eastern Baltic after 1815 between Russian pressures and Anglo-Swedish resistance and, by the beginning of this century, between German pressures and Russian resistance. Only the partition of the Polish core area made it possible to administer Poland among three powers. The prospect of the core area's unification and incorporation into the Russian Empire in the event of a victorious war was certain to take Russia beyond a line of an optimum of conquest; the ability to conquer must not be confused with the ability to rule. In the Russo-Ottoman frontier, Austria, despite its weakness, but with the support of first Britain and then Germany, had been able to contain Russia behind the Prut. The anticipated partition of Anatolia and the effective partition of the Persian core area were certain to create a backlash against the Russian advance. They would recreate within the Russian Empire the old rivalries over the frontier zones, now part of the empire's inner frontier, and require the deployment of troops beyond the range of effective action. Thus, a Russian victory in 1918 would have broken the stalemate and taken Russia far beyond a realistic line of an optimum of conquest. That realistic line, willy-nilly, had to run along the threshold of the Swedish, Polish, Turkish, and Persian core areas, while continuing to seek a political isobar from the Zungharian Gate to the Sea of Japan. Eventual success—should Russia reach the Heartland's periphery—contained the seeds of an inevitable disaster.

Notes

Preface

1. H. Mackinder, "The Geographical Pivot of History," *Geographical Journal*, 23:4 (1904): 421–44; *Democratic Ideals, passim*.
2. M. Sprout, "Mahan: Evangelist of Sea Power," in Earle, 415–45.
3. Ragsdale, 75–102.
4. Quoted in Florinsky, 604.

Introduction

1. Mackinder, *Democratic Ideals*, 92.
2. Parker, *Geopolitics*, 70–75; for the characteristic features of a core area see 66–67.
3. Ibid., 68.
4. Lattimore, *Studies*, 113–114.
5. Ibid., 115.
6. Ibid., 471. Alfred Rieber develops a similar approach to frontiers in Ragsdale, 315–59, here 329–35.
7. Bruce, *passim*.
8. Lattimore, *Studies*, 114.
9. Mahan, *Naval Strategy*, 385, 392–93.
10. Lattimore, *Studies*, 510–11.
11. It is not customary to speak of a Polish empire. There was, of course, no Polish emperor, but I do not see why the Swedes, with a Grand Duchy in Finland and other possessions in northern Germany, had an empire while the Poles did not.

Note: Because of the nature of this work and for reasons of space, references are limited to direct quotations.

12. Weigert et al., *Principles*, 73–75.
13. Mackinder, *Democratic Ideals*, 96.
14. The term is Dehio's, 113–14.
15. Weigert, *Generals*, 13.

Chapter 1

1. Articles 6–7; the text of the treaty is in *CTS*, 31:339–55.
2. Rousset, 1:347–56.
3. Ibid., 11:392–95.
4. Martens, 5:275–91.
5. Rousset, 16:486–90.
6. Ibid., 525–27.
7. Dickens to Newcastle, November 5/16, 1750, *SIRIO*, 148:146.
8. Solov'ev, *Istoriia Rossii*, 13:54
9. Martens, 6:42–43.
10. Kaplan, *First Partition*, 50–56, 59–66, 81–89, 185.

Chapter 2

1. Bowman, 7.
2. Kaplan, *First Partition*, 125.
3. Lord, 121.
4. Bonneville, 101.
5. Dickens to Newcastle, March 10/21, 1750, *SIRIO*, 148:26.
6. Florinsky, 532.
7. Martens, 2:228–35.
8. Lord, 478–82.
9. Bain, *Gustav III*, 2:213.
10. Lord, 448.

Chapter 3

1. Armfelt was a former favorite of Gustav III. He had commanded Swedish troops in Finland, but had been forced to flee to Russia for his opposition to the regent.
2. Romanov, *Diplomaticheskie snosheniia*, 1:113–15, 227–28.
3. Ibid., 3:211–12, 332–33.
4. Handelsman, 163.
5. Martens, 14:430–33, 2:301–303; Lord, 498.
6. *Polnoe Sobranie Zakonov Rossiiskoi Imperii*, 1832, N. 5165.
7. Martens, 12:48–49.

Chapter 4

1. Ramazani, 19–22.
2. Solov'ev, *Istoriia Rossii*, 10:7–10.
3. The term is Lybyer's, 12.
4. Kiniapina, 25–26.
5. Hurewitz, *Middle East and North Africa*, 1(1975):93.

6. A. Samoilov, "Zhizn' i deianiia general-fel'dmarshala kniazia G.A. Potemkina-Tavricheskogo," *Russkii Arkhiv*, 1867, col. 993–1027, here 1012–13.

7. Martens, 2:113–34.

8. Lord Lytton, viceroy of India (1876–1880), quoted in Alder, 115.

Chapter 5

1. Hurewitz, *Middle East and North Africa*, 1(1975):146–48.

2. Romanov, *Diplomaticheskie snosheniia*, 2:280; 3:42–44.

3. Rawlinson, 32–34.

4. Martens, 11:265–66.

5. Ibid., 11:414.

6. Quoted in Jelavich, *Balkan Entanglements*, 86.

7. Florinsky, 837.

8. Martens, 12:43.

9. Ibid., 12:39.

10. Hurewitz, *Middle East and North Africa*, 1(1975):262–65; emphasis mine.

11. Ibid., 279; emphasis mine.

12. Ibid., 290–92.

13. Ibid., 299–304.

14. Anderson, *Eastern Question*, 146–48.

15. Rawlinson, 84–87.

Chapter 6

1. Webb, *Great Frontier*, 2.

2. Rawlinson, 172.

3. Charykov, 160.

4. Greaves, 64–68.

5. Ibid., 138.

6. Kazemzadeh, 225.

7. Monasteries whose income went to support certain holy places and the patriarchates: Jelavich, *Balkan Entanglements*, 150–51.

8. Gorchakov, 2–6.

9. Jelavich, *Balkan Entanglements*, 165.

10. Florinsky, 999–1000.

11. Shotwell, 68.

12. Hurewitz, *Middle East and North Africa*, 2(1975):16–21.

13. Ibid., 1(1956):236.

14. Ramazani, 86.

Chapter 7

1. Cahen, 100.

2. Lamar and Thompson, 138.

3. Quoted in Dorpalen, 61. The original is in Ratzel, 386.

4. Lattimore, *Studies*, 117.

5. Golder, 170–71.

6. New Rules for the Russian-American Company in *Polnoe Sobranie Zakonov Rossiiskoi Imperii*, 1821, N. 28756, pt. 2.

7. Fu, 1:322–23.
8. Fairbank, 72–73.
9. Quested, 5.
10. Besprozvannykh, 202–203.
11. Quested, 10–11.
12. Fu, 1:367.
13. Ibid., 1:243–44.
14. G. Shtrandman, "Sibir' i eia nuzhdy v 1801 godu," *Russkaia Starina*, 1879, I (Jan.–April): 150–56, here 156.
15. Besprozvannykh, 231–32.

Chapter 8

1. Mamiya was a Japanese explorer who had sailed through the strait in 1808. The discovery was kept secret.
2. Besprozvannykh, 242.
3. Quested, 65.
4. See above, p. 122.
5. Besprozvannykh, 258–61.
6. Quested, 174.
7. Bilof, 16.
8. Romanov, *Russia*, 2, 5, 43.
9. Ibid., 45–48.
10. Alder, 22–24.
11. Hsu, *Ili Crisis*, 61.
12. Alder, 79.
13. Lensen, *Russian Push*, 329.
14. Ibid., 280–82, 291.
15. Ibid., 299, 301–302, 306.
16. Quoted in ibid., 367.
17. Ibid., 374–77.
18. Ibid., 451.

Chapter 9

1. *CTS*, 186:201–203, 257–58.
2. Fuller, 373.
3. Quoted in McNair and Lach, 77; Florinsky, 1266.
4. Quoted in Romanov, *Russia*, 444.
5. Nish, *Anglo-Japanese Alliance*, 41–42.
6. Trubetzkoi, 62.
7. *Cambridge History of China*, 11:116.
8. Ancel, 98.
9. Romanov, *Russia*, 218.
10. Ibid., 284.
11. Mackinder, *Democratic Ideals*, 78–79.
12. Romanov, *Russia*, 383.
13. Price, 39–58, 113–16.
14. Tang, 292, 295–97, 301–304.
15. Ibid., 311–14, 316, 327.

16. Ibid., 329.
17. Ibid., 357–58.

Chapter 10

1. Trachevsky, 35.
2. Martens, 5:337–38, 356–58.
3. Text in Martens, 1:202–12.
4. Stribrny, 9–12.
5. Ibid., 15–17.
6. Ibid., 20.
7. Ibid., 209.
8. Beer, 23.
9. Ibid., 24.
10. Ibid., 756.
11. Ibid., 39.
12. Trachevsky, 53.
13. Ibid., 115.
14. Stribrny, 217.
15. Martens, 6:132–34.

Chapter 11

1. *CHBFP*, 1:283.
2. Martens, 6:340.
3. Ibid., 6:310.
4. Ibid., 6:337–40.
5. Ibid., 2:375–76.
6. Jelavich, *Balkan Entanglements*, 13.
7. Martens, 3:19
8. Beer, 226.
9. Martens, 9:99–100.
10. Noailles to Richelieu, December 31, 1817, *SIRIO*, 119:530–31.
11. Martens, 8:376, 378–80.
12. Beer, 385–86.
13. Martens, 8:380–88.
14. Beer, 461–62.
15. Martens, 8:439.
16. Ibid., 8:454–55.
17. Ragsdale, 228.
18. *CHBFP*, 3:24–25.

Chapter 12

1. Schach, 449–52.
2. Ibid., 456–57.
3. Pribram, 2:189–91.
4. Ibid., 2:191–203.
5. Brennan, 130.
6. Pribram, 1:18–31.

7. Ibid., 1:50–55.

8. Ragsdale, 244.

9. Greaves, 81.

10. Pribram, 1:274–81.

11. Kennedy, *Rise and Fall of the Great Powers*, 232.

12. Romanov, *Russia*, 251.

13. Ibid., 356–59.

14. Quoted in Lieven, *Nicholas II*, 156–57.

15. Trubetzkoi, 113.

16. "Interior lines" are defined as "a central position prolonged in one or more directions": Mahan, *Naval Strategy*, 31.

17. Pribram, 1:184–95.

18. Charykov, 233.

19. Avetian, 43–45.

20. Jelavich, *Balkan Entanglements*, 252–57.

21. Lieven, *Russia*, 139–51.

22. Rohrbach, 71.

Chapter 13

1. Fu, 1:106.

2. Martens, 9:53–55.

3. Reading, vii–viii.

4. Martens, 13:120.

5. Clayton, 30–32.

6. Horn, 352, 367.

7. Anderson, *Britain's Discovery*, 131.

8. Cathcart to Rochefort, March 16, 1770, *SIRIO*, 19:42–43.

9. Anderson, *Britain's Discovery*, 134.

10. Martens, 13:145–46.

11. Martens, 2:119–20, 9:332–36; Madariaga, *Britain, Russia*, 59–60.

12. Halifax to Cathcart, April 5, 1771, *SIRIO*, 19:196.

13. *SIRIO*, 19:442–45.

14. Gerhard, 322.

15. Kennedy, *Rise and Fall of British Naval Mastery*, 89.

16. *CHBFP*, 1:205.

17. Gray, *Geopolitics of Super Power*, 46.

18. Anderson, *Britain's Discovery*, 172.

19. Gray, *Geopolitics of Super Power*, 76. I also borrow the term *decisive point* from him: 124.

20. Dehio, 145.

21. Article 10 of the treaty of January 1799, Hurewitz, *Middle East and North Africa*, 1(1975):132–33.

22. Martens, 13:302.

23. Temperley and Penson, 11–19.

24. Martens, 11:123.

25. Mahan, *Influence of Sea Power*, 239.

26. Rawlinson, 8–13.

27. Temperley and Penson, 242–43; *CHBFP*, 1:470–71.

Chapter 14

1. *SIRIO*, 119:678; *VPR*, 5/13:542–44.
2. Temperley and Penson, 54.
3. Anderson, *Britain's Discovery*, 235.
4. Ibid., 230–31.
5. Gleason, 50–56.
6. Ibid., 21–22.
7. Martens, 11:325–26.
8. *CHBFP*, 2:99.
9. Gleason, 85, 101–106.
10. *VPR*, 5/13:194–97.
11. Mahan, *Naval Strategy*, 31.
12. *VPR*, 5/13:372; emphasis in text.
13. Hurewitz, *Middle East and North Africa*, 1(1975):238–41.
14. Mackinder, 135.
15. Gleason, 132–34.
16. *CHBFP*, 2:169.
17. Temperley and Penson, 279–280.
18. Friedberg, 139.
19. Gleason, 155–56.
20. Guedalla, 206.
21. Martens, 12:65.
22. Gleason, 172–73.
23. Martens, 12:48–49.
24. P. Knaplund, "Finmark in British Diplomacy 1836–1855," *American Historical Review*, 30:3(1925):478–502, here 485.
25. Martens, 12:60; Gleason, 277–79.
26. Rawlinson, 70.
27. *CHBFP*, 2:202–203.
28. Kazemzadeh, 21.
29. Martens, 12:79.
30. Hurewitz, *Middle East and North Africa*, 1(1975):281.
31. Martens, 12:256–60.
32. Rawlinson, 265.
33. Clayton, 178.
34. Hurewitz, *Middle East and North Africa*, 1(1975):403–407.
35. Clayton, 126.
36. *CHBFP*, 3:122.
37. Ibid., 3:126.
38. Temperley and Penson, 384–85.
39. Wakeman, 156.

Chapter 15

1. Alder, 12–13.
2. Greaves, 39.
3. Nish, *Anglo-Japanese Alliance*, 17.
4. Dilke and Wilkinson, 156.
5. Greaves, 1–2.

6. Kennan, *Fateful Alliance*, 57.
7. Ibid., 264–68, 271–72.
8. Ibid., 265.
9. Alder, 224–30, 263–64.
10. Dilke and Wilkinson, 100–104.
11. Nish, *Anglo-Japanese Alliance*, 41.
12. Mahan, *Problems of Asia*, 42.
13. This is the thesis of Pratt's book.
14. Churchill, 15–16.
15. Temperley and Penson, 484.
16. Ibid., 497–501; Anderson, *Eastern Question*, 259.
17. Nish, *Anglo-Japanese Alliance*, 132.
18. Ibid., 55.
19. Friedberg, 298.
20. Nish, *Anglo-Japanese Alliance*, 378–79.
21. Ibid., 101–102.
22. Ibid., 2, 91.
23. Quoted in Hauner, 137.
24. Nish, *Anglo-Japanese Alliance*, 153–55, 175; emphasis in original.
25. Ibid., 381–85.
26. Romanov, *Russia*, 441.
27. Bruce, 324–26.
28. Nish, *Anglo-Japanese Alliance*, 205–206.
29. Greaves, 214.
30. Hurewitz, *Middle East and North Africa*, 1(1975):490–92.
31. Friedberg, 240–41.
32. Hurewitz, *Middle East and North Africa*, 1(1975):493–95.
33. Romanov, *Russia*, 330–31.
34. *CHBFP*, 3:329.
35. Nish, *Anglo-Japanese Alliance*, 303.
36. Ibid., 354–56.
37. Rawlinson, 133–35.
38. Shotwell, 74–77.
39. *CHBFP*, 3:424.
40. Romanov, Russia, 23–24.
41. Fuller, 423.
42. Clayton, 226.
43. Kennan, *Fateful Alliance*, 153.
44. Clayton, 203.

Conclusion

1. Weigert and Stefansson, *New Compass*, 150.
2. Luttwak, 162.
3. Martens, 4^1:63–64.
4. Quoted in ibid., 4^1:486.
5. Quoted in Alder, 309.
6. Temperley and Penson, 247.

References and Bibliography

Introduction

Ancel, J. *Géographie des frontières*. Paris, 1938.

Bowman, I. *The Pioneer Fringe*. New York, 1931.

Dehio, L. *The Precarious Balance: Four Centuries of European Power Struggles*. New York, 1962.

Dorpalen, A. *The World of General Haushofer: Geopolitics in Action*. New York, 1942.

Earle, E., ed. *Makers of Modern Strategy: Military Thought from Machiavelli to Hitler*. Princeton, N.J., 1944.

Gray, C. *The Geopolitics of Super Power*. Lexington, Ky., 1988.

———. *The Geopolitics of the Nuclear Era: Heartland, Rimland, and the Technological Revolution*. New York, 1977.

Kennedy, P. *The Rise and Fall of the Great Powers*. New York, 1987.

———. *The Rise and Fall of British Naval Mastery*. London, 1986.

Lamar, H. and Thompson, L., eds. *The Frontier in History: North America and Southern Africa Compared*. New Haven, Conn., 1981.

Lattimore, O. *Studies in Frontier History: Collected Papers, 1928–1958*. Paris, 1962.

———. *Inner Frontiers of China*. New York, 1940.

Luttwak, E. *Strategy and Politics: Collected Essays*. New Brunswick, N.J., 1980.

Mackinder, H. *Democratic Ideals and Reality: A Study in the Politics of Reconstruction*. New York, 1919.

Mahan, A. *Mahan on Naval Warfare: Selections from the Writings of Rear Admiral A. T. Mahan*. Boston, 1918.

———. *Naval Strategy*. Boston, 1911.

———. *The Problem of Asia and Its Effects Upon International Politics*. Boston, 1900.

———. *The Influence of Sea Power Upon History, 1660–1783*. Boston, 1890.

Parker, G. *The Geopolitics of Domination.* London, 1988.
Parker, W. *Mackinder. Geography as an Aid to Statecraft.* Oxford, 1982.
Pratt, E. *The Rise of Rail-Power in War and Conquest. 1833–1914.* London,
Ratzel, F. *Politische Geographie.* 3rd ed. Munich, 1923.
Webb, W. *The Great Frontier.* Austin, Tex., 1964.
Weigert, H. *Generals and Geographers: The Twilight of Geopolitics.* New York,
   1942.
——— and Stefansson, V., eds. *New Compass of the World.* New York, 1949.
——— et al., eds. *Principles of Political Geography.* New York, 1957.

General

Documents

British Documents on the Origin of the War, 1898–1914. G. Gooch and
   H. Temperley, eds. 11 vols. in 13. London, 1926–1938.
CTS. *Consolidated Treaty Series, 1648–1919,* C. Parry, ed. 231 vols. Dobbs
   Ferry, N.J., 1969-1981.
Die Grosse Politik der Europäischen Kabinette 1871–1914. J. Lepsius et al. eds.
   40 vols. in 54. Berlin, 1922–1927.
Gorchakov. *Sbornik izdannyi v pamiat' dvatsatipiatiletiia upravleniia Minister-
   stvom Inostrannykh Del gosudarstvennogo kantselera A. M. Gorchakova,
   1856–1881.* Petersburg, 1881.
Krasnyi Arkhiv. 106 vols. Moscow, 1922–1941.
Martens, F. *Recueil des traités et conventions conclus par la Russie avec les
   puissances étrangères.* 15 vols. Petersburg, 1874–1909.
Rousset. *Recueil historique d'actes, négociations, mémoires et traitéz.* 21 vols.
   The Hague, 1728–1755.
SIRIO. *Sbornik Imperatorskogo Russkogo Istoricheskogo Obshchestva.* 148 vols.
   Petersburg, 1876–1916.
Vneshniaia politika Rossii XIX i nachala XX veka (VPR). A. Narochnitsky,
   ed. 14 vols. (1801–1821). Moscow, 1960–1985.

Works

Charykov, N. *Glimpses of High Politics: Through War and Peace, 1855–1929.*
   New York, 1931.
Dallin, A., ed. *Russian Diplomacy and Eastern Europe, 1914–1917.* New York,
   1963.
Florinsky, M. *Russia: A History and an Interpretation.* 2 vols. New York, 1954.
Fuller, W. *Strategy and Power in Russia, 1600–1914.* New York, 1992.
Geyer, D. *Russian Imperialism. The Interaction of Domestic and Foreign Policy,
   1860–1914.* New Haven, Conn., 1987.
Grimsted, P. *The Foreign Ministers of Alexander I: Political Attitudes and the
   Conduct of Russian Diplomacy, 1801–1825.* Berkeley, Calif., 1969.
Historical Atlas of East Central Europe. P. Magosci, ed. Seattle, 1993.
Hunczak, T., ed. *Russian Imperialism from Ivan the Great to the Revolution.*
   New Brunswick, N.J., 1974.
Jelavich, B. *St. Petersburg and Moscow. Tsarist and Soviet Foreign Policy,
   1814–1974.* Bloomington, Ind., 1974.

Kerner, R. *The Urge to the Sea: The Course of Russian History.* Berkeley, Calif., 1942.

Lederer, I. ed. *Russian Foreign Policy: Essays in Historical Perspective.* New Haven, Conn., 1962.

Lieven, D. *Nicholas II. Emperor of All the Russias.* London, 1993.

MacKenzie, D. *Imperial Dreams, Harsh Realities, Tsarist Russian Foreign Policy, 1815–1917.* Fort Worth, Tex., 1994.

Madariaga, I. de. *Russia in the Age of Catherine the Great.* New Haven, Conn., 1981.

McDonald, D. *United Government and Foreign Policy in Russia, 1900–1914.* Cambridge, Mass., 1992.

Ragsdale, H., ed. *Imperial Russian Foreign Policy.* New York, 1993.

Solov'ev, S. *Istoriia Rossii s drevneishikh vremen.* 15 vols. Moscow, 1959–1966.

Trubetzkoi, G. *Russland als Grossmacht.* 2nd ed. Stuttgart, 1917.

Russia and Its Western Frontier

Bain, R. *Charles XII and the Collapse of the Swedish Empire 1682–1719.* New York, 1895.

———. *Gustav III and His Contemporaries (1742–1792).* 2 vols. London, 1894.

Bonneville, L. *Le Comte de Vergennes. Son Embassade en Suède 1771–1774.* Paris, 1898.

Handelsman, M. *Napoléon et la Pologne, 1806–1807.* Paris, 1909.

Kaplan, H. *The First Partition of Poland.* New York, 1962.

Lord, R. *The Second Partition of Poland. A Study in Diplomatic History.* Cambridge, Mass., 1915.

Ransel, D. *The Politics of Catherinian Russia. The Panin Party.* New Haven, Conn., 1975.

Roginsky, V. *Shvetsiia i Rossiia. Soiuz 1812 goda.* Moscow, 1978.

Tommila, P. *La Finlande dans la politique européenne en 1809–1815.* Helsinki, 1962.

Trulsson, S. *British and Swedish Policies and Strategies in the Baltic after the Peace of Tilsit in 1807.* Lund, Sweden, 1976.

Russia and Its Southern Frontier

Documents

Hurewitz, J., ed. *The Middle East and North Africa in World Politics. A Documentary Record*, 2nd ed., 2 vols. New Haven, Conn., 1975–1979.

———. *Diplomacy in the Near and Middle East, A Documentary Record.* New York, 1956.

Noradounghian, G., ed. *Recueil d'actes internationaux de l'empire ottoman, 1300–1902.* 4 vols. Paris, 1897–1903.

Works

Anderson, M. *The Eastern Question 1744–1923.* London, 1966.

Atkin, M. *Russia and Iran, 1780–1828.* Minneapolis, 1980.

Bruce, R. *The Forward Policy and Its Results.* London, 1900.

Druzhinina, E. *Kuchuk-Kainardzhiiskii mir 1774 goda.* Moscow, 1955.

Entner, M. *Russo-Persian Commercial Relations 1828–1914.* Gainesville, Fla., 1965.

Goldfrank, D. *The Origins of the Crimean War.* New York, 1994.

Greaves, R. *Persia and the Defense of India. 1884–1892.* London, 1959.

Habberton, W. *Anglo-Russian Relations Concerning Afghanistan, 1837–1907.* Urbana, Ill., 1937.

Hauner, M. *What Is Asia to Us? Russia's Asian Heartland Yesterday and Today.* Boston, 1990.

Jelavich, B. *Balkan Entanglements, 1806–1914.* Cambridge, 1991.

———. *A History of the Balkans.* 2 vols. Cambridge, 1983.

Kasemzadeh, F. *Russia and Britain in Persia 1864–1914. A Study in Imperialism.* New Haven, Conn., 1968.

Kiniapina, N. et al. *Kavkaz i Sredniaia Aziia vo vneshnei politike Rossii. Vtoraia polovina 18 v.-80-e gody 19 v.* Moscow, 1984.

Lang, D. *The Last Years of the Georgian Monarchy, 1658–1832.* New York, 1957.

Lockhart, L. *Nadir Shah: A Critical Study Based Mainly on Contemporary Sources.* London, 1938.

Lybyer, A. *The Government of the Ottoman Empire in the Time of Suleiman the Magnificent.* Cambridge, Mass., 1913.

Ramazani, R. *The Foreign Policy of Iran 1500–1941.* Charlottesville, Va., 1966.

Rawlinson, H. *England and Russia in the East.* London, 1875.

Saul, N. *Russia and the Mediterranean, 1797–1807.* Chicago, 1970.

Shotwell, J. and Deak, F. *Turkey at the Straits. A Short History.* New York, 1940.

Sumner, B. *Russia and the Balkans 1870–1880.* Oxford, 1937.

Russia and Its Eastern Frontier

Documents

Bantysh-Kamensky, N. *Diplomaticheskoe sobranie del mezhdu Rossiiskim i Kitaiskim gosudarstvami s 1619 po 1792-i god.* Kazan, 1882.·

Fu, Lo-shu, ed. *A Documentary Chronicle of Sino-Western Relations (1644–1820.* 2 vols. Tucson, Ariz., 1966.

MacMurray, J, ed. *Treaties and Agreements With and Concerning China 1894–1919.* 2 vols. New York, 1921.

Works

Appollova, N. *Prisoedinenie Kazakhstana k Rossii v 30kh gg. XVIII v.* Alma-Ata, 1948.

Barfield, Th. *The Perilous Frontier. Nomadic Empires and China.* Oxford, 1989.

Barsukov, I. *Graf Nikolai Nikolaevich Murav'ev-Amurskii.* 2 vols. Moscow, 1891.

Berton, P. "The Secret Russo-Japanese Alliance of 1916." Unpub. Ph.D. Diss., Columbia University, New York, 1956.

Besprozvannykh, E. *Priamur'e v sisteme russko-kitaiskikh otnoshenii XVII-seredine XIX v.* Khabarovsk, 1986.

Bilof, E. "The Imperial Russian General Staff and China in the Far East 1880–1888. A Study of the Operations of the General Staff." Unpub. Ph.D. diss., Syracuse University, N.Y., 1974.

Cahen, G. *Histoire des relations de la Russie avec la Chine sous Pierre le Grand (1689–1730).* Paris, 1912.

Cambridge History of China. vols. 10–11. Cambridge, 1978–1980.

Fairbank, J., ed. *The Chinese World Order. Traditional China's Foreign Relations.* Cambridge, Mass., 1968.

Foust, C. *Muscovite and Mandarin. Russia's Trade With China and Its Setting, 1727–1805.* Chapel Hill, N.C. 1969.

Golder, F. *Russian Expansion on the Pacific 1641–1850.* Cleveland, Oh., 1914.

Hsü, I. *The Ili Crisis. A Study of Sino-Russian Diplomacy 1871–1881.* Oxford, 1965.

Lensen, G. *The Russian Push toward Japan: Russo-Japanese Relations 1697–1875.* Princeton, N.J., 1959.

———. *Balance of Intrigue: International Rivalry in Korea and Manchuria, 1884–1899.* 2 vols. Tallahassee, Fla., 1982.

Malozemoff, A. *Russian Far Eastern Policy, 1881–1904.* Berkeley, Calif., 1958.

Mancall, M. *Russia and China: Their Diplomatic Relations to 1728.* Cambridge, Mass., 1971.

McNair, H. and Lach, D. *Modern Far Eastern Relations.* New York, 1950.

Paine, S. *Imperial Rivals: Russia, China and Their Disputed Frontier 1858–1924.* New York, 1996.

Price, E. *The Russo-Japanese Treaties of 1907–1916 Concerning Manchuria and Mongolia.* Baltimore, 1933.

Quested, R. *The Expansion of Russia in East Asia 1857–1860.* Kuala Lumpur, 1968.

Romanov, B. *Russia in Manchuria (1892–1906).* New York, 1974.

Tang, P. *Russian and Soviet Policy in Manchuria and Outer Mongolia 1911 to 1931.* Durham, N.C., 1959.

Wakeman, F. *The Fall of Imperial China.* New York, 1975.

Widmer, E. *The Russian Ecclesiastical Mission in Peking during the Eighteenth Century.* Cambridge, Mass., 1976.

Containment—The Germanic Powers

Documents

Arneth, A. von, ed. *Joseph II und Katharina von Russland: Ihr Briefwechsel.* Vienna, 1869.

Pribram, A. ed. *The Secret Treaties of Austria-Hungary, 1879–1914.* 2 vols. Cambridge, Mass., 1920–21.

Works

Avetian, A. *Germanskii imperializm na Blizhnem Vostoke.* Moscow, 1966.

Bagdasarian, N. der. *The Austro-German Rapprochement 1870–1879.* London, 1976.

Beer, A. *Die orientalische Politik Oesterreichs seit 1774.* Leipzig, 1883.

Brennan, W. "The Russian Foreign Ministry and the Alliance with Germany 1878–1884." Unpub. Ph.D. diss., University of Eugene, Oregon, 1971.

Fischer, F. *War of Illusions: German Policies from 1911 to 1914.* New York, 1975.

————. *Germany's Aims in the First World War.* New York, 1967.

Kaplan, H. *Russia and the Outbreak of the Seven Years' War.* Berkeley, Calif., 1968.

Lieven, D. *Russia and the Origins of the First World War.* New York, 1983.

Nerserov, G. *Politika Rossii na Teshenskom Kongresse, 1778–1779 gody.* Moscow, 1988.

Petrovich, M. *The Emergence of Russian Panslavism 1856–1870.* New York, 1956.

Rich, N. *Friedrich von Holstein. Politics and Diplomacy in the Era of Bismarck and William II.* 2 vols. Cambridge, 1965.

Rohrbach, P. *Russland und Wir.* Stuttgart, 1915.

Roider, K. *Austria's Eastern Question 1700–1790.* Princeton, N.J., 1982.

Schach, K. "Russian Foreign Policy under Prince Alexander N. Gorchakov. The Diplomatic Game Plan versus Austria 1856–1873." Unpub. Ph.D. diss., University of Nebraska, Omaha, 1974.

Stribrny, W. *Die Russlandpolitik Friedrichs des Grossen 1764–1786.* Wurzburg, 1966.

Thaden, E. *Russia and the Balkan Alliance of 1912.* University Park, Pa., 1965.

Trachevsky, A. *Soiuz kniazei i nemetskaia politika Ekateriny II, Fridrikha II, Iosifa II 1780–1790 gg.* Petersburg, 1877.

Williamson, S. *Austro-Hungary and the Origins of the First World War.* London, 1991.

Containment—The Coastland Powers

Documents

Romanov, Grand Prince Nikolai Mikhailovich, ed. *Diplomaticheskie snosheniia Rossii i Frantsii po doneseniam poslov imperatorov Aleksandra i Napoleona, 1808–1812.* 7 vols. Petersburg, 1905–1914.

Temperley, H. and Penson, L., eds. *Foundations of British Foreign Policy from Pitt (1792) to Salisbury (1902).* Cambridge, 1938.

Works

Albion, R. *Forests and Sea Power: The Timber Problem of the Royal Navy, 1652–1862.* Cambridge, Mass., 1926.

Alder, G. *British India's Northern Frontier, 1865–1895.* London, 1963.

Anderson, M. *Britain's Discovery of Russia, 1553–1815.* New York, 1959.

Chance, J. *George I and the Northern War.* London, 1909.

CHBFP. *The Cambridge History of British Foreign Policy 1783–1919.* A. Ward and G. Gooch, eds. 3 vols. New York, 1922–1923.

Churchill, R. *The Anglo-Russian Convention of 1907.* Cedar Rapids, Ia., 1939.

Clayton, G. *Britain and the Eastern Question: Missolonghi to Gallipoli.* London, 1971.

Dilke, C. and Wilkinson, S. *Imperial Defense.* London, 1892.

Friedberg, A. *The Weary Titan. Britain and the Experience of Relative Decline 1895–1905.* Princeton, N.J., 1988.

Gerhard, D. *England und der Aufstieg Russlands.* Munich, 1933.

Gleason, J. *The Genesis of Russophobia in Great Britain. A Study in the Inter-action of Policy and Opinion.* New York, 1972.

Guedalla, Ph. *Palmerston 1784–1865.* New York, 1927.

Horn, D. *Great Britain and Europe in the Eighteenth Century.* Oxford, 1967.

Kennan, G. *The Fateful Alliance. France, Russia and the Coming of the First World War.* New York, 1984.

———. *The Decline of Bismarck's World Order: Franco-Russian Relations 1875–1890.* Princeton, N.J., 1979.

Langer, W. *The Franco-Russian Alliance of 1890–1894.* Cambridge, Mass., 1929.

Madariaga, I. de. *Britain, Russia, and the Armed Neutrality of 1780.* New Haven, Conn., 1962.

Nish, I. *The Anglo-Japanese Alliance. The Diplomacy of Two Island Empires 1894–1907.* London, 1966.

———. *Alliance in Decline. A Study of Anglo-Japanese Relations 1908–23.* London, 1972.

Oliva, L. *Misalliance: A Study of French Policy in Russia during the Seven Years War.* New York, 1964.

Reading, D. *The Anglo-Russian Commercial Treaty of 1734.* New Haven, Conn., 1938.

Takeuchi, T. *War and Diplomacy in the Japanese Empire.* Garden City, N.J., 1935.

Vandal, A. *Napoléon et Alexandre Ier: l'alliance russe sous le premier empire.* 3 vols. Paris, 1896.

———. *Louis XV et Elizabeth de Russie.* Paris, 1882.

Webster, C. *The Foreign Policy of Palmerston, 1830–1841.* 2 vols. London, 1951.

Index